FLAMINGOS are found in warm areas on five different continents!

FEEDING Flamingos' bills have filters, which they use to strain mud and sand from their food.

FLOCKS Flamingos live in large colonies, which can have thousands of birds.

SIZE Flamingos grow to be 3-5 feet (1-1.5 meters) tall, but they only weigh 5-6 lbs.

HSP Kentucky

Science

Harcourt
SCHOOL PUBLISHERS

Visit *The Learning Site!*
www.harcourtschool.com

HSP Kentucky Science

American Flamingo

Excursion Photo Credits
Life: 40–41 © 2007 Newport Aquarium; **41** © 2007 Newport Aquarium; **42–43** (all) David Davis Photography; **44** © David Lutman/AFP/Getty Images; **44–45** © Kevib R. Morris/CORBIS; **45** (*t*) © Getty Images; **45** (inset) Getty Images.
Earth: 266–267 (*bg*) Chuck Summers; **266** (*bl*) Gary W. Carter/Corbis; **267** (*t*) Tom Uhlam Photography; **268–269** (all) Hazard Community & Technical College; **268** Hazard Community & Technical College; **269** Hazard Community & Technical College/Challenger Learner Center; **270** © 2007 Bin Dai; **270–271** © Digital Vision/Getty Images.
Physical: 444–445 Melissa Farlow/National Geographic Images; **445** (*l*) AP Wide World photo; **445** (*r*) Bill Bachmann/PhotoEdit, Inc.; **446** Getty Images; **447** © Masterfile; **448–449** Lee Thomas; **448** (*b*) Steven Brown.

Harcourt
SCHOOL PUBLISHERS

Printed in the United States of America

ISBN 10: 0-15-363859-1
ISBN 13: 978-0-15-363859-6

2 3 4 5 6 7 8 9 10 032 16 15 14 13 12 11 10 09 08

Consulting Authors

Michael J. Bell
Assistant Professor of Early Childhood Education
College of Education
West Chester University of Pennsylvania
West Chester, Pennsylvania

Michael A. DiSpezio
Curriculum Architect
JASON Academy
Cape Cod, Massachusetts

Marjorie Frank
Former Adjunct, Science Education
Hunter College
New York, New York

Gerald H. Krockover
Professor of Earth and Atmospheric Science Education
Purdue University
West Lafayette, Indiana

Joyce C. McLeod
Adjunct Professor
Rollins College
Winter Park, Florida

Barbara ten Brink
Science Specialist
Austin Independent School District
Austin, Texas

Carol J. Valenta
Senior Vice President
St. Louis Science Center
St. Louis, Missouri

Barry A. Van Deman
President and CEO
Museum of Life and Science
Durham, North Carolina

Senior Editorial Advisors

Napoleon Adebola Bryant, Jr.
Professor Emeritus of Education
Xavier University
Cincinnati, Ohio

Tyrone Howard
Associate Professor
Graduate School of Education and Information Studies
University of California, Los Angeles
Los Angeles, California

Robert M. Jones
Professor of Education Foundations
University of Houston–Clear Lake
Houston, Texas

Mozell P. Lang
Former Science Consultant
Michigan Department of Education
Science Consultant, Highland Park Schools
Highland Park, Michigan

Jerry D. Valadez
Science Coordinator
Fresno Unified School District
Fresno, California

Contents

Big Idea
You can answer your science questions by carrying out careful investigations.

Big Idea
Living things can be grouped according to their characteristics.

Big Idea
Living things inherit traits, grow, and develop according to life cycles.

Big Idea
Living things are adapted for survival in their environment.

Big Idea
To stay alive, people depend on body systems that work together.

Big Idea
Ecosystems are made up of both living and nonliving parts that all impact one another.

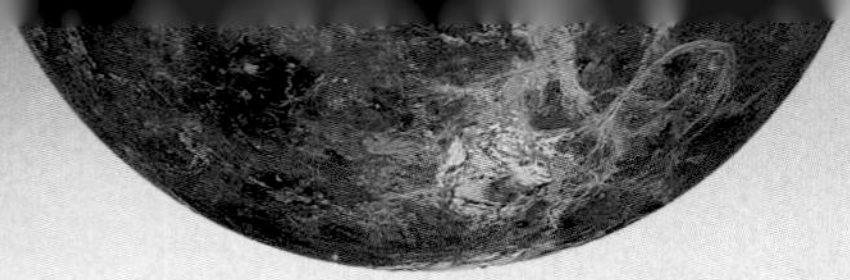

Big Idea
Living things get energy from the sun or from other living things.

Big Idea
Rocks and soil are formed and broken down by natural processes.

Big Idea
Earth's surface has landforms that have changed and continue to change.

Big Idea
Matter can undergo both physical and chemical changes.

Big Idea
Vibrations cause sounds, which travel in wave form.

Big Idea
Light and heat are useful forms of energy.

Getting Ready for Science

What's the Big Idea? You can answer your science questions by carrying out careful investigations.

Essential Questions

Lesson 1
What Are Tools for Inquiry?

Lesson 2
What Are Inquiry Skills?

Lesson 3
What Is the Scientific Method?

GO online ▸ Student eBook www.hspscience.com

What do YOU wonder?

Does doing science require special skills? How might this young snorkeler be answering a question she has about the shell?

Young snorkeler

LESSON

1

Essential Question

What Are Tools for Inquiry?

Investigate ways of measuring.

Read and Learn about different tools for inquiry.

Fast Fact

Out-of-This-World Tools

The wheels of the Mars Rovers were tools for exploration. They exposed layers of soil. Scientists used the soil data to draw conclusions about Mars. In the Investigate, you will draw conclusions about ways to measure.

Photo of Mars Rover on artist's backdrop

Vocabulary Preview

standard measure
[STAN•derd MEZH•er] An accepted measurement (p. 6)

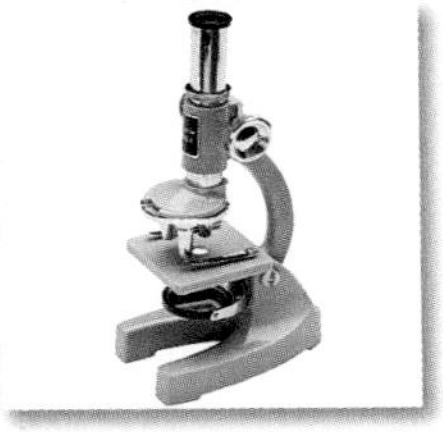

microscope
[MY•kruh•skohp] A tool that makes an object look several times bigger than it actually is (p. 8)

pan balance [PAN BAL•uhns]
A tool that measures mass (p. 11)

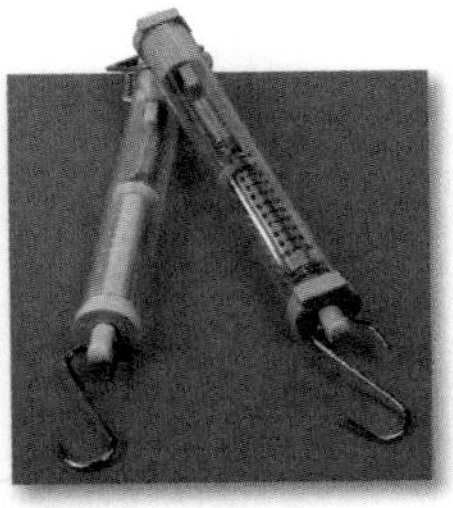

spring scale [SPRING SKAYL]
A tool that measures forces, such as weight (p. 11)

Measuring with Straws

Guided Inquiry

Start with Questions

Suppose you go to the grocery store. There, all of the products have been carefully measured based on government standards.

- What exactly is measuring?
- What are some different ways to measure objects?
- Are there standard ways to measure the same objects?

Investigate to find out. Then read to learn more.

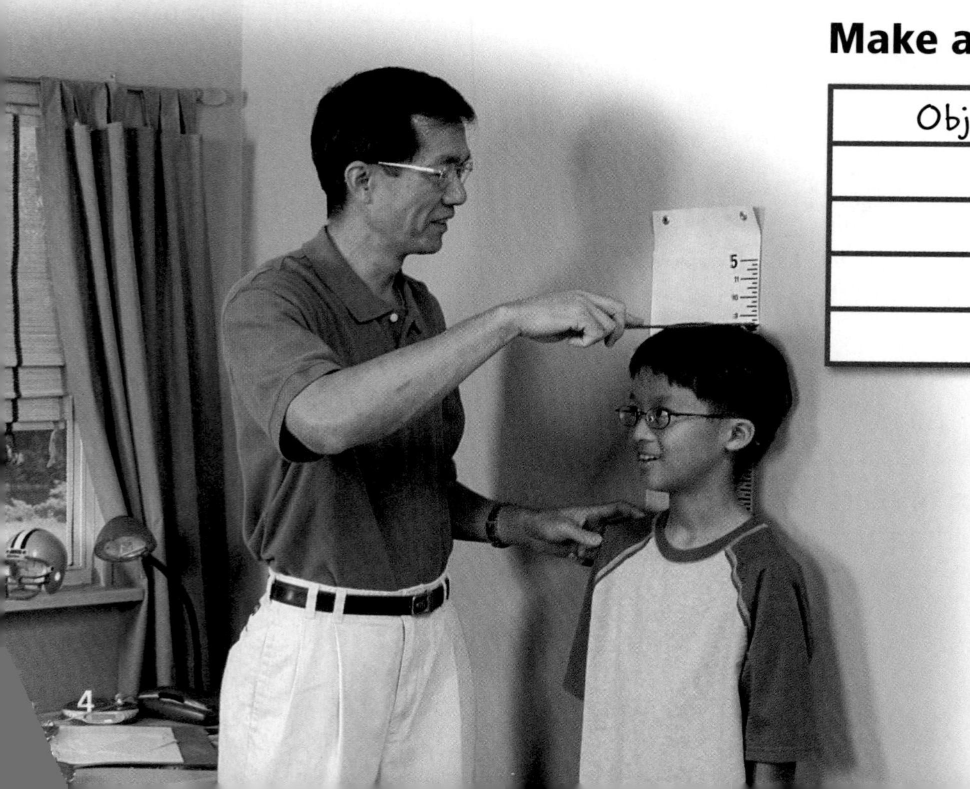

Prepare to Investigate

Inquiry Skill Tip

When you measure, you make observations by using numbers. Look for ways in which a straw can be used to measure things. Then think about other ways you might measure the same things.

Materials

- plastic straws
- classroom objects
- 2 cups
- water
- marker

Make a Data Table

Object	Measurement(s)

Follow This Procedure

1. Use straws to **measure** length and width (distance). For example, you might **measure** this textbook or another flat object. **Record** your measurements.

2. Now use straws to **measure** the distance around a round object (its circumference). Hint: Flatten the straws before you start. **Record** your measurements.

3. Next, work with a partner to find a way to use straws to **measure** the amount of water in a cup (its volume). **Record** your measurements.

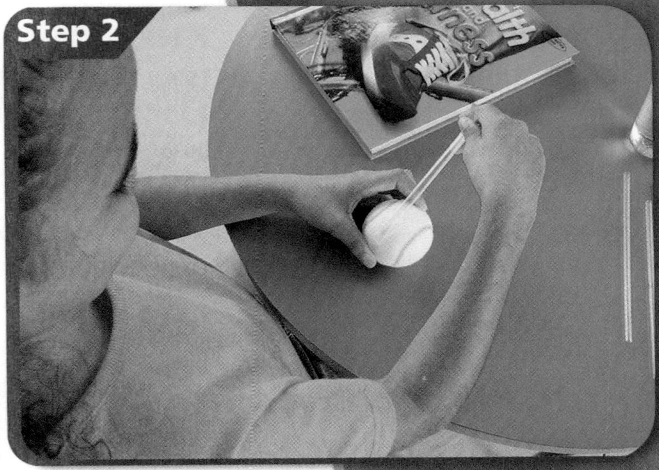

Step 2

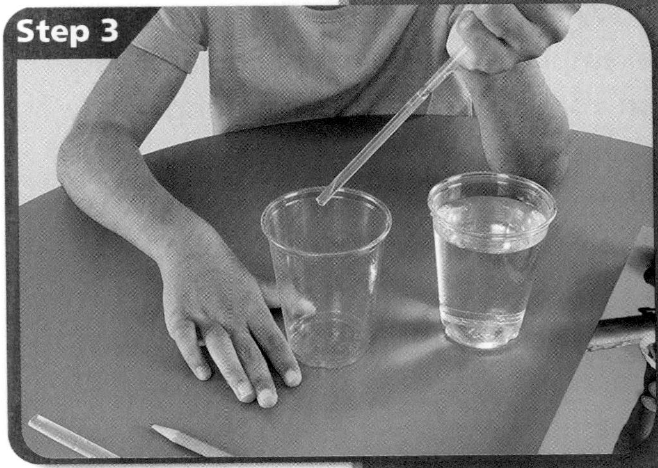

Step 3

Draw Conclusions

1. Compare your measurements with those of other students. What can you conclude?

2. **Inquiry Skill** Scientists **measure** carefully so they can record changes accurately. Why do all scientists need to use the same unit of **measurement** when working on the same problems?

Independent Inquiry

How could you mark a straw to divide it into smaller units? How would this change the way you collect data? What might be a reason to do this?

VOCABULARY
standard measure p. 6
microscope p. 8
pan balance p. 11
spring scale p. 11

SCIENCE CONCEPTS
- how scientists use tools to measure, observe, and manipulate
- how to use tools properly and safely

Focus Skill MAIN IDEA AND DETAILS
Look for tools that scientists use.

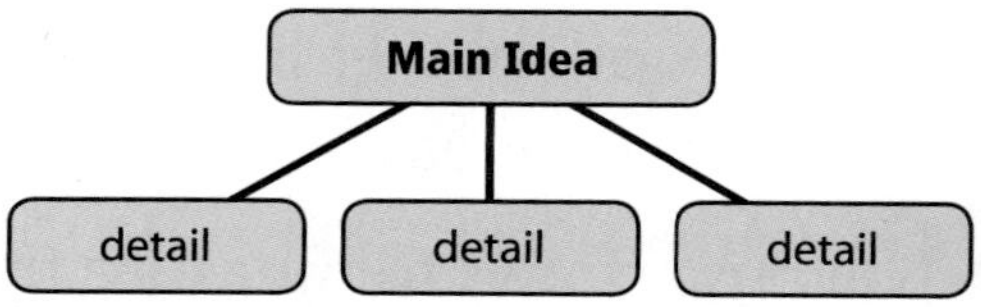

Tools for Measuring Distance

Long ago, people sometimes used body parts to measure distance. For example, King Henry I of England had an iron bar made. It was as long as the distance from his nose to the tips of his fingers. Copies of the bar were made. The king told everyone to use the bars to measure things. This bar became the standard length for one yard. A **standard measure** is an accepted measurement.

When it was introduced, the meter, another unit of length, was not based on a body part. It was defined as 1/10,000,000 of the distance from the North Pole to the equator. Imagine measuring that distance!

These units of measurement may seem strange. Yet they helped people agree on the lengths of objects and the distances between places.

Focus Skill MAIN IDEA AND DETAILS **Why do we have standard units of measure?**

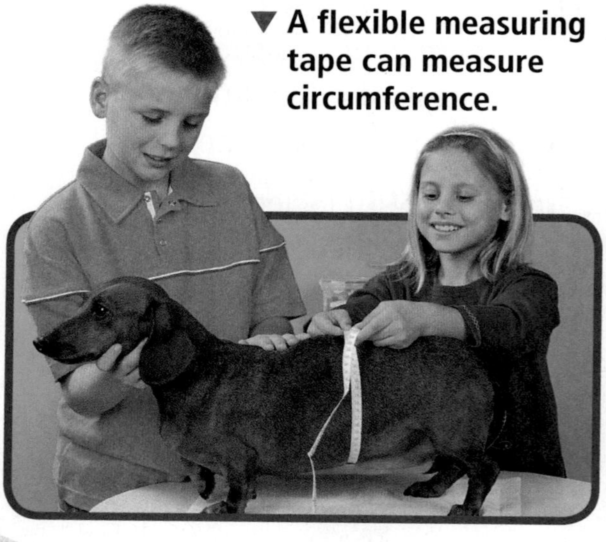

▼ A flexible measuring tape can measure circumference.

Geologists and surveyors use this tool to measure large distances.

◀ A ruler measures length. Place the first line of the ruler at one end of the object. The point on the ruler where the object ends is its length.

Tools for Measuring Volume

Cooks use cups and spoons to measure ingredients for a recipe. Scientists measure volume with tools, too. To find the volume of a liquid, you put it into a container such as a measuring cup, a beaker, or a graduate. The numbers on the side of the container show the volume of the liquid. Never use tools from your science lab for measuring food or medicine!

To measure the volume of a solid, multiply its length by its width by its height. For example, one box has a length of 4 centimeters and a width of 2 centimeters. Its height is 2 centimeters. The volume is 4 cm x 2 cm x 2 cm = 16 cubic centimeters.

Focus Skill MAIN IDEA AND DETAILS

How do you measure the volume of a solid? Of a liquid?

Insta-Lab

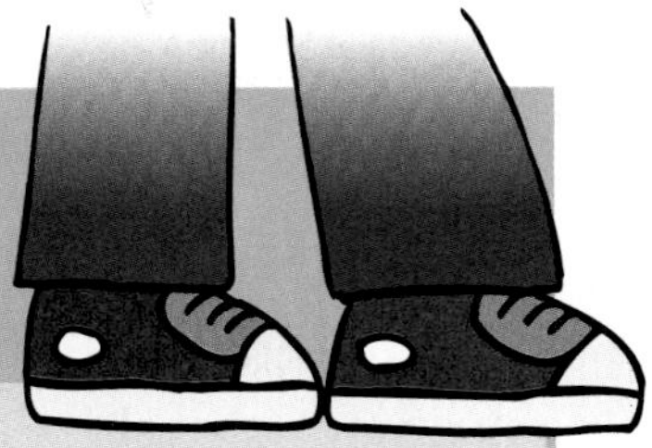

Personal Measuring Tools

Think of other ways that you could measure distance or volume, using items you have at home or in the classroom. Test your new measuring tools, and exchange ideas with other students.

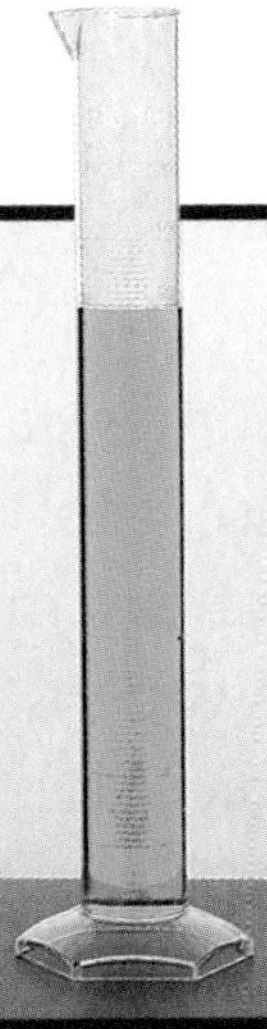

To measure a liquid, place the graduate on a flat surface. Your eyes should be even with the top of the liquid. The volume is the marking that is closest to the top of the liquid.

Droppers are used to measure small amounts of liquids.

Tools for Observing and Handling

Sometimes scientists need to observe an object closely. Certain tools can help them observe details they might not be able to see using just their eyes.

A hand lens makes things look larger than they are. It magnifies them. Hold the lens a few centimeters in front of your eye. Then move the object closer to the lens until you can see it clearly. Never let the lens touch your eye. Never use it to look at the sun!

Forceps let you pick up a sharp or prickly object without getting hurt. They can also protect a delicate object from too much handling. However, you must squeeze the forceps gently.

A magnifying box is sometimes called a bug box. Students often use it to observe live insects. An insect can move around in the box while you watch.

A microscope makes an object look several times bigger than it is. The **microscope** on the next page has several lenses that can magnify a little or a lot. Two knobs help you adjust the image until you can see it clearly.

A bug box lets you watch an insect move around—without it getting away.

Focus Skill MAIN IDEA AND DETAILS

How do the tools on these pages help scientists?

A hand lens allows you to see many details. When you use forceps to hold an object, you can observe it without your fingers getting in the way.

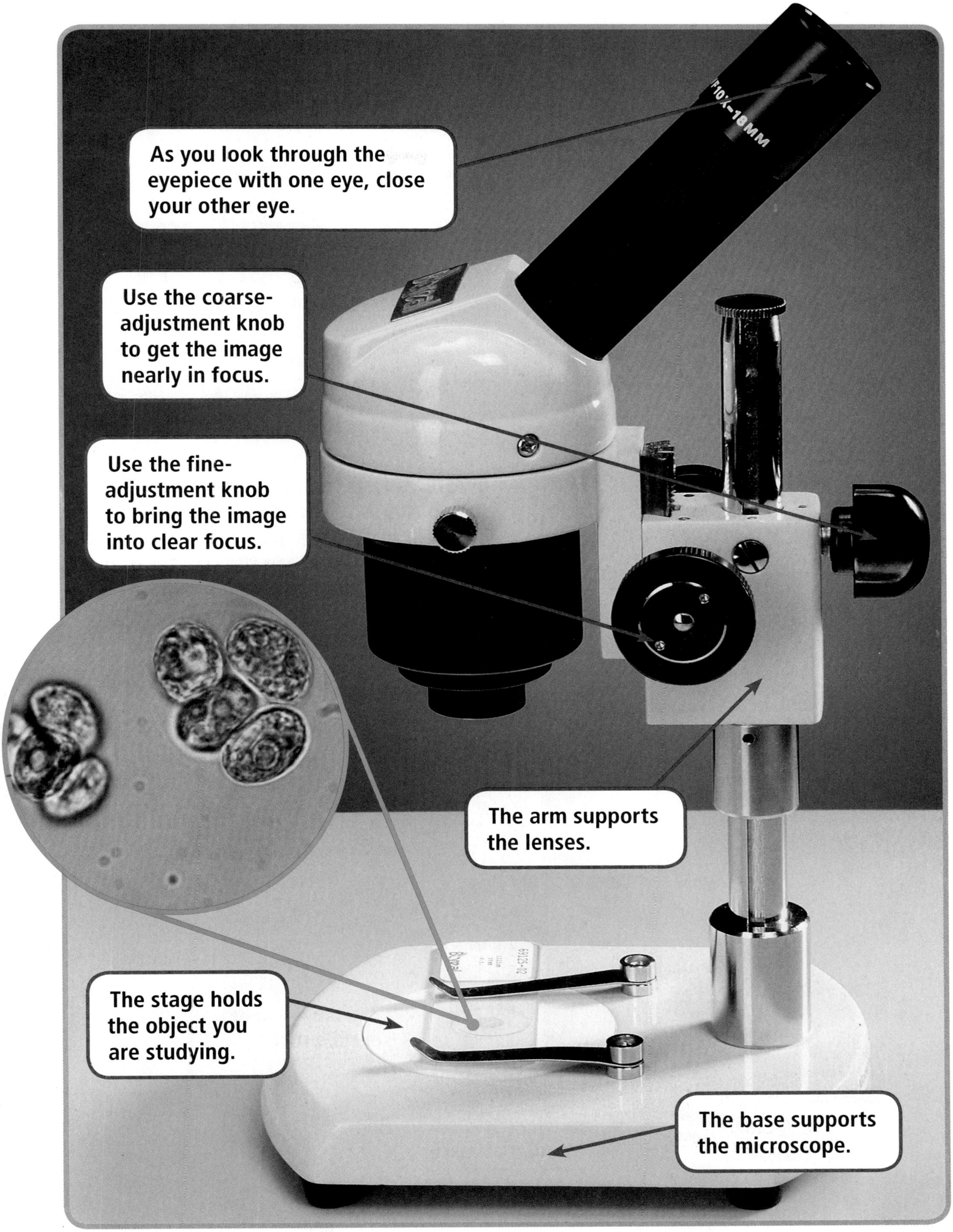
F10X-18MM
As you look through the eyepiece with one eye, close your other eye.
Use the coarse-adjustment knob to get the image nearly in focus.
Use the fine-adjustment knob to bring the image into clear focus.
The arm supports the lenses.
The stage holds the object you are studying.
The base supports the microscope.

Other Tools

Many other tools can help you measure. For example, a thermometer measures the temperature of the air or of a liquid. A thermometer is a hollow glass tube that has a bulb at one end. The bulb contains a liquid. The air or liquid around the bulb warms or cools the liquid inside the bulb. As the liquid inside the thermometer gets warmer, it expands and rises up the tube. Numbers on the thermometer tell how warm the air or liquid being measured is.

When you are using a thermometer, be sure to touch the bulb as little as possible. If your fingers are on the bulb, you will just measure the warmth of your fingers! Also, be careful—glass thermometers are very easy to break.

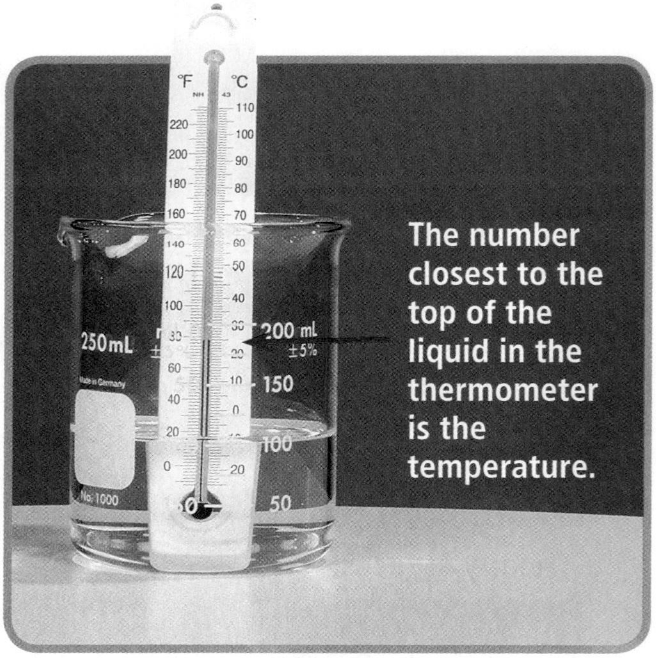

The number closest to the top of the liquid in the thermometer is the temperature.

Before you use a pan balance, make sure the pointer is at the middle mark. Place the object in one pan, and add standard masses to the other pan. When the pointer is at the middle mark again, add the numbers on the standard masses. The total is the mass of the object. ▼

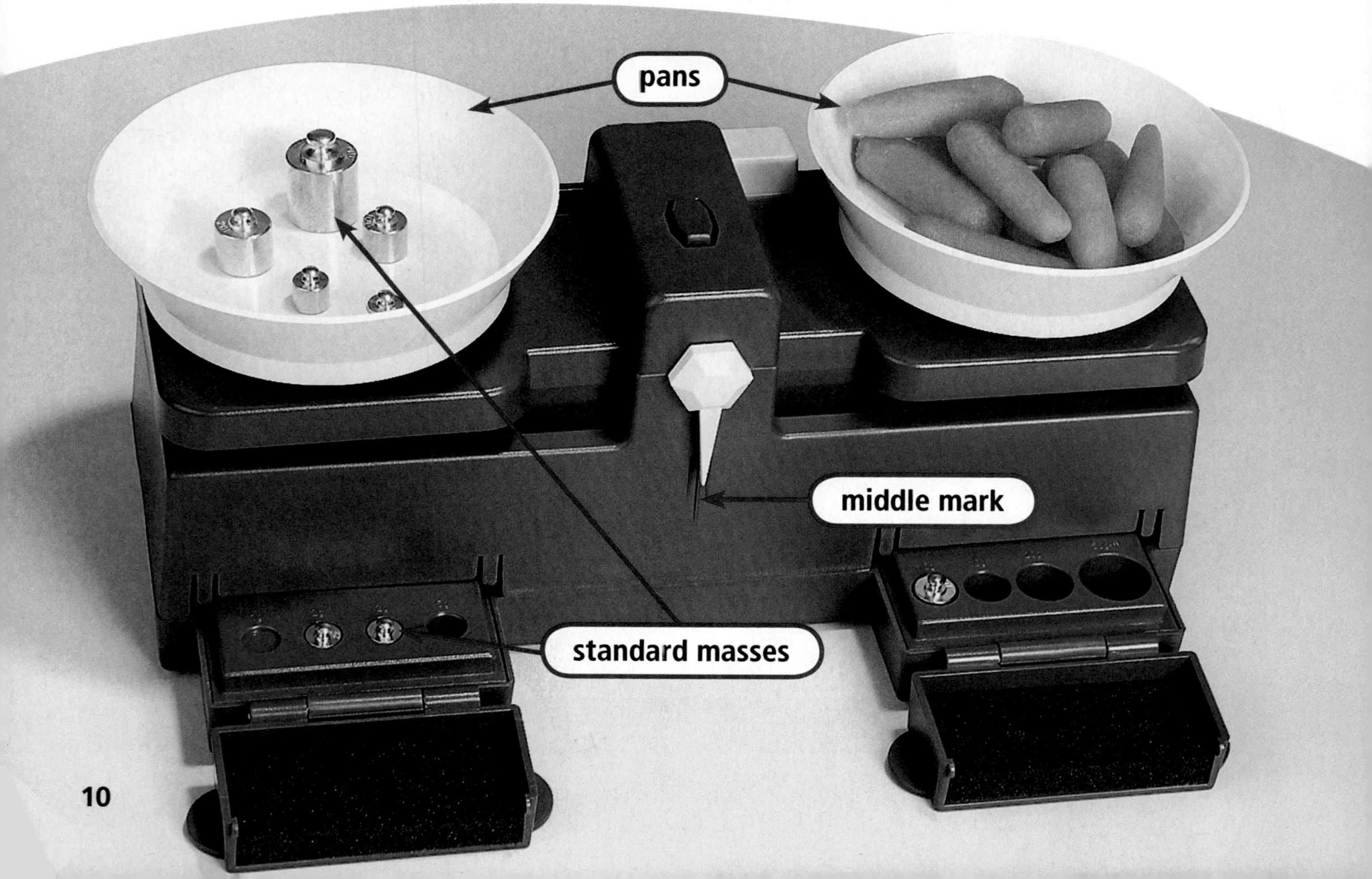

This girl is using a spring scale to measure the rabbit's weight. ▶

A rock hammer can chip away smaller samples from a large rock. How might you observe these samples?

If one breaks, tell your teacher or another adult right away.

A **pan balance** measures mass. Mass is the amount of matter in an object. It is measured in grams (g). A **spring scale** measures forces, such as weight. Force is measured in newtons (N).

Other tools help scientists as well. The rock hammer shown on this page can help scientists gather samples from larger rocks. The scientists then identify the rocks by using other tools, such as hand lenses, to observe the patterns of crystals and other properties.

Focus Skill MAIN IDEA AND DETAILS

What properties do a pan balance and a spring scale measure?

Timepieces

Sometimes, when you are carrying out inquiry, you will need to keep track of time that passes. You can do this with different kinds of timepieces.

Timepieces are tools that measure time. You might have a watch--that is a timepiece. It can tell you hours, minutes, and maybe seconds.

The clock on your classroom wall is another kind of timepiece. You can use it to measure hours, minutes, and seconds as well.

What if you need to start measuring time in a precise way? You can use a stopwatch! A stopwatch is a timepiece that is designed for measuring time. It has a counter that starts at zero and stops when you press a button. Then it tells you how long something took.

Focus Skill **MAIN IDEA AND DETAILS**

What kind of timepiece would you use to time a runner in a race?

The clock in your classroom will tell you what time it is.

This student is using a stopwatch to measure how long it takes for food coloring to dye water.

Lesson Review

Essential Question

What are investigation tools?

In this lesson, you measured length and volume and learned about the tools used to measure weight, length, and volume.

1. Focus Skill **MAIN IDEA AND DETAILS** Draw and complete a graphic organizer to summarize the main idea and list details that support it.

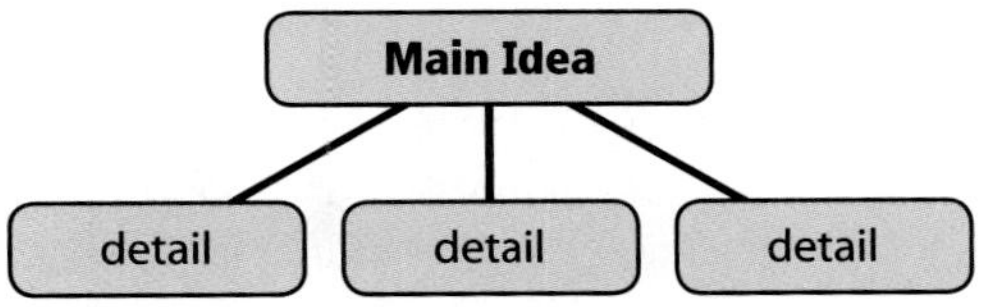

2. SUMMARIZE Write two sentences that tell what this lesson is mostly about.

3. DRAW CONCLUSIONS How would scientific experiments be different if scientists had no tools to use?

4. VOCABULARY Write a fill-in-the-blank sentence for each vocabulary word. Trade sentences with a partner.

Test Prep

5. CRITICAL THINKING How can you decide which tool to use in a certain experiment?

6. Which tool would help you measure how different colors absorb the energy in sunlight?

A. beaker
B. meterstick
C. pan balance
D. thermometer

Make Connections

Writing

Persuasive Writing

You are a scientist, but you can afford only two of the tools described in this lesson. Choose two tools, and write a persuasive **paragraph** about why they are the most important.

Math

Solve a Problem

You are using a measuring wheel to determine the width of a street. A rotation of the wheel is one meter (3.3 ft). The wheel rotates $9\frac{1}{2}$ times. About how wide is the street?

Art

Looking Closer

Draw an object as you would see it with your eyes. Then draw the same object as you think it would look under a hand lens. Now draw it as it looks under the highest-power microscope lens.

LESSON 2

Essential Question

What Are Inquiry Skills?

Investigate model buildings.

Read and Learn about different inquiry skills.

Fast Fact

Windows in the Roof
The clear, curving roof of Telstra Stadium in Sydney, Australia, lets in light but keeps out rain. Engineers built and tested many models before the final stadium was built. In the Investigate, you'll make a model building.

Telstra Stadium

Vocabulary Preview

observation [ahb•zuhr•VAY•shuhn] Information that you gather with your senses (p. 18)

inference [IN•fer•uhns] An untested interpretation of observations (p. 18)

hypothesis [hy•PAHTH•uh•sis] A scientific explanation that can be tested (p. 21)

experiment [ek•SPER•uh•muhnt] A controlled test of a hypothesis (p. 21)

Build a Straw Model

Guided Inquiry

Start with Questions

You use investigation skills every day. You observe the world around you. You predict what will happen. You compare objects and ideas. You also build models.

- What is a model?
- How can using models help you answer questions about science?

Investigate to find out. Then read to learn more.

Prepare to Investigate

Inquiry Skill Tip

A model is an object that looks or acts like the thing you are studying. Every model has limits. It can never be exactly the same as the thing you are studying.

Materials

- 16 plastic straws
- 30 paper clips
- 30-cm piece of masking tape

Make an Observation Chart

Step Number	Ideas and Observations

Follow This Procedure

1. You will work with a group to **construct a model** of a building. First, discuss questions such as these: What should the building look like? What are some ways to use the paper clips and the tape with the straws? What will keep the building from falling down?

2. Have one group member **record** all the ideas. Be sure to **communicate** well and respect each other's suggestions.

3. **Predict** which techniques will work best, and try them out. **Observe** what works, **draw conclusions**, and **record** them.

4. **Plan** how to construct a model building, and then carry out the plan.

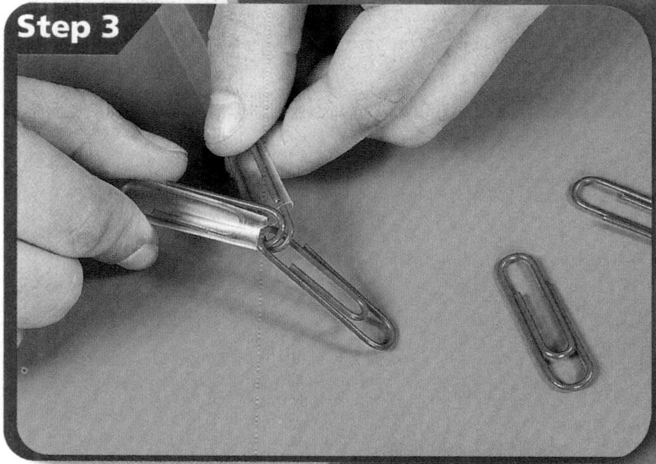

Draw Conclusions

1. Why was it important to share ideas before you began construction?

2. **Inquiry Skill** Scientists and engineers often **use models** to better understand how parts work together. Models help find problems before building. What did you learn about constructing a building by making the model?

Independent Inquiry

Choose one additional material or tool to use in constructing your model. Explain how it will improve your model.

Read and Learn

VOCABULARY
observation p. 18
inference p. 18
hypothesis p. 21
experiment p. 21

SCIENCE CONCEPTS
- how scientists think
- how asking questions helps scientists learn and understand

Focus Skill MAIN IDEA AND DETAILS
Look for inquiry skills scientists use.

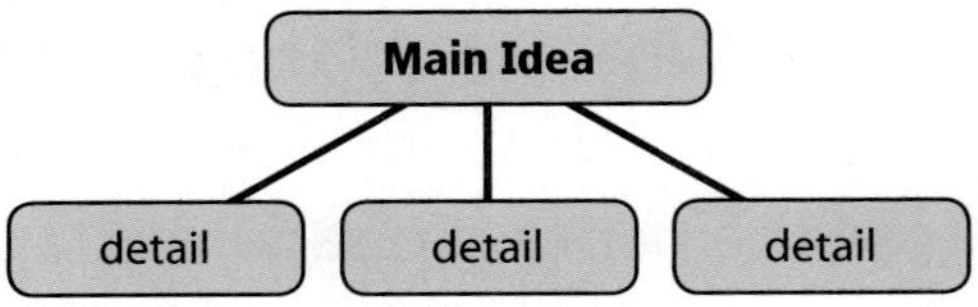

Scientists practice certain ways of thinking, or inquiry skills. You use these skills, too. Keep reading to learn more about inquiry skills.

Observe Did you notice the clouds when you woke up today? If so, you made an observation. An **observation** is information from your senses. You can observe how tall or smooth an object is.

Infer Did you ever try to explain why something is a certain color or why it smells like old socks? You were not observing. You were inferring. An **inference** is an untested conclusion based on your observations.

Scientists might observe that one star looks brighter than others. They could infer that the brighter star is bigger, hotter, or closer to Earth.

Predict You often use your knowledge to guess what will happen next. You are predicting. You figure out patterns of events. Then you say what will happen next. For example, scientists might observe a series of small earthquakes. Then they use that information to predict a nearby volcano eruption.

Focus Skill MAIN IDEA AND DETAILS **Why do scientists observe, infer, and predict?**

◀ **You use inquiry skills to infer when a flower's buds will open. You might even predict what color the flowers will be.**

▲ **How are these plants different and the same? What words and numbers can be used to describe them?**

Compare Scientists—and you—often compare things. You describe how the things are different and the same. For example, you learn about two rocks by comparing the minerals in them.

Classify/Order Is your music collection sorted in some way, such as by performer or type of music? Then you've classified it. You sorted it based on an observation. Scientists classify, or sort, things, too. For example, they might group rocks by color or texture.

You might also put objects or events in order. You could put planets in order by their size or their distance from the sun. You might put sounds in order by their pitch or their loudness. Putting things in order helps you see patterns.

Use Numbers Where would scientists be without numbers? They use exact numbers to show the mass of a seed. They use estimates to show the mass of a planet. Scientists—and you—use numbers to experiment and learn.

Focus Skill MAIN IDEA AND DETAILS

Name a way you use each skill on this page in your daily life.

Use Time and Space Relationships How do the orbits of planets relate to one another? What are the steps in the water cycle? How does a pulley work? To answer these questions, you need to understand time and space relationships. Scientists—and you—need to understand how objects and events affect each other. You also need to know the order in which events happen.

Measure You often need to measure the results of your experiments. How tall did each plant grow? How far did the block slide on sandpaper and on waxed paper? Measuring allows you to compare your results to those of others anywhere. Scientists use the International System (SI) of measurements. It is also called the *metric system.*

Formulate or Use Models Have you ever used a little ball and a big ball to show Earth orbiting the sun? Have you ever drawn the parts of a cell? You were making models. Models help you understand how something works. For example, a globe is a model of Earth.

Scientists often formulate, or make, models. Models help them understand things that are too big, small, fast, slow, or dangerous to observe in person.

Focus Skill MAIN IDEA AND DETAILS

How would you use these three skills to make a diorama of an ecosystem?

▼ **These students are measuring how fast loaded and unloaded toys move. Which variables are they controlling? Which variable changes?**

◀ **What is a possible hypothesis for an investigation using these materials?**

Plan and Conduct a Simple Investigation Your CD player will not work. You think of several possible causes, such as dead batteries. Then you plan and conduct a simple investigation. In this case, that means changing the batteries to see if that solves the problem. If it does not work, you can plan and conduct another simple investigation to find and fix the problem. Scientists also use this approach.

Hypothesize Suppose you have a more complex problem. Your class is making sandwiches to sell at a school fair. You must decide how to keep the sandwiches fresh.

A **hypothesis** is a statement of what you think will happen and why. You hypothesize that small, resealable bags work best because they keep air out. Next, you test your hypothesis.

You set up an **experiment** to test your hypothesis. You put different sandwiches in different wrappings. A day later, the meat and cheese sandwich in the resealable bag is freshest. However, maybe it was the cheese, and not the bag, that kept the sandwich fresh. You can't be sure! You might need to repeat your experiment to test your results.

Focus Skill MAIN IDEA AND DETAILS

Why would using a model be useful?

Insta-Lab

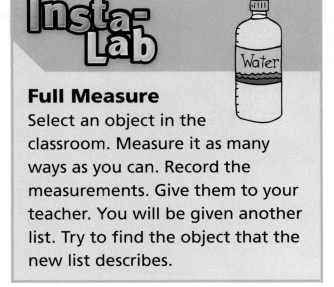

Full Measure

Select an object in the classroom. Measure it as many ways as you can. Record the measurements. Give them to your teacher. You will be given another list. Try to find the object that the new list describes.

Identify and Control Variables To make a fair test, you must identify the variables. Variables are the things that can change in an experiment. Then you need to control, or keep the same, all the variables except the one you are changing for your experiment. So, only the kind of sandwich wrapping should change.

Draw Conclusions After you have conducted your experiment, you need to decide what the results mean. This is called drawing conclusions. Look at all the information you gathered. What do your results tell you?

If the results do not support your hypothesis, you might need to come up with a different hypothesis. If the results do support your hypothesis, your conclusions will show how the results prove you right.

For the sandwich experiment, suppose the results support your hypothesis. You can draw a conclusion based on the data you collected. Small, resealable bags do keep sandwiches fresher than other wrappings. You are ready for the school fair!

▼ **These students are using words, objects, and pictures to communicate. They are sharing how they conducted their toy experiment and what conclusions they drew.**

Gather/Record/Interpret/ Display Data In this experiment, you gathered data by checking the freshness of each sandwich. You recorded the results for each wrapping so you would not mix them up. Then you interpreted the data by drawing a conclusion.

If this investigation were for a science class, you would display the results. You might organize the results into a graph, table, or map.

Graphs can help people understand your data. Line graphs, circle graphs, and bar graphs all display information in different ways. Line graphs are good for showing results over time. Circle graphs are good for showing percentages of a whole. Bar graphs help compare amounts of something.

Focus Skill MAIN IDEA AND DETAILS **Why is it important to control variables?**

These graphs display the same information.

Animal Groups Observed at the Park	
Animal Group	Number Observed
Mammals	7
Insects	63
Birds	22
Reptiles	5
Amphibians	3

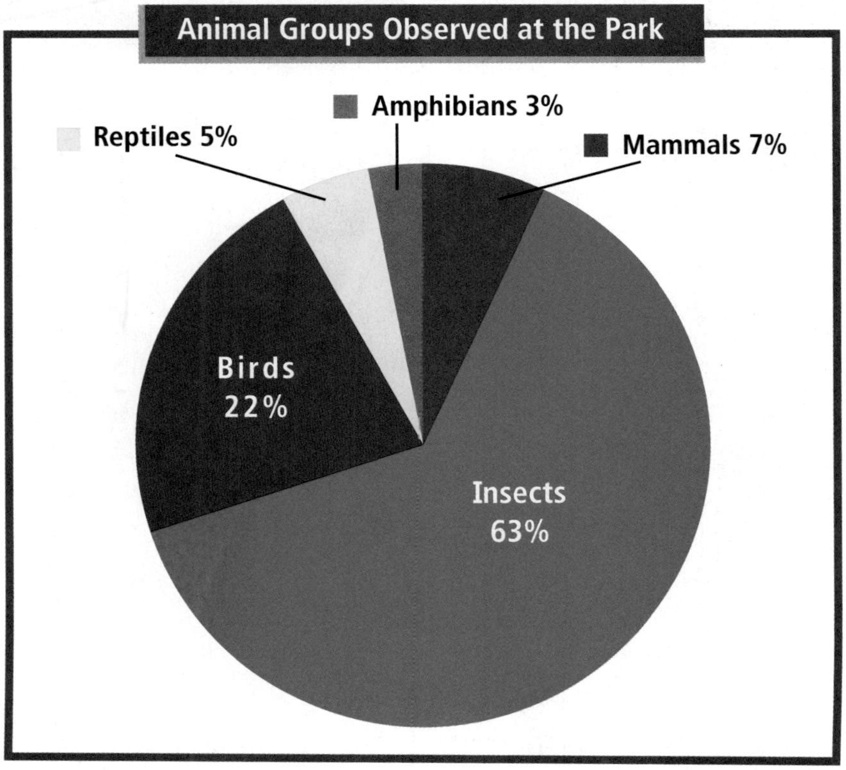

Communicate You would probably tell your friends which sandwich wrapping works best. If this experiment were for a science fair, you would use other tools to share information—writing, pictures, and graphs. You might even display some sandwiches. They would help communicate how well each kind of wrapping worked.

If your friends were far away, you might use the email program on your computer to share your results. You can attach charts you have made or send the results of your experiments.

Computers are useful tools for sharing information. You can use them to create graphics or reports.

Focus Skill MAIN IDEA AND DETAILS

Why is communication an important skill?

▼ **This girl is writing an email to communicate information.**

Essential Question

What are investigation skills?

In this lesson, you learned about important skills scientists use to explain the world around them. These skills include observing, inferring, predicting, measuring, and estimating. Scientists use these skills and others when they experiment to test a hypothesis.

1. Focus Skill MAIN IDEA AND DETAILS Draw and complete a graphic organizer to summarize the main idea and details that support it.

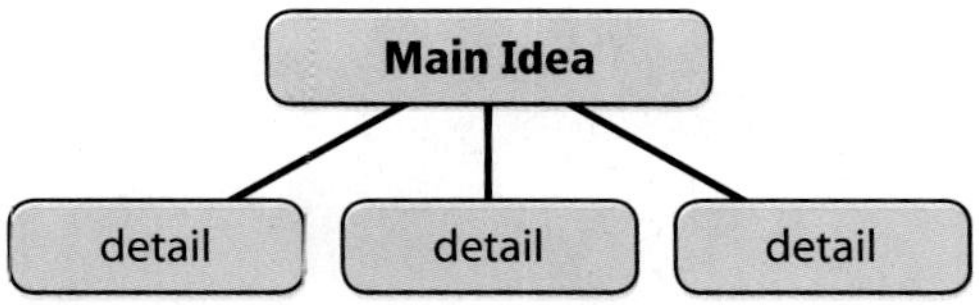

2. **SUMMARIZE** Write a sentence that tells the most important information in this lesson.

3. **DRAW CONCLUSIONS** You cannot understand a friend's science project. What inquiry skill or skills does your friend need to strengthen?

4. **VOCABULARY** Create a word puzzle with the vocabulary words.

Test Prep

5. **CRITICAL THINKING** Which skills could help you find out what kind of muscle tissue is on a microscope slide?

6. Which inquiry skill helps you notice a change?
   A. communicate
   B. hypothesize
   C. observe
   D. predict

Make Connections

Writing

Narrative Writing

Write a **story** about how you or an imaginary person your age uses several inquiry skills to solve a problem. At the end of the story, name the skills used.

Math

SI Units

Find out more about the International System (SI) of units. What SI units are most like these common units: inches, yards, miles, quarts?

Health

Get Moving

What do you believe is the main reason some people do not like to exercise? Now think of a way to find out whether your reason (hypothesis) is accurate. Write the steps you would take.

LESSON 3

Essential Question

What Is the Scientific Method?

Investigate the strength of your models.

Read and Learn about the scientific method.

Fast Fact

Olympic Wind Tunnels

Wind tunnels help scientists study how drag affects athletes. Smooth airflow means skiers can go faster. In the Investigate, you will study building strength by testing the straw models you made in Lesson 2.

Skier in a wind tunnel

Vocabulary Preview

scientific method
[sy•uhn•TIF•ik METH•uhd] A series of steps that scientists follow to test hypotheses and to find out answers to their science questions (p. 30)

Testing a Straw Model

Guided Inquiry

Start with Questions

You probably have questions about the world around you. For example, you might wonder what causes the weather to change. Scientists ask questions, too.

- How do scientists form their questions?
- How do scientists test their hypotheses?

Investigate to find out. Then read to learn more.

Prepare to Investigate

Inquiry Skill Tip

When you experiment, you test a hypothesis. You answer science questions by using controlled procedures to gather data. You then analyze the data and draw conclusions.

Materials

- paper clips
- straw model from Lesson 2
- paper cups
- pennies

Make a Data Table

Number of Pennies	Result

Follow This Procedure

1. Bend paper clips to make a handle for a paper cup, as shown.
2. With your group, **predict** how many pennies your straw model can support. Then hang the cup on your model and add one penny at a time. Was your prediction accurate?
3. Now work together to think of ways to strengthen your model. You might also look for other places on your model to hang the cup. **Record** your ideas.
4. **Form a hypothesis** about what will make the model stronger. Then **experiment** to see if the results support the hypothesis.
5. Discuss what made your straw model stronger, and **draw conclusions**.
6. **Communicate** your findings to the class.

Draw Conclusions

1. Were you able to increase the strength of your model? How?
2. **Inquiry Skill** Scientists **experiment** to test their hypotheses. What did you learn from your experiments in this activity?

Step 1

Step 2

Independent Inquiry

Will your model support more pennies if their weight is spread across the structure? Plan and conduct an experiment to find out.

Read and Learn

VOCABULARY
scientific method p. 30

SCIENCE CONCEPTS
- how to explain the steps in the scientific method
- how the scientific method helps scientists gain knowledge

Focus Skill MAIN IDEA AND DETAILS
Look for the steps in the scientific method.

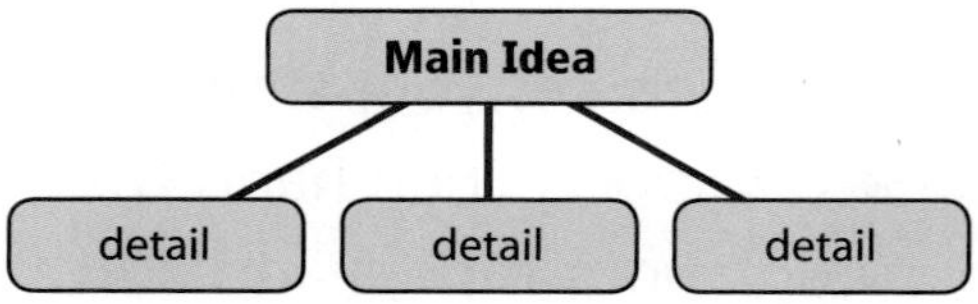

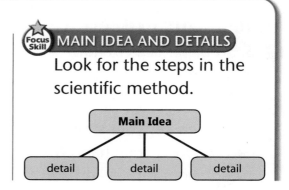

Using the Scientific Method

The **scientific method** is a way that scientists find out how things work and affect each other. The five steps of this method help test ideas. You learned the terms used in this method in Lesson 2. Now you will see how scientists—and you—can put these terms to work.

1 Observe and Ask Questions

After observing the straw models your class built, you might ask:

- Is a cube stronger than a triangle?
- Are straws more likely to bend if they are placed at an angle?
- Is a shorter straw stronger?
- Why do buildings use triangles?

Once you have a list of questions, you should pick one. Each question needs to be answered by a different experiment.

▼ **You can find triangle shapes in bridges and other structures. Why is that?**

2 Form a Hypothesis

Maybe you wonder whether a pyramid or a cube is stronger. Now form a hypothesis. A hypothesis is a statement that tells what will happen and why. It is not a guess. Your hypothesis is a possible answer to the question you thought of earlier.

Your hypothesis needs to make sense and be reasonable. A hypothesis must also be testable. Otherwise your experiment will not determine if your hypothesis is correct.

Here is a possible hypothesis: *Pyramids hold more weight than cubes because triangles are stronger than squares.*

This hypothesis makes sense and is reasonable. Triangles might be stronger than squares. This hypothesis is also testable. You can use your models to determine which shape is stronger.

Once you have written your hypothesis, write it down somewhere. You need to keep a record of it so that when your experiment is over you can go back and see if it was correct!

Focus Skill **MAIN IDEA AND DETAILS**

What is the scientific method?

You can use the scientific method to determine which of these structures is stronger.

❸ Plan an Experiment

How can you test your hypothesis? You think of a plan and then write it as steps. These steps are called your procedure. For example, you might hang a cup on each model, and then add one penny at a time to each cup.

Next, you need to think about all the variables. Make sure that you are changing only one each time you do the experiment. Remember, if you change more than one variable, you might not be able to tell what is causing your results. Your experiment would then need to be redesigned and redone!

In this experiment, both models are made of straws. Both are made the same way. The cups will be the same. The number of pennies added will be the same. Only one variable will be tested—the shape of the structures.

The complete plan should list all the materials. If you have everything you need on hand, it will be easier to conduct your experiment. After that, your plan should list what to do in order.

These students have planned an experiment. They have gathered the materials they will need to conduct their experiment.

These students are carrying out their planned experiment.

4 Conduct an Experiment

Now it's time to conduct, or carry out, your experiment. Make sure you have gathered all the materials listed in your plan so you have what you need.

Next, you follow the steps in the correct order. If you do not follow the steps, your results might not be accurate. Then you would have to do your experiment again!

At each step, record everything you observe. Do not try to just remember what happened. It is much easier to write things down so that you can check the data later. Keeping accurate records is important!

It is especially important to write down any results you did not expect. These results can tell you that your hypothesis is incorrect or that you have missed a step of your procedure.

Once you have finished your experiment, organize your records. This might mean rewriting some of them or putting them all in a notebook.

Focus Skill **MAIN IDEA AND DETAILS**

How do you plan an experiment?

Insta-Lab

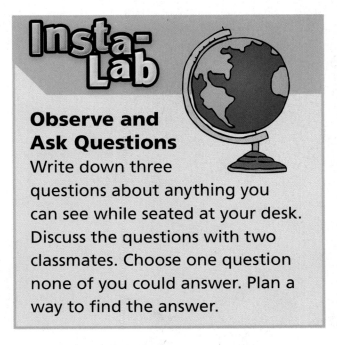

Observe and Ask Questions

Write down three questions about anything you can see while seated at your desk. Discuss the questions with two classmates. Choose one question none of you could answer. Plan a way to find the answer.

5 Draw Conclusions and Communicate Results

The final step is drawing conclusions. You look at the hypothesis again. Then you look at the observations you recorded. Do the results support your hypothesis? Was the pyramid able to support more pennies than the cube?

In this experiment, you could give the results in numbers. Other times, you might describe the results in other ways. For example, you might explain that a liquid turned blue or a plant wilted.

Scientists share the results of their investigations. That allows others to double-check the results. Then scientists can build new ideas on knowledge they are sure is reliable.

You can share your findings in a written or oral report. Charts, graphs, and diagrams help explain your results and conclusions. A written procedure allows others to repeat what you did.

Focus Skill MAIN IDEA AND DETAILS

Why should a report on an investigation be clear and detailed?

▼ Your report should describe your hypothesis, the steps you carried out, the results, and your conclusions. Another person should be able to read your report, repeat your investigation, and get similar results.

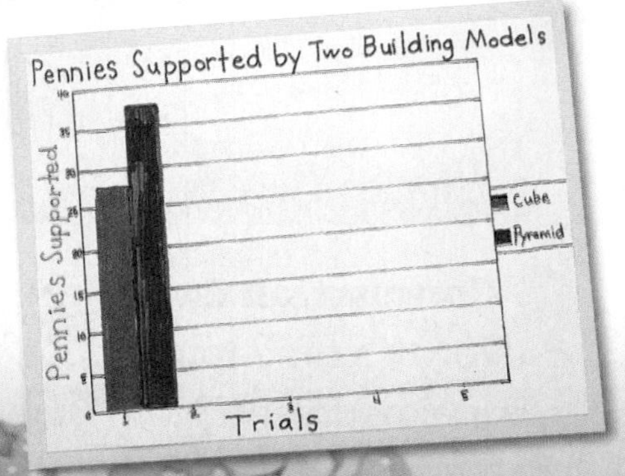

Lesson Review

Essential Question

What is the scientific method?

In this lesson, you learned that the scientific method is a way that scientists find answers to their questions. The five steps of the scientific method help scientists find the correct answers. Repeated trials help show that results are reliable.

1. **Focus Skill MAIN IDEA AND DETAILS** Draw and complete a graphic organizer to summarize the main idea and the details that support it.

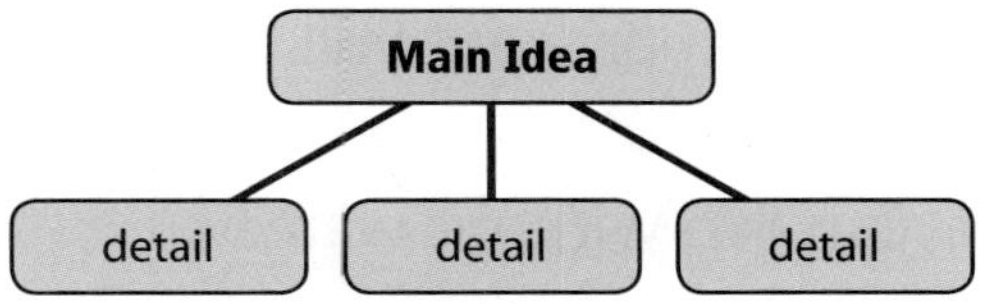

2. **SUMMARIZE** Write a summary of this lesson, beginning with this sentence: *The scientific method helps us gain new knowledge.*

3. **DRAW CONCLUSIONS** Will the scientific method be different 100 years from now? Why or why not?

4. **VOCABULARY** Write a fill-in-the-blank sentence for the vocabulary term.

Test Prep

5. **CRITICAL THINKING** Name a problem in a young person's life that could be solved using the scientific method.

6. When you use the scientific method, what are you testing?
   A. conclusions
   B. experiment
   C. hypothesis
   D. observations

Make Connections

Writing

Expository Writing

Choose an investigation you conducted or observed. Write a **report** on it. Describe how each step of the scientific method was completed—or how it should have been.

Math

Solve a Problem

A penny weighs 2.8 grams (0.1 oz). Let's say a pyramid supports 10 pennies, and a cube supports 6. How much more weight will the pyramid support than the cube?

Social Studies

Super Scientists

Choose a scientist who interests you, and research his or her life, challenges, and successes. Then make a poster to share interesting facts about this scientist with others.

Review and Test Preparation

GETTING READY FOR SCIENCE

Vocabulary Review

Use the terms below to complete the sentences. The page numbers tell you where to look in the chapter if you need help.

microscope p. 8
spring scale p. 11
inference p. 18
hypothesis p. 21
experiment p. 21
scientific method p. 30

1. Forces are measured by a _______.

2. A _______ is a testable explanation of an observation.

3. When you make an observation and then draw a conclusion, you make an _______.

4. To observe very small details, you might use a _______.

5. Scientists find out how things work and affect each other by using the _______.

6. A scientific test in which variables are carefully controlled is an _______.

Check Understanding

Write the letter of the best choice.

7. Which tool measures distance?
A. forceps
B. graduate
C. meterstick
D. microscope

8. Which of these is a hypothesis?
F. I wonder how long a cactus can live without water here on a sunny windowsill.
G. How long can a desert cactus live without water on a sunny windowsill?
H. This experiment will test how long a desert cactus can live without water on a sunny windowsill.
J. A cactus will live without water for a month on a sunny windowsill, since it can live in a desert.

9. Focus Skill **MAIN IDEA AND DETAILS** What is the main purpose of the scientific method?
A. to ask questions
B. to share information
C. to test ideas
D. to plan an experiment

10. In the scientific method, which of these do you do first?
F. draw conclusions
G. ask questions
H. communicate
J. hypothesize

11. Which of these is an observation?
A. The plant needs more water.
B. The plant wilted on the third day.
C. The plant will need water daily.
D. The plant will not live in a desert.

12. Which prediction for recycling in 2010 is based on the graph?

F. The rate will increase a little.
G. The rate will decrease a little.
H. The rate will level off.
J. The rate will decrease a lot.

13. Which tool measures volume?
A. hand lens
B. measuring cup
C. scale
D. ruler

14. Which inquiry skill is based on identifying common features?
F. classify
G. infer
H. predict
J. use numbers

15. Which of these is a possible inference based on seeing a bird eat seeds?
A. The bird ate only the seeds.
B. The bird has a thick beak.
C. The bird doesn't eat meat.
D. The males are quieter.

16. **MAIN IDEA AND DETAILS** Which of these is not an inquiry skill?
F. infer
G. communicate
H. scale
J. classify/order

Inquiry Skills

17. A model is not the real thing, so why do scientists **use a model**?

18. Which tool or tools would you use to **measure** and compare the mass of a cup of fresh water and a cup of salt water?

Critical Thinking

19. A scientist repeats another scientist's experiment but gets different results. What are possible causes?

The Big Idea

20. You want to find out how water temperature affects the movement of goldfish. Write a hypothesis for your investigation. Identify the variables you will control in your experiment and the variable you will change.

Safety in Science

Doing investigations in science can be fun, but you need to be sure you do them safely. Here are some rules to follow.

1. **Think ahead.** Study the steps of the investigation so you know what to expect. If you have any questions, ask your teacher. Be sure you understand any caution statements or safety reminders.
2. **Be neat.** Keep your work area clean. If you have long hair, pull it back so it doesn't get in the way. Roll or push up long sleeves to keep them away from your activity.
3. **Oops!** If you spill or break something, or get cut, tell your teacher right away.
4. **Watch your eyes.** Wear safety goggles anytime you are directed to do so. If you get anything in your eyes, tell your teacher right away.
5. **Yuck!** Never eat or drink anything during a science activity.
6. **Don't get shocked.** Be especially careful if an electric appliance is used. Be sure that electric cords are in a safe place where you can't trip over them. Don't ever pull a plug out of an outlet by pulling on the cord.
7. **Keep it clean.** Always clean up when you have finished. Put everything away and wipe your work area. Wash your hands.
8. **Play it Safe.** Always know where safety equipment, such as fire extinguishers, can be found. Be familiar with how to use the safety equipment around you.

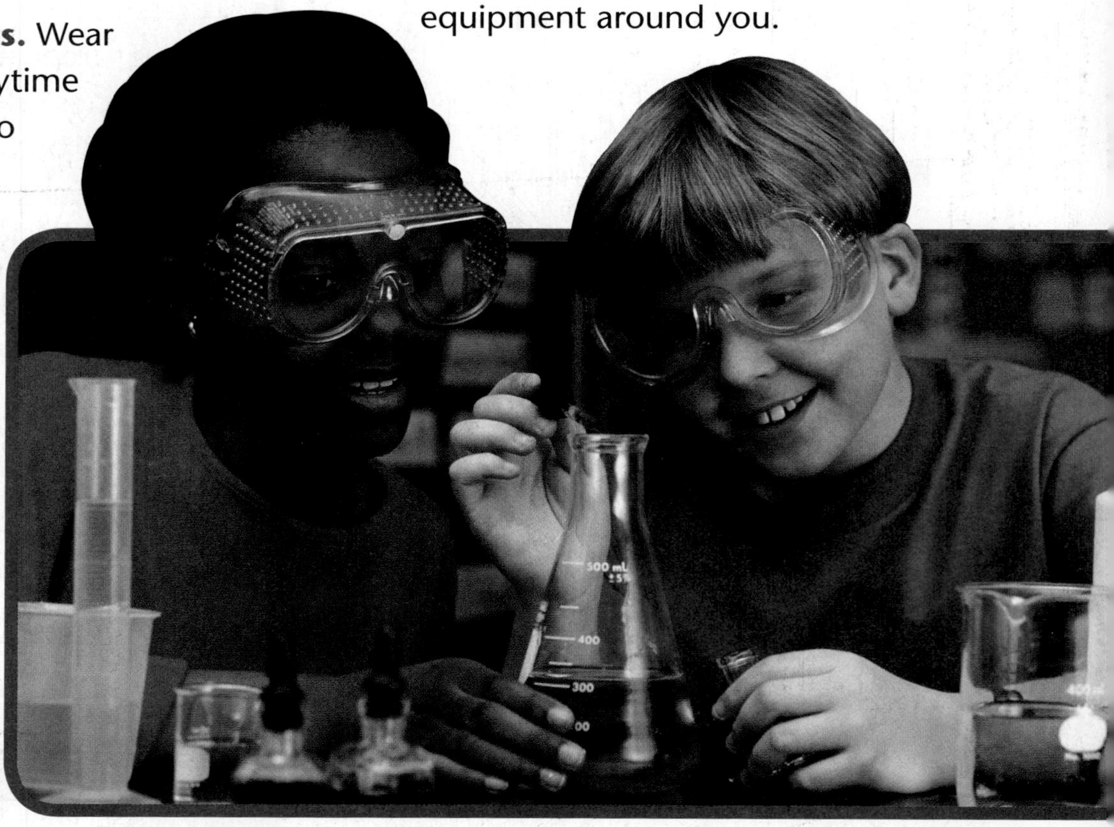

LIFE SCIENCE

Kentucky Standards

SC-04-3.4.1 Students will:
- compare the different structures and functions of plants and animals that contribute to the growth, survival and reproduction of the organisms;
- make inferences about the relationship between structure and function in organisms.

SC-04-3.4.2 Students will understand that things in the environment are classified as living, nonliving and once living. Living things differ from nonliving things. Organisms are classified into groups by using various characteristics (e.g., body coverings, body structures).

SC-04-3.4.3 Students will compare a variety of life cycles of plants and animals in order to classify and make inferences about an organism.

SC-04-3.4.4 Students will identify some characteristics of organisms that are inherited from the parents and others that are learned from interactions with the environment.

SC-04-3.5.1 Students will use representations of fossils to:
- draw conclusions about the nature of the organisms and the basic environments that existed at the time;
- make inferences about the relationships to organisms that are alive today.

SC-04-4.6.1 Students will analyze patterns and make generalizations about the basic relationships of plants and animals in an ecosystem (food chain).

SC-04-4.6.2 Students will:
- analyze data/evidence of the Sun providing light and heat to earth;
- use data/evidence to substantiate the conclusion that the Sun's light and heat are necessary to sustaining life on Earth.

SC-04-4.7.1 Students will make predictions and/or inferences based on patterns of evidence related to the survival and reproductive success of organisms in particular environments.

SC-04-4.7.2 Students will:
- describe human interactions in the environment where they live;
- classify the interactions as beneficial or harmful to the environment using data/evidence to support conclusions.

KENTUCKY

Kentucky Excursions and Projects

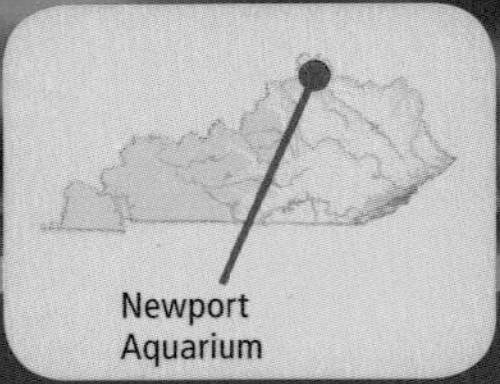

Newport Aquarium

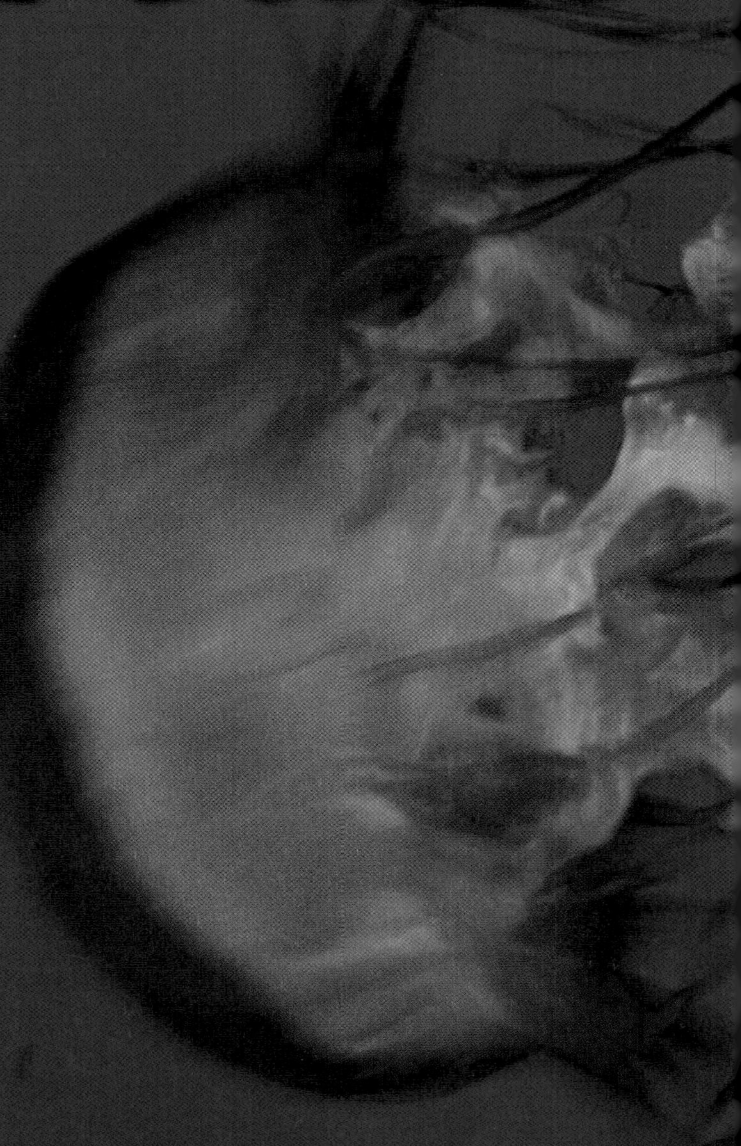

Have you ever wondered what it would be like to see a shark swimming beside you? You can find out at the Newport Aquarium. The aquarium has a communications system that lets you talk to divers as they swim in a tank full of sharks.

The aquarium also has giant octopods, poisonous stonefish, squirmy eels, ancient sea turtles, and much, much more. Visitors can walk through more than 60 meters (200 ft) of clear tunnels to see all kinds of aquatic life. You can watch animals being fed. You can even watch them getting a checkup from a veterinarian.

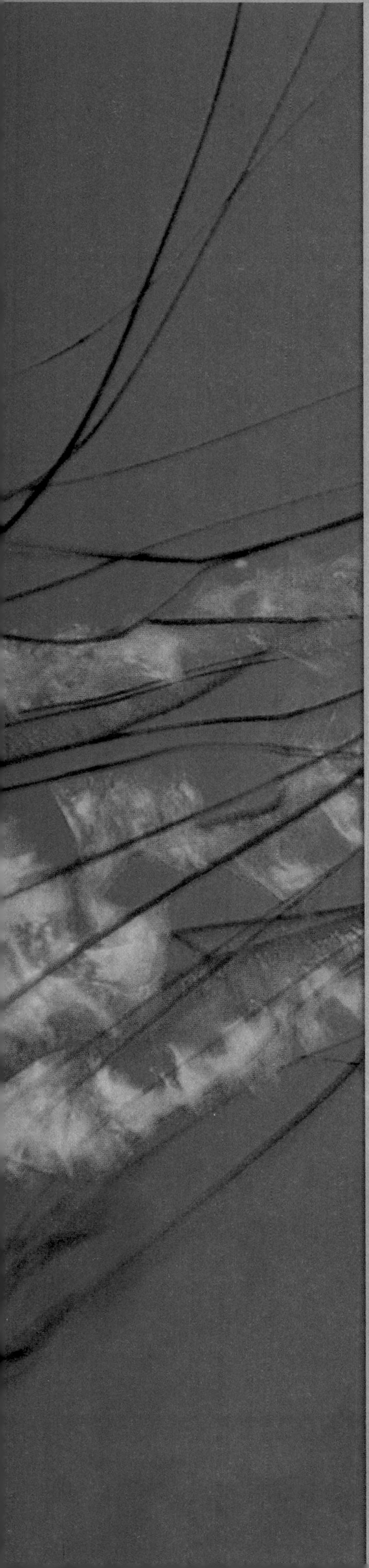

Aquatic Animals

From fins to fangs, the structures of aquatic animals help them survive in their environment. These structures might make it easier to find food, hide from predators, reproduce, or move around. For example, sharks have streamlined bodies that easily glide through water. This shape makes them strong swimmers.

Think and Write

1. **Scientific Inquiry** What would you ask a diver who was swimming with sharks?
2. **Scientific Thinking** Suppose your job is to build a model of a new aquatic animal. The animal will live in very cold water. What body structures might help the animal survive? How could you show those structures in your model?

Procedure

1. Study the photos your teacher gives you of two different aquatic animals.
2. Do research about the animals' life cycles.
3. How are the life cycles of the animals different? How are they the same?
4. Classify the animals by their life cycles.
5. Create a poster to share your findings.

Look out! There's a shark behind you!

Fort Boonesborough State Park

Fort Boonesborough STATE PARK

Many of Kentucky's early settlers came to the area with little more than the clothes on their backs. How did they survive?

Craftspeople at the Fort Boonesborough State Park show visitors exactly how Kentucky's pioneers got by. The craftspeople dress like settlers from the late 1700s. And just like the settlers, they use natural resources to make food, shelter, and other things. The craftspeople interact with visitors, demonstrating pioneer skills such as these:

- skinning animals for fur
- forging nails and axes to build cabins and furniture
- spinning wool for clothes
- dyeing cloth with bark and leaves
- starting a fire with flint
- using lard to make soap and candles
- growing crops
- making pottery from clay

Working Together

Kentucky's early settlers faced many hardships. The danger of attack by hostile groups was always present. Bad weather could spoil harvests. The pioneers thrived by working together to meet their needs. They shared a common fire. Instead of using money, people bartered, or traded, with one another. Even young children helped out by hauling water from nearby springs. People worked to change their environment so they could survive.

This person is starting a fire without matches!

Think and Write

1. **Scientific Thinking** What skills did the pioneers need to survive?
2. **Scientific Thinking** How do you think the pioneers learned these survival skills?

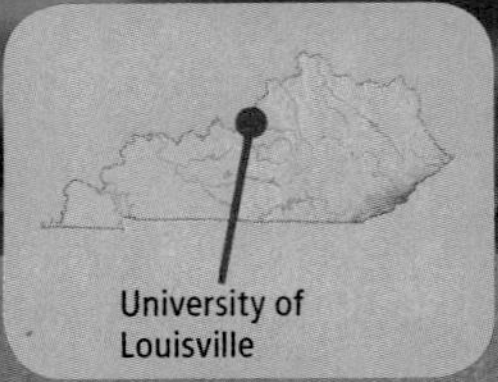

UNIVERSITY OF Louisville

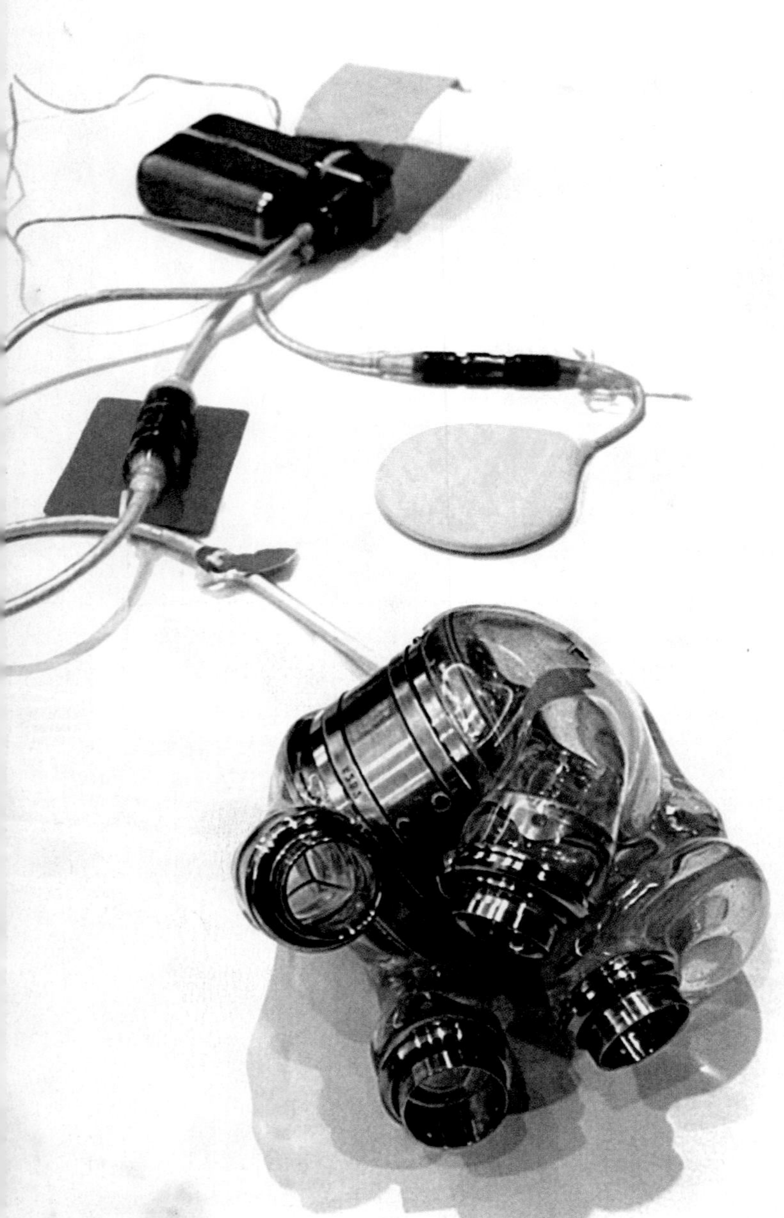

On July 2, 2001, a medical team at the University of Louisville gathered to do what no one had ever done before: put the first completely artificial heart into a patient.

It took seven hours for the 14-member team to do the surgery. They took out the patient's diseased heart. Then they replaced it with a 1-kilogram (2-lb) artificial heart.

The heart has a pump that moves blood throughout the body. It also has two batteries. One battery is located inside the patient's body. It is continually recharged by the second battery, which is worn around the patient's waist. When the second battery needs to be recharged, the system is plugged into an electrical outlet. This can be done at night when the patient is sleeping.

◀ **The artificial heart replaces the natural heart inside the body. But one of the batteries must remain outside of the body for charging.**

Hope for Heart Patients

In the years since that groundbreaking first operation, at least 14 patients have received artificial hearts. In 2006, the U.S. government officially approved the surgery for patients who are too old or too sick to receive natural heart transplants. In time, artificial hearts may save up to 100,000 people each year.

Think and Write

1. **Science and Technology** In your own words, explain how an artificial heart works.
2. **Scientific Thinking** Artificial heart surgery is very dangerous. Why do you think some people are willing to take the risk?

Fourteen medical professionals helped perform the seven-hour surgery that gave the man in the center a new heart.

The artificial heart weighs 1 kilogram (2 lb).

Project Learned and Inherited Behaviors

Materials
- pen or pencil and paper

Behavior	Learned	Inherited

Procedure
1. Make a table like the one shown, and list as many of your own behaviors as you can think of.
2. Think about each behavior. Decide whether you think it is learned or inherited, and make a check in the appropriate column.
3. Compare the number of learned behaviors with the number of behaviors you inherited.

Draw Conclusions
1. Choose one of the behaviors you learned. Communicate to a classmate how you learned that behavior.
2. Scientists often base inferences on their observations. Infer whether most human behaviors are learned or inherited. Explain.

UNIT A
LIFE SCIENCE

The World of Living Things

Unit Inquiry

Lung Capacity

In this unit, you will learn about living things. No two living things are exactly the same. People look different on the outside, but they also have differences inside. One difference inside people's bodies is how much air their lungs can hold. Are everyone's lungs about the same size? Do your lungs get larger as you get taller? Plan and conduct an experiment to find out.

CHAPTER 1

Classifying Living Things

What's the Big Idea?

Living things can be grouped according to their characteristics.

Essential Questions

GO online
Student eBook
www.hspscience.com

What do YOU wonder?

Which Is It? You might think that these sea anemones (uh•NEM•uh•neez) are beautiful flowers, but they are meat-eating animals. What characteristics cause them to be grouped with other animals? What characteristics make them animals? How does this relate to the **Big Idea?**

Sea anemones

LESSON 1

Essential Question

How Are Living Things Classified?

Investigate how models can help you understand cells.

Read and Learn how different living things are grouped according to their characteristics.

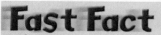

Fast Fact

Cute But Smelly

Don't bother these young skunks! If you do, you'll be covered with an oily liquid whose bad smell will stay with you for a long time. These animals are made up of cells. In the Investigate, you will make a model of a cell.

Young skunks

Vocabulary Preview

organism [AWR•guh•niz•uhm] A living thing (p. 54)

microscopic [my•kruh•SKAHP•ik] Too small to be seen with the eyes alone (p. 55)

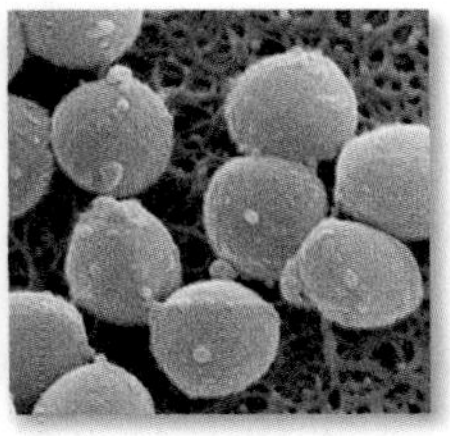

bacteria [bak•TIR•ee•uh] The kingdom of one-celled living things that lack nuclei (p. 59)

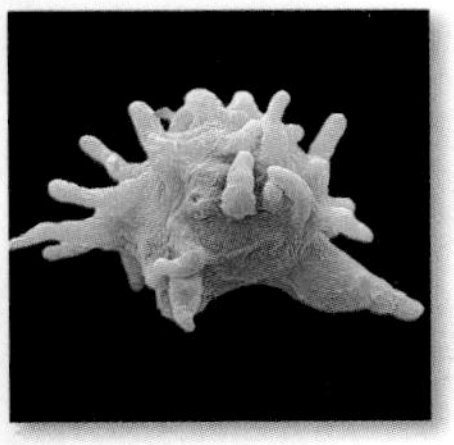

protist [PROHT•ist] One of the kingdoms of living things that can be one-celled (p. 60)

Make a Model Cell

Guided Inquiry

Start with Questions

Models can be used to represent things you can't examine in person. With a model, you can look at dangerous things or small things and draw conclusions about them.

- How could these blocks be used to make a model?
- What other things can be used to make models?

Investigate to find out. Then read and learn to find out more.

Prepare to Investigate

Inquiry Skill Tip

A model can be useful for studying things you would not otherwise get to examine. Remember that a model will not mimic the real thing in every detail.

Materials

- marker
- malted-milk ball
- raisins
- plastic cup
- plastic knife and plastic spoon
- liquid gelatin
- paper plate
- small jelly beans

Make an Observation Chart

Cell Model	Cell Pictures

Follow This Procedure

1. Write your name on a plastic cup. Pour liquid gelatin into the cup until it is two-thirds full. Allow the gelatin to set.
2. Carefully remove the gelatin. Use the plastic knife to slice the set gelatin in half. Place the halves on a paper plate.
3. Use a spoon to make a small hole in the center of one of the gelatin halves. Place the malted-milk ball in the hole.
4. Scatter a few raisins and jelly beans on the gelatin that has the malted-milk ball.
5. Place the plain gelatin half on top of the half that has the candy and raisins.
6. **Compare** your **model** to the pictures of animal cells in this lesson, which show a cell's parts. List your observations in a chart.

Step 3

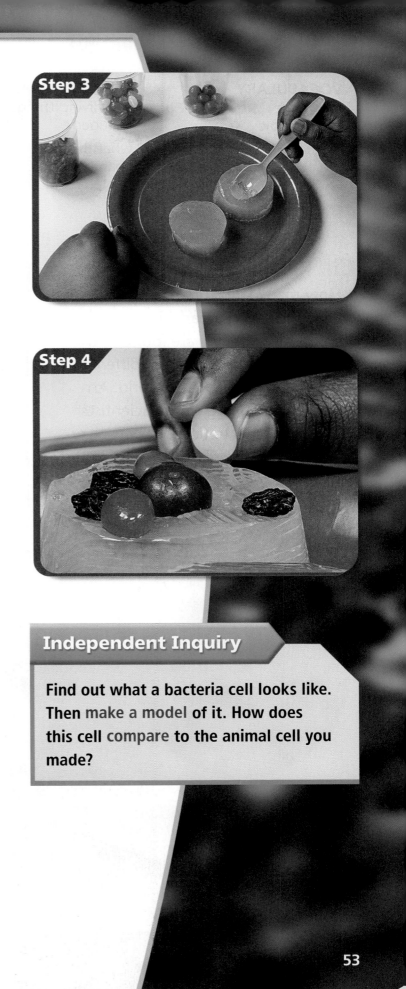

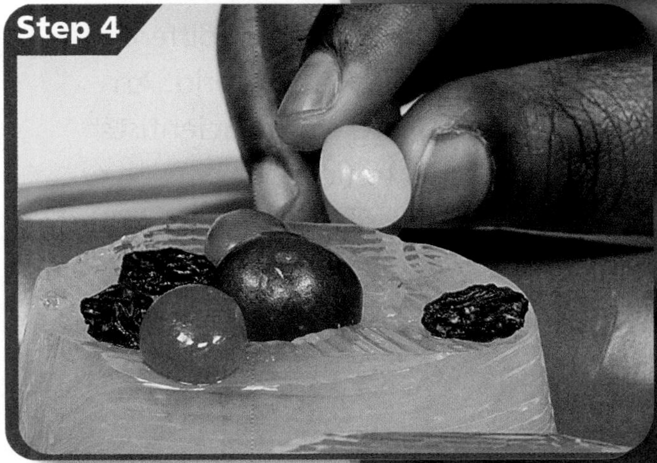

Step 4

Draw Conclusions

1. **Draw conclusions** about what the gelatin, raisins, jelly beans, and malted-milk ball each represent.
2. **Inquiry Skill** Scientists often **use models** to understand complex structures. How does the model help you understand some parts of an animal cell?

Independent Inquiry

Find out what a bacteria cell looks like. Then make a model of it. How does this cell compare to the animal cell you made?

VOCABULARY
organism p. 54
microscopic p. 55
bacteria p. 59
protist p. 60

SCIENCE CONCEPTS
- how living things are grouped
- what the characteristics are of bacteria and protists

Focus Skill MAIN IDEA AND DETAILS
Look for how living things are classified.

Main Idea
detail | detail | detail

Classifying Living Things

How many kinds of animals and plants would you see in a park? How many kinds of living things are found in the ocean? There are millions of different kinds of organisms in the world. An **organism** is a living thing. Scientists study organisms to find out how they live. Scientists classify organisms so they can study them. When you classify, you group things that are alike.

There are many ways to group organisms. Organisms that live in the ocean may be grouped together. You might group living things by how they move. Or you could group organisms that have the same kinds of body parts.

At first, scientists classified organisms by how they got their food. They put all living things into either the animal kingdom or the plant kingdom.

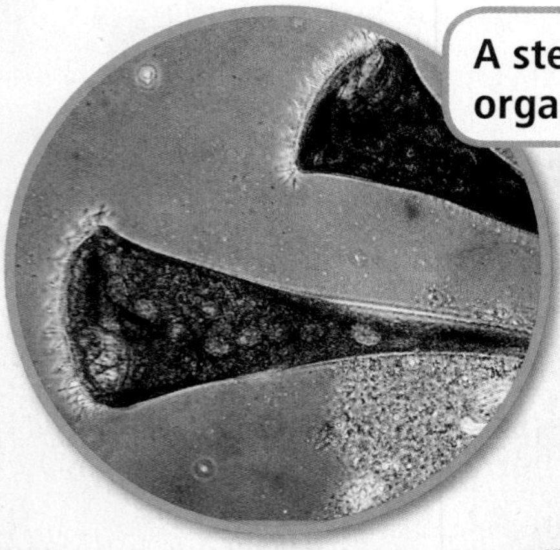
A stentor is a protist, a one-celled organism. It lives in ponds.

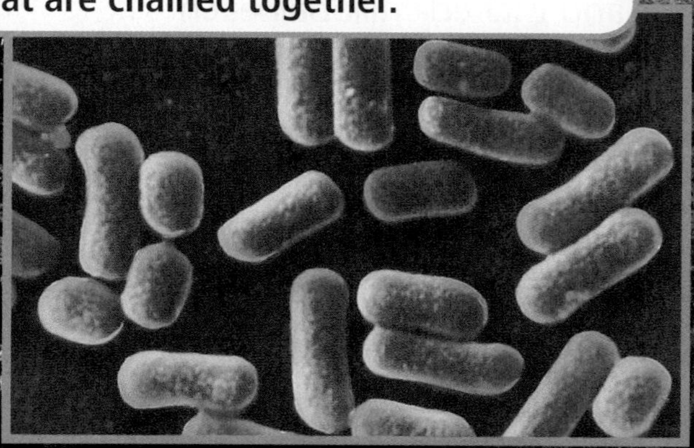
Streptobacillus (strep•tuh•buh•SIL•uhs) bacteria consist of rod-shaped cells that are chained together.

Organisms from every kingdom are found in every habitat.

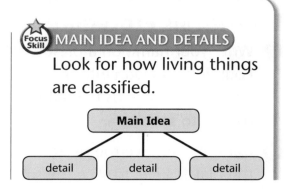

Most animals move to get their food. Plants make their own food, but they cannot move around. This way to classify worked for most living things, but not for all. For example, fungi (FUN•jy) can't move, but they also can't make food. So they became their own kingdom, the fungi kingdom.

When microscopes were invented, scientists found organisms that had never been seen before. Organisms that cannot be seen with the eyes alone are **microscopic**. Most microscopic organisms have one cell. Scientists compared one-celled organisms to animal cells and to plant cells. One-celled organisms were different. These organisms are in the bacteria and protist kingdoms.

Organisms are no longer classified by how they get food or move. Now organisms are also classified by what their cells look like.

Focus Skill **MAIN IDEA AND DETAILS** **Why are plants and fungi in separate kingdoms?**

Tree ferns are a type of plant that has been around for a long time. Ancient ferns could be 15 meters tall.

A chipmunk is in the animal kingdom. It holds food in its cheeks until it can store it in a burrow.

This bracket fungus is part of the fungi kingdom. Some brackets can mass 90 kilograms.

Cells

Every part of you is made of cells. An elephant's body is made of cells, too. Big or small, every organism is made of at least one cell.

Most cells have the same parts that you put in the model you made. All cells have a cell membrane. Materials needed by the cell pass into the cell through the cell membrane. Cells must also get rid of waste products. Waste products also pass through the cell membrane. In the mitochondria, activities are carried out that release energy for the cell. The nucleus controls many functions in the cell. It is surrounded by a nuclear membrane.

Cells make new cells by dividing. All the material in a cell is split between two new cells. Multicelled organisms grow as their cells divide. When the cells of some one-celled organisms divide, they make new organisms.

▼ **This is an animal cell photographed through a microscope. It is greatly magnified.**

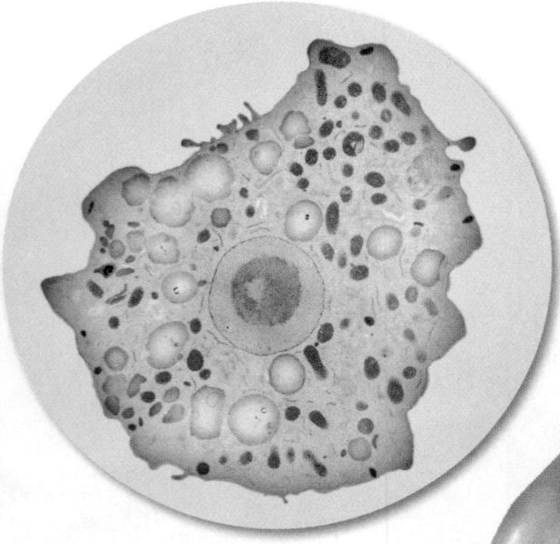

▼ **This diagram shows an animal cell. Almost every cell in an animal has these parts.**

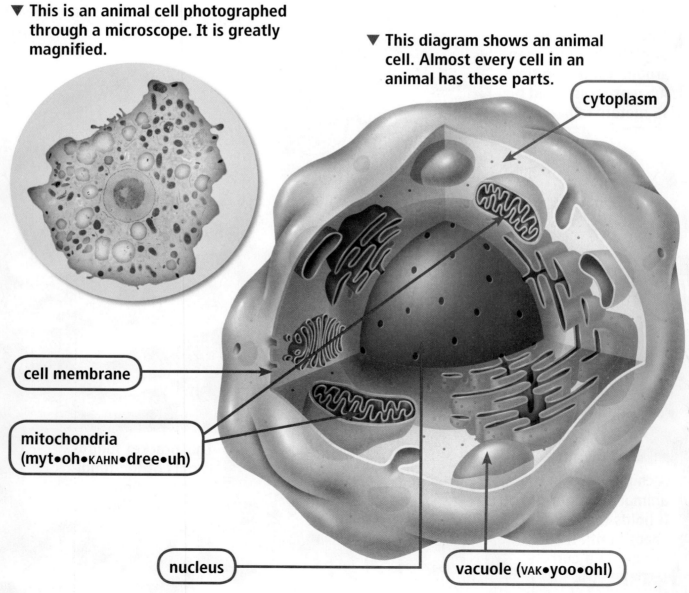

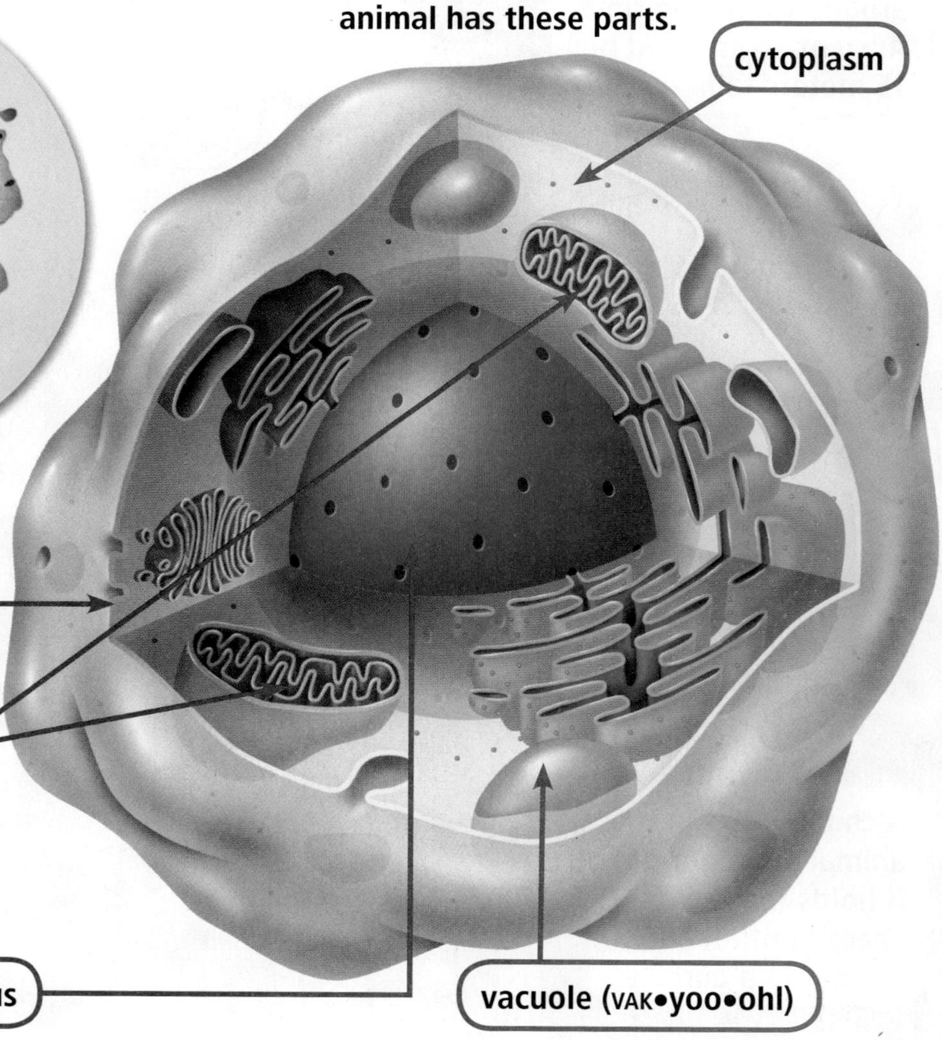

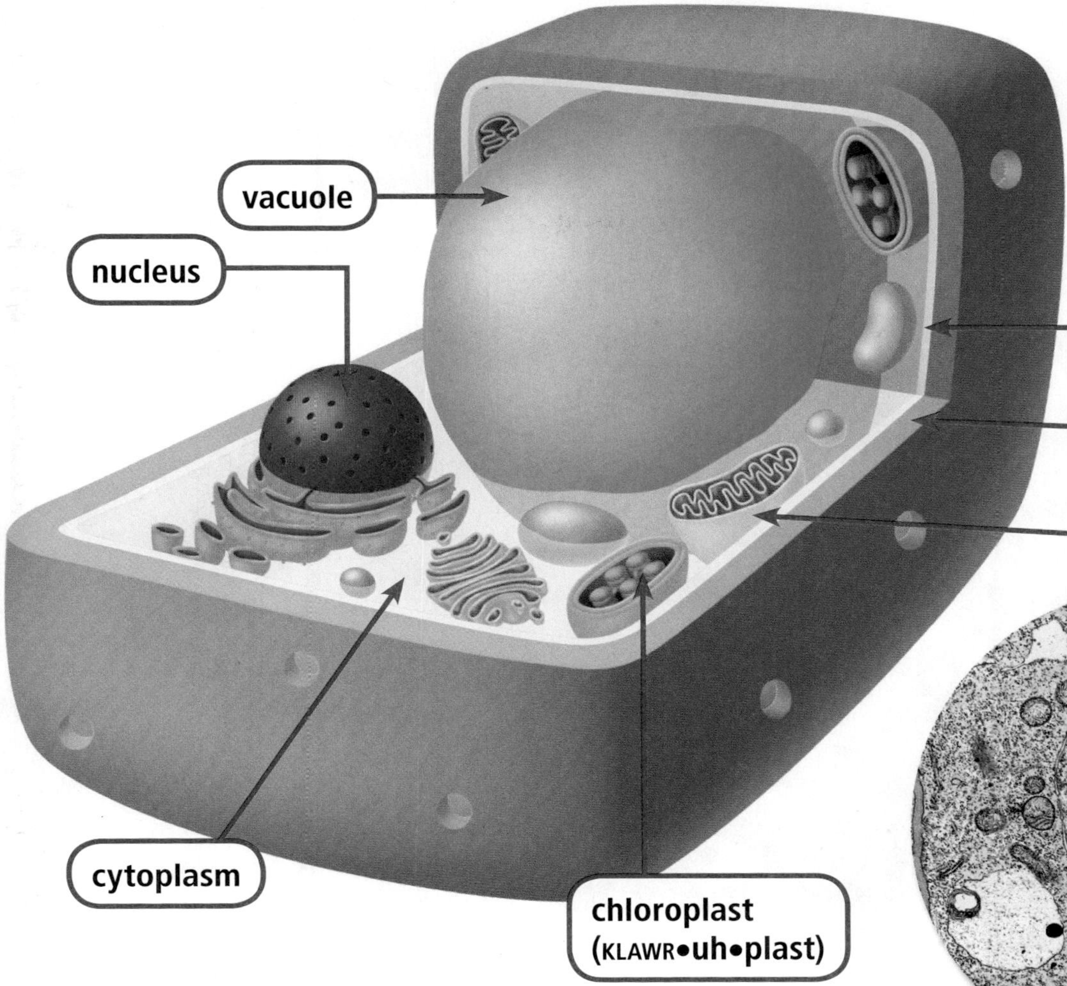

◀ This is a drawing of a plant cell. Notice how plant cells are similar to animal cells.

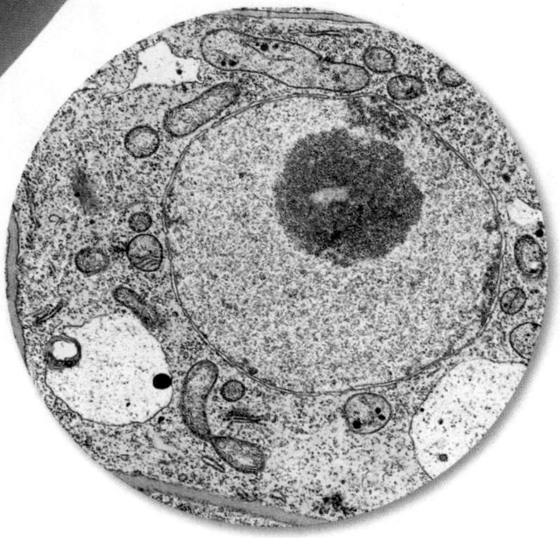

▲ This is a plant cell photographed through a microscope. It is greatly magnified.

Plant cells have all the same parts as animal cells. They take in materials, get rid of wastes, and divide, just as animal cells do. But plant cells differ in some ways. Plant cells are surrounded by a stiff cell wall. Plant cells also have chloroplasts, where food is made. Look at the pictures of plant cells to notice other parts that are different from those of animal cells.

Bacteria cells have cell walls, as do plant cells. But, bacteria cells are different from all other cells because they do not have a nucleus.

Focus Skill **MAIN IDEA AND DETAILS**

How are plant and animal cells alike?

Insta-Lab

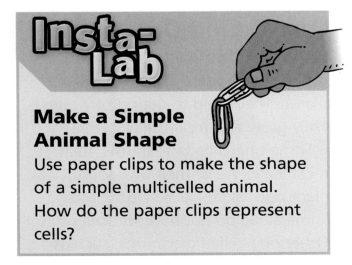

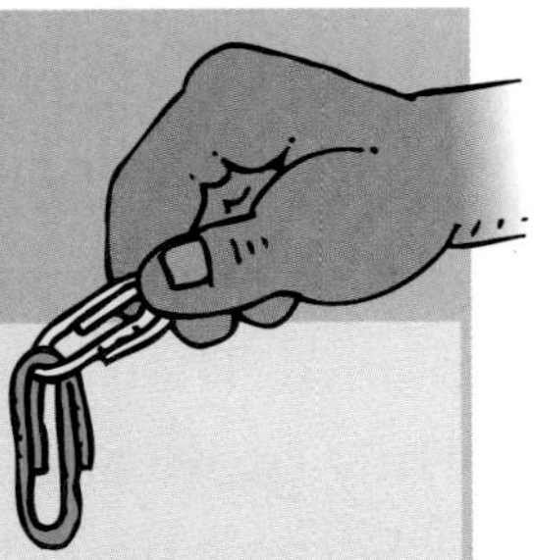

Make a Simple Animal Shape

Use paper clips to make the shape of a simple multicelled animal. How do the paper clips represent cells?

◀ A diatom is an alga with a hard shell made out of silica, or glass.

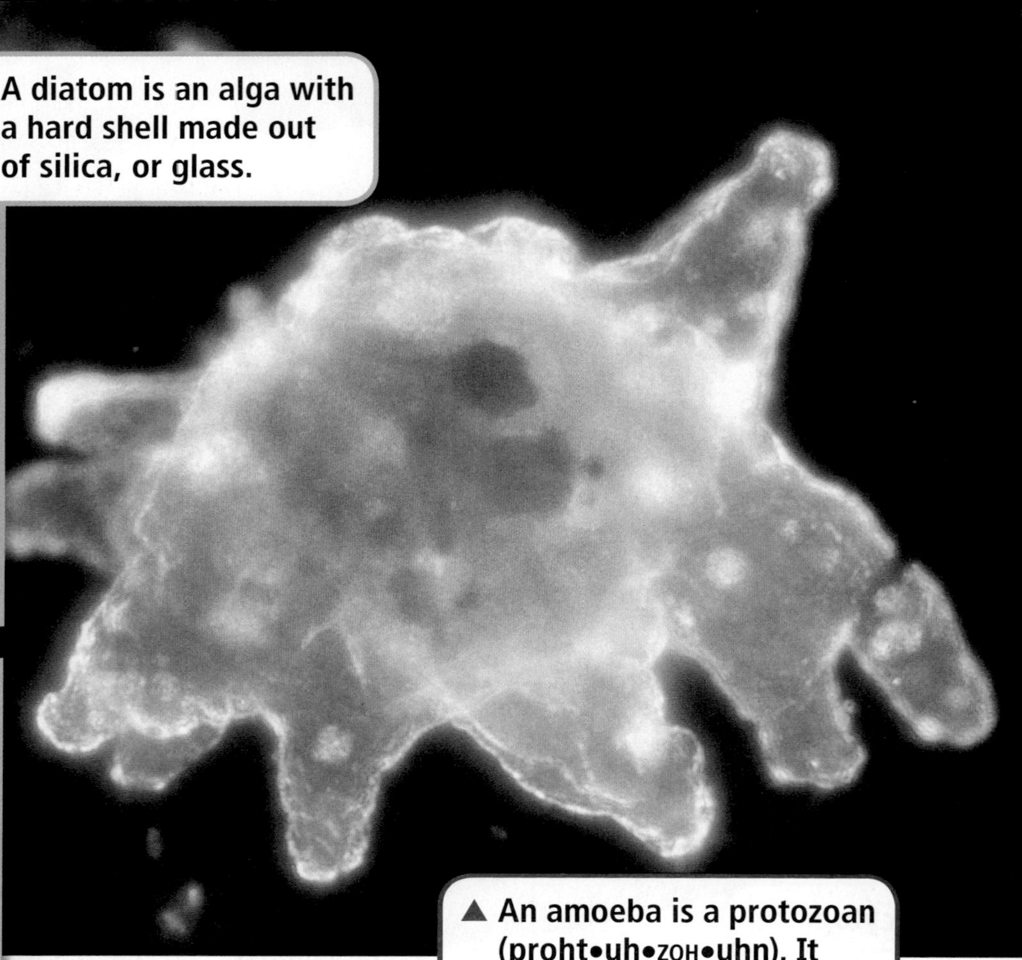

▲ An amoeba is a protozoan (proht•uh•ZOH•uhn). It surrounds its food, then digests it.

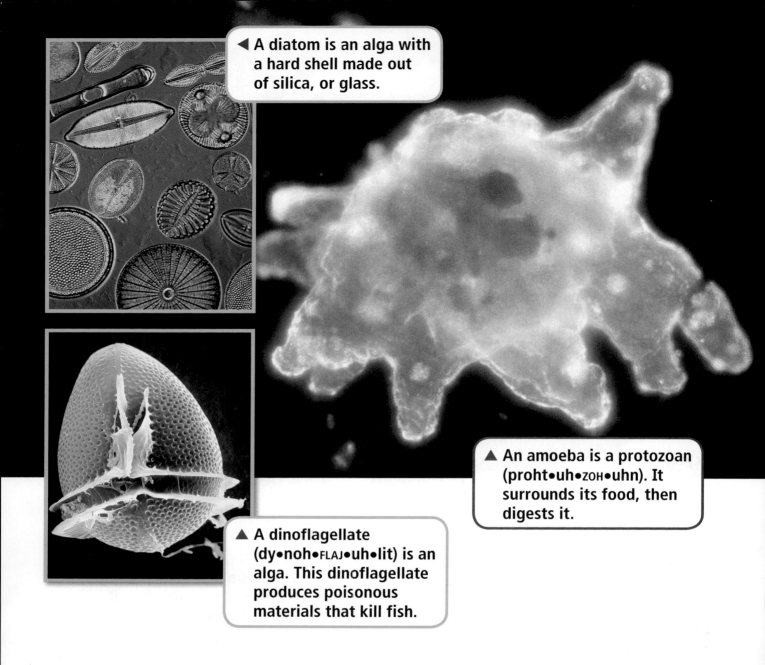

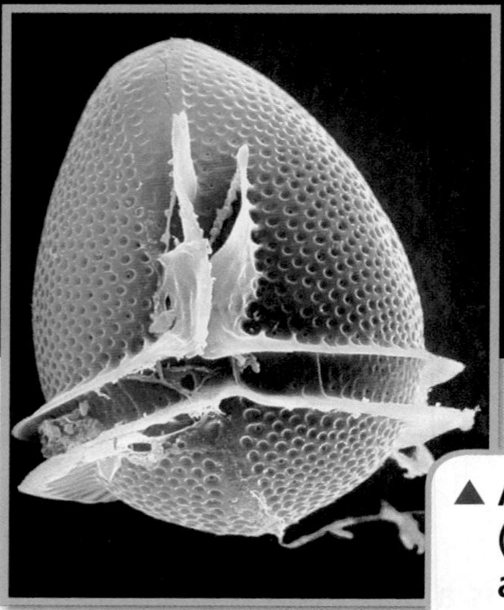

▲ A dinoflagellate (dy•noh•FLAJ•uh•lit) is an alga. This dinoflagellate produces poisonous materials that kill fish.

One-Celled Organisms

One-celled organisms need food, water, and oxygen, as do animals and plants. They need to get rid of wastes. They grow and reproduce.

Some one-celled organisms, such as most algae, make their own food. Like plant cells, algae have chloroplasts. Some algae do not have stiff cell walls. Other one-celled organisms, such as some amoebas, have no cell walls and no chloroplasts.

All one-celled organisms have a cell membrane. Most also have a nucleus that has its own membrane. Bacteria have no nucleus. They have the same material found in a nucleus, but the material is not inside its own membrane.

Focus Skill MAIN IDEA AND DETAILS

What do all one-celled organisms have?

Bacteria

Bacteria are the most numerous organisms on Earth. Billions of them can be found in just one handful of soil. Bacteria are commonly grouped by their shape. Some are rod-shaped. Some are shaped like balls. Others are spiral-shaped. Some bacteria live as individuals. Others cluster together in pairs or chains. Some colonies are large enough to be seen.

Bacteria have been found in $3\frac{1}{2}$-billion-year-old rock. They are probably the oldest living organisms.

Bacteria live in every part of the world. They live in ice at the North Pole and in hot springs. They live at the bottom of the oceans. And they live in your stomach and on your skin, too.

Some bacteria cause disease. When you scrape your knee, bacteria may cause infection. But not all bacteria are bad. Most of them are useful. They help digest food and are used to clean up oil spills.

Focus Skill MAIN IDEA AND DETAILS

How are bacteria commonly grouped?

Cyanobacteria (sy•uh•noh•bak•TIR•ee•uh) live in water and make their own food. They grow in ponds in colonies that are easy to see. ▶

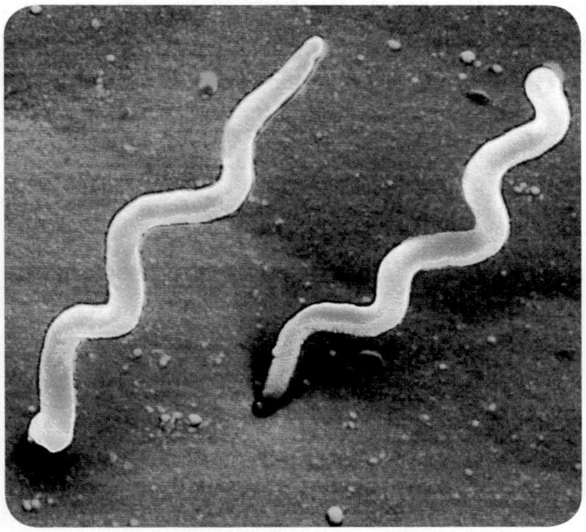

▲ These spirochetes (SPY•roh•keets), or spiral-shaped bacteria, cause Lyme disease.

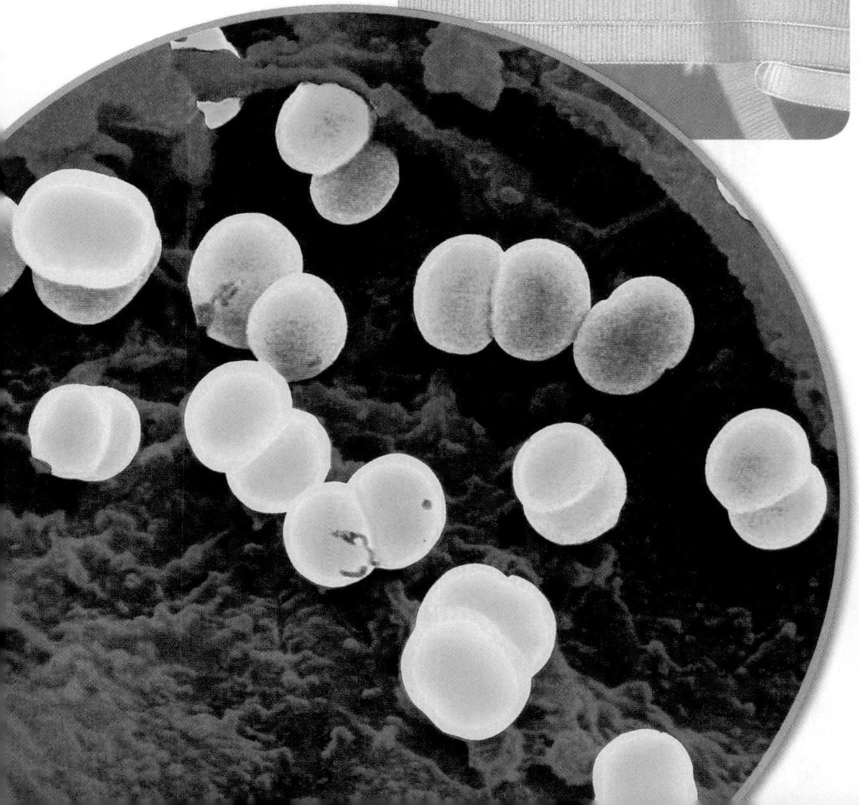

◀ *Diplococci* (dih•ploh•KAHK•sy) are spherical—or ball-shaped—bacteria that grow in pairs.

Protists

There are more than 80,000 kinds of protists. Algae and protozoans (proh•tuh•ZOH•unz) make up the **protists**.

Algae are found in fresh and salt water everywhere in the world. Algae also grow on rocks and trees and in moist soil. Most algae make food and put oxygen into the air. One type of alga that does not make food is the dinoflagellate. Instead, it stuns fish and then eats the fish's fluids.

▼ ***Chlamydomonas*** **(kluh•MID•uh•moh•nuhs) is an alga. It has a cell wall, one chloroplast, and an "eye" that "sees" light.**

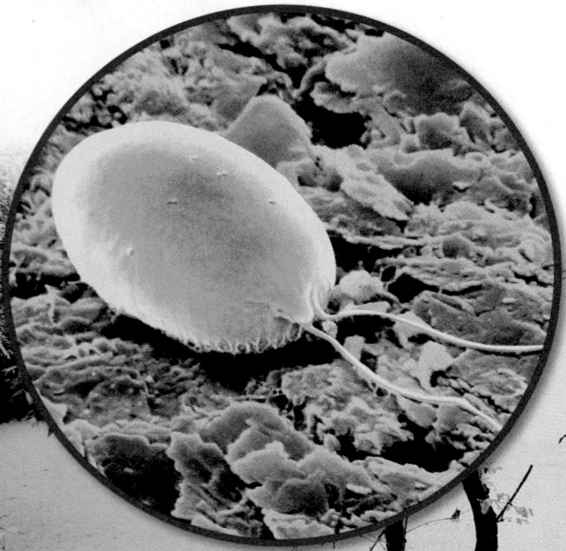

▼ **This *chromatium* (kroh•MAT•ee•uhm) lives in the pools of boiling water in Yellowstone National Park. It takes sulfur from the water for energy.**

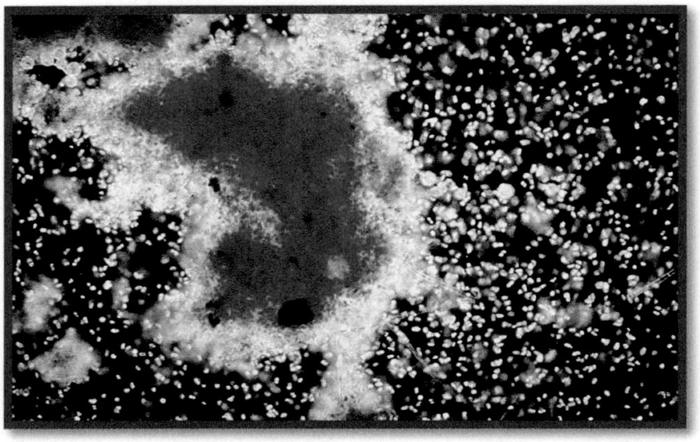

We use the shells of some algae, the diatoms, to make the grit in toothpaste and for the shiny paint used on roads. Diatoms come in all shapes. Some look like leaves, and some look like pinwheels.

Protozoans, like animals, hunt and gather food. They eat other protists and bacteria. The amoeba is a type of protozoan.

Focus Skill MAIN IDEA AND DETAILS

Which two groups make up the protists?

Look at a drop of this pond water through a microscope, and you can see protists moving about.

Essential Question

How Are Living Things Classified?

In this lesson, you learned how living things are classified and about the characteristics of some groups of organisms. You learned the differences between plant cells and animal cells. You also learned the characteristics of two kinds of one-celled organisms—bacteria and protists.

1. Focus Skill MAIN IDEA AND DETAILS Draw and complete a graphic organizer to summarize the main idea and the details that support it.

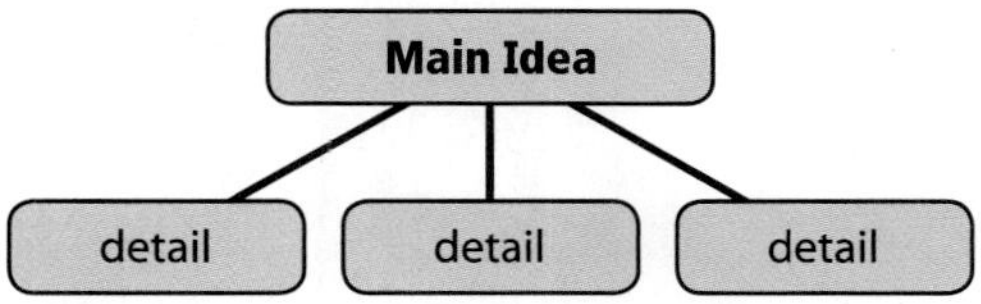

2. **SUMMARIZE** Write a summary of this lesson. Begin with this sentence: *Living things can be grouped according to their characteristics.*

3. **DRAW CONCLUSIONS** What would happen to animals if there were no more plants?

4. **VOCABULARY** Use vocabulary words and other science words to describe a diatom.

Test Prep

5. **CRITICAL THINKING** How might you protect yourself if your friend had an infection caused by bacteria?

6. Which statement is not true?
   A. All cells need food.
   B. Organisms are made of one or more cells.
   C. All cells are alike.
   D. All plant cells have stiff cell walls.

Make Connections

Writing

Write to Describe

Write a **letter** to a biologist to tell her about an organism you found and how you classified it. Explain why you classified the organism the way you did.

Math

Solve a Problem

A protozoan is $\frac{1}{50}$ of an inch long. How long would 25 protozoans in a row be?

Health

Bacteria Facts

Research bacteria to find the names of some bacteria that make people ill. Make a list of the bacteria and the illnesses they cause.

LESSON 2

Essential Question

How Are Plants and Fungi Classified?

Investigate how water moves through plant stems.

Read and Learn how plants and fungi are classified by their characteristics.

Fast Fact

Big and Little

Duckweed is covering this frog. It is the smallest flowering plant in the world. It floats on the water in ponds. The redwood tree is the tallest living plant. How do leaves at the top of a tall tree get water? In the Investigate, you will find out.

Frog in duckweed

Vocabulary Preview

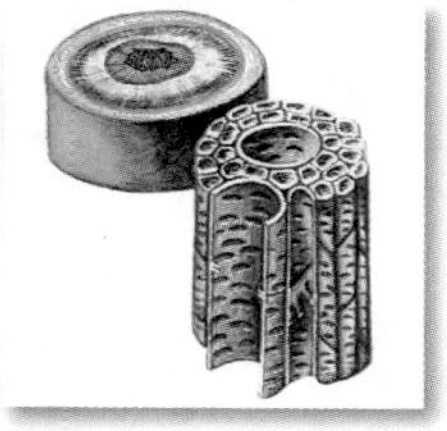

vascular [VAS•kyuh•ler] Having tubes or channels (p. 66)

nonvascular [nahn•VAS•kyuh•ler] Without tubes or channels (p. 68)

fungi [FUHN•jy] Organisms that can't make food and can't move about (p. 70)

Investigate

Plant Stems

Guided Inquiry

Start with Questions

Plants need nutrients and water, just like other living things. Different plants have different methods of getting nutrients and water to the parts that need them.

- These flowers were dyed in a vat. How else might flowers be dyed?
- Why do the petals turn a brighter color than the stem?

Investigate to find out. Then read and learn to find out more.

Prepare to Investigate

Inquiry Skill Tip

When you use space relationships, it is important to record your starting point. Otherwise you will not be able to judge any change that may occur.

Materials

- plastic knife
- paper towel
- two containers
- water
- hand lens
- two clothespins
- white carnation with stem
- blue and red food coloring

Make an Observation Chart

Time (min)	Observations
0	
15	
30	
45	
60	

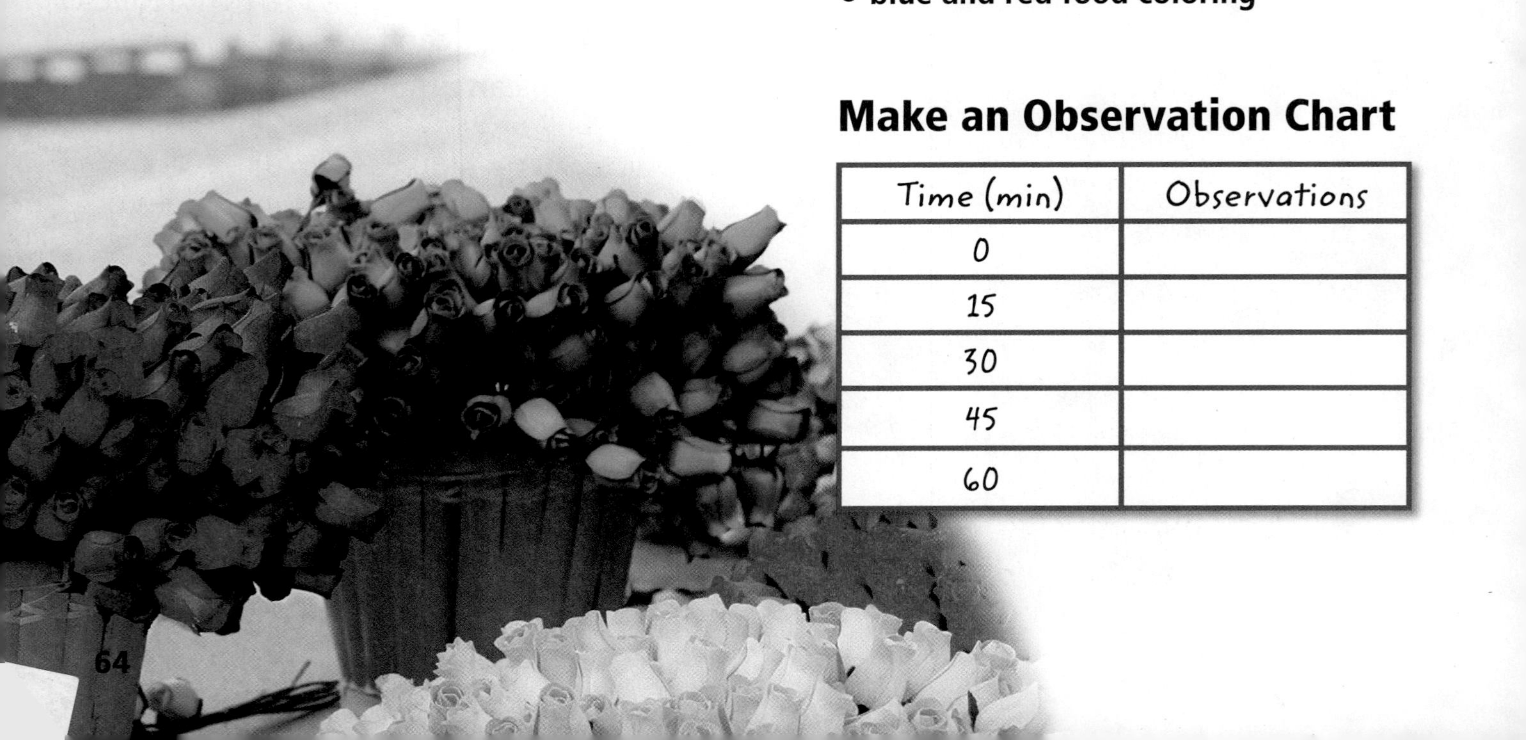

Follow This Procedure

1. Use the plastic knife to trim the end off the carnation stem. Split the stem from the middle to the bottom. Do not cut the stem completely in half.
2. Half-fill each container with water. Add 15 drops of blue food coloring to one container. Add 15 drops of red food coloring to the other container.
3. With the containers side by side, place one part of the stem in each container. Hold the stem parts in place with clothespins.
4. **Observe** the carnation every 15 minutes for an hour. **Record** your observations in a chart like the one here.
5. Put a paper towel on your desk. Cut 2 cm off the bottom of each stem part. Use the hand lens to **observe** the cut ends of the stem.

Draw Conclusions

1. What do you **observe** about the flower? What do you **observe** about the stem?
2. **Inquiry Skill** Scientists can **use space relationships** to better understand what happens in a process. Based on your observations, what can you conclude about the movement of water in a stem?

Independent Inquiry

Use tincture of iodine to test for starch in a carrot. Where there is starch, the carrot will turn dark. What can you conclude?

Read and Learn

VOCABULARY
vascular p. 66
nonvascular p. 68
fungi p. 70

SCIENCE CONCEPTS
- how vascular and nonvascular plants are structured
- how fungi are structured

Focus Skill MAIN IDEA AND DETAILS
Look for how plants and fungi are classified.

Main Idea
detail | detail | detail

Vascular Plants

How many plants can you name? There are about 270,000 kinds of plants in the world. That's too many to study in one group. The plant kingdom is divided into two groups.

One of the two large groups of the plant kingdom is made up of vascular plants. **Vascular** means "having tubes." Vascular plants have tubes that carry water and food to all their parts. In the Investigate, could you see the colored tubes? You were looking at the tubes that carry water through the plant.

Vascular plants are made up of three systems—roots, stems, and leaves. The roots help anchor the plant in the ground. They absorb water and nutrients from the soil. The plant needs both of these to live.

Stems connect the roots and the leaves. They carry water and food. Water in the stem helps keep the plant standing up straight.

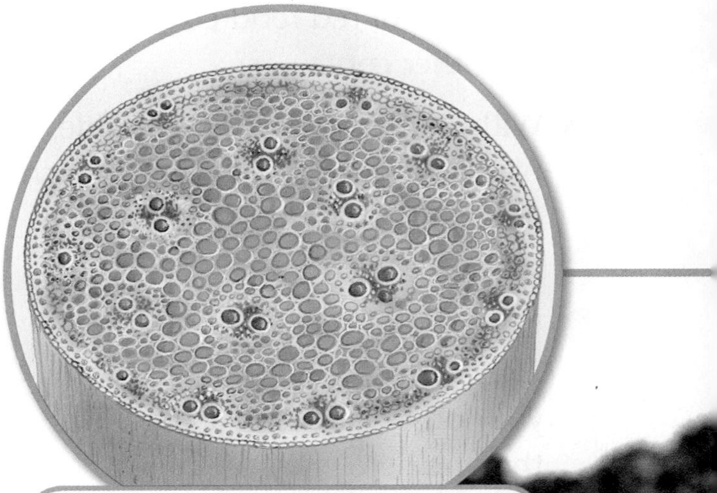

Tubes in the stem bring water up from the roots to the leaves. Food made in the leaves travels through tubes to the plant.

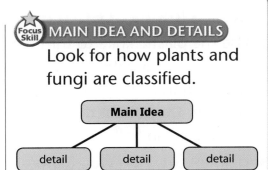

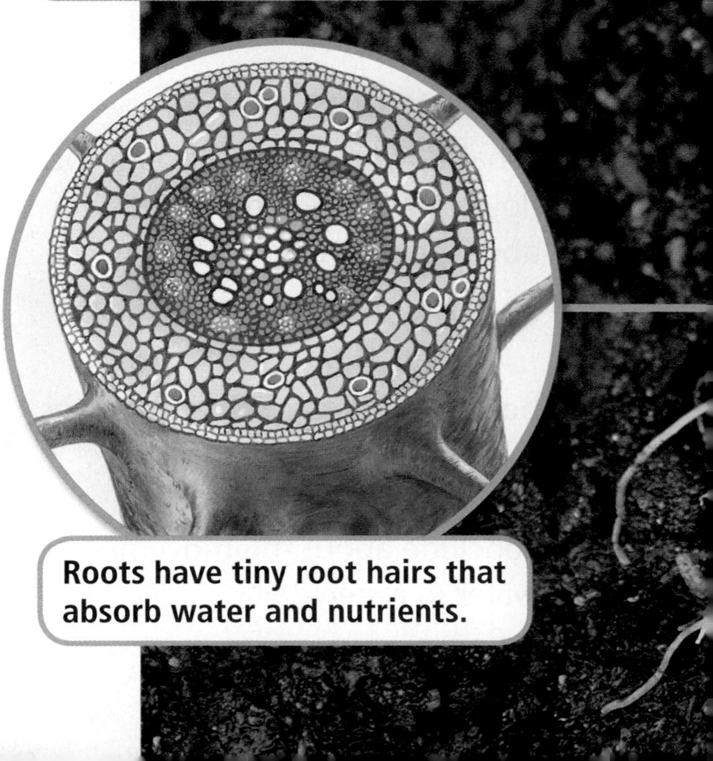

Roots have tiny root hairs that absorb water and nutrients.

The veins of a leaf are made up of small tubes. A leaf is covered with a waxy coating to keep in moisture.

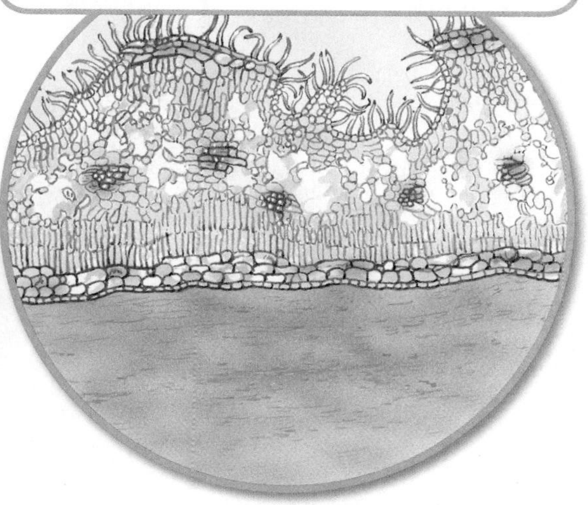

This coleus plant is a typical vascular plant. It has leaves, stems, and roots.

Leaves are like a factory. They make food and give off oxygen. The chloroplasts in plant cells contain *chlorophyll* (KLAWR•uh•fil). Chlorophyll is a green substance that absorbs sunlight. Chloroplasts use carbon dioxide, water, and light energy from the sun to make sugar. The sugar is food for the plant. This process is called *photosynthesis* (foht•oh•SIN•thuh•sis). In this process, plants take carbon dioxide from the air. They give off oxygen. Food made in the leaves is carried to all parts of the plant. Some food is also stored as starch in the roots.

Vascular plants are divided into three smaller groups. One group is the flowering plants, which make seeds in fruits. Another group is the cone-bearing plants, which make seeds in cones. The third group is the ferns, which do not make seeds.

Focus Skill **MAIN IDEA AND DETAILS**

What are the three systems that make up vascular plants?

▲ **Moss looks like a green carpet on decaying logs. It is really made up of many tiny plants.**

▲ **You can see tiny moss plants with a hand lens. These plants make spores, but do not make seeds.**

Nonvascular Plants

The second of the two large groups of the plant kingdom is made up of nonvascular plants. **Nonvascular** means "without tubes." Nonvascular plants do not have any tubes to carry water and food to parts of the plant. They absorb water directly, like a sponge. In fact, if you put water on a dried moss plant, a nonvascular plant, you would see it swell up and become green.

Nonvascular plants are very small. Plants in this group are called bryophytes (BRY•oh•fyts). Bryophytes grow in damp, shady places. They grow close to the ground, where they can absorb water and nutrients from their surroundings. Water moves from cell to cell in the tiny plant. Bryophytes don't have real roots, either. Instead, they have rootlike parts that anchor them to the ground. Their leaflike parts make food, which moves from cell to cell.

All bryophytes reproduce by spores and sex cells. The sex cells must travel in water to make new plants.

The hornwort gets its name from the hornlike part rising off the low, leafy plant. It splits open to spread spores. ▼

▲ The leaflike part of the liverwort plant is said to look like liver. The cuplike parts are full of spores.

The three groups of bryophytes include mosses, liverworts, and hornworts. Different groups have different ways of producing spores.

Mosses are the bryophytes that you probably know best. They grow where it is moist. You can find them growing on buildings, on brick walls, and on damp pavements. Liverworts and hornworts grow in damp forests and along rivers.

Focus Skill MAIN IDEA AND DETAILS

How do nonvascular plants get water and nutrients?

Insta-Lab

Soak It Up

Put some water in a dish. Take a dry sponge, and stand it on its edge in the dish. Observe how it absorbs water. How does this compare to a moss plant?

Fungi

Fungi are organisms that absorb food and can't move about. They were once classified in the plant kingdom. They look a little like plants and have stiff cell walls that let them grow upright. But in one important way, fungi are not at all like plants—fungi cannot make food. Their cells lack chloroplasts. Instead, fungi absorb nutrients from living things and from the remains of living things. They break down parts of these materials. This releases nutrients. The cells of the fungi take in the nutrients.

Fungi are divided into several groups. These include molds, mushrooms, and sac fungi.

Focus Skill **MAIN IDEA AND DETAILS**

How do fungi get their food?

Some puffballs crack open to send spores into the wind.

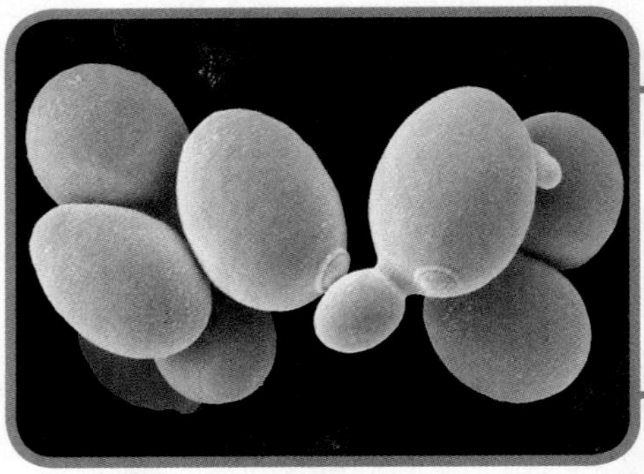

Yeast is a sac fungus used to help make bread rise.

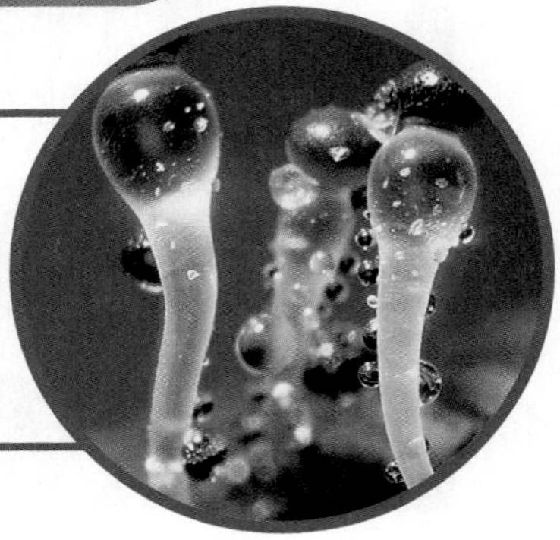

Pilobolus (py•LAHB•uh•luhs), a sac fungus, lives in cow dung and helps decompose it.

Oyster mushrooms grow in clusters on dead wood. They look and smell somewhat like oysters.

This amanita mushroom is very poisonous. Never touch or eat a wild mushroom!

If you leave bread in a dark place, mold will grow.

Lesson Review

Essential Question

How are plants and fungi classified?

In this lesson, you learned that plants can be vascular or nonvascular. You also learned that fungi cannot make their own food.

1. Focus Skill MAIN IDEA AND DETAILS Draw and complete a graphic organizer to summarize the main idea and the details that support it.

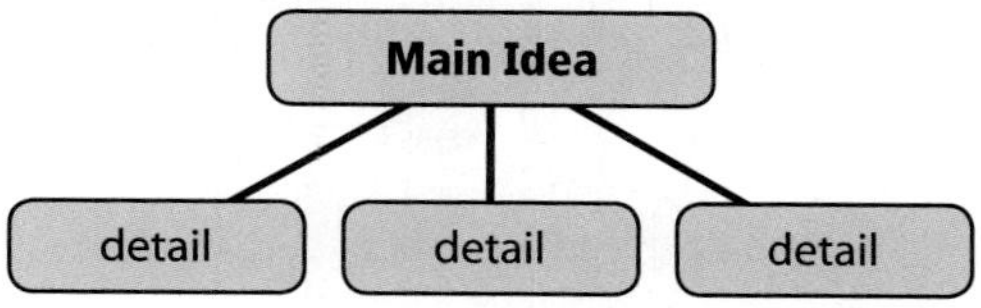

2. **SUMMARIZE** Use your vocabulary terms to write two or three sentences that sum up this lesson.

3. **DRAW CONCLUSIONS** What are some good reasons to plant trees?

4. **VOCABULARY** Write a paragraph that uses the vocabulary words.

Test Prep

5. **CRITICAL THINKING** What could you do to help if you saw a potted plant looking limp?

6. Which do all groups of plants have?
   A. chloroplasts
   B. roots
   C. spores
   D. tubes

Make Connections

Writing

Narrative Writing

Write a **story** for a school newspaper about a strange fungus you have found. Describe what it looks like, where it's growing, and why you think it's a fungus.

Math

Make a Bar Graph

Show the following in a bar graph. Nutrients in an edible mushroom: water 90%, proteins 3%, carbohydrates 5%, fats 1%, vitamins and minerals 1%.

Art

Draw Plants

Draw pictures of several kinds of plants to illustrate a children's book about plants. Choose at least one flowering plant.

LESSON 3

Essential Question

How Are Animals Classified?

Investigate the purpose of backbones.

Read and Learn how animals are grouped into different categories.

Fast Fact

A Sticky Subject

Banana slugs are animals without a backbone. They creep along on a cushion of slimy mucus. In the Investigate, you will compare models of an animal with a backbone and one without a backbone.

Banana slug feeding

Vocabulary Preview

vertebrates [VER•tuh•brits] The group of animals with a backbone (p. 76)

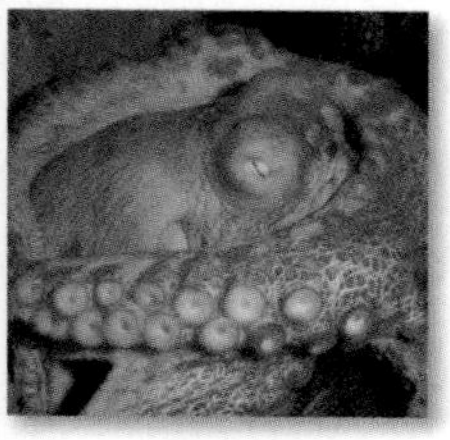

invertebrates [in•VER•tuh•brits] The group of animals without a backbone (p. 78)

Backbones

Guided Inquiry

Start with Questions

A center support beam can be found in all sorts of structures. It helps strengthen boats and houses and even living things!

- How does having a center support beam make a boat strong?
- How might having a center support beam affect the body of a living thing?

Investigate to find out. Then read and learn to find out more.

Prepare to Investigate

Inquiry Skill Tip

When you plan investigations, it is important to keep things simple. Limiting your variables makes it easier to interpret your results and draw conclusions.

Materials

- newspaper
- ruler
- modeling clay
- straight drinking straw

Make an Observation Chart

With Straw	Without Straw

Follow This Procedure

1. Cover your desk with newspaper. Work in pairs to make models to compare animals with and without a backbone.
2. Make a base 5 cm in diameter and 3 cm high, using modeling clay.
3. Next, cover a straight drinking straw with modeling clay. The clay should have a diameter of 3 cm to represent the body. The straw represents the backbone.
4. Poke the body into the base. You can build the base up around it to support it. The base represents legs. You can add arms and a head, too.
5. Repeat Steps 2–4 without the straw.
6. Compare the way the models stand. Record the data in chart form.

Draw Conclusions

1. What do you observe when you compare the two models?
2. **Inquiry Skill** Scientists plan simple investigations to test ideas. What steps would you follow to find out if the thickness of the backbone is important?

Independent Inquiry

Find a garden snail. Observe it. Record how it moves. What can you infer about whether this animal has a backbone?

Read and Learn

VOCABULARY
vertebrates p. 76
invertebrates p. 78

SCIENCE CONCEPTS
- which animals are vertebrates and which animals are invertebrates
- how vertebrates and invertebrates are structured

Focus Skill MAIN IDEA AND DETAILS
Look for characteristics of vertebrates and invertebrates.

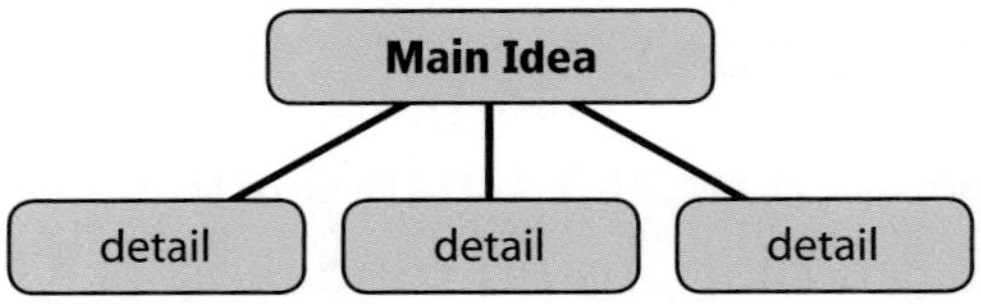

Vertebrates

How many animal pets can you name? What about wild animals? The animal kingdom is a large and diverse group of organisms. There are many different kinds of animals. The animal kingdom is divided into two groups—animals with a backbone and animals without a backbone.

Animals with a backbone belong to a group called **vertebrates**. You are a vertebrate. All vertebrates have bones inside their bodies that make up a skeleton.

Vertebrates are the most complex of all the animals. They have a system of nerves that carry messages to and from the brain. They have a system that brings nutrients, water, and oxygen in the blood to every cell of the body. The respiratory system brings oxygen to the blood and removes carbon dioxide. There is a system for digesting food and a system of muscles to move the body. There is a reproductive system.

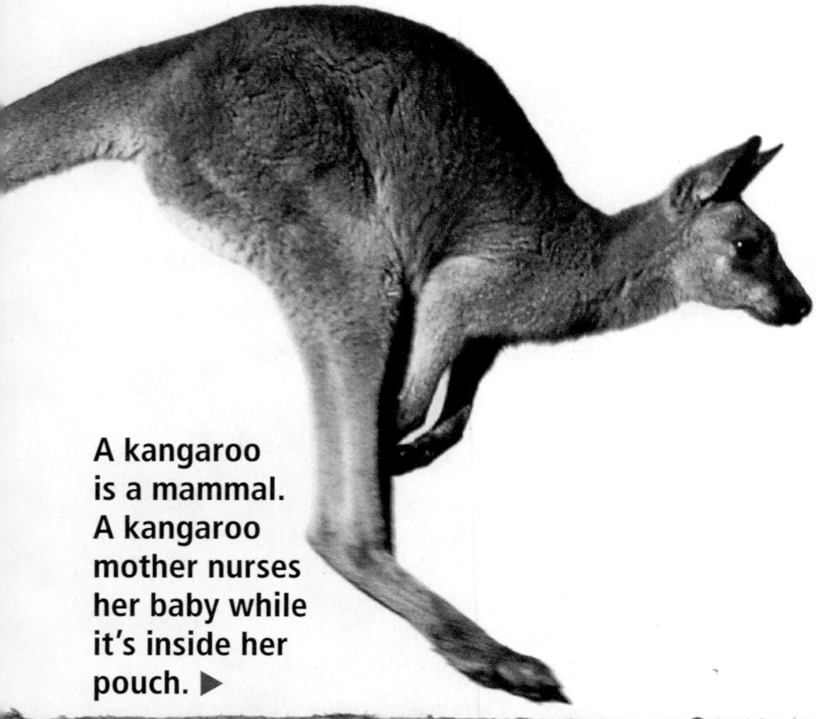

A kangaroo is a mammal. A kangaroo mother nurses her baby while it's inside her pouch. ▶

▲ A fish is a vertebrate, too. Its backbone supports it as it swims.

An iguana is a reptile. It suns itself to keep its body warm. ▶

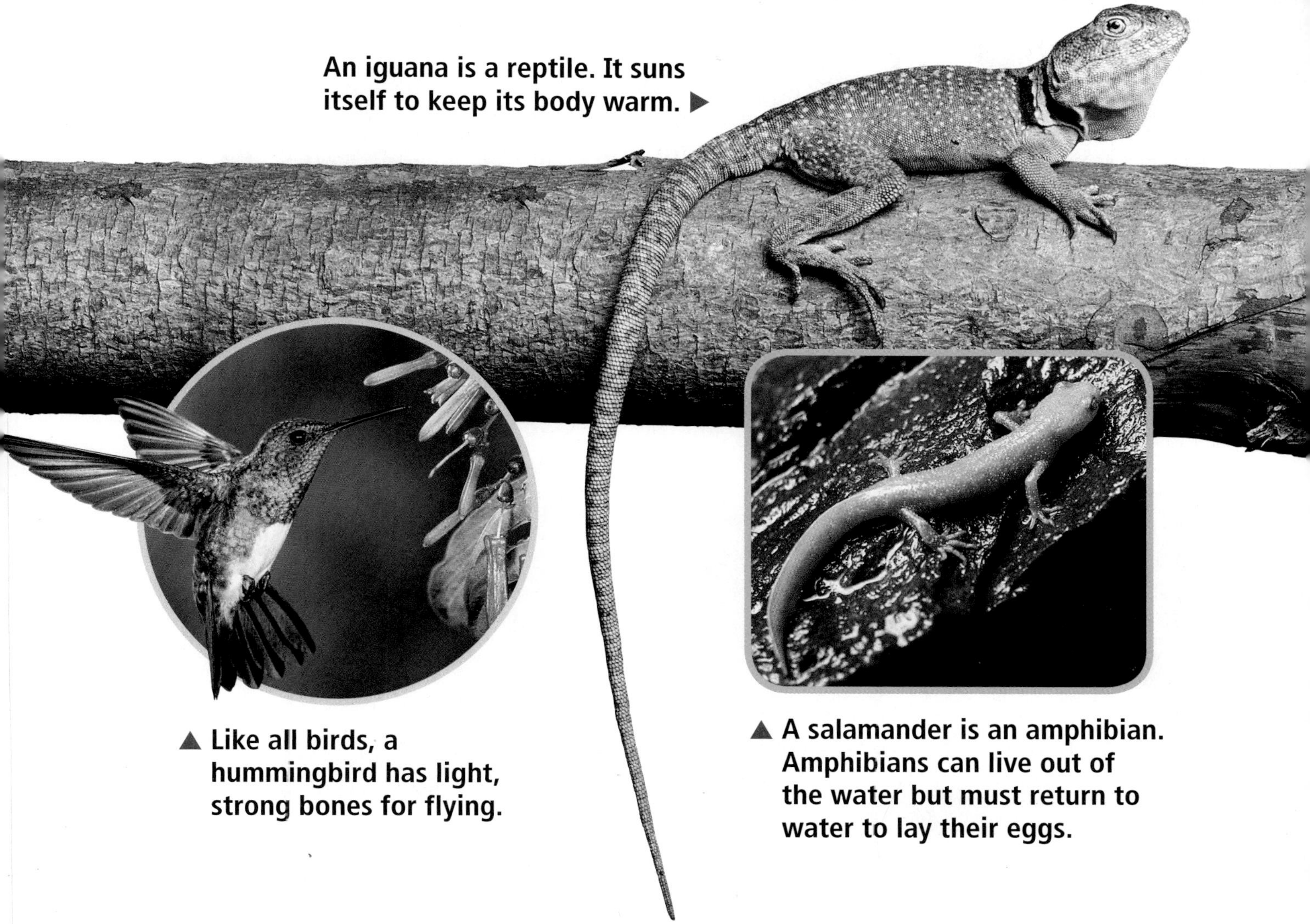

▲ Like all birds, a hummingbird has light, strong bones for flying.

▲ A salamander is an amphibian. Amphibians can live out of the water but must return to water to lay their eggs.

There are five groups of vertebrates—mammals, birds, reptiles, amphibians, and fish. Fish live in water. Their gills take oxygen from the water.

Amphibians have two lives—one in water and one on land. Most amphibians begin life in water. They grow lungs and legs and often lose their tails before they can live on land. They have smooth skin and lay eggs in water. Frogs, toads, and salamanders are amphibians.

Reptiles live on land. They don't have gills. Their bodies are the same temperature as what is around them. This is also true of fish and amphibians. Some reptiles lay eggs, and some have live young. Lizards, turtles, and snakes are reptiles.

Most birds can fly. They're covered with feathers, which keep them warm and dry and help them fly. Birds are warm-blooded. This means that their bodies stay at the same temperature no matter what the temperature around them is. All birds lay eggs.

You are a mammal. Female mammals nurse their young. All mammals are warm-blooded and have hair or fur. Their young are born live.

Focus Skill MAIN IDEA AND DETAILS

How are vertebrates complex?

◀ A snail is a mollusk. It uses its shell for protection.

A tarantula is an arachnid (uh•RAK•nid). It has eight legs and no antennae. ▶

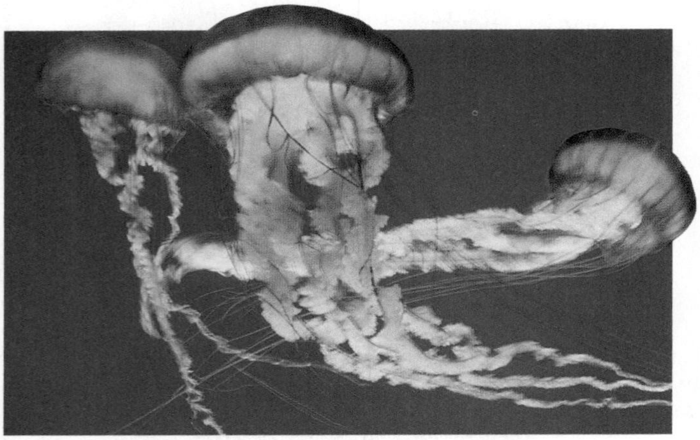

▲ A jellyfish stings its prey with tiny poison darts from its tentacles.

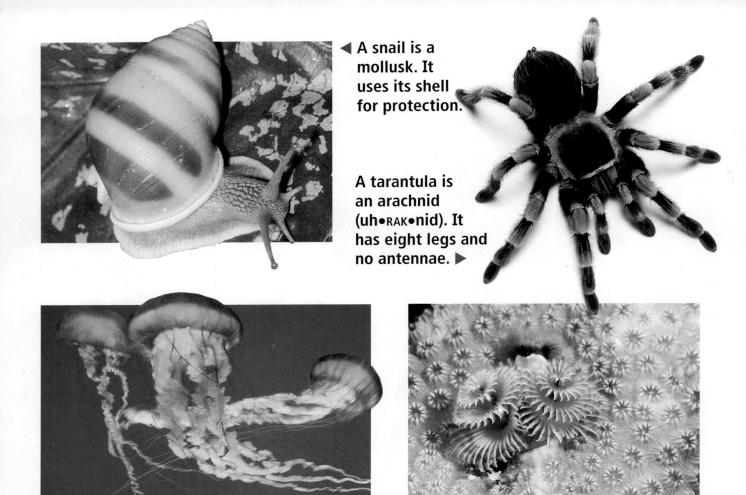

▲ A Christmas tree worm lives in a tube it builds on coral reefs. It filters food into its body with its tentacles.

Invertebrates

Animals without a backbone belong to a group called **invertebrates**. There are more than a million kinds of invertebrates, but scientists think that many more are yet to be found.

Many invertebrates live in the oceans. Water supports the bodies of underwater invertebrates.

Invertebrates have been divided into groups based on their body structures. Many groups have very simple body plans. Sponges are simple organisms with only a few types of cells. Members of the group that includes jellyfish and sea anemones are saclike organisms with a place for digesting food. Some corals are communities of tiny animals.

Mollusks are more complex. They include snails, slugs, mussels, and clams. A mollusk has a soft body and a muscular foot. It also has nerves that send messages through the body.

There are several groups of worms. Earthworms and fan worms have a brain and a system of nerves. An earthworm has five "hearts" that pump blood to all its parts.

A grasshopper is a typical insect because it has six legs and three main body parts. ▶

Crabs, which are crustaceans, walk on jointed legs and shed their shells as they grow. ▼

Arthropods are the largest group of invertebrates. They live almost everywhere on land and in water. All arthropods have jointed legs. They have a rigid body covering, called an exoskeleton, that covers the outside of their bodies. The exoskeleton doesn't grow. So when an arthropod grows, it molts, or sheds the old exoskeleton and grows a new one.

Insects are the largest group of arthropods. Crustaceans (kruhs•TAY•shuhnz), such as crabs and shrimps, are also arthropods. Spiders and scorpions are arthropods that belong to a subgroup called arachnids.

Focus Skill MAIN IDEA AND DETAILS

What supports the bodies of ocean invertebrates?

Math in Science
Interpret Data

Based on these circle graphs, what statement could you make about insects?

Invertebrates

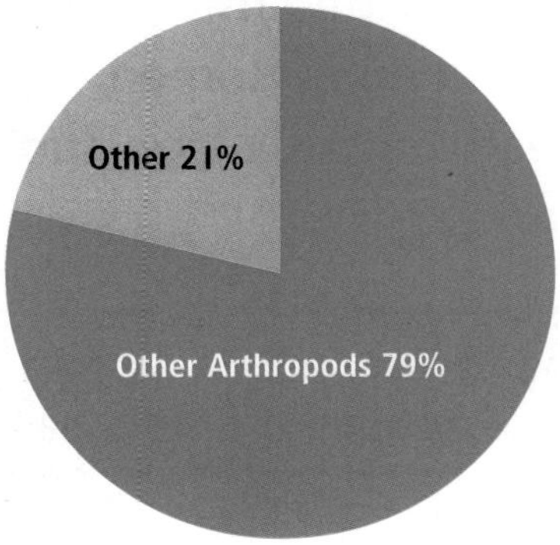

Animals

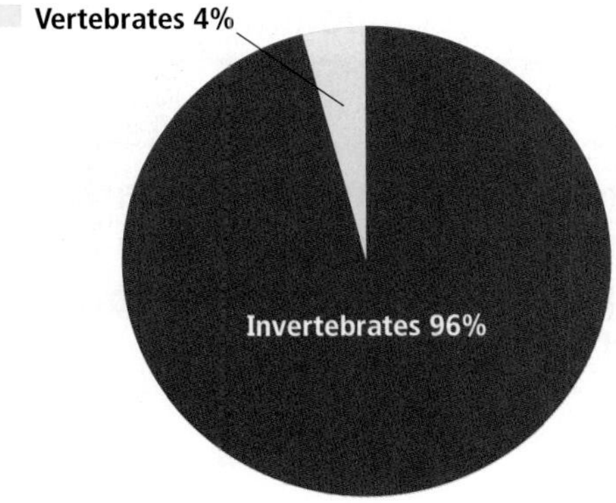

Insta-Lab

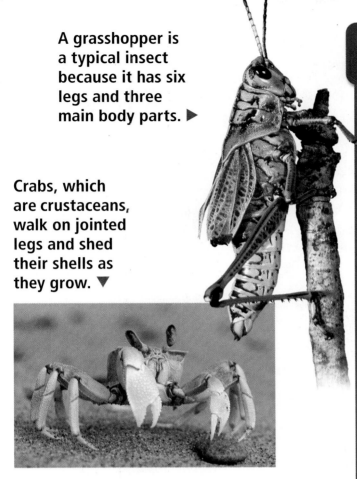

What Kinds of Animals?

Make a list of as many different kinds of animals in your community as you can. Then classify the animals. You can make up your own groups.

Science Up Close

For more links and animations, go to **www.hspscience.com**

A Typical Insect

A typical insect has an exoskeleton to protect its body. The body is divided into a head, a thorax, and an abdomen. Most insects have six legs and antennae.

Antennae can detect smells and sounds. Insects use antennae to find each other.
An insect's eyes have many lenses. They are called compound eyes.
The head has eyes and mouth parts. The mouth parts of some insects are adapted for chewing. Some are adapted for sucking.
The thorax is divided into three parts. A pair of legs is attached to each part of the thorax. If the insect has wings, the wings are also attached to the thorax.
The six legs are jointed.
The abdomen contains most of the insect's body systems. An insect breathes through the sides of its abdomen.

Essential Question

How are animals classified?

In this lesson, you learned that animals are grouped by whether they are vertebrates or invertebrates. Each of those groups is divided based on animal characteristics.

1. Focus Skill MAIN IDEA AND DETAILS Draw and complete a graphic organizer to summarize the main idea and the details that support it.

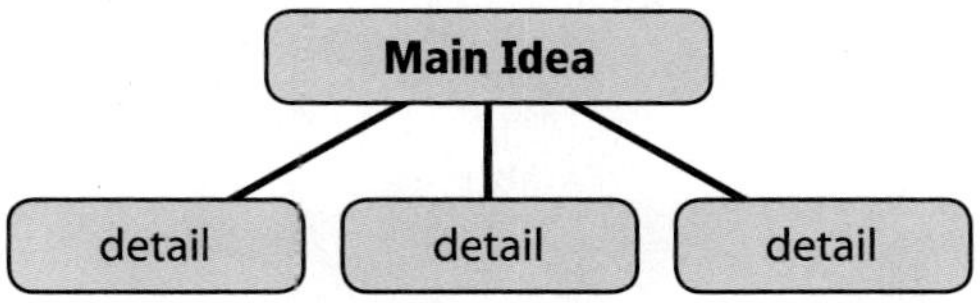

2. **SUMMARIZE** Write a summary of this lesson. Begin with this sentence: *Animals are grouped by the traits they have in common.*

3. **DRAW CONCLUSIONS** Why do you think a snake can move faster and in more directions than a slug?

4. **VOCABULARY** Use the vocabulary words as headings for a table. List at least three animals under each heading.

Test Prep

5. **CRITICAL THINKING** If you found a newborn squirrel and took it to a vet, what would the vet feed it? Why would the vet choose that food?

6. Which animal has an exoskeleton?
   A. fish
   B. grasshopper
   C. jellyfish
   D. snail

Make Connections

Writing

Expository Writing

Write a **description** of an animal you learned about in this chapter. Without naming the animal, see if a classmate can identify it.

Math

Using Percent

There were 100 arthropods in a garden. If 75 percent of them were insects, how many insects were there? How many other arthropods were in the garden?

Social Studies

Useful Insects

Research an insect that is used by farmers to control insect pests. Write a report about this insect.

Where the Wild Things Are

Divers search a lake in New York City during a recent BioBlitz.

Health Check

One of the goals of BioBlitz is to measure the health of city parks. Healthy parks should contain a variety of mammals, insects, fish, and reptiles. BioBlitz volunteers log every species that they locate in a park. Over time, scientists can compare current species counts with those from previous years to see whether some park creatures are in danger of dying out.

Don't bother looking for the yellow-billed cuckoo in a tropical forest. You won't find the bird there. But you might spot a rare creature like it in a city near you.

Recently, scientists discovered a yellow-billed cuckoo in a city park in Connecticut. The scientists were at the park to take part in BioBlitz, a 24-hour race to count every species, or type, of plant and animal in sight. By the end of the long day, they had found nearly 2,000 different species.

A Range of Life

BioBlitz is held in cities across the country. The program teaches people about the biodiversity of wildlife at their doorsteps. Biodiversity refers to the number and variety of life forms in a certain area. According to one BioBlitz organizer, you don't have to travel to a tropical forest to find a variety of life. "What we're saying is that there's biodiversity in our very own backyard."

Species Search

BioBlitz combines education with round-the-clock fun. The participants compete to collect the most—and the most unusual—species. Hundreds of people come to watch.

Teams use insect nets and special lights in their search. One volunteer brought a recording of a screeching owl. The noise attracted other owls for the team to count. Teams use microscopes and wildlife guides to help identify the species they find.

In many cases, computers play an important role in keeping track of the information gathered by scientists and students. In Vermont a running total of BioBlitz data was kept in a spreadsheet that had all the major classification groups, such as butterflies, worms, and lichens, that might be found in the area. In New York City, the BioBlitz data was input into a special software program created just for the event.

Perhaps the best part of BioBlitz is that everyone who participates sees something new. "We hope this event helps people pay closer attention to the world around them," another program organizer said.

Think and Write

1. Are projects like BioBlitz important to the environment? Why or why not?
2. In what other ways could computers be used to help the environment?

Spin-In™ Find out more. Log on to **www.hspscience.com**

Review and Test Preparation

Vocabulary Review

Use the terms below to complete the sentences. Some terms may be used twice. The page numbers tell you where to look in the chapter if you need help.

organism p. 54
microscopic p. 55
bacteria p. 59
protist p. 60
vascular p. 66
nonvascular p. 68
fungi p. 70
vertebrate p. 76
invertebrate p. 78

1. Organisms that grow on plant materials and absorb food from them are _______.
2. A plant with conducting tubes is called _______.
3. Anything that is too small to be seen with the eye alone is _______.
4. A one-celled organism that has a nucleus is a _______.
5. A multicelled animal without a backbone is an _______.
6. A living thing is an _______.
7. One-celled organisms without a nucleus are _______.
8. A multicelled animal with a backbone is a _______.
9. A plant that does not have conducting tubes is called _______.
10. A skunk is a _______.

Check Understanding

Write the letter of the best choice.

11. MAIN IDEA AND DETAILS Which statement is true of nonvascular plants?

Focus Skill

A. They absorb water that surrounds them.
B. They have conducting tubes.
C. They have stems and roots.
D. They reproduce by seeds.

12. What kind of cell does this picture show?

F. animal cell
G. bacteria
H. protist
J. plant cell

13. MAIN IDEA AND DETAILS Which statement is true of arthropods?

Focus Skill

A. They can live only in water.
B. They can't see or hear.
C. They have an internal skeleton.
D. They have an exoskeleton.

14. Which is **not** true of flowering plants?
   F. They are vascular plants.
   G. They produce oxygen.
   H. They produce seeds.
   J. They make cones.

15. What does this circle graph show?

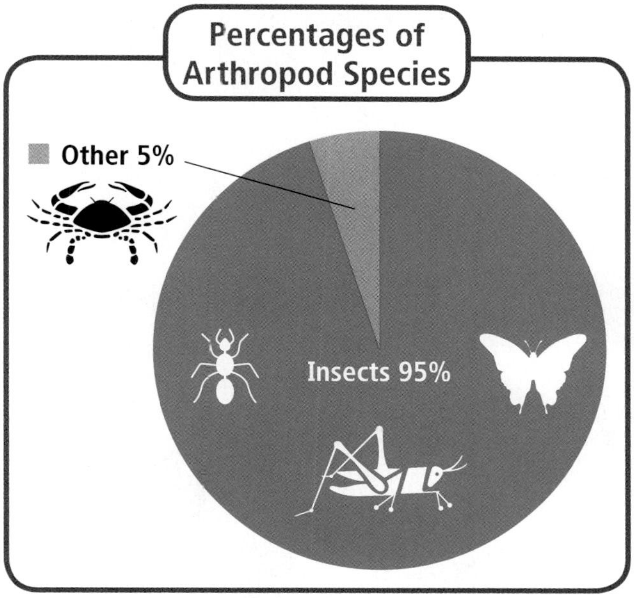

   A. Almost all arthropods are insects.
   B. Insects are more important than arthropods.
   C. Most insects must live on land.
   D. There are more insects than any other kind of animal.

16. Which would you plant on a hillside to stop soil from washing away?
   F. trees **H.** liverworts
   G. mosses **J.** fungi

Inquiry Skills

17. How can you **use models** to compare fungus cells and plant cells?

18. You observe a brown carpet of moss turn green after a rain. **Plan a simple investigation** to find out why the change occurs.

Critical Thinking

The Big Idea

19. Why do you think amphibians return to the water to lay their eggs?

20. You are walking through your neighborhood when you find a plant you have never seen before. It is very short and has flowers. What are some other characteristics you should look for in order to classify this plant? Based on how you classify the new plant, what can you infer about its root system?

CHAPTER

2 Life Cycles

What's the Big Idea? Living things inherit traits, grow, and develop according to life cycles.

Essential Questions

GO online Student eBook www.hspscience.com

What do YOU wonder?

How Long to Travel to the Sea? It took these sea turtle hatchlings two months to develop, hatch, and then dig out of the sandy hole where their mother had laid her eggs. Young sea turtles resemble their parents. Why do you think this happens? How does this relate to the **Big Idea?**

Recently hatched sea turtles

LESSON 1

Essential Question

What Is Heredity?

Investigate inherited characteristics.

Read and Learn how parents pass traits to their offspring.

Fast Fact

All Sizes and Shapes
All dogs belong to the same species. Fossils and genetic evidence show that all are descended from wolves. So why do dogs vary in size and shape? In the Investigate, you'll explore an answer–inherited traits.

Huskie with eyes of different colors

Vocabulary Preview

trait [TRAYT] A characteristic that makes one organism different from another (p. 92)

heredity [huh•RED•ih•tee] The process by which traits are passed from parents to offspring (p. 92)

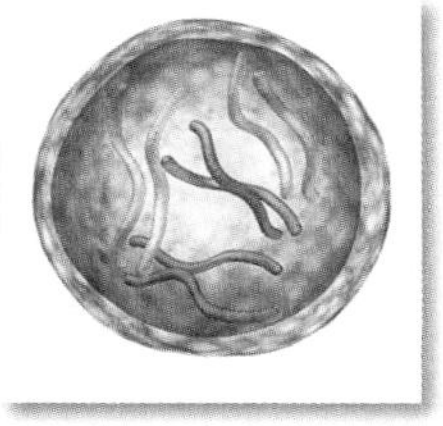

gene [JEEN] The basic unit of heredity (p. 93)

Inherited Characteristics

Guided Inquiry

Start with Questions

Observing is a useful tool for gathering information. Look at the picture of the cat and kittens. Pay attention to similarities and differences.

- Do the kittens look like the adult cat?
- What kinds of traits do parents pass to their offspring?

Investigate to find out. Then read and learn to find out more.

Prepare to Investigate

Inquiry Skill Tip

When you observe, look for things that are important to your investigation. If you are looking at hitchhiker thumbs, observing index fingers will not help you.

Materials

- hand mirror

Make an Observation Chart

Trait	Results (Circle one)	Class Totals
Hitchhiker thumb	Yes No	
Earlobes	Attached Free	

Follow This Procedure

1. Make a two-column table.
2. Make a fist with your thumb extended. Can you bend your thumb into the "hitchhiker position" as shown on the right? Record the results.
3. Use the mirror to observe your earlobes. Are they attached at the neck as shown on the left? Do they hang free as shown on the right? Record your observations.
4. Your teacher will ask members of the class to report their observations. Tally the results as your classmates report them.
5. Total the number of students who have each trait. Then use the numbers to find the fraction of the class that has each trait.

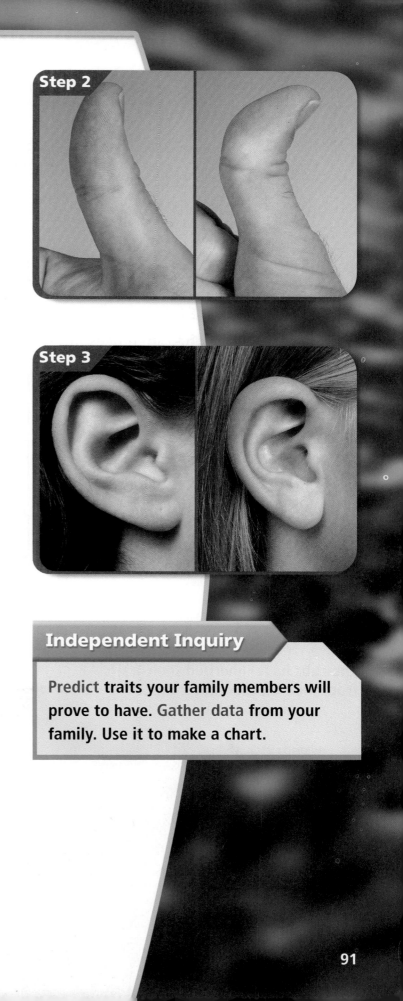

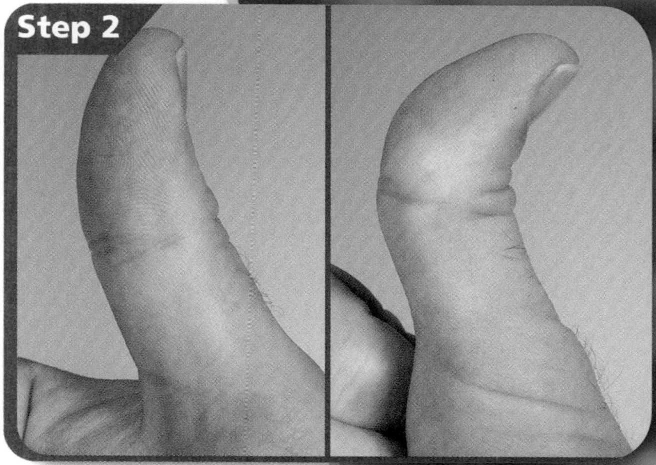

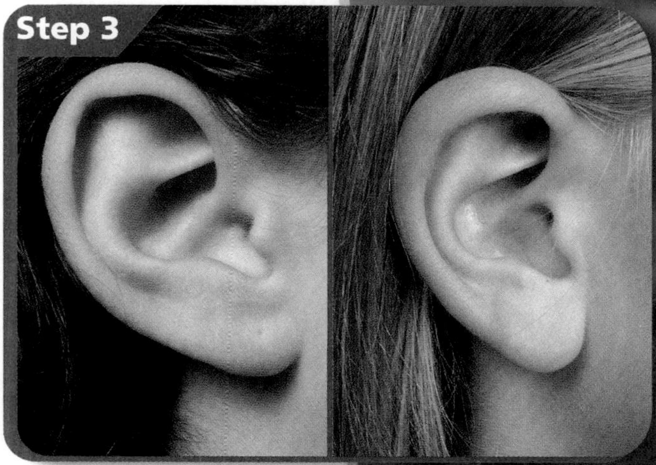

Draw Conclusions

1. Why would you infer that not all persons could learn to bend their thumbs into the hitchhiker position?
2. **Inquiry Skill** Based on your observations and inferences, what can you conclude about hitchhiker thumbs and attached earlobes?

Independent Inquiry

Predict traits your family members will prove to have. Gather data from your family. Use it to make a chart.

Read and Learn

VOCABULARY
trait p. 92
heredity p. 92
gene p. 93

SCIENCE CONCEPTS
- how traits are inherited
- how traits develop

Focus Skill **MAIN IDEA AND DETAILS**

Look for ways you get your traits.

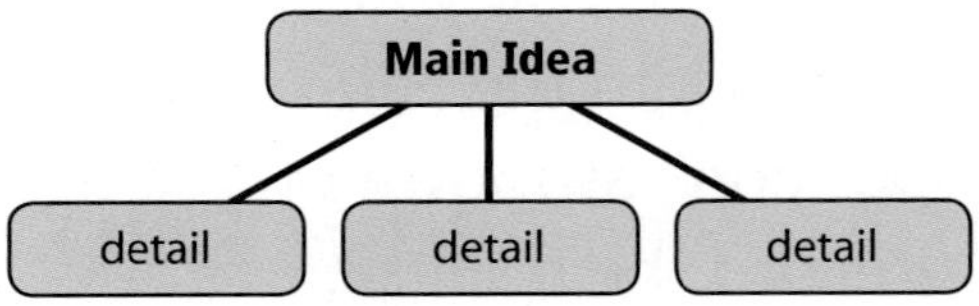

Parents and Offspring

Look around the room at your classmates. Notice ways you are all like one another. Notice the differences, too.

When living things breed, or *reproduce*, they make more of their own kind, or species. The offspring will also be able to reproduce. When bears reproduce, they produce bear cubs. Maple seeds grow into maple trees, and oak seeds grow into oak trees. But offspring also differ from one another. The members of the Asian family in the picture look like one another, but they are still unique individuals.

Children look more like their parents and grandparents than like people in other families. Do you have your mother's eyes or your grandfather's nose? Do your aunts and uncles look like your grandparents? Offspring look like parents because of similar traits.

A **trait** is a form of a characteristic that not all organisms have in common. All people have thumbs, but having a hitchhiker thumb is a trait. Where do our traits come from? Traits are passed on through heredity. **Heredity** is the process by which traits are passed from parents to offspring.

The cubs have inherited their traits from their mother and father. ▼

All the members of this Asian family have many similar traits.

This son looks very much like his father. ▶

A **gene** is a basic unit of heredity. Genes carry instructions for how a living thing will grow and develop. The genes in each cell determine what kind of cell it will become. Every human has the same number and type of genes, but the instructions on the genes vary. Different forms of genes cause people to have different traits. For example, everyone has genes for earlobe type. One form makes earlobes attached. Another form makes earlobes hang free.

Where did you get your gene set with all of its instructions? Genes are transferred from parents to offspring during *reproduction.* This is when a sperm cell and an egg cell join. Genes work in pairs. A sperm cell from the father carries only half of each pair. An egg cell from the mother also has only half of each pair. When the sperm and egg join, a new cell with a full set of genes forms. Half of the set comes from the mother, and half comes from the father. In the same way, the gene sets of the mother and father came from their parents.

So your genes came from your parents. But your combination of forms of genes differs from those of anyone else.

Focus Skill MAIN IDEA AND DETAILS

Why might a girl look like her mother's father?

Traits

Thousands of different traits make you who you are. Some traits, such as those determining eye color, are affected only by genes. Most traits, however, develop through a combination of heredity and nurture. *Nurture* is everything in your life—where you live, the people you know, and the activities you do.

The traits you studied in the Investigate are determined by heredity alone. No matter where you live, those traits will not change. The traits shown here are determined by heredity too.

Nurture influences many traits. For example, genes play a large role in determining how tall people will be. However, if people don't eat a healthful diet, they may not grow as tall. Their environment affects the trait. The gene for the trait does not change, and it will still be passed to offspring. In a similar way, people may dye their hair. Their genes for hair color do not change.

The people around you influence your behavior and traits, too. For example, you can learn to speak because of certain genes.

Eye color, hair color, the shape of the nose, and the shape of the lips are inherited traits.

You can identify a tree by its leaves. These leaves are from different trees: maple (top), oak (left), and palm (right).

A toucan (top) has a big beak for eating large fruit. A hawk (middle) tears at prey with its beak. A heron's beak (bottom) is suited for fishing.

However, the language you speak and the words you use are learned from the people in your life. You inherit the taste buds on your tongue, but many things influence the foods you like.

Some behaviors are not learned. Many animals hatch from eggs and never see their parents. They are born with a full set of instructions on how to survive. Animals with more-developed brains have more to learn. When they're young, they depend on their parents. They inherit traits for survival, but they have to learn how to use the traits. They learn from their parents or other adults.

Focus Skill **MAIN IDEA AND DETAILS**

How does dyeing the hair influence the genes for hair color?

Insta-Lab

A Family Tree

Draw your family tree or that of a friend. Start with the grandparents, and show their children. Then show the children's children. Ask family members for help. Do the people in the family tree look like one another?

Variations

Genes affect characteristics such as height, shape, and color. Some characteristics are affected by several genes. For instance, several genes control eye color. When a human sperm and egg cell join, many kinds of eye color are possible. Look at the variations of eye colors of students in your classroom. Eyes are usually not just blue or brown. They can be green or something different. This is because of the many possible gene combinations.

You can't change your eye color. But you can change some characteristics by the way you live. For example, genes carry information for how tall you can be. However, what you eat and how you take care of your body also influence your height. Eating healthful food and getting proper exercise enable your body to grow as tall as possible.

Focus Skill **MAIN IDEA AND DETAILS**

Why are there many different skin colors?

▼ When seeds from different colors of tulips are mixed, many colorful tulips result.

▲ Many dogs are bred so that they have certain traits. These three Labrador retrievers all have different mixes of genes.

Lesson Review

Essential Question

What is heredity?

In this lesson, you learned about traits that parents pass to their offspring. Genes pass on instructions for how living things grow and develop. Different gene combinations can cause variations.

1. Focus Skill **MAIN IDEA AND DETAILS** Draw and complete a graphic organizer to summarize the main idea and the details that support it.

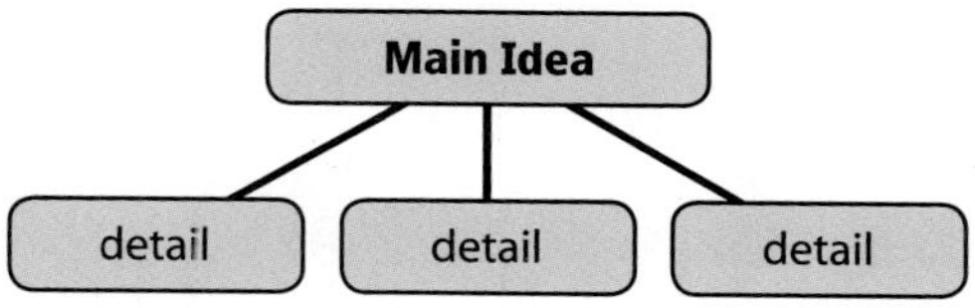

2. **SUMMARIZE** Write a summary of this lesson. Begin with this sentence: *Offspring resemble their parents.*

3. **DRAW CONCLUSIONS** What is wrong with the statement "You look exactly like your mother"?

4. **VOCABULARY** Complete the following sentence by using the lesson vocabulary words. By ____, a child's parents pass on their ____, which carry instructions for some ____ the child will have.

Test Prep

5. **CRITICAL THINKING** Why can't bears breed and produce monkeys?

6. Which trait is affected by behavior?
   - **A.** eye color
   - **B.** height
   - **C.** leaf shape
   - **D.** attached earlobes

Make Connections

Writing

Expository Writing

Write a **description** of how the dogs in the picture on the previous page are alike and different. Write why you think the dogs are the same.

Math

Make a Bar Graph

Review the data that you gathered during the Investigate. Use it to make a bar graph about your class's thumbs and earlobes. What does the data tell you?

Health

Healthy Bodies

Write a paragraph explaining how you could affect the development of your inherited traits by your health habits.

LESSON 2

Essential Question

What Are Some Life Cycles of Plants?

Investigate the best conditions for sprouting seeds.

Read and Learn how plants live and grow.

Fast Fact

Blowing in the Wind
When you blow on a head of dandelion seeds, the seeds sail through the air. They can travel on the wind across great distances. In the Investigate, you'll find out what seeds need to grow after they're in the ground.

Vocabulary Preview

photosynthesis [foht•oh•SIN•thuh•sis] The process that plants use to make sugar (p. 102)

life cycle [LYF CY•kuhl] All the stages a living thing goes through (p. 104)

Sprouting Seeds

Guided Inquiry

Start with Questions

Most plants start life as seeds. In order for the seeds to sprout and grow, they must have the right conditions.

- Do seeds need water to sprout?
- What is the purpose of the pod around these seeds?

Investigate to find out. Then read and learn to find out more.

Prepare to Investigate

Inquiry Skill Tip

The conclusions you draw must support or reject your hypothesis. If your conclusions do not support your hypothesis, you should write another one.

Materials

- radish seeds
- cup
- water
- 2 sponges
- 2 aluminum pie pans
- cardboard box

Make an Observation Chart

Day	Plant in Sun	Plant in Dark
1		
2		
3		
4		
5		

Follow This Procedure

1. Work in a group. Soak some radish seeds in a cup of water overnight. Write a **hypothesis** about whether seeds need light to sprout.
2. Place a wet sponge on a pie pan. Pour about 1 cm of water in the pan.
3. Poke some of the radish seeds into the holes of the sponge.
4. Place the pie pan in a warm, sunny place, and **observe** the sponge for the next 3 to 5 days. Be sure the sponge stays moist.
5. Repeat Steps 2 and 3 with the second pie pan. However, place the pan and sponge on a table, and cover them with a box so that no light gets in. Be sure the sponge stays wet, but keep it in the dark as much as possible.
6. **Compare** the growth on the two sponges, and **record** your **observations**.

Step 3

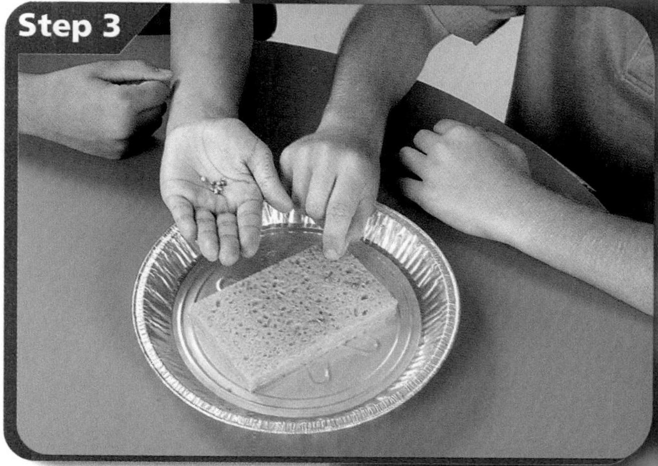

Step 5

Draw Conclusions

1. What do you **conclude** about light and the sprouting of seeds?
2. **Inquiry Skill** How did the experiment support or reject your **hypothesis**?

Independent Inquiry

Form a hypothesis about whether plants need soil to grow. For a test, use a radish seed on a moist sponge and a radish seed in soil in a pot.

VOCABULARY
photosynthesis p. 102
life cycle p. 104

SCIENCE CONCEPTS
- the stages in a plant's life cycle
- how plants reproduce

Focus Skill SEQUENCE
Look for stages in the life cycles of plants.

Food From the Sun

Think about what you feel when you raise your face to the sun. The warmth that you feel is part of the sun's energy. The sun is important to almost everything on Earth. Most living things get the energy to live from sunlight.

Green plants and algae (AL•jee) use solar energy—the energy of sunlight—and change it to chemical energy through a process called **photosynthesis** [foht•oh•SIN•thuh•sis]. In this process, water and carbon dioxide are combined in the presence of sunlight to form sugars and oxygen.

The sun provides energy for this producer.

The green leaves of this bush use photosynthesis to make food for the bush. The berries are a source of food for other living things.

Plants use the sugars for food. The sugars provide the energy the plants need for growth and good health. They use some of this energy right away. The rest is stored. The plants may later use that stored energy. Other organisms often use that energy by eating the plants. Plants would not have the energy for the various parts of their life cycle if they did not use photosynthesis.

Focus Skill SEQUENCE **What process do plants use to make food, using energy from the sun?**

The berries on this plant provide food for other organisms.
The bush's roots absorb nutrients from the soil.

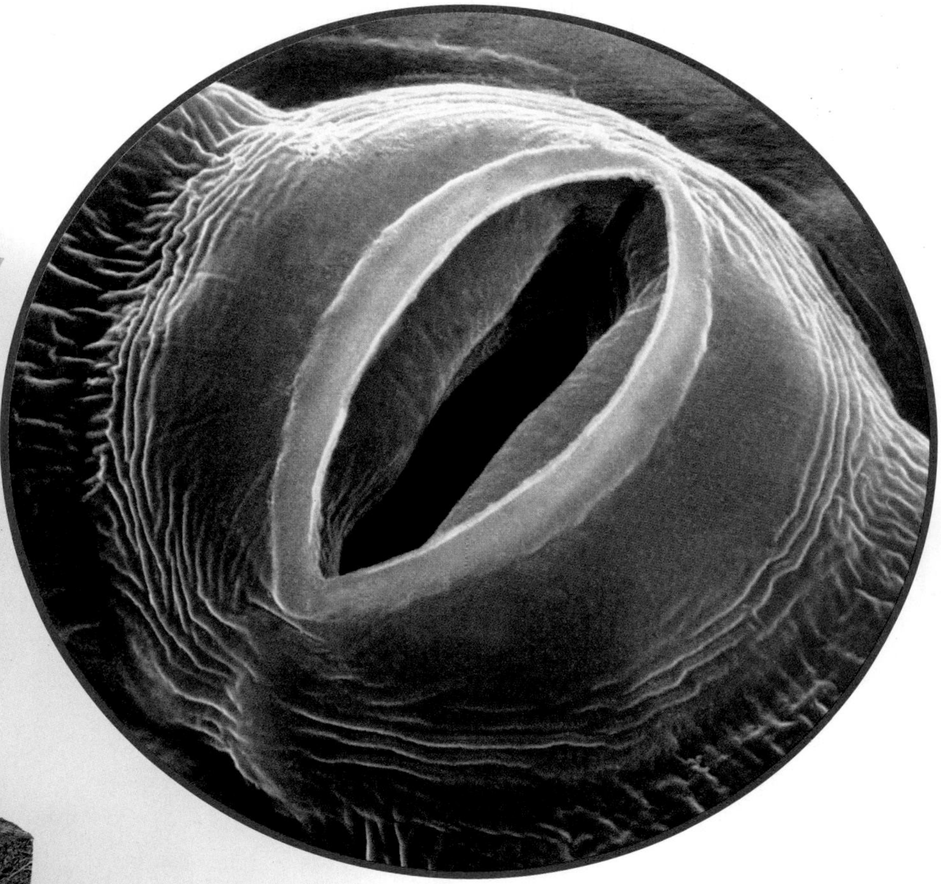

▲ **This small opening, or *stoma,* enables gases to pass into and out of the plant.**

Plants from Seeds

Flowering plants grow from seeds. A seed forms when an egg is fertilized. Each seed holds a tiny plant called an *embryo.* The tiny plant stays inside the seed until conditions are right for it to grow. When the soil is warm and there is enough moisture, the plant will *germinate* (JER•muh•nayt), or begin to grow.

Germination (jer•muh•NAY•shuhn) is one stage in a plant's life cycle. A **life cycle** is all of the stages a living thing goes through, from the beginning of one generation to the next.

When there is enough moisture, a seed swells and cracks open. Tiny roots begin to grow down into the soil. Inside the seed, the embryo is surrounded by food. This food gives the plant energy to grow until it can make its own food. After the roots begin to take up water, a tiny stem pushes up out of the soil. Leaves begin to grow, and the plant can now make its own food. A new plant, or seedling, is formed. The *seedling stage* is the next stage of a plant's life cycle.

Next, the plant grows and develops flowers. The *flowering stage* is the next stage of the life cycle.

◀ In pine trees, wind spreads pollen from the male cones to the female cones, where seeds develop.

▲ In orange trees, the flowers and fruit grow at the same time.

A coconut is the biggest seed. It can float in the ocean to a new island, where it will grow into a tree. ▶

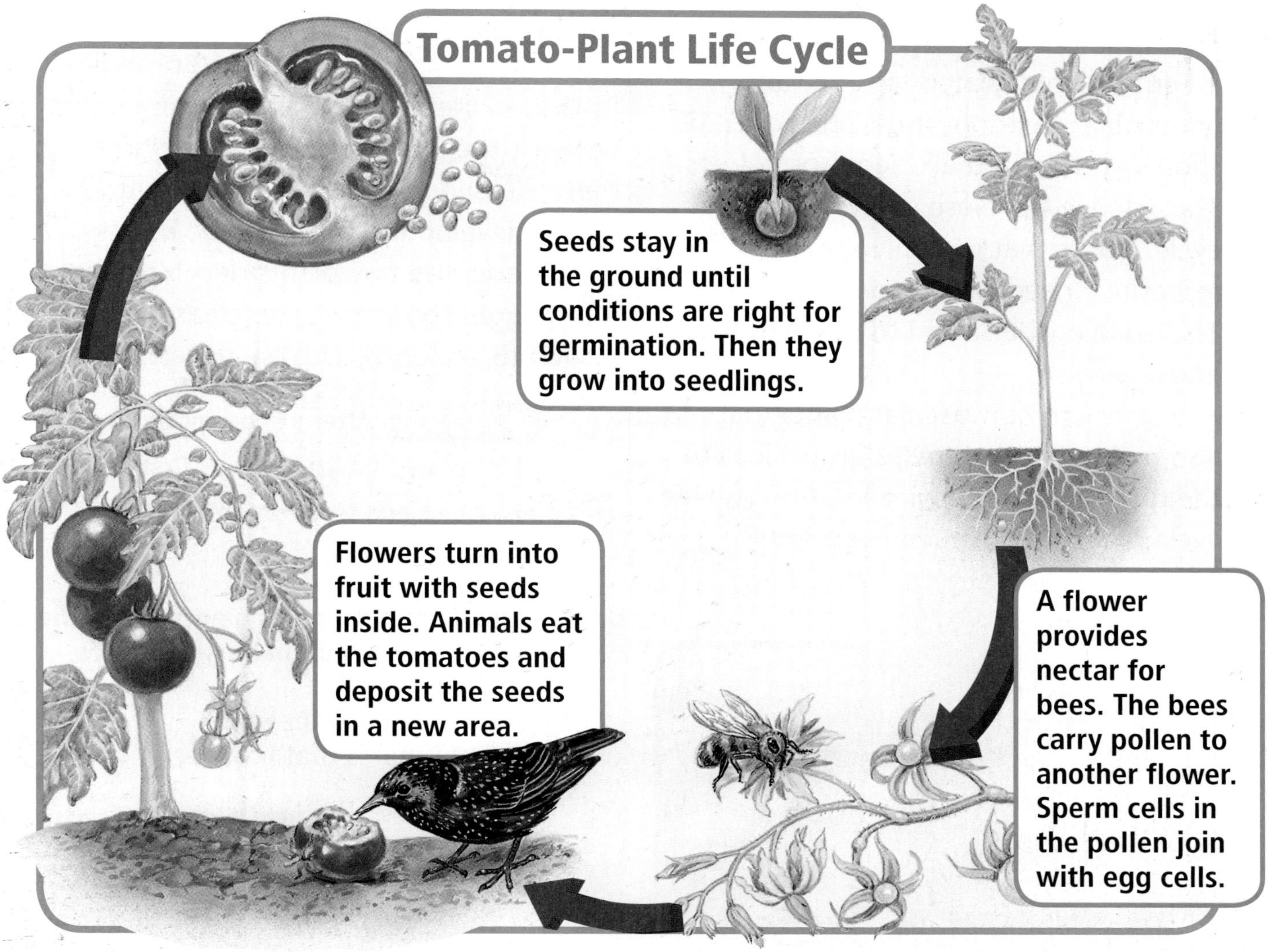

Tomato-Plant Life Cycle
Seeds stay in the ground until conditions are right for germination. Then they grow into seedlings.
A flower provides nectar for bees. The bees carry pollen to another flower. Sperm cells in the pollen join with egg cells.
Flowers turn into fruit with seeds inside. Animals eat the tomatoes and deposit the seeds in a new area.

Flowers produce pollen. It contains the male sex cells, or sperm cells, of the plant. The colors and scents of flowers attract birds and insects. As the birds and insects move from flower to flower, they *pollinate* (PAHL•uh•nayt), or bring pollen to, the flowers. Wind also carries pollen to other flowers and plants. A flower is pollinated when pollen grains are deposited onto the female part of the flower. Then sperm cells from the pollen grains join with egg cells inside the flower. New seeds develop, beginning a new life cycle.

A pollinated flower grows into a fruit that surrounds the seeds. When animals eat the fruit, the seeds go through their digestive systems. The seeds may be deposited far away from the parent plant. Other seeds are spread by wind. Still others are carried away in and drop from an animal's fur. When conditions are right, the seeds will grow into new plants.

Focus Skill SEQUENCE

After germination, which comes first—the flowers or the leaves?

Plants from Spores

Ferns, plants related to ferns, and other plants without roots reproduce by spores and don't make seeds or flowers. The Science Up Close shows a fern life cycle. Plants that use only spores to reproduce need moist environments. This enables the sperm to move to the eggs.

Mosses are nonvascular plants that also make spores. Mosses grow close to the ground in wet environments. The life cycle of a moss is much like a fern's.

First, fertilized eggs, or eggs that have joined with sperm, develop into small plants. When those plants become adult plants, they release spores. The spores are released into the moist environment. They develop into new plants. During this stage, the tiny plants develop sperm and eggs. The sperm are released and swim to the eggs. The cycle starts over.

Focus Skill SEQUENCE After a spore-producing plant grows, which happens first—spore release or egg fertilization?

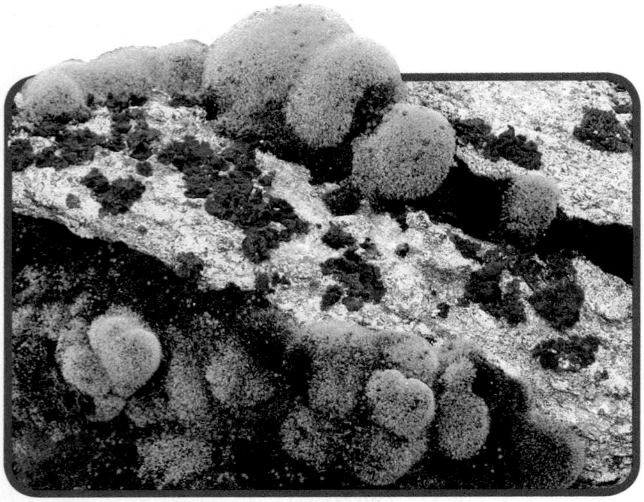

◀ Many tiny individual moss plants are in the moss you see growing on logs and trees.

▼ A takakia (tah•KAH•kee•uh) plant grows parts that produce sperm and eggs.

Spores on Leaves

Use a hand lens to look at the spore clusters on the back of a fern frond. Then rub the clusters over white paper, and look at the individual spores. How are spores different from seeds?

Fern Life Cycle
Ferns reproduce without seeds.

Clusters of spores grow on the fern fronds.

Spores are released from the clusters.

The fiddleheads uncurl and grow into fern fronds. This is the *sporophyte* (SPAWR•uh•fyt) *generation.*

Spores land on damp ground. They grow into heart-shaped plants. This is the *gametophyte* (guh•MEET•uh•fyt) *generation.*

The fertilized eggs develop into fiddleheads.

The gametophytes produce sperm and eggs. The sperm fertilize the eggs, beginning a new life cycle.

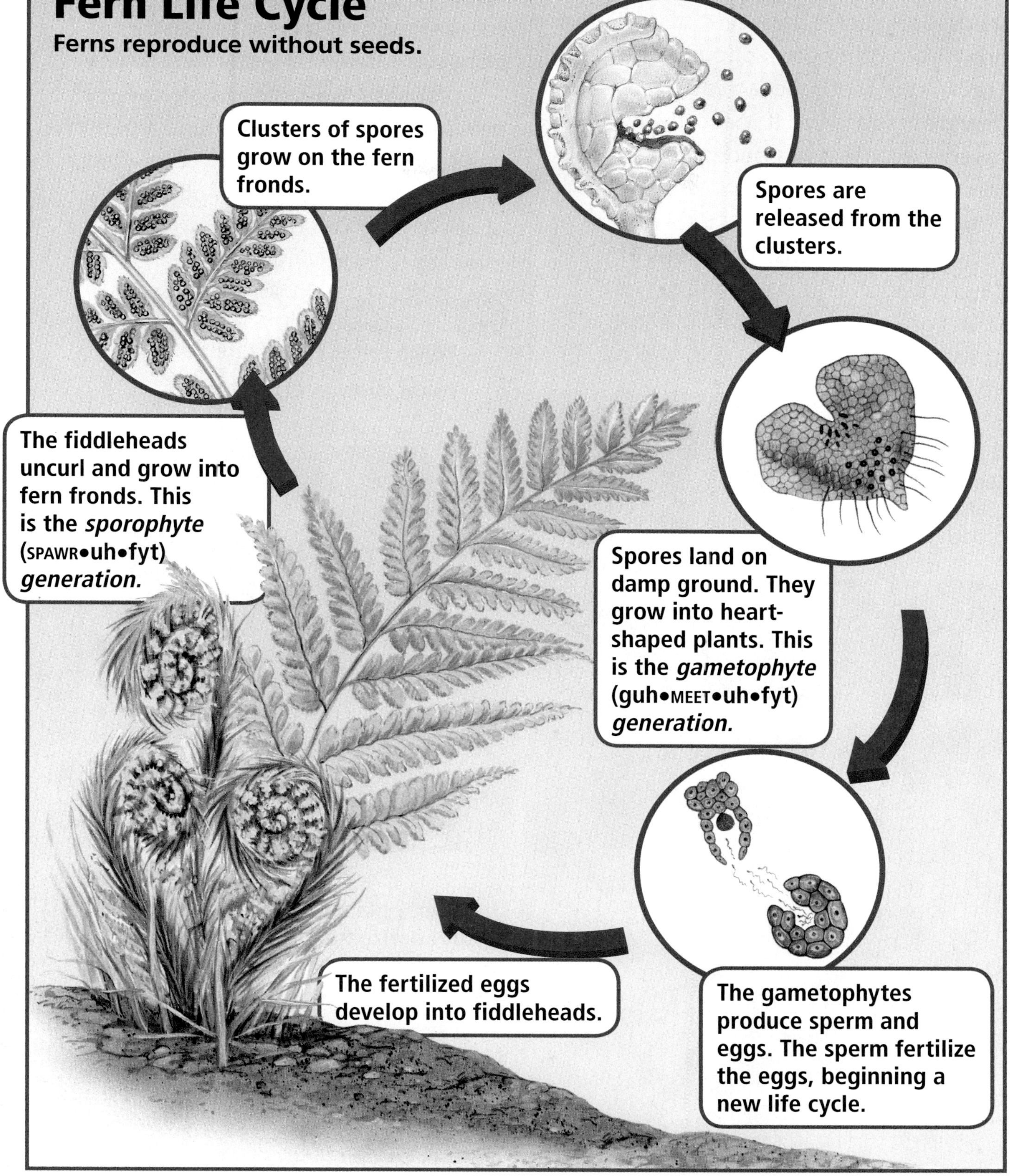

Other Ways for Plants to Grow

Most new flowering plants grow from seeds. Sometimes, however, new plants grow from other parts of parent plants. This kind of reproduction is *asexual.* The new plant is a *clone.* It is exactly like the parent because it has genes from only that one parent.

In some types of plants, new plants can grow from stems. The stems of parent plants send out runners. New plants grow from the runners. Most grasses grow from runners as well as from seeds.

Some plants grow from a storage stem called a *tuber.* Potatoes are tubers. Bulbs are underground storage stems that have complete miniature plants inside. If you cut open an onion bulb, you can see the plant surrounded by fleshy storage leaves.

Grafting is a way that people can make new plants grow. For example, a part of one type of apple tree may be grafted, or attached, onto part of a different type of apple tree. The grafted part keeps growing in its new place.

Focus Skill **SEQUENCE**

Which comes first—a runner or a new strawberry plant?

A daffodil flower has seeds, but daffodil plants are usually grown from bulbs.

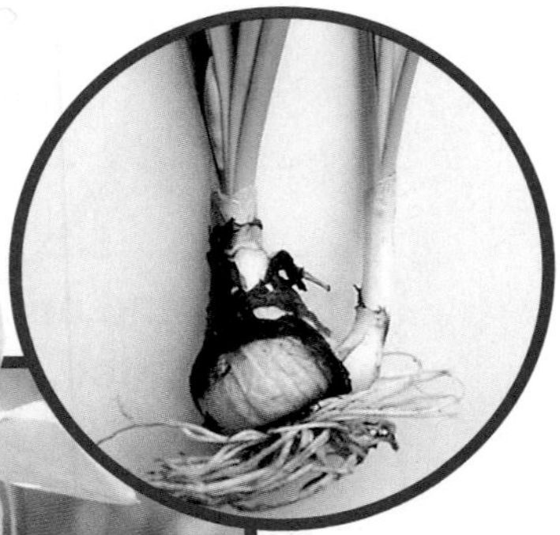

A potato plant grows from each "eye" on a potato.

A strawberry plant sends out horizontal runners on the ground.

Lesson Review

Essential Question

What are some life cycles of plants?

In this lesson, you learned that plants can grow from seeds. Some plants, such as ferns, grow from spores. Plants must reproduce as part of their life cycle.

1. Focus Skill **SEQUENCE** Draw and complete a graphic organizer to show the sequence of two plant life cycles.

   [ ] → [ ] → [ ]

2. **SUMMARIZE** Write a summary of this lesson. Begin with this sentence: *Plants grow in different ways.*

3. **DRAW CONCLUSIONS** Each kernel of corn is a seed that's part of a fruit. Seeds form from pollinated flowers. What can you conclude about the kernels on an ear of corn?

4. **VOCABULARY** Write definitions for *life* and *cycle,* and tell how they relate to the compound term *life cycle.*

Test Prep

5. **CRITICAL THINKING** How could you start a new grass plant?

6. Which of the following grows from a fern spore?
   A. seed
   B. flower
   C. fern clone
   D. a tiny heart-shaped plant

Make Connections

Writing

Narrative Writing

Write a **story** about a seed as it "wakes up." Tell what happens to it as it grows and has offspring.

9÷3 Math

Estimate

Potato plants grow from the eyes of potatoes. Count the eyes of a potato. Then estimate how many potatoes you would need to grow 100 potato plants.

Language Arts

Word Parts

Look up the meaning of the word part *-phyte.* Write a definition of it. Look up other word parts related to plants. Share them with the class.

LESSON 3

Essential Question

What Are Some Life Cycles of Animals?

Investigate the life cycles of animals.

Read and Learn how animals grow and reproduce.

Fast Fact

A "Comet" in the Forest

This comet moth from Madagascar did all its eating when it was a larva. Adult comet moths have no mouths and die in about 10 days. In the Investigate, you'll find out more about the life cycles of animals.

Comet moth laying eggs

Vocabulary Preview

direct development
[duh•REKT dih•VEL•uhp•muhnt] A kind of growth in which an organism gets larger but doesn't go through other changes (p. 116)

metamorphosis
[met•uh•MAWR•fuh•sis] Major changes in the body form during the life cycle of an animal (p. 118)

Animal Life Cycles

Guided Inquiry

Start with Questions

Animals can grow and change in unexpected ways. Things about animals change form as they grow.

- Do all animals grow in the same way?
- Do all animals go through the same number of stages?

Investigate to find out. Then read and learn to find out more.

Prepare to Investigate

Inquiry Skill Tip

When you compare two different life cycles, start by looking for ways in which they are similar. When you have written down all the ways life cycles are the same, look for ways the two life cycles are different.

Materials

- pictures of animal life cycles
- paper bag for whole class
- scissors

Make an Observation Chart

Life Cycle 1	Life Cycle 2

Math in Science
Interpret Data

Animal and Plant Life Spans

Each kind of animal and plant has a different life span, or amount of time to live. How does the average human life span compare to the life spans shown in the chart? Why do you think there is a big difference in life spans?

Fruit fly	37 days
Hummingbird	9 years
Galápagos Island land tortoise	150 years
Bristlecone pine	5000 years
Mouse	2 years
Sugar maple	300 years

▲ Bristlecone pines are the oldest living trees.

Galápagos Island land tortoises have the longest life span of any animal. ▲

A kangaroo's offspring develops inside its mother for about 33 days. Then the mother gives birth. In only about three minutes, the baby moves to its mother's pouch. It begins to drink its mother's milk as soon as it gets there. Inside the pouch, the tiny kangaroo continues to grow.

Another animal that grows in a pouch is a sea horse. The female sea horse deposits eggs in the male's pouch. There, the eggs are fertilized. After several weeks, young sea horses pop out of the pouch and swim away.

Many birds lay eggs in nests. The eggs have shells that protect the growing embryos inside. When many young birds hatch, they have no feathers. They need to be fed and kept warm.

Like birds, most reptiles also lay eggs. But when reptiles hatch, they are ready to survive on their own.

Most amphibians and fish lay their eggs in water. When fish hatch, they look just like their parents. They are ready to survive on their own. Amphibians usually go through changes in their bodies after they hatch. You'll read more about those changes later in the lesson. Many insects also go through complete body changes before they become adults.

Focus Skill COMPARE AND CONTRAST

How is a bird's life cycle similar to a reptile's life cycle? How is it different?

Growth and Development

Animals grow and develop in different ways. The bodies of many animals change as they grow older. Cats and dogs are born with very little fur. Their legs are wobbly, they have baby teeth, and their eyes are closed. They are tiny and cute. As they grow, their bodies lengthen and their faces change. However, their basic body plan is the same as an adult animal's.

Spiders also are very tiny when they hatch, but they are otherwise like their parents. They get larger, but they don't go through other major changes. The same is true of fish and other animals. This kind of growth is called **direct development**.

Shedding an outer covering is *molting.* A horseshoe crab sheds its shell 16 or 17 times in its lifetime. Each time it molts, the crab grows a little bigger. Then it grows a new and larger shell. Spiders, insects, and similar animals molt. Reptiles also shed their skins.

Animals grow at different rates. A fruit fly grows to be an adult in about 10 days. An elephant nurses for three years. An elephant is an adolescent at about 12 years. A dog develops about seven times faster than a human. A dog, depending on the breed, is an adult at about three years.

The stages in the human life cycle are infancy, childhood, adolescence, and adulthood. You began as a fertilized egg inside your mother.

◀ **Bald eagle young have dark brown feathers all over.**

◀ **Young deer are born with spots that help them hide in bushes and tall grass.**

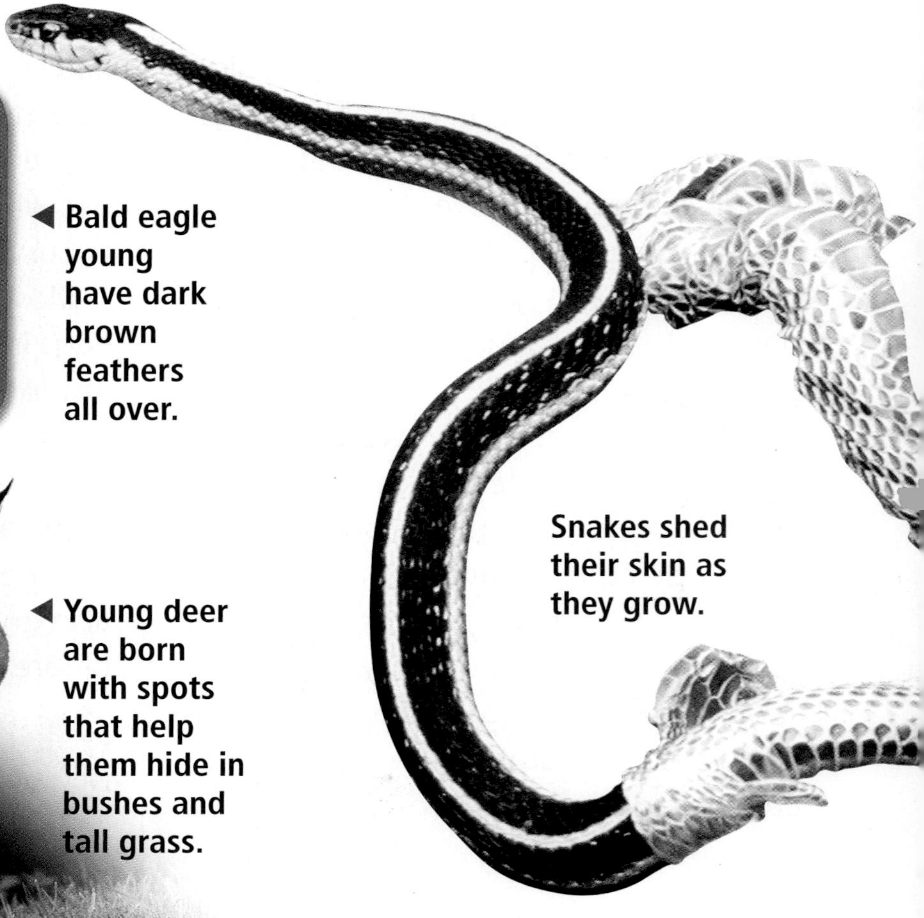

Snakes shed their skin as they grow.

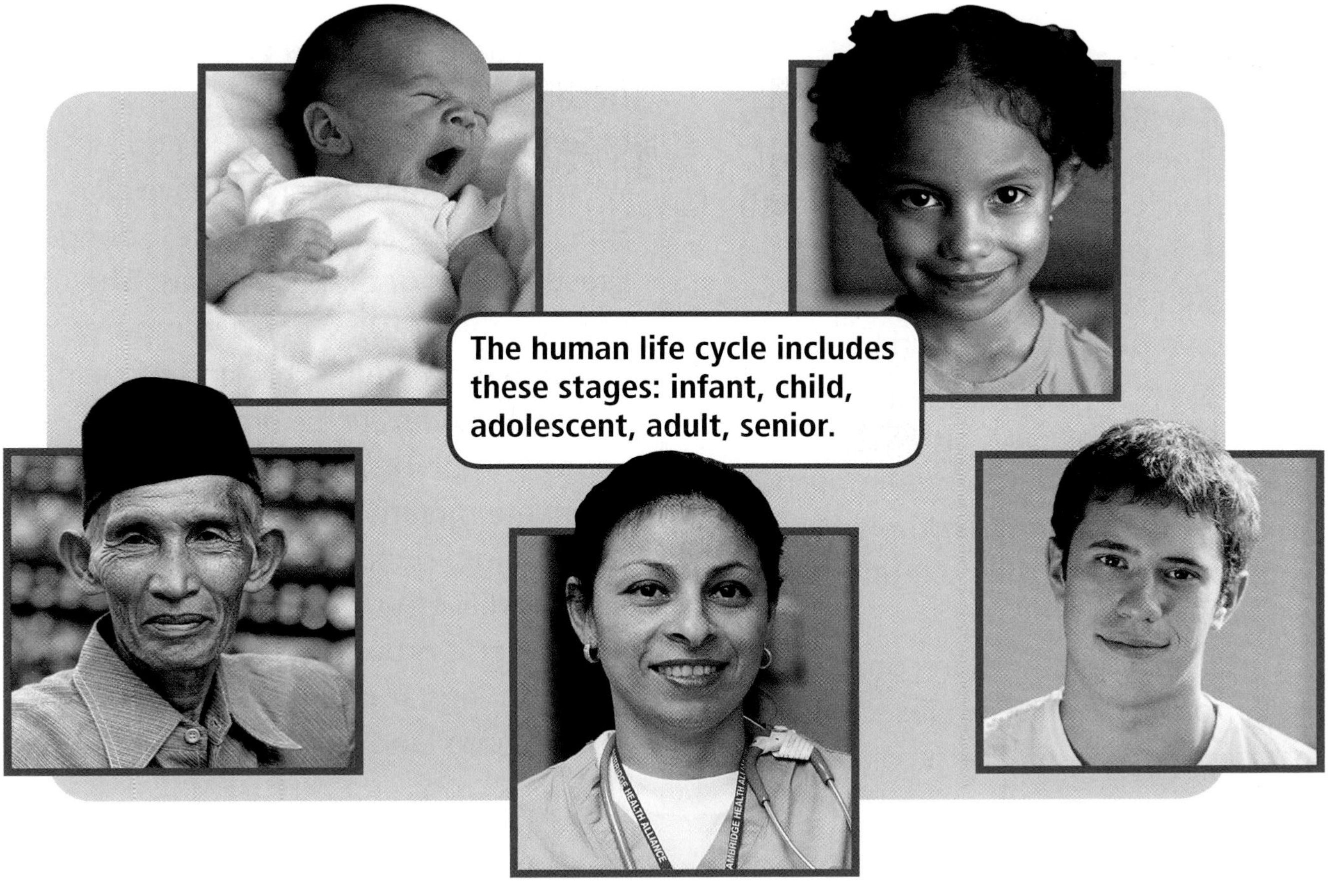

The human life cycle includes these stages: infant, child, adolescent, adult, senior.

When you were born, you were completely dependent on your parents. You were an infant from birth to two years. In those two years, you learned to walk and talk, and the size of your body changed.

Right now, you're in the childhood stage. During childhood, you grow a lot, but not quite as fast as during infancy. You lose some teeth and get some new ones. Your body changes, and you learn many new things.

Next you'll become an adolescent. Adolescents go through many changes in their bodies as they move toward adulthood. Not everyone reaches adolescence at the same time.

When you reach adulthood, your body will be fully developed. You will have reached your full height. A person over the age of 50 is considered a senior.

Focus Skill COMPARE AND CONTRAST

List similarities and differences between human adult and child stages.

Insta-Lab

What Will You Look Like as an Adult?

Draw a picture of yourself as you think you will look when you're about 50 years old. How tall will you be, and what might you be doing in life?

Metamorphosis

Did you know that a caterpillar is an insect? Look at the pictures showing the life cycle of a sphinx (SFINGKS) moth. Notice the caterpillar and other stages of the life cycle. Major changes in the body form of an animal during its life cycle are called **metamorphosis** (met•uh•MAWR•fuh•sis). Butterflies, moths, bees, and flies undergo metamorphosis. An insect that changes completely from one stage to the next undergoes *complete metamorphosis.*

There are four stages in complete metamorphosis. First, an insect lays fertilized eggs. A tiny caterpillar, or larva, hatches from each egg. The larva eats, grows, and then rolls up and becomes a pupa (PYOO•puh) in a chrysalis (KRIS•uh•lis) or a cocoon. The pupa changes to become the adult insect.

Some animals look like the adults when they hatch but don't have all the adults' parts. For example, young grasshoppers don't have wings. They are *nymphs* (NIMFS). Once a nymph grows wings, it is an adult. This kind of change is called *incomplete metamorphosis.*

Most amphibians, such as frogs, show complete metamorphosis. When a tadpole, or young frog, hatches, it has a tail and lives in water, breathing with gills. Later it grows legs and loses its tail. When its legs and lungs are fully grown, it hops onto land as an adult frog.

Focus Skill COMPARE AND CONTRAST

Compare the life cycle stages of a moth with those of a grasshopper.

Life Cycle of a Moth

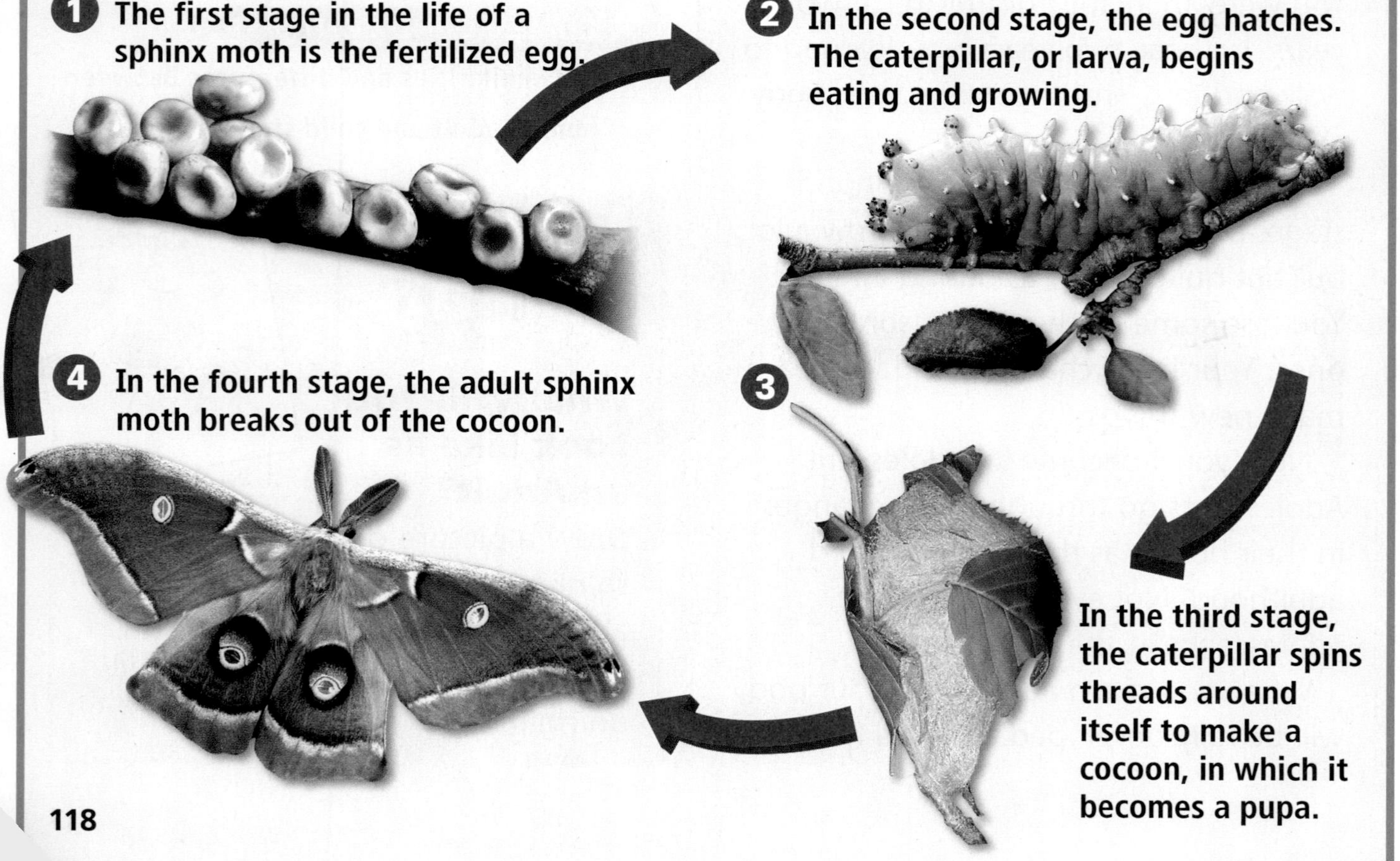

1 The first stage in the life of a sphinx moth is the fertilized egg.

2 In the second stage, the egg hatches. The caterpillar, or larva, begins eating and growing.

3 In the third stage, the caterpillar spins threads around itself to make a cocoon, in which it becomes a pupa.

4 In the fourth stage, the adult sphinx moth breaks out of the cocoon.

Lesson Review

Essential Question

What are some life cycles of animals?

In this lesson, you learned that animals have different life cycles. Some grow by direct development. Some undergo metamorphosis and change forms.

1. Focus Skill **COMPARE AND CONTRAST** Draw and complete a graphic organizer to show similarities and differences in direct development and metamorphosis.

   alike — different

2. **SUMMARIZE** Write your own definitions, using information from this lesson, for the vocabulary terms *direct development* and *metamorphosis.*

3. **DRAW CONCLUSIONS** What kind of habitat does a tadpole need in order to survive?

4. **VOCABULARY** Use the vocabulary terms to describe the way a fish develops and the way a fly develops.

Test Prep

5. **CRITICAL THINKING** Why would your parents want you to be a good helper if there was a new baby in your family?

6. Which animal goes through the most body shape changes in its life cycle?

   A. grasshopper
   B. kitten
   C. moth
   D. spider

Make Connections

Writing

Narrative Writing

Write a **biography** (life story) of a pet. The pet can belong to you or to someone you know. Start with how it was born.

Math

Calculate Stages

One year in the life of a human is like seven years in a dog's life. What stage is a dog in at the age of two? At age nine, is it an adult or an older adult?

Art

Make a Mobile

Research the life cycle of a monarch butterfly. Then make a mobile illustrating the four stages of its life cycle. Share your mobile with the class.

Dian Fossey

▶ **DIAN FOSSEY**

▶ Ethologist

Dian Fossey was a scientist who did not work in a lab. Instead, she worked in the mountain forests of Rwanda, a country in Africa. Fossey went to Africa to study mountain gorillas. These animals live in forests about 10,000 feet above sea level.

Fossey studied gorillas in their habitat, where they lived. That way she could observe their natural behavior.

Much of what is known about mountain gorillas comes from Fossey's work. For example, Fossey showed that the gorillas have a complex family structure. Fossey also worked to stop the illegal hunting of gorillas.

When Fossey later returned to the United States, she wrote a book. *Gorillas in the Mist* tells about her life in the jungle. She died in 1985 in Africa.

Think and Write

1. What did Dian Fossey discover about gorilla families?
2. Why was it important that she study gorillas in their habitat?

▶ **LYDIA VILLA-KOMAROFF**

▶ Biologist

Lydia Villa-Komaroff

Lydia Villa-Komaroff grew up in a big family in New Mexico. When Villa-Komaroff was five, her father brought home a set of encyclopedias. He told her that all she needed to know was in those books.

She must have listened to her dad, because Villa-Komaroff grew up to be one of the top scientists in her field. She has made many important discoveries in the field of biology.

Her most important discovery was in 1978 when she proved that bacterial cells could be changed to make **insulin**. Insulin is important in treating diabetes. Villa-Komaroff's discovery made it easier and cheaper to get insulin.

Think and Write

1. What did Lydia Villa-Komaroff receive from her father when she was a child?
2. What is her most important discovery?

Career Biologist

When a drug company develops a new drug, biologists usually take part in the important first steps. Biologists study living things and how those things interact with their environments. These scientists work on a wide range of projects, including developing new drugs, increasing crop yields, and protecting the environment.

CHAPTER 2

Review and Test Preparation

Vocabulary Review

Use the terms below to complete the sentences. The page numbers tell you where to look in the chapter if you need help.

trait p. 92
heredity p. 92
genes p. 93
photosynthesis p. 102
life cycle p. 104
direct development p. 116
metamorphosis p. 118

1. The stages a plant or an animal goes through from the beginning of one generation to the beginning of a new generation is a _______.

2. The passing on of characteristics from parents to offspring is _______.

3. The change from a larva stage to a nymph stage is a kind of _______.

4. The basic units of heredity are _______.

5. Fish grow and develop in a process known as _______.

6. A characteristic that is passed from parent to child is a _______.

7. The process by which plants make sugar for energy is called _______.

Check Understanding

Write the letter of the best choice.

8. Which of the following plant structures are on a moss plant?
F. leaves
G. roots
H. seeds
J. spores

9. How can you **best** explain the resemblance between offspring and parents?
A. eating habits
B. heredity
C. daily activity
D. behavior

10. Which of this girl's characteristics is **not** controlled by genes?

F. the color of her hair
G. her dimples
H. the shape of her earlobes
J. her hairstyle

11. In which stage of the human life cycle is the body completely developed?
A. adolescent
B. adult
C. child
D. infant

12. What makes Grant such a fast runner?

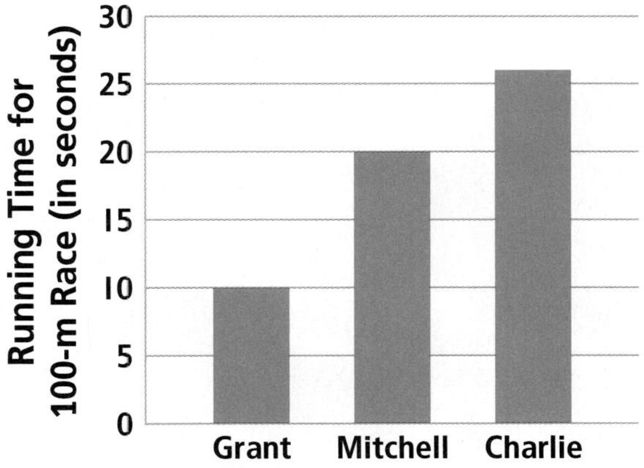

F. behavior
G. behavior and inherited traits
H. direct development
J. inherited traits

13. **COMPARE AND CONTRAST** Sexual and asexual production both result in more plants. What makes the product of asexual reproduction different?
Focus Skill
A. The new plant is a different species.
B. The new plant is a clone.
C. The new plant cannot reproduce.
D. The new plant is a different color.

14. **SEQUENCE** Which stage is missing from this plant life cycle?
Focus Skill

F. embryo
G. flower
H. leaves
J. roots

15. Which stage of a moss plant's life cycle produces sperm and eggs?
A. gametophyte
B. plant
C. seed
D. sporophyte

16. Which is the first stage of incomplete metamorphosis?
F. adult
G. egg
H. larva
J. nymph

Inquiry Skills

17. Describe an **experiment** that would help you **conclude** whether or not a plant needs water to grow.

18. Suppose you **observe** a tadpole grow into a frog. What can you **infer** about its life cycle?

Critical Thinking

19. How can you explain why the eyes of different humans can be many different colors?
The Big Idea

20. Humans need to be cared for until they can care for themselves. Why do you think humans need to be taken care of much longer than all other animals? List some of the things you need to learn before you can take care of yourself completely.

CHAPTER 3

Adaptations

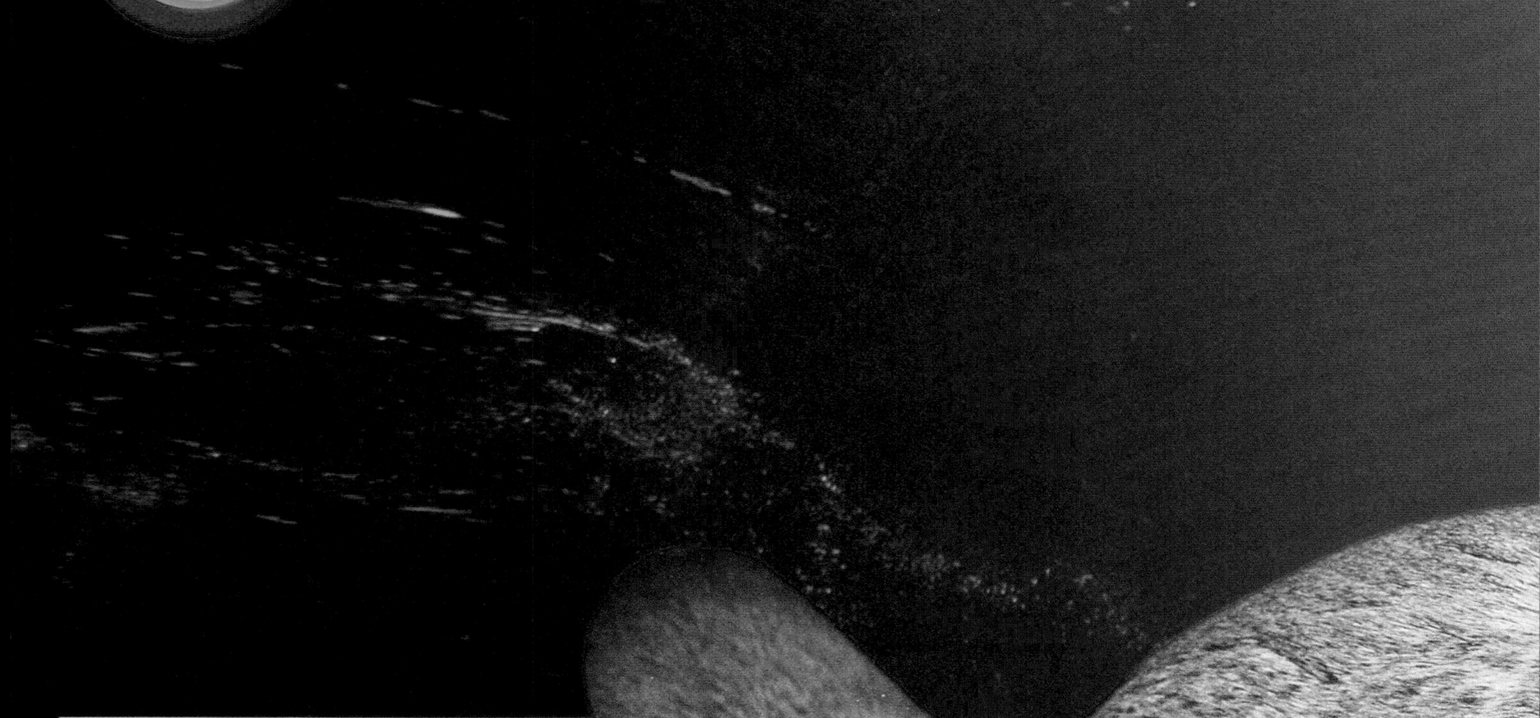

What's the Big Idea? Living things are adapted for survival in their environment.

Essential Questions

Lesson 1
How Do the Bodies of Animals Help Them Meet Their Needs?

Lesson 2
How Do the Behaviors of Animals Help Them Meet Their Needs?

Lesson 3
How Do Living Things of the Past Compare with Those of Today?

Go online
Student eBook
www.hspscience.com

Platypus swimming

What do YOU wonder?

One or the Other? The platypus (PLAT•uh•puhs) is a mammal that lays eggs. It has special body parts for swimming and for eating in water. How might the adaptation of its webbed feet help it survive in its environment? How does this relate to the **Big Idea?**

LESSON 1

Essential Question

How Do the Bodies of Animals Help Them Meet Their Needs?

Investigate how different beak shapes handle different foods.

Read and Learn how the bodies of animals help them meet their basic needs.

Fast Fact

Big Beak!
This toucan is an eye-catching sight! Its long, colorful beak looks heavy, but it's really very light. The long beak helps the toucan reach fruit at the ends of branches. In the Investigate, you will explore characteristics that help birds survive in their ecosystems.

Toucan with fruit

Vocabulary Preview

basic needs [BAY•sik NEEDZ] Food, water, air, and shelter that an organism needs to survive (p. 130)

adaptation [ad•uhp•TAY•shuhn] A body part or behavior that helps an organism survive (p. 132)

natural selection [NACH•er•uhl suh•LEK•shuhn] A process in which the best adapted organisms in an ecosystem are able to survive and reproduce (p. 135)

Investigate

Eating Like a Bird

Guided Inquiry

Start with Questions

Birds' beaks help them get and eat food. Think about the different birds you have seen in this book and the different shapes of their beaks.

- How does beak shape help the egret in the picture?
- What beak shape would make it hard for this bird to get food?

Investigate to find out. Then read and learn to find out more.

Prepare to Investigate

Inquiry Skill Tip

Look at your data chart before you start to draw conclusions. Consider all your observations.

Materials

tools—
- 2 chopsticks or unsharpened pencils
- clothespin
- pliers
- spoon
- forceps

food—
- plastic worms
- raisins
- cooked spaghetti
- peanuts in shells
- water in a cup
- cooked rice
- birdseed

- small paper plates

Make an Observation Chart

Food	Best Tool (Beak)	Observations

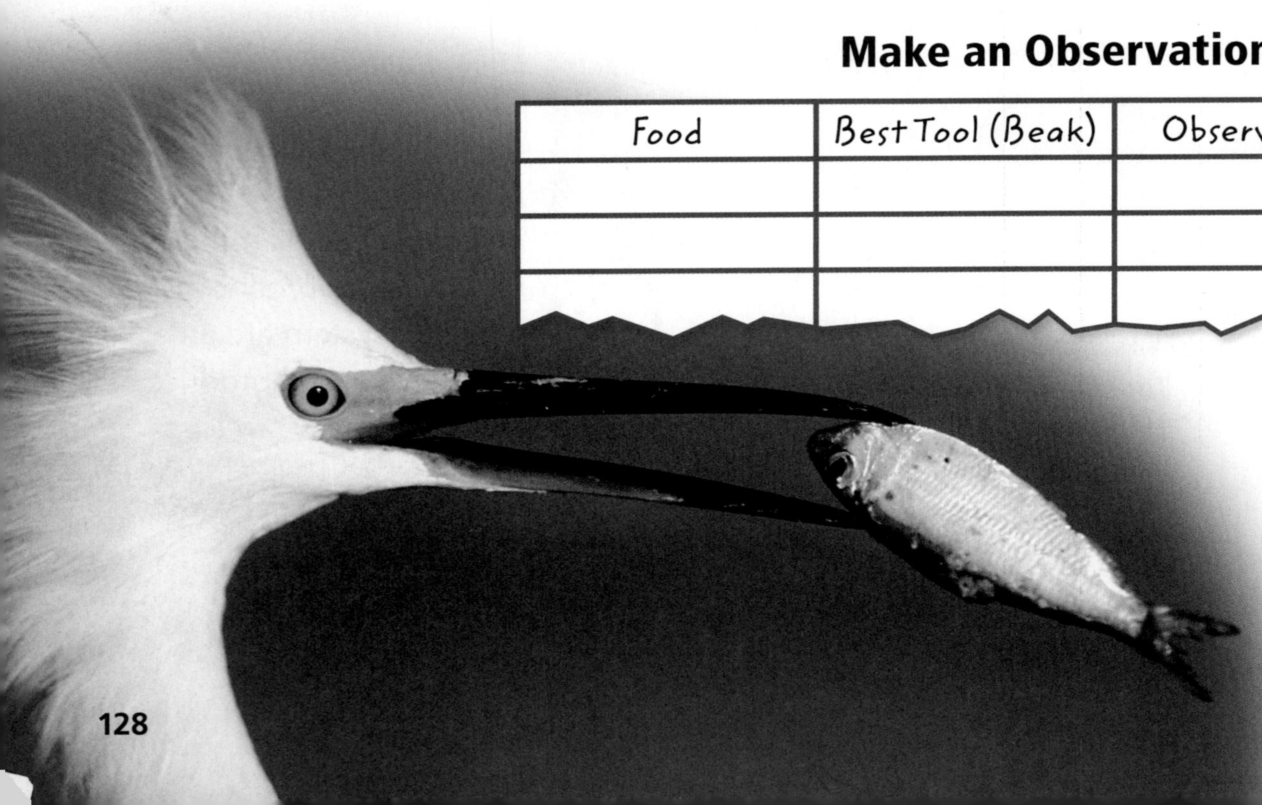

Follow This Procedure

1. Make a chart like the one shown on page 128.
2. Put the tools on one side of your desk, and think of them as bird beaks. Put each kind of food on a paper plate.
3. Place one type of food in the middle of your desk. Try picking up the food with each tool (beak), and decide which kind of beak works best.
4. Test all the beaks with all the foods and with the water. Use the table to **record** your **observations** and conclusions.

Draw Conclusions

1. Which kind of beak is best for picking up small seeds? Which kind is best for crushing large seeds?
2. **Inquiry Skill** Scientists experiment and then **draw conclusions** about what they have learned. After experimenting, what conclusions can you draw about why bird beaks are different shapes?

Independent Inquiry

Use a reference book about birds. Match the tools you used with real bird beaks. Make a hypothesis about how beak shape relates to food. Then read your book to find out if you are correct.

Read and Learn

VOCABULARY
basic needs p. 130
adaptation p. 132
natural selection p. 135

SCIENCE CONCEPTS
- what basic needs are shared by all living things
- how adaptations allow living things to meet their needs

Focus Skill MAIN IDEA AND DETAILS
Look for different kinds of basic needs.

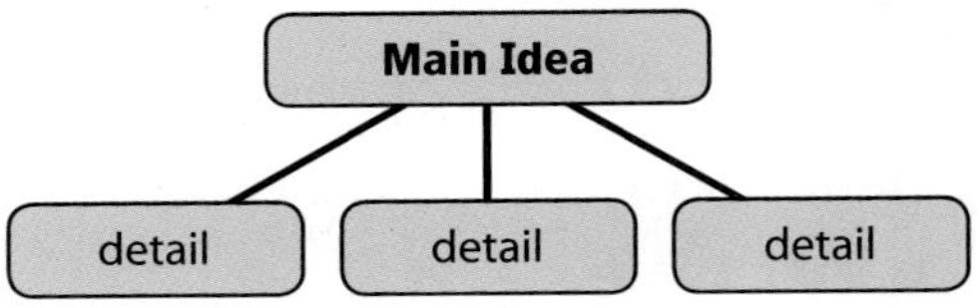

Basic Needs

What do you need to survive? You might want to have jeans in the latest style. You might want to eat pizza for dinner every night. But you do not really need these things to survive.

All living things, from ants to tigers to you, have the same basic needs. These **basic needs** are food, water, air, and shelter.

Living things meet their needs in a variety of ways. Plants can make their own food, but they must have sunlight to do it. Most other living things depend on plants—or on animals that eat plants—for food.

Many animals, such as frogs and wolves, get their food by catching it. Some animals, such as vultures, wait until another animal has killed something. Then they eat the leftovers. Humans get most of their food by growing plants and raising animals.

Plants get water from rain and from moist soil. Many animals drink water from streams and puddles, but some desert animals obtain enough water to survive from the foods they eat.

Like every other living thing, a tiger needs water.

All animals must take in oxygen. Animals that live on land and some animals that live in water get oxygen from air. Other animals that live in water get oxygen from the water.

Shelter can take many forms. Some insects live under rocks, while foxes make dens in hollow logs. Prairie dogs dig burrows in the ground, and eels hide in coral reefs. Delicate plants grow in protected places. People build homes of many sizes and shapes.

Hunger and thirst signal the need to eat and drink. Rain and cold tell many animals to find shelter. Meeting basic needs isn't always easy, but living things must do it to survive.

Focus Skill MAIN IDEA AND DETAILS

How do you meet your basic needs?

After beavers cut sticks and twigs from trees, they eat the leaves and bark. Then they use the sticks to build shelters. ▶

▲ Like other living things, this alligator needs air. It keeps its nostrils above water while it watches for food.

▼ The heron's long beak helps it catch frogs and fish in shallow water.

Adaptations

Plants and animals have adaptations that help them meet their needs. An **adaptation** is a body part or a behavior that a living thing gets from its parents and that helps it survive.

One adaptation is fur color. For example, during the summer, the snowshoe hare is rusty brown. This helps it blend with the ground. In the winter, the rabbit's fur turns white. This helps it blend with the snow. The color change helps the rabbit hide from enemies.

Instead of fur, fish and reptiles have scales. Their scales help protect them from injury and from drying out. Often, the color and pattern of their scales help them hide from enemies. A snake's scales help it slide along the ground to find food, water, and shelter.

Many frogs and lizards have long tongues that help them catch insects. Imagine how such a long tongue would look on a lion. Lions have other adaptations that help them catch their food, such as speed, strength, long claws, and sharp teeth.

You have explored differences in bird beaks. Different kinds of feet also help birds meet their needs. A robin's feet allow it to perch on a branch. An eagle's claws help it snatch up food, while a penguin's feet help it swim.

◀ **Vampire bats live in Central and South America. They need about 20 grams (about 2 tablespoons) of blood a day. They get the blood mostly from cattle.**

▼ **A vampire bat's tiny, razor-sharp teeth easily pierce the skin of its prey. The bat doesn't suck the blood. Instead, it laps up the blood with its tongue.**

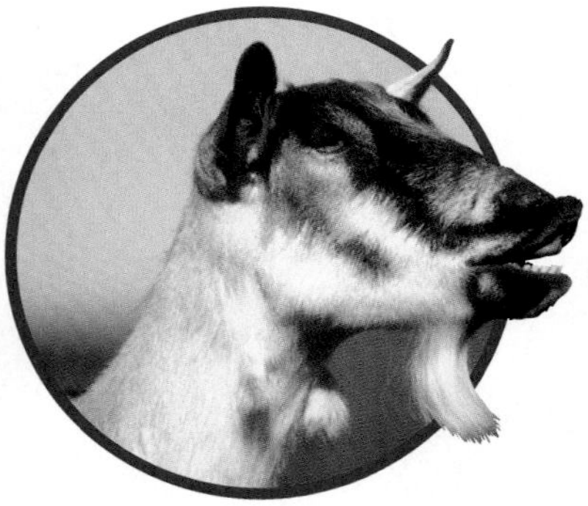

◀ **A goat's teeth are adapted for the food it eats. Large and flat, these teeth are just right for grinding up grasses.**

▼ **Most goats eat grasses during the summer. During the winter, they eat hay, which is a dried grass. All these grasses require a lot of chewing.**

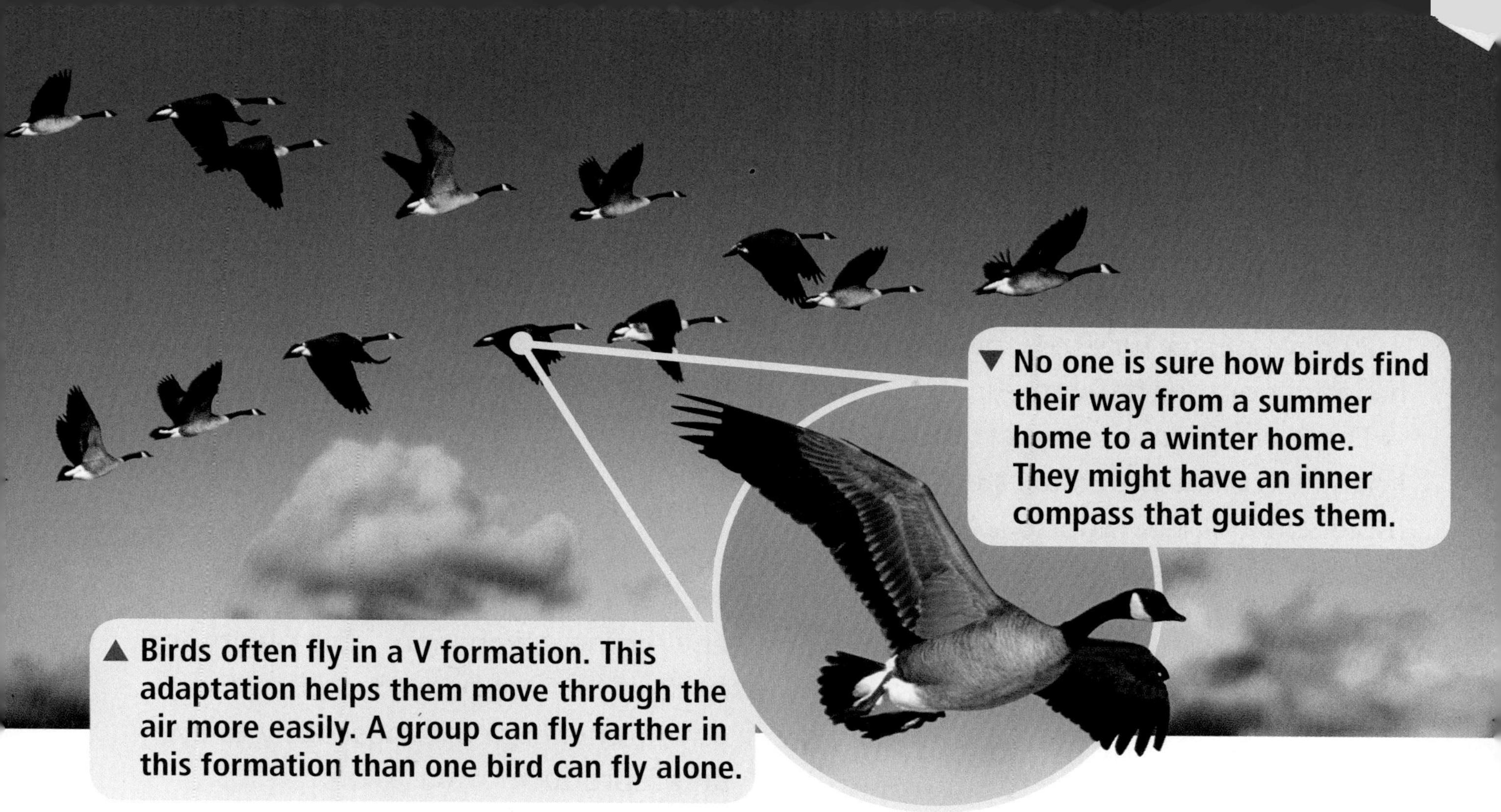

▼ No one is sure how birds find their way from a summer home to a winter home. They might have an inner compass that guides them.

▲ Birds often fly in a V formation. This adaptation helps them move through the air more easily. A group can fly farther in this formation than one bird can fly alone.

During a long, cold winter, food and water can be scarce. Animals need more shelter. Many have adapted to winter by migrating or hibernating.

Migration means "moving from a summer home to a winter home and back again." Gray whales' bodies allow them to swim 16,000 to 23,000 kilometers (10,000 to 14,000 mi) a year. They spend summer in the Arctic. In the fall, they swim to warmer waters. There, they give birth to their young.

Monarch butterflies migrate up to 4,800 kilometers (3,000 mi). As the weather cools, monarchs west of the Rocky Mountains fly to the west coast. Monarchs east of the Rockies fly to Mexico. There, they rest for the winter.

During *hibernation,* an animal's heart rate and breathing rate slow almost to a stop. Bats, ground squirrels, and woodchucks hibernate. Their bodies are adapted to survive for long periods on a tiny amount of food and oxygen.

Bears, skunks, and chipmunks sleep a lot. This helps them survive the cold winter months. Yet their body systems are still active. These animals do not hibernate.

Focus Skill **MAIN IDEA AND DETAILS**

What are three examples of adaptations?

Insta-Lab

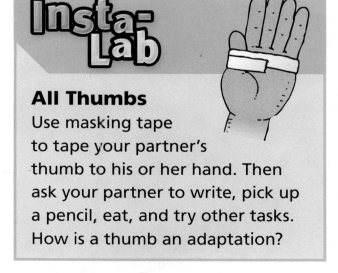

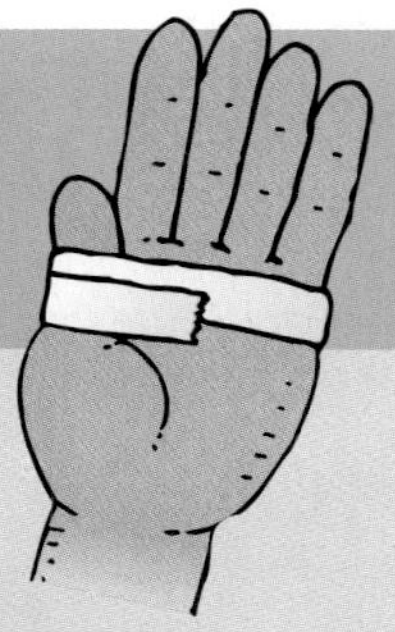

All Thumbs

Use masking tape to tape your partner's thumb to his or her hand. Then ask your partner to write, pick up a pencil, eat, and try other tasks. How is a thumb an adaptation?

Biological Change

Have you ever seen a litter of kittens or mice? The young animals in a litter have the same parents. Yet they may look different. Some may be striped. Some may have darker fur. Every population has variations, or differences.

These variations are important. Imagine a plant with a tall stem. It gets more sunlight than shorter plants. As a result, it can gather more energy. Tall-stemmed plants grow better in this environment.

Maybe the plant's stem grew tall because it was in the perfect soil type and had the right amount of water. It grew tall because of its environment. If so, the plant would not pass this trait to its offspring.

However, the plant may have had special codes in its cells that made it grow tall. The plant could pass on this tall-stem trait to its offspring. Over time, there would be more tall-stemmed plants.

Passing on these traits makes this type of plant better able to cope with environmental changes. The plants and animals that are best adapted to their environment are the most likely to live and reproduce.

Look at the kittens. Even though they have the same mother, they do not look the same. Diversity is an important part of a population. It helps the population adapt, or change, as the environment changes.

Dark gray moths are better able to blend in with the bark of dark trees. The light gray moths can only blend in with lighter bark.

A good example of adaptation is the peppered moth. Long ago, most peppered moths were light gray. Their color helped them blend with their environment. This hid them from birds that would try to eat them.

After a time, people built many factories. The factories filled the air with dark soot. The soot darkened the trees, plants, and other things. The tree trunks got darker. The ground was darker.

What do you think happened to the moths? Now, the dark gray moths were better hidden. The light gray moths stood out. They were easier for the birds to see and eat. Over time, there were more dark gray moths. The light gray moths became rare. The population of moths was adapting to change over time.

The moths are an example of natural selection. **Natural selection** is the process by which organisms with favorable traits are more likely to survive and produce offspring. The moths' environment changed. The new environment made dark gray coloring an advantage to the moths. So the dark-colored moths were more likely to live and to make more moths.

Over time, populations, such as the moths, change and adapt to their environment. This type of biological change occurs in many plants and animals.

Focus Skill **MAIN IDEA AND DETAILS**

How might change benefit an organism?

Growth and Decay

All plants and animals follow a cycle of life. It begins with a fertilized egg. Sprouting, being born, or hatching comes next. Then the seedling or baby grows into an adult. Adult living things reproduce in many ways. Some make seeds, some give birth to babies, and some lay eggs.

Living things are being born all the time. They are also dying and decaying. Fungi, insects, bacteria, and plants all help dead organisms decay, or decompose. The nutrients in a dead organism often become part of the soil. This makes the soil richer, which helps new plants grow.

Living things can complete their life cycles only if they are able to meet all their basic needs. Adaptations help living things meet their basic needs.

If a plant or an animal can't meet its needs, it might die before it can reproduce. If this continues for every member of the species, this kind of living thing will no longer survive on Earth.

Focus Skill **MAIN IDEA AND DETAILS**

What parts make up the cycle of life?

◀ This tree fell years ago in the rain forest. As the log decayed, seeds blew onto it and sprouted. Now the dead tree is a "nurse log" for new trees. The new trees will grow in a row.

Adult trees stretch their roots around the nurse log and into the soil.

Essential Question

Lesson Review

How Do the Bodies of Animals Help Them Meet Their Needs?

In this lesson, you learned that animals have developed special body parts to help them meet their needs. Unless animals meet their basic needs, they will not survive.

1. Focus Skill **MAIN IDEA AND DETAILS** Draw and complete a graphic organizer to show how adaptations help animals survive.

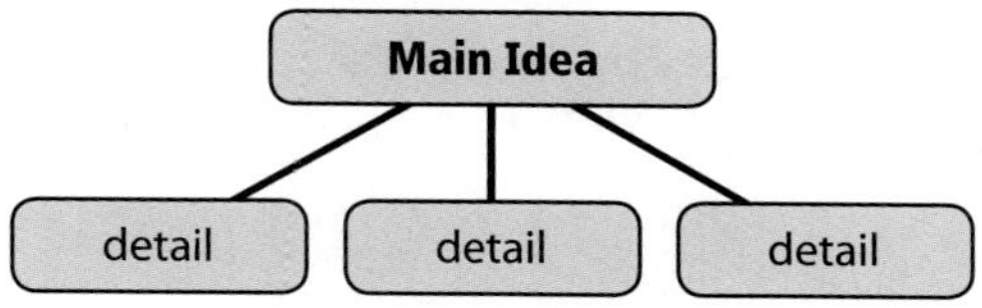

2. **SUMMARIZE** Write a summary of this lesson. Begin with this sentence: *Animals need food, water, air, and shelter to survive.*

3. **DRAW CONCLUSIONS** Name three adaptations in behavior that some animals show during winter.

4. **VOCABULARY** Write a paragraph that includes a blank for each vocabulary term. Have a partner fill in the terms.

Test Prep

5. **CRITICAL THINKING** Explain two ways that a body covering can help an animal meet its basic needs.

6. Which adaptation helps a robin catch a worm?
   A. sharp eyesight
   B. feather coloring
   C. perching feet
   D. nest building

Make Connections

Writing

Narrative Writing

Write a **story** about how a real animal in a forest uses an adaptation to meet its needs in some way. Make your story exciting!

Math

Solve a Problem

A deer must have about 20 acres of land to meet its needs for food, water, and shelter. One square mile has 640 acres. How many deer could live on 2 square miles of land?

Art

Collage

Cut out magazine pictures, or use your own drawings, to make a collage of the basic needs of a person or a specific animal. Then display your work.

LESSON 2

Essential Question

How Do the Behaviors of Animals Help Them Meet Their Needs?

Investigate how to change the behavior of a goldfish.

Read and Learn how the ways animals behave can help them survive.

Fast Fact

Whale Song

Some people call beluga whales the canaries of the sea. Beluga songs can be heard even above the water! Young belugas learn how to survive by watching adult belugas. In the Investigate, you will see if a goldfish has the ability to learn.

Adult beluga whale with young whale

Vocabulary Preview

instinct [IN•stinkt] A behavior that an animal begins life with (p. 142)

hibernation [hy•ber•NAY•shuhn] A dormant, inactive state in which normal body activities slow (p. 143)

migration [my•GRAY•shuhn] The movement of animals from one region to another and back (p. 144)

learned behavior [LERND bee•HAYV•yer] A behavior that an organism doesn't begin life with (p. 146)

Train a Fish

Guided Inquiry

Start with Questions

Animals can learn more than tricks. This chipmunk has learned to hide food to help it survive. Animals can learn new things and change the way they behave.

- How do animals learn new things?
- How does hiding food help the chipmunk survive?

Investigate to find out. Then read and learn to find out more.

Prepare to Investigate

Inquiry Skill Tip

When you observed your fish, were you careful to do so under the same conditions each time? Changing the way in which you observe things can change your observations.

Materials

- goldfish in a bowl
- goldfish food

Make an Observation Chart

Day	Observations of the Fish's Behavior
1	
2	
3	
4	
5	

Follow This Procedure

1. Work in a group of three or four classmates to train a goldfish. On the first day, **observe** the behavior of the fish when you hold your hand above the bowl. Then feed the fish by dropping some food into the bowl. **Record** the fish's behavior.
2. The next day, hold your hand a little closer above the bowl. Then drop the pellet. **Record** the fish's behavior.
3. Each day, repeat Step 2, moving your hand nearer the water.
4. Use your **observations** to plan how to continue the **experiment**.

Draw Conclusions

1. From your **observations**, what can you **infer** about a fish's ability to learn?
2. **Inquiry Skill** When scientists experiment, they design procedures to gather data. How did **observing** the fish help you plan the experiment?

Independent Inquiry

Observe a pet's behavior. List things that the pet does that no one taught it to do. Also list things it may have learned.

Read and Learn

VOCABULARY
instinct p. 142
hibernation p. 143
migration p. 144
learned behavior p. 146

SCIENCE CONCEPTS
- how instinctive behaviors help animals meet their needs
- how learned behaviors help animals meet their needs

Focus Skill: MAIN IDEA AND DETAILS
Look for ways animals fill their basic needs.

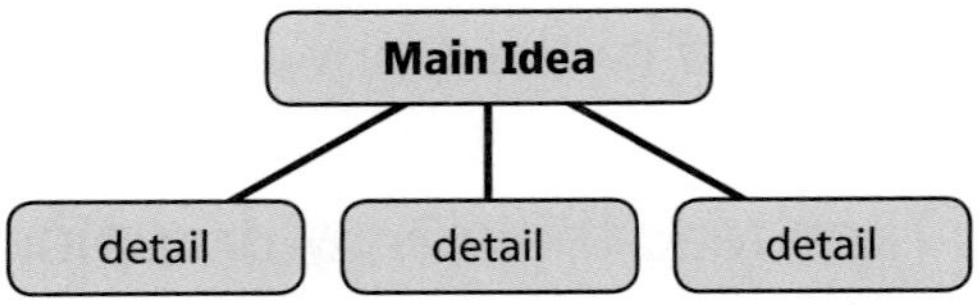

Instincts

When you were born, you already knew how to suck to get milk. You knew how to cry. Other animals already know things, too. A spider knows how to spin a web to catch food. Some animals, like zebras, know that living together in herds helps protect them from predators. Some animals know how to protect themselves from the weather. Each of these behaviors is an **instinct**—a behavior that animals begin life with that helps them meet their needs.

Focus Skill: MAIN IDEA AND DETAILS
What are some instinctive behaviors?

▼ **Orb-weaver spiders spin new webs every night. Each kind of spider begins life knowing the pattern for its own kind of web.**

▲ **Weaverbirds build complex nests from grasses and other materials. They hatch knowing how to weave their nests.**

Hibernation

Some animals live where winters are very cold. Many of them know by instinct how to get ready for winter. First, they eat more food than normal, so they can gain fat. Then, they find dens or build shelters. When the days become short and cold, the animals move to shelters. They enter a dormant, inactive state called **hibernation** (hy•ber•NAY•shuhn). Normal body activities slow. The heart barely beats, and breathing almost stops. The body temperature drops to just above freezing.

Since the body is barely working, a hibernating animal doesn't use much energy and doesn't need to eat. There is enough fat stored in the animal's body to keep it alive through the winter. By springtime, hibernating animals are thin and they're very hungry!

Focus Skill MAIN IDEA AND DETAILS

Why do some animals hibernate?

◀ When the weather is cold, koi fish hibernate at the bottom of a pond.

A bat's normal heartbeat rate is 400 beats per minute. When the bat hibernates, its heart beats only 11 to 25 times per minute. ▶

▼ A woodchuck digs a winter burrow. Its body temperature drops from 36°C (97°F) to less than 8°C (47°F).

Some male frogs hibernate at the bottom of ponds. The female frogs and their young stay in holes or dens on land. ▼

Migration

Every year, people gather to watch whales. People also like to watch caribou travel. It's possible to predict when to watch whales and caribou. These animals travel every year at about the same time.

Migrate means "to move from one region to another." When animals regularly move as a group from one region to another and back, it's a **migration**. Animal migrations can depend on seasons or on other factors.

Migration is an instinctive behavior. Generally, animals migrate to a place that has more food and a better climate. Some migrations are puzzling. For example, young salmon go out to sea. Adults return to lay eggs in the mountain stream where they were hatched.

Focus Skill MAIN IDEA AND DETAILS

How do animals know when to migrate?

Math in Science
Interpret Data

Which Animal Migrates the Farthest?

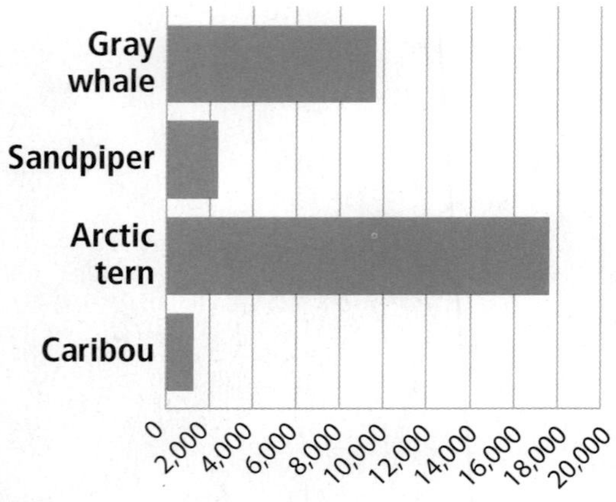

Migration Distances (in kilometers)

Science Up Close

Animal Migration Routes

Gray whales feed in cold northern waters in winter and travel south in summer to look for mates and to give birth.

Caribou spend the winter in forests in northern Canada. Then, in early spring, they move further north.

The sandpiper spends summers in eastern Canada. In winter, it flies nonstop over the Atlantic to South America.

The Arctic tern travels farther than any other animal. It breeds in the summer, north of the Arctic Circle. In fall, it migrates to the Antarctic ice packs.

For more links and animations, go to **www.hspscience.com**

Learned Behaviors

Many animals have only instinctive behaviors to help them meet their needs. But some animals can use a **learned behavior** to help them survive. What instincts did you have when you were born? Did you have to learn how to eat, drink, and sleep? What other behaviors have you learned? You learned to walk and to feed yourself. Now you can write and play sports. Most behaviors are learned. Who helped you learn these things? Older animals usually teach young animals learned behaviors.

Most mammals raise their young. Mammal mothers usually teach their young how to get food and how to protect themselves. Among some animals, both parents care for and teach their young.

Some animals can be trained to change their behaviors. Dogs often instinctively bark at strangers, but people can train them not to do so. Horses are trained to respond to their riders. These are learned behaviors.

Focus Skill **MAIN IDEA AND DETAILS** **What are some behaviors bears learn?**

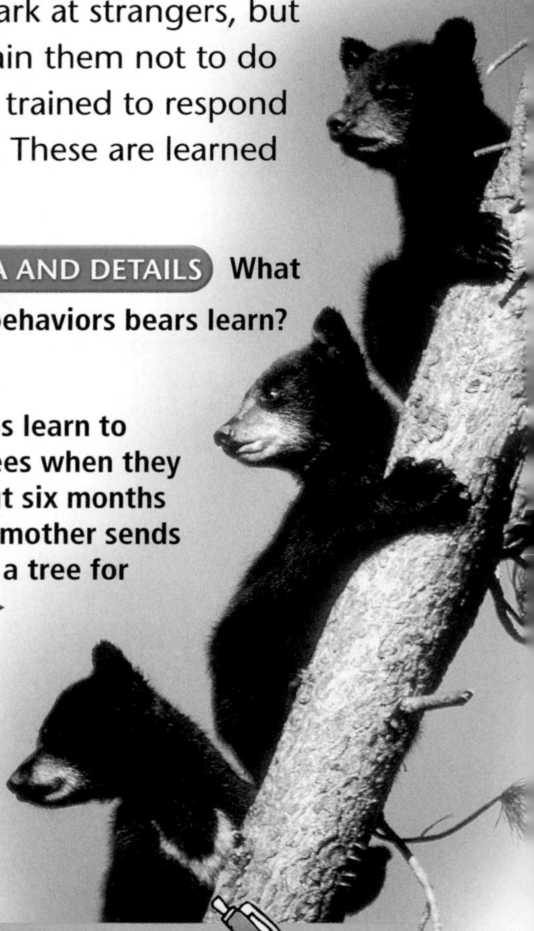

Bear cubs learn to climb trees when they are about six months old. The mother sends them up a tree for safety. ▶

Robins are ready to leave the nest two weeks after hatching. Then the parents teach them how to fly. ▶

▼ Tiger cubs imitate their mother's every move while she hunts. They learn from her example.

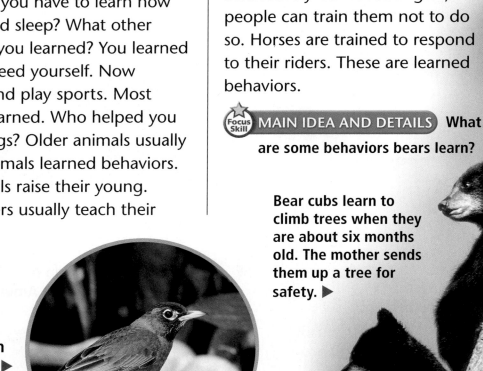

Insta-Lab

Learn How

Make a list of behaviors you have learned in order to meet your basic needs. Compare your list with a classmate's. Why do you think humans have many more learned behaviors than most other animals?

Essential Question

How do the behaviors of animals help them meet their needs?

In this lesson, you learned that animals learn new things and change the ways they behave to help them survive. Animals can migrate or hibernate to avoid severe weather. Instinct causes some actions, and others are learned behaviors.

1. Focus Skill MAIN IDEA AND DETAILS Draw and complete a graphic organizer to define instincts.

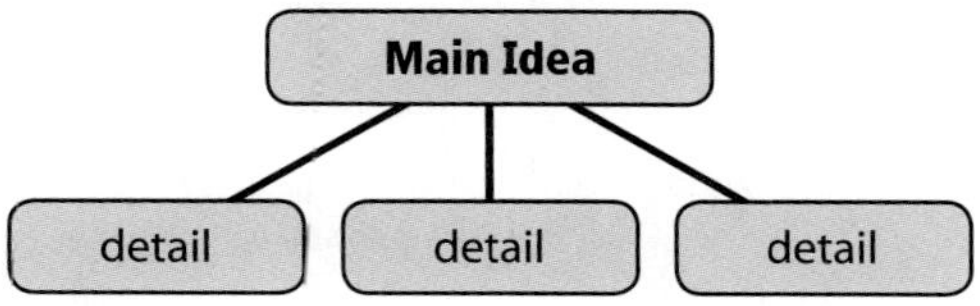

2. **SUMMARIZE** Write a sentence that tells the main idea of this lesson.

3. **DRAW CONCLUSIONS** Does a butterfly meet its basic needs by instinct or by learned behavior? What leads you to your conclusion?

4. **VOCABULARY** Write a paragraph, using all the vocabulary terms from this lesson.

Test Prep

5. **CRITICAL THINKING** Why would you **not** feed koi in a pond in winter?

6. Why does a hibernating animal's temperature drop?
   - **A.** to gain energy
   - **B.** to provide food
   - **C.** to protect its young
   - **D.** to conserve energy

Make Connections

Writing

Narrative Writing

Choose an animal that migrates. Research its migration path. Then write a **story** about its migration.

Math

Multiply Whole Numbers

A gray whale eats for only four months of the year. Then it eats 300 kilograms (660 lb) of food each day. How many pounds of food does it eat in one week?

Health

Basic Needs

Make a list of behaviors you have learned to keep yourself healthy and meet your basic needs.

LESSON 3

Essential Question

How Do Living Things of the Past Compare with Those of Today?

Investigate how fossils form.

Read and Learn how animals of the past compare with those of today.

Fast Fact

Step Back in Time
Thousands of fossils have been found at Thomas Farm in central Florida. More are still being discovered. In the Investigate, you will learn more about fossils.

Uncovering fossils

Vocabulary Preview

fossil [FAHS•uhl] The remains or traces of a plant or an animal that lived long ago (p. 152)

extinction [ek•STINGK•shuhn] The death of all the members of a certain group of organisms (p. 156)

Investigate

Make a Fossil

Guided Inquiry

Start with Questions

The remains of ancient animals were sometimes preserved as fossils. Fossils can show how animals of the past looked. They can also tell what those animals might have eaten and how they might have behaved.

- What kind of animal was the fossil that is pictured below?
- Does it look like any present-day animals?

Investigate to find out. Then read and learn to find out more.

Prepare to Investigate

Inquiry Skill Tip

When you infer an explanation, make it specific. If your explanation is too broad, it can be hard to test in an experiment.

Materials

- white glue
- 8 sugar cubes
- strainer
- sink or large bowl
- warm water

Make an Observation Chart

Observations	
Sugar	Glue

Follow This Procedure

1. Use the glue to put together 4 sugar cubes, making a 2 × 2 layer.
2. Glue the other 4 cubes together to make a second layer. Let both layers dry separately for 5 minutes.
3. Spread glue in the shape of a shell on one layer, and place the other layer on top. Let them dry overnight.
4. Put the two-layer structure in the strainer. Hold the strainer over a sink or bowl.
5. Pour warm water over the structure. **Observe** what happens to the sugar and the glue. **Record** your observations.

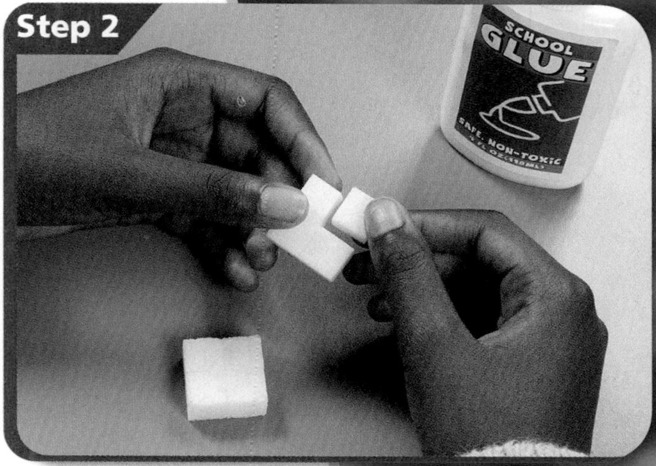

Draw Conclusions

1. You **made a model** of a fossil. What parts of a plant or an animal did the sugar cubes stand for? What parts did the dried glue stand for?
2. **Inquiry Skill** Scientists infer and then explain, based on what they observe. Based on your observations, what can you **infer** about how fossils form?

Independent Inquiry

Why might fossil skeletons break apart? Hypothesize what will happen if you put your fossil in a bag with rocks and shake it. Try it. Record your results.

Read and Learn

VOCABULARY
fossil p. 152
extinction p. 156

SCIENCE CONCEPTS
▶ how living things of long ago compare with those of today

Focus Skill COMPARE AND CONTRAST
Look for ways animals of long ago are like those of today.

alike	different

Animals Then and Now

A **fossil** is evidence of a plant or an animal that lived long ago. Footprints that formed when an animal stepped in mud are one kind of fossil. Over a long time, the mud hardened into rock. Footprints tell us about an animal's size. They also can tell how it moved.

Many fossils are bones that became buried before they could decay. Minerals replaced the bones, but the shapes remain.

Scientists compare these fossils with the footprints and bones of animals that are alive today. Using the comparisons, they can infer how animals have changed.

Although they are not at all related, fossils show that the triceratops (try•SAIR•uh•tahps) and today's rhinoceros (ry•NAHS•er•uhs) share the same body shape and a horned nose. Dinosaurs were reptiles, while rhinos are mammals.

Triceratops fossil skeleton

Modern-day rhinoceros

Triceratops

Camels lived in North America many years ago. Fossils tell us that some ancient camels were about the size of a rabbit. Others were about 4.5 meters (15 ft) tall at their shoulders!

A few animals, such as turtles, are much like ones from long ago. Others are very different now. By a careful study of their fossils, scientists can link animals of long ago with those of today. However, many ancient animals are now gone.

Focus Skill COMPARE AND CONTRAST How is the study of ancient animals different from the study of animals that live today?

By the early part of the twentieth century, the coelacanth (SEE•luh•kanth) fish shown in this fossil was thought to exist no longer. But a live coelacanth was caught near South Africa in 1938. ▶

Plants Then and Now

You might have found a plant fossil on a flat rock in a park or in your own yard. Some of these fossils formed when plant leaves fell on muddy ground millions of years ago. The leaves made an impression in the mud. When the mud dried, the imprint of the leaf was still there. This imprint shows the size, shape, and details of the leaf.

Have you ever held a piece of wood that felt like a rock? Petrified wood is another kind of plant fossil. It formed when a tree fell on the ground and was buried in mud before it could decay. Minerals slowly replaced the wood. In time, the wood became rock.

Like some animals of long ago, many plants of long ago are no longer living. Scientists know about them only because of fossils. You can also find fossils that look much like some plants that still grow today.

Many other plants have survived, but they have changed over time. In fact, plants are still changing. For example, farmers are now growing new kinds of corn that resist insects.

Focus Skill COMPARE AND CONTRAST

How are plants of long ago like animals of long ago?

About 300 million years ago, most of the plants on Earth were ferns. These plants and others died and were buried under many layers of soil. ▼

Insta-Lab

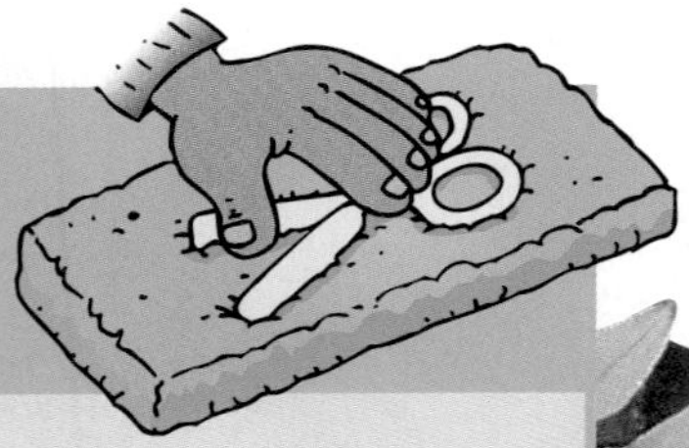

Fossil Quiz

Flatten some clay, and lightly press an object into it. Don't let anyone see the object you used. Then challenge others to identify the object you used by looking only at the imprint. How is your imprint like a fossil imprint?

◀ Ginkgo trees are often called living fossils because they have not changed much in 100 million years. Some types of ginkgo trees growing in China have existed more than 3000 years.

Bristlecone pine trees were growing 100 million years ago. The oldest tree living today is almost 5000 years old! Fossils show that these trees have changed very little. ▶

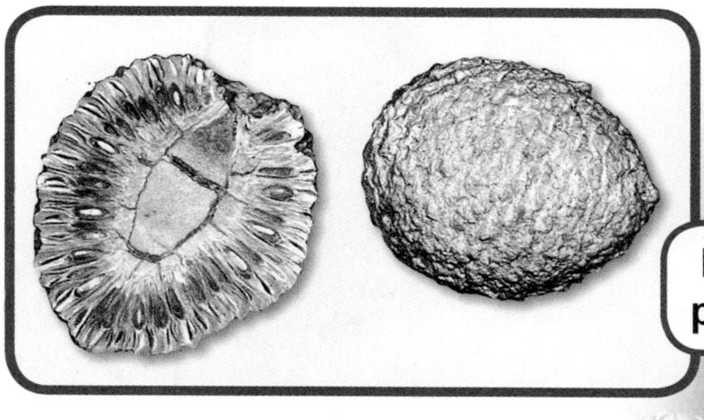

Extinction

Many plants and animals are now extinct (ek•STINGKT). **Extinction** means that all the members of a certain kind of living thing have died. Extinction can happen when a habitat changes. For example, a habitat may become drier. Then the habitat may no longer meet the needs of some living things. Plants in these places die. Animals must find new places to live or they will die, too.

Extinction can also happen for other reasons. One reason is an increase in predators. Another is a decrease in the food supply. About 65 million years ago, 70 percent of all living things became extinct. It is possible that an asteroid hit Earth, changing the environment and reducing the food supply.

Extinction is still happening. People may cause extinction when they cut forests or fill in wetlands. This change in the environment can cause living things to lose their habitats.

Focus Skill **COMPARE AND CONTRAST** **How might a change in the environment affect plants differently than it would animals?**

The last woolly mammoth died about 30,000 years ago. ▼

▼ **The last great auk died in 1844. These birds, which could not fly, were killed for food and bait.**

▼ **Fossils of saber-toothed cats have been found in California's La Brea (BRAY•uh) tar pits. The last saber-toothed cat died about 10,000 years ago.**

Essential Question

How Do Living Things of the Past Compare with Those of Today?

In this lesson, you learned that animals of the past were like animals of today in many ways. This does not mean they were related. Plants of the past were much like plants of today. Some plants and animals have not changed much over time.

1. Focus Skill **COMPARE AND CONTRAST** Draw and complete a graphic organizer to show how organisms of the past are like those of today.

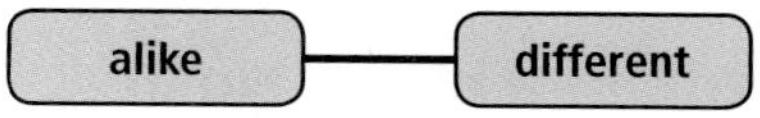

2. **SUMMARIZE** Write a summary of this lesson. Begin with this sentence: *Fossils can show how animals of the past may have looked and acted.*

3. **DRAW CONCLUSIONS** Suppose you have found a fossil. Why should you be careful with it?

4. **VOCABULARY** Write a paragraph, leaving spaces for this lesson's two vocabulary words. Have a partner fill in the words.

Test Prep

5. **CRITICAL THINKING** Why are fossils important?

6. Which of these could be called a living fossil?
   A. woolly mammoth
   B. rhinoceros
   C. camel
   D. bristlecone pine

Make Connections

Writing

Persuasive Writing

Suppose you find an unusual fossil. Write a **letter** to a scientist, describing your fossil. Try to persuade him or her to come to see it. Explain why the fossil might be important.

Math

Make a Bar Graph

Make a bar graph to show how many plants and animals are close to extinction in these states: Hawai'i, 317; California, 299; Florida, 111; Tennessee, 96; Texas, 91.

Social Studies

Then and Now

Research what your region may have looked like 65 million years ago. What kinds of plants and animals lived in your neighborhood then?

Slithering Through the Air

Look, up in the sky. It's a bird. It's a plane. No, it's a snake. That's right, a snake. The paradise tree snake can soar through the air, even though it doesn't have wings.

The paradise tree snake can glide through the air to move from one tree to another, to chase prey, or to avoid being eaten by a predator. Until recently, scientists were not sure how the snake managed to move through the air.

A Soaring Serpent

Scientist Jake Socha has been studying this "flying snake" for several years. He has tried to learn how it performs its aerial feats. Socha traveled to Southeast Asia, where he built a *scaffold,* or support structure. He attached a branch to the top of the scaffold and placed still cameras and video cameras around the branch. He also used a *theodolite* to set up the platform. A theodolite is a tool used by engineers to determine the horizontal or vertical angle of a structure being built.

After his "tree" was complete, Socha placed a paradise tree snake on the branch and waited for it to take off. "Occasionally, when the snake wouldn't move, I'd give it a prod," he said, "and sit there and wait and hope it would jump off."

As soon as the snake began to move, the cameras started snapping photos. The photos show that as the snake soars through the air, it flattens itself out and forms an S shape. The snake then begins twisting back and forth and from top to bottom. The motion helps it control its path through the air and glide to a smooth landing.

Not Really a Flier

The paradise tree snake is one of several kinds of flying snakes. According to Socha, the snake is more of a parachuter than a flier, which means that it can only glide downward.

But you shouldn't worry too much about a paradise tree snake falling on you from the sky. Not only has Socha never heard of that happening, but the paradise tree snake can only be found in a remote part of Southeast Asia.

Think and Write

1. Do you know of any other animals, other than birds, that fly from tree to tree?
2. In what other ways can cameras be used in doing scientific research?

Spin-In™ Find out more. Log on to **www.hspscience.com**

Chapter 3 Review and Test Preparation

Vocabulary Review

Use the terms below to complete the sentences. The page numbers tell where to look in the chapter if you need help.

basic needs p. 130
adaptation p. 132
instinct p. 142
hibernation p. 143
migration p. 144
learned behavior p. 146
fossil p. 152
extinction p. 156

1. Both breathing rate and body temperature change during ________.
2. The development of a thick beak for grinding seeds is an ________.
3. Behaviors that you begin life with are ________.
4. Air and water are ________.
5. When all the members of a species have died out completely, the result is called ________.
6. Speaking is a ________.
7. When you see a flock of geese fly south in the fall, you are watching a ________.
8. An imprint of an ancient fern in rock is a type of ________.

Check Understanding

Write the letter of the best choice.

9. Why does a whale surface?
   A. for fun
   B. for food
   C. for air
   D. to see

10. **MAIN IDEA AND DETAILS** Which detail relates to learned behavior?
   Focus Skill
   F. A mother feeds her baby.
   G. A fish swims in a pond.
   H. You yawn.
   J. A kitten watches its mother hunt.

11. Which animal on this bar graph has the shortest migration route?

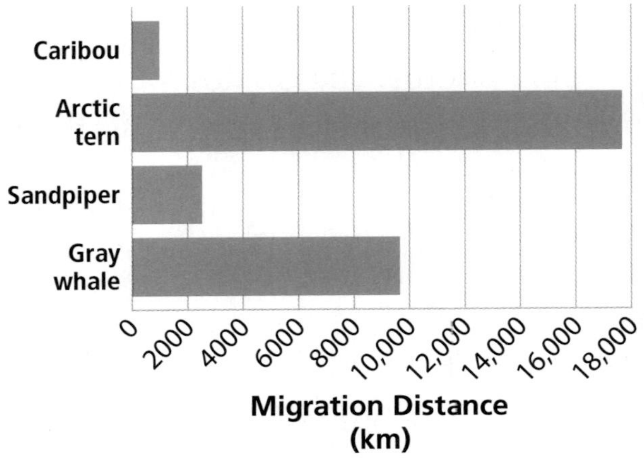

   A. Arctic tern
   B. caribou
   C. sandpiper
   D. gray whale

12. **COMPARE AND CONTRAST** Which statement compares the camels of long ago with camels of today?

Focus Skill

F. Camels that live in Africa have hooves.
G. Skeletons of camels of long ago are similar to those of camels today.
H. Ancient camels ate grass.
J. The bones of ancient camels are fossils.

13. Notice the beak pictured here. What is it an adaptation for?

A. eating fruit
B. eating leaves
C. grinding seeds
D. spearing fish

14. Why don't you see any ground squirrels in winter?
F. They are migrating.
G. They don't like the cold.
H. They are hiding.
J. They are hibernating.

15. What can you learn by studying fossils of an organism?
A. how long it lived
B. how well-adapted it was
C. its color
D. how it compares with modern-day organisms

16. What will probably happen to a tiger that isn't raised with other tigers?
F. It will become friendly.
G. It will never learn to hunt.
H. It will live longer.
J. It will lose its instincts.

Inquiry Skills

17. Explain how your **observations** of the goldfish's behavior helped you plan how to train it.

18. What tool would you use for a **model** of a beak of a bird that eats seeds?

Critical Thinking

The Big Idea

19. Why do you think caribou grow hair on the bottom of each foot in winter and lose it in summer?

20. Suppose you want to help save a bird that is threatened with extinction. What things should you study about its habitat? Why would it be a good idea to find out if the birds are laying eggs and how many chicks are hatching?

CHAPTER 4

The Human Body

What's the Big Idea?

To stay alive, people depend on body systems that work together.

Essential Questions

Lesson 1
How Does Your Body Get Oxygen and Nutrients?

Lesson 2
How Does Your Body Think and Move?

GO online ▸ Student eBook www.hspscience.com

Women practicing judo

What do YOU wonder?

Do Muscles Work Together? These women are practicing judo, a Japanese martial art that people do for fitness, sport, and fun. Judo makes the heart stronger and helps it send oxygen to muscles. How does this relate to the **Big Idea?**

LESSON 1

Essential Question

How Does Your Body Get Oxygen and Nutrients?

Investigate the different ways your heart responds to activity.

Read and Learn how your body gets the oxygen and nutrients it needs.

Fast Fact

Going the Distance

If you were to lay all of your body's blood vessels end to end, they would reach a length of more than 100,000 kilometers (62,000 mi)! In the Investigate, you'll find out more about the pumping of your blood.

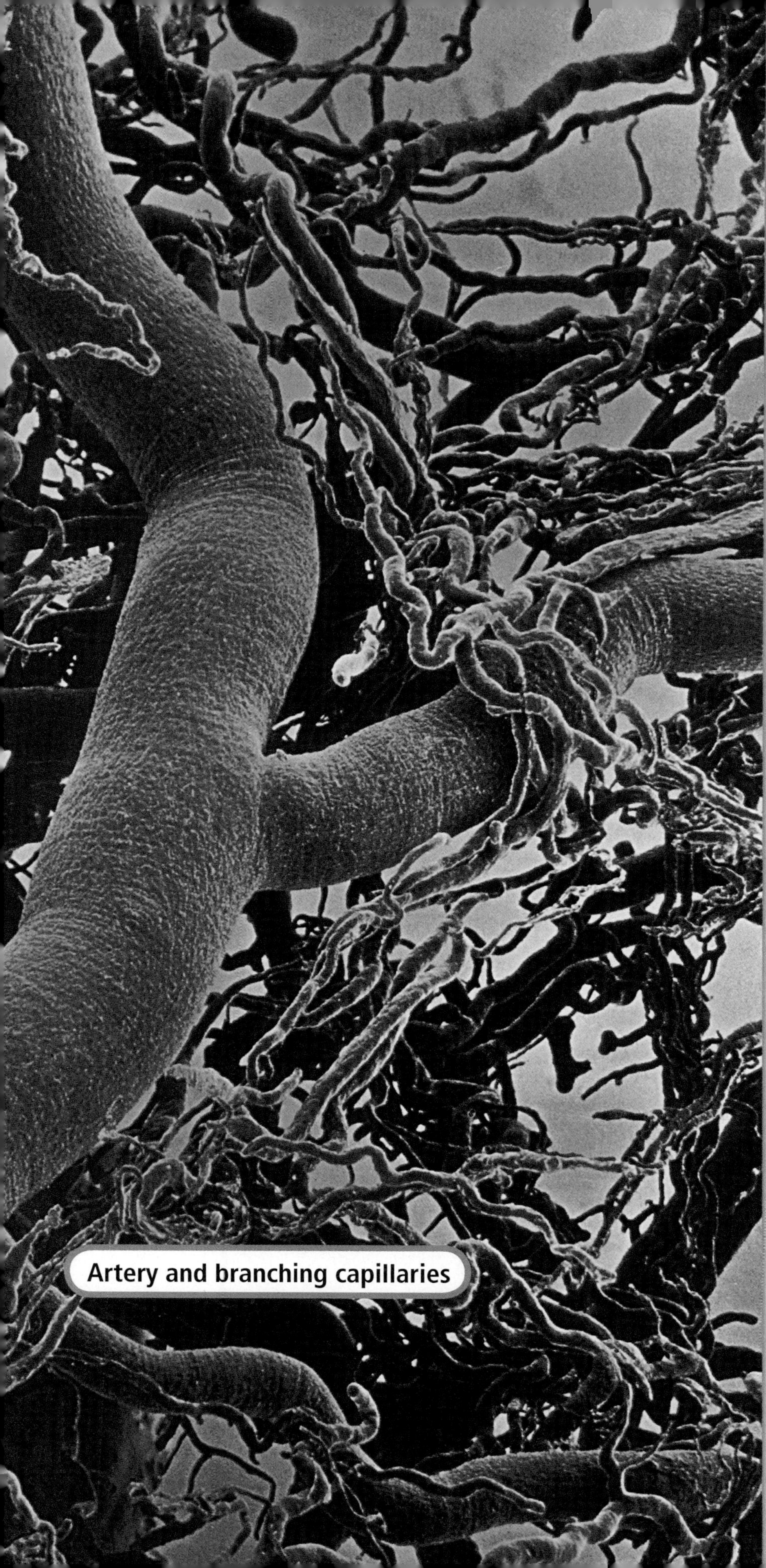
Artery and branching capillaries

Vocabulary Previe

tissue [TISH•oo] A group of cells of the same type that work together to perform a certain job (p. 168)

organ [AWR•gun] A body part made of different kinds of tissues that work together to perform a particular job (p. 169)

esophagus [ih•SAHF•uh•guhs] A muscular tube that connects your mouth with your stomach (p. 170)

stomach [STUHM•uhk] A baglike organ in which food is mixed with digestive juices and squeezed by muscles (p. 170)

diaphragm [DY•uh•fram] The muscle in your body that enables you to inhale and exhale (p. 172)

artery [ART•er•ee] A blood vessel that carries blood away from the heart (p. 174)

capillary [KAP•uh•lair•ee] A blood vessel with very thin walls that allows oxygen and carbon dioxide to pass through (p. 174)

vein [VAYN] A blood vessel that carries blood back to the heart from another part of the body (p. 174)

Pulse Rates

Guided Inquiry

Start with Questions

When you are active, your heart responds by working harder. You might breathe harder as well. Your body needs more oxygen to continue your activity.

- What does your heart do?
- Why does it sometimes need to work harder?

Investigate to find out. Then read and learn to find out more.

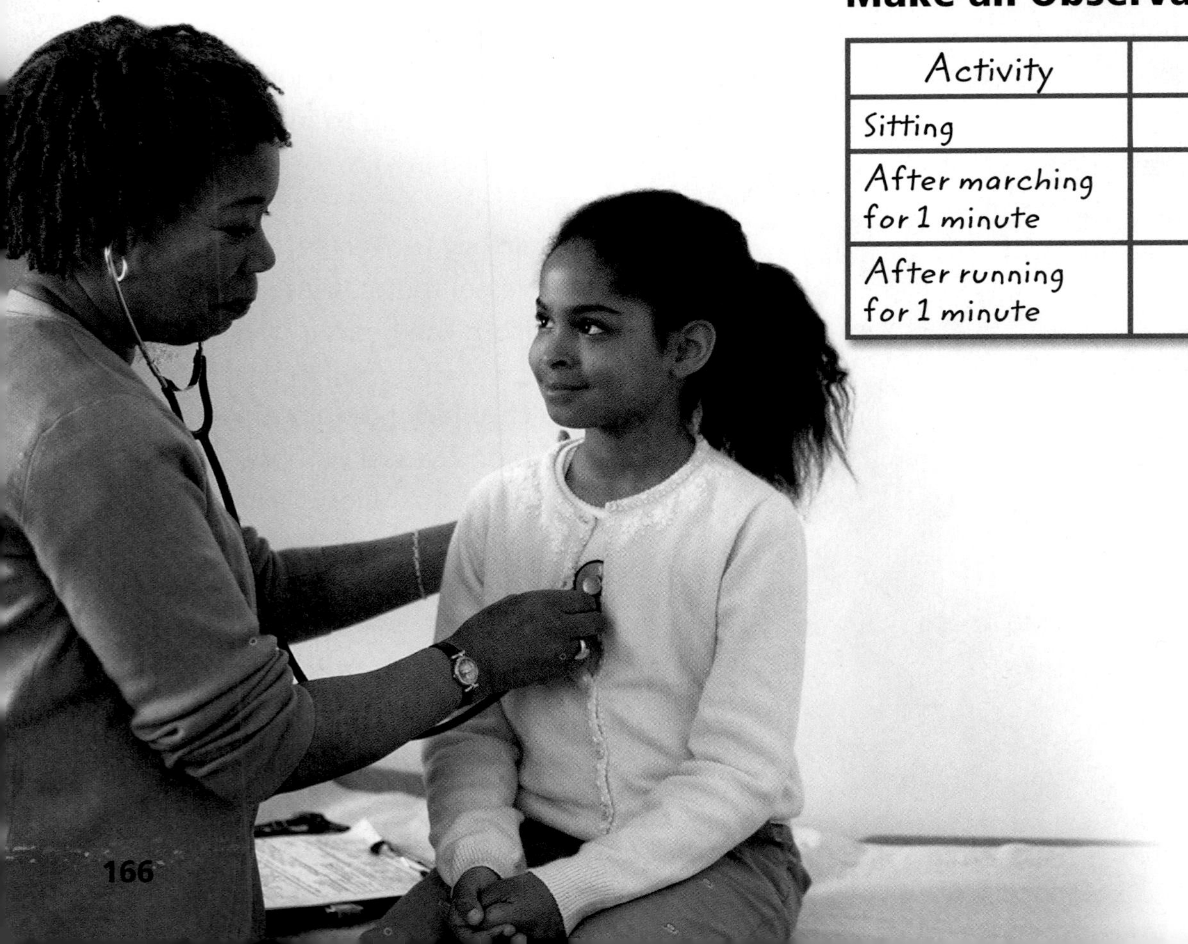

Prepare to Investigate

Inquiry Skill Tip

When you plan an investigation, you should make a list of the materials you will need. That way, you will not be missing any equipment!

Materials

- stopwatch, timer, or clock with second hand

Make an Observation Table

Activity	Pulse Rate
Sitting	
After marching for 1 minute	
After running for 1 minute	

Follow the Procedure

1. Make a table like the one shown on page 166.
2. While you're sitting, find the pulse on your wrist. Count the number of times your heart beats in 15 seconds. Multiply that **number** by 4 to find how often your heart beats in a minute while resting. **Record** the result in your table.
3. Stand up and march in place for 1 minute. As soon as you stop, find your pulse. Count your heartbeats for 15 seconds, and **use the number** to calculate the beats per minute. **Record** the result.
4. Rest for a few minutes, and then run in place for 1 minute. As soon as you stop, find your pulse. Count your heartbeats for 15 seconds. Then **use the number** to find the beats per minute. **Record** the result.

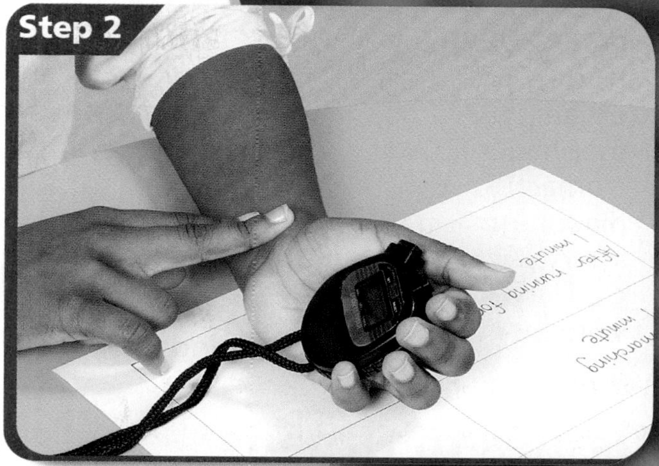

Draw Conclusions

1. Which activity increased your heart rate the least? Which increased it the most?
2. **Inquiry Skill** **Plan an investigation** to find out which activity elevates your heart rate for a longer time.

Independent Inquiry

How do you think exercise affects your breathing rate? Make a prediction, and design an experiment to find out.

Read and Learn

VOCABULARY

tissue p. 168
organ p. 169
esophagus p. 170
stomach p. 170
diaphragm p. 172
artery p. 174
capillary p. 174
vein p. 174

SCIENCE CONCEPTS

- how tissues and organs form systems
- how the respiratory and digestive systems work
- how the circulatory system carries oxygen and nutrients

Focus Skill SEQUENCE

Note the order of events of respiration and circulation.

Tissues to Organs

Have you ever made something out of blocks? Many blocks can be put together to form something bigger. The same thing happens in your body. Many smaller parts work together. Cells are some of these smaller parts. They are the body's building blocks.

A **tissue** is a group of many cells of the same type that work together to perform a certain job. Your body is made up of four types of tissues. You have skin tissue. You also have muscle tissue, nerve tissue, and connective tissue. Each tissue has a different purpose.

Skin tissue is made of skin cells. Your skin protects your body. What makes up other types of tissue? Muscle cells make up muscle tissue. Neurons make up nerve tissue.

Connective tissue gives your body support. It includes the bones in your skeleton and the ligaments that hold joints together.

▼ **These blocks form a model of a building, much like tissues form organs.**

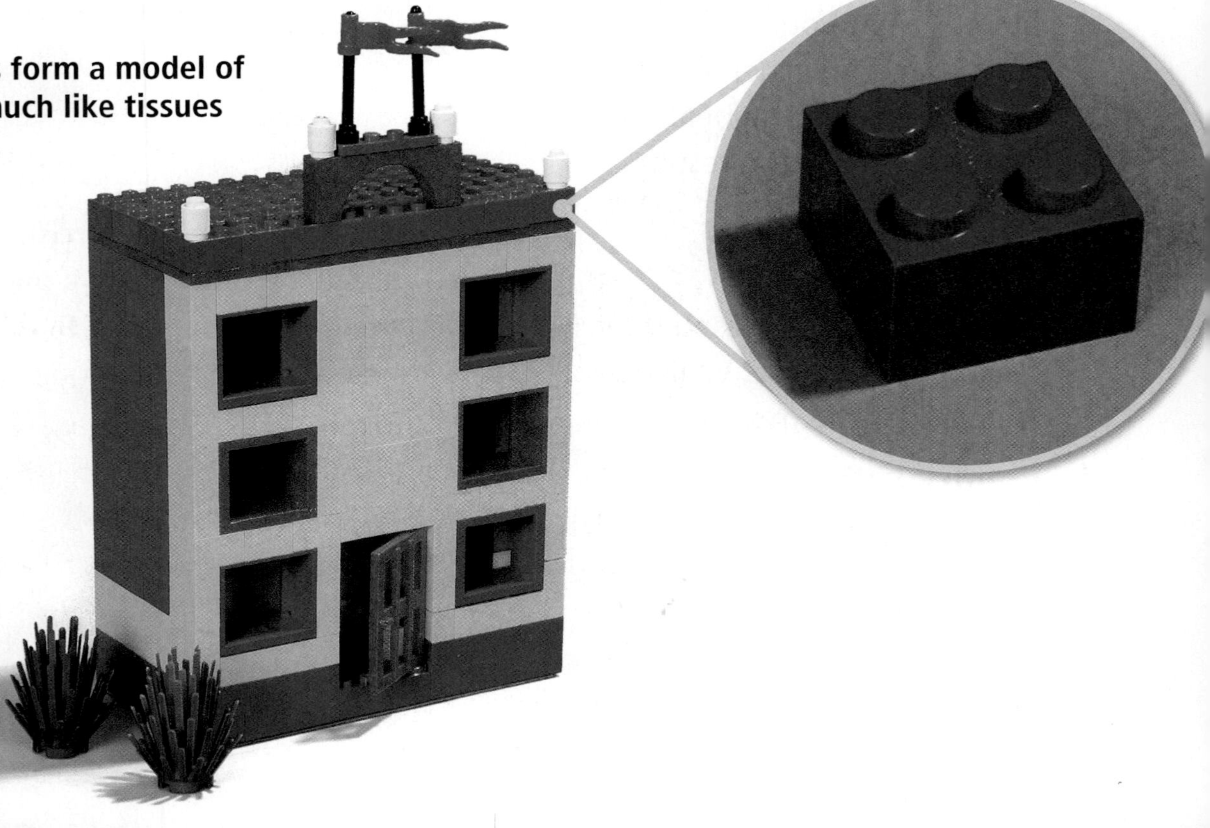

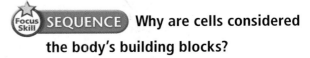

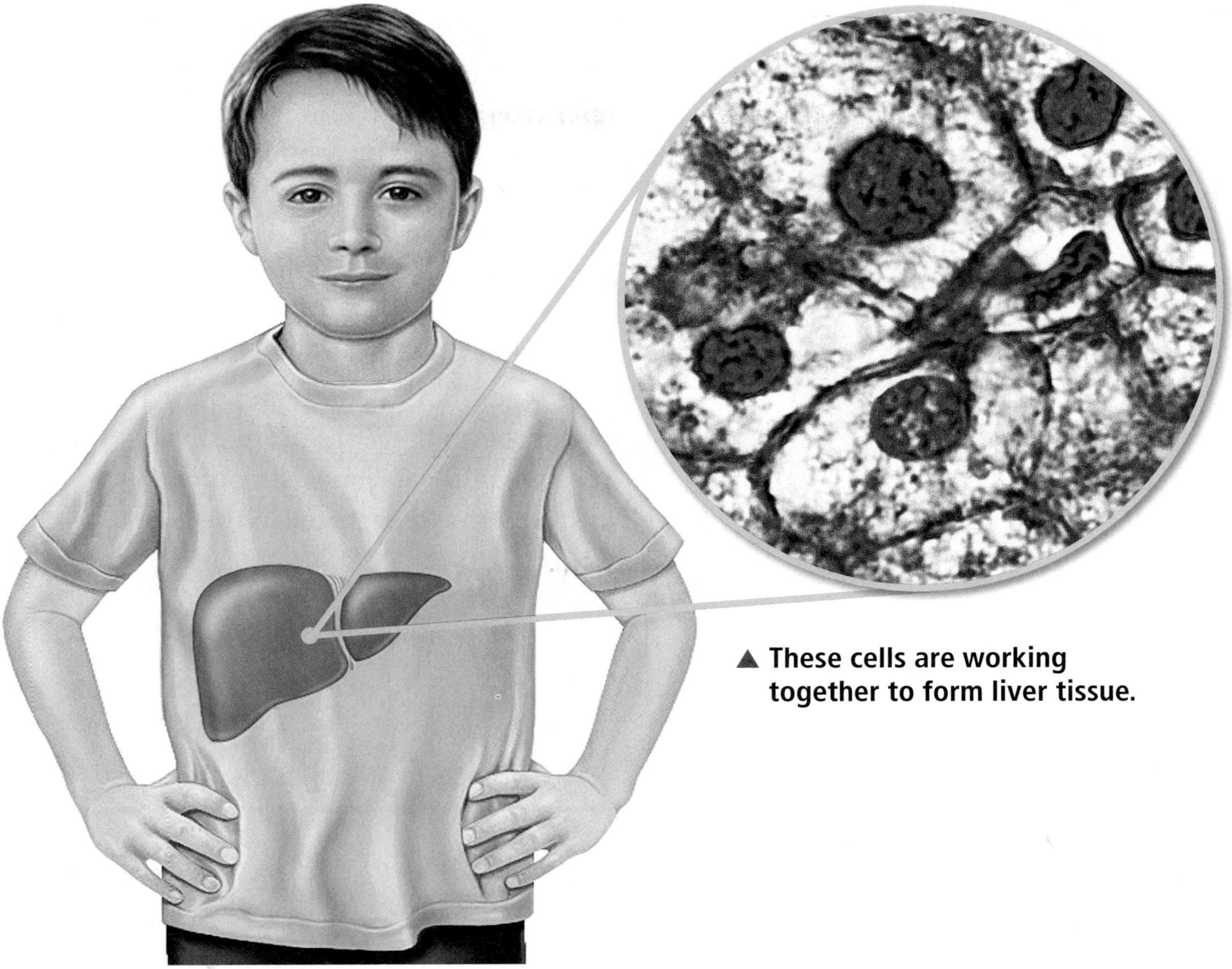

▲ These cells are working together to form liver tissue.

In the same way that cells work together to form tissues, tissues work together to form organs. An **organ** is a group of tissues that does a particular job. Each organ in your body is made up of many different kinds of tissue.

Your skin is your body's largest organ. Layers of skin tissue cover and line the body. Skin is also made up of muscle, nerve, and connective tissue. The different kinds of tissue work together so that your skin can do many things. The outer layer of your skin protects you. The middle layer, or dermis, has oil glands to make you "waterproof." The inner layer of skin is made of connective tissue and fat. Its job is to keep your body warm.

Groups of organs that work together to do major jobs for the body are systems. The human body has ten body systems. For example, bones work together and make up the skeletal system. Muscles work together and make up the muscular system. The organs that work together to digest the food you eat make up the digestive system.

Focus Skill SEQUENCE **Why are cells considered the body's building blocks?**

The Digestive System

You know that the cells of your body need oxygen. They also need nutrients, which come from food.

The digestive system breaks down food into nutrients that can be used by the body. The mouth, esophagus (ih•SAHF•uh•guhs), stomach, and small intestine are parts of the digestive system.

Digestion begins in the mouth. When you chew, your teeth grind up your food. Saliva softens it and begins to break it down. After you swallow, the food travels down the **esophagus**, a muscular tube that connects your mouth to the next organ, the stomach.

The **stomach** is a baglike organ with walls of smooth muscle. The stomach squeezes your food and mixes it with digestive juices. The food becomes almost liquid.

From the stomach, food passes into another long tube of muscle. This organ is the small intestine. The small intestine adds other digestive juices to the food. When digestion is complete, nutrients pass through the walls of the small intestine into capillaries. Blood carries the nutrients to each cell in the body.

Focus Skill SEQUENCE **How do nutrients from the food you eat get to your body's cells?**

Math in Science
Interpret Data

Not So Small
How does body size relate to the length of the small intestine? Infer the reason.

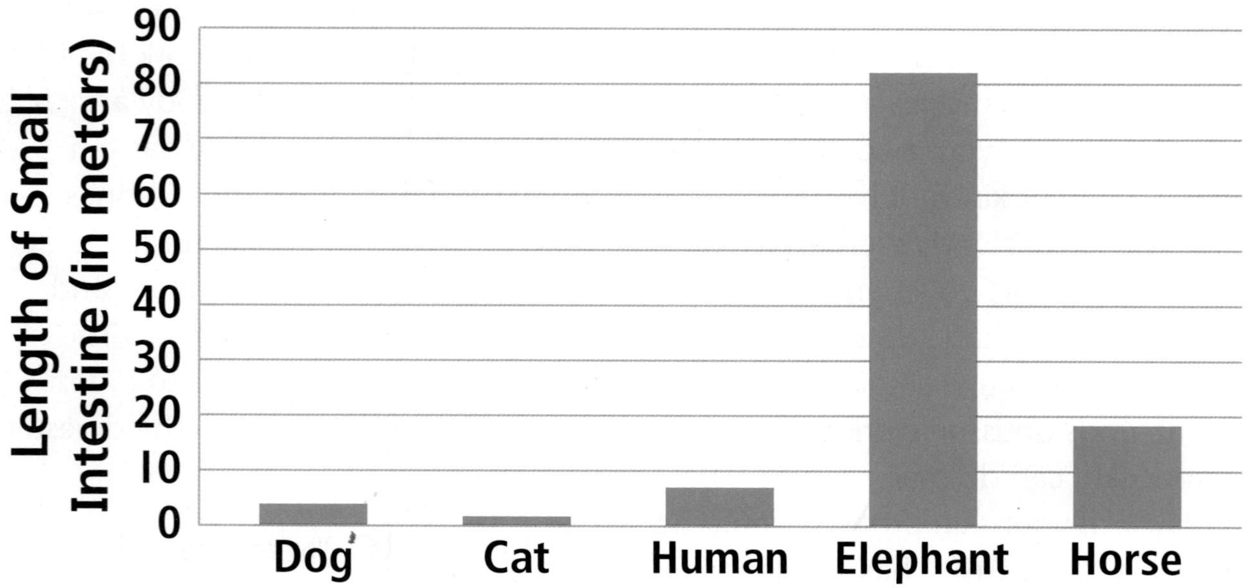

The Digestive System

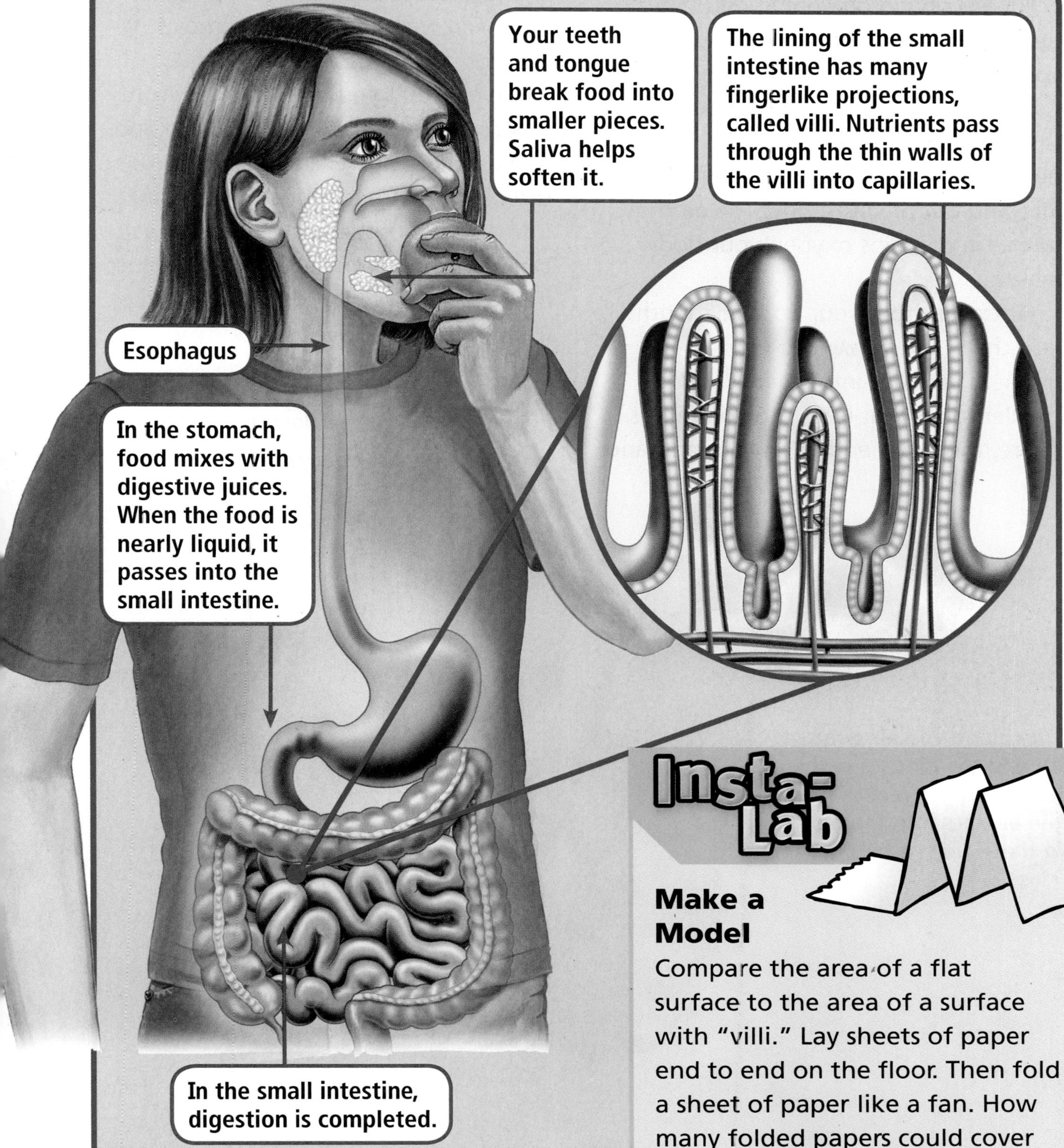

Your teeth and tongue break food into smaller pieces. Saliva helps soften it.
The lining of the small intestine has many fingerlike projections, called villi. Nutrients pass through the thin walls of the villi into capillaries.
Esophagus
In the stomach, food mixes with digestive juices. When the food is nearly liquid, it passes into the small intestine.
In the small intestine, digestion is completed.

Insta-Lab

Make a Model

Compare the area of a flat surface to the area of a surface with "villi." Lay sheets of paper end to end on the floor. Then fold a sheet of paper like a fan. How many folded papers could cover the flat "intestine"? How do you think villi help take in more nutrients?

The Respiratory System

Put your hand on your chest, take a deep breath, and let it out. Do you feel your chest rise and fall? This movement is caused by breathing. A muscle called the **diaphragm** (DY•uh•fram), located below your lungs, causes air to move into and out of your body. The air that comes in contains oxygen your body needs.

Air travels from your nose or mouth into the *trachea* (TRAY•kee•uh). The trachea branches into smaller and smaller tubes that lead into your lungs. There, the tubes end in tiny air sacs, and tiny blood vessels wrap around the air sacs. The air sacs and the blood vessels have thin walls that let gases move through them.

Oxygen that you inhale moves from the air sacs into the blood. Then blood moves to the heart. The heart pumps the blood that has a lot of oxygen in it to all parts of the body. Blood also carries carbon dioxide, a waste product made in the body's cells, to the air sacs. Carbon dioxide leaves the body when you exhale, or breathe out.

Focus Skill SEQUENCE **How does oxygen get to the cells of the body?**

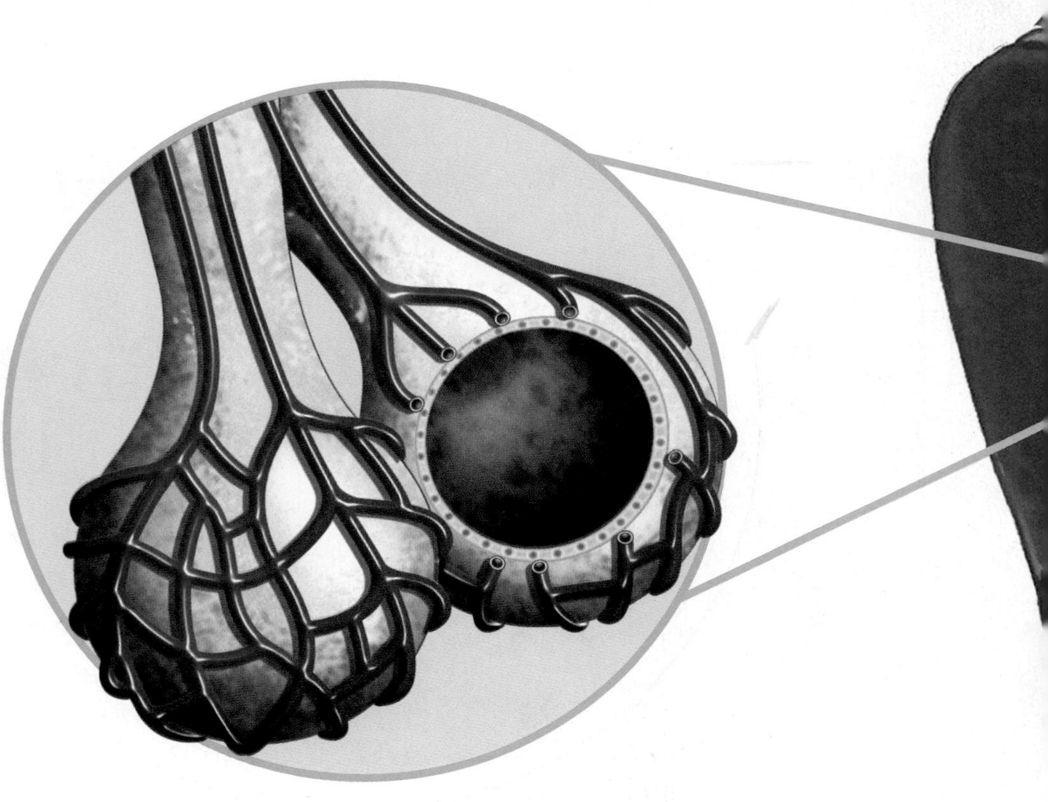

Tiny blood vessels wrap around the air sacs in the lungs. Oxygen moves from the air sacs into the blood in these tiny vessels. ▶

The Respiratory System

Before blowing into his trumpet, this musician takes a deep breath. How does the oxygen travel to the rest of his body?

The Circulatory System

Blood gets oxygen from the lungs. The blood then travels to the heart. The heart pumps the blood through the body. A blood vessel that carries blood away from the heart is called an **artery**. Arteries keep branching into smaller and smaller blood vessels, until they become **capillaries** (KAP•uh•lair•eez). Oxygen moves across capillary walls to reach the body's cells. **Veins** are vessels that return blood to the heart.

Focus Skill SEQUENCE How does the circulatory system get oxygen to each cell?

Science Up Close

For more links and animations, go to **www.hspscience.com**

The Heart

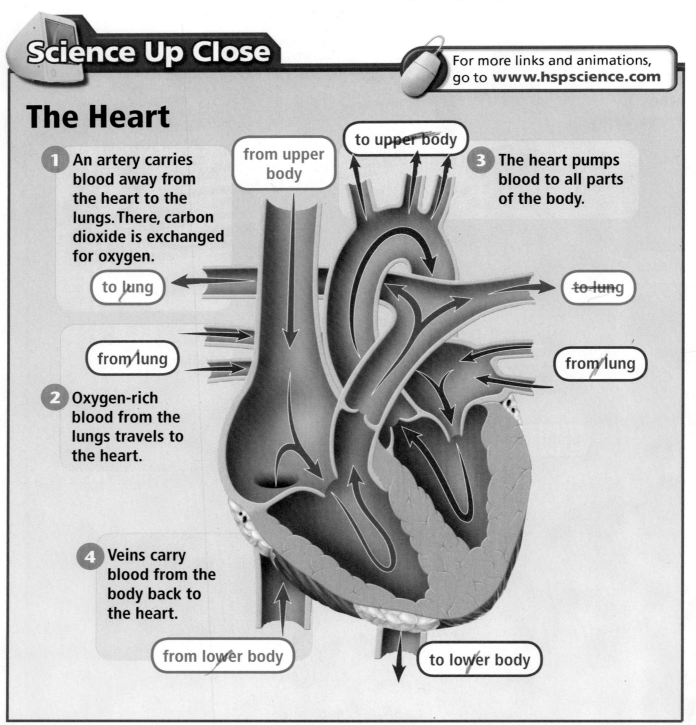

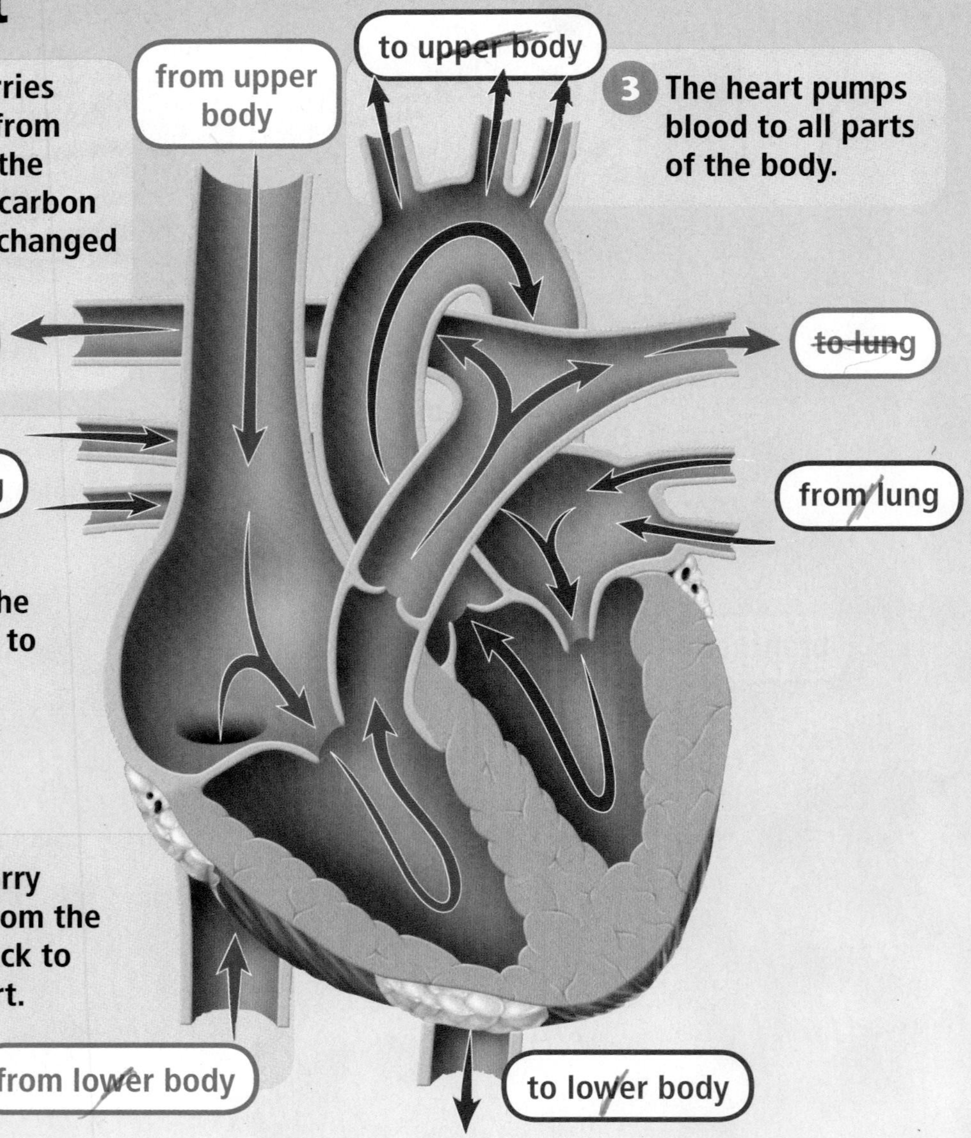

1 An artery carries blood away from the heart to the lungs. There, carbon dioxide is exchanged for oxygen.

2 Oxygen-rich blood from the lungs travels to the heart.

3 The heart pumps blood to all parts of the body.

4 Veins carry blood from the body back to the heart.

The Circulatory System

Blood is carried away from the heart through arteries. Blood returns to the heart through veins.

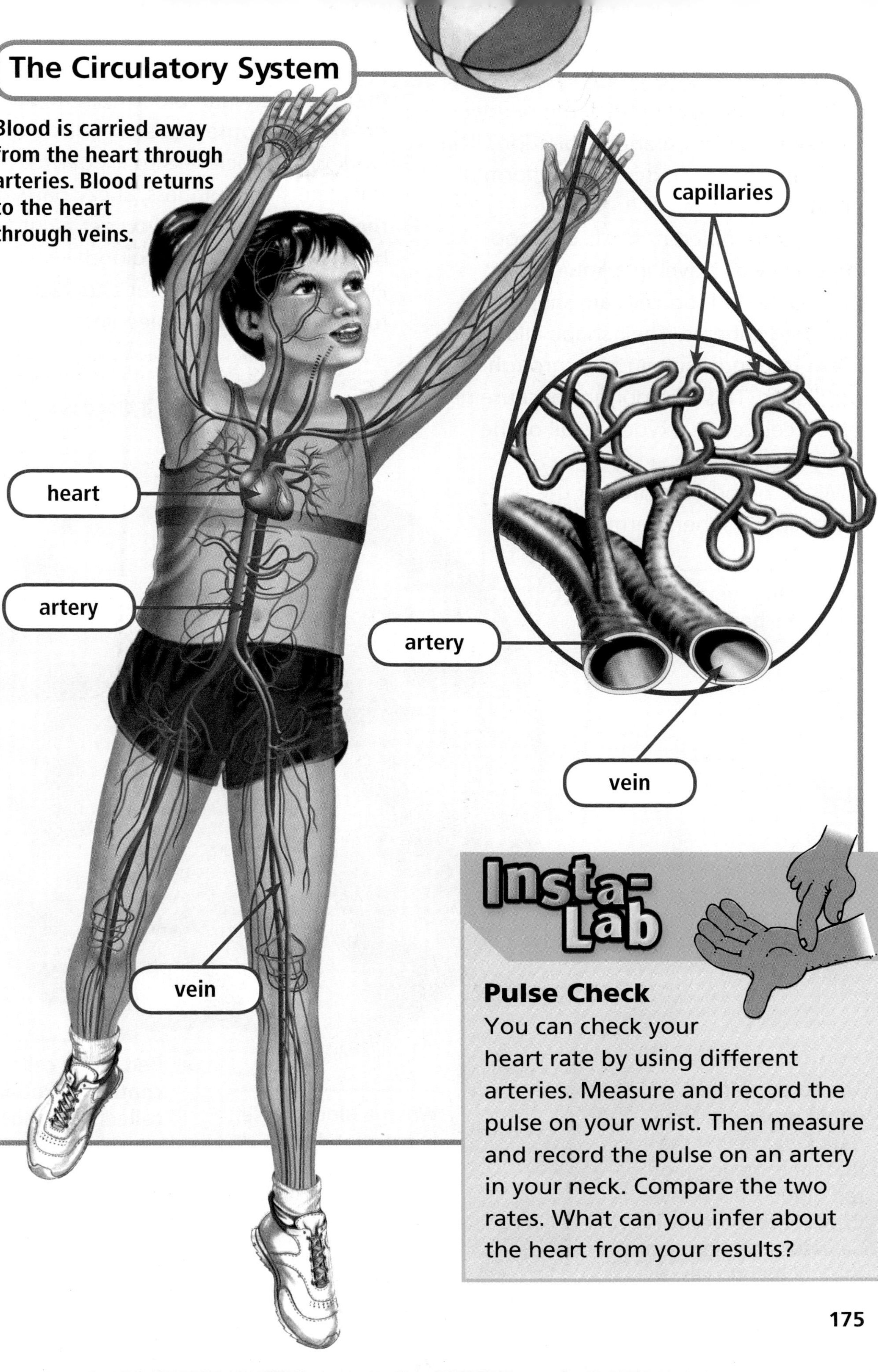

Insta-Lab

Pulse Check

You can check your heart rate by using different arteries. Measure and record the pulse on your wrist. Then measure and record the pulse on an artery in your neck. Compare the two rates. What can you infer about the heart from your results?

Blood

Can you guess what tissue is needed for both circulation and respiration? That tissue is *blood.* Blood is a liquid form of connective tissue.

There are different kinds of blood cells. They all travel in a liquid called *plasma.* Red blood cells are shaped like flattened spheres. Their shape allows them to bend and squeeze through tiny capillaries. This is important because red blood cells carry oxygen to all of the body's cells.

White blood cells protect the body from illness. When germs enter the body, white blood cells work to destroy them. Some white blood cells attack the germs, and some make proteins that work with attack cells to kill germs.

Platelets are colorless, sticky parts of the blood. Whenever you get a cut and bleed, you have torn a blood vessel. Platelets move to the cut and stick together to stop the bleeding.

Focus Skill **SEQUENCE**

What happens when a blood vessel is cut?

White blood cells protect the body from sickness.
When a blood vessel is cut, platelets stick together to form a clot. This stops the bleeding.
Red blood cells contain a protein called hemoglobin, which carries oxygen.

The straw-colored liquid is plasma. The dark layer below the plasma is made up of red blood cells. A layer of white blood cells is between the plasma and the red blood cells. ▶

Lesson Review

Essential Question

How Does Your Body Get Oxygen and Nutrients?

In this lesson, you learned that your body has systems whose parts work together to move oxygen and nutrients to the parts of your body that need them. Organs made up of tissues make up these systems.

1. **Focus Skill SEQUENCE** Draw and complete a graphic organizer to show the path blood takes in the circulatory system.

2. **SUMMARIZE** Write a summary of this lesson. Begin with this sentence: *Tissues are the fabrics of the human body.*

3. **DRAW CONCLUSIONS** Why is it easy for oxygen to move from the air sacs to the blood?

4. **VOCABULARY** Use the lesson vocabulary to make a word puzzle.

Test Prep

5. **CRITICAL THINKING** What would happen if blood entering the heart mixed with blood leaving it?

6. Which of these carry blood away from the heart?

   A. air sacs
   B. arteries
   C. capillaries
   D. veins

Make Connections

Writing

Narrative Writing

Write a **story** describing the travels of a blood cell through arteries, capillaries, veins, and the heart.

Math

Multiply Whole Numbers

Count the number of breaths you take in one minute. Then **calculate** the number of breaths you are likely to take in one hour.

Health

Healthy Lungs and Heart

Use reference materials to investigate the relationship between exercise and a healthy heart and lungs. How does exercise help you?

LESSON 2

Essential Question

How Does Your Body Think and Move?

Investigate how the sense of touch works on different parts of your arm.

Read and Learn how your brain works and how your body moves around.

Fast Fact

Amazing Feats

Men and women all over the world compete to find out who is the strongest by pulling such huge and heavy objects as airplanes and trucks. In the Investigate, you'll make a model of how bones and muscles move to help us do amazing things!

Man pulling a large truck

Vocabulary Preview

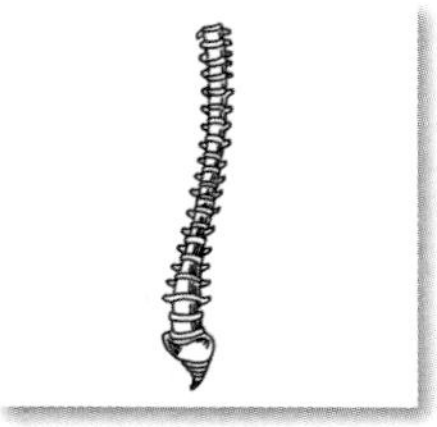

spinal cord [SPY•nuhl KAWRD] A tube of nerves that runs through your backbone to your brain (p. 182)

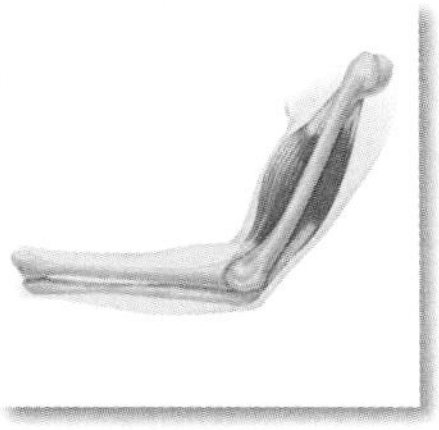

bone [BOHN] A hard organ made of a hard outer covering tissue and a softer inside tissue (p. 184)

joint [JOYNT] A place in the body where two bones meet (p. 184)

muscle [MUHS•uhl] An organ that is made of bundles of long fibers and works with bones to help you move (p. 186)

The Sense of Touch

Guided Inquiry

Start with Questions

Your sense of touch tells you about the world. In the picture, a person is using Braille to read. To read Braille, you feel the writing instead of looking at it.

- Why might people need a way to read without looking at the words?
- Why do people reading Braille use their fingertips instead of another part of their hand?

Investigate to find out. Then read and learn to find out more.

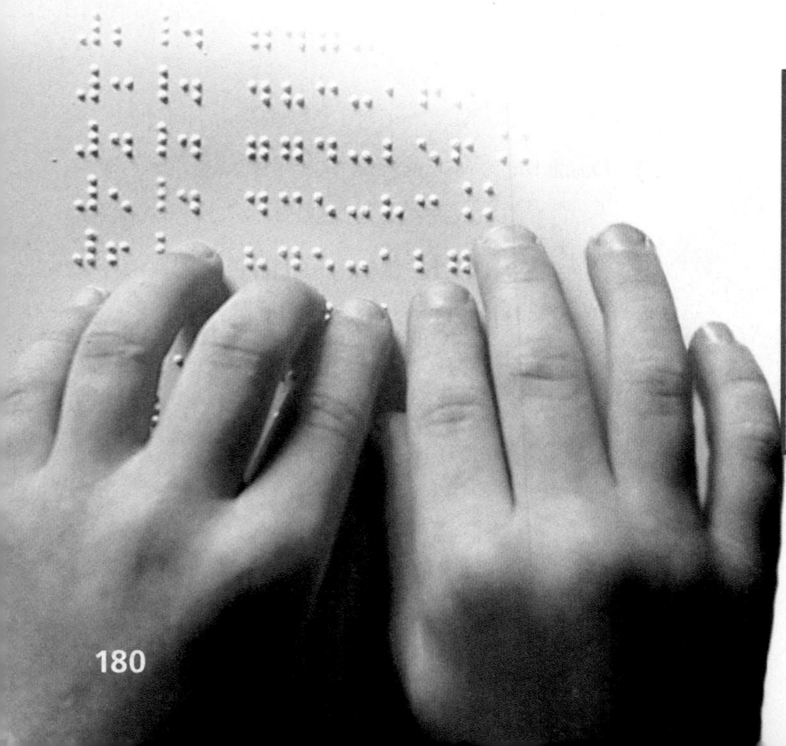

Prepare to Investigate

Inquiry Skill Tip

When you have carried out an experiment and inferred an explanation from your observations, you can test that inference. Design another experiment to see if you are right. One experiment leads to another because of inferences.

Materials

- index card
- ruler
- tape
- 8 toothpicks

Make an Observation Chart

Prediction:			
	Distance Apart When Two Toothpicks Are First Felt		
	Palm	Lower Arm	Upper Arm
Prediction			
Actual			

Follow This Procedure

CAUTION: **Toothpicks are sharp. Do not play with them. Use them only as directed.**

1. Copy the chart. Then **predict** which of the body parts that are named has the best sense of touch. **Record** your prediction.
2. Along one edge of the index card, make two marks 1 cm apart. Use the ruler. Tape a toothpick to each mark. The toothpicks should stick out 1 cm from the edge.
3. Repeat Step 2 for the other three edges of the index card. This time, space the toothpicks 2 cm, 5 cm, and 8 cm apart.
4. Look away while a partner *lightly* touches each pair of toothpicks to a body part named in the table. At each part, begin with the 1-cm distance and then try the greater distances in turn.
5. For each body part, **predict** the shortest distance at which you'll feel two separate toothpicks. When you do feel two, tell your partner. **Record** the distance.

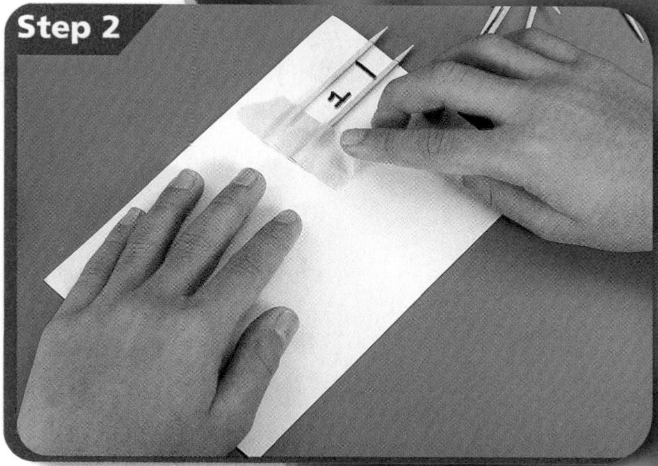
Step 2

Step 4

Independent Inquiry

Use your results to predict which will be more sensitive, your fingertip or the back of your neck. Test your prediction.

Draw Conclusions

1. On which body part did you feel two toothpicks at the shortest distance?

2. Inquiry Skill Based on the results of this test, which body part would you **infer** has the best sense of touch? Explain.

Read and Learn

VOCABULARY
spinal cord p. 182
bone p. 184
joint p. 184
muscle p. 186

SCIENCE CONCEPTS
- how the nervous system acts as the body's control system
- that bones support the body, protect organs, and make blood cells
- how muscles work with bones to move the body

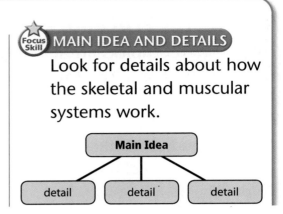

Focus Skill MAIN IDEA AND DETAILS
Look for details about how the skeletal and muscular systems work.

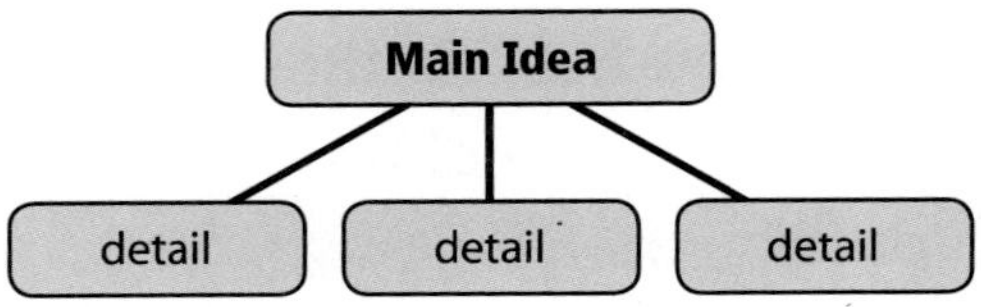

The Nervous System

Has a doctor ever tapped on your knee with a small rubber mallet or checked your eyes with a light? Doctors use these tools to check the nervous system. The nervous system is very important. None of the other body systems could work without its help.

Your brain is the control center of your nervous system. There are billions of nerve cells in your brain. Signals from the brain direct your body's activities.

Your brain receives information from all parts of your body. Messages from your body travel along nerves to the spinal cord. The **spinal cord** is a bundle of nerve tissue that runs through your backbone to your brain. The brain acts on information it gets from the body. Then it sends messages back out through the spinal cord.

Focus Skill MAIN IDEA AND DETAILS **How do messages from the body reach the brain?**

Messages to and from the brain travel along nerve cells, or neurons. Groups of neurons are called nerves.

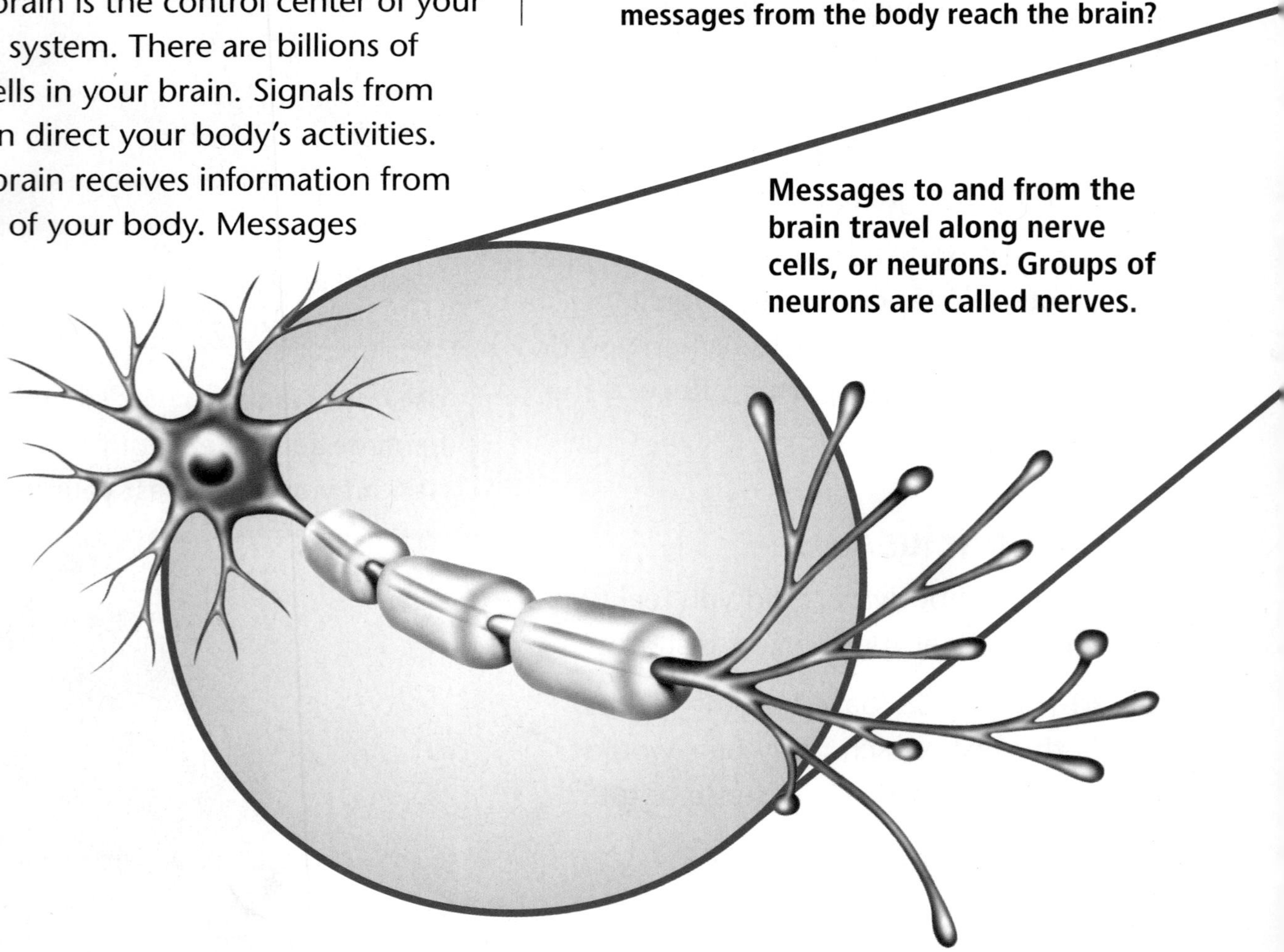

The Nervous System

Messages from the brain travel down the guitar player's spinal cord. They are signals that direct his fingers how to move.

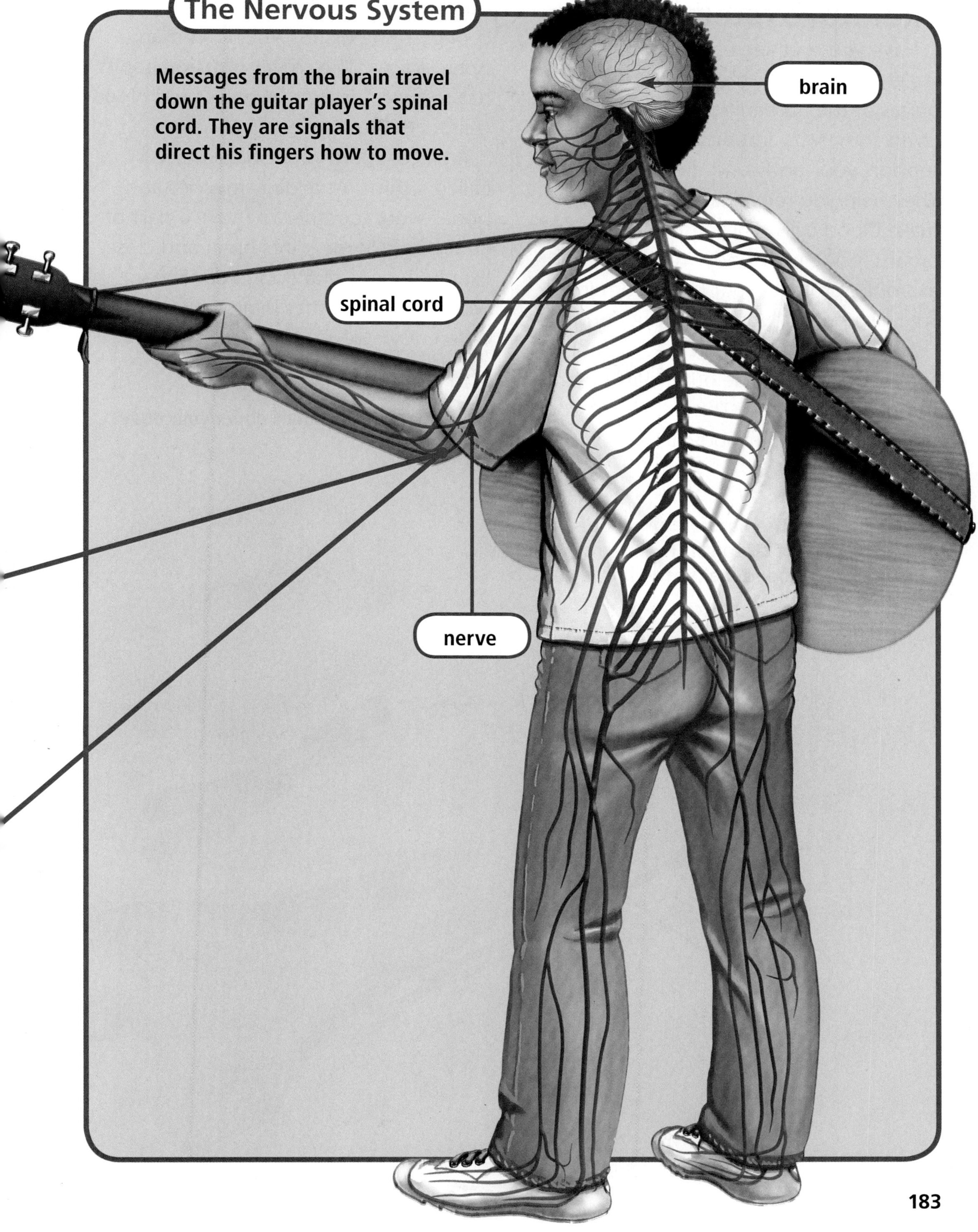

Skeletal System

Have you ever seen a skeleton? A skeleton may look strange, but the bones of the human body work together to do some very important jobs. Bones support your body and give it shape. They help you move, and some bones make blood cells. They also protect the organs inside your body. Your skull, for example, protects your brain from injury. Your ribs protect your heart and lungs.

A **bone** is a hard organ made up of connective tissue. The outer part is hard, smooth, and strong. This part helps your bones support your body. It gives your body its shape. The bone is lined with spongy bone tissue, which has many open spaces. The center of many bones has marrow, tissue that makes red blood cells.

A place where your bones meet is called a **joint**. At a joint, muscles and bones work together to move a part of your body. Some joints open and close, like the hinges of a door. Your knees work this way. Other joints move in different ways.

Focus Skill MAIN IDEA AND DETAILS

What jobs do bones do for your body?

The hard outer part of a bone gives it strength. The marrow inside the bone makes red blood cells. ▶

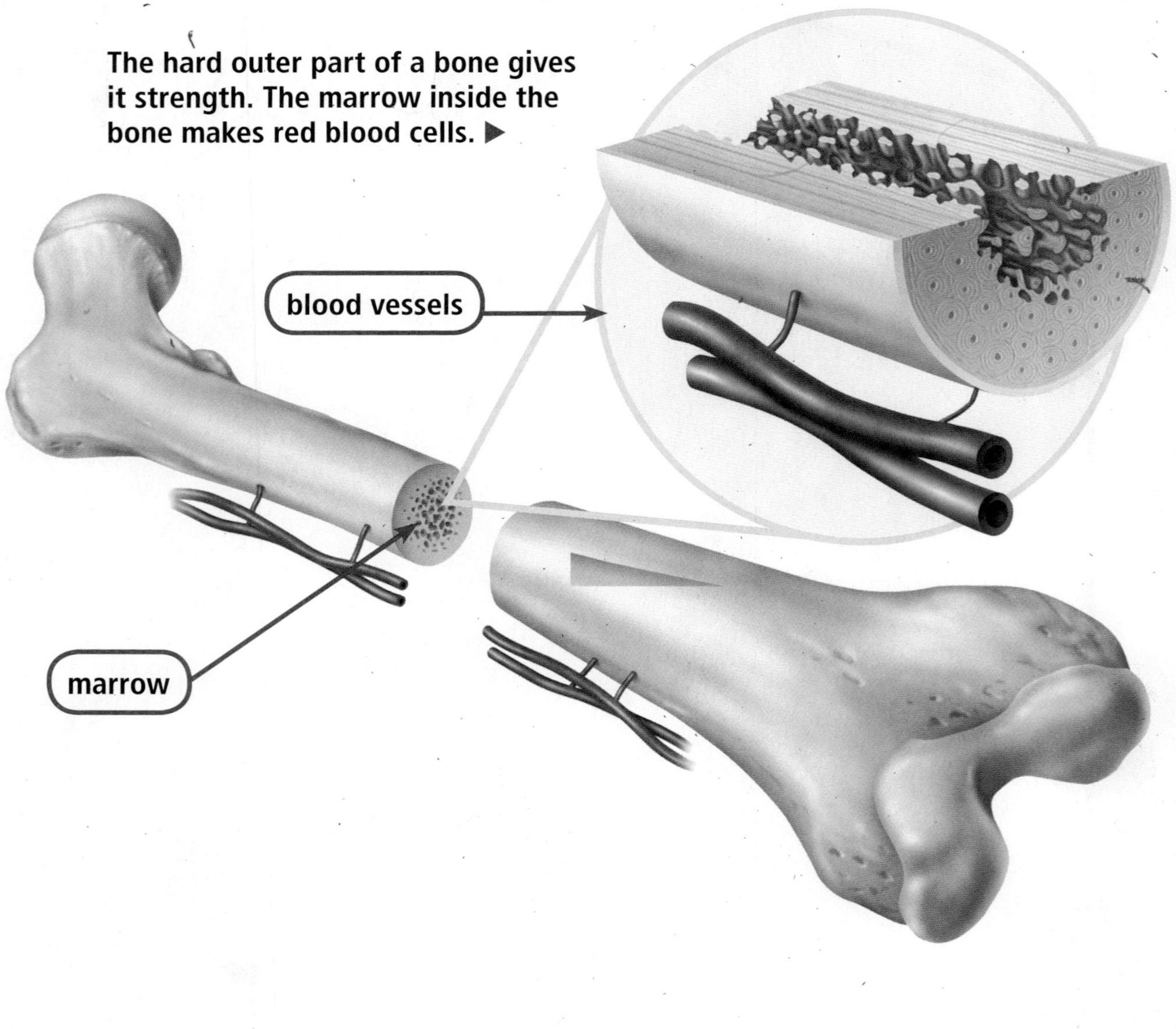

Skeletal System

Bones give your body support, help you move, protect your organs, and make blood cells.

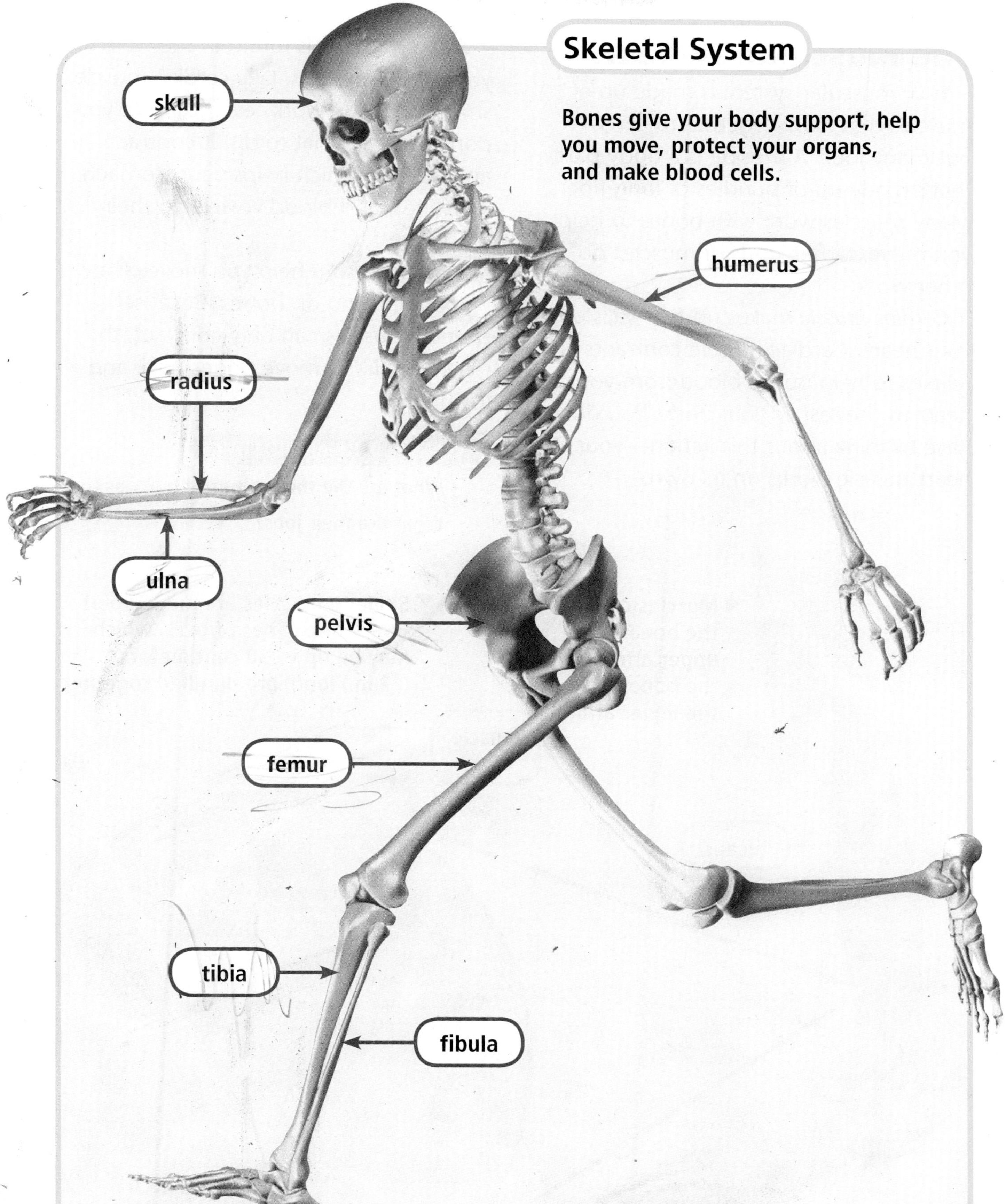

The Muscular System

Your muscular system is made up of muscles that work together to carry out many jobs. A **muscle** is a body part that's made up of bundles of long fibers. Many muscles work with bones to help you move. Other kinds of muscles do other work.

Cardiac muscle makes up the walls of your heart. Cardiac muscle contracts and relaxes to help pump blood from your heart to the rest of your body. You don't have to think about this action—your heart muscle works on its own.

Smooth muscle is found in the walls of your body's organs. Like cardiac muscle, smooth muscle works even though you don't "tell" it what to do. It contracts and relaxes, which helps your stomach, intestines, and blood vessels do their jobs.

Skeletal muscles help you move. They work by pulling on bones. Because skeletal muscles can only contract, they work in pairs to move bones back and forth.

Focus Skill MAIN IDEA AND DETAILS

What are the three types of muscles? What are their jobs?

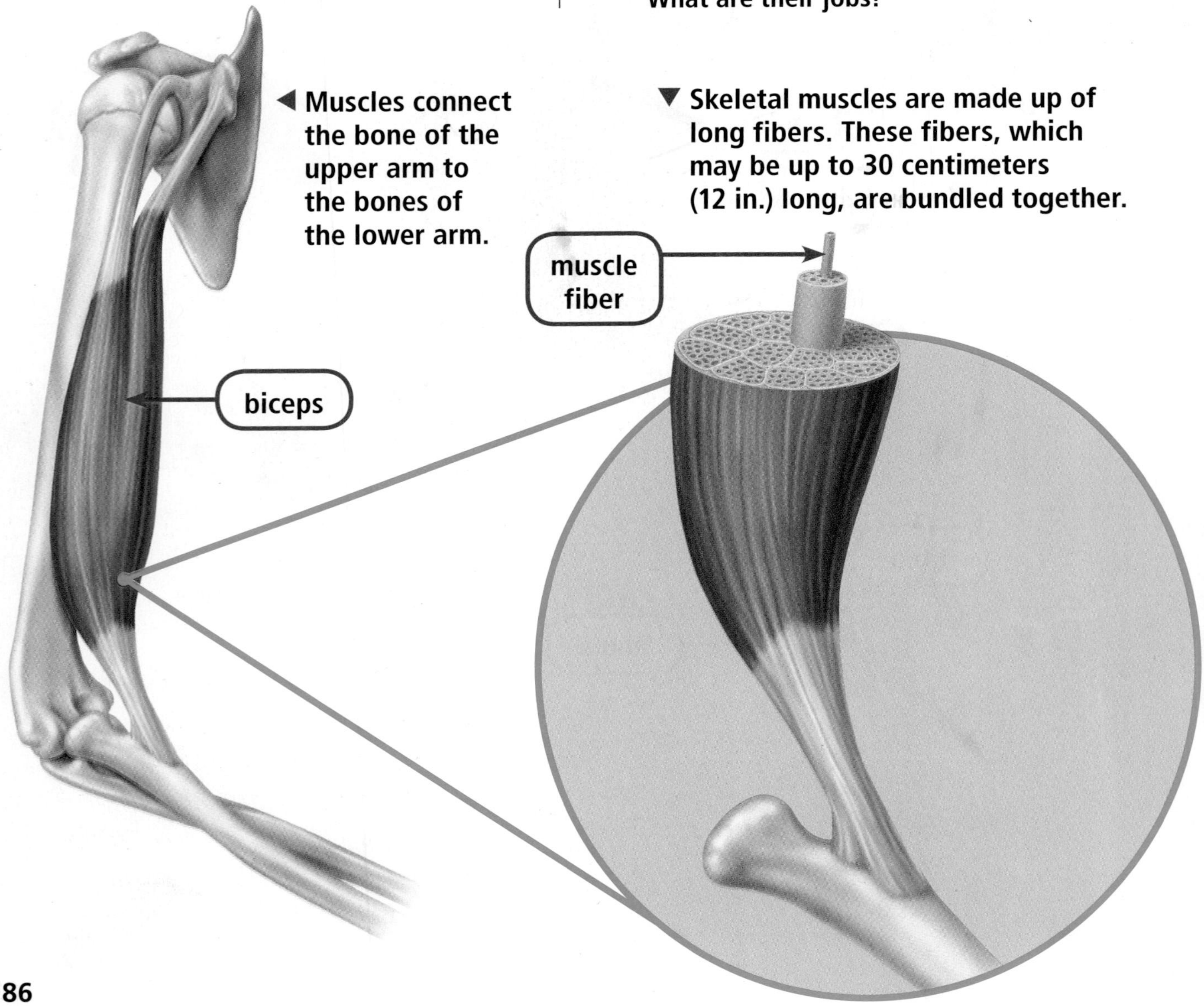

◄ **Muscles connect the bone of the upper arm to the bones of the lower arm.**

▼ **Skeletal muscles are made up of long fibers. These fibers, which may be up to 30 centimeters (12 in.) long, are bundled together.**

Muscular System

Skeletal muscles work in pairs. One muscle in a pair pulls a bone in one direction. The other muscle pulls it in the opposite direction.

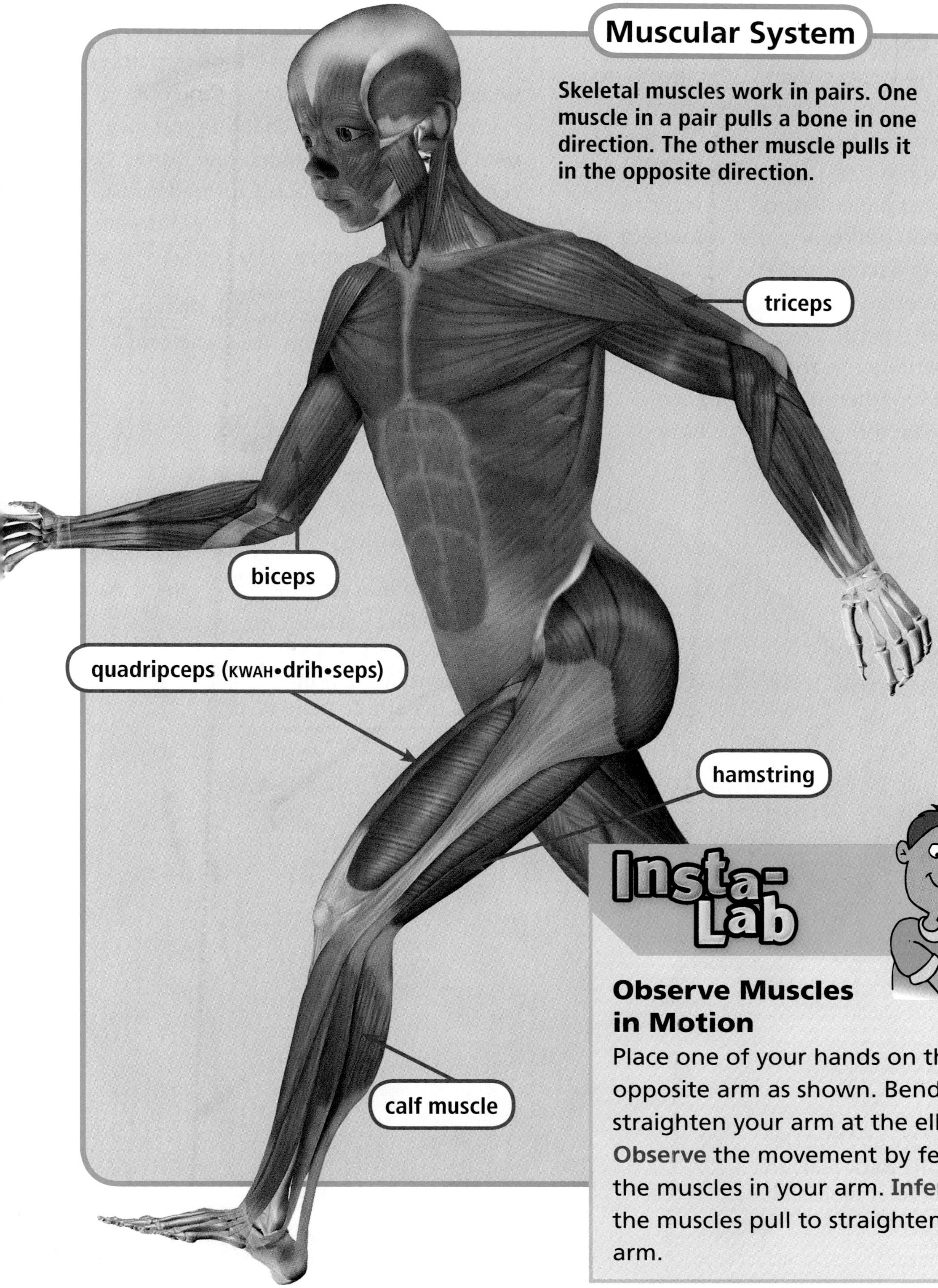

Insta-Lab

Observe Muscles in Motion

Place one of your hands on the opposite arm as shown. Bend and straighten your arm at the elbow. **Observe** the movement by feeling the muscles in your arm. **Infer** how the muscles pull to straighten your arm.

Joints

You have more than 230 joints in your body. Most of these places where bones meet are movable. They let your body change position.

In most joints, *ligaments*—which are tough bands of tissue—connect bones to each other. The muscles are connected to the bones by *tendons,* another type of tough connective tissue.

Depending on their shape, bones can fit together in different ways. Some joints, like those in your knees and elbows, move like the hinges on a door. In other joints, one bone stays in place while the other turns, or *pivots.* Your neck has a pivot joint that lets you turn your head. In other joints, one bone rolls like a ball in a socket formed by the other bone. Your shoulders and hips are ball-and-socket joints.

Focus Skill MAIN IDEA AND DETAILS **What is a joint? How do joints move your body?**

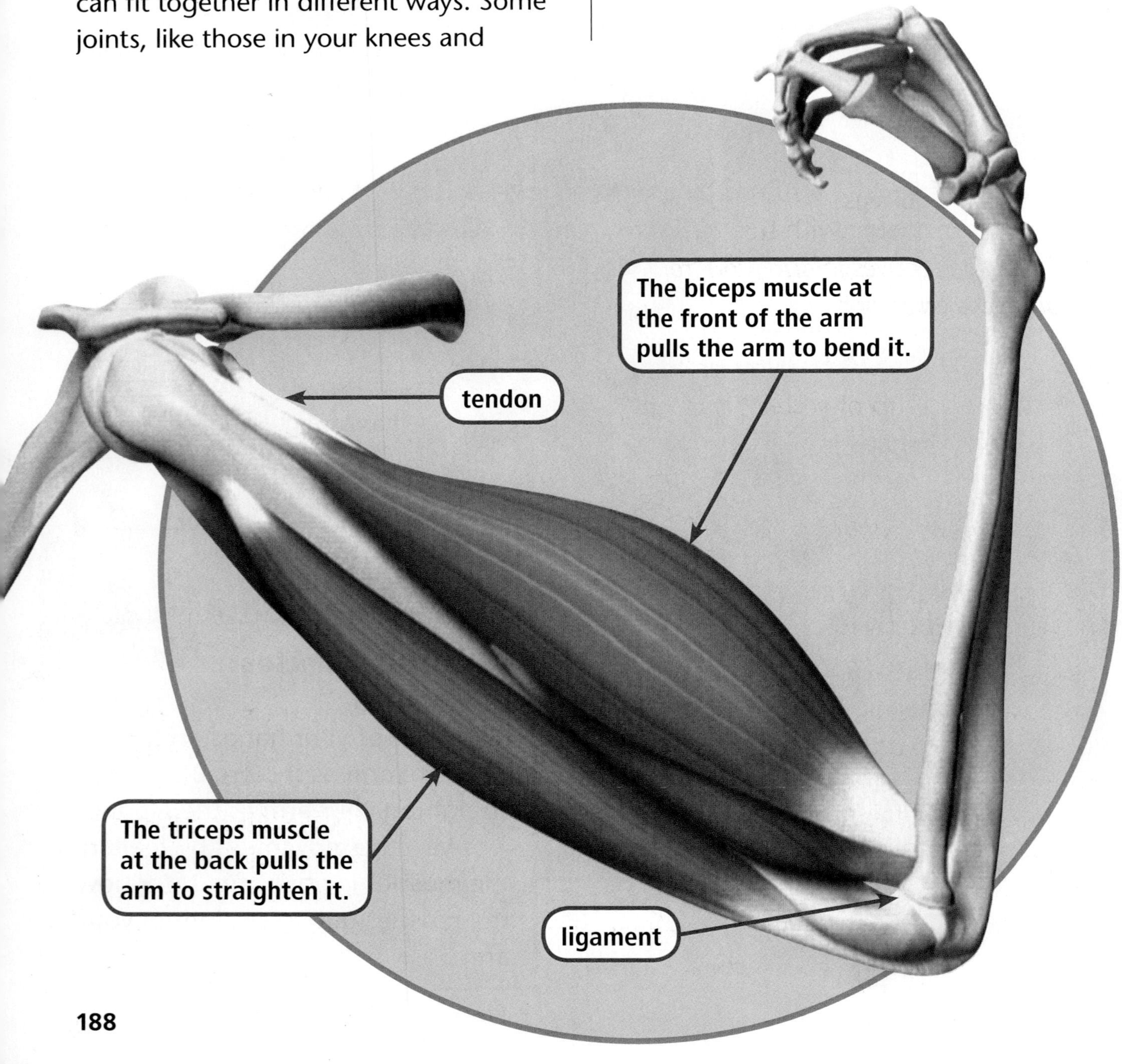

The biceps muscle at the front of the arm pulls the arm to bend it.
tendon
The triceps muscle at the back pulls the arm to straighten it.
ligament

Lesson Review

Essential Question

How Does Your Body Think and Move?

In this lesson, you learned that your nervous system collects information about the world from your senses. Your skeletal and muscular systems work together to provide shape for your body and to help you move.

1. **Focus Skill MAIN IDEA AND DETAILS** Draw and complete a graphic organizer to show the details of the muscular system.

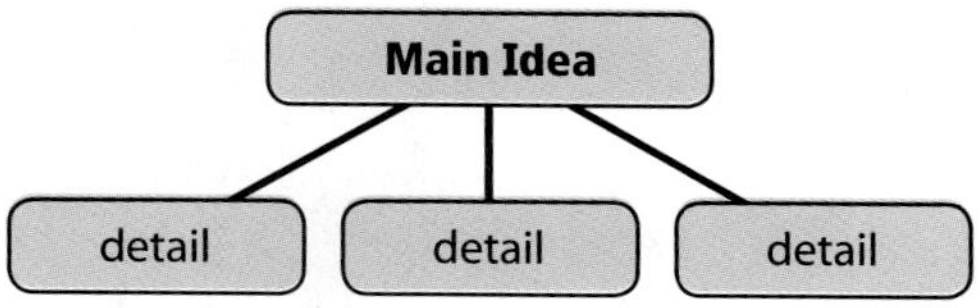

2. **SUMMARIZE** Write a summary of this lesson. Begin with this sentence: *The brain receives information from all parts of the body.*

3. **DRAW CONCLUSIONS** Why isn't the heart made up of smooth muscle like other organs in your body?

4. **VOCABULARY** Use the lesson vocabulary to write a sentence about how the body moves.

Test Prep

5. **CRITICAL THINKING** In what ways do the skeletal and muscular systems work together?

6. What type of joint bends and straightens the knee?
   A. ball joint
   B. hinge joint
   C. pivot joint
   D. socket joint

Make Connections

Writing

Narrative Writing

Suppose you take a long hike. Write a **story** describing the hike from the point of view of your muscles. How would your skeletal muscles respond? What about your cardiac muscle?

Math

Multiply Whole Numbers

Count your heartbeats for 15 seconds. Multiply this number by 4 to see how often your heart beats each minute. How often does your heart beat in one hour?

Physical Education

Make a Plan

Experts say that you should exercise each day to stay healthy. What activities can you do each day to get 30 minutes of exercise? Make a plan.

Prosthetic Limbs and Organs

What if you could pick up a pencil without lifting a finger? What if all you had to do was think about it? Would you use such a mind-powered machine? You might not, but millions of people who are missing hands, arms, or legs would welcome such an invention. Some people are born with a missing body part. Others lose a limb to accidents or diseases. Whatever the cause, prosthetic limbs can help.

Artificial hand

This runner has a prosthetic leg, but it doesn't slow her down.

Prosthetic Limbs

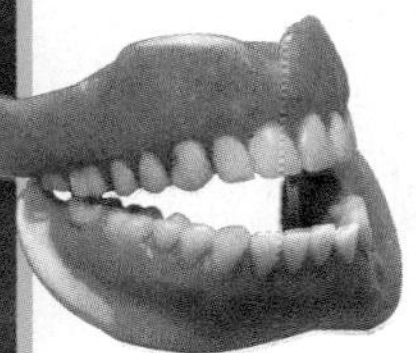

A prosthesis (prahs•THEE•suhs) is any device that substitutes for a body part. Dentures and bridges are prostheses (prahs•THEE•seez) for missing teeth. Many people have them. Artificial knee and hip joints are also common. These replacement joints help athletes who have injured their knees and older people whose joints have worn away over time.

People who lose arms and legs often get prosthetic (prahs•THEH•tik) limbs. Most limbs today are mechanical. Muscles power them. Cables drive them. It takes a lot of work to learn to use them well. Some scientists are trying to invent prostheses that are easier to use. These prostheses are driven by electrical power and controlled by the nervous system. One such experiment was performed at Duke University, in North Carolina. Researchers there fit a robotic arm to an owl monkey. Using signals from its brain alone, the monkey moved the arm.

Prosthetic Organs

Arms and legs aren't the only prosthetic devices. Human-made bone substitutes, artificial blood, and kidney machines are prostheses, too. So are prosthetic organs. They are artificial devices that can replace organs lost to an accident or a disease.

The artificial heart is a prosthetic organ. A few people who cannot receive a real human heart have received an artificial one. More people have received a prosthesis called a left ventricular assist device (LVAD). It does not replace the entire heart, but it helps a weak heart pump better. Many scientists are working to invent and test better LVADs.

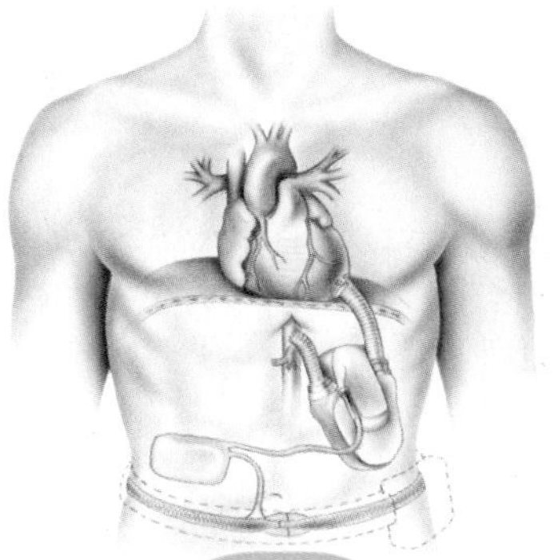

LVAD

Other researchers are trying to develop a group of tiny electrodes to replace the retina. The retina is the structure in the back of the eye on which images form. It contains cells that detect light and color. Diseases can destroy the retina but leave a healthy optic nerve, which carries the retina's signals to the brain. In such cases, a prosthetic retina could restore vision to people who have lost their sight.

Think and Write

1. Is a hearing aid a prosthesis? Explain your answer.
2. If you wanted to invent a prosthetic replacement for a limb or an organ, which one would it be? Why?

Artificial hip joint and socket

Spin-In Find out more. Log on to www.hspscience.com

Review and Test Preparation

Vocabulary Review

Use the terms below to complete the sentences. The page numbers tell you where to look in the chapter if you need help.

esophagus p. 170	**vein** p. 174
stomach p. 170	**spinal cord** p. 182
diaphragm p. 172	**bone** p. 184
capillary p. 174	**joint** p. 184
artery p. 174	**muscle** p. 186

1. A tiny, thin-walled blood vessel is a _______.

2. The bundle of nerve tissue that carries messages to and from the brain is the _______.

3. A hard organ that helps support and move the body is a _______.

4. A place where two bones meet is a _______.

5. The main muscle that controls the movement of air into and out of the body is the _______.

6. Smooth, cardiac, and skeletal are types of _______.

7. A blood vessel that carries blood away from the heart is an _______.

8. The muscular organ that turns food into almost a liquid is the _______.

9. The tube between the mouth and the stomach is the _______.

10. A blood vessel that carries blood to the heart is a _______.

Check Understanding

Write the letter of the best choice.

11. **MAIN IDEA** What are these fingerlike projections in the small intestine?

Focus Skill

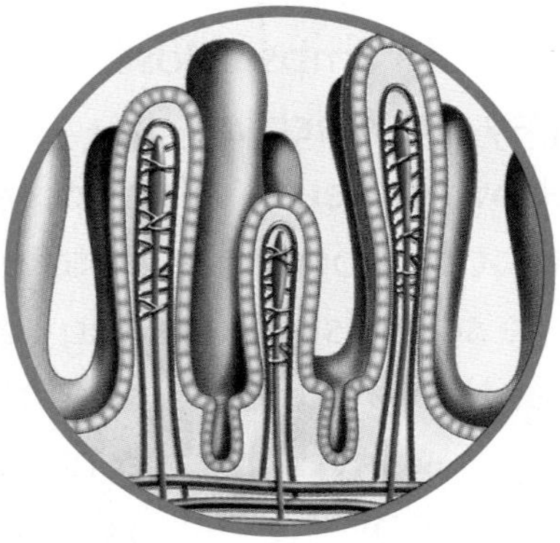

A. capillaries
B. nerve tissue
C. nerves
D. villi

12. **SEQUENCE** What is the path that blood follows through the body, beginning at the heart?

Focus Skill

F. heart, capillaries, arteries, veins, heart
G. heart, arteries, capillaries, veins, heart
H. heart, veins, capillaries, arteries, heart
J. heart, capillaries, veins, arteries, heart

13. What are organs made of?
   A. large, individual cells
   B. specialized tissues
   C. muscle
   D. bone

14. Which two organs run parallel to each other?
   F. stomach and esophagus
   G. esophagus and intestine
   H. eyes and ears
   J. spinal cord and esophagus

15. Which is the main sense being used to catch the ball?
   A. hearing
   B. sight
   C. smell
   D. taste

16. Which systems work together to provide the body's cells with nutrients?
   F. circulatory and digestive
   G. circulatory and respiratory
   H. respiratory and circulatory
   J. respiratory and nervous

Inquiry Skills

17. **Compare** digestion and respiration.

18. Draw and complete the graphic organizer to show the following order of events. A message from a touch receptor reaches the brain, which then directs a leg muscle to move. Use the completed graphic organizer to **infer** what happens when you touch something soft.

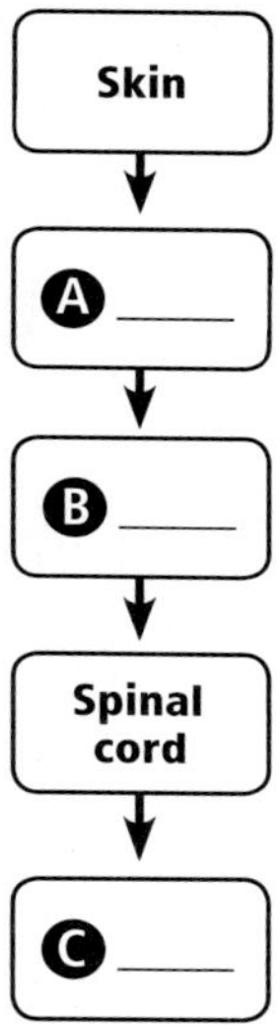

Critical Thinking

The Big Idea

19. How would unhealthy teeth or gums affect digestion?

20. Different body systems work together to keep us healthy. How are the digestive and circulatory systems related? Explain how the heart and lungs help each other provide oxygen to the body.

Unit A Life Science: Visual Summary

Tell how each picture shows the **Big Idea** for its chapter.

Chapter 1 Big Idea

Living things can be grouped according to their characteristics.

Chapter 2 Big Idea

Living things inherit traits, grow, and develop according to life cycles.

Chapter 3 Big Idea

Living things are adapted for survival in their environment.

Chapter 4 Big Idea

To stay alive, people depend on body systems that work together.

Looking at Ecosystems

UNIT B
LIFE SCIENCE

Unit Inquiry

Counting Species

When people develop land and build new houses, the environment that was already there is changed. The animals living in the habitat must find new places to live. Is there a difference between natural habitats and habitats that humans have developed? Are there more types of living things in one of the two kinds of environments? Plan and conduct an experiment to find out.

CHAPTER 5
Understanding Ecosystems

What's the Big Idea? Ecosystems are made up of both living and nonliving parts that all impact one another.

Essential Questions

Lesson 1
What Are the Parts of an Ecosystem?

Lesson 2
What Factors Influence Ecosystems?

Lesson 3
How Do Humans Affect Ecosystems?

GO online ▸ Student eBook www.hspscience.com

Osprey catching a fish

What do YOU wonder?

Catching Dinner? This osprey has very sharp claws, called talons. The osprey's talons help it catch fish. What impact does the osprey have on the fish population? How does this relate to the **Big Idea?**

LESSON

1

Essential Question

What Are the Parts of an Ecosystem?

Investigate how plants grow together in an ecosystem.

Read and Learn how living things group together to make up different ecosystems.

Fast Fact

Silver Kings

The tarpon in this photograph are not yet full-grown! These fish don't become adults until they are between 7 and 13 years old, when they can weigh more than 91 kilograms (200 lb). Tarpon live in salt water, but they can survive in a variety of ecosystems. In the Investigate, you will observe how sunlight affects plants in another ecosystem.

Tarpon in an aquarium

Vocabulary Preview

environment [en•VY•ruhn•muhnt] All of the living and nonliving things that affect an organism (p. 202)

ecosystem [EE•koh•sis•tuhm] A community and its physical environment together (p. 202)

population [pahp•yuh•LAY•shuhn] All the individuals of the same kind living in the same environment (p. 204)

community [kuh•MYOO•nuh•tee] All the populations of organisms living together in an environment (p. 206)

Investigate

Modeling an Ecosystem

Guided Inquiry

Start with Questions

This plant is growing in a small garden ecosystem.

- Does the plant depend on other living things?
- If the ecosystem were larger, could more plants grow there?

Investigate to find out. Then read and learn to find out more.

Prepare to Investigate

Inquiry Skill Tip

Models, such as terrariums, can show how living things work together. Terrariums are small versions of large ecosystems found around the world.

Materials

- gravel
- 6 small plants
- 2 empty 2-L soda bottles with tops cut off
- sand
- water in a spray bottle
- soil
- clear plastic wrap
- 2 rubber bands

Make an Observation Chart

Plants	Observations
In sun	
In dark	

Follow This Procedure

1. Pour a layer of gravel, a layer of sand, and then a layer of soil into the bottom of each bottle.
2. Plant three plants in each bottle.
3. Spray the plants and the soil with water. Cover the top of each bottle with plastic wrap. If necessary, hold the wrap in place with a rubber band.
4. Put one of the terrariums you just made in a sunny spot. Put the other one in a dark closet or cabinet.
5. After three days, **observe** each terrarium and **record** what you see.

Step 2

Step 3

Draw Conclusions

1. What did you **observe** about each of your ecosystems after three days? What part was missing from one ecosystem?
2. **Inquiry Skill** Scientists often learn more about how things affect one another by **making a model**. What did you learn by making a model and observing how its parts interact?

Independent Inquiry

What effect does sunlight have on seeds that have just been planted? First, write your hypothesis. Then plan an experiment to see if your hypothesis is supported.

VOCABULARY

environment p. 202
ecosystem p. 202
population p. 204
community p. 206

SCIENCE CONCEPTS

▶ how living and nonliving parts of an ecosystem interact
▶ what populations and communities are

Focus Skill — MAIN IDEA AND DETAILS

Look for the parts that make up an ecosystem.

Main Idea
detail | detail | detail

Ecosystems

Where do you live? You might name your street and town. You also live in an environment. An **environment** is all the living and nonliving things that surround you. The living things in your environment are people, other animals, and plants. The nonliving things around you include water, air, soil, and weather.

The parts of an environment affect one another in many ways. For example, animals eat plants. The soil affects which plants can live in a place. Clean air and clean water help keep both plants and animals healthy. All the living and nonliving things in an area form an **ecosystem** (EE•koh•sis•tuhm).

An ecosystem can be very small. It might be the space under a rock. That space might be home to insects and tiny plants. You might need a microscope to see some of the things living there.

This prairie smoke plant grows well in the hot, dry climate of prairies and grasslands. ▼

Prairie dogs also live on the prairies and grasslands. ▼

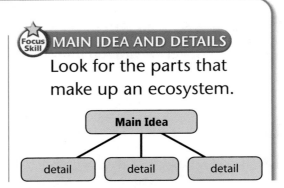

Moose thrive in a coniferous forest ecosystem.

The small ecosystem found under a rock has nonliving parts, too. They include pockets of air and the soil under the rock. You might find a few drops of water or maybe just damp soil. All ecosystems must have at least a little water.

The ecosystem under a rock has a climate. The *climate* in an area is the average weather over many years. Climate includes temperature and rainfall. The climate of an ecosystem depends on where the ecosystem is. If the rock is in Florida, its climate is warm and wet. If the rock is in Maine, its climate is cold in winter.

An ecosystem can also be as large as a forest. A forest can provide many kinds of food and shelter. This ecosystem may include hundreds of kinds of plants and animals. Each organism finds what it needs in the forest.

Like all ecosystems, a forest has nonliving parts. They include water, air, soil, and climate. Later, you will read more about ways living and nonliving parts of an ecosystem affect one another.

Focus Skill MAIN IDEA AND DETAILS

Name the two parts of an ecosystem, and give two examples of each part.

This individual waterlily is part of a large population of waterlilies.

Individuals and Populations

One plant or animal is an *individual.* For example, one blueberry bush is an individual. One honeybee is an individual. One blue jay is an individual. You are an individual.

A group made up of the same kind of individuals living in the same ecosystem is a **population**. A group of blueberry bushes is a population. So is a hive of bees. So are all the blue jays living in one forest. So are all the people living in one city.

Robins might live in the same forest as the blue jays. Robins are a different kind of bird. That makes them a different population.

The members of a population might not live in a group. For example, frogs don't live in families. Still, a number of green tree frogs may live near the same pond. They belong to the same population. Bullfrogs might also live near that pond. They are a different population.

Many animals live in groups. People live in families. How many people are in your family? Wolves live in packs. A pack can have from 3 to 20 wolves. A wolf population may have several packs. The wolf population in Yellowstone National Park includes 19 packs.

Some populations can live in more than one kind of ecosystem. For instance, red-winged blackbirds often live in wetlands, but they are also found in other areas. Red-winged blackbirds can live in different ecosystems. If one ecosystem no longer meets the needs of these birds, they fly to another one.

Some populations can live in only one kind of ecosystem. One such animal is the Hine's emerald dragonfly. This insect can live only in certain wetlands. It can't survive in other places. Because this dragonfly can live only in specific places, its total number is very small.

Ecosystems are often named for the main population that lives there. For example, one kind of ecosystem forms where a river flows into the ocean. There, fresh water mixes with salt water. Many trees can't live in salty water. But mangrove trees have roots that allow them to get rid of the salt in the water. When many mangrove trees live in a salty ecosystem, the area is called a *mangrove swamp.*

Focus Skill **MAIN IDEA AND DETAILS**

Name an individual and a population that are not mentioned on these two pages.

Insta-Lab

Eeek! Oh System!

Work with a partner to list some of the populations in your school ecosystem. Think about the building and the land around it. Then compare lists with other students. Did you list the same populations?

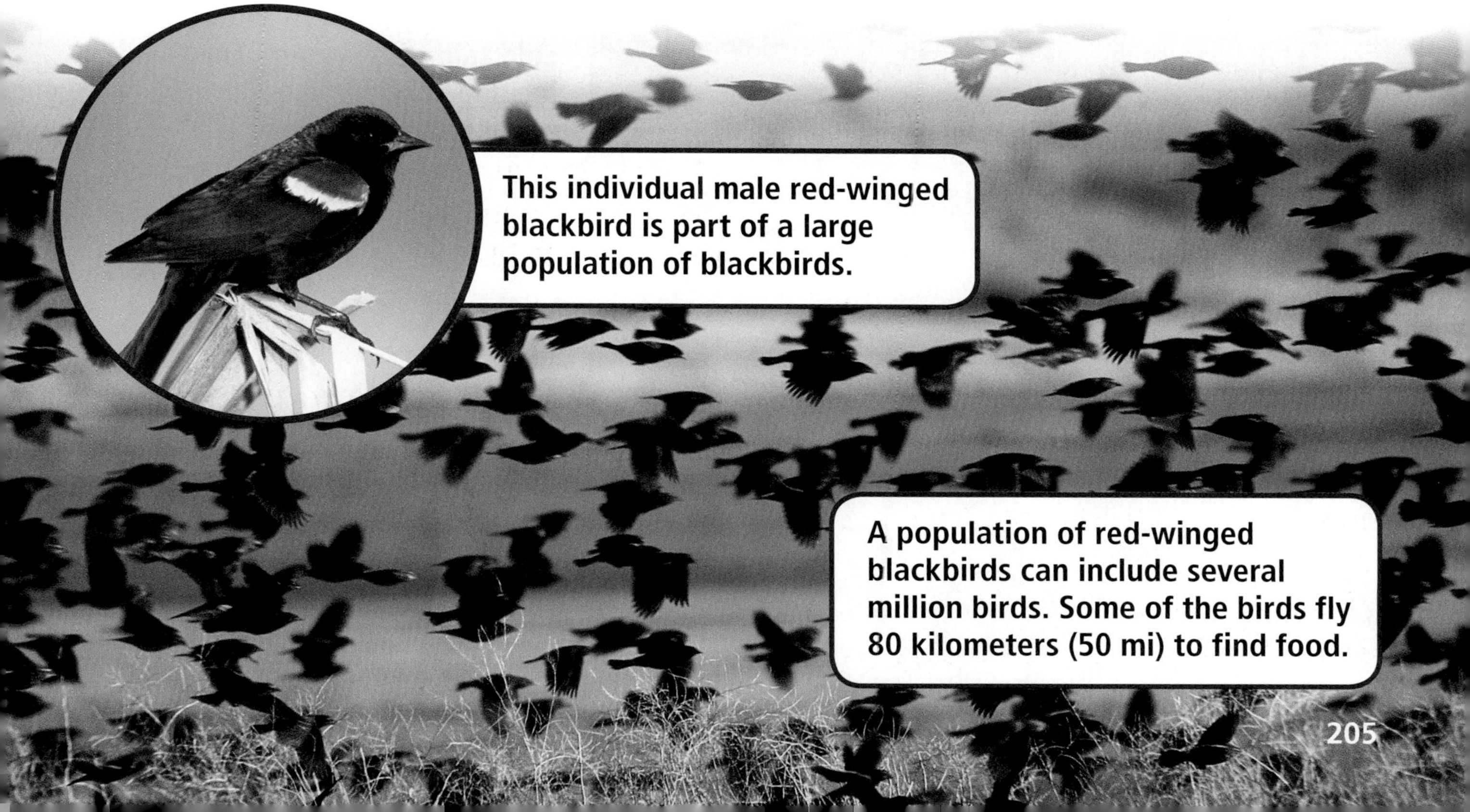

This individual male red-winged blackbird is part of a large population of blackbirds.

A population of red-winged blackbirds can include several million birds. Some of the birds fly 80 kilometers (50 mi) to find food.

Communities

You live in a community. Other animals and plants do, too. A **community** is made up of all the populations that live in the same place.

Have you ever visited or seen pictures of the Everglades National Park? Many different populations make up this community. The plants include mangrove trees, cypress trees, and sawgrass. If you have been to the Everglades, you may know about the mosquitoes from getting bitten! The area has 43 kinds. And 50 kinds of butterflies live there.

Animals found in the Everglades community include alligators, bobcats, and raccoons. Bird-watchers like to visit the Everglades. They try to see some of the 350 kinds of land birds and 16 kinds of wading birds that live there.

In some ways, the Everglades is like all communities. The plants and animals there depend on one another. Some animals eat the plants. Other animals eat the plant eaters. The animals help spread the plants' seeds. The plants provide shelter for the animals.

Focus Skill MAIN IDEA AND DETAILS

Name three populations that might be found in a forest community.

Many populations make up the communities in this cold taiga ecosystem. They include conifers, moose, and many kinds of birds.

Lesson Review

Essential Question

What Are the Parts of an Ecosystem?

In this lesson, you learned that living things group together in different ways to make up ecosystems. All the living and nonliving parts of an ecosystem affect one another.

1. **MAIN IDEA AND DETAILS** Use a graphic organizer to list the parts of an ecosystem.

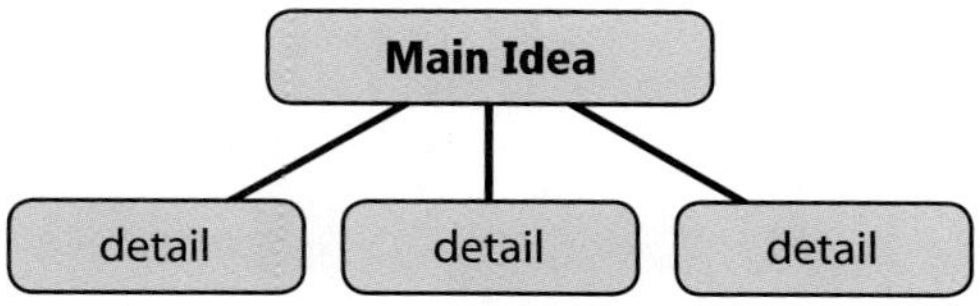

2. **SUMMARIZE** Write a sentence for each main idea presented in this lesson. Use the vocabulary terms where appropriate.

3. **DRAW CONCLUSIONS** Why do some ecosystems include more living things than other ecosystems?

4. **VOCABULARY** Use the lesson vocabulary words to create a matching quiz.

Test Prep

5. **CRITICAL THINKING** How is a population different from a community?

6. Which word describes a group of cows that share a field?
   A. community
   B. ecosystem
   C. individual
   D. population

Make Connections

Writing

Expository Writing

You are a scientist planning an ecosystem on the moon. Write **two paragraphs** explaining what this ecosystem should include.

Math

Solve a Problem

The Everglades includes many "rivers of grass." The water in these rivers moves slowly, only about 30 meters (100 ft) a day. About how many meters would the water move in June? In February?

Social Studies

Ecosystems and People

Choose a group of people who live in an ecosystem different from yours. Find out how that ecosystem affects the people. Share what you learn in an oral or a written report.

LESSON 2

Essential Question

What Factors Influence Ecosystems?

Investigate how water affects plants.

Read and Learn how living and nonliving things influence ecosystems.

Fast Fact

That's Dry!
This photograph shows the Atacama Desert in Chile. It's the driest place on Earth. Less than 0.01 centimeter (0.004 in.) of rain falls there every year. It hasn't rained in some parts of this desert for 400 years! In the Investigate, you will explore what happens when there is no rain.

Atacama Desert, Chile

Vocabulary Preview

biotic [by•AHT•ik] Of the living parts of an ecosystem (p. 212)

abiotic [ay•by•AHT•ik] Of the nonliving parts of an ecosystem (p. 214)

diversity [duh•VER•suh•tee] A measure of the number and variety of species in an ecosystem (p. 218)

Observing the Effects of Water

Guided Inquiry

Start with Questions

These plants are watered with sprinklers to help them grow.

- Why do plants need water?
- Can plants have too much water?

Investigate to find out. Then read and learn to find out more.

Prepare to Investigate

Inquiry Skill Tip

When you compare your plants, look at all the different parts of the plants. Examine the leaves on each plant, and note the differences you see. Examine the stems, and write down how they are the same and how they are different.

Materials

- 4 small identical plants in clay pots
- water
- large labels

Make an Observation Chart

	Day 1	Day 4	Day 7	Day 10
Plant 1 (watered)				
Plant 2 (watered)				
Plant 3 (not watered)				
Plant 4 (not watered)				

Follow This Procedure

1. Use the labels to number the pots 1, 2, 3, and 4. Label pots 1 and 2 *watered.* Label pots 3 and 4 *not watered.*
2. Make a table like the one shown here. Draw a picture of each plant under Day 1.
3. Place all four pots in a sunny window.
4. Water all four pots until the soil is a little moist. Keep the soil of pots 1 and 2 moist during the whole experiment. Don't water pots 3 and 4 again.
5. Wait three days. Then **observe** and **record** how each plant looks. Draw a picture of each one under Day 4.
6. Repeat Step 5 twice. Draw pictures of the plants on Days 7 and 10.

Draw Conclusions

1. What changes did you **observe** during this Investigate? What do they tell you?
2. **Inquiry Skill** Scientists **compare** changes to determine how one thing affects another. How could you **compare** how fast the soil dries out in a clay pot with how fast it dries out in a plastic pot?

Independent Inquiry

How does covering a plant with plastic wrap affect the plant's need to be watered? Write your hypothesis. Then design and carry out an experiment to check your hypothesis.

VOCABULARY
biotic p. 212
abiotic p. 214
diversity p. 218

SCIENCE CONCEPTS
- how biotic and abiotic factors affect ecosystems
- how climate influences an ecosystem

Focus Skill CAUSE AND EFFECT
Look for ways in which factors affect ecosystems.

cause → effect

Living Things Affect Ecosystems

Do plants and animals need each other? Yes, they do! Plants and animals are living parts of an ecosystem. These living parts are **biotic** factors. *Bio* means "life." Biotic factors affect the ecosystem and one another in many ways.

For example, plants provide food for caterpillars, birds, sheep, and other animals. People eat plants every day—at least they should.

Plants also provide shelter for animals. For instance, many insects live in grasses. Squirrels make dens in trees. Your home likely contains wood from trees.

Animals help plants, too. When animals eat one kind of plant, it can't spread and take over all the available space. This gives other kinds of plants room to grow.

A gypsy moth can lay 1000 eggs or more. Most of the eggs hatch into hungry caterpillars like this one. ▶

A healthy tree isn't hurt when a few insects nibble on it.

Gypsy moth caterpillars can eat all the leaves on a tree. Bad weather or an attack by other insects may kill trees.

Animals help plants in other ways. Animal droppings make the soil richer. Earthworms help loosen the soil. Rich, loose soil helps plants grow.

At the same time, too many plant eaters can be harmful. A herd of hungry deer can eat enough of a tree's leaves to kill the tree. A huge swarm of locusts can leave a field bare of plants.

You know that animals affect one another. For example, wolves eat rabbits. If the wolf population becomes too large, wolves can wipe out the rabbits. Then the wolves go hungry. Without the rabbits to eat them, the grasses spread.

In this case, an increase in wolves causes a decrease in rabbits. Fewer rabbits causes an increase in plants.

A change in plants can also cause a change in animals. If dry weather or disease kills the grasses, the rabbits starve. Then the wolves go hungry, too. Disease can also kill animals in an ecosystem.

Sometimes, a new kind of plant or animal changes an ecosystem. For example, people brought the skunk vine to the United States from Asia in 1897. For a time, they planted it as a crop. Now it grows wild. This smelly vine can grow 9 meters (30 ft) long! It crowds out other plants, and it can even grow underwater.

CAUSE AND EFFECT **Explain how an increase in plants could affect an ecosystem.**

Math in Science
Interpret Data

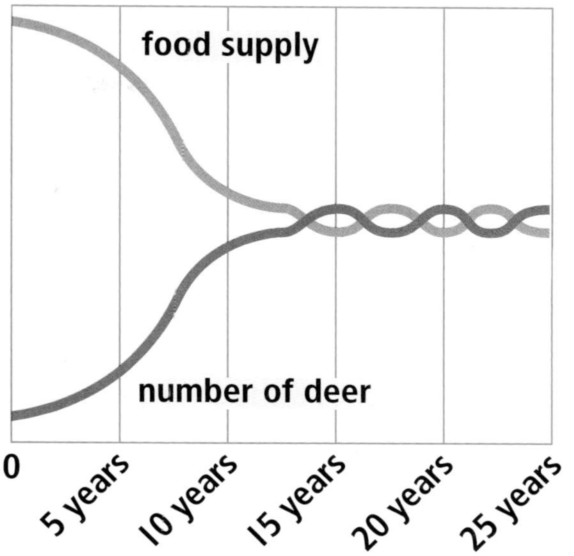

What happened to the population of deer as the food supply got smaller?

Tree leaves are a main source of food for deer. It takes 15 to 30 acres of land to provide enough food for one deer.

Nonliving Things Affect Ecosystems

Plants and animals are the living parts of an ecosystem. The nonliving parts include sunlight, air, water, and soil. Abiotic means nonliving, so the **abiotic** factors are the nonliving parts of an ecosystem. They are just as important as the biotic factors.

For example, a change in the water supply can affect all the living things in an ecosystem. Too little rain causes many plants to wilt and die. Animals must find other homes. Some may die.

An ecosystem with rich soil has many plants. Where the soil is poor, few plants grow. An ecosystem with few plants will have few animals.

Air, water, and soil can contain harmful substances. They can affect all living things. You will learn more about this problem later in the chapter.

Focus Skill CAUSE AND EFFECT

How might a change in the water supply affect a rabbit?

Insta-Lab

Super Soil!

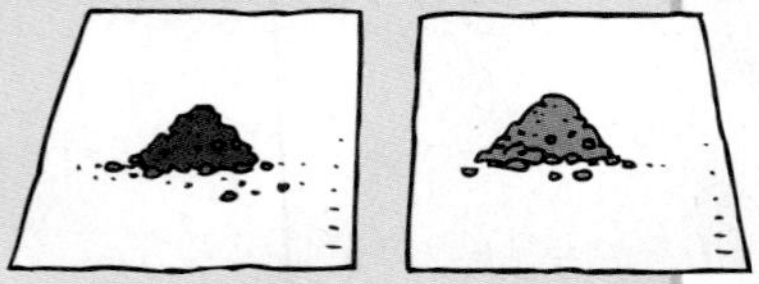

With a partner or a group, compare two different soil samples. How might each soil affect its ecosystem?

Science Up Close

Nonliving Factors

Without the nonliving parts of an ecosystem, there would be no living parts.

For more links and animations, go to **www.hspscience.com**

Sunlight

Plants need sunlight to produce food. Where trees shade the ground, not many other plants can grow.

Water

Almost all living things need water. Plant roots absorb water, and animals drink it.

Soil

Most plants need soil to grow. The kind of soil in an ecosystem is one of the factors that determine which plants grow there.

Climate Affects Ecosystems

What is the climate like where you live? Is it warm and sunny, or is it cool and rainy? Maybe it's something in between.

Climate is an abiotic factor. It's a combination of other abiotic factors. Climate includes the amount of rainfall and sunlight in a region. It also includes the repeating patterns of the temperature of the air during the year.

Climate affects the soil. Some climates allow many plants to grow and help dead plants decay. Animals that eat the plants leave behind their droppings. The decaying plants and droppings make the soil richer.

Climate affects the kinds of plants and animals in an ecosystem. For example, warm, wet climates support tropical rain forests. Hot summers and cold winters result in temperate forests.

The frozen tundra suits the hardy caribou. The mosses they eat thrive there. Zebras could not survive in the tundra. They need the mild climate and tender grasses of the savanna.

Focus Skill **CAUSE AND EFFECT**

What would happen to an ecosystem if its climate changed?

World Climate Zones

This map shows six climate zones around the world.

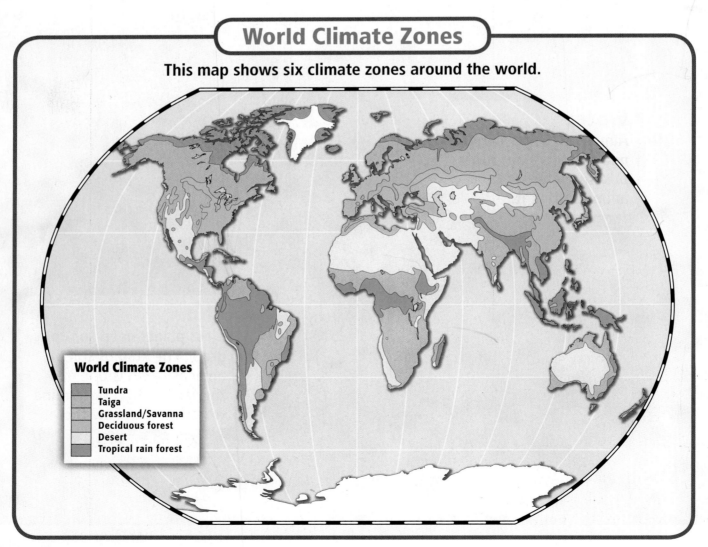

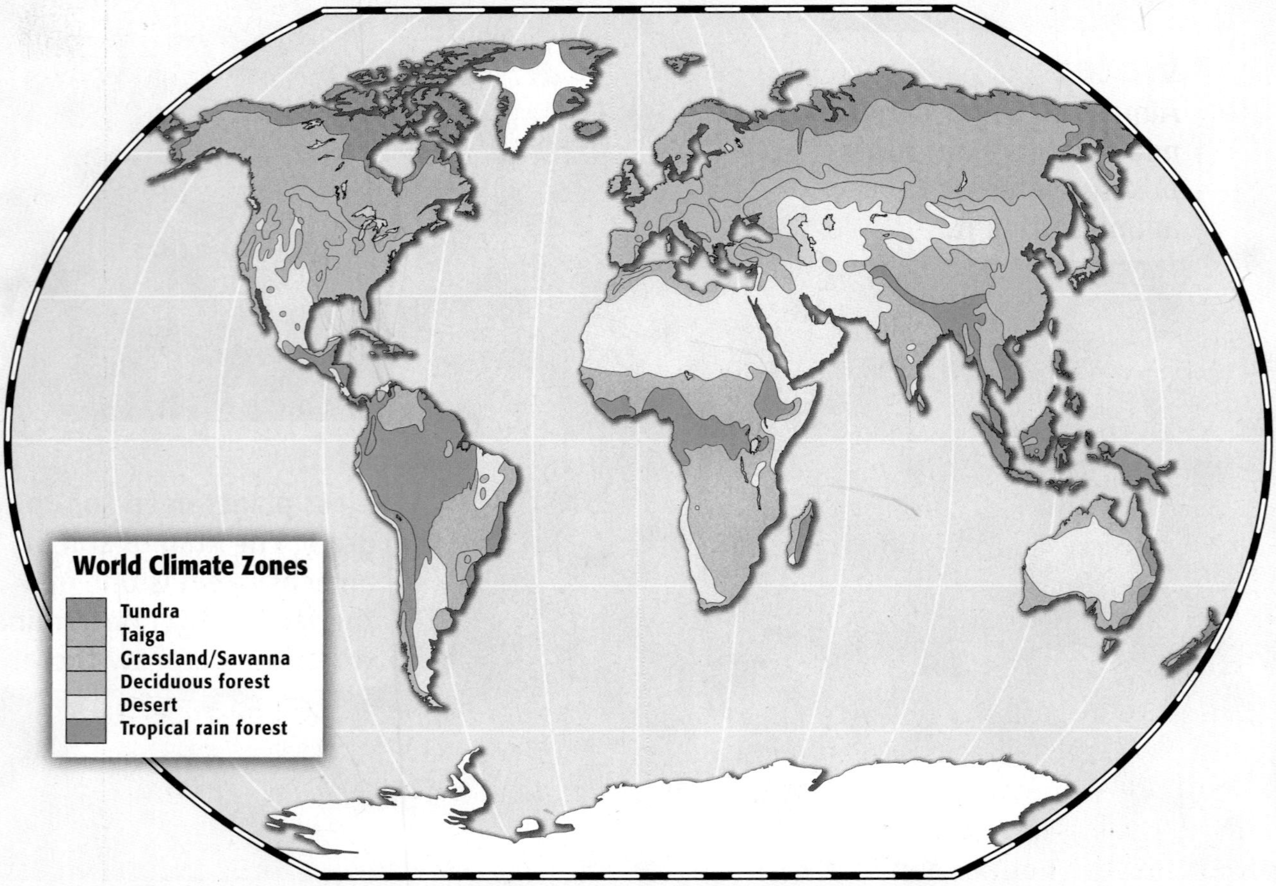

Deciduous forests have four seasons. The trees, such as oaks and maples, lose their leaves in the fall. This helps them survive the cold winters.

Rain forests receive 2000 to 10,000 millimeters (7 to 33 ft) of rain each year! Tropical rain forests are near the equator.

The climate in the grassy savanna is nearly the same all year. The temperature stays between 18°C and 22°C (64°F and 72°F).

Deserts get only about 250 millimeters (10 in.) of rain a year. Plants there grow very quickly after a rain. Their seeds can survive for years as they wait for more rain.

The taiga covers more of Earth than any other kind of plant community. The taiga is mostly just south of the tundra and is very cold in winter. Most of its trees are conifers.

The tundra has the coldest climate: –40°C to 18°C (–40°F to 64°F). *Tundra* means "treeless plain."

There are layers in a rain forest.

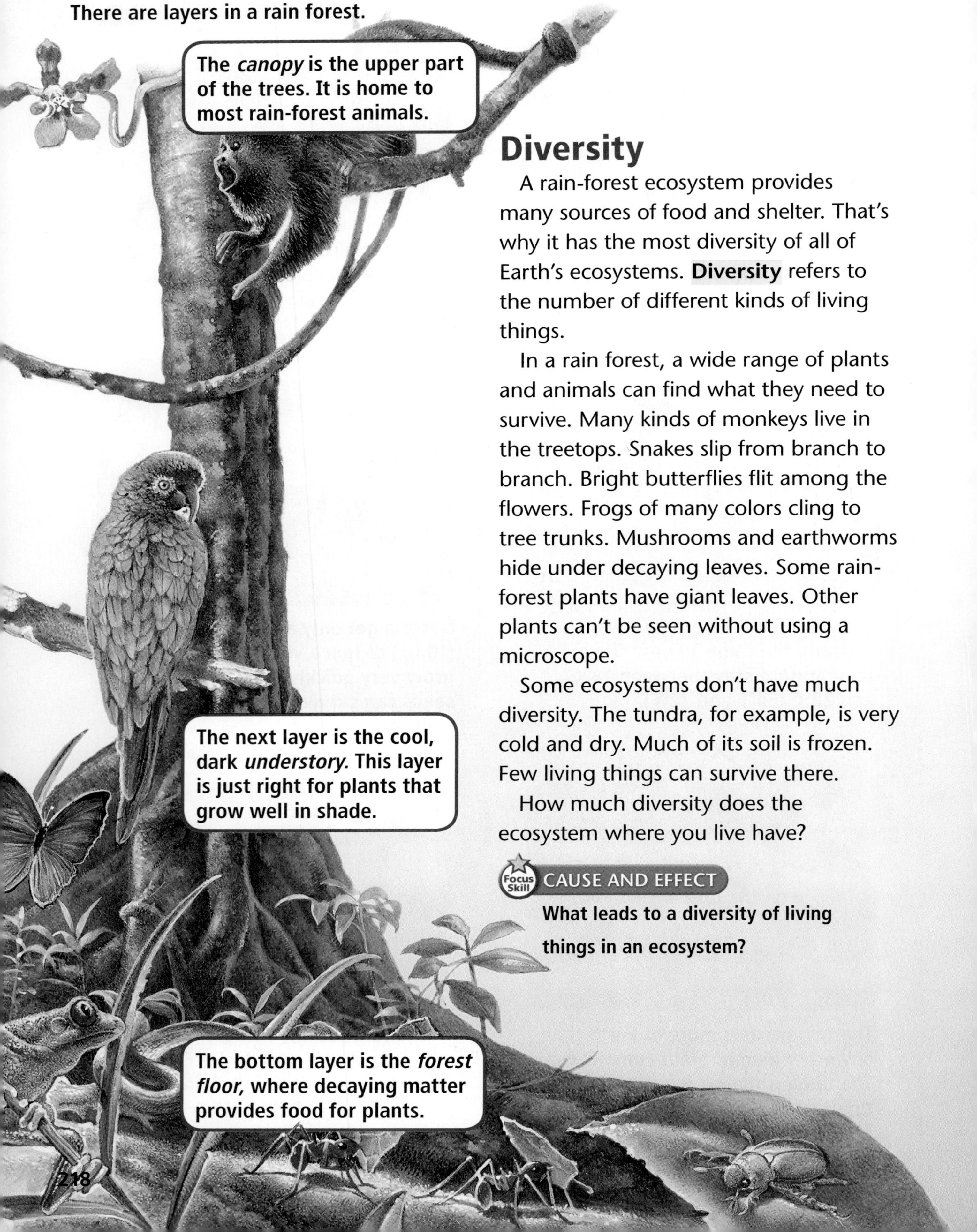

The *canopy* is the upper part of the trees. It is home to most rain-forest animals.
The next layer is the cool, dark *understory.* This layer is just right for plants that grow well in shade.
The bottom layer is the *forest floor,* where decaying matter provides food for plants.

Diversity

A rain-forest ecosystem provides many sources of food and shelter. That's why it has the most diversity of all of Earth's ecosystems. **Diversity** refers to the number of different kinds of living things.

In a rain forest, a wide range of plants and animals can find what they need to survive. Many kinds of monkeys live in the treetops. Snakes slip from branch to branch. Bright butterflies flit among the flowers. Frogs of many colors cling to tree trunks. Mushrooms and earthworms hide under decaying leaves. Some rain-forest plants have giant leaves. Other plants can't be seen without using a microscope.

Some ecosystems don't have much diversity. The tundra, for example, is very cold and dry. Much of its soil is frozen. Few living things can survive there.

How much diversity does the ecosystem where you live have?

Focus Skill CAUSE AND EFFECT

What leads to a diversity of living things in an ecosystem?

Lesson Review

Essential Question

What Factors Influence Ecosystems?

In this lesson, you learned that biotic factors are the living parts of an ecosystem. Abiotic factors are the nonliving parts of an ecosystem. Both affect the ecosystem and its diversity, or variety, of life.

1. Focus Skill **CAUSE AND EFFECT** Use a graphic organizer to show what happens when there is a lack of water.

   cause → effect

2. **SUMMARIZE** Write a summary of this lesson. Begin with this sentence: *Plants provide food for many animals.*

3. **DRAW CONCLUSIONS** Which can exist without the other—biotic factors or abiotic factors? Explain your answer.

4. **VOCABULARY** Write a quiz-show-type question for each of the vocabulary words.

Test Prep

5. **CRITICAL THINKING** How might flooding in their ecosystem affect some robins?

6. Which of these is an abiotic factor in an ecosystem?
   A. ant
   B. decaying plant
   C. earthworm
   D. sand

Make Connections

Writing

Persuasive Writing

Write a **travel brochure** for a climate zone where few people vacation, such as the tundra or taiga. Tell your readers what interesting things they can see and experience there.

9÷3 Math

Make a Graph

Find the average rainfall in five of the six world climate zones, including your own region. Then make a bar graph that compares the amounts.

Literature

Learn More

Read a current nonfiction book about one of the world climate zones, such as the desert. After learning more about that climate zone, share what you know by making a display or a written report.

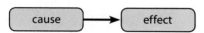

LESSON 3

Essential Question

How Do Humans Affect Ecosystems?

Investigate how erosion carries away soil.

Read and Learn how humans can have an impact on ecosystems.

Fast Fact

Saving Soil
Contour-plowing slopes helps keep rain from washing away the soil. It can reduce erosion by as much as 75 percent! In the Investigate, you will experiment with "rain" and erosion.

Field with contour plowing and strip cropping

Vocabulary Preview

pollution [puh•LOO•shuhn] Waste products that damage an ecosystem (p. 226)

habitat restoration [HAB•ih•tat res•tuh•RAY•shuhn] Returning a natural environment to its original condition (p. 227)

Losing It: Observing Erosion

Guided Inquiry

Start with Questions

This bank has suffered from erosion. The soil that used to form the bank has been carried away.

- What might have caused this erosion?
- How might people prevent erosion?

Investigate to find out. Then read and learn to find out more.

Prepare to Investigate

Inquiry Skill Tip

Think about your experiment. Pay attention to what you control and what you change. Change only one thing at a time.

Materials

- marker
- soil and small rocks
- 2 paper cups
- water
- 2 clean plastic foam trays
- sharpened pencil
- measuring cup

Make an Observation Chart

	Before being watered	After being watered
Tray A Cup A		
Tray B Cup B		

Follow This Procedure

1. Use the marker to write *A* on one tray and on one paper cup. Write *B* on the second tray and on the second paper cup.
2. In each tray, make an identical slope out of soil and rocks.
3. Carefully use the pencil to make three small holes in the bottom of cup A. Make six larger holes in the bottom of cup B.
4. **Record** how the two slopes look now. Label your drawings *A* and *B*.
5. Hold cup A over the slope in tray A. Slowly pour 1 cup of water into the paper cup, and let it run down the slope. **Record** how the slope looks now.
6. **Repeat** Step 5, using cup B and tray B. Then record how the slope looks.

Draw Conclusions

1. At the end of the activity, compare the slopes. What did each cup represent?
2. **Inquiry Skill** An **experiment** is a careful, controlled test. What were you testing and what did you control in the activity?

Independent Inquiry

Try the same activity, using only rocks, using level soil, or using plants growing in the soil. Make a prediction about what will happen, and then do the activity to see if your prediction was accurate.

Read and Learn

VOCABULARY
pollution p. 226
habitat restoration p. 227

SCIENCE CONCEPTS
- how humans use the resources in ecosystems
- the positive and negative ways humans affect ecosystems

Focus Skill **COMPARE AND CONTRAST**
Compare positive and negative effects that humans have on ecosystems.

alike — different

Humans Within Ecosystems

Do you use any natural resources? You do if you breathe! Natural resources are the parts of ecosystems that humans use, including air.

What other natural resources do you use? Do you ever go to the seashore or a park? Those are natural resources. When you turn on a light, you use natural resources. Most electricity is produced by burning coal. Coal is a natural resource that is taken from under the ground.

Do you ride a bus to school? The fuel that makes the bus run is made from oil. Oil is a natural resource that is also taken from under the ground.

Minerals are natural resources, too. Iron, copper, and aluminum are examples of mineral resources.

Some natural resources can be replaced. Sunlight, air, and water are renewable resources. People can grow more trees and plant more crops.

▼ **Natural resources include lakes, fresh air, and sunlight.**

Fish and other living things are also natural resources.

More than 2000 years ago, people drank tea made from the bark of the white willow tree to help ease pain. In 1829, scientists discovered the chemical in the willow that reduces pain. They used it to make aspirin tablets.

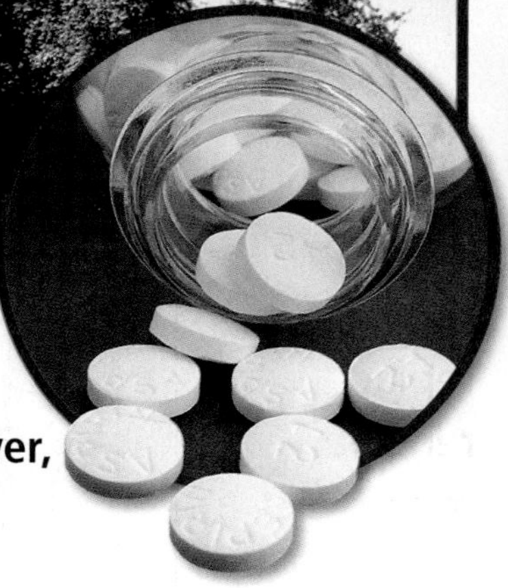

Aspirin can be bought without a prescription. However, it is a powerful and valuable drug.

People have been growing wheat for 10,000 years.

Making bread is just one way wheat is used. This grain is also used in cakes, cookies, cereals, and pastas. Parts of the wheat plant are fed to cattle.

Some natural resources can't be replaced. They include coal, gas, and oil. After the supplies buried underground are used, these resources will be gone.

Humans use natural resources in many ways. People build homes and furniture from wood. They make bricks from clay, and glass from sand. They use iron to make steel, which they then use to make cars and many other things.

People raise crops to feed themselves and their animals. They use plants as medicines, too. Humans learned long ago that plants could help treat or cure some illnesses. More than 40 percent of the medicines used today originally came from plants.

For example, a medicine made from a plant called foxglove can help treat heart disease. Scientists use the bark of the Pacific yew tree to make a medicine to treat cancer.

Scientists have tested only 2 percent of all plants to see if they can be used as medicines. Who knows how many more medicines plants may provide?

Focus Skill **COMPARE AND CONTRAST**

Compare the supply of crops with the supply of coal.

Negative and Positive Changes

Humans make many negative changes in ecosystems. When people clear land for houses and shopping malls, they destroy habitats. As a result, the animals that lived there can no longer meet all their basic needs. They must move or die.

Farmers plow land to plant crops. Plowing loosens soil. That makes it easier for rain and wind to carry away the soil. Humans also cause some kinds of pollution. **Pollution** happens when harmful substances mix with water, air, or soil.

Storms washing chemicals off fields can cause water pollution. These chemicals flow into streams and rivers. Trash and waste from homes and businesses can also enter the water supply.

Much air pollution comes from burning gasoline. Fumes from car engines carry chemicals into the air. Factory smokestacks release more chemicals. Some of these chemicals form acid rain. Acid rain can burn trees and other plants. It can poison lakes and rivers.

Soil pollution can come from fertilizers and trash. Wastes, such as old paint and drain cleaners, can poison the soil.

Cars and other vehicles are a major source of air pollution in cities. This pollution causes smog and breathing problems.

Bicycles don't release pollution. They also provide a good way to get exercise.

Many laws are designed to prevent water pollution, but it still happens.

Water treatment plants remove harmful substances from water before it reaches people's homes. ▶

Without plant roots to hold soil in place, much of the soil can wash away.

These people are helping prevent beach erosion by planting dune grasses.

Humans also make positive changes. Many groups are working to repair damage to ecosystems. They plant new trees and create new wetlands. They build parks over closed landfills. This process is known as **habitat restoration**.

People are also polluting less. Cars now have special devices on their tailpipes. These devices reduce the harmful gases that escape. Factories now release fewer chemicals. They don't dump wastes into rivers and streams.

Many people now use natural ways to get rid of weeds and insects. They spread fewer chemicals on fields and lawns.

People also recycle paper, glass, metal, and plastic. Recycling uses less energy than making new products. That means less coal is burned. Burning less coal means less pollution.

People are learning other ways to help reduce pollution. Science is one way of finding solutions to the problems caused by pollution.

Focus Skill COMPARE AND CONTRAST

Which kind of pollution is most harmful—water, air, or soil? Why?

Insta-Lab

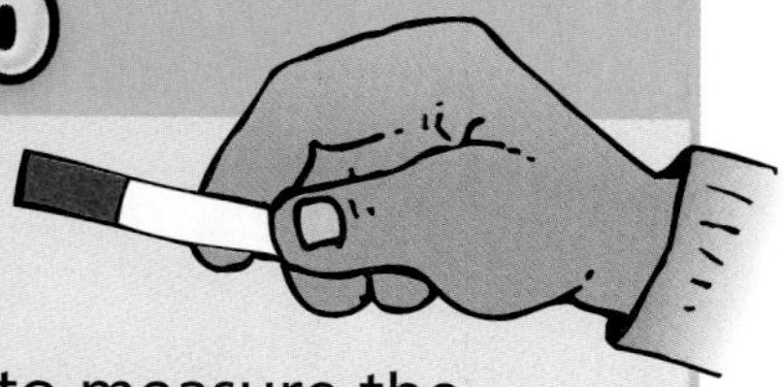

Acid or Not?

Use pH paper to measure the acidity in rainwater or in water from a stream or lake. The redder the strip turns, the more acid the water contains. What might be the source of this acid?

Clean Air and Water

Living things need clean air and clean water. Human activities can pollute the air, dirty the water, and reduce fresh water supplies. What can people do to protect the air and water? Nations, governments, businesses, and communities all have responsibilities. So do you.

There's a lot you can do to prevent air pollution. Turn off the lights when you leave a room. Every bit of electricity you save means less fuel must be burned at the power plant. That means less pollution in the air and a saving of fuel, too. You achieve the same goal when you walk, ride a bike, or take a bus instead of riding in a car. You protect clean air and water when you use grocery bags over again or set your home heat at a lower temperature in winter. Many people use fans instead of air-conditioning to cut down on energy costs in the summer.

Many states have passed clean air laws that require businesses to be responsible for the environment. For example, factories must use scrubbers in their towers to clean the smoke that would otherwise pollute the air.

▼ **Factories have had to install scrubbers to clean the smoke they release into the air.**

Before

After

▲ **The blue water might look clean but it is full of chemicals. People cleaned the water up and now the ecosystem is healthier.**

There are also many ways to save water. Repairing dripping faucets means that less water is wasted. Taking short showers and using water-saving showerheads and toilets help in the same way. Dishwashers and clothes washers should be run only when there is a full load. Don't let the faucet run every time you want a cool glass of water. Instead, store drinking water in the refrigerator.

Some communities have rules about watering lawns. Residents may be asked to turn off sprinkler systems for at least a week after a rain. They may be asked not to let sprinklers water sidewalks and driveways. That's a waste.

People who are adding plants to their yards can save water by planting drought-tolerant flowers, grasses, shrubs, and trees. Some trees that stand up well in heat and drought are the juniper and the Russian olive. Flowers that don't need a lot of water include cosmos, bachelor buttons, marigolds, and zinnias.

Focus Skill COMPARE AND CONTRAST

How are the steps you can take to protect air the same as the steps you can take to protect water?

Planning for Change

Earth's human population keeps growing. People need more space for places to work and live. But before we build, we have to consider both abiotic and biotic factors. Some abiotic factors include the type of soil, the amount of rain, and the climate. A building set on soft soil will not stand. A home must also be able to withstand the weather of the area where it is built.

Biotic factors can affect more than humans. Building new structures often means destroying wildlife habitats. Builders should plan new projects in ways that protect ecosystems. A building near a river must not pollute the water. Even working close to a river can cause problems. Soil can wash into the water. Too much soil in the water can harm fish and plants.

Wetlands near the river must not be filled in. Wetlands help keep the water clean and provide homes for many plants and animals. Builders often leave or create ponds or pockets of forest. These habitats provide homes for some wildlife. Every ecosystem has a delicate balance. People must do their part to protect that balance.

Focus Skill COMPARE AND CONTRAST **Compare a human and an animal seeking a new habitat. How are they the same?**

Construction must be carefully planned to protect natural ecosystems. ▶

◀ Land-use planners must consider the biotic and abiotic factors in an ecosystem.

Essential Question

How do humans affect ecosystems?

In this lesson, you learned that people both hurt and help ecosystems. Planning for the changes that occur when humans move into an area prevents problems.

1. Focus Skill **MAIN IDEA AND DETAILS** Use the graphic organizer to show the positive and negative effects humans can have on ecosystems.

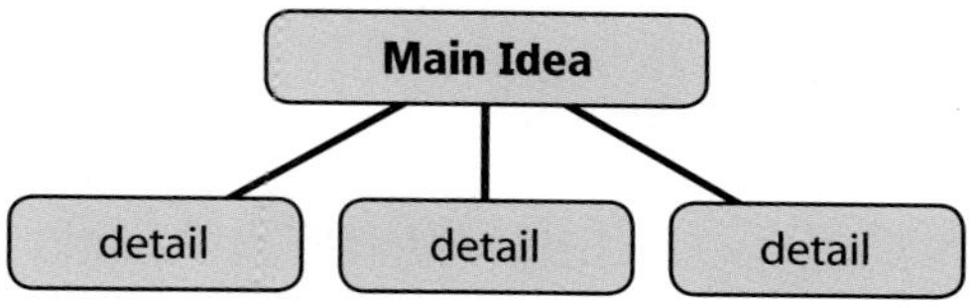

2. **SUMMARIZE** Write one sentence that answers the question presented in the lesson title. Write three more sentences that provide supporting details.

3. **DRAW CONCLUSIONS** Why do humans affect natural ecosystems in negative ways?

4. **VOCABULARY** Make an acrostic for *pollution*. Each letter begins a sentence about that term.

Test Prep

5. **CRITICAL THINKING** How can a weedkiller used on a cornfield pollute a lake miles away?

6. Which of these is soil pollution likely to cause?

   A. air pollution
   B. biotic factors
   C. abiotic factors
   D. water pollution

Make Connections

Writing

Persuasive Writing

Think of a way your community has had a negative effect on an ecosystem. Write a **letter** you might send to the editor of a local newspaper describing the problem.

Math

Comparing Gas Use

An older, larger car gets 10 miles per gallon of gasoline. A newer, smaller car gets 35 miles per gallon. How many fewer gallons would the newer car use on a 70-mile trip?

Health

Pollution and You

With a small group, research the health effects of water, air, or soil pollution. Then share what you learn in a written report, an oral presentation, or a poster.

Raman Sukumar

In India, adult Asian elephants have no natural enemies. However, humans have killed many elephants. Now elephants are close to dying out. Raman Sukumar wants to save them.

Sukumar studied how building things changes or destroys elephant habitats. New dams, roads, and railways force elephants closer to towns. He also studied elephant deaths. He found that illegal hunting has killed many elephants.

Sukumar has found ways to help humans and elephants live together. Wild areas are being linked so elephants can move safely. They don't have to go through farms or towns. Farmers now use different types of fences so that elephants will not eat crops.

▶ **RAMAN SUKUMAR**

▶ Deputy Chairman of the Asian Elephant Specialist Group of IUCN (World Conservation Union)

Think and Write

1. Why do you think elephants are eating people's crops?
2. Why do you think it is important to Raman Sukumar to save the elephants?

Career Paleobotanist

If you like old plants, then you may want to become a paleobotanist. These scientists study the fossils of ancient plants. As a result, paleontologists often can figure out why some species disappeared long ago, while other species still exist today.

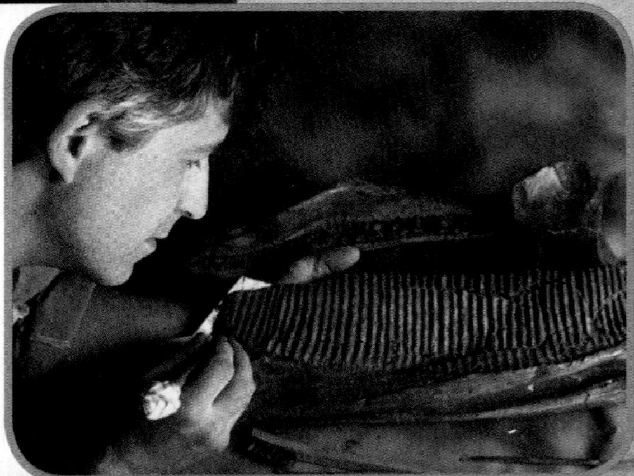

Wangari Maathai

▶ **WANGARI MAATHAI**

▶ Assistant Minister for the Environment and Natural Resources, Kenya

Can ordinary people help the environment? Wangari Maathai knows that they can. She was the first woman in East and Central Africa to earn a doctorate degree. Maathai works to protect both Kenya's forests and its people's rights. She is best known for starting the Green Belt Movement.

In Africa, too many trees have been cut for wood and fuel. This has harmed the environment. In 1977, Maathai began organizing groups of women to plant new trees. Maathai's organization became known as the Green Belt Movement. At least 30 million new trees are growing in Kenya because of what the women have done. Other African nations are starting their own Green Belt Movements.

The new forests provide shelter for many living things. They also show the people who plant and protect them how they can change their world. The women work to improve the environment. At the same time, they improve their own lives.

In 2004, Wangari Maathai received the Nobel Peace Prize for bringing people together to plant millions of trees.

Think and Write

1. Why do you think the leaders of the Green Belt Movement carefully choose the kinds of trees they plant?
2. How do more forests lead to more animals for Kenya?

CHAPTER 5 Review and Test Preparation

Vocabulary Review

Use the terms below to complete the sentences. The page numbers tell you where to look in the chapter if you need help.

environment p. 202
ecosystem p. 202
population p. 204
community p. 206
biotic p. 212
abiotic p. 214
diversity p. 218
pollution p. 226

1. A group of maple trees is an example of a _______.

2. The living parts of an ecosystem are _______.

3. All the living and nonliving things in an area interact to form an _______.

4. An ecosystem that includes many kinds of living things has _______.

5. Several kinds of plants and animals living in the same place form a _______.

6. Trash in a stream is one kind of _______.

7. Nonliving factors in an ecosystem are _______ factors.

8. An _______ includes all the living things and nonliving things in an area.

Check Understanding

Write the letter of the best choice.

9. Which of these is an abiotic factor?
A. lack of food
B. disease
C. cold temperatures
D. introduction of a new plant

10. Which of these is **not** an abiotic factor?
F. air
G. soil
H. mushrooms
J. water

11. **MAIN IDEA AND DETAILS** Focus Skill What is the main idea behind planting trees in an area that has been logged?
A. pollution
B. habitat restoration
C. harvesting natural resources
D. preserving an ecosystem

12. **CAUSE AND EFFECT** Focus Skill Which statement is true about an ecosystem?
F. Biotic factors are the climate.
G. The climate affects biotic factors.
H. Biotic factors cause abiotic factors.
J. Biotic factors never change.

13. What does the picture show?

A. abiotic factors
B. diversity
C. habitat restoration
D. pollution

14. Which of these has the greatest effect on an ecosystem?
F. communities
G. biotic factors
H. climate
J. population

15. Which of these is **never** a result of human actions?
A. population increases
B. changes in abiotic factors
C. natural increase in diversity
D. pollution

16. Which climate zone is probably shown in the photo?

F. savanna
G. taiga
H. temperate forest
J. tundra

Inquiry Skills

17. **Compare** an environment and an ecosystem.

18. A scientist has tracked the migration route of a Yellowstone elk herd every winter for 10 years. The table shows how far south the elk herd has traveled each year. **Write a hypothesis** as to find out why the distances increased.

Year	Kilometers Migrated
1990	122
1991	122
1992	130
1993	126
1994	130
1995	133
1996	132
1997	133
1998	133
1999	136

Critical Thinking

19. Imagine that a new kind of animal has suddenly appeared. How might it affect the local ecosystem?

The Big Idea

20. A builder has bought land that includes a forest. The builder is planning to put in a housing development. Name two possible negative effects the builder and other humans might have on this forest. Now name two possible positive effects the builder and other humans might have on this ecosystem.

CHAPTER 6

Energy Transfer in Ecosystems

What's the Big Idea? **Living things get energy from the sun or from other living things.**

Essential Questions

Lesson 1
What Are the Roles of Living Things?

Lesson 2
How Do Living Things Get Energy?

GO online ▶ **Student eBook**
www.hspscience.com

What do YOU wonder?

Energy for Living This lynx must catch and eat hares and many other small animals in order to live. This hare may provide energy for the lynx. Where do hares get the energy they need to live? How does this relate to the **Big Idea?**

Predator and prey

LESSON 1

Essential Question

What Are the Roles of Living Things?

Investigate how living things decompose.

Read and Learn how living things fill certain roles.

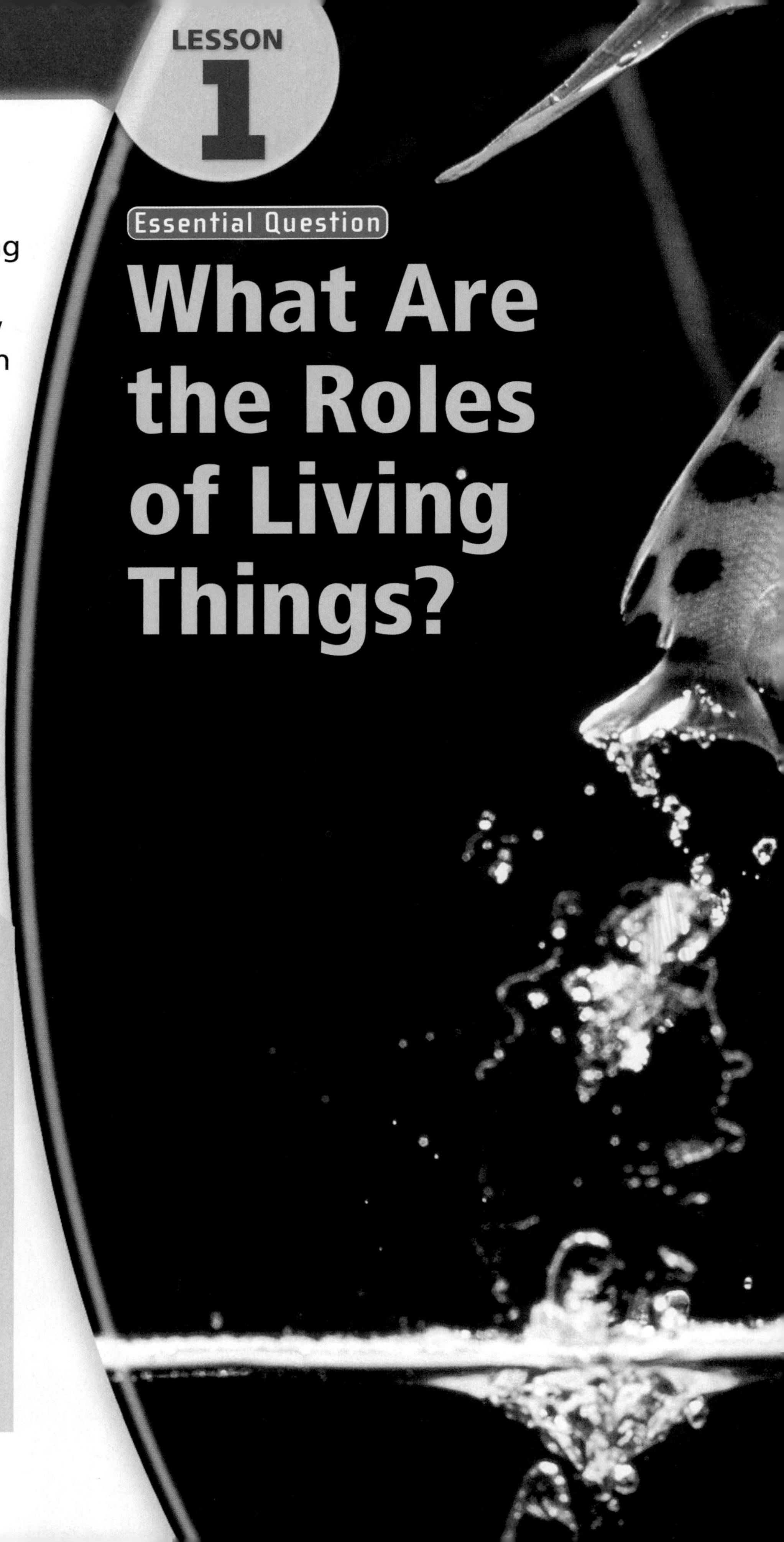

Fast Fact

Nothing Fishy About Eating

This archerfish is leaping for its prey. It eats insects to get energy for living. Archerfish also hunt by spitting at insects to knock them into the water. Some archerfish are eaten by other animals or die and then decay in the water. In the Investigate, you will find out how decomposers (dee•kuhm•POHZ•ers) help once-living matter decay.

Archerfish leaping for its prey

Vocabulary Preview

producer [pruh•DOOS•er] A living thing, such as a plant, that can make its own food (p. 242)

---

consumer [kuhn•SOOM•er] A living thing that can't make its own food and must eat other living things (p. 242)

---

herbivore [HER•buh•vawr] An animal that eats only plants, or producers (p. 244)

carnivore [KAHR•nuh•vawr] An animal that eats only other animals (p. 244)

---

omnivore [AHM•nih•vawr] An animal that eats both plants and other animals (p. 244)

---

decomposer [dee•kuhm•POHZ•er] A living thing that feeds on the wastes of plants and animals (p. 246)

Decomposing Bananas

Guided Inquiry

Start with Questions

The food in this container has gone bad! It is no longer good to eat.

- Why is this food changing?
- Is it becoming food for organisms other than you?

Investigate to find out. Then read and learn to find out more.

Prepare to Investigate

Inquiry Skill Tip

Scientists use time relationships to measure change. Think about the amount of time it takes for any changes that you observe.

Materials

- 2 slices of banana
- 2 zip-top plastic bags
- spoon
- package of dry yeast
- marker

Make an Observation Chart

Day	Banana Without Yeast	Banana With Yeast
1		
2		
3		
4		
5		

Follow This Procedure

1. Put a banana slice in each bag.
2. Sprinkle $\frac{2}{3}$ spoonful of dry yeast on one banana slice. Yeast is a decomposer, so use the marker to label this bag *D*.
3. Close both bags. Put the bags in the same place.
4. Check both bags every day for a week. **Observe** and **record** the changes you see in each bag.

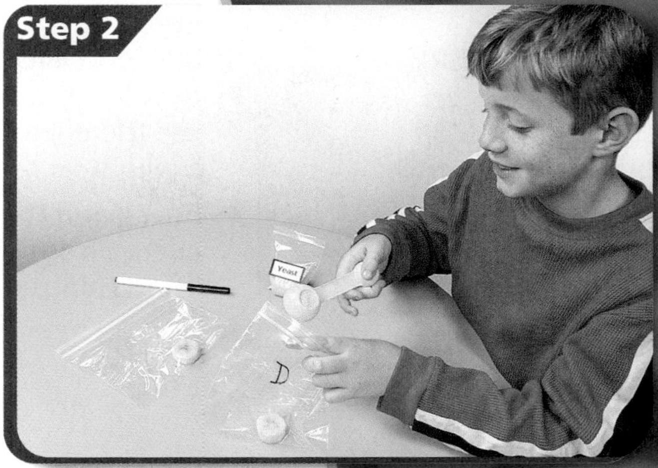

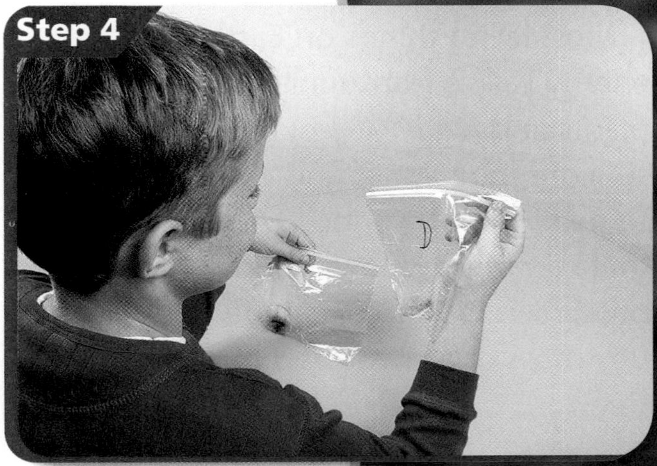

Draw Conclusions

1. Which banana slice shows more changes? What is the cause of these changes?
2. **Inquiry Skill** Scientists **use time relationships** to measure progress. How long did it take for your banana slice to begin showing signs of decomposition? How long do you think it would take for your banana slices to completely decompose?

Independent Inquiry

What will happen if you put flour, instead of yeast, on one banana slice? Write down your prediction, and then try it.

Read and Learn

VOCABULARY
producer p. 242
consumer p. 242
herbivore p. 244
carnivore p. 244
omnivore p. 244
decomposer p. 246

SCIENCE CONCEPTS
- how living things use the energy from sunlight
- how living things get energy from other living things

Focus Skill MAIN IDEA AND DETAILS
Look for details about the movement of energy among living things.

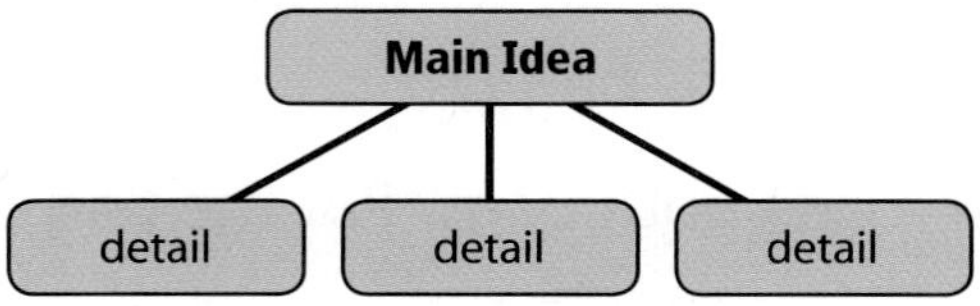

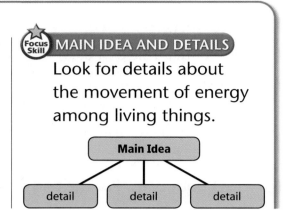

Producers and Consumers

Most living things on Earth get the energy to live from sunlight. Green plants and algae (AL•jee) use energy in sunlight, plus water and carbon dioxide, to make their own food. Any living thing that can make its own food is called a **producer**. Producers can be as small as a tiny moss or as large as a huge redwood tree.

Some animals, such as deer and cattle, get the energy they need to live by eating plants. When these animals eat, the energy stored in the plants moves into the animals' bodies.

Not all animals eat plants. Lions and hawks, for example, get the energy they need by eating other animals.

An animal that eats plants or other animals is called a **consumer**. Consumers can't make their own food, so they must eat other living things.

These plants are using energy in sunlight to produce food. Without sunlight, the plants would die.

Which animal gets its energy directly from producers? Which one gets its energy from other consumers? Which one gets its energy from both?

Some consumers eat the same kind of food all year. Horses, for example, eat grass during warm weather. During winter, they eat hay, a kind of dried grass.

Other consumers eat different things in different seasons. For example, black bears eat grass in spring. Later on, they might eat birds' eggs. Bears might also dig up tasty roots or eat fish from streams. In fall, bears eat ripe berries.

Florida panthers eat other consumers, but their diet varies. Mostly, panthers consume wild hogs, which are easy for them to catch. Another common meal is deer. Panthers also eat rabbits, raccoons, rats, birds, and sometimes even alligators.

Focus Skill MAIN IDEA AND DETAILS

What is a producer? What is a consumer? Give two examples of each.

Kinds of Consumers

Consumers are not all the same. In fact, there are three kinds—herbivores, carnivores, and omnivores.

A **herbivore** is an animal that eats only plants, or producers. Horses are herbivores. So are giraffes, squirrels, and rabbits.

A **carnivore** is an animal that eats only other animals. The Florida panther and the lion are carnivores. A carnivore can be as large as a whale or as small as a frog.

An **omnivore** is an animal that eats both plants and other animals. That is, omnivores eat both producers and other consumers. Bears and hyenas are omnivores. Do any omnivores live in your home?

Producers and all three kinds of consumers can be found living in water. Algae are producers that live in water. They use sunlight to make their own food. Tadpoles, small fish, and other small herbivores eat algae. Larger fish that are carnivores eat the tadpoles. Some animals, including green sea turtles, are omnivores. Green sea turtles eat seaweed, algae, and fish. In fact, algae make the flesh of the green sea turtle green!

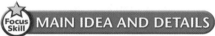

Focus Skill **MAIN IDEA AND DETAILS**

Name the three kinds of consumers. Give two examples of each.

This diagram shows how the different kinds of consumers get energy to live. The arrows show the direction of energy flow.

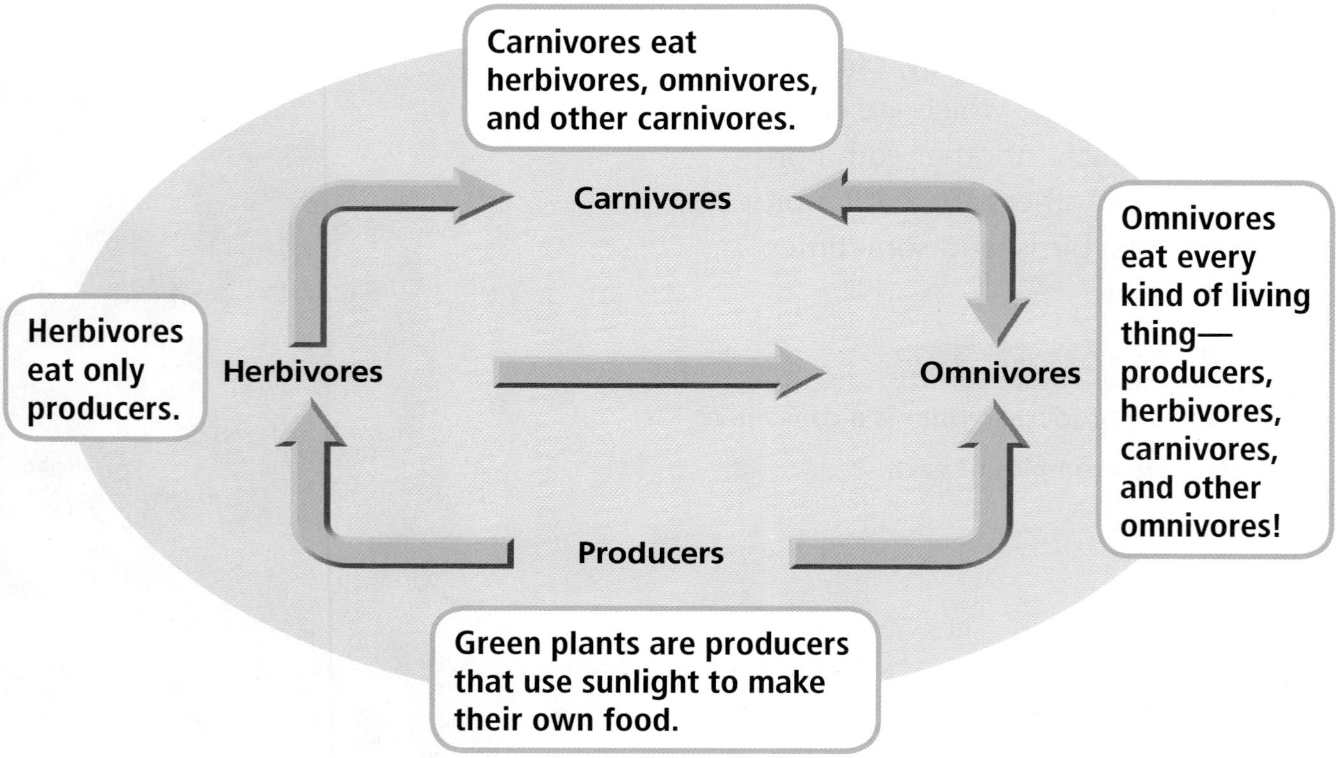

Carnivores eat herbivores, omnivores, and other carnivores.
Carnivores
Herbivores eat only producers.
Herbivores
Omnivores
Omnivores eat every kind of living thing—producers, herbivores, carnivores, and other omnivores!
Producers
Green plants are producers that use sunlight to make their own food.

▲ The jaguar, a carnivore, eats tapirs, river hogs, and other consumers.

▲ The tapir, a herbivore, eats only producers. It eats tender buds and twigs.

▲ River hogs are omnivores. They eat producers, consumers, and herbivores.

▲ This plant is a producer. It makes its own food and provides stored energy for consumers.

Insta-Lab

Who's an Omnivore?

Read the nutrition labels on several food containers. Think about the source of each kind of food. What does the food's source tell about consumers who eat it?

Decomposers

A **decomposer** is a living thing that feeds on wastes and on the remains of dead plants and animals. Decomposers break down wastes into nutrients, substances that are taken in by living things to help them grow. These nutrients become part of the soil. Next, plants take up the nutrients through their roots. Animals eat the plants. When plants and animals die, decomposers break down their bodies into nutrients. This cycle is repeated again and again.

Decomposers come in many shapes and sizes. Some are tiny bacteria that you can see only with a microscope. Other decomposers are as big as mushrooms and earthworms.

Without decomposers, Earth would be covered with dead plants and animals. Instead, decomposers turn wastes into nutrients. They allow living things to recycle nutrients.

Focus Skill MAIN IDEA AND DETAILS

Name two kinds of decomposers, and describe their role in nature.

Sow bugs

Sow bugs are related to lobsters. They help plant matter decay faster than it would without them.

Millipede

In the forest, millipedes chew up dead plant material. Like sow bugs, millipedes aren't insects.

Bracket fungus

The bracket fungus is one of a group of fungi (FUN•jy) that includes mushrooms. Bracket fungi often grow on dead tree trunks and help them decay quickly.

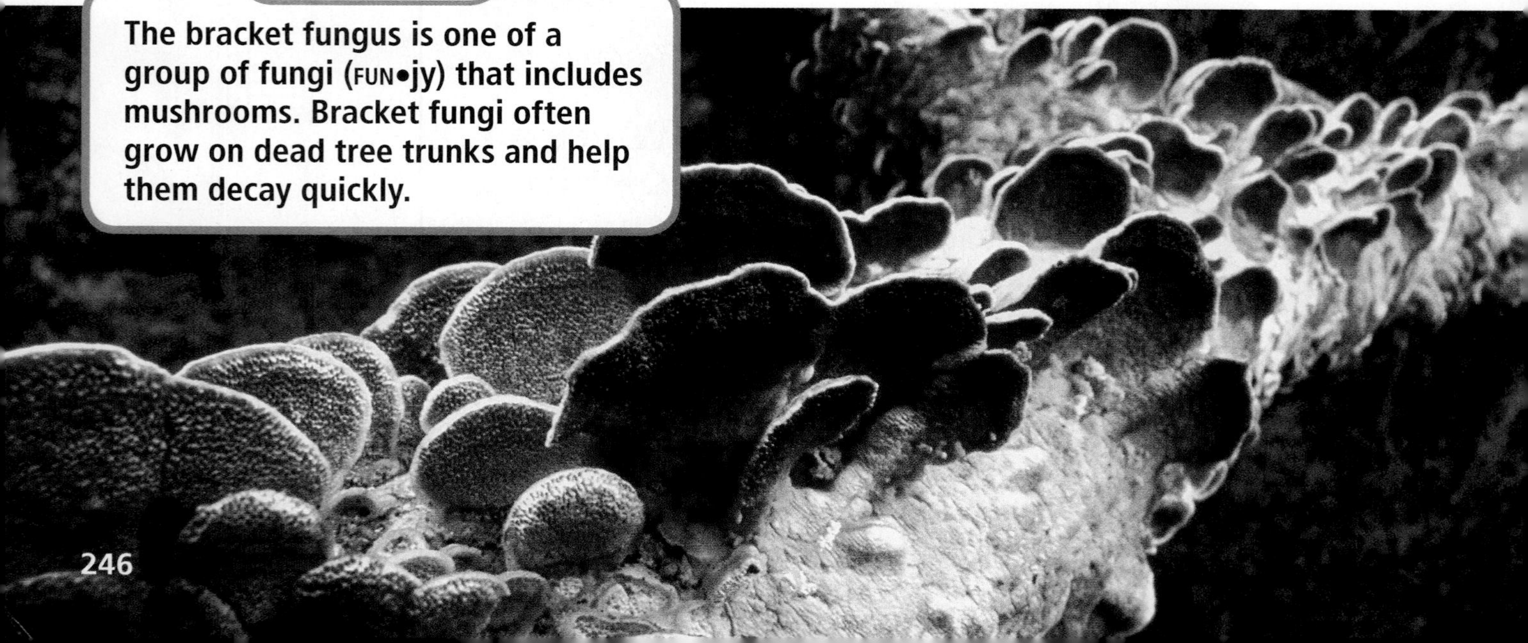

Lesson Review

Essential Question

What are the roles of living things?

In this lesson, you learned that living things fill certain roles. Producers use energy from the sun to grow. Consumers eat producers or other consumers for energy. Decomposers return energy to the soil.

1. Focus Skill MAIN IDEA AND DETAILS Use a graphic organizer to list the kinds of producers and consumers.

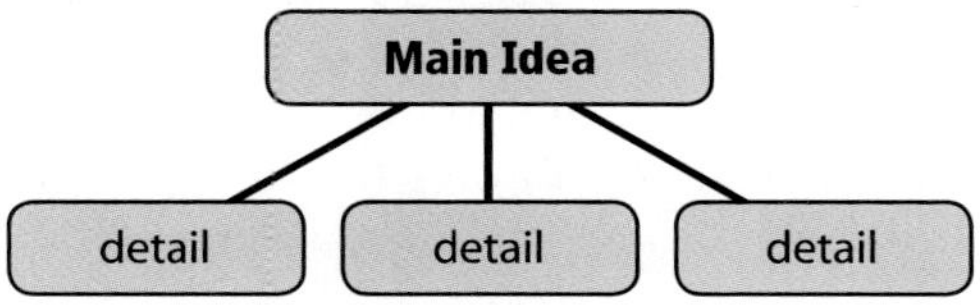

2. **SUMMARIZE** Write a summary of this lesson. Begin with this sentence: *Energy for life comes from the sun.*

3. **DRAW CONCLUSIONS** How are decomposers consumers?

4. **VOCABULARY** Construct a crossword puzzle using this lesson's vocabulary words.

Test Prep

5. **CRITICAL THINKING** How do eagles depend on sunlight for their energy?

6. Which term describes a hyena?
   A. carnivore
   B. herbivore
   C. omnivore
   D. producer

Make Connections

Writing

Narrative Writing

Write a **science fiction story.** Tell about a time when all the producers on Earth disappear. Describe what happens to the consumers.

Math

Solve a Problem

A shrew eats about $\frac{2}{3}$ of its body weight daily. Suppose a child who weighed 30 kilograms (66 lb) could eat $\frac{2}{3}$ of his or her body weight. How many kilograms of food is that?

Health

Eating Decomposers

Find out what vitamins and minerals are in mushrooms. Find healthful recipes that have mushrooms as one of the ingredients.

LESSON 2

Essential Question

How Do Living Things Get Energy?

Investigate how food chains link living things together.

Read and Learn how living things pass energy through an ecosystem.

Fast Fact

Ouch!
Only female mosquitoes bite people and other animals. They need the blood to produce eggs. In the Investigate, you will make food chains. You might include a mosquito in yours!

Mosquito drinking blood.

Vocabulary Preview

habitat [HAB•ih•tat] An environment that meets the needs of an organism (p. 252)

niche [NICH] The role of an organism in its habitat (p. 253)

food chain [FOOD CHAYN] The movement of food energy in a sequence of living things (p. 254)

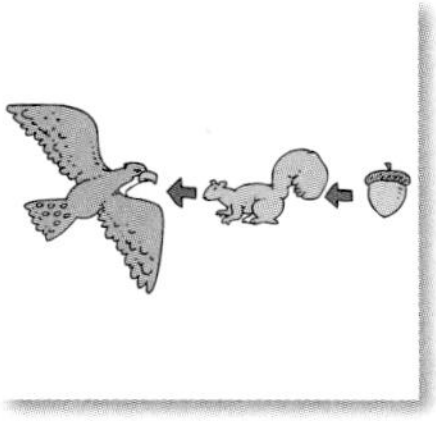

prey [PRAY] Consumers that are eaten by predators (p. 254)

predator [PRED•uh•ter] A consumer that eats prey (p. 254)

food web [FOOD WEB] A group of food chains that overlap (p. 256)

energy pyramid [EN•er•jee PIR•uh•mid] A diagram showing how much energy is passed from one organism to the next in a food chain (p. 258)

Make a Food Chain

Guided Inquiry

Start with Questions

A snake can swallow prey that is much larger than its mouth because its jaw unhinges.

- Why would a snake need to eat such a large animal?
- What kinds of animals eat snakes?

Investigate to find out. Then read and learn to find out more.

Prepare to Investigate

Inquiry Skill Tip

Scientists communicate ideas in many ways. Before you communicate, think about ways to present the ideas, such as the order in which to put things.

Materials

- 8 to 10 blank index cards
- colored pencils or markers
- reference books about animals

Make an Observation Chart

Your food chain	Other food chain

Follow This Procedure

1. Choose a place where animals live. Some examples are pine forest, rain forest, desert, wetland, and ocean.
2. On an index card, draw a living thing that lives in the place you have chosen. Draw more living things, one kind on each card. Include large animals, small animals, and producers. Look up information about plants and animals if you need help.
3. Put your cards in an order that shows what eats what. You might have more than one set of cards. If one of your animals doesn't fit anywhere, trade cards with someone. You can also draw another animal to link two of your cards. For example, you could draw a rabbit to link a grass card and a hawk card.

Step 2

Step 3

Draw Conclusions

1. Could the same animal fit into more than one set of cards? Explain your answer.
2. **Inquiry Skill** Scientists communicate their ideas in many ways. What do your cards communicate about the relationships of these living things to one another?

Independent Inquiry

Draw a series of cards in order, with yourself as the last consumer. Compare your role with the roles of other consumers.

VOCABULARY
habitat p. 252
niche p. 253
food chain p. 254
prey p. 254
predator p. 254
food web p. 256
energy pyramid p. 258

SCIENCE CONCEPTS
- how consumers depend on other living things
- how energy moves through food chains and food webs

Focus Skill SEQUENCE
Look for the order in which things happen.

Habitats

You probably wouldn't see a heron in a desert or a penguin in a swamp. Animals must live in places that meet their needs. A **habitat** is an environment that meets the needs of a living thing. An insect's habitat can be as small as the space under a rock. A migrating bird's habitat can cross a continent.

Many habitats can overlap. For example, the three living things pictured on this page all live in a desert habitat. This desert habitat meets all their needs. Sagebrush grows well here. Sidewinders and tarantulas find many small consumers to eat.

Sidewinder

The venomous sidewinder eats mice, rats, lizards, and birds. ▶

Tarantula

◀ **Tarantulas are venomous, too. They eat insects, other spiders, and small lizards.**

Sagebrush

Sagebrush can grow where other plants can't. Sheep and cattle often eat sagebrush in the winter. ▶

These living things thrive in the desert habitat, even though it's hot and has little water.

Each living thing in a habitat has a role, or **niche** (nich). The term *niche* describes how a living thing interacts with its habitat. Part of a living thing's niche is how it gets food and shelter. Its niche also includes how it reproduces, cares for its young, and avoids danger. Each animal has body parts that help it carry out its role. For example, a cat's sharp claws and excellent eyesight help it catch its food.

Part of the sidewinder's niche is to eat small animals in its habitat. If all these snakes died, the desert would have too many mice, birds, and lizards. These small animals would eat all the available food and would soon starve. The sidewinder's niche helps keep the number of small desert animals in balance.

Focus Skill SEQUENCE What would happen next if all the sagebrush disappeared from a desert?

This coral reef habitat has a balance of producers and consumers. All of the organisms in the picture are consumers.

Food Chains

Living things depend on one another to live. A **food chain** is the movement of food energy in a sequence of living things. Every food chain starts with producers. Some consumers, such as deer, eat these producers. Then the deer are eaten by other consumers, such as mountain lions. Consumers that are eaten are called **prey**. A consumer that eats prey is a predator. Prey are animals that are hunted. **Predators** are the hunters.

Some animals in a habitat are prey, while other animals are predators. Predators limit the number of prey animals in a habitat. Wolves are predators of antelope. They keep the population of antelope from increasing too much, so the antelope don't eat all of the producers. Predators often compete for the same prey. This limits the number of predators in a habitat.

Focus Skill SEQUENCE **What would happen next if the number of predators in a habitat increased too much?**

A mangrove swamp is one kind of habitat. Special prop roots hold mangrove trees in the muddy soil. Fresh water and salt water mix in this habitat.

Many organisms live in and around the mangrove roots.

A mullet is a kind of fish that can live in fresh water or salt water. Mullet are a part of the food chain.

Without hawks, the chipmunk population would get very large. The chipmunks would eat all the acorns and then starve.

Acorns provide energy for the chipmunk, which in turn provides energy for the hawk.

An alligator is just one of the predators in a mangrove swamp. Food energy moves to them through the prey that they eat.

Insta-Lab

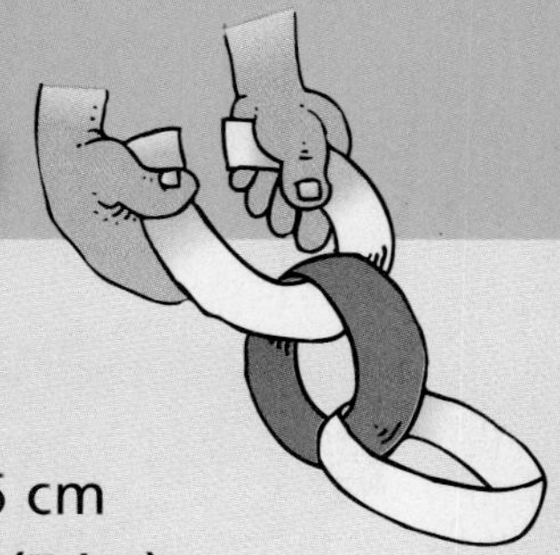

Chain of Life

Cut paper into strips that are 2.5 cm (1 in.) by 12.5 cm (5 in.) On each strip, write the name of a producer or a consumer. Then use glue or tape to combine the strips into paper food chains. Which food chains end with you?

Food Webs

A food chain shows how an animal gets energy from one food source. But food chains can overlap. One kind of producer may be food for different kinds of consumers. Some consumers may eat different kinds of food. For example, hawks eat sparrows, mice, and snakes.

Several food chains that overlap form a **food web**. There are food webs in water habitats, too. For example, herons eat snails, fish, and other birds.

On the next page, you can see an ocean food web. It shows that energy moves from plankton, small producers in the ocean, to small shrimp. These shrimp are called *first-level consumers.*

These shrimp then become prey for fish and other *second-level consumers.* They, in turn, are eaten by the biggest fish and mammals in the ocean, called *top-level consumers.*

Focus Skill SEQUENCE **What happens after a first-level consumer eats a producer?**

Follow several paths in this food web. Begin at the bottom, with a producer, and trace the movement of energy through the web.

For more links and animations, go to **www.hspscience.com**

Antarctic Ocean Food Web

This food web begins with energy from the sun. The producers are tiny plants called phytoplankton (fyt•oh•PLANGK•tuhn). They float near the water's surface because sunlight can't reach deep underwater. No plants grow at the bottom of the ocean. Where would decomposers fit in this food web?

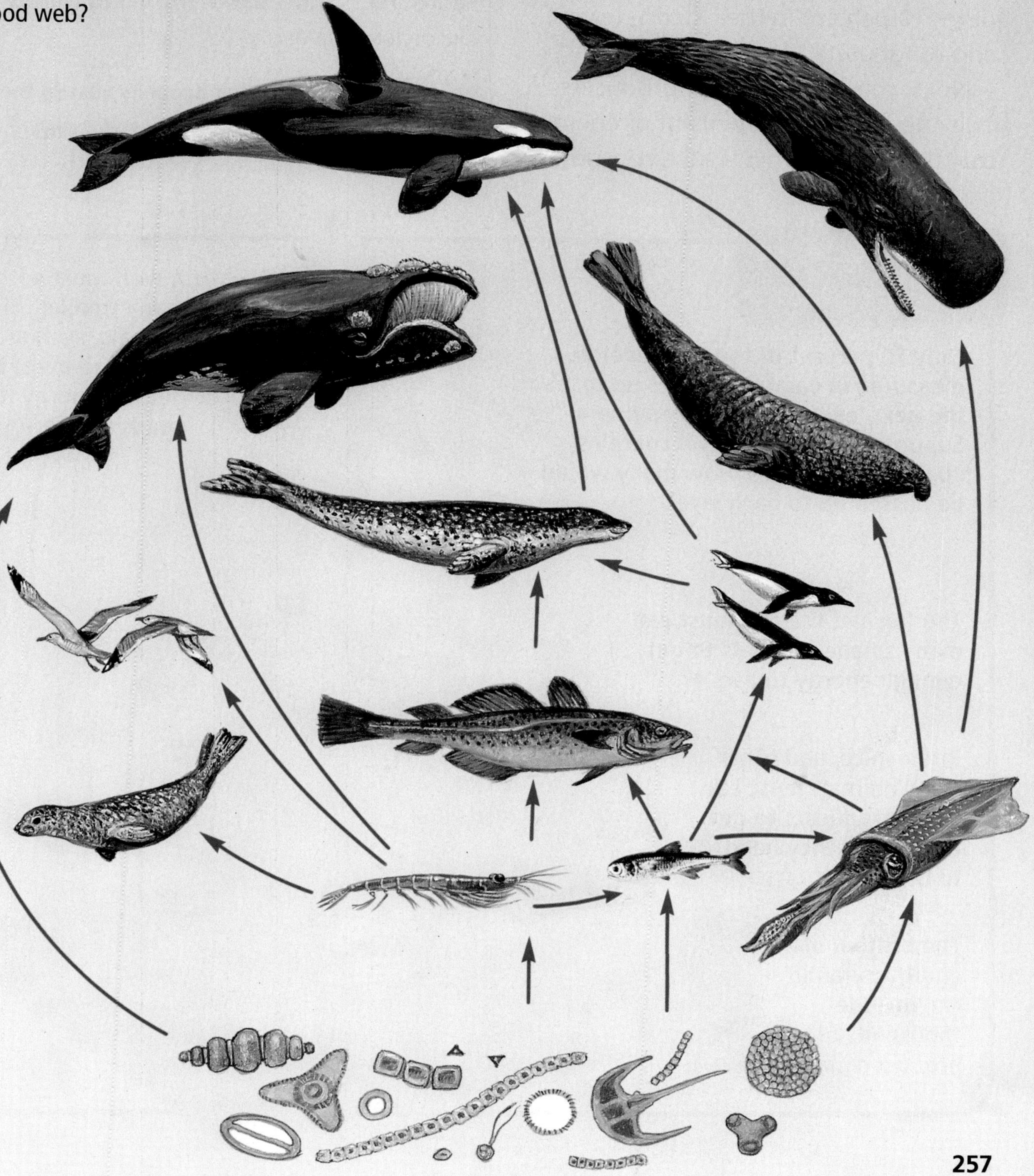

Energy Pyramids

An **energy pyramid** shows how much energy is passed from one living thing to another along a food chain. Producers form the base of the pyramid. They use about 90 percent of the energy they get from the sun to grow. They store the other 10 percent in their stems, leaves, and other parts.

Next, consumers eat the producers. They get only the 10 percent of energy that the plants stored. These consumers use about 90 percent of the energy they get from the producers to grow and then store the other 10 percent in their bodies. That 10 percent is passed on to the consumers that eat them.

You can see how little energy is passed from one level to the next. That's why consumers must eat many living things in order to live.

Focus Skill SEQUENCE **What happens next to the energy that plants get from the sun?**

Math in Science
Interpret Data

Only 10 percent of the food energy, measured in calories, passes up to the next level in an energy pyramid. Suppose the bottom level contains 10,000,000 calories. How many would be passed up to each level?

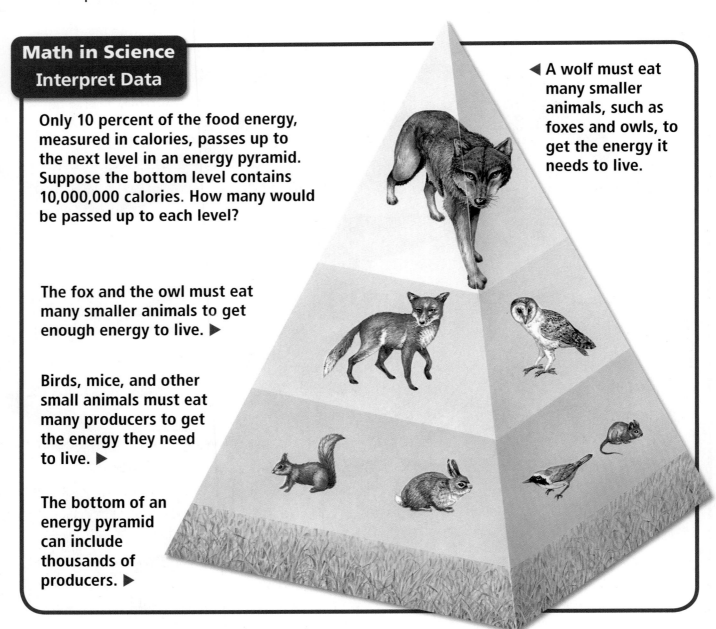

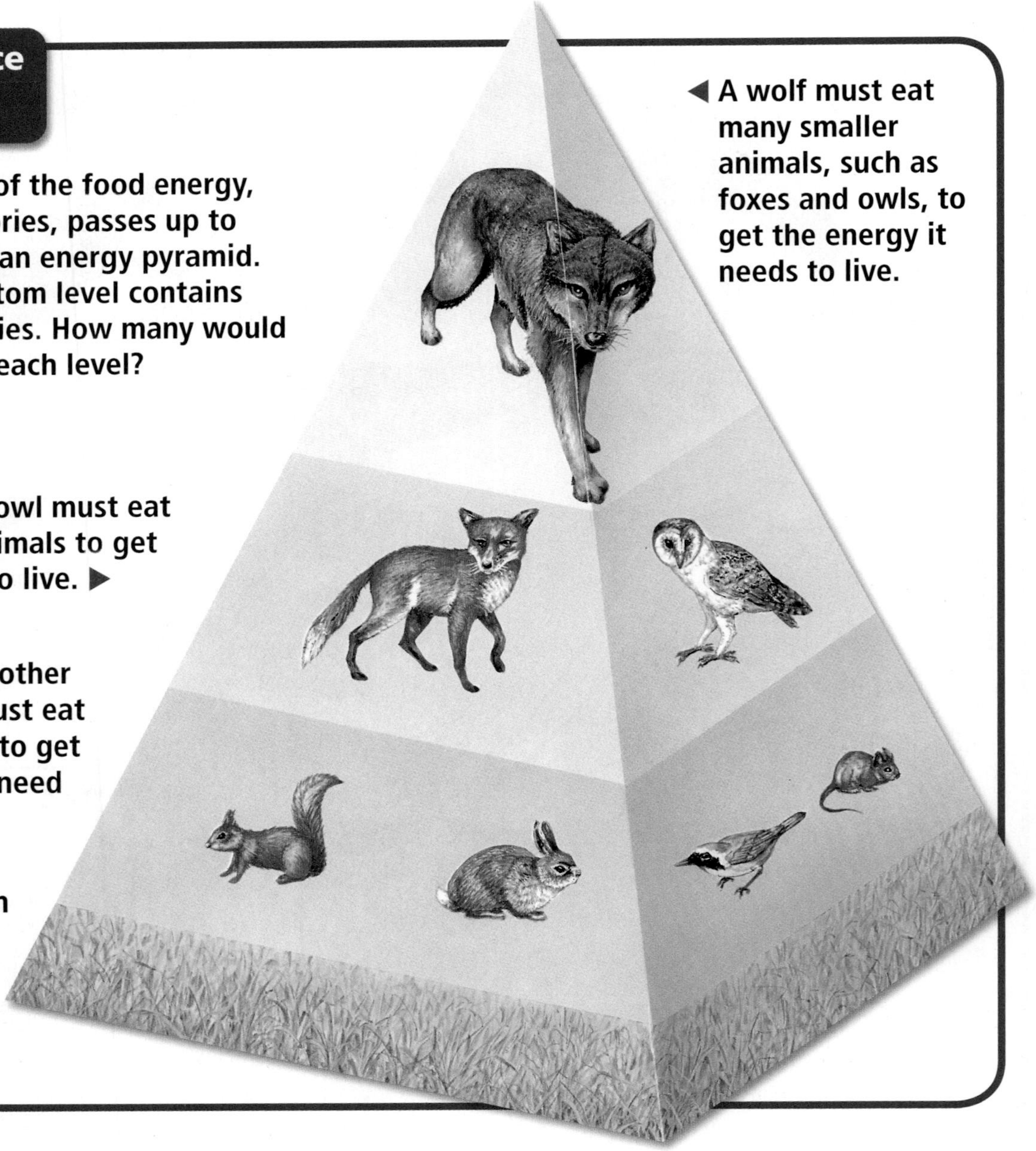

◀ A wolf must eat many smaller animals, such as foxes and owls, to get the energy it needs to live.

The fox and the owl must eat many smaller animals to get enough energy to live. ▶

Birds, mice, and other small animals must eat many producers to get the energy they need to live. ▶

The bottom of an energy pyramid can include thousands of producers. ▶

Lesson Review

Essential Question

How do living things get energy?

In this lesson, you learned that every organism has a role, called a niche, to fill in its habitat. Producers make their own energy while consumers must get energy by eating organisms. Organisms that depend on one another in this way make up food chains.

1. **Focus Skill SEQUENCE** Use a graphic organizer to show how energy moves in a food chain.

2. **SUMMARIZE** Write a summary of this lesson. Begin with this sentence: *An animal's habitat must meet its basic needs.*

3. **DRAW CONCLUSIONS** How are predators good for prey?

4. **VOCABULARY** Use the vocabulary terms to make a quiz. Then trade quizzes with a partner.

Test Prep

5. **CRITICAL THINKING** How would the deaths of all of one kind of consumer affect a food web?

6. Which of these best shows why deer must eat grass all day long?
   A. diagram
   B. energy pyramid
   C. food chain
   D. food web

Make Connections

Writing

Expository Writing

Write a **description** of ways humans might affect a food web and what would then change. For example, people might clear trees for a housing development or feed the deer in a park.

Math

Solve a Problem

Producers in a field have stored 20,000 calories. Herbivores get 2000 calories by eating the producers. How much energy is available to the next level of the energy pyramid?

Art

Food Chains

Choose any art medium, such as watercolor, charcoal, collage, or torn paper, and show the living things in a food web. (You don't have to show them eating one another!)

Creepy Crawly Surgeons

There you are, taking a walk through the park. You look down. You see the remains of a mouse. You look closer and see other things—tiny, white crawling things. The sight of them may make your stomach flip, but those crawly organisms have a place in modern medicine. Welcome to the world of maggot therapy.

Maggots are helping thousands of people each year.

Eating Machines

Blowflies lay their eggs in rotting animal matter. When the eggs hatch, they become maggots. Maggots are "eating machines." They make quick work of decaying animal matter—including human flesh!

Soldiers' Friends

Long ago, army doctors noticed that wounds with maggots were cleaner. Those wounds were less likely to get infected than untreated wounds were. During the Civil War and World War I, maggots were commonly used to treat wounds.

After World War II, antibiotics became popular. Now some bacteria are resistant to antibiotics. Some doctors are looking to the past for proven treatments.

Nature's Surgeons

Dr. Ronald A. Sherman works at the University of California, Irvine. He has researched the use of maggots for decades. Sherman has found that maggots break down infected tissue. When they eat the infected tissue, they also kill bacteria. As the maggots chomp away, the patient feels no pain. The patient doesn't need pain-killing drugs. Recovery time is also faster. The maggots' removal of diseased tissue helps healthy tissue grow.

Many people are uncomfortable with the idea of using maggots. Sherman knows that. He approaches maggot therapy with a sense of humor. He wants people to see the benefits of using nature's surgeons.

Think and Write

1. How does the maggot's role as a decomposer enable it to help people?
2. How might using maggots in medicine help people conserve resources?

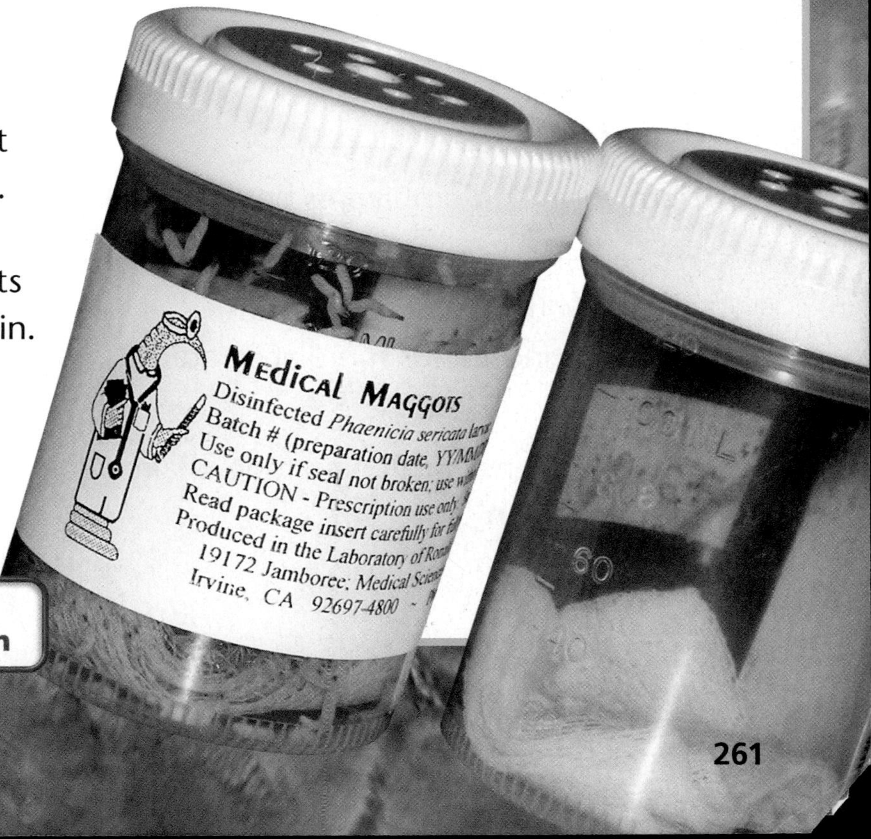

Spin-In
Find out more. Log on to **www.hspscience.com**

CHAPTER 6 Review and Test Preparation

Vocabulary Review

Use the terms below to complete the sentences. The page numbers tell you where to look in the chapter if you need help.

producers p. 242
consumer p. 242
omnivores p. 244
decomposers p. 246
niche p. 253
predators p. 254
food chain p. 254
energy pyramid p. 258

1. An animal that eats other living things is a _______.
2. Nutrients would be lost without _______.
3. The animals at the top of a food chain are always _______.
4. The kind of food that an animal eats is part of its _______.
5. Animals that eat both producers and other consumers are _______.
6. Herbivores and omnivores both eat _______.
7. A food web shows relationships among living things more accurately than a _______.
8. The loss of energy along a food chain is shown in an _______.

Check Understanding

Write the letter of the best choice.

9. Which of these must a pond food chain have?
   A. algae **C.** tiny fish
   B. sunlight **D.** whales

10. **MAIN IDEA AND DETAILS** Which term includes herbivores, carnivores, and omnivores?
   F. consumers **H.** prey
   G. predators **J.** producers

11. How much energy is used at each level of the energy pyramid and not passed on?
   A. 10 percent **C.** 80 percent
   B. 20 percent **D.** 90 percent

12. Which of the following do herbivores eat?
   F. consumers **H.** predators
   G. omnivores **J.** producers

13. What is shown below?

   A. niche **C.** habitat
   B. food chain **D.** food web

14. What are robins, which eat worms and insects?

F. carnivores **H.** omnivores
G. herbivores **J.** prey

15. Antelopes are herbivores. What other term describes them?

A. omnivores **C.** prey
B. predators **D.** producers

16. **SEQUENCE** What is the first organism on a food chain?

Focus Skill

F. a consumer
G. a decomposer
H. a producer
J. a predator

Inquiry Skills

17. **Compare** a carnivore and a predator. How are these living things the same? How are they different?

18. While hiking with your family, you follow a trail that leads past many dead plants. Even the trees seem to be dying. The soil is very dry. What can you **infer** is happening to the consumers in this area?

Critical Thinking

The Big Idea

19. Which of these could survive without being part of a food chain—a strawberry plant, a chicken, or a dog? Explain your answer.

20. Different types of diagrams are used to show the relationships among living things. Study the diagram below.

Would this diagram be correct if there were two snakes at the top? Explain your answer. How is this diagram different from a food chain?

Visual Summary

UNIT B LIFE SCIENCE

Tell how each picture shows the **Big Idea** for its chapter.

CHAPTER 5 Big Idea

Ecosystems are made up of both living and nonliving parts that all impact each other.

CHAPTER 6 Big Idea

Living things get energy from the sun or from other living things.

EARTH SCIENCE

Kentucky Standards

SC-04-2.3.1 Students will:
- classify earth materials by the ways that they are used;
- explain how their properties make them useful for different purposes.

SC-04-2.3.2 Students will describe and explain consequences of changes to the surface of the Earth, including some common fast changes (e.g., landslides, volcanic eruptions, earthquakes), and some common slow changes (e.g., erosion, weathering).

SC-04-2.3.3 Students will make generalizations and/or predictions about weather changes from day to day and over seasons based on weather data.

SC-04-2.3.4 Students will identify patterns, recognize relationships and draw conclusions about the Earth-Sun system by interpreting a variety of representations/models (e.g., diagrams, sundials, distance of sun above horizon) of the sun's apparent movement in the sky.

SC-04-2.3.5 Students will understand that the moon moves across the sky on a daily basis much like the Sun. The observable shape of the moon can be described as it changes from day to day in a cycle that lasts about a month.

SC-04-3.5.1 Students will use representations of fossils to:
- draw conclusions about the nature of the organisms and the basic environments that existed at the time;
- make inferences about the relationships to organisms that are alive today.

KENTUCKY

Kentucky Excursions and Projects

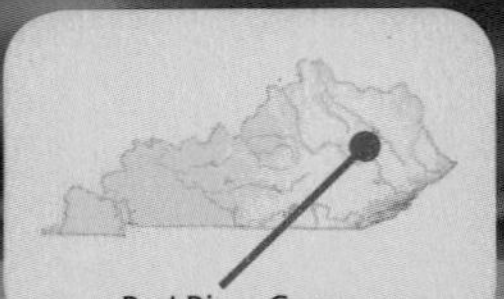

Red River Gorge
Geological Area

One little raindrop cannot change Earth's surface very much. But billions of raindrops over hundreds of millions of years can carve deep valleys and high cliffs. You can see the evidence at the Red River Gorge Geological Area.

Located within Daniel Boone National Forest, the Red River Gorge Geological Area has a spectacular variety of features, such as twisting ridges, breathtaking cliffs, and more than 80 natural arches. The features were formed over 300 million years, as wind and water shaped layers of sandstone rock.

This arch was formed by erosion.

Weathering and Erosion

Wind and water are agents of both weathering and erosion. Weathering is the process in which rocks are broken into smaller pieces, called sediments. Flowing water, for example, can tumble rocks in a riverbed, which breaks some of them apart. Erosion is the process that moves the sediments from place to place. A strong wind erodes sediments when it carries them away.

These fossil crinoid stems tell scientists what the area was like long ago.

Think and Write

1. **Scientific Thinking** Compare and contrast weathering and erosion.
2. **Scientific Inquiry** Design an experiment to show how water erodes soil. Write down each step of your procedure. Include any materials you would need, as well as safety measures you should take.

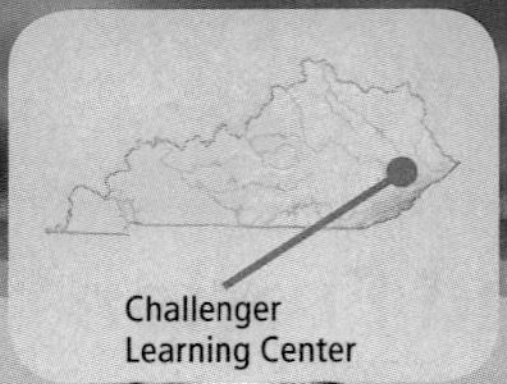

CHALLENGER LEARNING CENTER of Kentucky

10, 9, 8, 7, 6, 5, 4, 3, 2, 1... Blast off!

At the Challenger Learning Center of Kentucky, students perform the countdown for missions to space. First, they train in their classrooms for five to six weeks. They study science, math, and space technology. Then it's off to the Challenger Learning Center to put their knowledge to use.

Each member of a class is assigned a role. It might be astronaut, engineer, mission controller, or scientist. The team members work together, using real NASA technology such as remote gloveboxes, computers, and video cameras. Their goal might be to build a space probe or explore the surface of Mars.

The Learning Center is full of interactive exhibits for visitors to explore.

The Sun-Earth-Moon System

You can explore space, too, right in your backyard. With an adult, go outside at night several times during a month and observe the changing phases of the moon. At school, work with a partner to record changes in the position of the sun during the day.

Think and Write

1. **Scientific Thinking** Describe how the moon's appearance changed throughout the month.
2. **Scientific Thinking** Earth's rotation causes the sun to appear to move across the sky. It also causes night and day. Write a letter to a younger student, explaining the relationship between Earth's rotation and night and day.

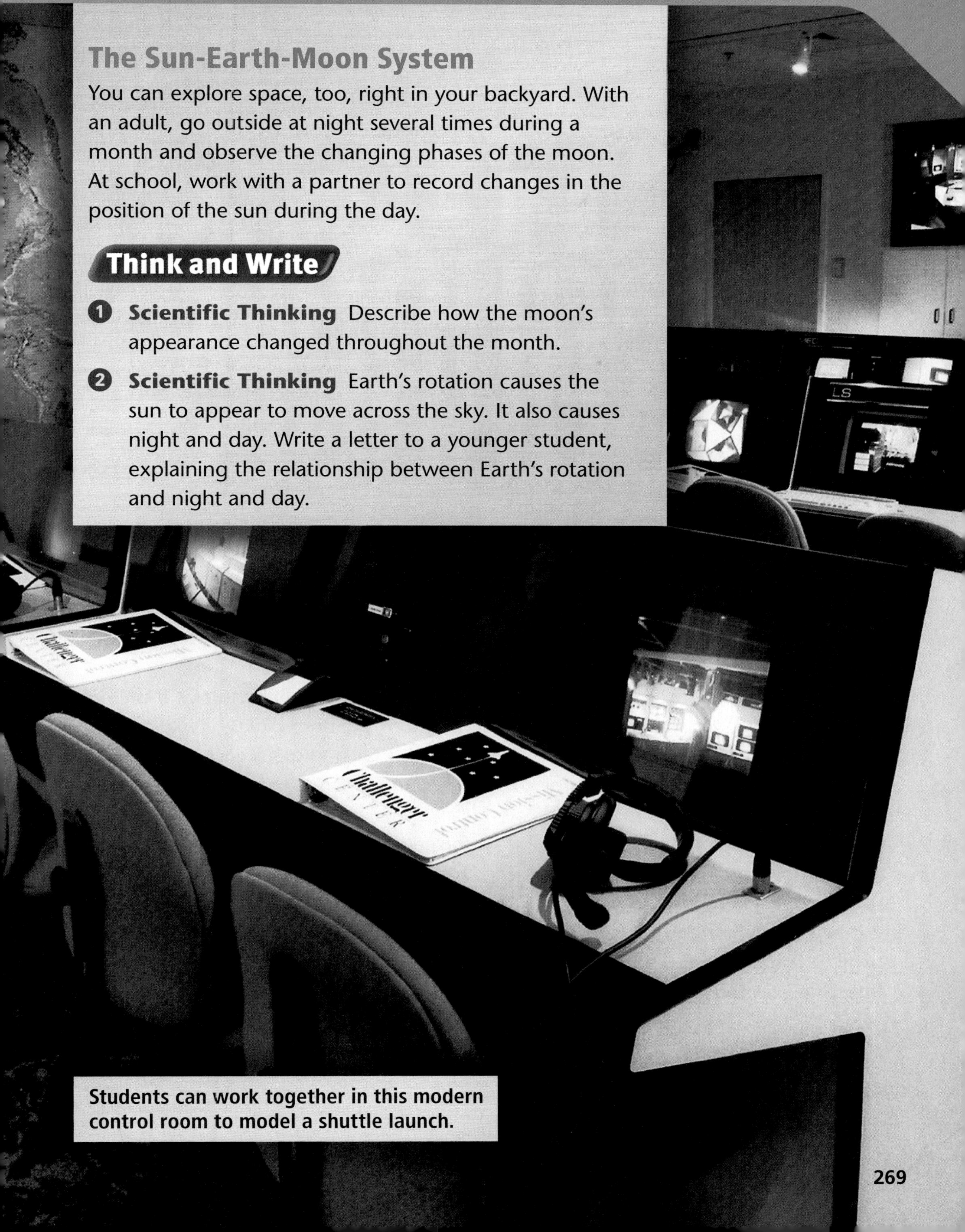

Students can work together in this modern control room to model a shuttle launch.

KENTUCKY RESOURCES

Under your feet is a wealth of natural resources, ranging from the soil you stand on to deep deposits of oil and gas.

Kentucky's fertile soils are used to grow hay, corn, soybeans, and other crops. One of the richest soils in the state is called Crider soil. It is found in about 35 counties.

The western and central parts of Kentucky produce large amounts of limestone and dolomite. In fact, the biggest stone quarry in the United States is in western Kentucky. The stones are used for construction, farming, and mining. One kind of limestone, Kentucky "marble," is found in cliffs along the Kentucky River. It was used to build the Old State Capitol in Frankfort. You can visit it and see the marble for yourself!

Other Resources

Clay is also mined in Kentucky. It is used to make bricks, tiles, china, and cat litter. Oil and gas are found in 65 counties across the state. Oil and gas are called fossil fuels because they formed hundreds of millions of years ago from the remains of once-living things. They are used to produce electricity, to heat buildings, and to make gasoline.

Crider soils are clay soils. They have deep layers that are well-drained. Crider soils are excellent for farming.

Think and Write

1. **Scientific Inquiry** New oil and gas wells in Kentucky are much deeper than older wells. Infer why new wells have to be drilled deeper.
2. **Scientific Thinking** Write a paragraph explaining how you use some of the resources mentioned in this article.

Procedure

1. Use the media center or the Internet to make a list of at least five Kentucky resources. Write down where each resource is found.
2. Study the map your teacher gives you. Plot on the map the locations of the resources. Use a symbol for each resource. For example, you can use a brick to represent clay. Make a key to show what each symbol represents.
3. What resources are found in your county?
4. Describe any patterns you see on the map. Do some areas have more resources than others?

The Old State Capitol is made of Kentucky marble.

Project Make a Fossil

Materials
- clay
- plastic foam pellets

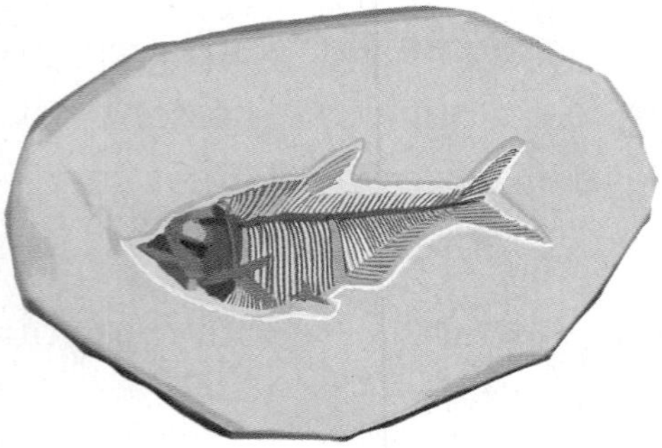

Procedure
1. Use clay to make a layer of sediment about 12 cm square and 2 cm thick.
2. Place the plastic foam pellets on top of the sediment layer.
3. Use the clay to make a second layer of sediment. Place it over the pellet layer.
4. Press gently to encase the pellets in the clay.
5. Peel the layers of sediment apart and remove the plastic foam pellets. Examine the depressions left by the pellets.

Draw Conclusions
1. What type of fossil is being modeled?
2. How might fossils of this type provide information about the animals that left them?

UNIT C EARTH SCIENCE

Earth's Changing Surface

Unit Inquiry

Earthquake-Resistant Buildings

Many people find beauty in the formations that make up Earth's surface. But a calm scene can quickly become frightening during events like earthquakes and volcano eruptions. Scientists and engineers work together to design buildings that can withstand the forces of an earthquake. What types of structures and materials are more likely to fall over during an earthquake? Plan and conduct an experiment to find out.

CHAPTER 7

The Rock Cycle

What's the Big Idea?

Rocks and soils are formed and broken down by natural processes.

Essential Questions

Lesson 1
What Are the Types of Rocks?

Lesson 2
What Is the Rock Cycle?

Lesson 3
How Do Weathering and Erosion Affect Rocks?

Lesson 4
What Is Soil?

GO online **Student eBook www.hspscience.com**

What do YOU wonder?

A Forest of Rocks These formations are part of the Stone Forest, near Kunming, China. How does the way they formed relate to the **Big Idea**?

LESSON 1

Essential Question

What Are the Types of Rocks?

Investigate how sedimentary rocks form.

Read and Learn about minerals and the different kinds of rock.

Fast Fact

Tiny Particles
Sandstone is made of tiny grains of sand. You would need to line up more than 315 grains to reach 2 centimeters (0.8 in.). The picture shows layers of sandstone rock. In the Investigate, you'll look at one way rocks can form.

Layers of sandstone

Vocabulary Preview

mineral [MIN•er•uhl] A solid substance that occurs naturally in rocks or in the ground (p. 280)

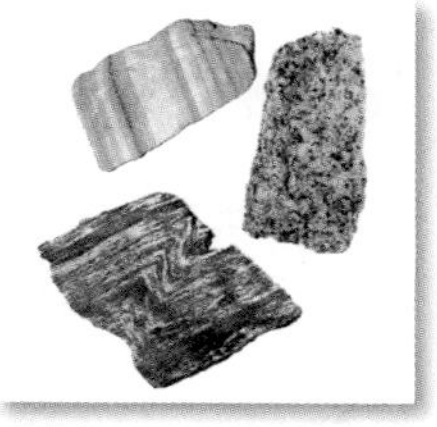

rock [RAHK] A solid substance made of one or more minerals (p. 280)

igneous rock [IG•nee•uhs RAHK] A type of rock that forms from melted rock that cools and hardens (p. 282)

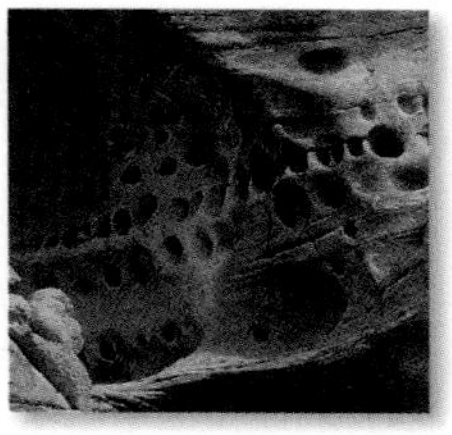

sedimentary rock [sed•uh•MEN•ter•ee RAHK] A type of rock that forms when layers of sediment are pressed together (p. 283)

metamorphic rock [met•uh•MAWR•fik RAHK] A type of rock that forms when heat or pressure change an existing rock (p. 284)

Making Sedimentary Rock

Guided Inquiry

Start with Questions

These rocks have smooth edges and are shiny.

- Do you think the rocks are this way naturally?
- How are these rocks different from each other?

Investigate to find out. Then read to find out more.

Prepare to Investigate

Inquiry Skill Tip

Compare what you read about the formation of sedimentary rocks with your model. Look for ways the natural process is different and the same.

Materials

- sand
- measuring cup
- white glue
- water
- 2 small plastic cups
- plastic stirrer for mixing
- pushpin
- scissors
- large plastic cup

Make an Observation Chart

Step	Observations

Follow This Procedure

1. Use the pushpin to make a small hole in the bottom of the large cup. The hole should be big enough to let water out but not sand.
2. Place 60 mL water and 60 mL white glue in the first small cup. Mix and set aside.
3. Fill the large cup with sand.
4. Set the large cup inside the second small cup.
5. Pour the glue mixture into the sand. Let the liquid drain into the small cup. Let the glue dry. This could take two or three days.
6. When the liquid stops draining, remove the cup with the sand in it. Cut away the plastic cup with the scissors.

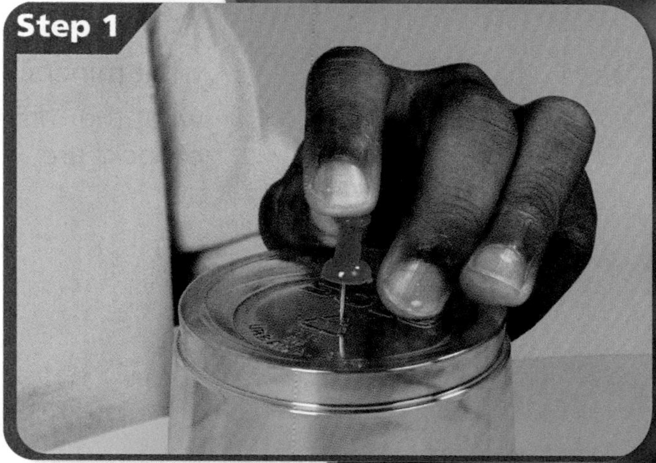

Draw Conclusions

1. Observe and describe the structure that has formed in the cup. Use a hand lens.
2. **Inquiry Skill** Compare the way you made your "rock" with the way you think an actual rock would form. Check your answer when you finish the lesson.

Independent Inquiry

Make a sandstone rock with several layers. Plan the investigation so you can easily observe each layer in the rock.

Read and Learn

VOCABULARY
mineral p. 280
rock p. 280
igneous rock p. 282
sedimentary rock p. 283
metamorphic rock p. 284

SCIENCE CONCEPTS
- what minerals are
- what the three types of rocks are

Focus Skill MAIN IDEA AND DETAILS

Look for details about the three types of rock.

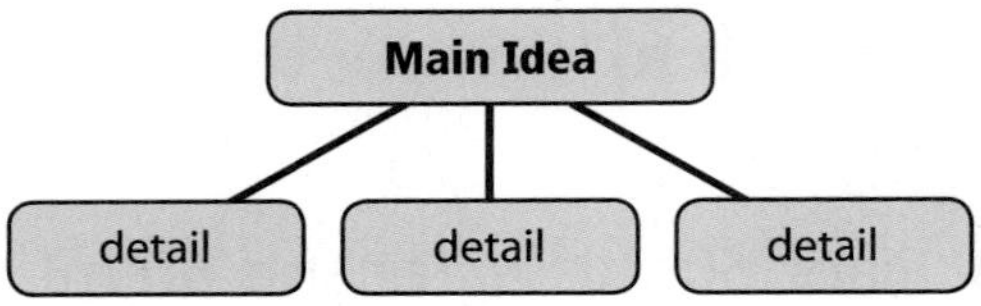

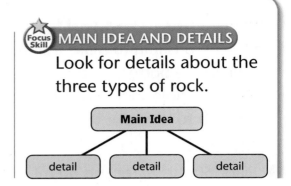

Minerals

Do you remember the last time you picked up a pebble? Maybe it had sparkling specks or wavy lines. Maybe it was as clear as glass.

Minerals formed the colors and patterns in the pebble. A **mineral** (MIN•er•uhl) is a solid, nonliving substance that occurs naturally in rocks or in the ground. Every mineral has unique properties. Earth's surface is **rock**, a solid substance made of minerals. Rock can be made of many minerals or of many different grains of one mineral. For example, look at granite. Each of its colors is a different mineral.

There are more than 4000 minerals. Many of them look alike. Scientists use the minerals' physical properties to tell them apart. For example, scientists can compare the hardness of two minerals by how easily they can be scratched. Gypsum and calcite can look alike, but gypsum is easier to scratch than calcite.

Fluorite often forms cube-shaped crystals of blue, purple, green, yellow, and white.

Calcite is a soft mineral. It can be white or perfectly clear, as this sample is. It makes up most limestone and marble rocks.

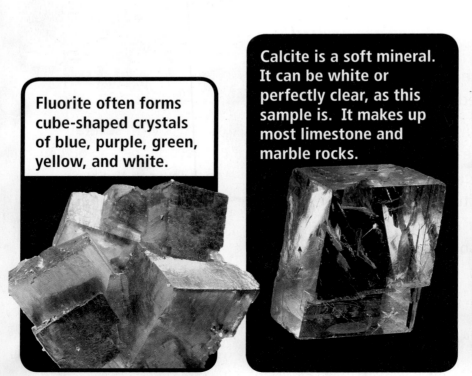

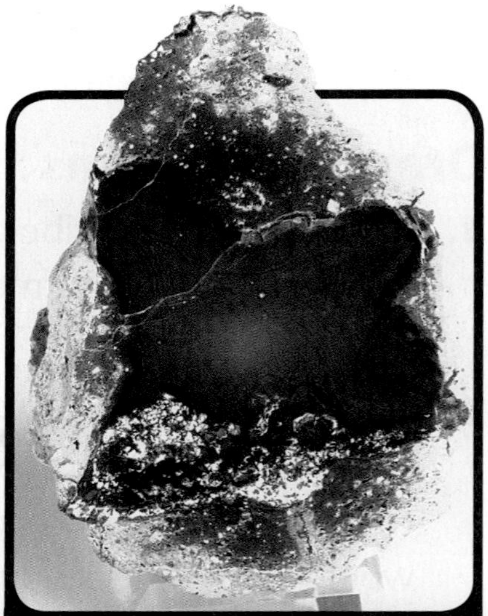

Agate is a type of quartz. It forms in cracks and holes in other rocks. The colored bands take the shape of the hole in which it formed.

▼ Silvery galena is a common mineral from which we get lead.

These two minerals are types of mica. The darker one is biotite. The yellowish one is muscovite.

▲ Hornblende is one of a group of hard green, black, and brown minerals.

▼ Copper is produced from the mineral chalcopyrite (kal•koh•PY•ryt).

The way a mineral reflects light is its *luster.* Two minerals may be the same color, but one may have a shiny luster and the other a dull luster.

When you rub a mineral across a surface, the mineral leaves a *streak* of powder. This colored streak can help scientists identify two minerals that look alike.

Minerals have other properties, too. Is the mineral magnetic? What shape are its crystals?

Two minerals might look alike and share some properties, but they don't share all properties. Gold and pyrite are both shiny and gold in color. Pyrite is sometimes called "fool's gold," because people have mistaken it for gold. Gold is much softer than pyrite. Gold leaves a golden streak. Pyrite's streak is greenish black.

Focus Skill MAIN IDEA AND DETAILS

What properties can scientists use to identify minerals?

Igneous Rocks

Scientists classify rocks into three groups, based on how they form. One group is **igneous rock** (IG•nee•uhs RAHK). Igneous rocks form when melted rock cools and hardens.

The idea of melted rock might seem strange. Deep inside Earth, it is so hot that some rock is liquid, like syrup. This melted rock is *magma.* Inside Earth's crust, magma cools slowly. Volcanic eruptions release magma. Magma on Earth's surface is *lava.* Lava cools quickly.

Focus Skill MAIN IDEA AND DETAILS

How does igneous rock form?

Two or more igneous rocks can form from the same magma. How they look depends partly on how deep in Earth they form. On Earth's surface, lava cools quickly, and grains don't have time to grow big. Inside Earth's surface, magma cools slowly, giving grains time to grow big.

▼ Conglomerate contains very large sediments. Notice the grains have rounded edges.

Shale is Earth's most common sedimentary rock. It forms from very fine sediments of silt and clay.

▼ Sandstone rock forms from sand-sized sediment.

▲ Scientists group sedimentary rocks by how they form and the size of the sediment grains that form them. This picture shows grains of sand, silt, and clay.

Sedimentary Rocks

Another group of rocks is very common on Earth's surface. **Sedimentary rock** (sed•uh•MEN•ter•ee RAHK) forms from sediment. *Sediment* is pieces of rock that have been broken down and moved. Water, wind, and ice break down rock and then carry the sediment. When the wind or water slows down, the sediment falls. It piles up in layers. The layers get pressed together. Water, carrying minerals, moves through the sediment. Over time, the minerals cause the sediment to stick together. This is what you modeled in the Investigate.

Focus Skill MAIN IDEA AND DETAILS

How does sedimentary rock form?

Insta-Lab

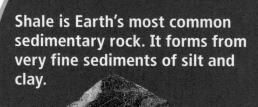

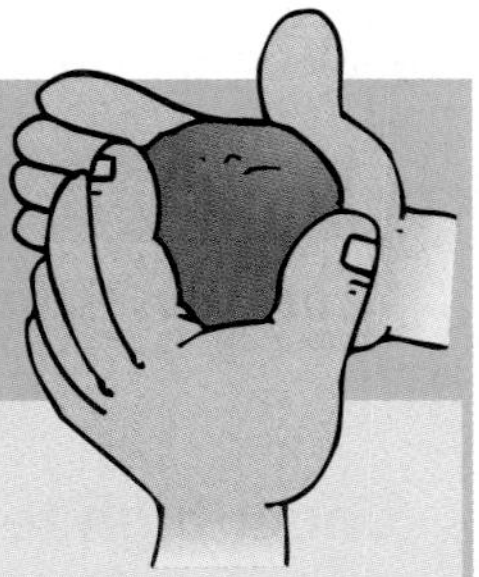

Making Layered Rock

Use small round pieces of clay to make a model of a sedimentary rock. How are these layers like the layers of real sedimentary rocks? How are they different?

Metamorphic Rocks

Another group of rocks is metamorphic (met•uh•MAWR•fik). **Metamorphic rock** is rock that has been changed from another type of rock. High temperature and pressure can cause this type of rock to form.

Mountain building often causes metamorphic rock to form. Mountains form when plates that make up Earth's surface push together. Rock near the surface can get pushed down. Pressure on the rock squeezes it. Mineral grains in the rock get pressed more tightly together. If pressure is great enough, minerals in the rock change.

As natural forces push the rock deeper into Earth's crust, the temperature around it rises. High temperatures can change the minerals in rock. But the rock must not melt if it is to become metamorphic rock. If the rock melts, it becomes magma and eventually igneous rock.

Metamorphic rock can form from any type of rock. This includes other metamorphic rock.

Focus Skill **MAIN IDEA AND DETAILS** **What two processes form metamorphic rock?**

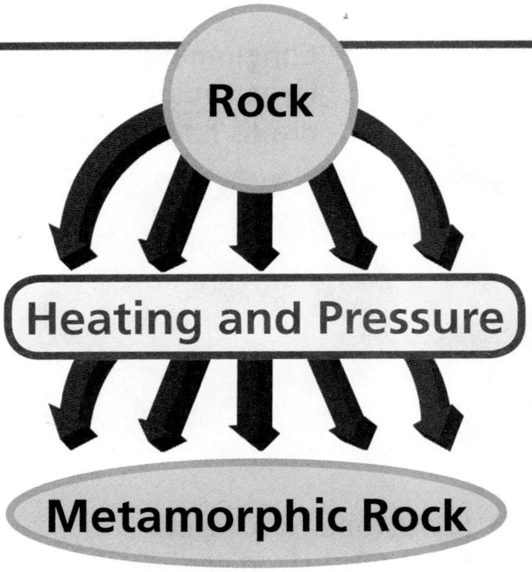

High temperature and pressure can change one type of rock into metamorphic rock.

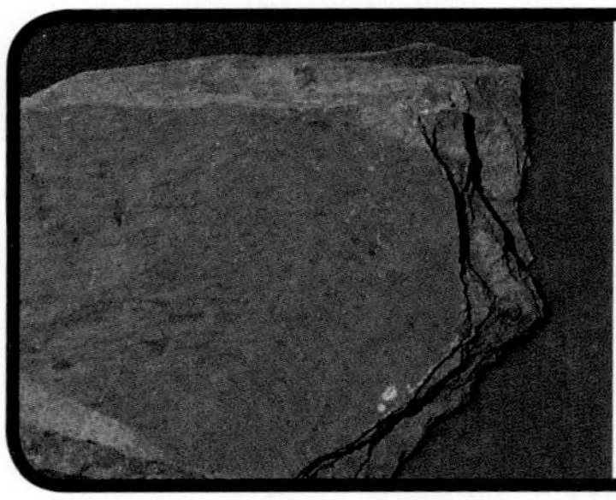

Metamorphic slate forms from shale or mudstone.

Gneiss (NYS) is a metamorphic rock that forms from schist or granite.

Under high temperature and pressure, sedimentary limestone becomes metamorphic marble.

The grains in the rock show the effect of pressure on this metaconglomerate rock.

Lesson Review

Essential Question

What Are the Types of Rocks?

In this lesson, you learned that rock is a solid substance made of minerals. The three different groups of rock (metamorphic, sedimentary, and igneous) are named for how they form.

1. **Focus Skill MAIN IDEA AND DETAILS** Draw and complete a graphic organizer showing the three kinds of rock.

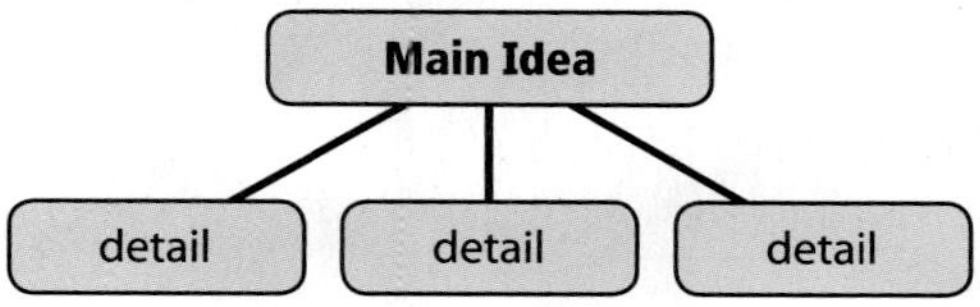

2. **SUMMARIZE** Write a summary of this lesson. Begin with this sentence: *Earth's surface is made of rock.*

3. **DRAW CONCLUSIONS** Igneous rock is the most common type of rock in Earth's crust. Why do you think this is so?

4. **VOCABULARY** In your own words, write definitions of the three types of rock.

Test Prep

5. **CRITICAL THINKING** You find a mineral that is shiny and a golden color. How can you tell if it is gold?

6. Under which of these conditions would igneous rock form?
   A. water breaks down rock
   B. pressure builds
   C. magma cools
   D. sediment collects

Make Connections

Writing

Expository Writing

Choose a type of mineral or rock. Write an explanation of how it forms, where it is found, and what it is used for.

Math

Make a Circle Graph

About 75 percent of rock on Earth's surface is sedimentary. Together, what percent are the other two types? Draw a circle graph to show the relationship.

Art

Rock Art

Draw a picture of the type of rock or mineral you wrote about in your explanation. Include details that would help someone else identify it.

LESSON 2

Essential Question

What Is the Rock Cycle?

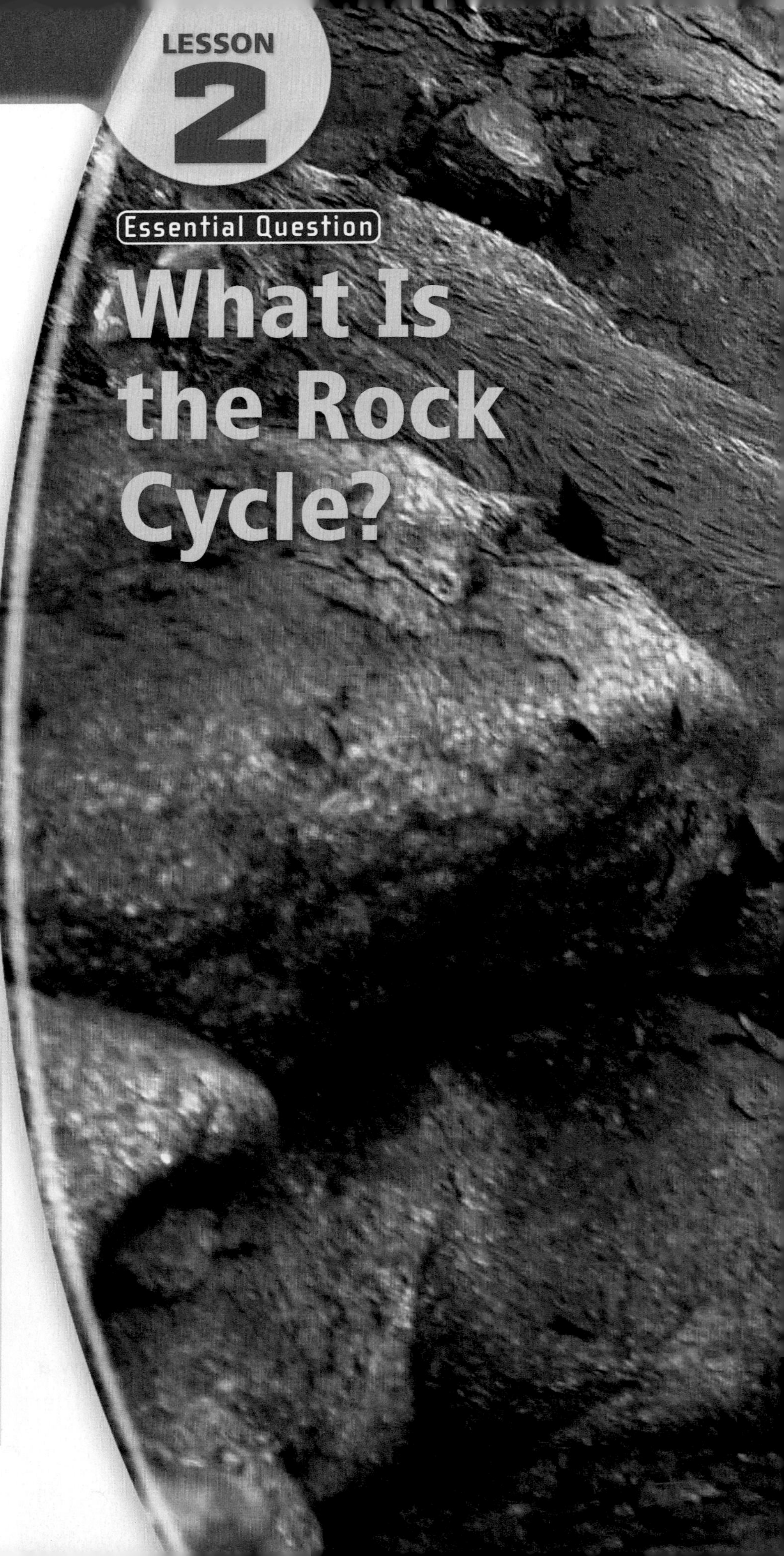

Investigate how heat and pressure work to form rocks.

Read and Learn how rocks form as part of a cycle.

Fast Fact

Hot Rock

Basalt rock doesn't melt easily. It can stay solid at 1000°C (1832°F). This basalt lava flowed from a Hawaiian volcano. The Hawaiians call this páhoehoe (pah•HOH•ee•hoh•ee) lava. In the Investigate, you'll model how rocks change over time.

Flowing lava

Vocabulary Preview

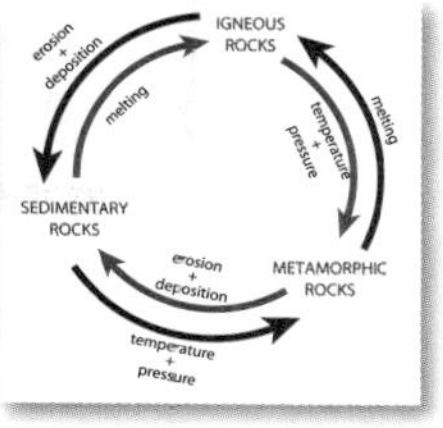

rock cycle [RAHK SY•kuhl] The sequence of processes that change rocks from one type to another over long periods (p. 290)

Investigate

Model a Rock Cycle

Guided Inquiry

Start with Questions

The rocks this child is picking up and the sand on the beach are part of the same cycle.

- How are rocks and sand related?
- Does the ocean water affect the rocks?

Investigate to find out. Then read to find out more.

Prepare to Investigate

Inquiry Skill Tip

The heat and pressure that are part of the rock cycle would be impossible for you to observe—you could not survive working in those conditions! However, you can plan and conduct an investigation to observe how the process works.

Materials

- small pencil sharpener
- crayons of three colors
- metal cookie sheet
- wax paper
- iron
- aluminum pie pan
- toaster oven

Make an Observation Chart

Material	Result
Step 2	
Step 3	
Step 4	

Follow This Procedure

1. Use a sharpener to make three piles of crayon shavings, each a different color.
2. Place the crayon shavings in three layers, on a cookie sheet. Press down the layers with your hand. Draw what you **observe**.
3. Place wax paper over the shavings. Your teacher will press down on the shavings lightly with a warm iron. The teacher will leave the iron for a few seconds, until the shavings soften. They should not melt completely. Let the shavings cool for a few minutes. Draw what you **observe**.
4. Place the block of shavings into a pie pan. CAUTION: **Your teacher will put the pan in the toaster oven. Let the shavings melt. Your teacher will remove the shavings and let them cool.** Draw what you **observe**.

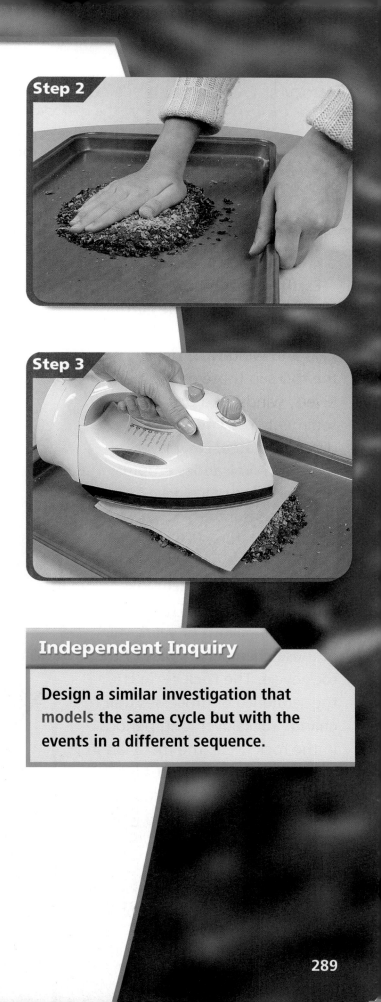

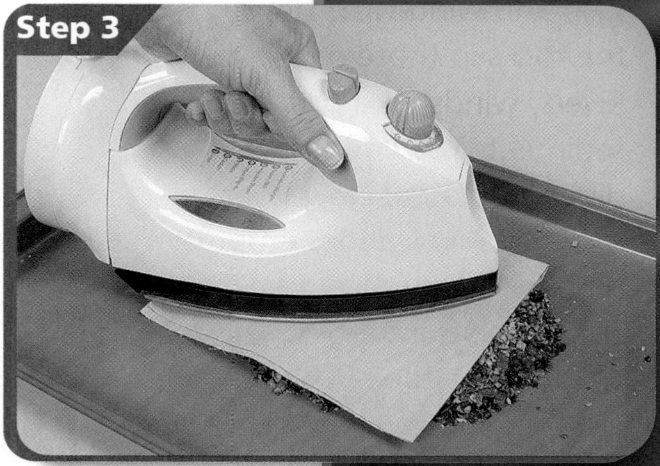

Draw Conclusions

1. What type of rock does Step 2 represent? What type of rock does Step 3 represent? How about Step 4?
2. **Inquiry Skill** How would you **plan and conduct a simple investigation** that uses the "rock" from Step 4 to model how sedimentary rock forms?

Independent Inquiry

Design a similar investigation that models the same cycle but with the events in a different sequence.

VOCABULARY
rock cycle p. 290

SCIENCE CONCEPTS
- what the rock cycle is
- what processes take place during the rock cycle

Focus Skill SEQUENCE
Look for the steps of the rock cycle.

The Rock Cycle

Earth's surface is always changing. Forces inside Earth push mountains upward. Rain and wind wear down the rocks in those mountains. Rivers, winds, and oceans carry sediment. They deposit it in different places. New layers of rock form. Volcanoes erupt lava onto Earth's surface. Lava cools and hardens into rock. This rock wears away, too.

Often you can't see these changes. Many of them take thousands of years. They can even take millions of years. All of these changes are part of the rock cycle. The **rock cycle** is the sequence of processes that change rocks over long periods. In the rock cycle, the materials in rocks change again and again.

The rock cycle can follow many paths. There is a close-up look at one of them later in the lesson.

Focus Skill SEQUENCE

Are there a first and last step in the rock cycle? Explain.

The Rock Cycle

During the rock cycle, each type of rock can be changed into any of the others. Notice that there is more than one path to each type of rock. Also, each type of rock can move through the rock cycle and wind up back where it began!

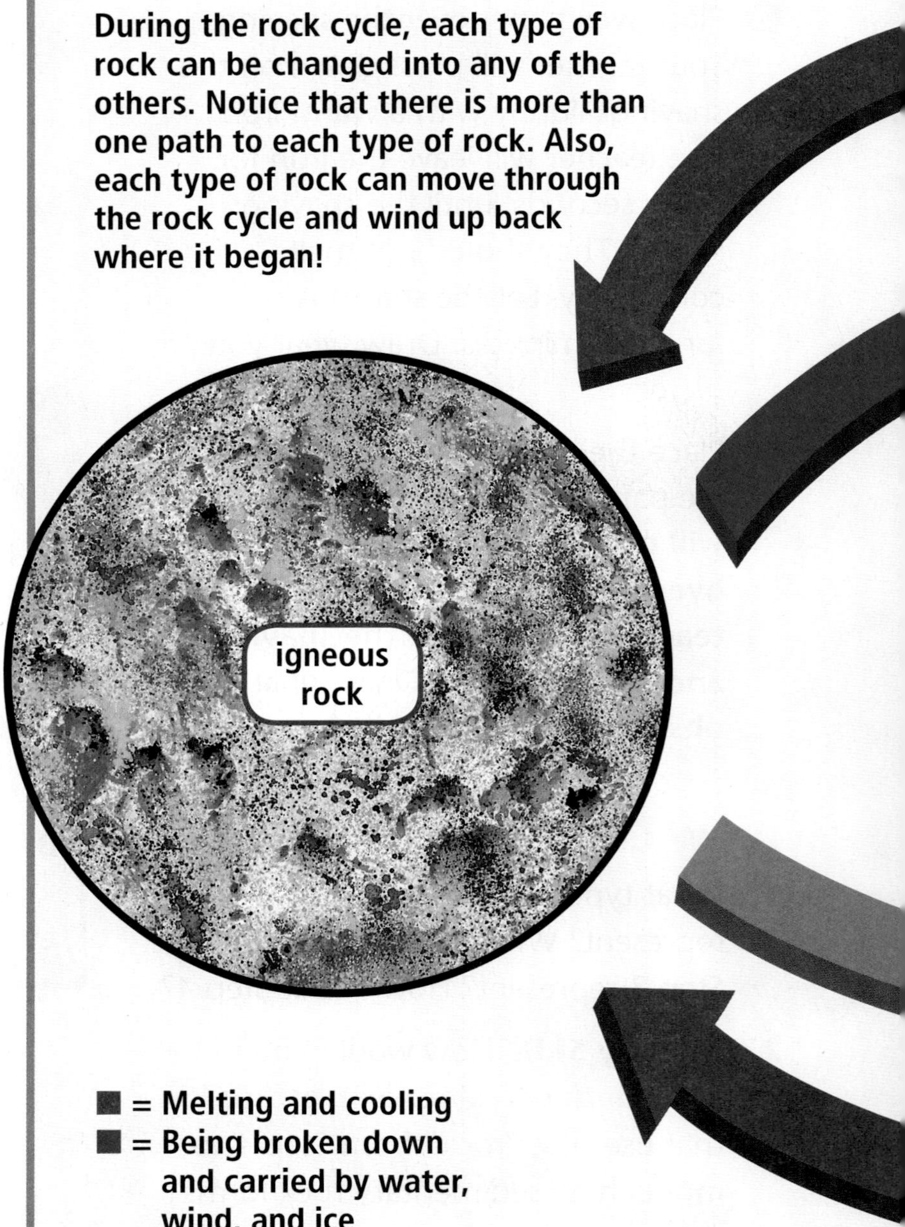

■ = Melting and cooling
■ = Being broken down and carried by water, wind, and ice
■ = Pressure and heat

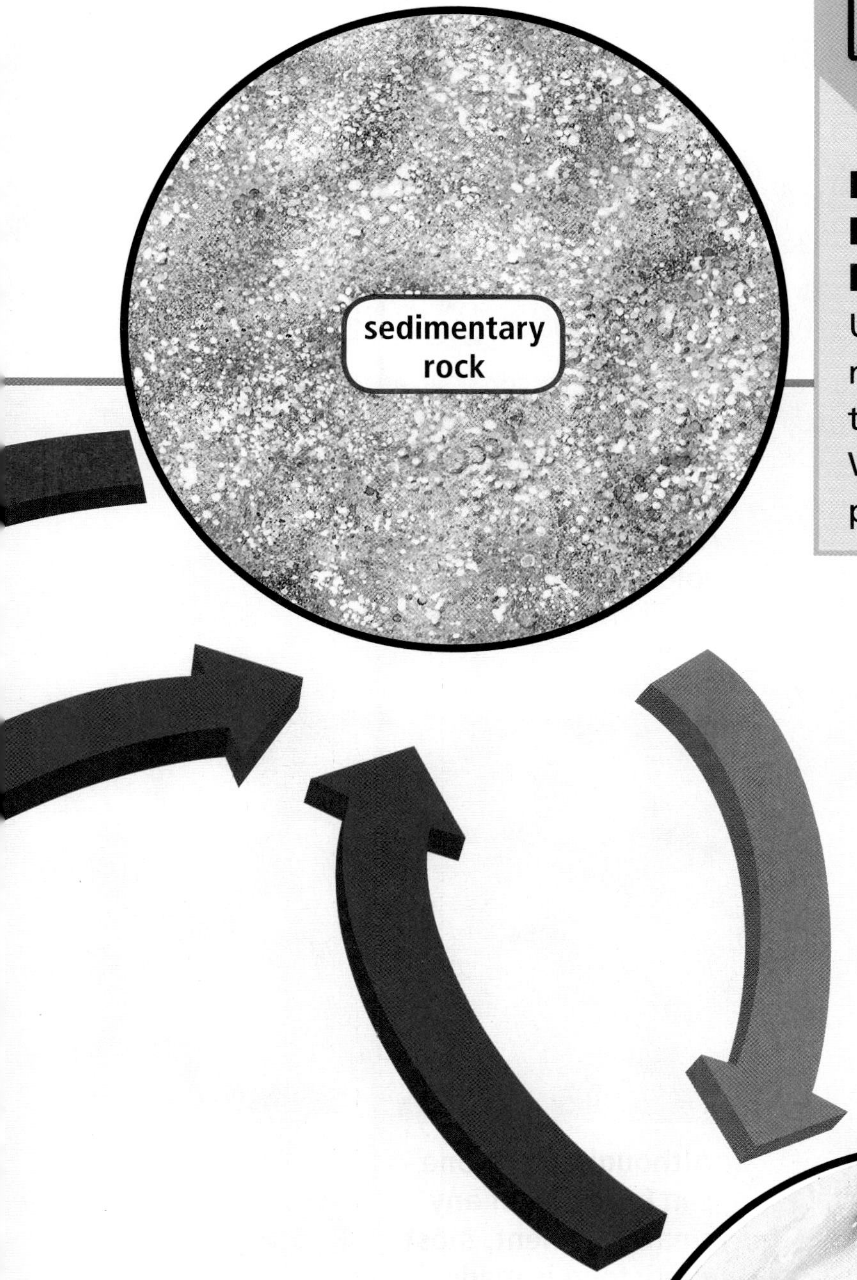

Insta-Lab

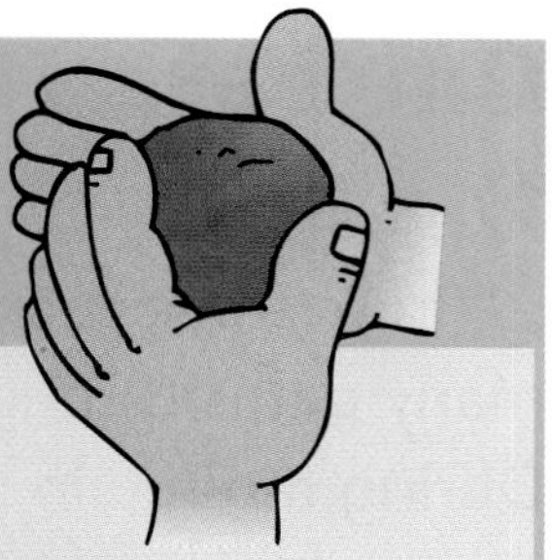

Make a Metamorphic Rock

Use the clay sedimentary rock you made in the Lesson 1 Insta-Lab to model a metamorphic rock. What would you do to model the process? Explain why.

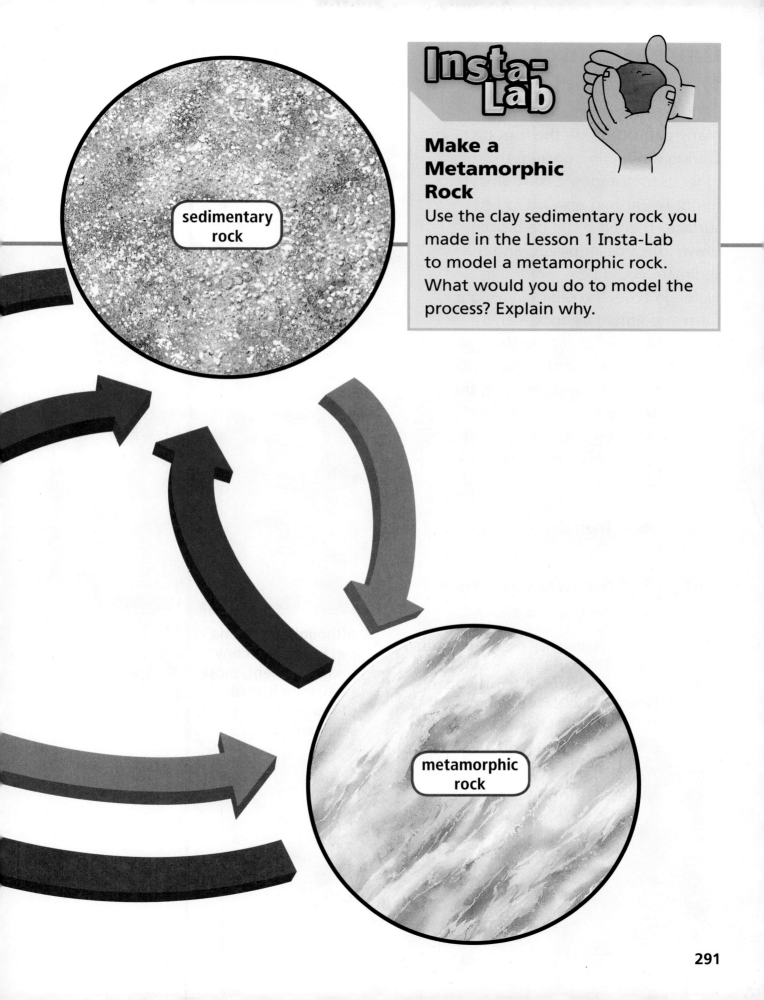

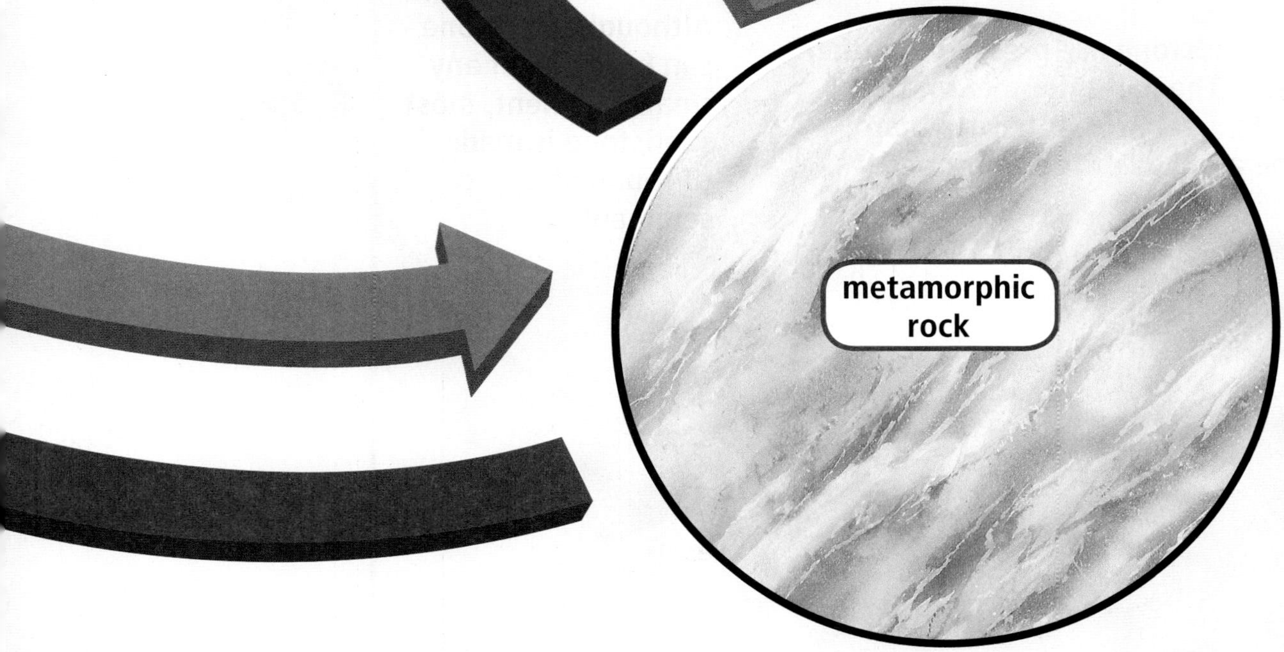

One Path Through the Rock Cycle

These three rocks show one of many paths through the rock cycle. During mountain building, the igneous rock andesite (AN•duh•zyt) might be pushed upward to Earth's surface. There it could be broken down into smaller pieces, and this sediment could be deposited in water. In time, the sediment might form a sedimentary rock such as sandstone. This sandstone may get pushed deep into Earth's crust. With high temperature and pressure, the sandstone may become quartzite (KWAWRT•syt). Suppose even higher temperature acts on quartzite. The rock would melt, and eventually it would cool. It could harden as an igneous rock. Then the rock cycle continues.

Focus Skill **SEQUENCE** **What new type of rock can form after quartzite melts?**

▲ Andesite is a common rock that forms from volcanic lava.

▲ Although sandstone can be made of any small sediment, most sandstone is made of rounded quartz sediment.

▼ Grains in sandstone are pressed together and heated. The metamorphic rock that results, quartzite, is harder than sandstone and has different properties.

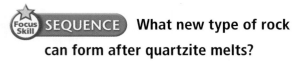

Lesson Review

Essential Question

What Is the Rock Cycle?

In this lesson, you learned that rocks are constantly moving through the rock cycle. Rocks of one kind are changed into rocks of another kind, depending on the conditions around them.

1. **Focus Skill SEQUENCE** Draw and complete a graphic organizer showing how sedimentary rock becomes igneous rock.

2. **SUMMARIZE** Write a summary of this lesson. Begin with this sentence: *Rocks can be changed.*

3. **DRAW CONCLUSIONS** How might igneous rock become metamorphic rock?

4. **VOCABULARY** Define the term *rock cycle* in your own words without using the word *cycle.*

Test Prep

5. **CRITICAL THINKING** Identify a part of the rock cycle that you might see near your home.

6. Which of these isn't produced by the rock cycle?
   A. lava
   B. sand
   C. sediment
   D. fungi

Make Connections

Writing

Expository Writing

Choose one path through the rock cycle. Write a step-by-step **explanation** of the way one rock changes into another. Don't choose the path explained on the opposite page.

9÷3 Math

Solve Problems

A layer of sedimentary rock is 5 meters thick. The layer was deposited at a rate of 1 centimeter per year. How many years did it take to form?

Language Arts

Word Origins

Research the origins of the words *igneous, sedimentary,* and *metamorphic.* Write a short explanation about each one.

LESSON 3

Essential Question

How Do Weathering and Erosion Affect Rocks?

Investigate how rocks can break softer rocks.

Read and Learn how the environment can change rocks.

Fast Fact

Rising Seas

The Giant's Causeway in Ireland is made of basalt, a kind of rock that can form five- or six-sided columns as it cools and shrinks. The sea is wearing away these cliffs. In the Investigate, you'll get an up-close look at one way rock breaks down.

Vocabulary Preview

weathering [WETH•er•ing]
The breaking down of rocks on Earth's surface into smaller pieces (p. 298)

erosion [ee•ROH•zhuhn]
The process of moving sediment from one place to another (p. 302)

Investigate

Shake Things Up

Guided Inquiry

Start with Questions

Water can have interesting effects on rock.

- How long did it take water to change the rocks below?
- Why might it be a bad thing for water to change rock?

Investigate to find out. Then read to find out more.

Prepare to Investigate

Inquiry Skill Tip

Before you infer why some materials in your experiment break down faster than others, closely examine the materials. Remember what they were like before. Look for characteristics of the materials that might determine how quickly they break down.

Materials

- 6 medium-size rocks
- 2 pieces of chalk
- empty clear 2-qt plastic juice container with lid

Make an Observation Chart

Observations	
Start	
After 1 minute	
After 2 minutes	
After 3 minutes	
After 4 minutes	

Follow This Procedure

1. Make a model of the way rocks break down in nature. Add two pieces of chalk to the container.
2. Place six rocks in the container.
3. Put the lid on the container.
4. Shake the container so that the rocks and chalk rub against each other. Do this for several minutes. You can take turns with your lab partner.

Draw Conclusions

1. **Compare** the way the rocks and chalk looked at the start and at the end of the investigation.
2. **Inquiry Skill** Scientists often infer the reasons for an investigation's results. Why did some of the materials in the container break down faster than other materials? How do you think this relates to rocks in nature?

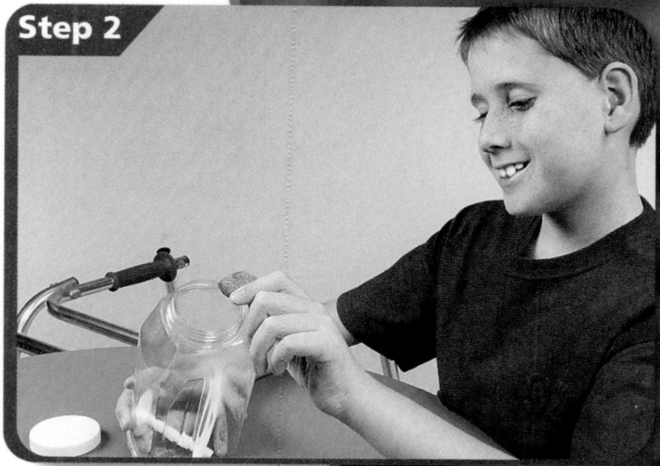

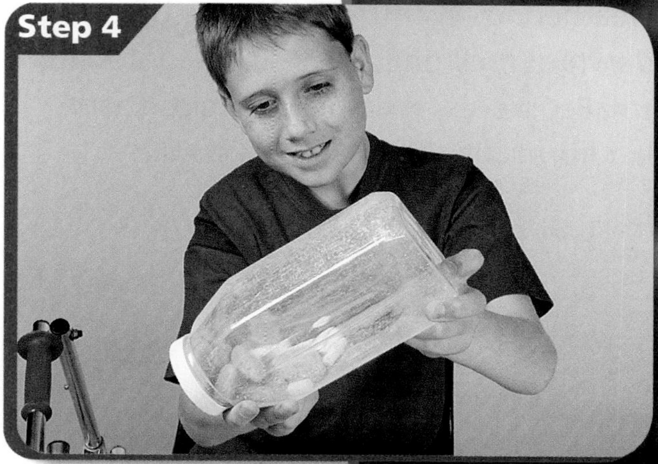

Independent Inquiry

First, weigh the chalk that is left after the investigation. Then, add water to the container and repeat the test. Compare the mass of the chalk before and after the test. What conclusion can you draw?

Read and Learn

VOCABULARY
weathering p. 298
erosion p. 302

SCIENCE CONCEPTS
- how weathering affects rock
- how erosion affects rock

Focus Skill CAUSE AND EFFECT
Look for the causes of weathering.

cause → effect

Weathering

Have you ever seen a weed growing through a crack in a sidewalk? Maybe you've seen a statue with its features worn away. These are examples of weathering. **Weathering** is the breaking down of rock on Earth's surface into smaller pieces. Weathering helps shape landforms. It also helps make soil.

One type of weathering changes the chemical makeup of rock. This softens and weakens the rock, helping water wear it away. Water causes most weathering. It can break down some rock by itself. For example, water can wear away rock salt, calcite, and limestone.

Sinkholes are the result of weathering. They form when water slowly dissolves underground rock.

▼ **Water can help wear away bits of surface rock.**

A chemical change has turned the surface of this rock brown. Iron oxide, or rust, breaks down the outer layer of some kinds of rock.

Some rocks break down when oxygen combines with minerals in them. This often happens in rocks that have iron. When iron mixes with oxygen, iron oxide, or rust, forms. Rust makes it easier for other processes to weather the rock.

Focus Skill CAUSE AND EFFECT

What is the effect of weathering?

Science Up Close

For more links and animations, go to **www.hspscience.com**

Formation of a Sinkhole

1 Rain soaks into the ground. The rainwater dissolves limestone under the surface. Water carries away the dissolved rock. A small opening forms.

2 The opening in the rock becomes larger as time passes.

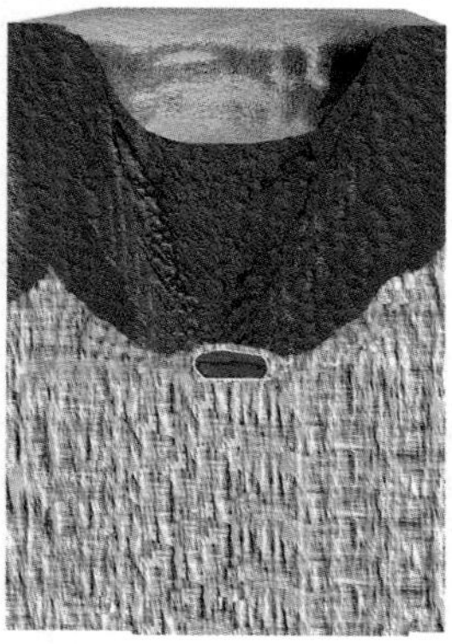

3 Rock and soil that covered the underground opening cave in. A sinkhole forms on the surface. Do you think this process happens quickly or slowly? Explain.

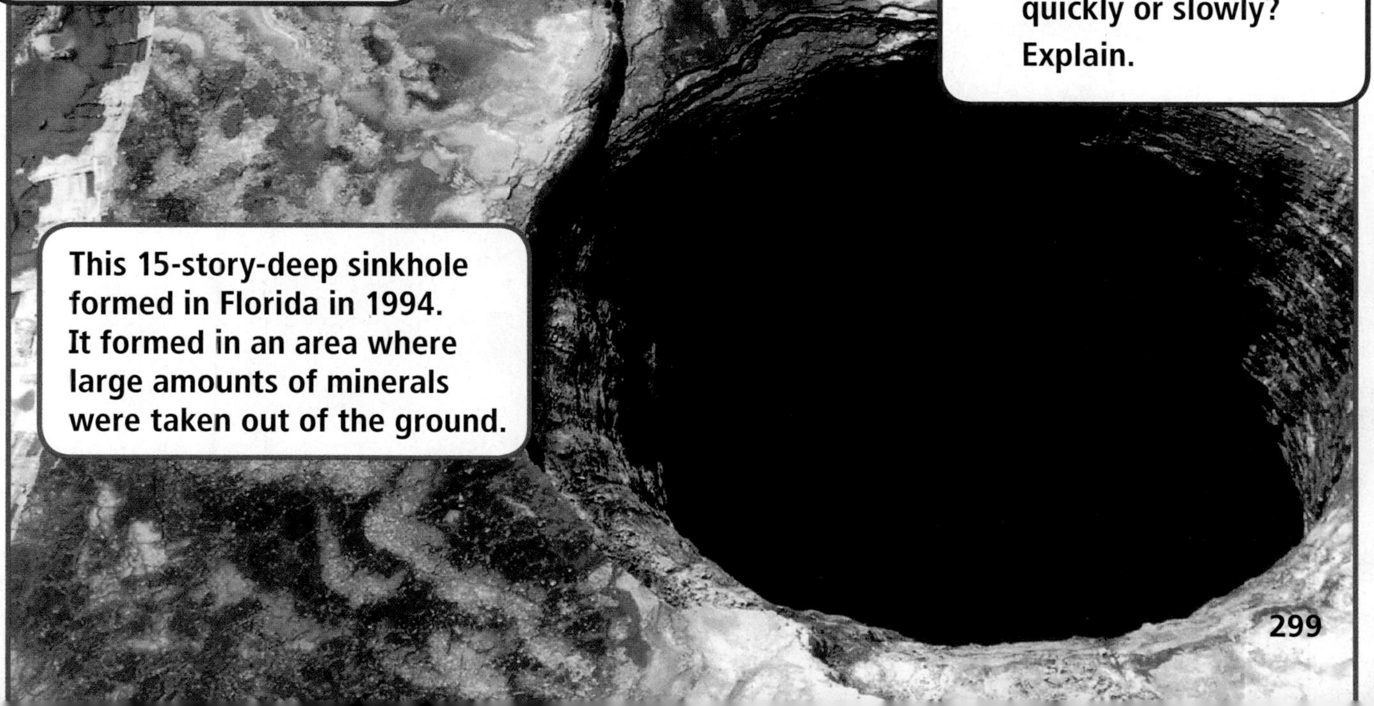

This 15-story-deep sinkhole formed in Florida in 1994. It formed in an area where large amounts of minerals were taken out of the ground.

Weathering by Physical Processes

A second type of weathering doesn't change rock chemically. It breaks rock down through physical processes. Water, ice, living things, and wind are causes of this type of weathering.

You see the results of this weathering around you each day. It can cause cracks in sidewalks and potholes in streets. Rain enters cracks in rock and cement. If the water freezes into ice, it expands. The ice cracks and breaks rock around it. Stones in streams are also a sign of weathering. These stones were broken from larger pieces of rock. As they tumble against each other, they break down even more.

Large ocean waves weather coastlines. Waves smash into the bottom of a cliff. The rock that the waves hit cracks and breaks. In time, rock at the top of the cliff falls into the sea.

Even temperature changes can weather rock. Rock expands when it heats up. It contracts when it cools. Repeated heating and cooling can weaken some rock. The rock can then crack or break.

Pounding waves force air into cracks. This helps split the rock. Water also carries sediment. This scrapes rock like sandpaper.

▼ Waves hit cliffs like this with great force. Thousands of tons of water smash into coastal rocks during storms.

▲ **Running water carries sediment. The sediment scrapes against itself and against rocks in the streambed as the water moves.**

Scraping and bumping against each other in a moving stream gives these rocks rounded edges.

Living things can cause weathering. You have probably seen plants grow through cracks in rocks. The roots wedge into the rocks, splitting the rock around them as they grow. Animals can cause weathering, too. When animals dig in soil, they move rocks closer to Earth's surface. Then rainwater can reach them more easily.

Wind also causes weathering. Wind picks up bits of rock and soil and throws them against other rocks. This chips away the rocks' surface bit by bit.

Focus Skill CAUSE AND EFFECT

How does ice cause weathering?

Insta-Lab

Observe Weathering

Use a large rock or brick to press down on a handful of rock salt. What happens to the rock salt? What kind of weathering does this model?

Erosion

What happens after weathering breaks down rock into sediment? Erosion takes over. **Erosion** is the process of moving sediment.

Water can cause erosion. Rivers carry sediment downstream. They drop it on their banks or at their mouths. Ocean waves pick up sediment and leave it on the shore as sand.

Wind erosion is most common in deserts. With few plants to hold sediment in place, wind picks it up easily. Wind stacks sand into huge mounds called sand dunes.

Glaciers are important causes of erosion. As these giant sheets of ice move, they scrape the ground. They pick up rocks and soil. During the last Ice Age, huge glaciers covered large parts of what is now the northern United States. They eroded and helped shape the plains and other landforms we see today. As glaciers moved over land, they also formed lakes. When the glaciers melted, they left behind huge ridges of sediment and large amounts of water.

Focus Skill **CAUSE AND EFFECT**

What are the main causes of erosion?

Water that washes over areas of bare soil can form gullies. Planting vegetation can help prevent this type of soil erosion.

Math in Science
Interpret Data

What is the largest type of sediment? What is the smallest? Which would erosion affect more, boulders and cobbles or silt and clay? Why is that?

SEDIMENT COMES IN ALL SIZES		
256 mm and up	BOULDERS	GRAVEL
64-256 mm	COBBLES	
2-64 mm	PEBBLES	
0.0625-2 mm	SAND	
0.002-0.0625 mm	SILT	
0.002 mm and under	CLAY	

This photo shows one river flowing into another. Sediment washes into rivers from areas along their banks. One of these rivers is carrying much more sediment than the other. The sediment has turned parts of the water brown.

Essential Question

How Do Weathering and Erosion Affect Rocks?

In this lesson, you learned that weathering is the process by which rocks are broken down into smaller rocks. Erosion is the movement of sediment. These processes can change landforms.

1. Focus Skill **CAUSE AND EFFECT** Draw and complete a graphic organizer showing the effects of erosion.

2. **SUMMARIZE** Write a summary of this lesson. Begin with this sentence: *There are two kinds of weathering—chemical and physical.*

3. **DRAW CONCLUSIONS** The Colorado River flows through the bottom of the Grand Canyon. Does the river cause weathering or erosion? Explain.

4. **VOCABULARY** Make a crossword puzzle by using the vocabulary for the first three lessons in this chapter.

Test Prep

5. **CRITICAL THINKING** You see a marble sign. Its letters are too worn to read. What caused this?

6. Which of these doesn't cause weathering?
   A. wind
   B. magma
   C. water
   D. plants

Make Connections

Writing

Narrative Writing

Write the **story** of a grain of sediment that has been weathered from a mountain, carried to the sea by a river, and left on a beach. Write from the sediment's point of view.

Math

Solve Problems

A farmer plants $\frac{1}{5}$ of his land with trees to stop erosion. If he plants trees on 525 hectares, how much land does he have? Show your work.

Social Studies

Famous Features

Research a famous natural feature, such as a canyon, a mountain, or a rock formation. Explain how it formed. Draw a map that shows where the feature is located. Share with the class what you find.

LESSON 4

Essential Question

What Is Soil?

Investigate the different sizes of soil particles.

Read and Learn what soil is made of and why it is an important resource.

Fast Fact

Forming Soil

This tree is starting soil formation by weathering rock. Over a long time, the rock will be broken down into soil. It can take up to 1000 years for 2 centimeters ($\frac{3}{4}$ in.) of topsoil to form!

Rock split by tree

Vocabulary Preview

humus [HYOO•muhs] The remains of decayed plants or animals in the soil (p. 308)

horizon [huh•RY•zuhn] A layer in the soil (p. 308)

bedrock [BED•rahk] The solid rock that forms Earth's surface (p. 309)

sand [SAND] The largest particles that make up soil (p. 310)

clay [KLAY] The smallest particles that make up soil (p. 310)

Investigate

Testing Soil

Guided Inquiry

Start with Questions

This plant is being potted in potting soil. The potting soil will help the plant's roots get water and nutrients.

- Why is potting soil a better carrier for moisture than sand is?
- Why don't people pot plants in mud?

Investigate to find out. Then read to find out more.

Prepare to Investigate

Inquiry Skill Tip

In order to make valid comparisons of your results, you need to record your information accurately. Begin by measuring your water carefully.

Materials

- measuring scoop
- sand
- 2 large jars with wide mouths
- potting soil
- 250-mL measuring cup
- water

Make an Observation Chart

Material	Water Used
Sand	
Potting Soil	

Follow This Procedure

1. Place several scoops of sand in a jar. Place an equal amount of potting soil in another jar.
2. Put 200 mL of water in a measuring cup.
3. Slowly pour the water into the sand. Stop when water starts to puddle on top.
4. Record how much water you used.
5. Repeat steps 2, 3, and 4 for the potting soil.

Step 2

Step 3

Draw Conclusions

1. Compare the amounts of water the two types of soil absorbed. Infer where the water you poured into them went.
2. **Inquiry Skill** When scientists do an experiment, they often do it in more than one way and compare results. What do your results tell you about how the size of particles and the spaces between them compare in sand and potting soil?

Independent Inquiry

Repeat the investigation, using a different type of soil. Predict how the new results will compare with the results of the Investigate. Is your prediction correct?

Read and Learn

VOCABULARY
humus p. 308
horizon p. 308
bedrock p. 309
sand p. 310
clay p. 310

SCIENCE CONCEPTS
- what soil is
- how soil forms and how soils differ

Focus Skill COMPARE AND CONTRAST
Look for ways that soils are alike and different.

alike — different

Soil Formation

If you walk in the woods, you are walking on soil. If you grow flowers on a windowsill, you use soil. Soil is one of the most important things on Earth. Plants can't grow without soil. Without plants, animals could not exist.

So what is soil? The largest part of soil is weathered rock. Sediment makes up almost 50 percent of soil.

Soil has living and nonliving parts. It contains **humus** (HYOO•muhs), or the remains of decayed plants and animals. Soil is crawling with living organisms. There are worms and insects as well as bacteria, fungi, and roots that you can't see with just your eyes.

Water and air make up about half the volume of a soil sample. Water and air are in the spaces between soil particles.

Most soil has **horizons**, or layers. Some soils have several horizons that are easy to see. Other soils have few horizons.

▼ **These three pictures show steps of soil formation.**

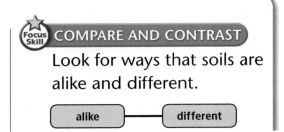

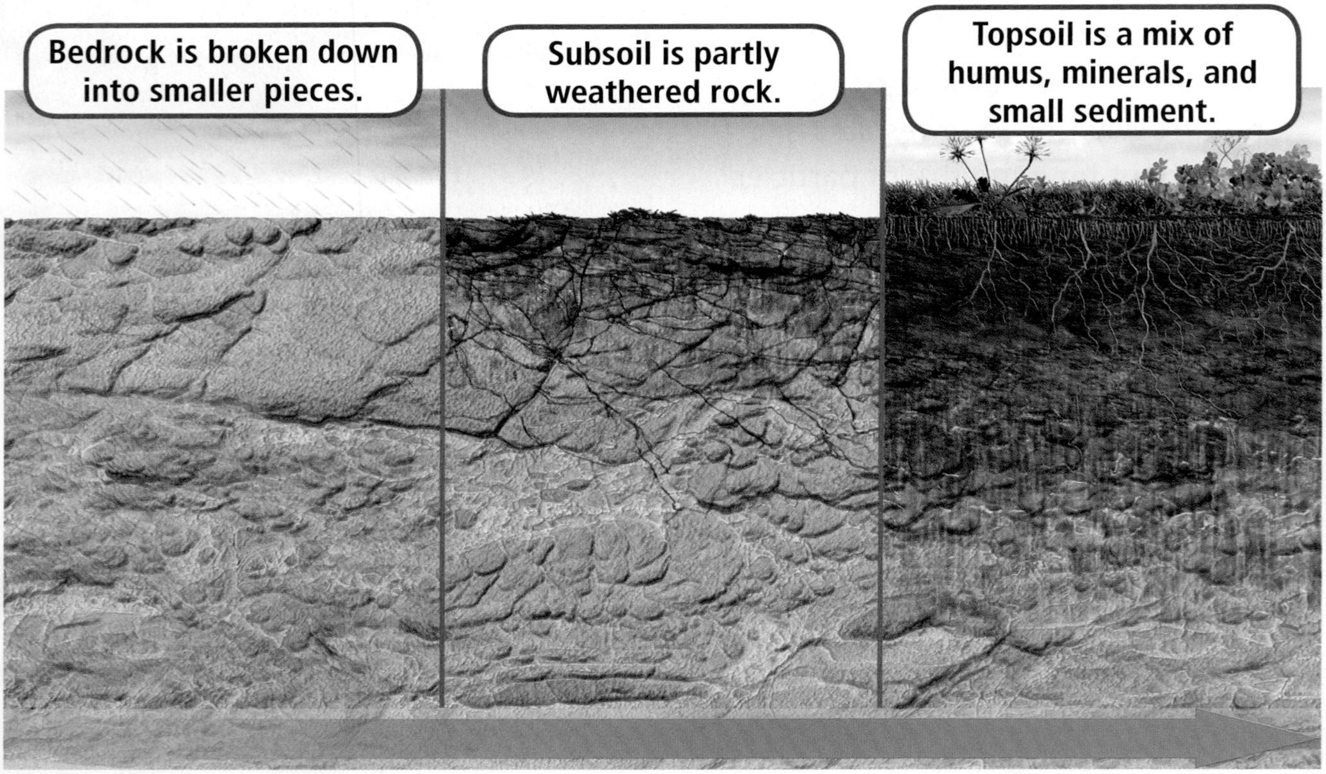

Bedrock is broken down into smaller pieces.
Subsoil is partly weathered rock.
Topsoil is a mix of humus, minerals, and small sediment.

Because horizons form differently, each has particles of different sizes. Horizons also may have different minerals. Horizons all share some properties. The upper layer is topsoil. It includes humus. The lower horizons have partly weathered rock. The lower horizons also contain minerals that rain has carried from upper layers. The bottom horizon is **bedrock**, or the solid rock that forms Earth's surface.

Soil is always forming, but it takes a long time. Some soils take thousands of years to form. That is one reason why it is important to take steps to care for soil.

Focus Skill COMPARE AND CONTRAST

How are the top and bottom horizons of soil different?

This well-developed soil has several horizons.

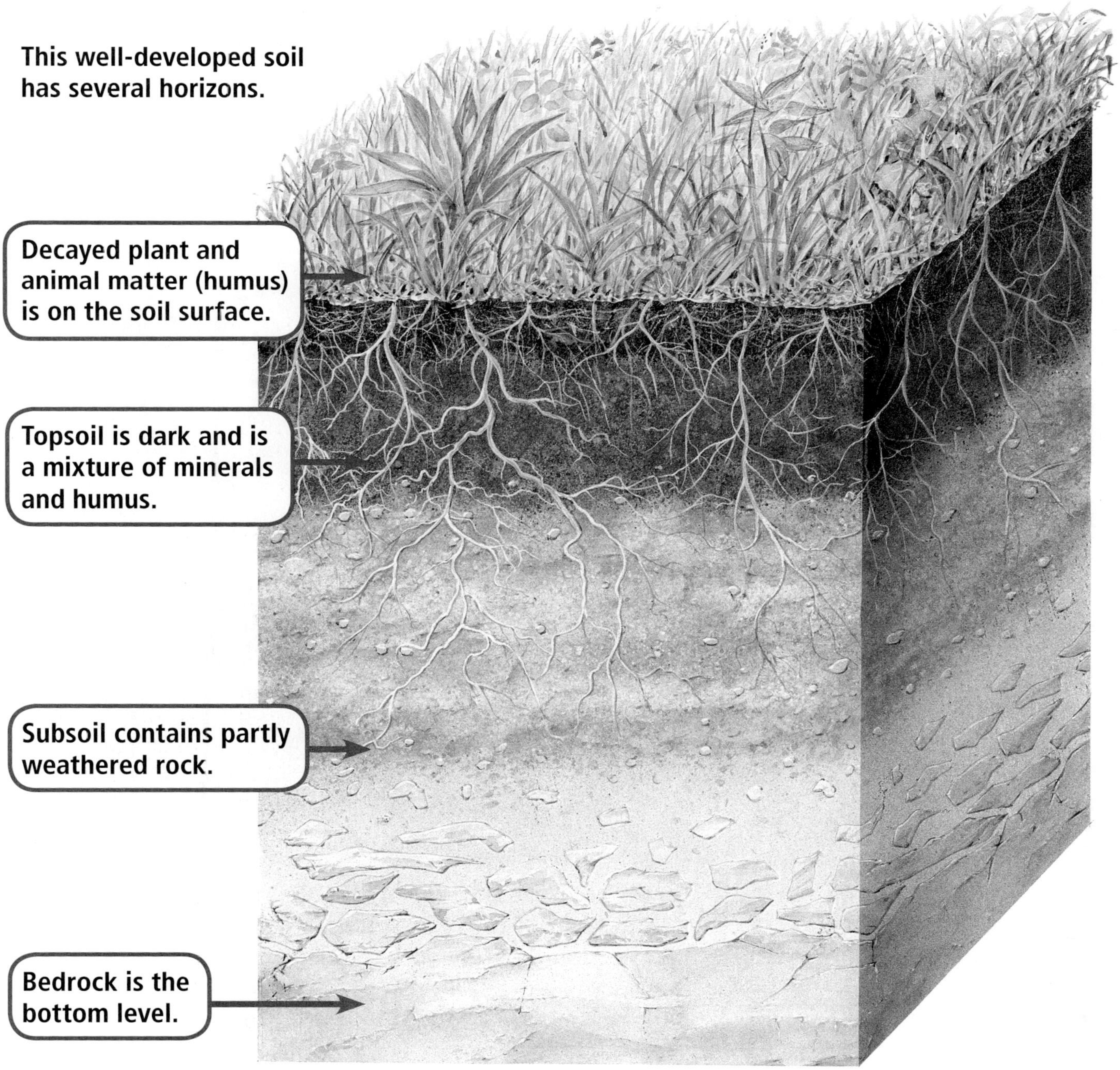

Decayed plant and animal matter (humus) is on the soil surface.
Topsoil is dark and is a mixture of minerals and humus.
Subsoil contains partly weathered rock.
Bedrock is the bottom level.

Types of Soil

You might think that one type of soil is very much like another, but there are many types of soil. Soils are classified by their physical properties. The size of soil particles is one property. Each type of soil is a mix of particles of different sizes. The largest particles are **sand**. A sand particle might be 1 to 2 millimeters (0.04 to 0.08 in.) across. The smallest soil particles are **clay**. Clay particles might be $\frac{1}{1000}$ the size of sand particles. The size of silt is between sand and clay.

Different amounts of sand, silt, and clay in soil give it texture. Texture is how the soil feels in your hands. Soil with more sand feels rough, while soil with more clay feels smooth. Soils differ in other ways, also. They have different compositions. Soil under a desert has less humus than grassland soil. Some soils hold water well, while others don't. Soil horizons can be just a few centimeters thick, or they can reach several meters underground.

Sandy soils have large particles. Water passes through quickly. They can be good for growing crops.

Fertile soils often have a thick layer of topsoil. Large amounts of humus make the soil dark.

Clay soils have tiny particles. They hold nutrients and water so well it's hard for plants to grow.

Soil Horizons in Three Different Places

Soils of grasslands often have a thick top horizon that is full of humus. They are loose, soft, and fertile.

Desert soils don't have much humus. They are pale gray to red in color and high in salts. Horizons are not well developed.

This typical Florida soil is sandy, with a thin layer of humus. It forms from limestone bedrock.

Soil type depends on the area where it forms. Bedrock breaks down to form the soil above it. Granite bedrock forms coarse soil. Soil formed by basalt bedrock is fine-grained.

A soil's color is also dependent on where the soil forms. A dark soil may have formed in a place with a lot of humus, such as a forest. A light-colored soil may have little organic matter, such as in a desert.

Focus Skill COMPARE AND CONTRAST

How might desert soil and forest soil be alike? Different?

Insta-Lab

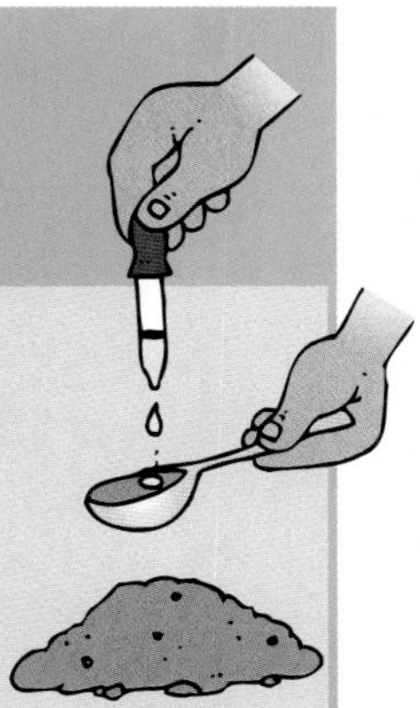

How Much Water?

With a dropper, drop water onto a tablespoon of soil and onto a small sponge. Compare how much water soaks in and how much runs off in each case. What property of soil are you modeling?

Soil and Plants

Most plants need soil. Their roots draw nutrients, water, and oxygen from soil.

Some soils are fertile. They are good for growing plants. Other soils lack nutrients. To make the soil better for growing plants, many farmers and gardeners add nutrients to soil. The nutrients they add are fertilizer (FERT•uhl•eye•zer).

There are natural fertilizers and artificial fertilizers. Artificial fertilizers are human-made mixtures of chemicals. They add to the soil nutrients that plants need. Natural fertilizers include compost and animal waste. People make compost by putting food and plant scraps in a pile. The scraps decay to make fertilizer.

Some soils hold more moisture than other soils. Humus helps soil hold water. Soils with small particles hold water better than soils with large particles. When soil is too dry for plants, people add water. They pump water from wells and other sources and sprinkle it on soil.

Focus Skill **COMPARE AND CONTRAST** **Compare and contrast the two types of fertilizers.**

Soils can lose nutrients because of erosion or heavy use. Fertilizers put back important nutrients, such as phosphorus, nitrogen, and potassium.

Many farmers use fertilizers on their soil.

Many farmers and gardeners use compost to give soil nutrients. Compost is a natural fertilizer that adds humus to soil.

Lesson Review

Essential Question

What Is Soil?

In this lesson, you learned that soil is made up of once-living and nonliving parts. Different kinds of soil are found in different areas and can support different kinds of life.

1. Focus Skill **COMPARE AND CONTRAST** Draw and complete a graphic organizer that compares sandy soil with fertile soil.

   alike — different

2. **SUMMARIZE** Write a summary of this lesson. Begin with this sentence: *The largest part of soil is weathered rock.*

3. **DRAW CONCLUSIONS** Erosion can wash away soil. Why is it important to control this type of erosion?

4. **VOCABULARY** Make a page for a picture dictionary, using the five lesson vocabulary words.

Test Prep

5. **CRITICAL THINKING** Why is understanding soil and how it forms useful to all people?

6. Which of these makes up the largest part of soil?
   A. water
   B. humus
   C. air
   D. sediment

Make Connections

Writing

Persuasive Writing

Write a short **e-mail** to the editor of a newspaper. Persuade gardeners to use compost instead of other fertilizers in their gardens. Explain why compost is a better choice.

Math

Solving a Problem

Soil in a certain area erodes at a rate of 3.2 centimeters per month. How much soil erodes over a period of 5 years?

Social Studies

Report

Write a **report** about the problems of drought and soil erosion that led to the Dust Bowl. If possible, interview someone who was affected by the Dust Bowl. Include a map.

Crumbling HISTORY

WILL THE GREAT SPHINX CRUMBLE LIKE A COOKIE?

The Great Sphinx in Egypt has stood the test of time. For at least 4,500 years, the sphinx has towered over a desert in Egypt. Now, however, rising groundwater may cause the ancient statue to crumble.

Wind has blown desert sand into the Great Sphinx, wearing away the monument.

The Mysterious Sphinx

A sphinx is a figure with the head of a person and the body of a lion. No one knows for sure why the Great Sphinx was built. Some say it honors an ancient king named Khafre. Others say the sphinx was made to represent an ancient Egyptian god.

The sphinx was built at about the same time that the Great Pyramid was built. Even though scientists know little about the sphinx, they do know something about the Great Pyramid and the other nearby pyramids.

The ancient Egyptians built the pyramids as tombs for their kings. When an Egyptian king died, his body was mummified. The body was then placed in the tomb. Many of the king's belongings were also placed in the tomb.

Damaging History

The sphinx and pyramids have suffered damage over time. For example, wind has blown the desert sand into the monuments, causing them to wear away. Some of the blocks that make up the monuments have come loose and fallen.

Now the ancient monuments are facing the most serious threat ever—water. A dam built near the monuments traps water. That water is used to irrigate farm crops grown nearby. Irrigation has caused the level of groundwater to increase. The water is filled with salts. The salts and water react with the stone that makes up the monuments. The chemical reaction causes the stones to crumble and turn into dust.

Two scientists are now trying to protect the ancient monuments. They want to find ways to keep groundwater from flowing under the monuments. If the water isn't stopped, the Great Sphinx and pyramids may one day crumble into dust blown by the desert wind.

Think and Write

1. Why did the ancient Egyptians build the pyramids?
2. Can you think of any monuments in the United States that need protecting?

THE GREAT SPHINX

20 meters (66 ft) high
73 meters (240 ft) long
4-meter-wide (13-ft-wide) face
2-meter-high (7-ft-high) eyes

Spin-In™ Find out more. Log on to **www.hspscience.com**

CHAPTER 7 Review and Test Preparation

Vocabulary Review

Use the terms below to complete the sentences. The page numbers tell where to look in the chapter if you need help.

mineral p. 280
igneous p. 282
sedimentary p. 283
metamorphic p. 284
rock cycle p. 290
weathering p. 298
erosion p. 302
humus p. 308
horizon p. 308
bedrock p. 309

1. Rock that formed from other weathered rock is _______.
2. The process of moving sediment from one place to another is _______.
3. Rock that forms when melted rock cools and hardens is _______.
4. A group of processes that change rocks over a long time is the _______.
5. A soil layer is a _______.
6. A solid substance that occurs naturally in rocks or in the ground is a _______.
7. The breaking down of rock on Earth's surface into smaller pieces is _______.
8. The solid rock that forms Earth's surface is _______.
9. Rock that has changed from another type of rock is _______.
10. The decayed remains of dead plants and animals is _______.

Check Understanding

Write the letter of the best choice.

11. Of which substance are rocks made?
    - **A.** water
    - **B.** horizons
    - **C.** humus
    - **D.** minerals

12. Identify the rock below.

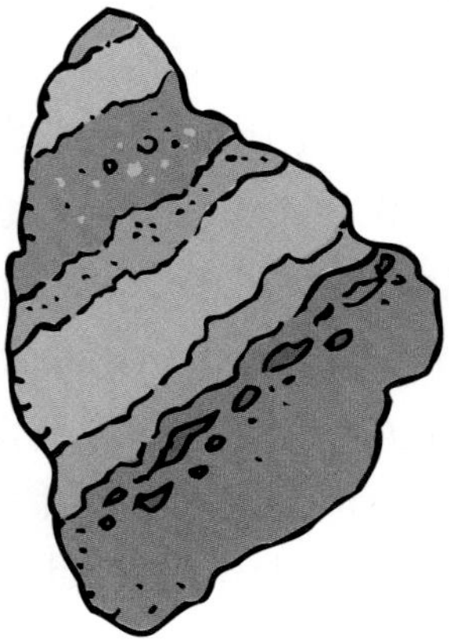

- **F.** igneous granite
- **G.** metamorphic quartzite
- **H.** sedimentary conglomerate
- **J.** sedimentary sandstone

13. **MAIN IDEA AND DETAILS** Which of these is **not** a part of the rock cycle? (Focus Skill)
    - **A.** Metamorphic rock melts.
    - **B.** Lava hardens into rock.
    - **C.** Nitrogen enters soil.
    - **D.** Plants weather rock.

14. COMPARE AND CONTRAST Which describes how some igneous rock forms?

Focus Skill

F. Water freezes in cracks in rock.
G. Magma cools underground.
H. Pressure changes minerals in rock.
J. Water erodes sediment.

15. What is the name of the lowest soil horizon?

A. bedrock
B. magma
C. subsoil
D. topsoil

16. What makes up humus?

F. decayed plants and animals
G. fertilizer
H. minerals
J. sediment

Inquiry Skills

17. Why is the ability to **use models** important when studying processes that are part of the rock cycle?

18. What are you looking for when you **compare** rocks?

Critical Thinking

The Big Idea

19. Why is most metamorphic rock harder than the sedimentary rock from which it formed?

20. Jameer is on vacation with his family in Hawai'i. He sees rock formations all around the Kīlauea volcano. Some of these look like the image below. Help Jameer identify the part of the rock cycle shown in the image. What happened just before this step? List two possible steps in the cycle after this one.

CHAPTER 8 Changes to Earth's Surface

What's the Big Idea? **Earth's surface has landforms that have changed and continue to change.**

Essential Questions

Lesson 1
What Are Some of Earth's Landforms?

Lesson 2
What Causes Changes to Earth's Landforms?

Lesson 3
What Are Fossils?

Go online **Student eBook www.hspscience.com**

What do YOU wonder?

Ride the Wave? This formation, near Hyden, Australia, looks like a tumbling wave. But rock can't flow like water. How do you think this landform came to look like a wave? How does this relate to the **Big Idea?**

Wave Rock in Australia

LESSON 1

Essential Question

What Are Some of Earth's Landforms?

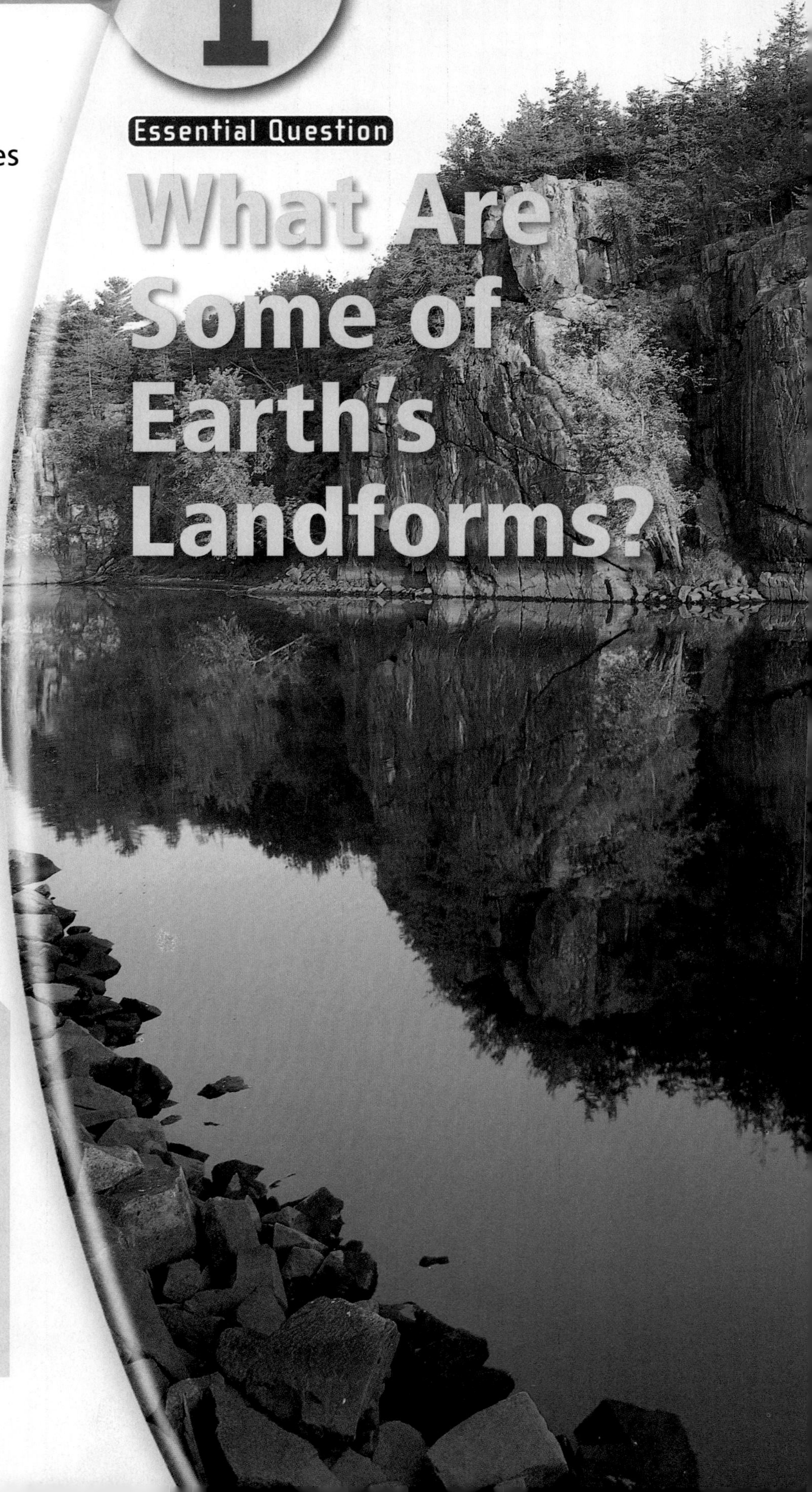

Investigate the shapes of local landforms.

Read and Learn about the different kinds of landforms found on Earth.

Fast Fact

Deep Valley

About 10,000 years ago, water from melting glaciers cut through Earth's crust to form what is now the Upper St. Croix River gorge in Wisconsin. In the Investigate, you will choose a natural landform and make a model of it.

Cliffs along the St. Croix river

Vocabulary Preview

landform [LAND•fawrm] A natural feature on Earth's surface (p. 324)

mountain [MOUNT•uhn] An area that is higher than the land around it (p. 324)

topography [tuh•PAHG•ruh•fee] The shape of landforms in an area (p. 326)

Investigate

Make a Landform Model

Guided Inquiry

Start with Questions

There is a huge gap in the glacier these penguins are crossing! The penguins will have to find a way around it.

- What do you think caused the crack in the glacier?
- What might cause cracks in rock?

Investigate to find out. Then read to find out more.

Prepare to Investigate

Inquiry Skill Tip

As you build your model, pay attention to the way it looks. Observe the changes that occur as you build a model that resembles a local landform.

Materials

- paper
- pencil
- modeling clay
- heavy cardboard

Make a Data Table

Sketch of Landform	Predictions

Follow This Procedure

1. Look for a landform in your area. It might be a mountain, hill, dune, valley, plateau, canyon, or cliff.
2. **Observe** the landform's shape and size. Sketch the landform on a sheet of paper.
3. Get a piece of modeling clay from your teacher. Place it on a sheet of cardboard.
4. Use clay and your sketch of the landform to **make a model**.

Draw Conclusions

1. Which type of landform did you **make a model** of with the clay?
2. **Predict** how the landform might change in the future. What might cause the change? Write your predictions down.
3. **Inquiry Skill** Scientists often **observe** objects in nature and then use models to understand them better. How did **observing** the model help you understand the landform you chose?

Independent Inquiry

Use the information on a topographic map to make a model of one of the landforms shown on the map.

Read and Learn

VOCABULARY
landform p. 324
mountain p. 324
topography p. 326

SCIENCE CONCEPTS
- what major landforms are
- how some landforms form

Focus Skill **COMPARE AND CONTRAST**
Look for ways that landforms differ.

alike — different

Mountains and Hills

Earth's surface looks flat from space. However, it is wrinkled, cracked, and folded into many landforms. A **landform** is a natural feature on Earth's surface.

Mountains are some of Earth's most spectacular landforms. A **mountain** is an area that is higher than the land around it. Mountains are usually at least 500 meters (1,600 ft) tall. Hills look like mountains, but they are smaller.

Mountains form in many ways. Some mountains are volcanoes. Other mountains form when forces bend and fold Earth's crust. Blocks of Earth's crust can get pushed upward to form mountains. It can take millions of years for a chain, or group, of mountains to form.

Focus Skill **COMPARE AND CONTRAST**

How are mountains and hills different?

▼ **The temperature of the air decreases as you move up a mountain. Snow and ice always cover the tops of the highest mountains.**

▼ **These hills are green because of plentiful rainfall. Hills in dry areas can be bare and rocky.**

This wide, green valley is in Scotland. Its wide floor and gently sloping sides are different from those of a canyon.

Palo Duro Canyon in Texas is 193 kilometers (120 mi) long, as much as 32 kilometers (20 mi) wide, and more than 240 meters (790 ft) deep.

Valleys and Canyons

You have learned that mountains are highlands. There are also lowland areas called valleys. A *valley* is an area with higher land around it. Valleys stretch between mountains and between hills.

The bottom of a valley is its floor, and its sides are its walls. There are different kinds of valleys. A canyon is a valley with steep walls. Some canyons are so deep and narrow that sunlight barely reaches the floor. Other canyons, like the one shown here, are wide and open.

Rivers or glaciers form most valleys. The moving water or ice cuts through rock and soil. Erosion from rainfall moves soil and rock from valley walls. Some of this rock and soil settle on valley floors. The floors of many valleys have fertile soil that is excellent for farming.

Focus Skill COMPARE AND CONTRAST

How are a valley and a canyon alike?

Plains and Plateaus

Some parts of Earth's surface are mostly flat. These large, flat landforms are called plains. A plain can have a gently rolling surface. It can even have a slight slope. Plains don't have highlands or deep valleys.

Some plains are inland and others are along coasts. A plain that slopes toward the sea along a coast is a coastal plain.

Some plains extend along rivers. Sometimes rivers overflow their banks, causing floods. When the floods go down, soil and sediment are left behind. This soil helps form plains called floodplains.

A *plateau* (pla•TOH) is also a flat area, but it is higher than the land around it. The edges of plateaus can form steep cliffs. As plateaus erode, they can become other landforms. A much smaller landform with the shape of a plateau is a mesa (MAY•suh). A smaller mesa is a butte (BYOOT). These landforms sometimes make unusual topography (tuh•PAHG•ruh•fee). **Topography** is the shape of landforms in an area.

Focus Skill **COMPARE AND CONTRAST**

How are plateaus and plains alike?

This plateau is in Australia. Weathering and erosion are wearing away parts of it.

▼ Many farms are located on plains. This wide plain in Asia has rich soil.

Deltas can look like different things from space. Some deltas resemble fans or triangles, while another delta might resemble a bird's foot.

Deltas and Dunes

Deltas and dunes look very different, but both are formed by the movement of sand and sediment.

Deltas form at the ends of rivers. Fast-moving rivers carry away bits of soil and rock. When a river enters a lake or an ocean, it slows down. When this happens, the water can't carry as much material. It drops most of the rock and soil where it meets the lake or ocean, forming a delta.

Dunes form in dry areas or along sandy coasts. They form where wind carries sand. As the wind flows over rocks or other barriers, its speed slows. The wind drops the sand around the object. Over time, a dune forms.

Focus Skill COMPARE AND CONTRAST

What is different about the way deltas and dunes form?

The dunes of White Sands, New Mexico, are made of the mineral gypsum. The highest dunes are about 18 meters (60 ft) tall.

Islands

Every *island* is a body of land surrounded by water. Islands differ in the way they form. Some were once linked to a mainland. When the sea level rose thousands of years ago, water covered the land that formed the link. The British Isles formed this way.

Other islands are the tops of volcanoes that have been built up from the sea floor. Alaska's Aleutian Islands formed this way. Barrier islands are thin, sandy islands that build up along coasts. Barrier islands form where waves deposit sand near the shore.

Coral islands form from the remains of tiny sea animals. The remains form huge structures of limestone in the sea. There are many coral islands in the Pacific Ocean.

Focus Skill **COMPARE AND CONTRAST**

How are coral islands different from all other types of islands?

Insta-Lab

Make an Island

Build a hill out of clay. Place it in the middle of an aluminum pan. Pour water into the pan until only the top is above water. How is your model like the islands shown on this page?

This view from the air shows a chain, or group, of islands.

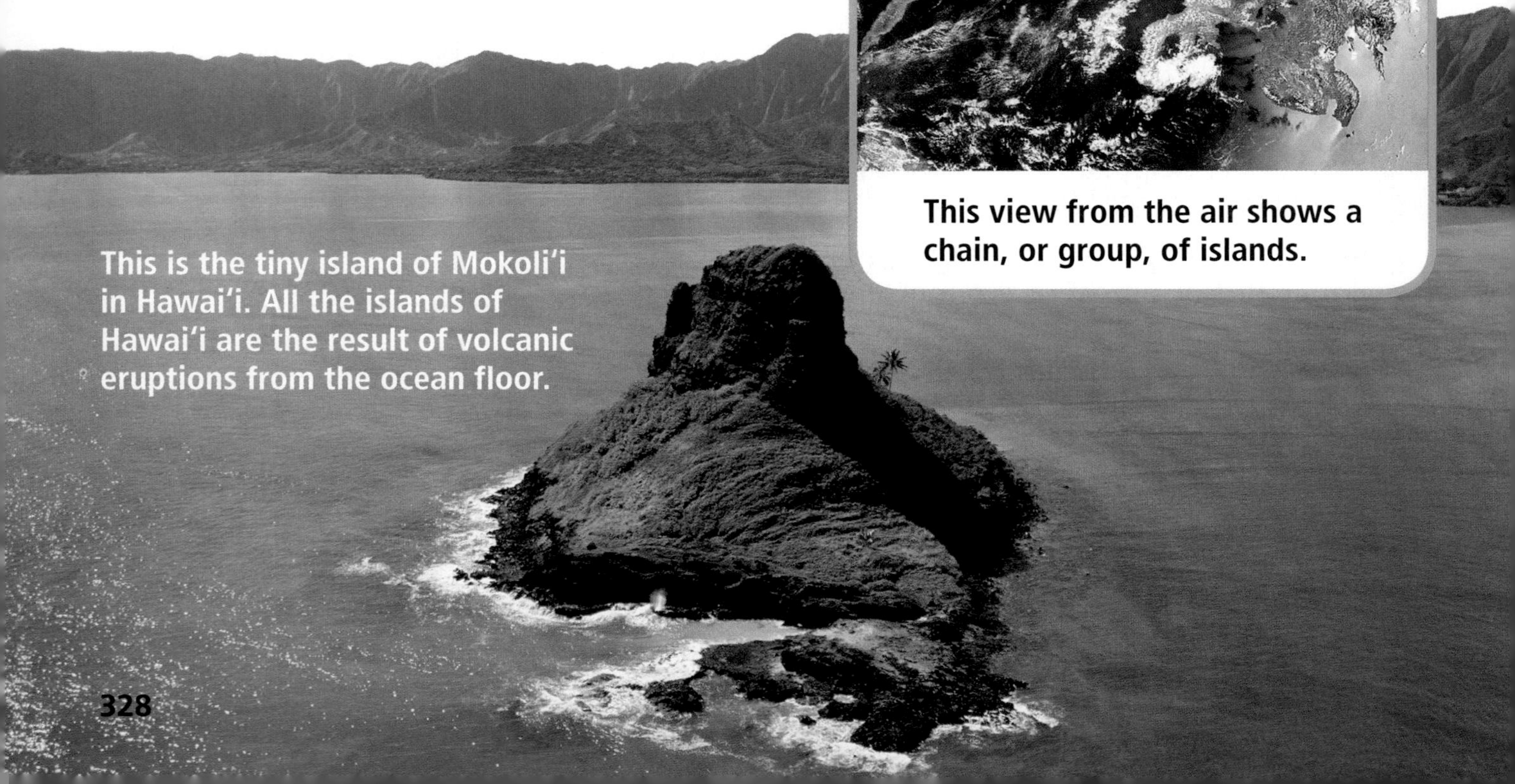

This is the tiny island of Mokoli'i in Hawai'i. All the islands of Hawai'i are the result of volcanic eruptions from the ocean floor.

Essential Question

What Are Some of Earth's Landforms?

In this lesson, you learned that Earth's surface takes many shapes—that is, it has different landforms. Most of these landforms were formed by natural processes.

1. Focus Skill COMPARE AND CONTRAST Draw and complete a graphic organizer to show how mountains and hills are different.

alike	different

2. **SUMMARIZE** Write a summary of this lesson. Begin with this sentence: *Mountains are one kind of landform on Earth.*

3. **DRAW CONCLUSIONS** How might a mountain become a plain over a long time?

4. **VOCABULARY** Write a definition of one of the vocabulary terms. Use your own words.

Test Prep

5. **CRITICAL THINKING** You want to start a farm. Should you choose land on a mountain or in a valley? Explain your answer.

6. Which of these landforms is flat or partly flat?
   A. hill
   B. plateau
   C. dune
   D. mountain

Make Connections

Writing

Expository Writing

Choose an important landform outside the United States. Write an **explanation** of how it formed. Share your explanation with classmates.

9÷3 Math

Organize Data

Look in an encyclopedia to find the world's five largest islands. Arrange them in a table in order from the largest to the smallest.

Social Studies

Use a Map

Locate two major landforms on a map of the United States. They can be a mountain, a valley, a canyon, a plateau, a plain, a delta, or an island. Write a one-sentence caption to identify each landform.

LESSON 2

Essential Question

What Causes Changes to Earth's Landforms?

Investigate how volcanoes erupt.

Read and Learn what causes changes to Earth's landforms.

Fast Fact

Rocky Coast

These tall rocks along the Australian coast are sea stacks. They are all that is left of a rocky cliff that was pounded to pieces by ocean waves. In the Investigate, you will find out about the forces that shape volcanoes.

Sea stacks along the Australian coast

Vocabulary Preview

volcano [vahl•KAY•noh] A mountain that forms as lava flows through a crack onto Earth's surface (p. 336)

earthquake [ERTH•kwayk] The shaking of Earth's surface caused by movement of rock in the crust (p. 337)

deposition [dep•uh•ZISH•uhn] The dropping of bits of rock and soil by a river as it flows (p. 338)

glacier [GLAY•sher] A large, moving block of ice (p. 339)

Volcanic Eruptions

Guided Inquiry

Start with Questions

This lava might look cool and solid, but underneath the black crust, there is still hot molten rock. Warning signs are posted so people do not try to walk on it.

- What happens when volcanoes erupt?
- What happens when lava meets water?

Investigate to find out. Then read to find out more.

Prepare to Investigate

Inquiry Skill Tip

It can be difficult to study volcanoes. Observing the movement of lava is dangerous because of the heat. As you use a model in this Investigate, remember that lava is a liquid, not a solid.

Materials

- 2-L plastic bottle
- small pieces of modeling clay
- aluminum pie plate
- puffed rice cereal
- funnel
- air pump

Make an Observation Chart

Action	Observation

Follow This Procedure

1. Ask your teacher to make a hole near the bottom of a bottle. Stick the bottom of the bottle to a pie plate with clay.
2. Use a funnel to add cereal to the bottle until it is one-fourth full.
3. Attach an air pump to the hole in the bottle. Make sure the nozzle points down. Put a piece of clay around the hole to make it airtight.
4. Pump air into the bottle. **Observe** what happens.

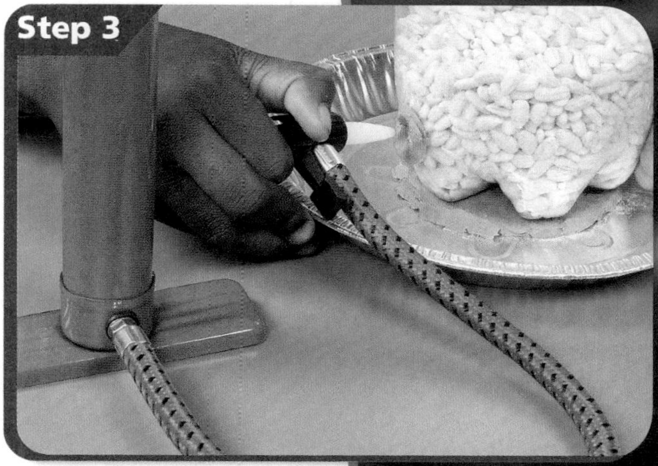

Draw Conclusions

1. What happened to the cereal when you pumped air into the bottle?
2. **Predict** how the model would change if you made it larger.
3. **Inquiry Skill** Scientists often **use models** to help them understand things that happen in nature. How does the bottle model an erupting volcano?

Independent Inquiry

Make models using fine sand and gravel to test this hypothesis: A volcano that forms from thick lava is steeper than one that forms from thin lava.

VOCABULARY
volcano p. 336
earthquake p. 337
deposition p. 338
glacier p. 339

SCIENCE CONCEPTS
- characteristics of Earth's structure
- what forces change Earth's surface

Focus Skill CAUSE AND EFFECT
Look for causes of changes to Earth's surface.

cause → effect

Layers of Earth

Every minute of every day, you are on Earth's surface. If you could cut open Earth and look inside, you would find the four layers shown in the diagram below.

Earth's thin outer layer is the crust. The crust includes the land that makes up the continents as well as the land under the oceans.

The mantle is the rock layer below the crust. Deep below Earth's surface, the temperature rises. The upper parts of the mantle are so hot that the rock can flow. In some places the rock is melted to form *magma.*

At Earth's center is the core. The core is made mostly of iron and nickel. The outer core is liquid. The inner core is solid. The inner core is almost as hot as the surface of the sun. It is solid because there is so much pressure on it.

Earth's crust and upper mantle are broken into large slabs of rock called plates. The plates move on a layer of the mantle that can flow like taffy.

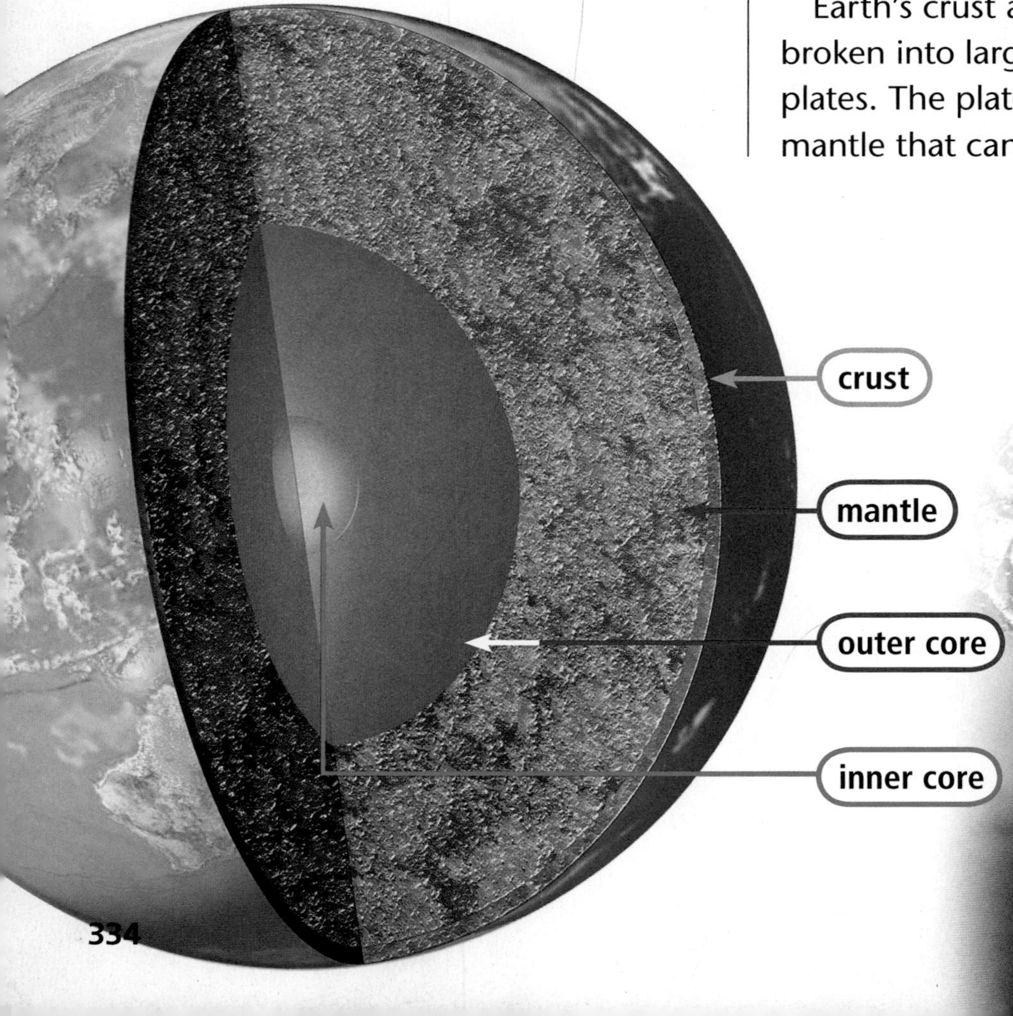

◀ **The crust is Earth's thinnest layer. It is solid rock. The crust sits on top of the mantle, which is Earth's thickest layer. Earth's core is mostly metal, and it's very hot. Temperatures in the core reach as high as 5000°C (9000°F).**

You can't see the movement of these plates. The plates move only a few centimeters per year. Over a long time, this movement leads to the formation of different landforms.

Plates move in several ways. Some move toward each other. When two land plates meet, the edges crush and fold as one is pushed down under the other, forming mountain chains. Where a land plate and an ocean plate or two ocean plates meet, islands made of volcanic mountains can result.

Some plates travel away from each other. Large cracks can form where the two plates are moving apart. Magma from the mantle oozes up through these cracks. It hardens and makes new crust. Often this happens in the oceans.

Plates can also slide past each other. Where this happens, huge cracks appear at Earth's surface.

Focus Skill **CAUSE AND EFFECT** **What landform can form where two land plates collide?**

Insta-Lab

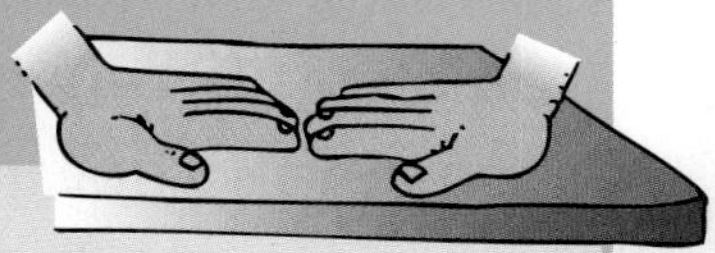

How Mountains Grow

Place both hands flat on a table, with the fingertips facing each other. Keep moving your hands toward each other until your fingertips are pushing against each other. What happens to your fingers? How does this model mountain formation?

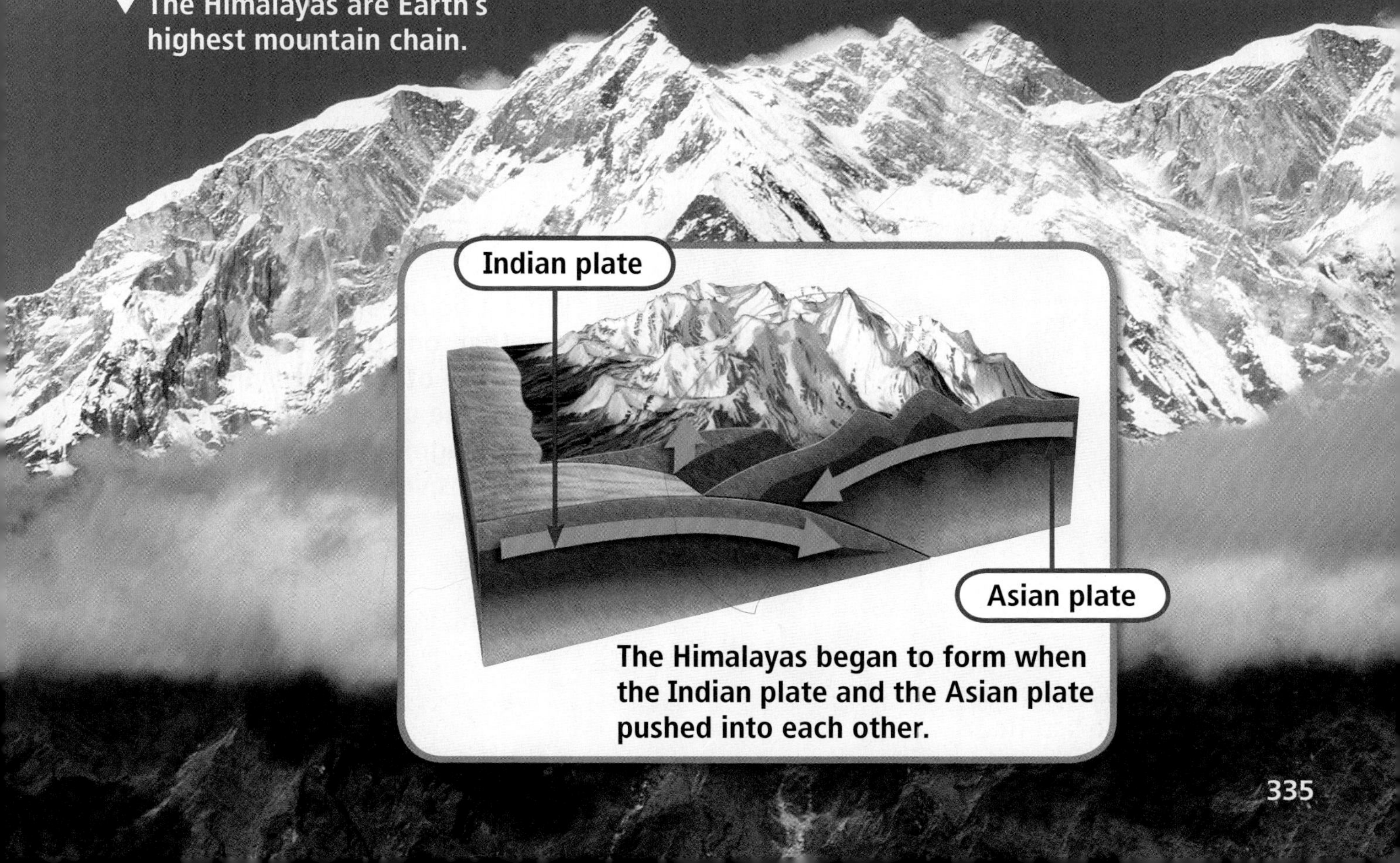

▼ **The Himalayas are Earth's highest mountain chain.**

The Himalayas began to form when the Indian plate and the Asian plate pushed into each other.

Volcanoes and Earthquakes

On the morning of May 18, 1980, the volcano Mount St. Helens, in the state of Washington, erupted. A **volcano** is a mountain that forms as lava flows through a crack onto Earth's surface. This major eruption threw ash 19 kilometers (12 mi) into the air. The lava, ash, rock, and hot gases that shoot out of volcanoes change the land. Hot rock and gas from Mount St. Helens covered the land, filled in streams, and destroyed forests around the volcano. Since 1980, there have been many small eruptions of Mount St. Helens.

There are different types of volcanoes. One type is *composite volcanoes.* They are made of layers of lava, rock, and ash. They can have steep peaks and are usually explosive when they erupt. Hawai`i has *shield volcanoes.* These huge mountains erupt slowly, and lava flows steadily down their gently sloping sides. *Cinder cone volcanoes* are small and have steep sides. They shoot cinders, ash and chunks of rock into the air and down their slopes.

When two ocean plates push together, one plate is forced under the other. In the process, part of the upper plate melts and forms magma. This magma rises and forms volcanoes.

The base of this Indonesian volcano is on the sea floor.

Science Up Close

For more links and animations, go to **www.hspscience.com**

Strike-Slip Fault

A seismogram shows the movement of Earth's surface during an earthquake. ▶

At a strike-slip fault, slabs of rock slide past each other. Movement at the fault can rip apart roads, bridges, pipelines, and other structures. ▼

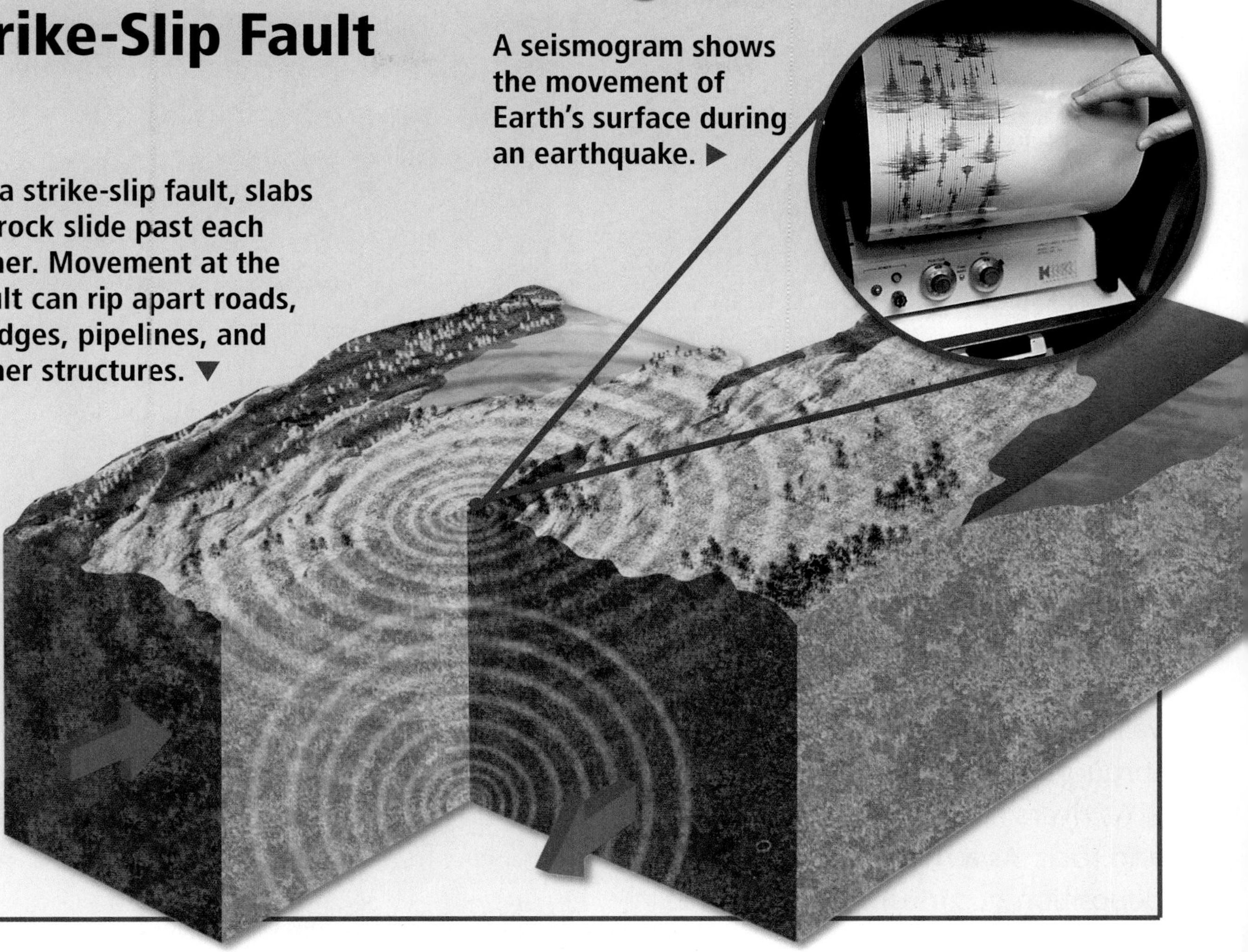

Movement between two plates can cause earthquakes. An **earthquake** is the shaking of Earth's surface caused by movement of rock in the crust.

Most earthquakes occur along faults. A *fault* is a break in the crust, where rock moves. If the movement is sudden, it can send out waves of energy that move through the crust. This energy can cause shaking and cracking in the crust and Earth's surface.

▲ The motion of an earthquake tore this Californian highway into several pieces.

Focus Skill CAUSE AND EFFECT

What is the cause of most earthquakes?

Rivers

Rivers are found all over Earth. Although they aren't as dramatic as volcanoes or earthquakes, rivers can cause big changes to Earth's surface. Rivers often take longer to affect the land around them.

Rivers flow through valleys. The shape of a valley depends on the way the river runs through it. In steep areas, rivers move quickly. The rushing water cuts into the soil and rock. These valleys are narrow and V-shaped.

As a river gets older, its valley becomes less steep. The floor of the river becomes more level. The valley walls become farther apart. As a result, older rivers often have wide valleys with flat floors. They flow through the valleys in wide curves.

As rivers flow, they carry soil and rock. As a river moves, deposition occurs. In **deposition** (dep•uh•ZISH•uhn), water that carries sediment drops bits of rock and soil. As water slows down, more deposition occurs. Deposition builds landforms such as deltas and floodplains.

Focus Skill CAUSE AND EFFECT

What causes deposition to increase?

Rivers on wide plains flow in large curves like these.

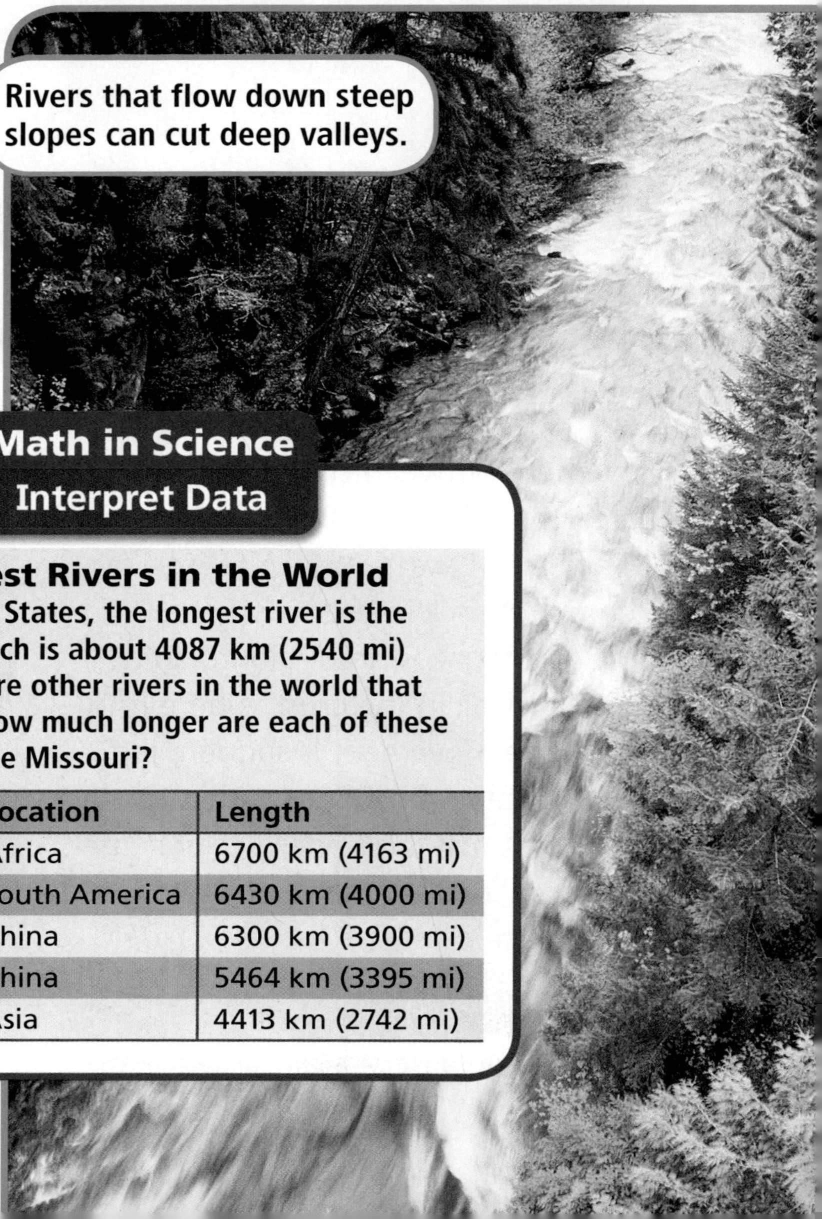

Rivers that flow down steep slopes can cut deep valleys.

Math in Science
Interpret Data

Longest Rivers in the World

In the United States, the longest river is the Missouri, which is about 4087 km (2540 mi) long. There are other rivers in the world that are longer. How much longer are each of these rivers than the Missouri?

River	Location	Length
Nile	Africa	6700 km (4163 mi)
Amazon	South America	6430 km (4000 mi)
Yangtze	China	6300 km (3900 mi)
Huang He	China	5464 km (3395 mi)
Amur	Asia	4413 km (2742 mi)

Cracks appear in this glacier as it flows slowly down a mountain valley. Glaciers may move as little as a few centimeters or as much as several meters per day.

Fiords form where the sea has flooded valleys formed by glaciers.

Glaciers

In some places, snowfall is high and temperature is low. Sometimes more snow falls in winter than melts in summer. The snow piles up year after year. As it thickens, it turns to ice. If the mass of ice starts to move downhill, it becomes a glacier (GLAY•sher). A **glacier** is a large, moving mass of ice.

There are two main types of glaciers—alpine glaciers and ice sheets. Alpine glaciers flow down mountain valleys. The ice scrapes the floor and sides of the valley as it moves. The glacier widens the valley, giving it a U shape. *Fiords* (FYAWRDZ) form where these valleys reach the coast. Ice sheets are huge glaciers that cover large areas, such as Antarctica and Greenland.

Thousands of years ago, ice sheets covered much of Earth. As these ice sheets moved over the land, they shaped many landforms people see today.

Focus Skill CAUSE AND EFFECT

What causes glaciers to form?

Wind and Waves

You have seen trees bend and move on a windy day. Wind can affect the way Earth's surface looks. In dry areas and along sandy coasts, soil is dry and loose. There aren't many plants. Wind lifts particles and carries them.

Wind slams sand into rocky surfaces. The wind-blown sand makes pits and grooves in rock. Wind also carries sand and deposits it in dunes, as you learned in Lesson 1.

Waves break down rocky cliffs. As the cliffs crumble, the land moves further back. Structures such as sea arches and sea stacks are left behind. As the sea moves further in, the structures are left offshore.

Waves also change the shape of sandy coastlines. They remove sand from some areas and deposit it in other places. This erosion and deposition of sand creates beaches, sand bars, and barrier islands along the shore.

Focus Skill **CAUSE AND EFFECT** **What conditions are needed for wind erosion?**

▼ The pounding of waves carved this sea arch. The hole formed when water wore away rock at the center of a solid formation sticking out into the sea.

Erosion from waves has washed away the cliff under this house. It will soon topple onto the shore below.

Essential Question

What Causes Changes to Earth's Landforms?

In this lesson, you learned that Earth's landforms can change. These changes can be fast, like changes caused by volcanoes and earthquakes, or slow, like changes caused by rivers, glaciers, and wind.

1. Focus Skill **CAUSE AND EFFECT** Draw and complete a graphic organizer showing the effects of plate movement.

2. **SUMMARIZE** Write a summary of this lesson. Begin with this sentence: *The Himalayas are young mountains.*

3. **DRAW CONCLUSIONS** Which has a greater effect on landforms—wind or water? Why do you think that?

4. **VOCABULARY** Make a crossword puzzle, using the vocabulary terms from Lessons 1 and 2.

Test Prep

5. **CRITICAL THINKING** What evidence of wave erosion might be seen in landforms along the shore?

6. What is magma?
   A. hot gases
   B. hard rock
   C. melted rock
   D. hot metals

Make Connections

Writing

Descriptive Writing

Write a **report** that describes the journey of a piece of rock that erupts from a volcano. Follow the rock from the mantle until it shoots out of the volcano onto Earth's surface.

Math

Make a Bar Graph

Use an encyclopedia to identify the world's five most deadly earthquakes during the past 100 years. Use the number of people who died as the measure. Make a bar graph to compare the earthquakes.

Art

Illustration

Read in a science book or an encyclopedia about a major earthquake or volcanic eruption. Make a drawing that shows some part of what happened. Write a caption to describe it.

LESSON 3

Essential Question

What Are Fossils?

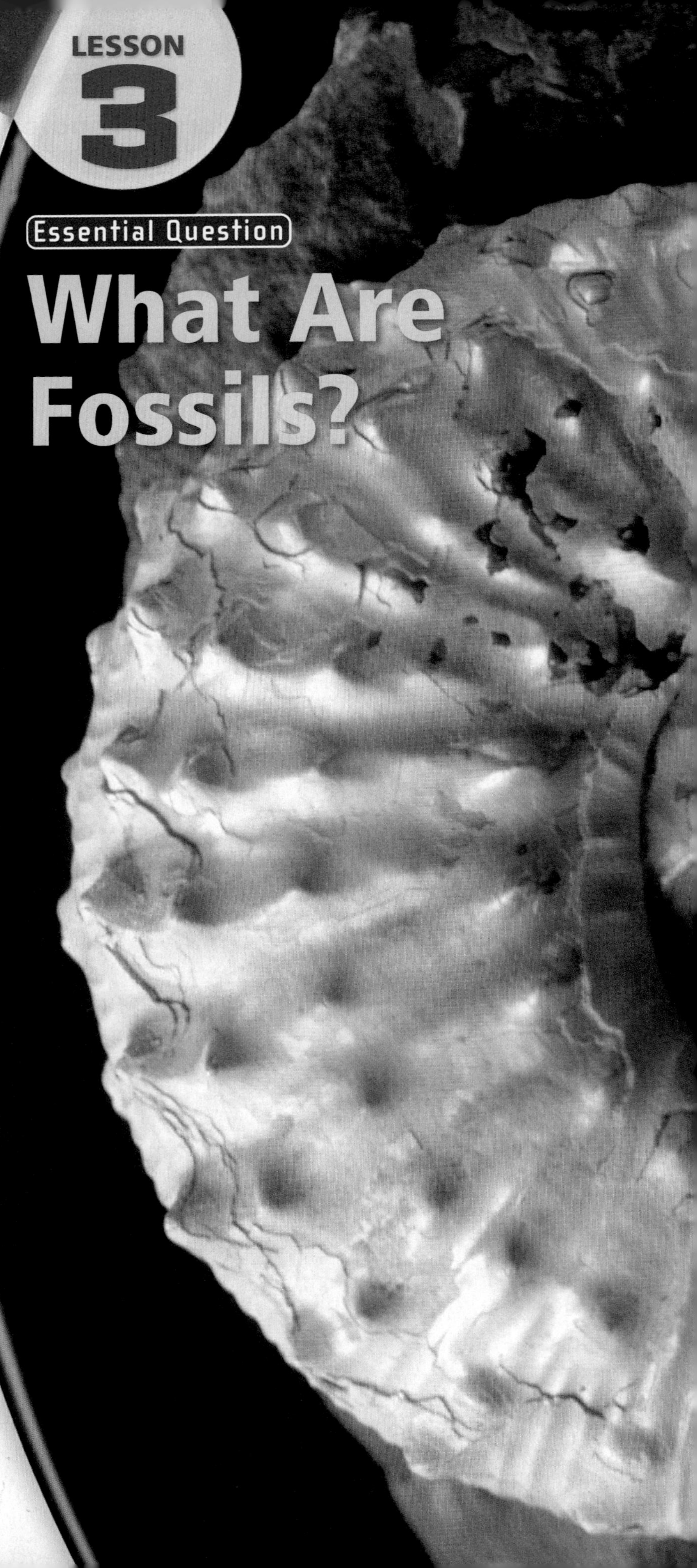

Investigate what an animal's tracks can tell you about the animal.

Read and Learn how fossils form and what we can learn from them.

Fast Fact

Big Shell
Ammonites (AM•uh•nyts) were animals similar to squids with shells. They lived millions of years ago. The largest ammonite fossil found so far has a shell almost 2 meters ($6\frac{1}{2}$ ft) across. In the Investigate, you will model another type of fossil.

Ammonite fossil

Vocabulary Preview

fossil [FAHS•uhl] The remains or traces of a plant or animal that lived long ago (p. 346)

fossil record [FAHS•uhl REK•erd] The information about Earth's history that is contained in fossils (p. 348)

Sets of Animal Tracks

Guided Inquiry

Start with Questions

An animal left this track in the sand as it walked.

- Can you tell what kind of animal it is from just its tracks?
- What information could we gather from an old track?

Investigate to find out. Then read to find out more.

Prepare to Investigate

Inquiry Skill Tip

Use your knowledge of the ecosystem to predict which animal tracks you would see in a nighttime version of your picture.

Materials

- poster board
- markers, crayons, or colored pencils
- animal footprint stamps
- ink pad

Make an Observation Chart

Order in Which the Other Group's Tracks Were Made	Reasons for the Order You Chose

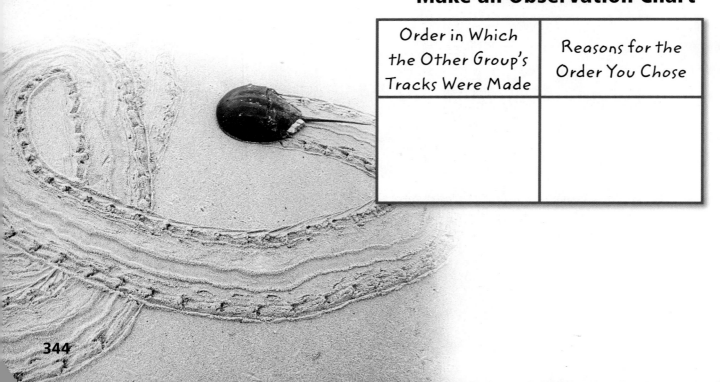

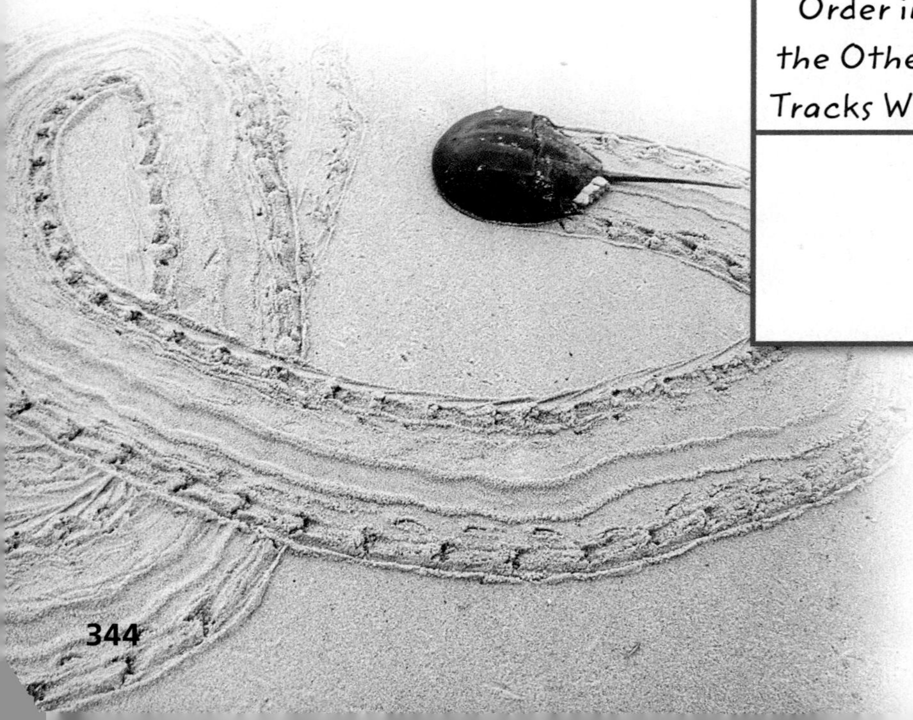

Follow This Procedure

1. Old animal tracks, or fossil footprints, help scientists learn about animals from the past. On poster board, draw a picture of an area where you might find animal tracks, such as a riverbank or a sandy beach.

2. Each person in your group should choose a different animal. Using an ink pad and stamps or other materials, mark the animal's tracks on the poster board. Keep a record of which animal made tracks first, second, third, and so on.

3. Trade finished poster boards with another group. Figure out the order in which the other group's tracks were made. **Record** your conclusions in an ordered list. Give reasons for the order you choose.

Draw Conclusions

1. Did all the animals move in the same way? How could you tell what kind of animal made the tracks?
2. **Inquiry Skill** Scientists often examine an ecosystem at different times of day to see different animals that are out at different times. **Predict** which tracks you might see if the picture showed tracks of night animals.

Independent Inquiry

Make animal tracks on a sheet of paper. Have a classmate infer from the tracks how the animal moves. Does it slither, walk, or jump?

VOCABULARY
fossil p. 346
fossil record p. 348

SCIENCE CONCEPTS
- what fossils are and how they form
- what the fossil record is

Focus Skill SEQUENCE
Look for the steps in the formation of fossils.

Fossils

Have you ever seen a movie about dinosaurs? The movie probably showed how dinosaurs looked, how they moved, and what they ate. Dinosaurs became extinct millions of years ago. That was long before there were people on Earth. So how do people today know so much about dinosaurs?

People today know about many plants and animals of the past because of fossils. A **fossil** is the remains or traces of an organism that lived long ago.

Most fossils form in sedimentary rock. First, sediment covers an organism. Then, the sediment hardens into rock, preserving the fossil shape. The soft parts of organisms break down quickly and decay.

Molds and casts, like those of this trilobite, are common fossil types.

Mold and Cast Formation

1 Sediment covers a clam. The soft parts of the clam decay.

2 Its shell leaves a clam-shaped hole in the sedimentary rock that forms. This is a fossil *mold*.

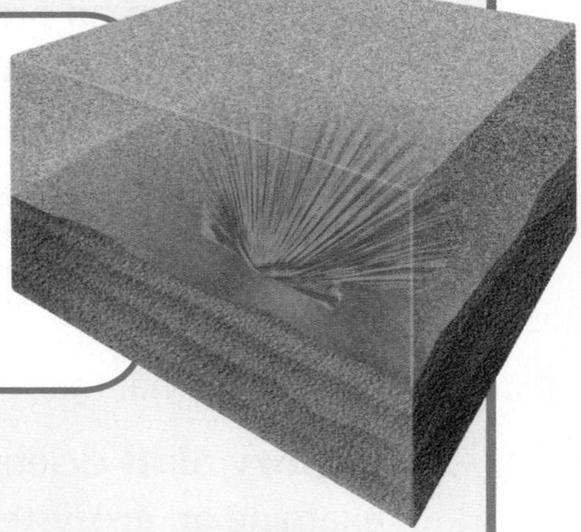

3 The mold fills with minerals. They form a *cast* in the shape of the clam inside the rock.

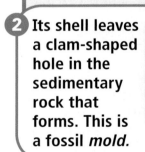

▲ Minerals have seeped into these dinosaur eggs and turned them into stone.

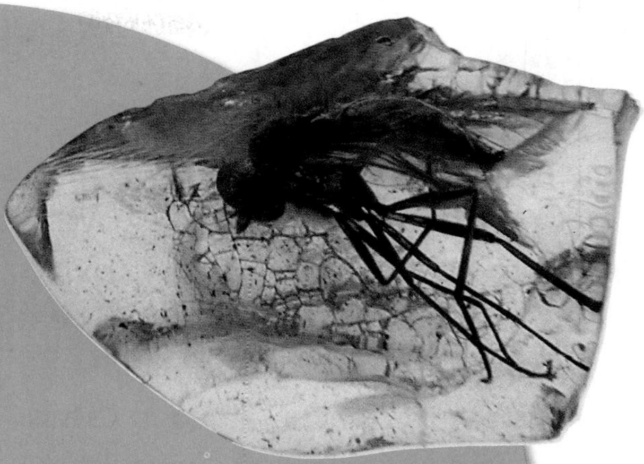

▲ Amber has encased this insect. Amber is sticky tree sap that trapped a living insect and then hardened around it.

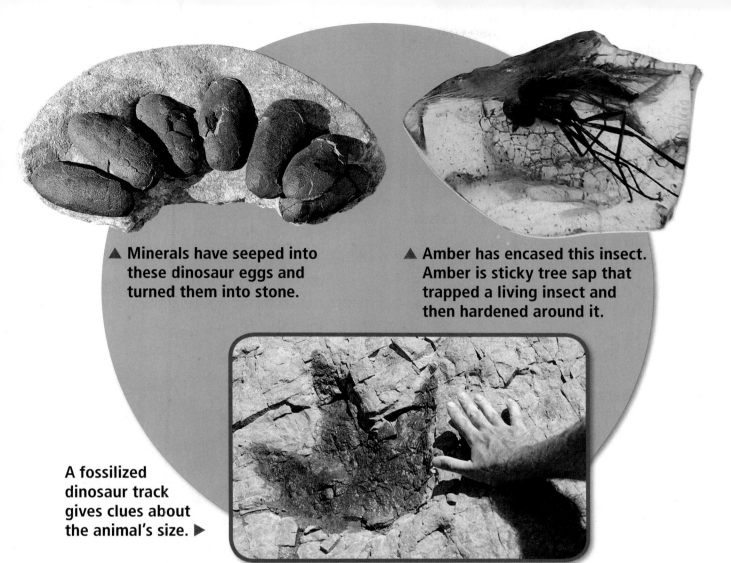

A fossilized dinosaur track gives clues about the animal's size. ▶

Because of this, most fossils are formed from only the hard parts of living things, such as shells, bones, and teeth. The numbered diagram shows the steps of forming a mold and cast fossil.

There are other kinds of fossils. When minerals fill the cells of once-living things, a different kind of fossil forms. Petrified wood is an example. It is the wood of a tree that has been replaced by rock. The Petrified Forest, in Arizona, has thousands of stone logs that were trees millions of years ago.

Another type of fossil is a trace fossil. It doesn't show how a whole plant or animal looked, but it tells something about it. A fossil footprint is a trace fossil that helps tell about an animal's size or how it moved. Fossils of animal droppings show what an animal ate.

Some fossils are the remains of whole animals. They were trapped in ice or tree sap that hardened. Scientists have found woolly mammoths preserved in ice in Siberia. These animals died long ago. People know about them because of fossil evidence.

Focus Skill SEQUENCE

How do a mold and a cast form?

Fossil Record

Earth is about 4.5 billion years old. People have lived on Earth for a very small part of that time. Scientists have found clues about Earth's past by using fossils as a record of ancient times. The **fossil record** is the information about Earth's history that is contained in fossils. It's the main source of clues about Earth's past life and environment.

Because of the fossil record, we know about animals that lived and died long, long ago. Dinosaurs and trilobites are examples of such animals. No one has ever seen a living one. We know about them because people have found and studied their fossils.

The fossil record also shows how some species changed over time. Mammoths lived during the last Ice Age. At that time, ice sheets covered much of Earth. The Ice Age ended, and the mammoths died out. Other animals much like them continued to live. It is likely that the elephants of today are related to some of these animals.

Sediment covered the reef, and it became fossilized over millions of years. ▼

Millions of years ago, this reef was home to corals and many other sea animals. ▶

Scientists study reef fossils to find out about animals that lived in oceans and on reefs long ago.

▲ **A dinosaur laid these eggs millions of years ago.**

The eggs have become part of the fossil record. The size and number of eggs tell scientists about the dinosaur that laid them. ▶

The fossil record helps scientists learn how Earth's environment has changed over time. Today, palm trees live in warm areas. Scientists have found fossils of palm trees in Wyoming, where it's too cold for palms to grow today. From this evidence, scientists infer that the climate there must have been much warmer in the past.

Scientists have also found fossils of sea animals in Kansas. Today, Kansas is far from any ocean. Scientists have inferred that a shallow sea covered parts of Kansas long ago.

Focus Skill SEQUENCE

What does the fossil record tell us about climate change in Wyoming?

Insta-Lab

Fossil Hunt

Get a cupful of soil from outside. Examine it closely with a hand lens. Describe what you see. Can you see any evidence of fossils? Why or why not?

Geologic Time Scale

Many living things have lived and died out during Earth's long history. Scientists use the *geologic time scale* to understand better what was living during each part of this history.

The scale has several divisions. The table here shows the four eras of the time scale. Each era is millions of years long. In the middle of the Paleozoic (pay•lee•uh•ZOH•ik) Era, there were more fish than any other vertebrate. In the next era, the dinosaurs became the most common land vertebrate.

Why is the geologic time scale divided the way it is? The scale shows the way life has changed over time. The fossil record shows that animals died out at certain times during Earth's history. Scientists use these times to mark when eras start and end. For example, trilobites were common at the start of the Paleozoic Era. They died out about 248 million years ago. That marks the end of the Paleozoic Era and the start of the next era. Dinosaurs became extinct about 65 million years ago. That time marks the end of the Mesozoic Era and the start of the present era.

Focus Skill **SEQUENCE** **What are the four main eras of the geologic time scale, from earliest to the present?**

Geologic Time Scale

▼ **The geologic time scale showing eras**

Cenozoic Era

Mesozoic Era

Paleozoic Era

Precambrian Time

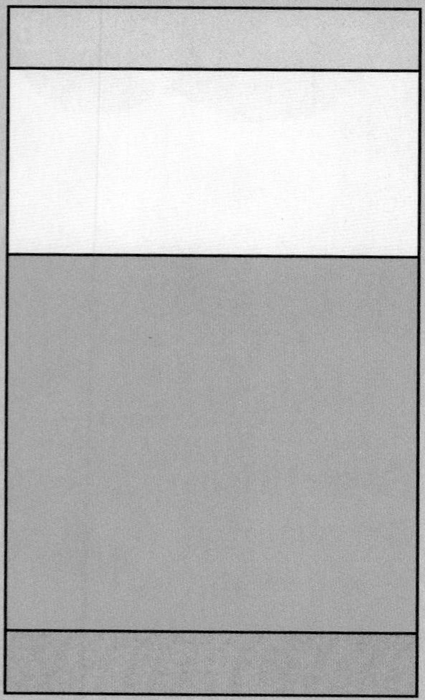

◀ **The Cenozoic Era includes the present. Humans first appeared during this era.**

◀ **Dinosaurs were dominant during the Mesozoic Era. Scientists are still researching what caused them to die out.**

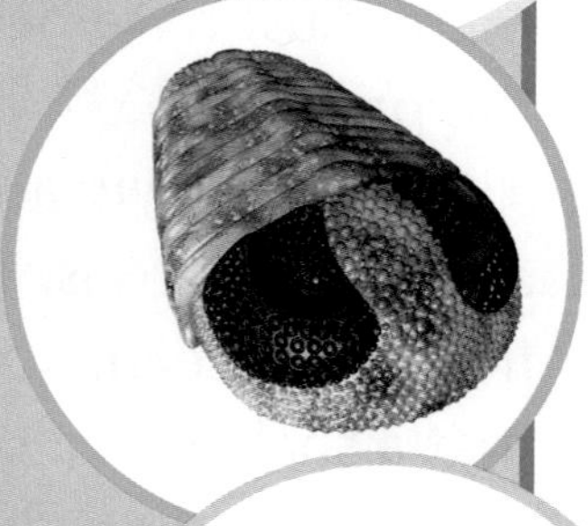

◀ **Trilobites were dominant during part of the Paleozoic Era, but they died out at the end of it.**

◀ **One-celled organisms were dominant during the Precambrian Era, which covers Earth's early history.**

Lesson Review

Essential Question

What Are Fossils?

In this lesson, you learned that fossils are records of animals and plants that lived on Earth long ago. Fossils can provide information about the kinds of animals that lived in an area and about how they lived.

1. **Focus Skill SEQUENCE** Draw and complete a graphic organizer to show how fossil footprints are formed.

2. **SUMMARIZE** Write a summary of this lesson. Begin with this sentence: *Without fossils, people wouldn't know about organisms that lived long ago.*

3. **DRAW CONCLUSIONS** Are fossils being formed today? Explain.

4. **VOCABULARY** Use each of the lesson's vocabulary terms in a sentence.

Test Prep

5. **CRITICAL THINKING** In which type of rock are you most likely to find a fossil? Why?

6. Which kind of fossil is a dinosaur footprint?
   A. tar pit fossil
   B. cast fossil
   C. petrified fossil
   D. trace fossil

Make Connections

Writing

Narrative Writing

Suppose you are hiking near a cliff. You see a large bone trapped in rock. Write a **story** that describes the animal whose fossil you found. Tell how you think it lived and how the fossil formed.

Math

Compare Two Whole Numbers

Ammonites were like squids with shells. Use an encyclopedia to find the size of squids today. Compare their size with the size of the largest ammonite.

Social Studies

Make a Brochure

Research a place in the United States where people can see fossils. It could be a national park, a museum, or another type of area. Design a brochure that encourages people to visit it. Share it with the class.

Michael Ballard

People use telescopes most often to study the planets or stars. But Michael Ballard is using a telescope to look at Earth. He is looking at a special type of Earth landform—a volcano. A volcano is an opening in the crust of the Earth from which hot lava and steam erupt.

Michael is studying a volcano named Mount St. Helens in Washington State. He is watching the volcano as steam erupts from its top. In 1980, the top of Mount St. Helens blew off in a huge eruption.

Since then, the volcano has had a few small eruptions, but nothing like in 1980. Recently, Mount St. Helens became active again, sending smoke and steam many kilometers up into the sky. Michael continues to watch the volcano for activity like this with his telescope.

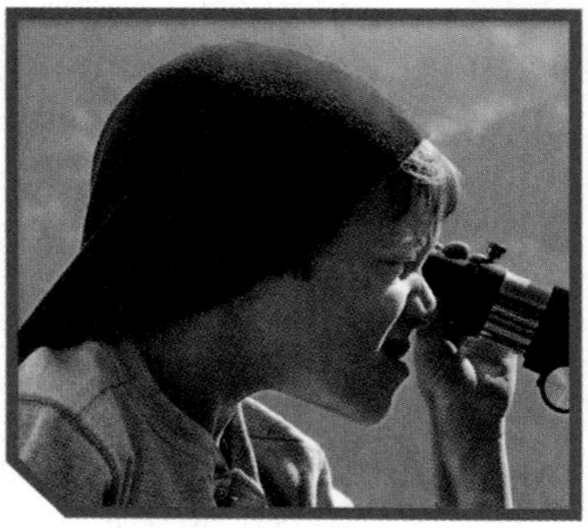

▶ **MICHAEL BALLARD**

▶ Volcano watcher

Think and Write

1. What can Michael learn by watching Mount St. Helens?
2. Is Michael doing science when he watches the volcano?

Career Landscaper

What kind of grass would grow best in this yard? This is a question for a landscaper! Landscapers study how plants live in different areas and how landforms can be changed or used to help plants grow.

▶ **RICHARD HOBLITT**

▶ Volcanologist at Hawai'i Volcanoes Observatory of the United States Geological Survey

Richard Hoblitt

Richard Hoblitt knows a lot about volcanoes. That's because he studies them for a living. He is a volcanologist (vahl•kuh•NAHL•uh•jist).

Dr. Hoblitt actually works on an active volcano. He is on the staff of the Hawai'i Volcanoes Observatory (HVO). Each of the islands of Hawai'i is a volcano sitting on the ocean floor.

At HVO, Hoblitt monitors active volcanoes, such as Kīlauea (kee•low•AY•uh). This Hawaiian volcano has erupted nonstop for many years. Hoblitt also studies the dangers the volcanoes present for people nearby. The scientists at HVO can then warn the public if their instruments tell them a volcano is about to erupt.

Before coming to Hawai'i, Dr. Hoblitt worked at the Cascades Volcano Observatory in the state of Washington. There, he studied the volcanoes of the Cascade Range of Washington, Oregon, and California. One of those volcanoes is Mount St. Helens.

The volcanoes of Hawai'i and those of the Cascades are different. But Dr. Hoblitt finds all volcanoes fascinating—no matter where they are.

Think and Write

1. What does Dr. Hoblitt study?
2. How does Dr. Hoblitt help people by doing his job?

CHAPTER 8

Review and Test Preparation

Vocabulary Review

Use the terms below to complete the sentences. The page numbers tell you where to look in the chapter if you need help.

landform p. 324	**earthquake** p. 337
mountain p. 324	**deposition** p. 338
topography p. 326	**glacier** p. 339
volcano p. 336	**fossil** p. 346

1. A mountain that forms as lava flows through a crack onto Earth's surface is a _______.

2. When water slows down, it drops sediment in a process called _______.

3. Any natural shape on Earth's surface is a _______.

4. The traces or remains of an organism that lived long ago is a _______.

5. The shape of the landforms in an area is _______.

6. The shaking of Earth's surface caused by movement of rock in the crust is an _______.

7. An area that is higher than the land around it is a _______.

8. A huge, moving mass of ice is a _______.

Check Understanding

Write the letter of the best choice.

9. **COMPARE AND CONTRAST** In which pair are the landforms most alike? (Focus Skill)

A. plain/plateau
B. canyon/mesa
C. valley/fault
D. butte/mountain

10. **CAUSE AND EFFECT** Which kind of landform is formed by deposition? (Focus Skill)

F. mountain
G. valley
H. delta
J. plateau

11. Which is the name of the layer of Earth indicated by X?

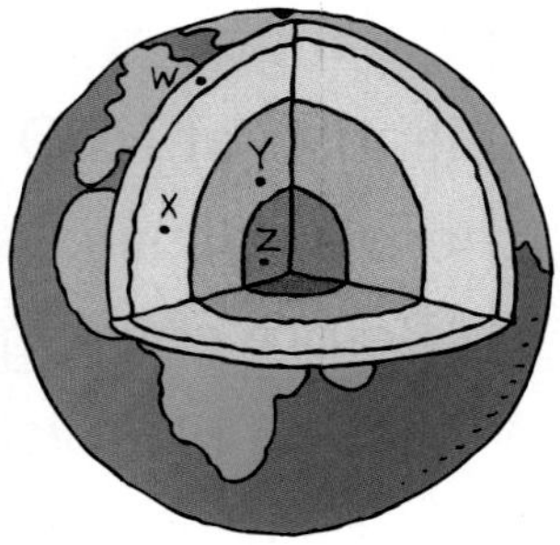

A. inner core
B. crust
C. outer core
D. mantle

12. What happens where two land plates push against each other?

F. glaciers form
G. mountains form
H. islands form
J. new sea floor forms

13. What is happening where these two plates meet?

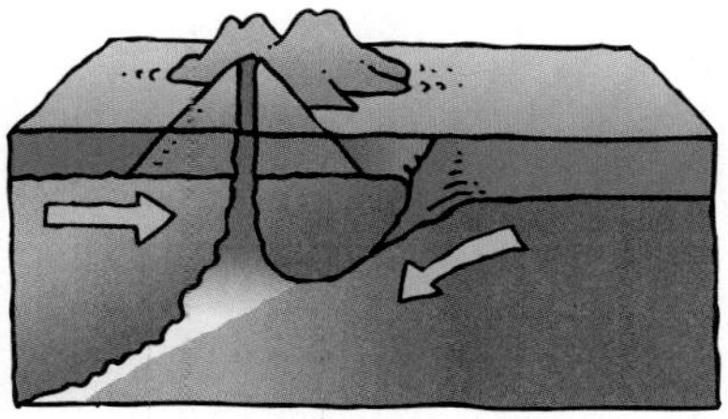

A. The sea floor is spreading apart.
B. An undersea canyon is forming.
C. Volcanic islands are forming.
D. The coast is eroding.

14. Which of these does **not** come from an erupting volcano?
F. ice H. lava
G. gases J. ashes

15. Which of these changes to land does an earthquake cause?
A. Soil is deposited.
B. River valleys become wider.
C. Rocks split in Earth's crust.
D. Lava covers the surface.

16. Which kind of fossil is illustrated by this picture?

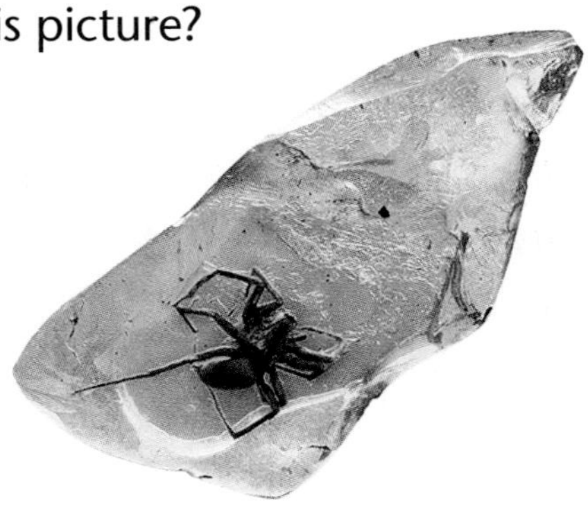

F. amber fossil H. fossil cast
G. trace fossil J. petrified wood

Inquiry Skills

17. Why is it useful to **use a model** to study processes such as stream and river deposition?

18. What would be the importance of being able to **predict** when a volcano will erupt?

Critical Thinking

The Big Idea

19. You discover a fossil in the bottom layer of a canyon wall. You identify the fossil as an animal that lived between 250 and 230 million years ago. What information can this fossil give you about the area where the canyon is located?

20.

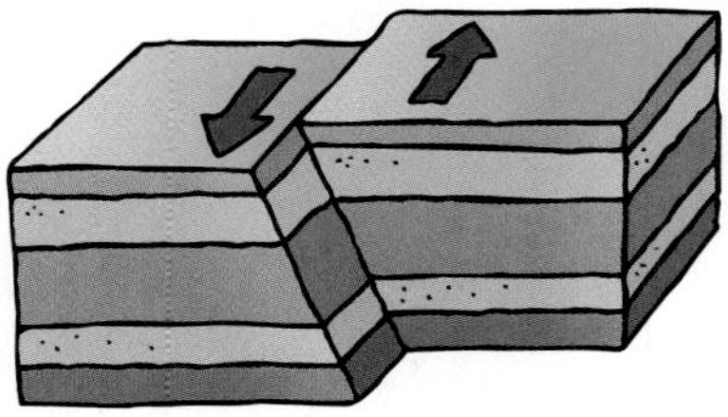

Describe what is happening in the diagram. How is the event changing Earth's surface in the area right around it? How could this affect Earth's surface several kilometers away?

Visual Summary

Tell how each picture shows the **Big Idea** for its chapter.

CHAPTER 7 Big Idea

Rocks and soils are formed and broken down by natural processes.

CHAPTER 8 Big Idea

Earth's surface has landforms that have changed and continue to change.

UNIT D

EARTH SCIENCE

Weather and Space

Unit Inquiry

Model of Solar System

Our solar system is made up of eight unique planets. It takes Earth 365.26 days, which we call one year, to travel around the sun. Do the other planets take the same amount of time to orbit the sun? Build a model of the solar system. Plan and conduct an experiment to find out.

CHAPTER 9

The Water Cycle

What's the Big Idea?

Water moves in a regular cycle that influences the weather.

Essential Questions

Lesson 1
What Is the Water Cycle?

Lesson 2
How Is the Water Cycle Related to Weather?

Lesson 3
How Do Land Features Affect the Water Cycle?

Lesson 4
How Can Weather Be Predicted?

GO online ▶ **Student eBook www.hspscience.com**

Stream during the spring thaw

What do YOU wonder?

Seasons Changing? Each spring as the weather warms, snow and ice in the Yukon begin to melt. The snow and ice turn into millions of gallons of moving water. How does this relate to the **Big Idea?**

LESSON 1

Essential Question

What Is the Water Cycle?

Investigate how to make fresh water from salt water.

Read and Learn about the cycle through which water moves.

Fast Fact

Got Water?

Almost all of Earth's water is in the oceans. In fact, more than 97 percent of Earth's water is ocean water! In the Investigate, you will find out what ocean water is like.

Storm clouds over the ocean

Vocabulary Preview

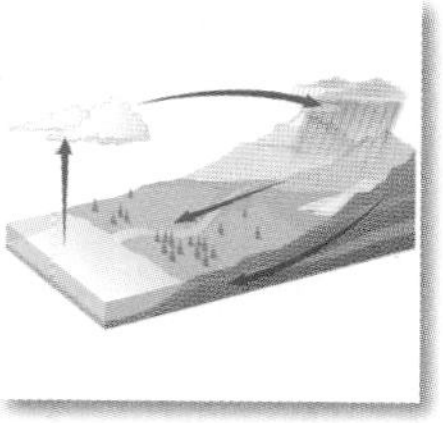

water cycle [WAW•ter SY•kuhl] The movement of water from the surface of Earth into the air and back again (p. 364)

precipitation [pree•sip•uh•TAY•shuhn] Water that falls to Earth (p. 364)

evaporation [ee•vap•uh•RAY•shuhn] The process by which a liquid changes into a gas (p. 366)

condensation [kahn•duhn•SAY•shuhn] The process by which a gas changes into a liquid (p. 367)

From Salt Water to Fresh Water

Guided Inquiry

Start with Questions

These white-water rafters are enjoying water in its liquid state.

- How did the river water get there?
- How does water change forms?

Investigate to find out. Then read to find out more.

Prepare to Investigate

Inquiry Skill Tip

Carry out your entire experiment, and organize your observations before you begin to infer. It is important to have all the information you can gather.

Materials

- 500 mL warm water
- cotton swabs
- plastic wrap
- salt
- large bowl
- large rubber band
- masking tape
- spoon
- small glass jar
- small ball

Make an Observation Chart

Liquid	Taste
Water with salt	
Water in jar	
Water in bowl	

Follow This Procedure

1. Stir two spoonfuls of salt into the warm water. Dip a cotton swab into the mixture. Touch the swab to your tongue. Record what you observe. CAUTION: **Do not share swabs. Throw away the swab.**
2. Put the jar in the center of the bowl. Pour the salt water into the bowl. Be careful not to get any salt water in the jar.
3. Put plastic wrap over the bowl. The wrap should not touch the jar. Use the rubber band to hold the wrap in place.
4. Put the ball on the wrap over the jar. Make sure the wrap doesn't touch the jar.
5. Mark the level of the salt water with a piece of tape on the outside of the bowl. Put the bowl in a sunny spot for one day.
6. Remove the wrap and the ball. Use clean swabs to taste the water in the jar and in the bowl. Record what you observe.

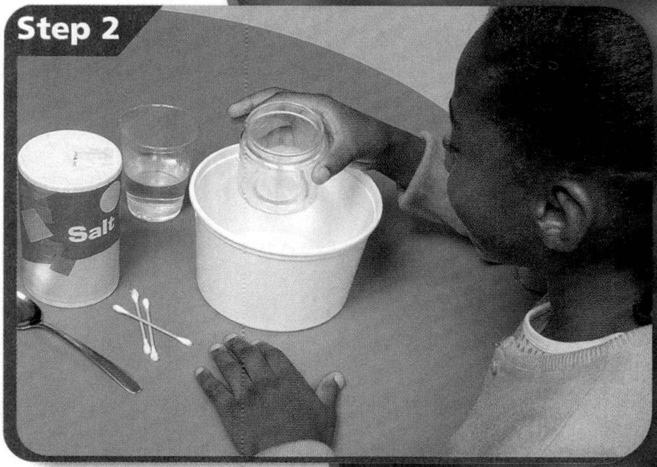

Draw Conclusions

1. What did you observe during the investigation?
2. **Inquiry Skill** Scientists infer based on what they observe. What can you infer is a source of fresh water for Earth?

Independent Inquiry

What would happen if you left the bowl and jar in the sun for several days? Write a hypothesis. Try it!

VOCABULARY
water cycle p. 364
precipitation p. 364
evaporation p. 366
condensation p. 367

SCIENCE CONCEPTS
- what processes make up the water cycle
- how a raindrop forms

Focus Skill SEQUENCE
Look for the order in which events of the water cycle occur.

The Water Cycle

As you are on the way home from school, it suddenly starts raining. Where does rain come from? When rain reaches the ground, where does it go?

Water is constantly moving through the environment. Water moves from the surface of Earth to the air and then back to Earth's surface again in a never-ending process called the **water cycle.**

Energy from the sun drives the water cycle. When the sun's energy warms water on Earth's surface, the water changes from a liquid to a gas.

The gas form of water, known as water vapor, goes into the air. If the water vapor cools, it becomes liquid water again and falls back to Earth. Water that falls back to Earth is called **precipitation** (pree•sip•uh•TAY•shuhn). Precipitation can be rain, snow, sleet, or hail. Rain is liquid water. Snow, sleet, and hail are frozen water. Energy from the sun changes precipitation to water vapor once again. This continues the water cycle.

Focus Skill SEQUENCE **What steps must take place in order for ocean water to become rain?**

A cloud forms when water vapor cools. The water vapor becomes liquid again in a process known as condensation. The liquid water in clouds is in the form of tiny droplets that can stay up in the air.
When the sun warms the surface of water, the water changes to water vapor, a gas. The gas then becomes part of the air.

In the clouds, water droplets can bump into each other and join to make larger droplets. Soon the droplets become heavy and fall to Earth as precipitation.
Some precipitation soaks into the ground. Precipitation can also run over the ground and flow into streams, rivers, lakes, and eventually the ocean.

Parts of the Water Cycle

It's a hot day. To cool off, you take a swim. When you get out of the water, you dry yourself with a towel. You leave the towel in the sunlight while you play with your friends. When you come back, the towel is dry. Where did the water in the towel go?

The water evaporated. **Evaporation** (ee•vap•uh•RAY•shuhn) is the process by which a liquid changes into a gas. A large amount of water evaporates from Earth's oceans, lakes, and rivers every day. But water also evaporates from the soil, from puddles, and even from your skin as you sweat.

Water vapor mixes with other gases in the air. When the wind blows, air moves. The water vapor moves with the air. Sometimes, the water vapor can move very long distances. The water vapor can also move high up into the air.

Science Up Close

How Precipitation Forms

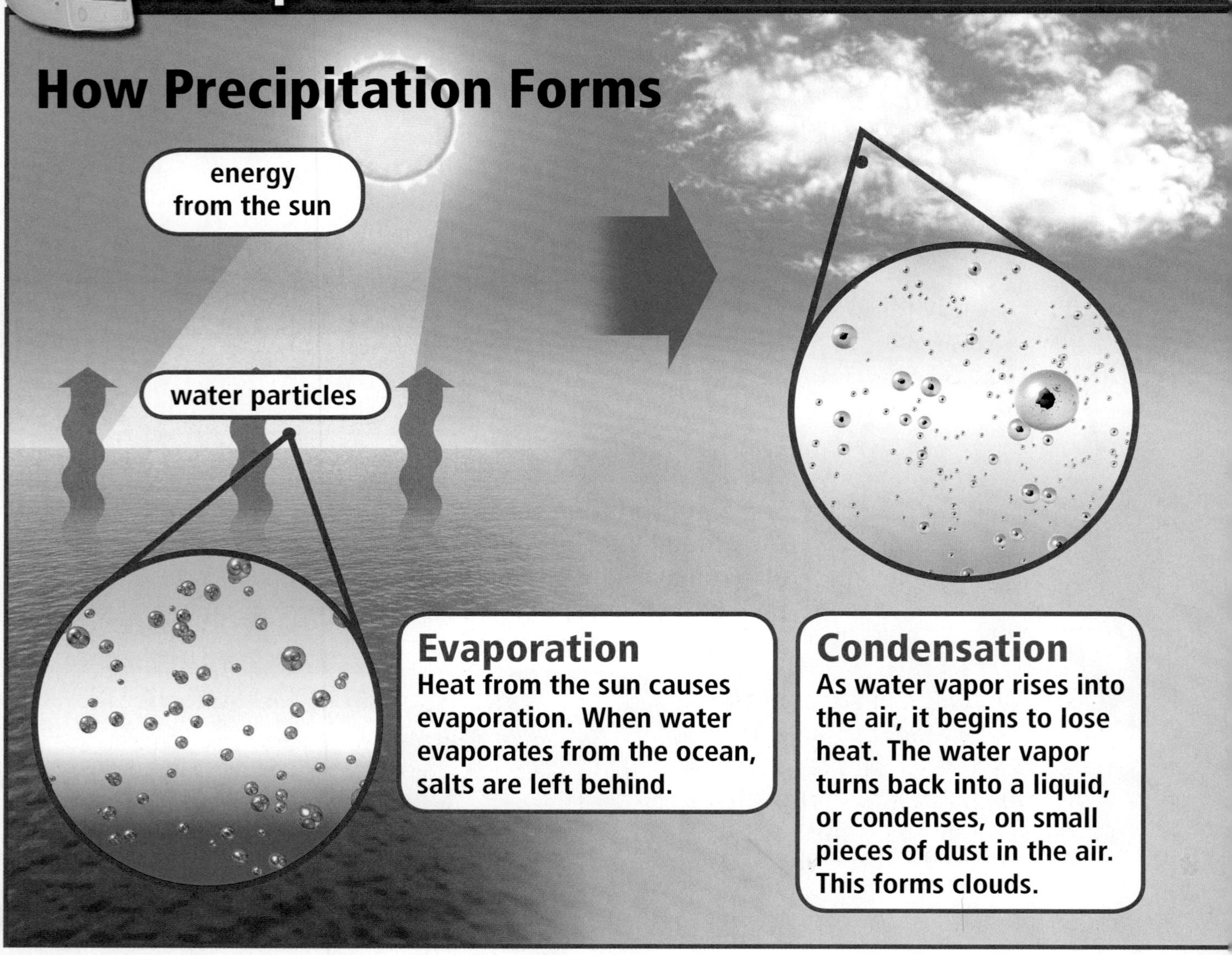

Evaporation
Heat from the sun causes evaporation. When water evaporates from the ocean, salts are left behind.

Condensation
As water vapor rises into the air, it begins to lose heat. The water vapor turns back into a liquid, or condenses, on small pieces of dust in the air. This forms clouds.

When the water vapor moves up in the air, it becomes cooler. If the water vapor cools enough, condensation (kahn•duhn•SAY•shuhn) happens. **Condensation** is the process by which a gas changes into a liquid. Have you ever seen water dripping from an air conditioner? The dripping water is from water vapor that condensed as it cooled.

Air has many small bits of dust in it. When water vapor cools, it condenses on the dust particles. The condensed water and dust particles form clouds. Inside clouds, tiny droplets of water can join to make larger droplets. These droplets can join to make even larger, heavier droplets. When the droplets become too heavy to stay in the air, they fall to Earth as precipitation. The type of precipitation that falls depends on the temperature of the air around it.

Focus Skill **SEQUENCE** **Heat causes a piece of ice to melt. What will happen next?**

For more links and animations, go to **www.hspscience.com**

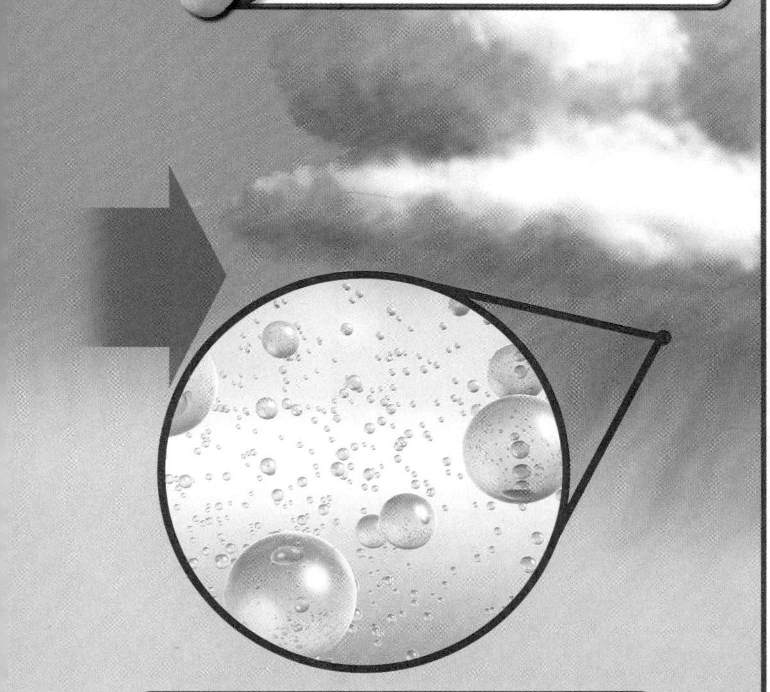

Precipitation

Inside clouds, small water droplets join to form larger droplets. In time, these larger droplets become raindrops that fall to Earth. The water in raindrops is fresh water.

Insta-Lab

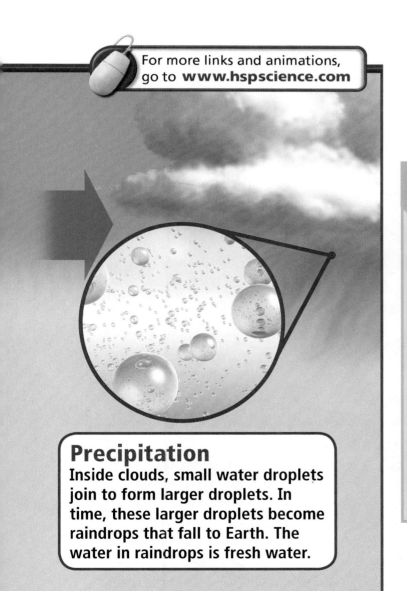

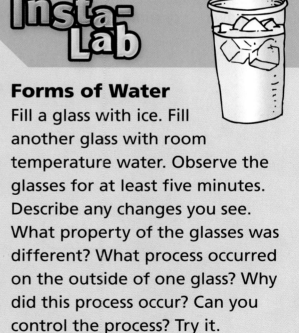

Forms of Water

Fill a glass with ice. Fill another glass with room temperature water. Observe the glasses for at least five minutes. Describe any changes you see. What property of the glasses was different? What process occurred on the outside of one glass? Why did this process occur? Can you control the process? Try it.

Groundwater and Runoff

When rain falls on land, some of it soaks into the soil. Plants use much of this water. Also, some of the water in the soil evaporates back into the air. But not all of the water in soil evaporates or is used by plants.

Some of the water that goes into soil moves deeper into the ground. The water in the ground moves down until it gets to solid rock. The water flows through small holes in some kinds of rock, like an underground river. Groundwater is water that flows through rock underground.

Many people rely on groundwater for their drinking water. They dig wells to reach the groundwater. Then they pump the water up to the surface.

Rain that is not soaked up by the soil becomes runoff. The runoff flows into creeks and streams, which flow into rivers. Large rivers, such as the Mississippi River and the Columbia River, flow into larger bodies of water.

Focus Skill SEQUENCE **In what sequence of events does groundwater form?**

Some precipitation that falls on the land becomes either groundwater or runoff. ▼

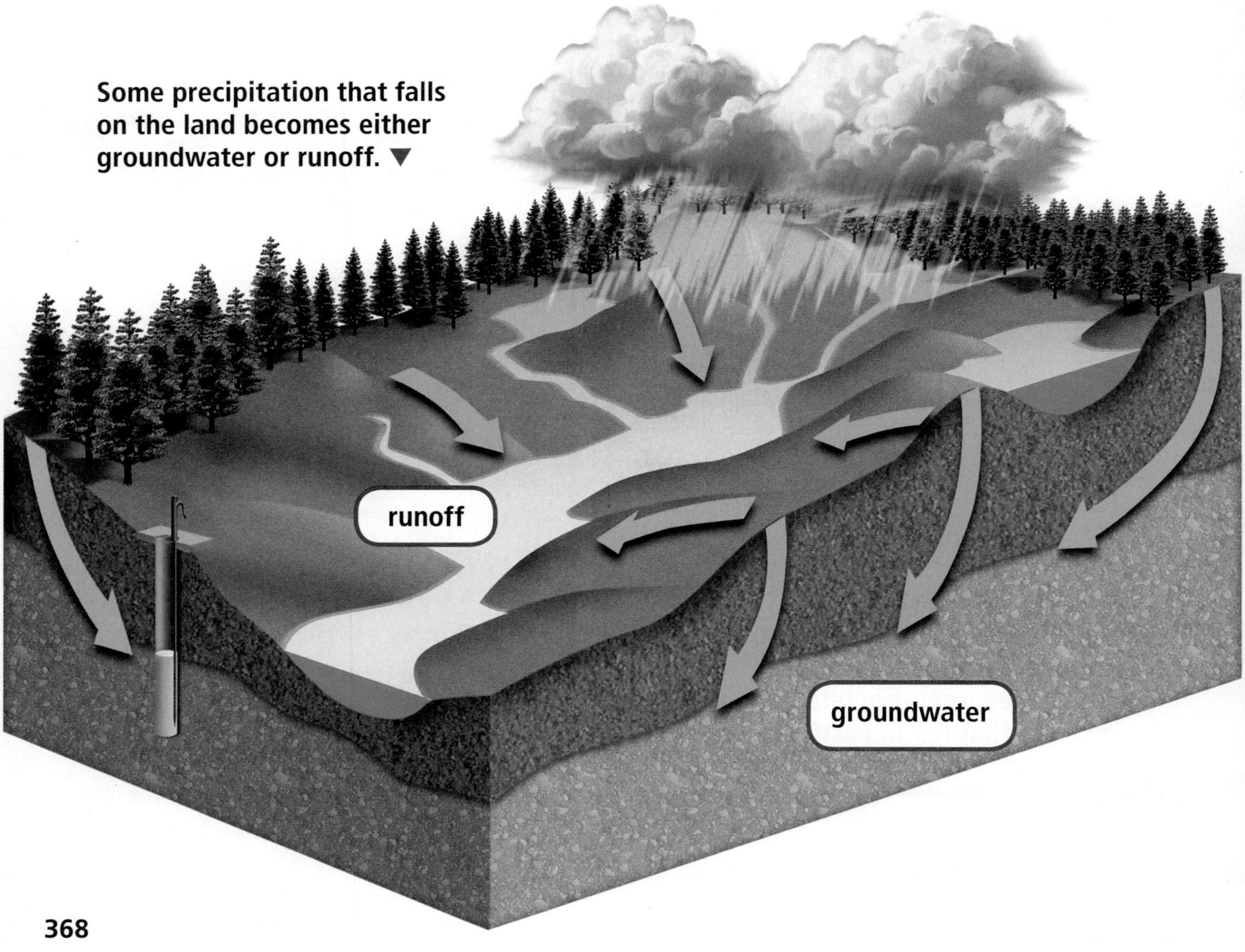

Lesson Review

Essential Question

What Is the Water Cycle?

In this lesson, you learned that the water cycle is the process by which water moves from the surface of Earth to the air and back. Water can be solid, liquid, or gas.

1. Focus Skill SEQUENCE Draw and complete a graphic organizer showing the steps of the water cycle.

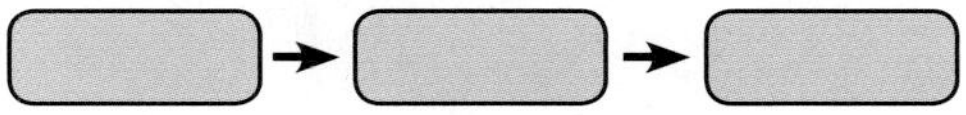

2. **SUMMARIZE** Write two sentences that sum up the main idea of this lesson.

3. **DRAW CONCLUSIONS** Will pond water evaporate faster on a warm, sunny day or on a warm, cloudy day? Explain.

4. **VOCABULARY** Write one sentence that uses all the vocabulary terms for the lesson.

Test Prep

5. **CRITICAL THINKING** Most rainwater comes from the ocean, but rainwater is not salty. Why not?

6. Which of the following happens when water vapor cools?
   A. condensation
   B. evaporation
   C. heating
   D. vaporization

Make Connections

Writing

Persuasive Writing

Less than 3 percent of Earth's water is fresh. Write a **speech** that explains to people why it's important to protect Earth's freshwater resources. Present your speech to the class.

Math

Make a Circle Graph

Earth is known as "the water planet." Find out how much of Earth's surface is covered by water. Make a circle graph that shows this information.

Social Studies

Where Is Water?

Find a world map. Make a list of all the major bodies of water you see. Research one of the bodies of water, and report on it. Include information such as how the body of water formed.

LESSON 2

Essential Question

How Is the Water Cycle Related to Weather?

Investigate how a flood moves.

Read and Learn how water and the weather cycle are related.

Fast Fact

When It Rains, It Pours

Floods cause billions of dollars in damage to property every year. It takes only 60 cm (2 ft) of moving floodwater to sweep away a car. Higher waters sweep away trees, bridges, and even buildings! In the Investigate activity, you will model a flood.

Flooded neighborhood

Vocabulary Preview

rain [RAYN] Precipitation that is liquid water (p. 374)

sleet [SLEET] Precipitation made when rain falls through freezing air and turns into ice (p. 375)

snow [SNOH] Precipitation caused when water vapor turns directly into ice and forms ice crystals (p. 375)

hail [HAYL] Round pieces of ice formed when frozen rain is coated with water and refreezes (p. 375)

tornado [tawr•NAY•doh] A fast-spinning spiral of wind that touches the ground (p. 376)

hurricane [HER•ih•kayn] A large tropical storm that has winds of at least 74 miles per hour (p. 376)

Modeling a Flood

Guided Inquiry

Start with Questions

These sand bags are holding back rising floodwaters. Rapid changes in the weather can cause flooding and other serious problems.

- What can people do to be prepared for severe weather?
- What can cause a flood?

Investigate to find out. Then read to find out more.

Prepare to Investigate

Inquiry Skill Tip

When you gather, record, and interpret data, it is very important to be accurate. If you do not keep precise records of your information, your conclusions could be wrong.

Materials

- aluminum baking pan
- plastic bag
- plastic gloves
- soil
- water
- toothpick
- beaker

Make an Observation Table

Rainy Day	Observations
1	
2	
3	
4	

Follow This Procedure

1. Put on gloves and half-fill an aluminum baking pan with soil. Make a path in the soil to form a "river channel" that runs through the center of the pan. Build up some small hills around the river channel. Press the soil in place.
2. Use a toothpick to poke several holes in the bottom of a plastic bag.
3. **Measure** 150 mL of water in a beaker. One partner should hold the plastic bag over the pan while the other partner slowly pours the water into the bag. Let the water drip over the pan to **model** a rainy day. **Record** what you **observe**.
4. Repeat Step 3 several times until the pan becomes three-fourths full of water.

Draw Conclusions

1. What happened to the soil in the pan after the first "rainy day"? What happened after the last "rainy day"?
2. **Inquiry Skill** Scientists often **gather, record, and interpret data** to understand how things work. **Interpret** what you observed and recorded by using your model. What do you think causes floods?

Independent Inquiry

Would the results be the same if there were several days between each rainfall? Plan and conduct a simple investigation to find out.

Read and Learn

VOCABULARY
rain p. 374
sleet p. 375
snow p. 375
hail p. 375
tornado p. 376
hurricane p. 376

SCIENCE CONCEPTS
- what some kinds of precipitation are
- what causes different kinds of weather

Focus Skill CAUSE AND EFFECT
Look for the causes of certain types of weather.

cause → effect

Kinds of Precipitation

You may think of precipitation as bad weather. After all, rain keeps you from playing outdoors. It can also cause floods. Hail can damage cars and homes. Sleet can make roads dangerous. Snow can pile up on driveways and on sidewalks. However, all of these kinds of precipitation are simply part of the water cycle.

What causes different kinds of precipitation? Most water on Earth, such as ocean water, is liquid. You learned in Lesson 1 that if water is heated enough, it becomes water vapor, a gas. If water is cooled enough, it freezes.

Rain, the most common kind of precipitation, is liquid water. Rain falls if the air temperature is higher than 0°C (32°F).

Kinds of Precipitation

Types	Causes
Rain	Water vapor condenses in air.
Snow	Water vapor turns into ice crystals instead of a liquid.
Sleet	Falling rain passes through a layer of freezing-cold air and turns into ice.
Hail	Rain freezes and then falls to a warmer pocket of air. The frozen rain is coated with liquid water and then carried back up to a cold pocket of air, where the liquid coating also freezes.

RAIN
Rain is liquid precipitation. Tiny raindrops are called drizzle. Heavy rain can cause floods.

Sleet is frozen rain. Sleet is caused when rain falls through a layer of freezing-cold air. This turns the rain into ice pellets. **Snow** is made of ice crystals. Snow is caused when the air temperature is so cold that water vapor turns directly into ice. **Hail** is round pieces of ice. Hail is caused when rain freezes and then falls to a warmer part of the air. Raindrops coat the frozen rain before it is carried back up to a colder part of the air by wind. The new liquid coating then freezes also. This happens over and over until the hail is so heavy that it falls to the ground.

Focus Skill CAUSE AND EFFECT

What causes rain to become sleet?

▲ **SLEET**
Sleet is made of frozen raindrops. It forms when rain falls through a pocket of cold air.

▲ **HAIL**
Hail can be as small as a pea or as large as a grapefruit. The size of a piece of hail depends on how many times it is carried up and down in a storm cloud.

SNOW
Snow is made of ice crystals. The crystals, which come in many different shapes, form high in the air.

Severe Storms

Heat from the sun powers the water cycle. This same energy causes severe storms.

One type of severe storm is a thunderstorm. Thunderstorms are storms with lightning, strong winds, and heavy rain. Sometimes tornadoes form during thunderstorms. A **tornado** is a fast-spinning spiral of wind that stretches from the clouds of a thunderstorm to the ground. Tornadoes can have wind speeds greater than 400 kilometers (250 mi) per hour! Every year, there are about 800 to 1000 tornadoes in the United States.

Another kind of severe storm is a hurricane. **Hurricanes** are large tropical storms with wind speeds of 119 kilometers (74 mi) per hour or more.

▲ **The United States has more tornadoes per year than any other country in the world.**

Blizzards are severe snowstorms that can last for hours. Blizzards have strong winds, blowing snow, and very low air temperatures. ▼

Math in Science
Interpret Data

Hurricanes are categorized by their wind speed. Does a hurricane's wind speed relate to the amount of damage it causes?

Hurricane Strength

Category/ Wind Speed	Hurricanes	Cost of damage in dollars
5 (>155 mph)	Hurricane Andrew, 1992	$34.1 billion
4 (131–155 mph)	Hurricane Charley, 2004	$14 billion
3 (111–130 mph)	Hurricane Betsy, 1965	$9 billion
2 (96–110 mph)	Hurricane Floyd, 1999	$4.9 billion
1 (74–95 mph)	Hurricane Agnes, 1972	$9.1 billion

Three pictures of Hurricane Andrew

Hurricanes form over warm water in the tropical oceans. These storms can last for weeks out at sea. But when a hurricane reaches land, it no longer gets energy from warm water. It soon becomes weaker.

The winds of a hurricane spin around the calm center of the storm, called the "eye." Rain, waves, and "storm surge," a huge bulge of water pushed onto the land by the storm, can cause flooding.

Focus Skill CAUSE AND EFFECT

What causes flooding during a hurricane?

Insta-Lab

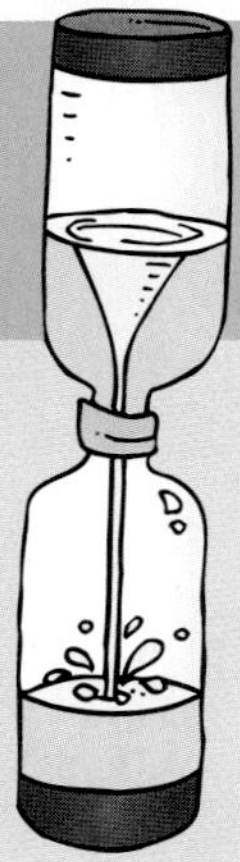

Tornado in a Bottle

Fill a clear, plastic bottle three-fourths full of water. Tape a washer over the mouth of the bottle. Tape a second clear, plastic bottle upside down on top of the first bottle. Turn the bottles over and swirl the top bottle around quickly. What do you observe?

Weather Safety

Severe storms are dangerous. Injuries can be caused by downed power lines and trees. Floods can occur. It's important to keep yourself safe during severe weather. One way to stay safe is to follow safety rules in your community. Local radio or TV stations will tell you if there is a severe storm in your area.

There are other ways to warn people about severe weather. For example, some areas have weather sirens that are turned on when a severe storm is detected. Some sirens can even detect nearby tornadoes on their own and warn people in the area.

When there is a severe storm, stay inside a building unless officials tell you to leave. Sometimes, people are asked to leave an area before a storm strikes. If that happens, people will follow a safe route away from the area.

Focus Skill CAUSE AND EFFECT

How might a severe storm affect you?

Weather siren ▶

▲ Watch TV during severe weather to get directions about what to do.

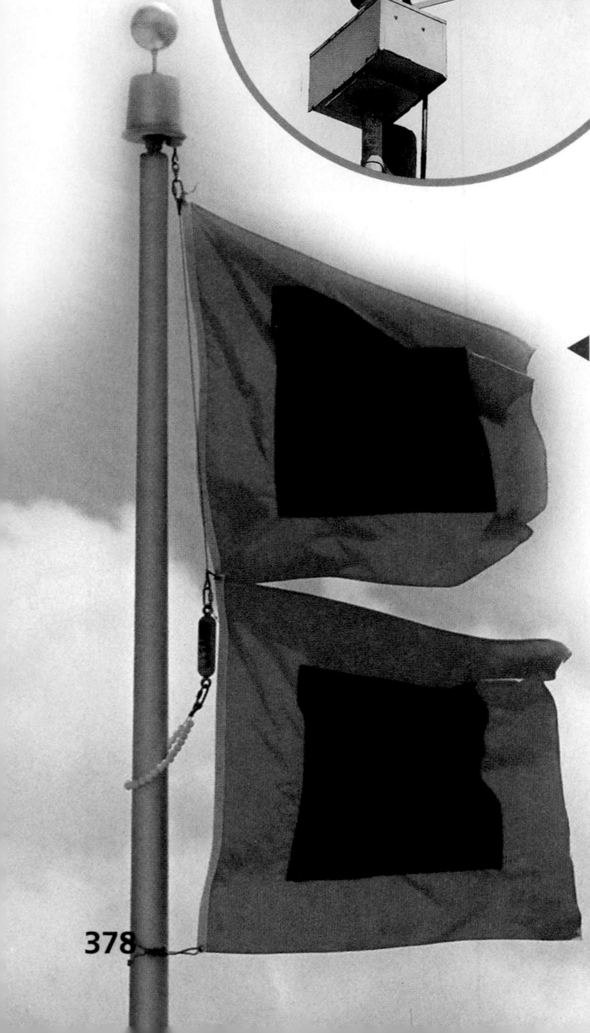

◀ These flags warn that a hurricane is coming.

Follow signs like these if you are asked to leave an area when a hurricane is coming. ▶

Essential Question

How Is the Water Cycle Related to Weather?

In this lesson, you learned that the water cycle can determine the kind of weather an area gets. The amount of water in the air and the form water takes can result in hail, snow, or rain.

1. Focus Skill CAUSE AND EFFECT Draw and complete a graphic organizer showing the effects of severe weather.

2. **SUMMARIZE** Write a summary of this lesson. Use vocabulary words to organize your ideas.

3. **DRAW CONCLUSIONS** What affects the kind of precipitation that falls?

4. **VOCABULARY** Write a weather report that uses at least four vocabulary terms from this lesson.

Test Prep

5. **CRITICAL THINKING** Explain how weather is related to the water cycle.

6. Which of the following is not a kind of precipitation?
   - **A.** air
   - **B.** hail
   - **C.** rain
   - **D.** sleet

Make Connections

Writing

Expository Writing

Suppose that you're a drop of water in a cloud. Write a **story** that describes what you experience as you continue your travel through the water cycle.

Math

Solve a Problem

Measure the outdoor temperature. Based on the temperature you found, what kind of precipitation is most likely to fall now in your area?

Health

Weather and Health

Make a booklet that shows what to do to stay safe during severe weather, such as tornadoes, thunderstorms, and hurricanes.

LESSON 3

Essential Question

How Do Land Features Affect the Water Cycle?

Investigate how soil and water are warmed by the sun.

Read and Learn how the water cycle can be affected by landforms.

Fast Fact

Thunderstorms in a Row

When cold air over the ocean meets warm air over the land, squall lines can form. A squall line is a long line of moving thunderstorms. Squall lines can stretch across the land for hundreds of kilometers! In the Investigate, you will observe how land and water heat up.

Vocabulary Preview

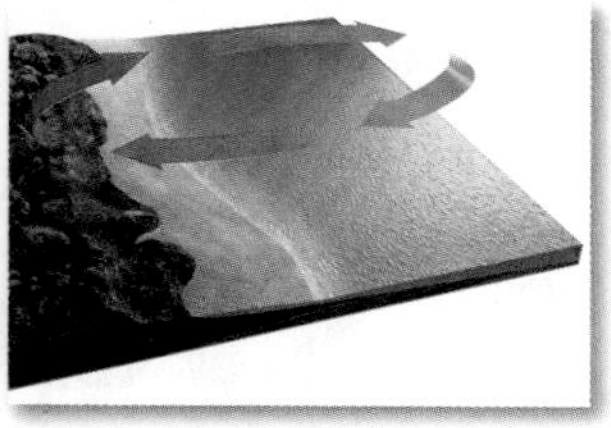

sea breeze [SEE BREEZ] A breeze that moves from the water to the land (p. 384)

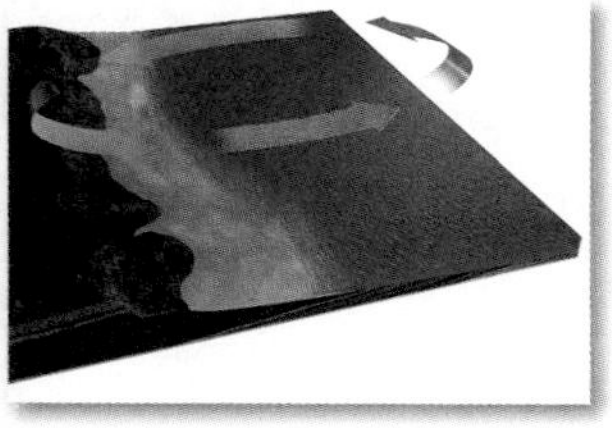

land breeze [LAND BREEZ] A breeze that moves from the land to the water (p. 384)

rain shadow [RAYN SHAD•oh] The area on the side of a mountain range that gets little or no rain or cloud cover (p. 386)

Heating Land and Water

Guided Inquiry

Start with Questions

You would probably want to wear your shoes if you walked across this black beach on a sunny day!

- Why is this sand black?
- Why is it warmer than sand that is not black?

Investigate to find out. Then read to find out more.

Prepare to Investigate

Inquiry Skill Tip

When you hypothesize which thermometer will reflect the higher temperature and why, remember that your explanation must be testable.

Materials

- 2 small plastic or foam cups
- water
- 2 thermometers
- stopwatch
- dark soil or sand
- light source with 100-W bulb or greater

Make an Observation Chart

	Lamp On Time (min)					Lamp Off Time (min)		
Contents of Cup	0	5	10	15	20	5	10	15
Soil or sand								
Water								

Follow This Procedure

1. Fill one cup with dark soil or sand. Fill the second cup with water. Place a thermometer upright in each cup.
2. Time 1 minute, using the stopwatch. Then **measure** and **record** the temperatures of the two cups.
3. Remove the thermometer after every measurement. Place the cups under the light. Make sure that both cups get an equal amount of light.
4. After the cups have been under the light for 5 minutes, **measure** and **record** their temperatures. Repeat this step three times.
5. Turn off the lamp. Time 5 minutes, and then **measure** and **record** the temperatures of the cups. Repeat this step twice.

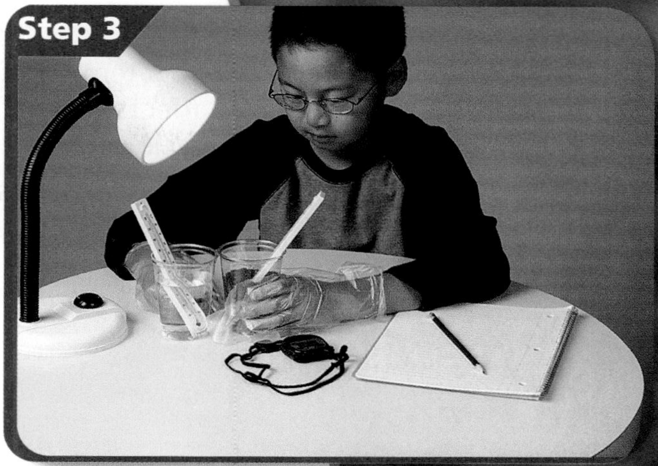

Draw Conclusions

1. Describe how the soil and water heated differently. How did they cool differently?
2. **Inquiry Skill** Scientists use what they observe to form a **hypothesis**. Use your observations from this investigation to **hypothesize** how the weather on Earth would be different if Earth's surface were mostly land instead of mostly water.

Independent Inquiry

Does wet soil heat differently from dry soil? Conduct an experiment to find out.

Read and Learn

VOCABULARY
sea breeze p. 384
land breeze p. 384
rain shadow p. 386

SCIENCE CONCEPTS
- how temperature affects the water cycle
- how landforms affect the water cycle

Focus Skill CAUSE AND EFFECT
Look for ways that landforms affect the water cycle.

cause → effect

Sea Breezes and Land Breezes

Have you ever been to the beach on a hot day? It might be so hot that your feet burn when you walk on the sand. But when you go into the water, you quickly cool off. That's because the water is cooler than the sand.

Land heats up much more quickly than water. Land also cools down more quickly than water. Because of this, the temperature of the air over land is almost always different from the temperature of air over nearby water. During the day, the air over water is cooler than the air over land. The hot air over a beach is pushed upward by the cool air moving in from over the water. This causes a sea breeze. A **sea breeze** is a breeze moving from the water to the land. During the night, the land becomes cooler than the water. This causes a land breeze. A **land breeze** is a breeze moving from the land to the water.

Focus Skill CAUSE AND EFFECT
What causes a land breeze?

Warm air is pushed upward as cool air moves into its place. During the day, the air over land is warmer than the air over water, which causes a sea breeze.

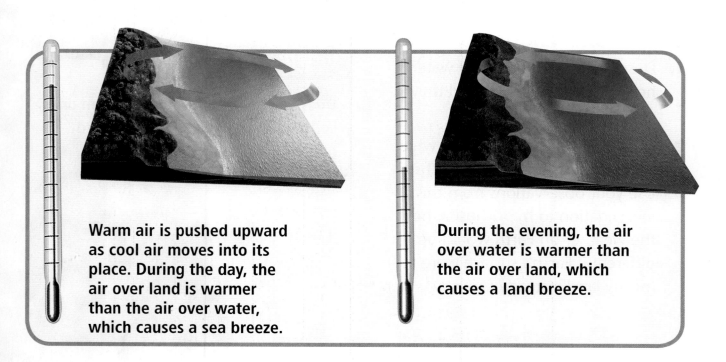

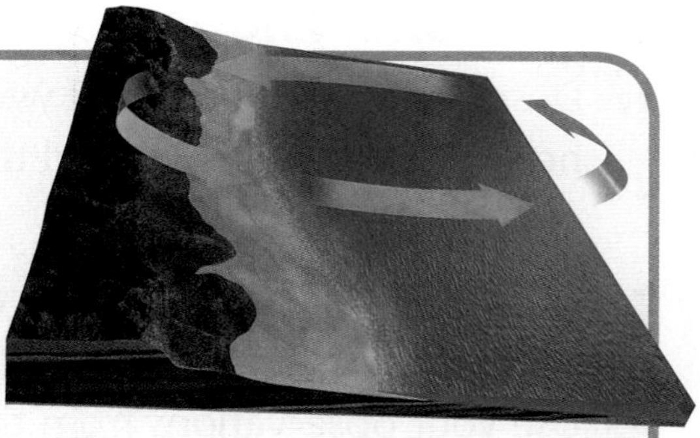

During the evening, the air over water is warmer than the air over land, which causes a land breeze.

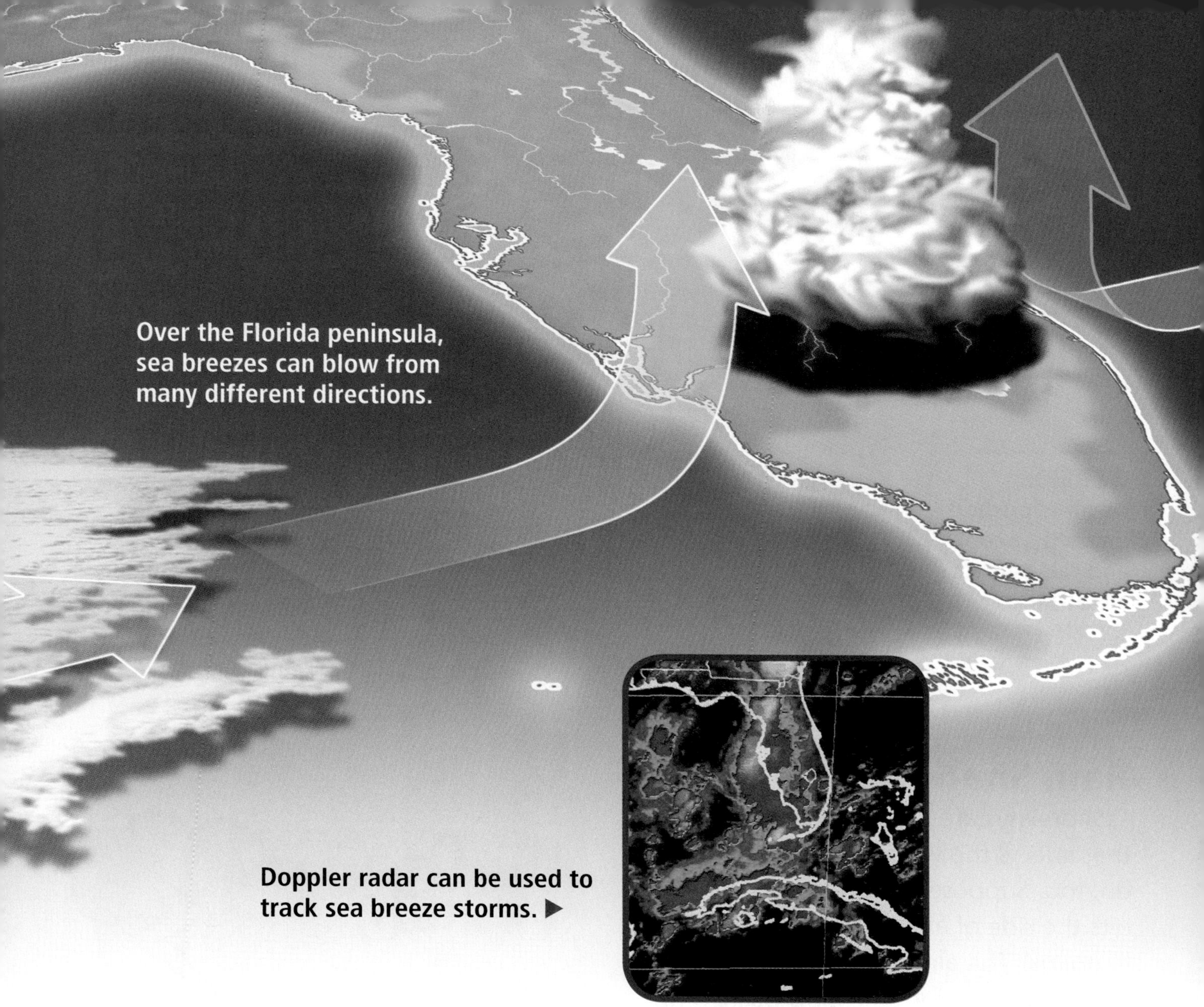

Over the Florida peninsula, sea breezes can blow from many different directions.

Doppler radar can be used to track sea breeze storms. ▶

Sea Breeze Storms

You learned in Lesson 1 that when water vapor cools, it condenses to form precipitation. Sometimes, cool sea breezes push clouds toward the shore. The clouds can then produce storms over the land. These storms are called sea breeze storms.

A peninsula is a piece of land that is surrounded by water on all sides but one. Over a peninsula like Florida, sea breezes can come in from the east and from the west. The collision of the two sea breezes causes the air to become unstable. If the two bodies of air have a lot of water vapor, a very strong sea breeze storm could form over the center of the peninsula. This type of sea breeze storm happens often in Florida during the summer.

Focus Skill CAUSE AND EFFECT

What causes a sea breeze storm?

WET SIDE
As air is pushed upward, it cools and releases its moisture.
DRY SIDE
As the cool air moves downward, it warms and dries out as it spreads over land.

Rain Shadows

Shorelines are not the only landform that affects the water cycle. Mountains do, too. Suppose a moving body of air hits the side of a mountain range. What happens? The air can't move through the mountains. Instead, the air is pushed up the side of the mountains and then over them. As the air moves up, it cools. The water vapor in the cooler air condenses and brings rain to that side of the mountains. By the time the air reaches the other side, the air is dry. So, it doesn't rain on the other side. This causes a rain shadow. A **rain shadow** is the area on the side of a mountain range that gets little or no rain or cloud cover.

Focus Skill **CAUSE AND EFFECT**

What is the effect of a rain shadow?

Insta-Lab

Lightning and Thunder

The next time a thunderstorm is in your area, watch for lightning. When you see the lightning, start counting, "One-Mississippi, two-Mississippi, . . ." and so on. When you hear the thunder, stop counting. For every three seconds you count, the thunderstorm is about one kilometer from you. How far away is the thunderstorm?

Essential Question

Lesson Review

How Do Land Features Affect the Water Cycle?

In this lesson, you learned that land features can influence the weather. Mountains affect the water cycle and make some places drier than others. Land heats and cools faster than water, causing sea breezes and land breezes.

1. Focus Skill **CAUSE AND EFFECT** Draw and complete a graphic organizer to show what happens when air over water is cooler than air over land.

   cause → effect

2. **SUMMARIZE** Write a summary of this lesson. Begin with this sentence: *Walking barefoot in a parking lot on a sunny day can result in hot feet!*

3. **DRAW CONCLUSIONS** Will sea breeze storms happen more often in warm places or cool places? Explain.

4. **VOCABULARY** Explain the difference between a land breeze and a sea breeze.

Test Prep

5. **CRITICAL THINKING** Explain why a mountain may be green on one side and desertlike on the other.

6. How does warm air move?
   A. It falls.
   B. It is pushed upward.
   C. It spins.
   D. It stays still.

Make Connections

Writing

Expository Writing
Suppose that you are an early explorer of a mountain range that experiences the rain shadow effect. Write a **journal** describing your explorations of the range.

9÷3 Math

Solve Problems
A sea breeze storm is moving across Florida from the northeast to the southwest at 23 km/hr. How long does the storm take to reach Tampa if it started above Orlando, which is 137 km away?

Physical Education

Water Sports
Many water sports, such as sailing, make use of sea breezes. Choose a sport that uses sea breezes, and write a simple how-to guide for this sport.

LESSON 4

Essential Question

How Can Weather Be Predicted?

Investigate how to make a barometer.

Read and Learn how people predict the weather.

Fast Fact

A Winter Wonderland

Ice storms deposit huge amounts of ice over everything. During a severe ice storm, about 45,000 kilograms (99,000 lb) of ice can pile up on a 15-meter-tall (50-ft-tall) pine tree! In the Investigate, you will make and use a weather instrument to help predict weather.

Ice hanging from tree

Vocabulary Preview

air mass [AIR MAS] A large body of air that has a similar temperature and moisture level (p. 392)

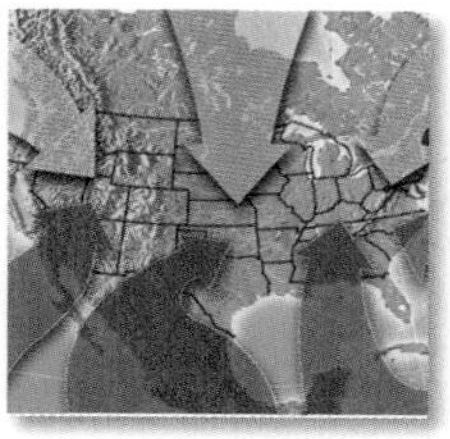

cold front [KOHLD FRUHNT] The boundary where a cold air mass moves under a warm air mass (p. 394)

warm front [WAWRM FRUHNT] The boundary where a warm air mass moves over a cold air mass (p. 394)

barometer [buh•RAHM•uh•ter] A weather instrument used to measure air pressure (p. 398)

anemometer [an•uh•MAHM•uht•er] A weather instrument that measures wind speed (p. 398)

Investigate

Making a Barometer

Guided Inquiry

Start with Questions

This child isn't dressed for a summer day!

- Why is it important to dress for the weather?
- Why might this child have known to choose these clothes?

Investigate to find out. Then read to find out more.

Prepare to Investigate

Inquiry Skill Tip

Use the same tools in the same way each time you measure. Otherwise, you may get inaccurate measurements.

Materials

- plastic jar
- safety goggles
- wooden craft stick
- scissors
- large rubber band
- large index card
- large round balloon
- masking tape
- ruler

Make an Observation Chart

Day	Air Pressure	Weather Observations
1		
2		
3		
4		
5		

Follow This Procedure

1. CAUTION: **Wear safety goggles.** Be careful when using scissors. Use the scissors to cut the neck off a balloon.
2. Have your partner hold a jar while you stretch the balloon over the open end. Secure the balloon with a rubber band.
3. Tape a craft stick to the top of the balloon. More than half of the craft stick should extend beyond the jar's edge.
4. On the blank side of an index card, draw a line and label it *Day 1.* Tape the card to a wall. The line should be at the same height as the stick on your barometer. Next to it, **record** the current weather.
5. Air pressure is the force of air pressing down on Earth. **Measure** air pressure by marking the position of the wooden stick on the index card for the next four days. Label the marks *Days 2–5.* **Record** the pressure and weather each day.

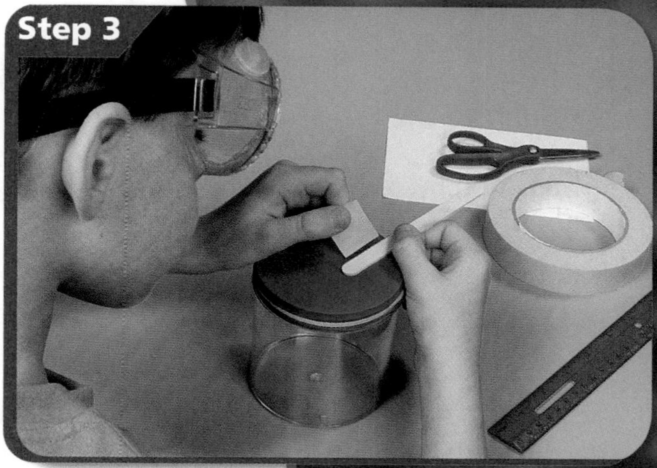

Draw Conclusions

1. How did the air pressure change? What might cause changes in air pressure?
2. **Inquiry Skill** Scientists use instruments to **measure** weather data. Infer how a barometer works.

Independent Inquiry

Track changes in air pressure and weather for five more days. What can you infer about the relationship between air pressure and type of weather?

Read and Learn

VOCABULARY
air mass p. 392
cold front p. 394
warm front p. 394
barometer p. 398
anemometer p. 398

SCIENCE CONCEPTS
- what makes an air mass
- how to read a weather map

Focus Skill **CAUSE AND EFFECT**
Look for the causes of changes in weather.

cause → effect

Air Masses

Have you ever wondered why the weather can be sunny one day and rainy the next? Movements of air masses cause weather changes. An **air mass** is a large body of air. All the air in an air mass has a similar temperature and moisture level. Moisture level means the amount of water that is in air.

The temperature and moisture levels of an air mass depend on where the air mass formed. Air masses that form over land are dry. Air masses that form over water have a lot of moisture in them. In the United States, cold air masses come from the north. Warm air masses come from the south.

The temperature and moisture levels of an air mass affect the kind of weather the air mass brings. Cold, wet air masses can bring snow to an area. But cold, dry air masses can bring cool weather with little or no precipitation.

The map shows where the air masses that affect North America form. Cool air masses are in blue. Warm air masses are in red. ▼

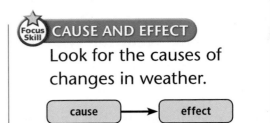

▲ **Air masses do not mix very much with each other. Instead, they stay separate as they move.**

Warm air masses with a lot of moisture usually bring precipitation. But warm, dry masses can bring warm weather with little or no precipitation.

As air masses move, they tend to stay separate from each other. That's because warm air is lighter than cold air. When they come in contact with each other, warm air masses are pushed upward and cold air masses sink.

Focus Skill CAUSE AND EFFECT

What causes the weather to change?

Insta-Lab

Making an Air Mass

Fill a cup halfway with ice cubes. Wait five minutes. With one hand, pour chilled water into the cup. Hold the other hand over the cup as you pour the water. What do you feel? If the air you felt were an air mass, how would you describe it? In a cold front, the air is colder behind the front than ahead of it.

Fronts

When air masses move, they come into contact with other air masses. The border between one air mass and another is called a front. Most storms happen at fronts.

There are two main types of fronts: cold fronts and warm fronts. A **cold front** forms where a cold air mass moves under a warm air mass. This causes the warm air mass to move upward. As the warm air mass moves up, it begins to cool. Remember that water vapor condenses when it cools. The condensing water vapor in the upward-moving air mass forms clouds. It might begin to rain along the front. Thunderstorms will often develop. Also, the air temperature will become cooler as the cold air mass moves forward.

A **warm front** forms where warm air moves over cold air. The warm air slides up over the cold air as it moves forward. Warm fronts generally move slowly. Because of this, warm fronts bring steady rain instead of thunderstorms. Warm fronts are then followed by clear, warm weather as the warm air mass moves over the area.

Fronts do not always move. A front that stays in one place for many days is called a stationary front. Stationary fronts happen when the two air masses along a front do not have enough energy to move. The weather along a stationary front is often cloudy and wet. This kind of front can leave many inches of snow or cause flooding rains. For this reason, stationary fronts can be dangerous.

Different kinds of fronts move differently. Because of this, they cause different kinds of clouds to form. The types of clouds in an area can help you predict the weather.

Focus Skill CAUSE AND EFFECT

What are the effects of a cold front?

▲ In a warm front, the air is warmer behind the front than ahead of it.

In a cold front, the air is colder behind the front than ahead of it. ▼

◀ STRATUS CLOUDS
Stratus clouds often occur along warm fronts.

Stratus clouds can develop into nimbostratus clouds. Nimbostratus clouds bring light rain or snow showers. ▶

◀ CUMULUS CLOUDS
Cumulus (KYOO•myuh•luhs) clouds are common on clear, warm days.

Cumulus clouds can develop into cumulonimbus, or thunderstorm, clouds. ▶

CIRRUS CLOUDS
Cirrus (SIR•uhs) clouds usually indicate cool, fair weather.

Weather Maps

Have you ever used a street map to find a friend's house? Have you ever used a trail map while hiking? Another kind of map you can use is a weather map. A weather map helps you know what the weather is like in an area.

Weather maps use symbols to show the weather. A sun symbol means it is sunny in the area. A symbol of a cloud with rain means it is raining in the area.

Fronts are also shown on weather maps. The symbol for a warm front is a red line with half circles along it. A blue line with triangles shows a cold front.

Many weather maps show temperature. Sometimes the temperature is written on the map. In the United States, the temperature is given in degrees Fahrenheit. Almost all other countries give the temperature in degrees Celsius. When the temperature is not written on the weather map, it may be shown by using colors. When an area is warm, it is colored red (very hot), orange (warm), or yellow (mild). When an area is cold, it is colored green (cool) or blue (very cold).

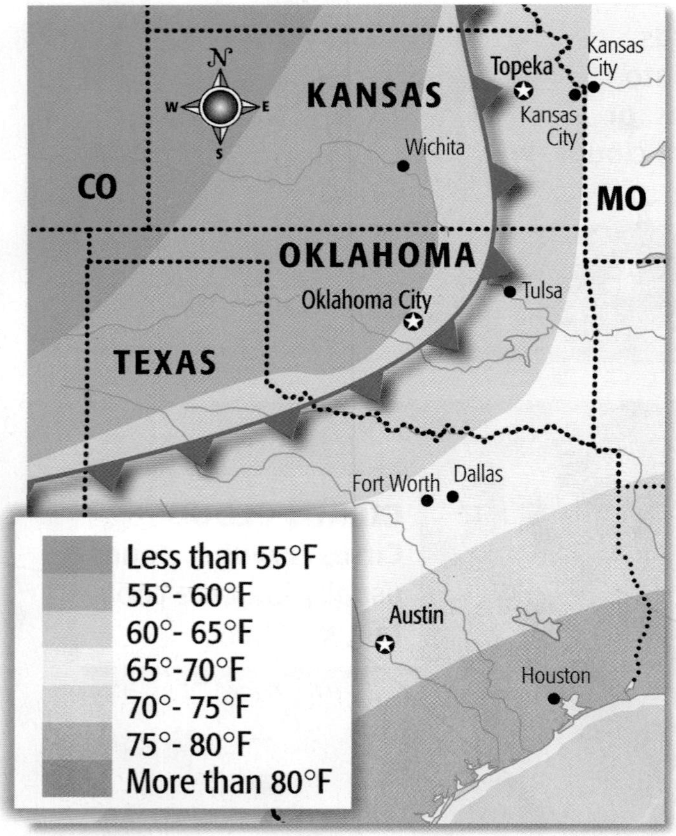

▲ **A line with triangles is the symbol for a cold front. The triangles point in the direction of movement.**

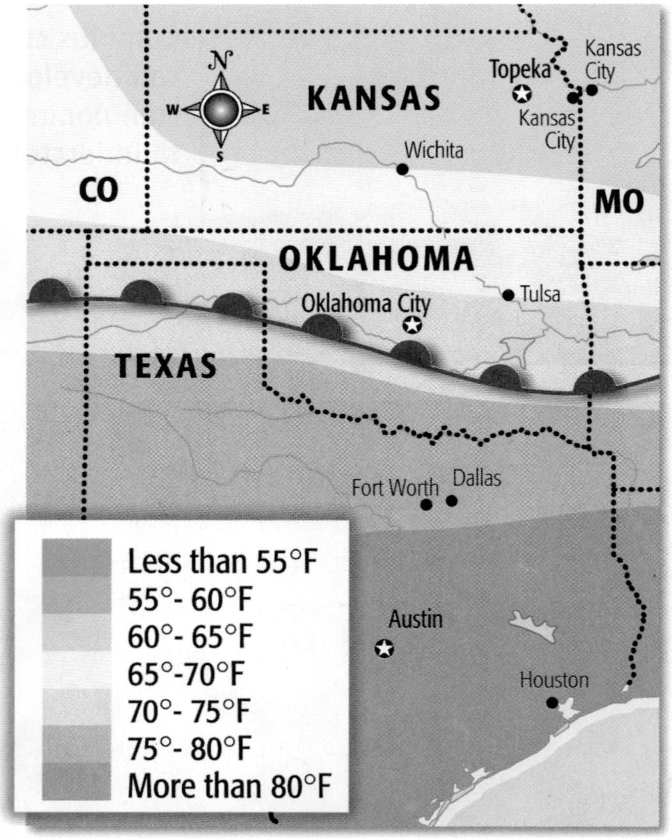

▲ **A line with half circles is the symbol for a warm front. The half circles point in the direction the front is moving.**

Math in Science
Interpret Data

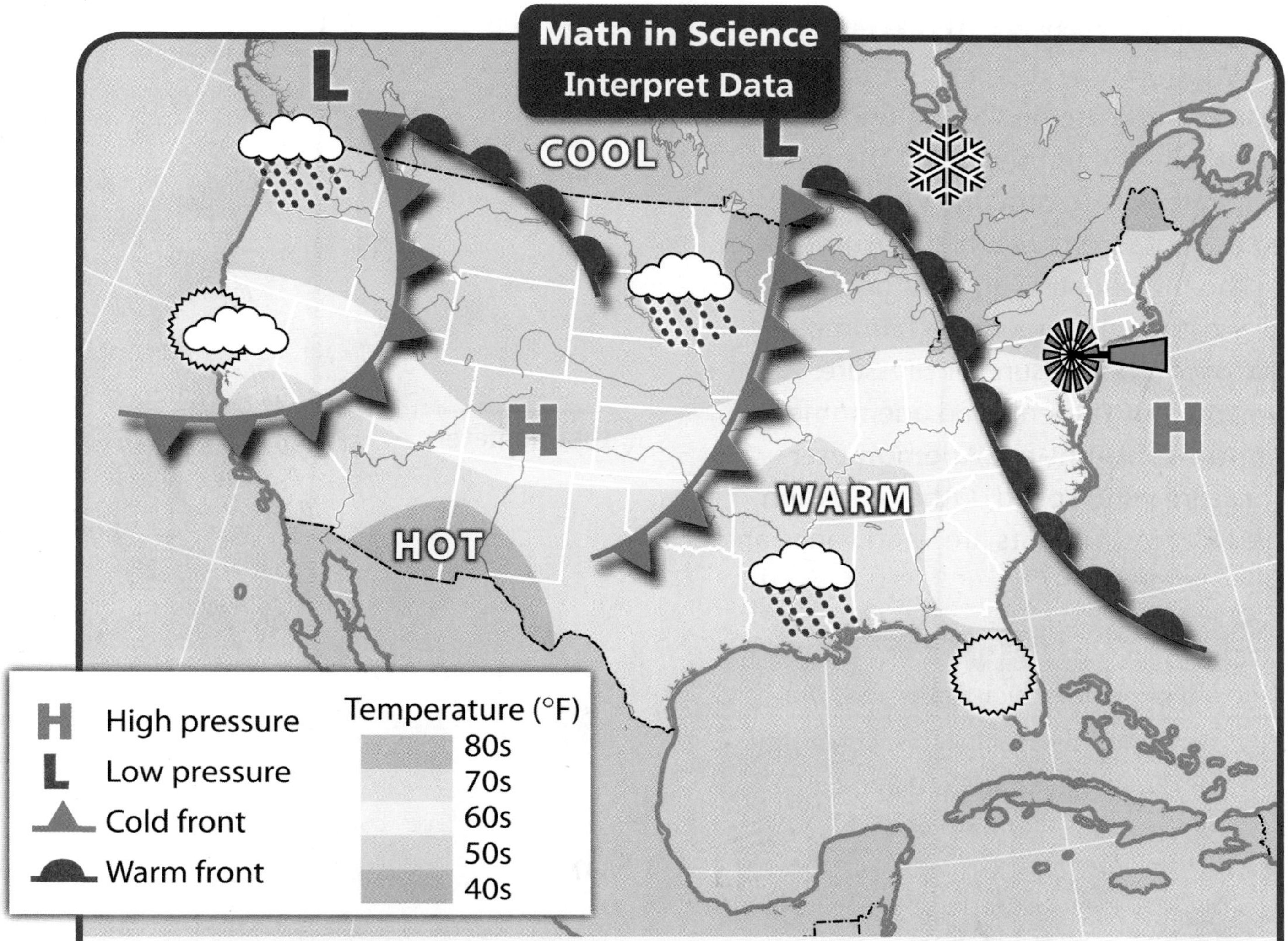

Use the key to read the weather map. What is the weather in Washington, D.C.?

Other information you may see on a weather map includes wind speed and direction, air pressure, and the highest and lowest temperature in an area for that day.

Where does all the information on a weather map come from? Weather information is collected at thousands of weather stations across the country. A weather station is a place that has many different instruments that measure weather. The information from the weather stations is reported to the National Weather Service (NWS). The NWS then studies the weather data from all the weather stations. Each day, the NWS makes weather maps based on the information collected at all the weather stations.

Focus Skill CAUSE AND EFFECT **How would the weather map above look if a warm front were moving through Florida?**

Measuring Weather

When you say that it is hot or cold outside, you are describing one part of weather—the temperature. The most accurate way to describe weather is to use data from weather instruments. In the Investigate, you built one kind of weather instrument—a barometer. **Barometers** measure air pressure. Another weather instrument is an anemometer (an•uh•MAHM•uht•er). **Anemometers** measure wind speed. Other common weather instruments are wind vanes and rain gauges.

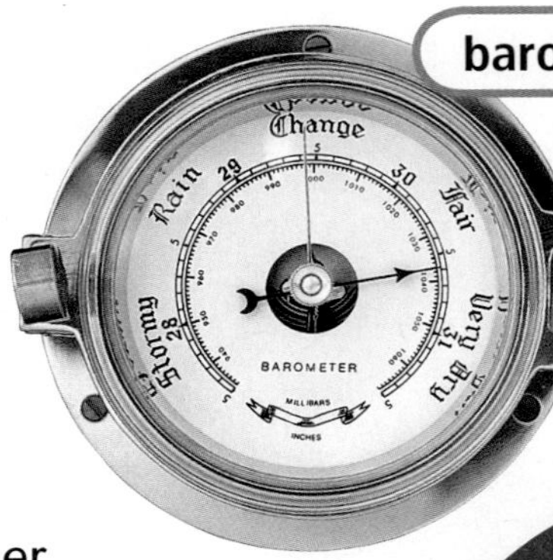

Focus Skill CAUSE AND EFFECT **While reading a thermometer, you notice that the temperature has fallen throughout the day. What might be causing this?**

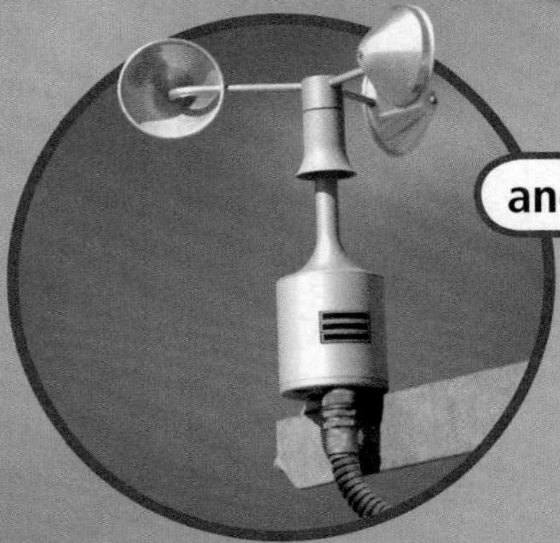

This school weather station collects data for students. The data is shared with other schools. ▶

Lesson Review

Essential Question

How Can Weather Be Predicted?

In this lesson, you learned about different ways in which people can try to predict the weather. Analyzing air masses and fronts can help people know what the temperature is going to be like and if it is going to rain. Weather maps can show what is going on over the whole country.

1. Focus Skill **CAUSE AND EFFECT** Draw and complete a graphic orgranizer to show what happens when a cold front forms.

   cause → effect

2. **SUMMARIZE** Write a summary of this lesson. Begin with this sentence: *When I wake up in the morning, I need to know what the weather is going to be like.*

3. **DRAW CONCLUSIONS** Why might it have been more difficult to predict weather years ago?

4. **VOCABULARY** Use each vocabulary term from the lesson in a sentence.

Test Prep

5. **CRITICAL THINKING** You hear on the radio that a cold front is headed toward your town. What type of weather can you expect?

6. Which of the following instruments measures wind speed?
   A. anemometer
   B. barometer
   C. rain gauge
   D. thermometer

Make Connections

Writing

Narrative Writing

Use what you have learned in this chapter to write a short **poem** about weather and the water cycle. Use these terms in your poem: *air mass, front, rain, clouds.*

9÷3 Math

Subtract Decimals

Suppose you record a rainfall of 0.3 cm in the gauge in the morning. You don't empty the gauge. In the afternoon, the gauge reads 1.5 cm. How much new rain fell?

Language Arts

Be a Weather Forecaster

Make up a weather map of your state. Present your forecast to the class. Be sure to use the correct vocabulary for the weather you are describing.

INTO THE EYE OF THE STORM

Hurricane Charley occurred in August 2004. Normally, during such a deadly storm, many people run, drive, or fly away as fast and as far as possible. One flight crew working for the National Weather Service, however, flew into (yes, into) the storm. Called Hurricane Hunters, they actually flew a plane into the center of Charley.

Hurricanes are powerful, whirling storms that form over warm oceans and cause torrential rains and heavy winds. The eye of a hurricane is the calm center of the storm. The eye has little wind and few clouds. Swirling around the eye are heavy winds.

Hurricane Hunters fly directly into the eye of a hurricane—not above it. The reason is that a hurricane can be more than 15,000 meters (50,000 ft) high, and the planes can fly only as high as 9000 meters (30,000 ft).

Hurricanes are rated on a scale of 1 to 5. The ratings are based on a storm's wind speed and potential for destruction.	
CATEGORY 1	74 to 95 miles per hour (mph) Minor damage to trees and shrubs; minor flooding
CATEGORY 2	96 to 110 mph Some trees and signs blown down; some flooding; no major damage to buildings; some evacuations
CATEGORY 3	111 to 130 mph Some large trees and signs destroyed; some damage to small buildings; some evacuations
CATEGORY 4	131 to 155 mph Extreme damage to buildings; major beach erosion; evacuations up to 2 miles from shore
CATEGORY 5	Greater than 155 mph Severe damage to buildings; some small buildings knocked down; evacuations up to 10 miles from shore

A Hurricane Hunter drops a tube into the eye of a storm.

As the plane "punched through" the eye wall of Charley, crew members experienced a rocky ride. The eye wall is a solid ring of thunderstorms around the eye. The strongest winds and heaviest rains are located here.

The plane contained equipment that recorded weather. In the eye of the storm, Hurricane Hunters released small tubes attached to parachutes. Each tube was about the size of a can of tennis balls. The tubes sent information about wind speed, power, and moisture back to the crew.

Accurate Forecasting

As part of their job, Hurricane Hunters help forecasters rate storms. Hurricanes are rated on a scale of 1 to 5.

A storm's rating is based on wind speed and potential for damage. Before hitting land, Charley was a Category 4 storm.

Charley packed winds of up to 230 kilometers (145 mi) per hour by the time it hit land. The storm first walloped Jamaica and Cuba before slamming into Florida.

Hurricane Charley left about a million Florida households without electricity. The storm destroyed or severely damaged at least 16,000 homes and left thousands of residents without running water.

Think and Write

1. Why is it important that forecasters accurately predict the path of a hurricane?
2. How do you think hurricanes can cause flooding on land?

Spin-In™ Find out more. Log on to **www.hspscience.com**

CHAPTER 9 Review and Test Preparation

Vocabulary Review

Use the terms below to complete the sentences. The page numbers tell you where to look in the chapter if you need help.

water cycle p. 364
precipitation p. 364
evaporation p. 366
condensation p. 367
hurricane p. 376
land breeze p. 384
air mass p. 392
warm front p. 394
barometer p. 398
anemometer p. 398

1. A breeze moving from the land to the sea is a _______.
2. A large tropical storm with high wind speeds is called a _______.
3. Air pressure is measured with a _______.
4. A gas changes to a liquid during the process of _______.
5. A large body of air is called an _______.
6. Water that falls to Earth from the air is known as _______.
7. A liquid changes to a gas during the process of _______.
8. Warm air pushes forward and moves over cold air along a _______.
9. Wind speed is measured with an _______.
10. The movement of water through the environment is known as the _______.

Check Understanding

Write the letter of the best choice.

11. **SEQUENCE** (Focus Skill) In the water cycle, what happens before water condenses in clouds?

A. Water dissolves salt.
B. Water evaporates.
C. Water falls as precipitation.
D. Water vapor changes to a gas.

12. **CAUSE AND EFFECT** (Focus Skill) Look at the diagram below. What is shown?

F. evaporation
G. groundwater formation
H. cirrus clouds
J. sea breeze

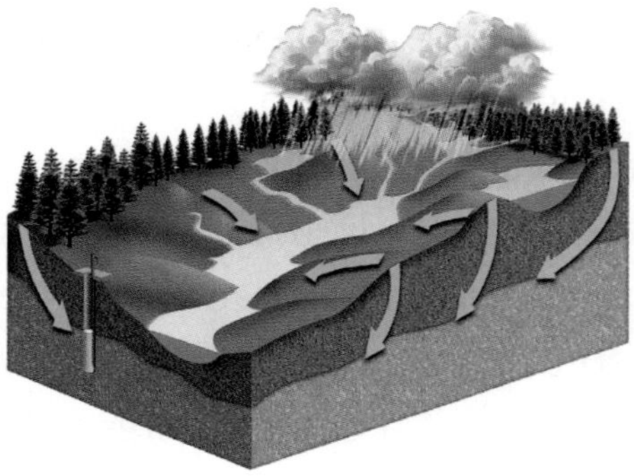

13. What type of precipitation is shown in the picture?

A. hail
B. rain
C. sleet
D. snow

14. Landforms such as mountains affect the water cycle.

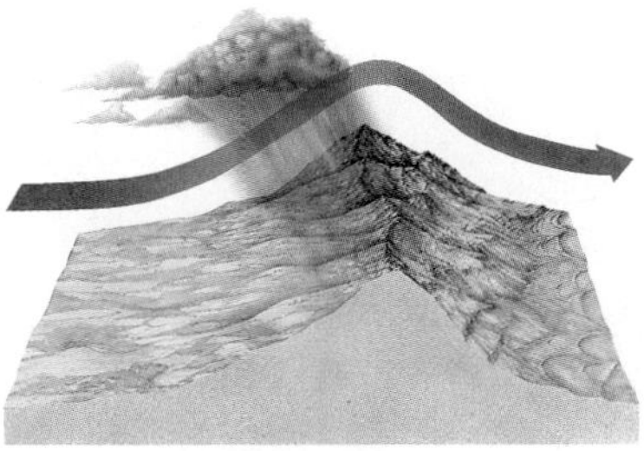

What is it called when one side of a mountain is dry?

F. a land breeze **H.** a sea breeze
G. a rain shadow **J.** a tornado

15. There is a stationary front over Centerville. What kind of weather is Centerville most likely having?

A. a few hours of drizzly rain
B. a few hours of thunderstorms
C. clear weather
D. several days of rain or snow

16. How would an air mass that forms over the Gulf of Mexico most likely be described?

F. cold and dry
G. cold and moist
H. warm and dry
J. warm and moist

Inquiry Skills

17. You **observe** clouds forming on a warm, sunny day. What can you **infer** is happening in the atmosphere? What may happen later in the day?

18. Suppose you plan to **measure** weather conditions over the next week. What will you measure, and what equipment will help you?

Critical Thinking

19. Look at the weather map below. Describe the weather in Miami.

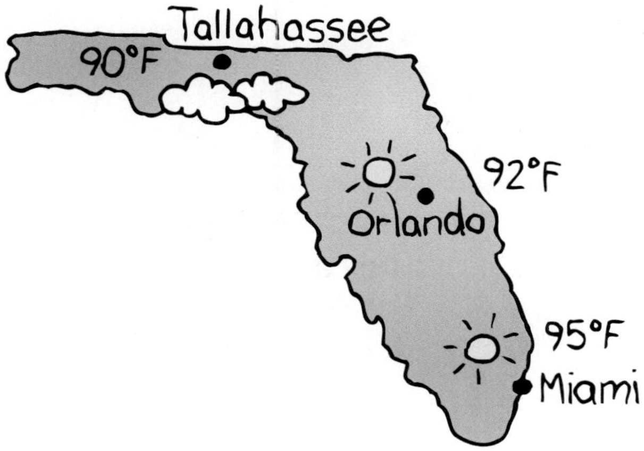

20. Tonya watches the weather report every day for a week. Each day, the average temperature is the same, and the air pressure doesn't change. Explain what might be happening to cause the weather in Tonya's town. How would the weather change if a warm front came through the area?

The Big Idea

CHAPTER 10

Planets and Other Objects in Space

What's the Big Idea?

Objects in space, including Earth and its moon, move in regular and observable patterns.

Essential Questions

Lesson 1
How Do Earth and Its Moon Move?

Lesson 2
How Do Objects Move in the Solar System?

Lesson 3
What Other Objects Can Be Seen in the Sky?

Go online Student eBook www.hspscience.com

Stars in the night sky

What do YOU wonder?

Stars like sand? On a clear night, away from city lights, about 3000 stars are visible. The stars seem to move with the seasons through the night sky. How does this relate to the **Big Idea?**

LESSON 1

Essential Question

How Do Earth and Its Moon Move?

Investigate sunlight and the seasons.

Read and Learn about how Earth and its moon move.

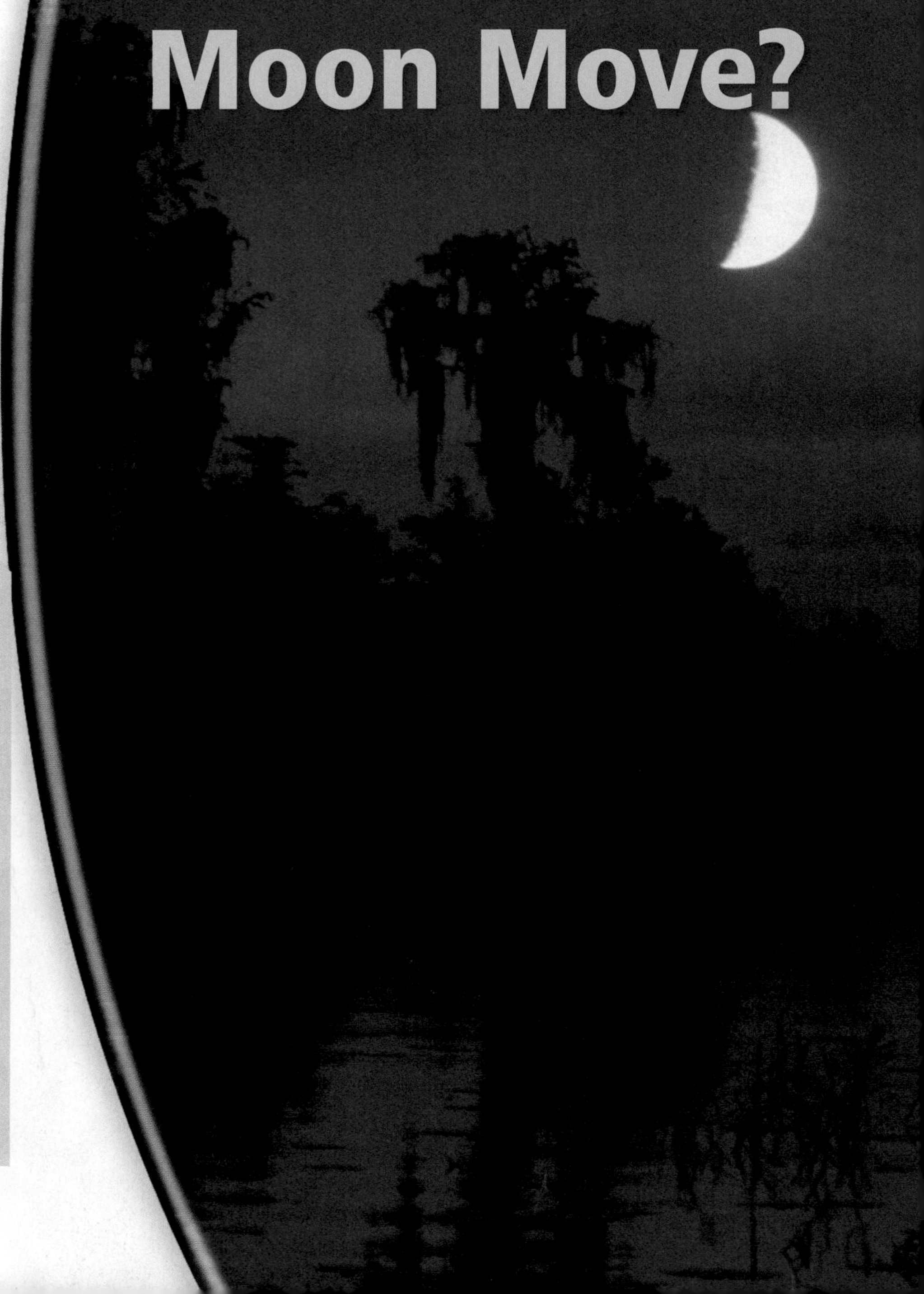

Fast Fact

Sun, Moon, and Myths

To the ancient Romans, Diana was the goddess of the moon. They honored Apollo as the sun god. The ancient Romans believed that their gods caused day and night and brought about changes in weather and seasons. In the Investigate, you will learn more about what really causes the seasons on Earth.

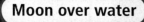

Moon over water

Vocabulary Preview

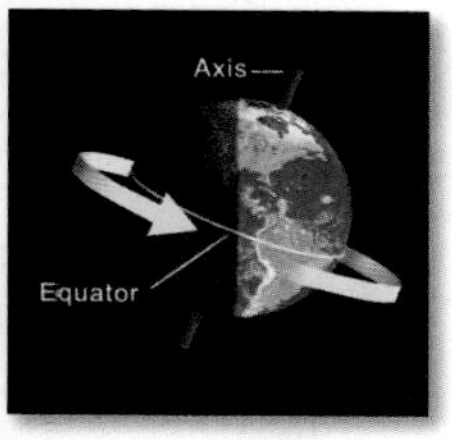

axis [AK•sis] The imaginary line that Earth spins around as it rotates (p. 410)

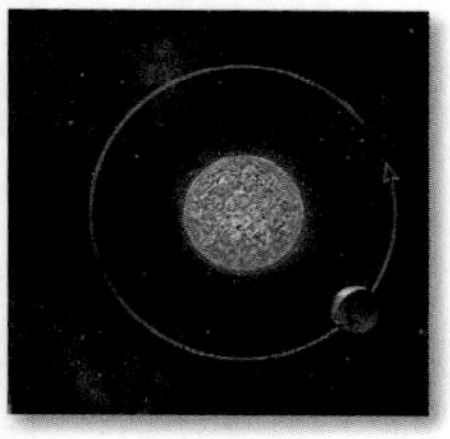

orbit [AWR•bit] The path of one object in space around another object (p. 410)

telescope [TEL•uh•skohp] A device people use to observe distant objects with their eyes (p. 412)

moon [MOON] Any natural body that revolves around a planet (p. 414)

phases [FAYZ•uhz] The different shapes that Earth's moon seems to have (p. 414)

Investigate

Seasons and Sunlight

Guided Inquiry

Start with Questions

The sun moves through the sky throughout the day.

- Is the sun moving around Earth?
- Does the sun move in a regular pattern in the sky?

Investigate to find out. Then read to find out more.

Prepare to Investigate

Inquiry Skill Tip

Some things are harder to measure than others. When using the thermometer, read the temperatures precisely.

Materials

- small 60-W table lamp
- ruler
- graph paper
- black construction paper
- thermometer

Make an Observation Chart

Step	Lamp Angle	Temperature
1	straight down	
2	tilted	

Follow This Procedure

1. Work with a partner. Shine the lamp straight down from a height of 30 cm onto a sheet of graph paper. Draw an outline of the lit area, and label it Step 1.
2. Repeat Step 1 with a new sheet of graph paper, this time placing the lamp at an angle. Label this outline Step 2.
3. Shine the lamp straight onto a sheet of black paper. After 15 minutes, **measure** the temperature of the paper in the lit area. **Record** the temperature on the sheet of graph paper labeled Step 1.
4. Now use another sheet of black paper, and angle the light as you did in Step 2. Again, **measure** the temperature of the lit area after 15 minutes. **Record** the temperature on the sheet of graph paper labeled Step 2.

Draw Conclusions

1. How did the area covered by the light change? How did the temperature in that area change? Explain why these changes occurred.
2. **Inquiry Skill** How could scientists **measure** the effect that the sun has on seasons?

Independent Inquiry

Try your experiment on the real thing! Choose a sunny spot outdoors, and measure and record its temperature throughout the day. Why does it change?

Read and Learn

VOCABULARY
axis p. 410
orbit p. 410
telescope p. 412
moon p. 414
phases p. 414

SCIENCE CONCEPTS
- why there are seasons on Earth
- why the moon appears to change shape

Focus Skill **SEQUENCE**
Events in a sequence happen in a certain order.

Earth's Tilt and the Seasons

Night follows day. Spring follows winter. The changes of night and day, as well as the seasons, occur because of the ways Earth moves.

Earth moves in two ways. Earth rotates, or spins, on its axis. An **axis** is an imaginary line through both poles. It takes about 24 hours for Earth to completely rotate on its axis. The second way Earth moves is by revolving, or following a path, around the sun. The path of one object in space around another object is its **orbit**.

As Earth revolves around the sun, part of it is tilted toward the sun. That part of Earth takes in more energy from the sun. This energy is in the form of heat. The part of Earth that is tilted away from the sun takes in less energy from the sun.

In this illustration, the sun's rays shine more directly on the Northern Hemisphere than on the Southern Hemisphere because of Earth's tilt. So the Northern Hemisphere has summer.

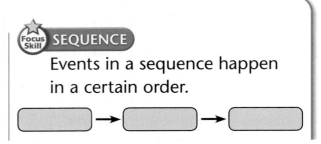

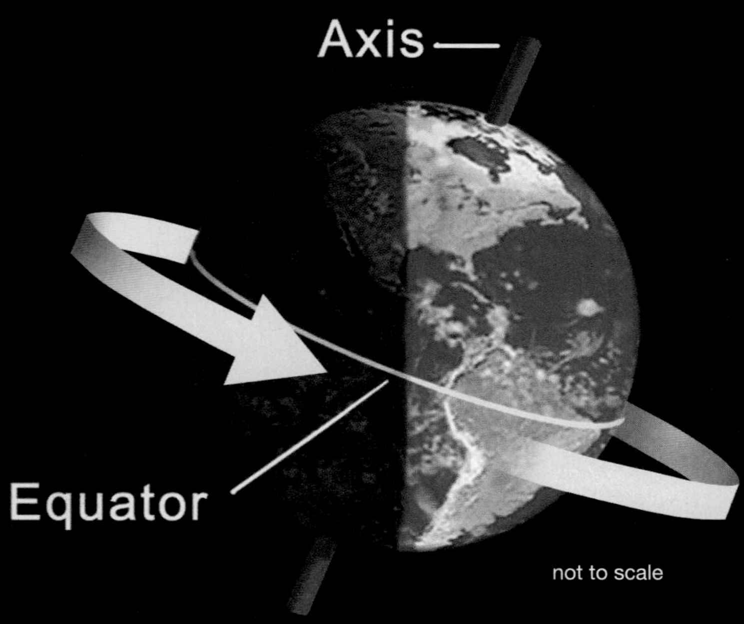

1 The summer *solstice* (SAHL•stis), about June 21 in the Northern Hemisphere, is the day of the year that has the most hours of daylight. 3 The winter solstice, about December 21, is the day that has the most hours of darkness.

2 On the autumn *equinox* (EE•kwih•nahks), about September 21, and the 4 spring equinox, about March 21, the hours of daylight and darkness are the same. These dates mark the beginning of autumn and of spring.

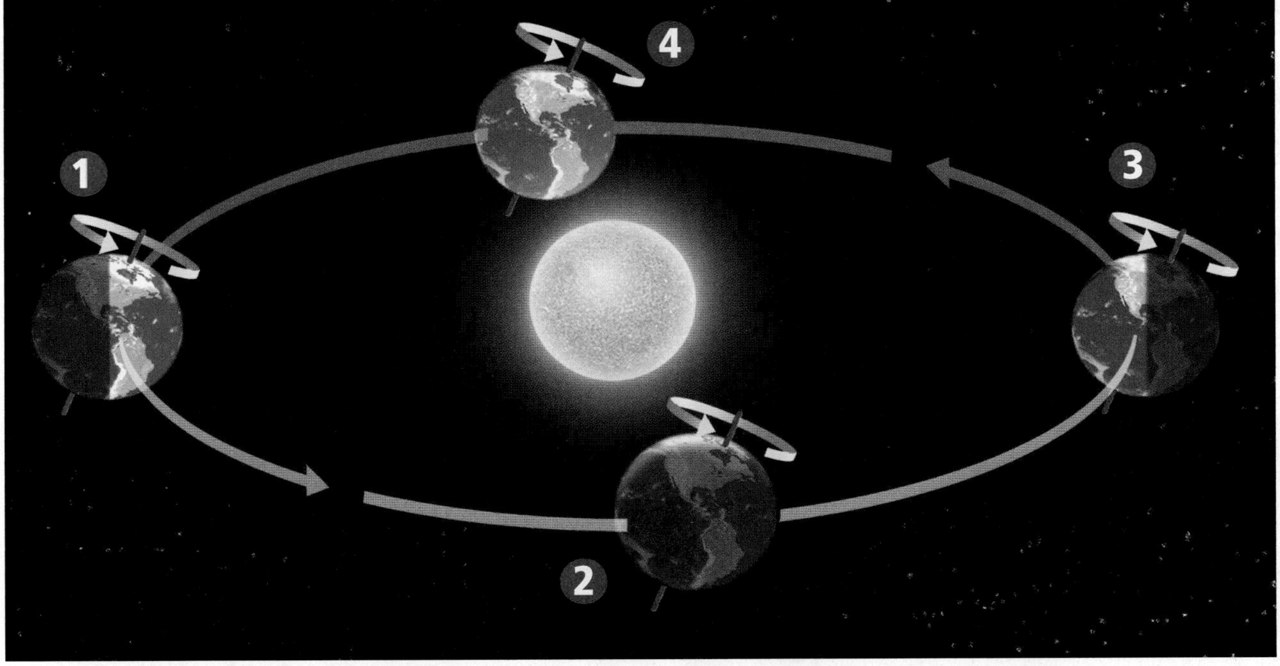

During June, July, and August, the Northern Hemisphere of Earth is tilted toward the sun and the Southern Hemisphere is tilted away. The sun's rays shine more directly on the Northern Hemisphere, which has summer, than on the Southern Hemisphere, which has winter. As Earth continues its orbit, the Northern Hemisphere is tilted away from the sun, causing winter. The Southern Hemisphere is tilted toward it, causing summer. This cycle continues as Earth orbits the sun.

Focus Skill SEQUENCE **What happens next after the Northern Hemisphere has been tilted away from the sun?**

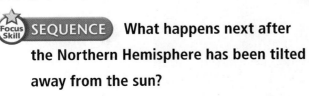

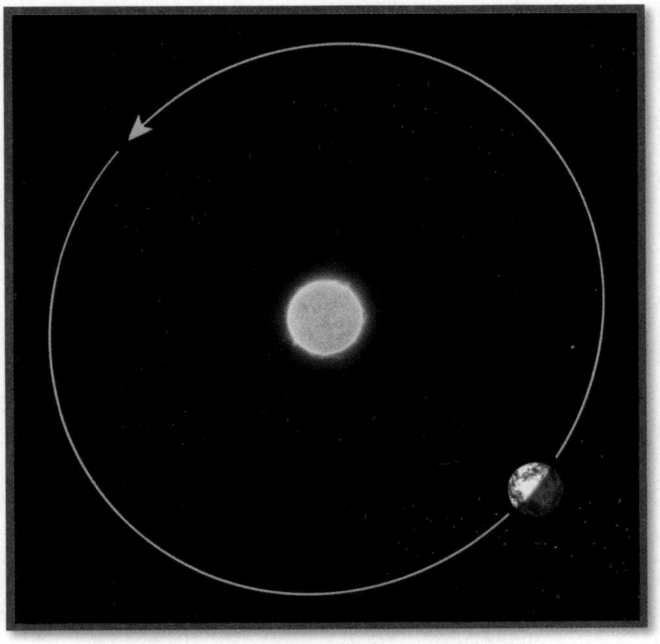

▲ **Earth's orbit around the sun is almost a perfect circle.**

Telescopes

You don't have to be an astronaut to see the moon's surface up close. You could use a telescope. A **telescope** is a tool that makes distant objects look larger.

A *refracting* telescope uses a curved piece of glass, called a lens, to bend light. This makes a distant object seem larger. In 1609, an Italian astronomer named Galileo Galilei was the first person to use this kind of telescope to look at the moon.

In 1668 another scientist, Isaac Newton, invented the *reflecting* telescope. This type of telescope uses mirrors to reflect light and make an object seem larger. The Hubble Space Telescope, launched in 1990, is a reflecting telescope that orbits Earth. It can take clear pictures of objects in our solar system and beyond.

Focus Skill SEQUENCE

Which type of telescope was invented first? When was it first used to see objects in space?

Large telescopes are located in observatories. Smaller telescopes can be used at home.

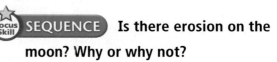

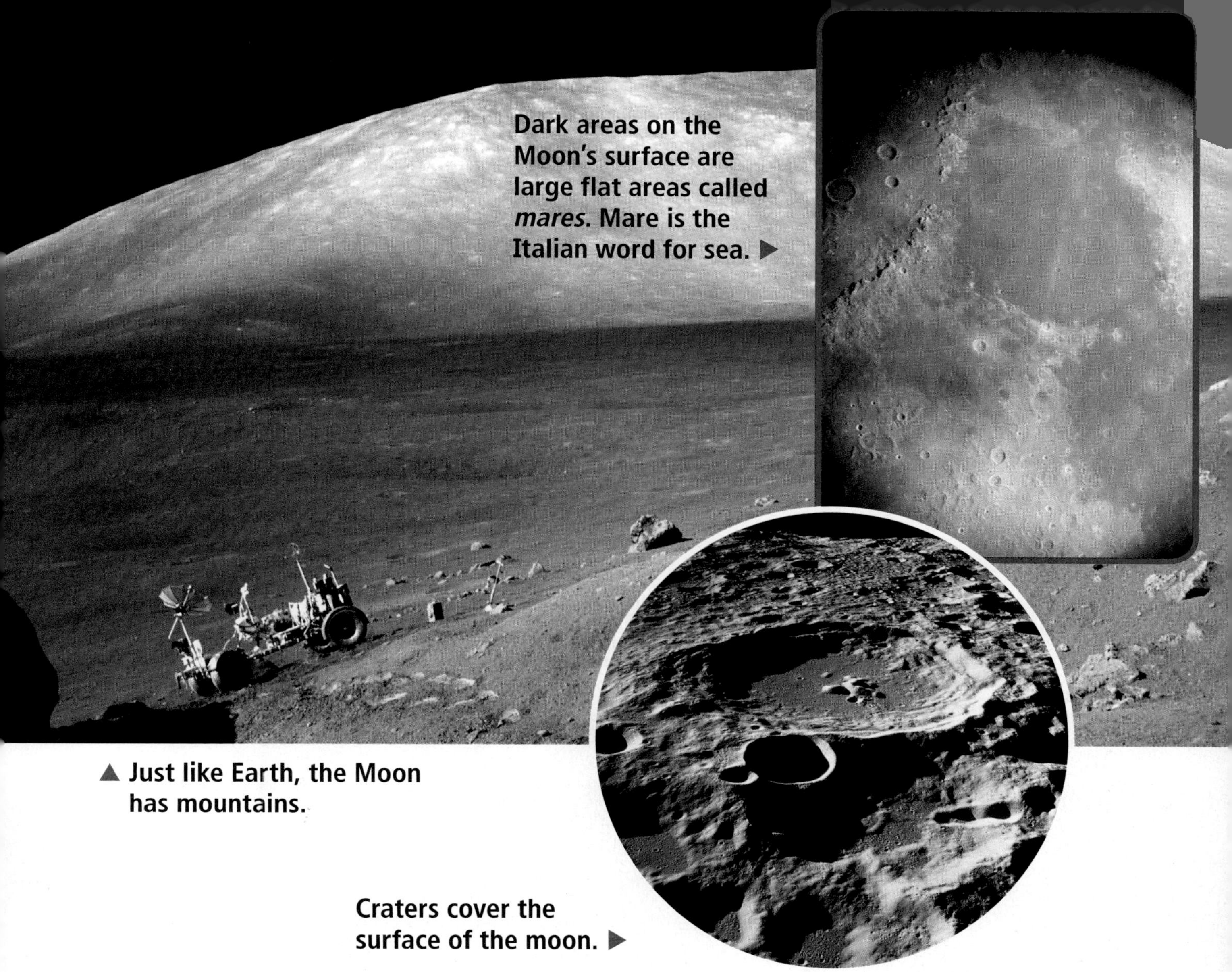

▲ **Just like Earth, the Moon has mountains.**

Dark areas on the Moon's surface are large flat areas called *mares.* Mare is the Italian word for sea. ▶

Craters cover the surface of the moon. ▶

Earth's Moon

Just as Earth orbits the sun, Earth's moon orbits Earth. It may look like a shining disk in the night sky, but up close, it looks very different. It has a rocky, dusty surface. There is no liquid water and very little ice. There are mountains and valleys, flat areas, and areas that are full of hills.

Unlike Earth, which has a thick layer of air around it, the moon has almost no atmosphere. When rocks from space enter Earth's atmosphere, they often burn up before they hit the ground. The moon does not have this protection. Its surface is covered with craters. Craters are low areas with high rims that form when rocks and other objects crash into the moon. There is no water to wear the rims down, so these craters last for a long time.

Focus Skill SEQUENCE **Is there erosion on the moon? Why or why not?**

Moon Phases

The **moon** is a small planetlike body that revolves around Earth, instead of the sun. As Earth revolves around the sun, the moon revolves around Earth.

The moon seems to shine, but the light you see is actually reflected light from the sun. As the moon revolves around Earth, different amounts of its lit surface can be seen. That's why the moon seems to have different shapes, or **phases**.

The phases of the moon follow the same pattern about every $29\frac{1}{2}$ days. On one of those days, all of the lit side of the moon can be seen from Earth. When this happens, we say there is a full moon. Then, as the days pass and the position of the moon changes, from Earth we see less of the lit side. Finally, we see none of the lit side at all. On that night, the moon is called a new moon.

Focus Skill SEQUENCE

What phase of the moon happens after we see less and less of the moon at night?

During the first half of the moon's cycle, the amount of the lit side of the moon seen from Earth *waxes,* or increases.

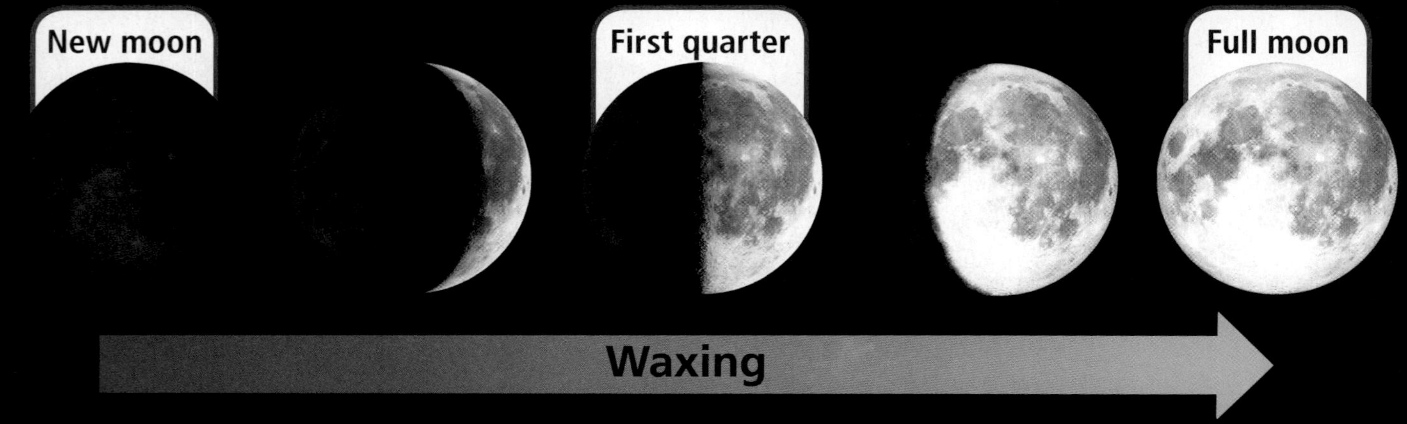

During the second half of the moon's cycle, the amount of the lit side of the moon seen from Earth *wanes,* or decreases. Then the cycle begins again.

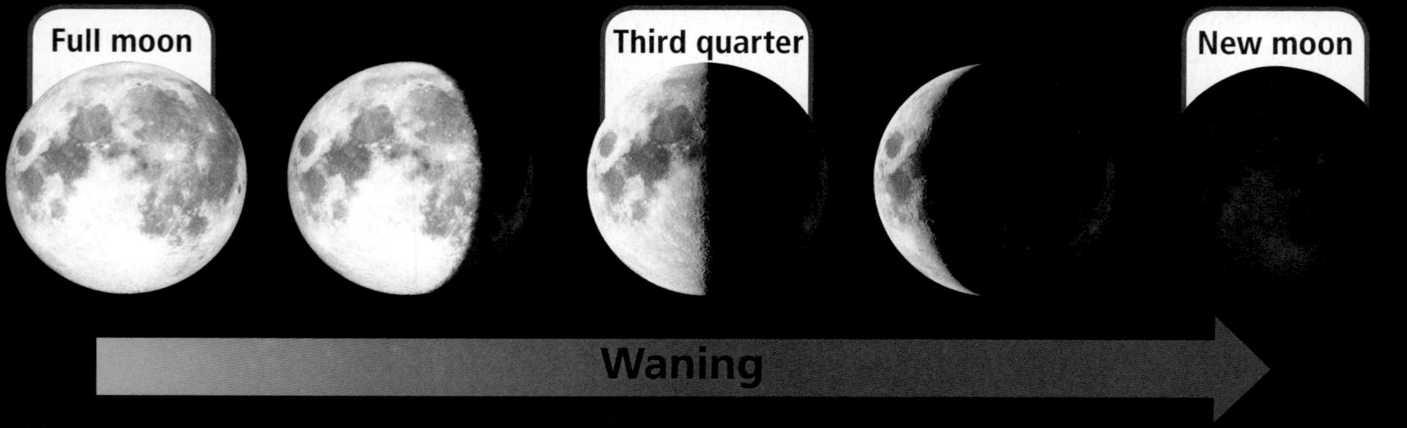

Science Up Close

For more links and animations, go to **www.hspscience.com**

One half of the moon is always being lit by the sun. Whether people can see all, some, or none of the lit side depends on the positions of the moon and Earth.
During the new moon phase, the lit side of the moon can't be seen from Earth.
The full moon phase occurs about 15 days after the new moon phase.

New Moon To Full Moon

When the moon's orbit brings it between Earth and the sun, its lit side can't be seen from Earth. This phase is called the new moon. Later in the month, when Earth is between the moon and the sun, we see the sun's light reflected from one whole side of the moon. When this happens, we see a full moon.

Insta-Lab

Sun, Moon, and Earth

Model the moon phases in a dark room. Use a flashlight for your "sun" and two balls for your "moon" and "Earth." Shine the sun toward Earth, and move the moon around Earth. What causes changes in how much of the moon's lit side can be seen from Earth?

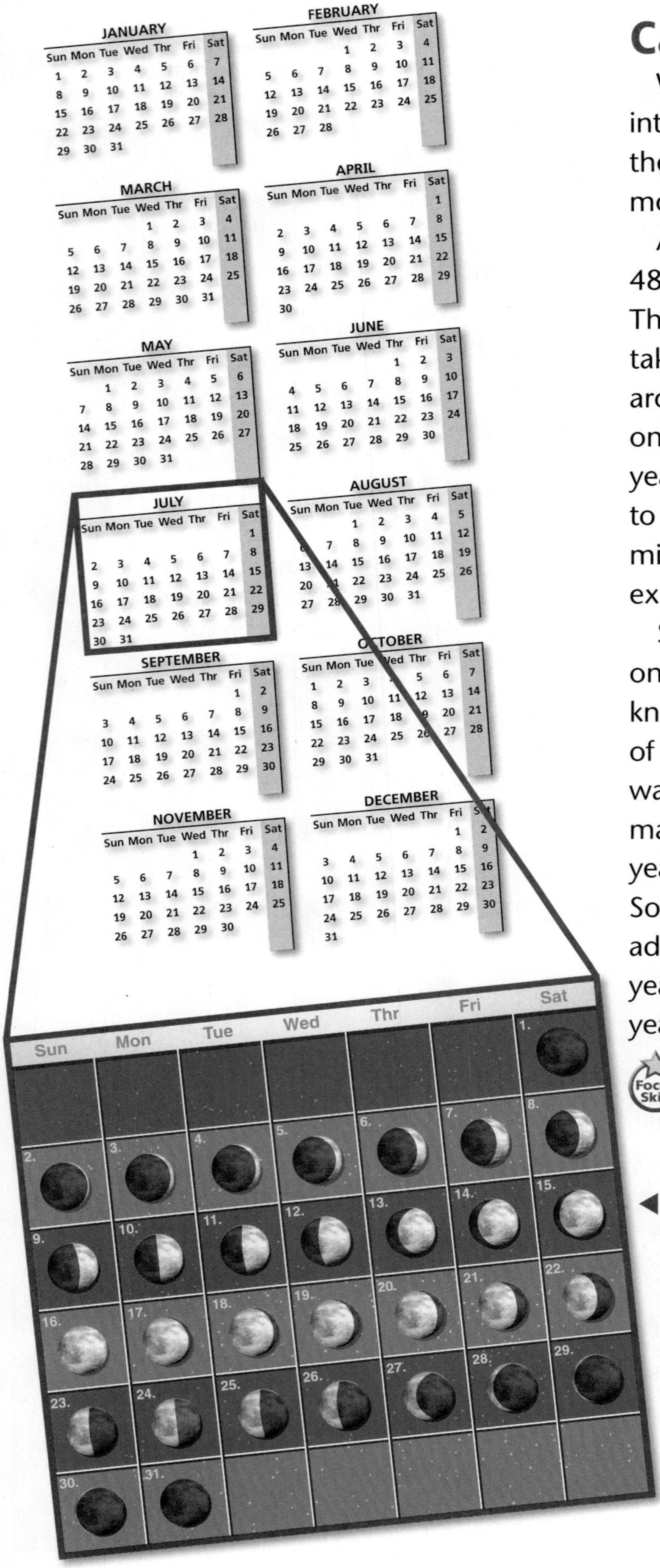

Calendars

We use calendars to divide time into days, months, and years. All of these units of time are based on the movements of Earth.

A solar year is 365 days, 5 hours, 48 minutes, and $45\frac{1}{2}$ seconds long. This is based on the amount of time it takes Earth to make one complete orbit around the sun. Today's calendars have only 365 days in a year. So every four years, an extra day is added in February to make up for the extra hours and minutes in a solar year. Years with an extra day are called leap years.

Some ancient people based months on the movements of the moon. They knew that the moon completes a cycle of phases in about $29\frac{1}{2}$ days. Each cycle was considered a month, and 12 months made a lunar year. However, a lunar year is $11\frac{1}{2}$ days shorter than a solar year. Some cultures that use lunar calendars add a month to their calendar every few years to make up for the shorter lunar year.

Focus Skill **SEQUENCE** **What occurs after three years have 365 days each?**

◀ **Most calendars are based on the solar year. Many also show the phases of the moon, which don't happen on the same day each month.**

Essential Question

How Do Earth and Its Moon Move?

In this lesson, you learned that Earth moves in a regular path through space. This movement and the tilt of Earth cause seasons. Earth rotates around its axis, which causes day and night. The moon also moves through space, around Earth. This movement causes the phases of the moon.

1. Focus Skill **SEQUENCE** Draw and complete a graphic organizer that shows the phases of the moon.

2. **SUMMARIZE** Write a summary of this lesson. Begin with this sentence: *The sun seems to move through Earth's sky.*

3. **DRAW CONCLUSIONS** If Earth took 500 days instead of 365 to orbit the sun, how would the seasons be different? Why?

4. **VOCABULARY** Use *axis* in a sentence that explains its meaning.

Test Prep

5. **CRITICAL THINKING** How would day and night be different if Earth's axis were not tilted?

6. If you live in the Southern Hemisphere, what season do you have in August?
   A. spring
   B. summer
   C. fall
   D. winter

Make Connections

Writing

Expository Writing

Suppose a friend from the Southern Hemisphere plans to visit you in December. Write a **letter** explaining what kind of clothes to pack and why.

Math

Use Data

A normal year has 365 days. In a normal year, on average, how many days are in a month? How many days, on average, are there in each season?

Social Studies

Different Calendars

Research and report on a calendar other than the one you use. It can be an ancient calendar or one that is used today in a different part of the world.

LESSON 2

Essential Question

How Do Objects Move in the Solar System?

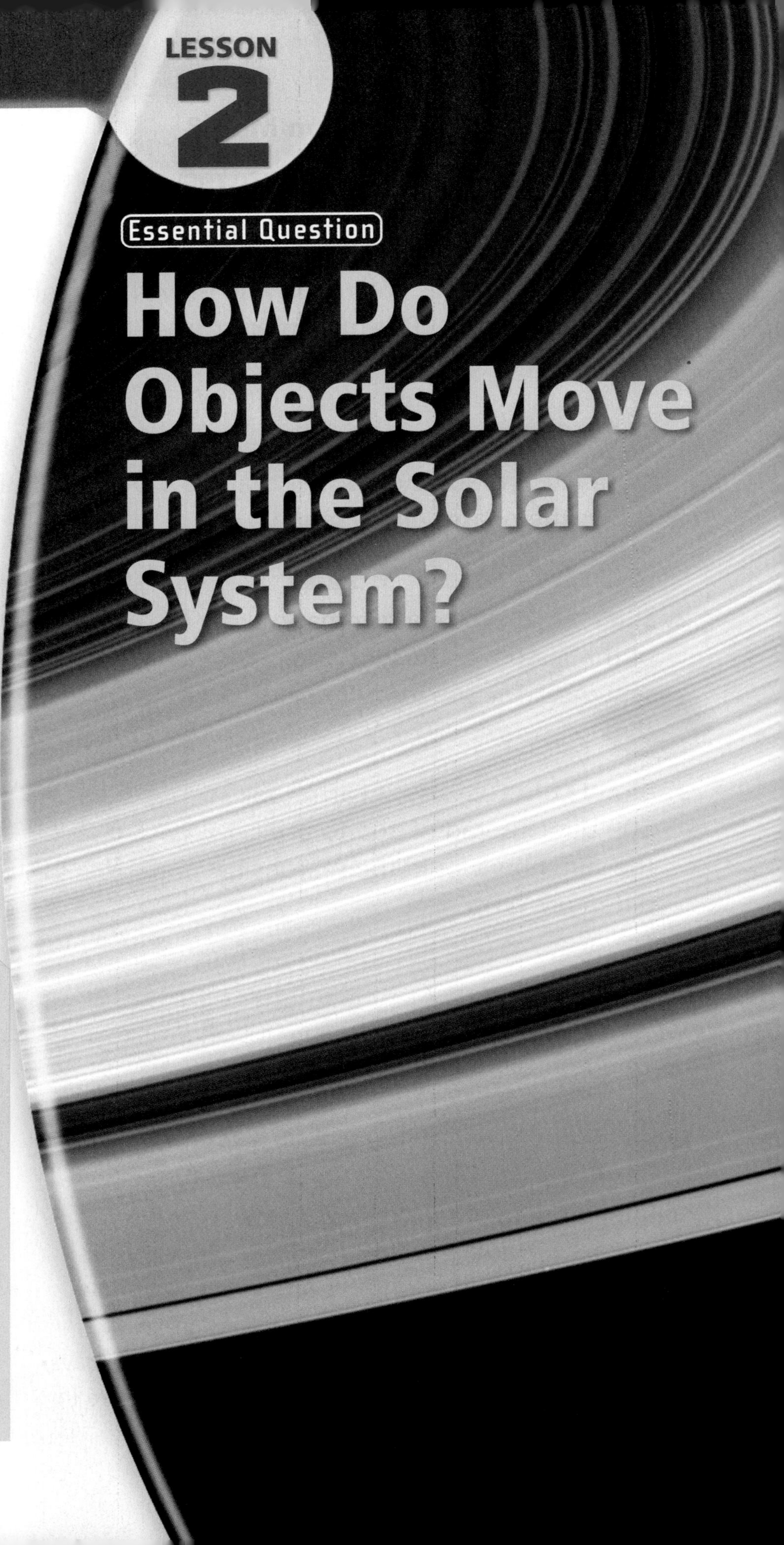

Investigate the distance between planets.

Read and Learn how objects in the solar system move.

Fast Fact

Rings Around a Planet

Saturn's rings have fascinated sky gazers since the astronomer Galileo (gal•uh•LAY•oh) first saw them in 1610. We've learned that the rings are made of rock, gas, and ice. Saturn is millions of kilometers from Earth. In the Investigate, you will make a model to help you understand that distance.

The rings of Saturn

Vocabulary Preview

solar system [SOH•ler SIS•tuhm] A group of objects in space that revolve around a central star (p. 422)

planet [PLAN•it] A large object that moves around a star (p. 422)

comet [KAHM•it] A ball of rock, ice, and frozen gases in space (p. 426)

Distances Between Planets

Guided Inquiry

Start with Questions

This child is looking through a telescope. Telescopes help people examine the objects in our solar system.

- How much detail can a telescope show?
- Do more powerful telescopes show more detail?

Investigate to find out. Then read to find out more.

Prepare to Investigate

Inquiry Skill Tip

Some distances are so large that calculations with them are tricky. Using numbers that are smaller instead of real distances will make your calculations simpler.

Materials

- 4-m length of string
- 9 markers of different colors
- tape measure

Make a Data Table

Planet Data				
Planet	Distance from Sun (km)	Distance from Sun (AU)	Scale Distance (cm)	Planet's Diameter (km)
Mercury	58 million	$\frac{4}{10}$	4	4876
Venus	108 million	$\frac{7}{10}$	7	12,104
Earth	150 million	1		12,756
Mars	228 million	2		6794
Jupiter	778 million	5		142,984
Saturn	1429 million	10		120,536
Uranus	2871 million	19		51,118
Neptune	4500 million	30		49,532
Pluto*	5900 million	39		2274

*In 2006, scientists classified Pluto as a "dwarf planet."

Follow This Procedure

1. Copy the table.
2. At one end of the string, make a large knot. This knot will stand for the sun as you make your model.
3. An AU (astronomical unit) is Earth's average distance from the sun. In your model, 10 cm will represent 1 AU. Use a tape measure to measure Earth's distance from the knot that represents the sun. Use a marker to mark this point on the string. Record on the table which color you used for Earth by placing a small dot with the marker next to the planet name.
4. Complete the Scale Distance column of the table. Repeat Step 3 for each planet. Use a different color for each planet.

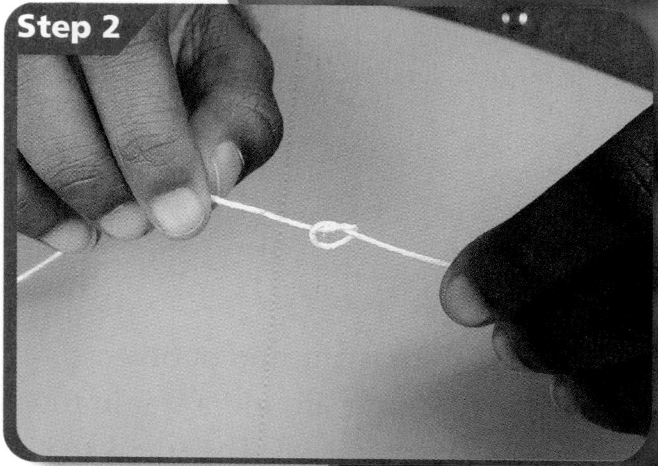

Step 2

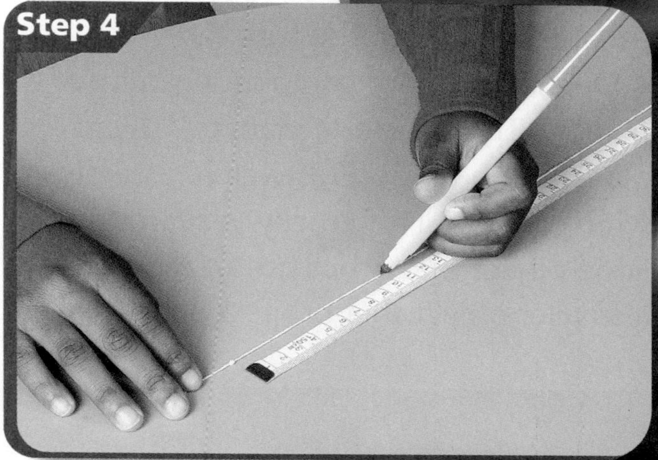

Step 4

Draw Conclusions

1. In your model, how far away from the sun is Mercury? How far away is Pluto?
2. Why do scientists use AUs to measure distances in the solar system?
3. **Inquiry Skill** How does it help to use numbers instead of using real distances?

Independent Inquiry

Use a calculator to make a model of planet diameters. Use 1 cm to represent Earth's diameter. Then divide the other planets' diameters by Earth's. Make a scale drawing.

Read and Learn

VOCABULARY
solar system p. 422
planet p. 422
comet p. 426

SCIENCE CONCEPTS
- what makes up our solar system
- what the inner and outer planets are

Focus Skill COMPARE AND CONTRAST

Look for phrases such as by contrast and in common.

alike — different

Our Solar System

A **solar system** is a group of objects in space that revolve around a star in the center, plus the star itself. The sun is the star in the center of our solar system. Everything else in the solar system is small compared to the sun.

Our solar system contains a variety of objects. These include planets, "dwarf planets," and moons as well as asteroids, which are small and rocky. A **planet** is a large object that orbits a star. A moon is a smaller object that orbits a planet.

In our solar system, there are eight planets. Often, scientists group them as the inner planets, which are closer to the sun, and the outer planets, which are farther from the sun. These groups of planets are separated by a ring of asteroids that orbit the sun between Mars and Jupiter.

Focus Skill COMPARE AND CONTRAST

How are moons and planets similar and different?

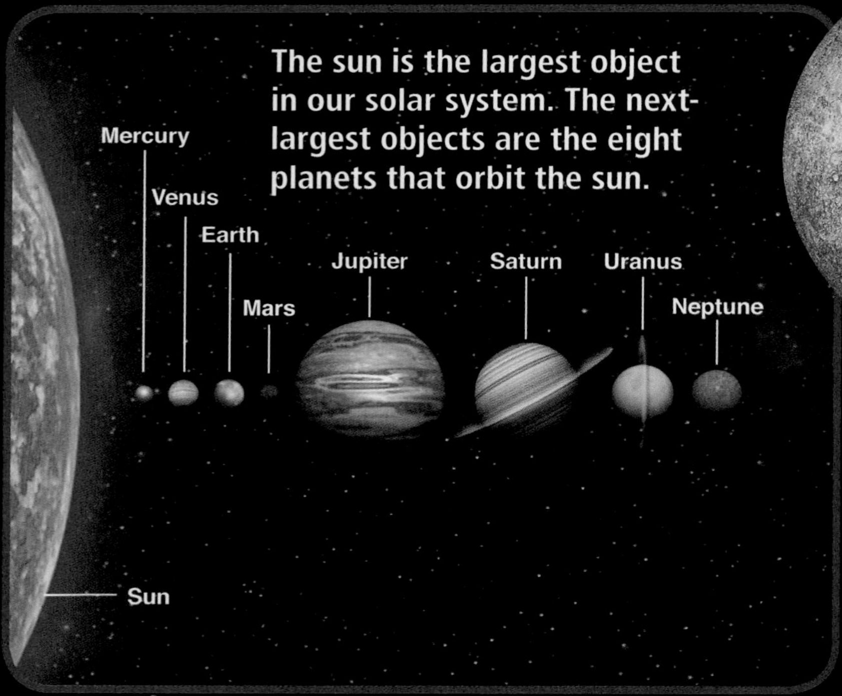

The sun is the largest object in our solar system. The next-largest objects are the eight planets that orbit the sun.

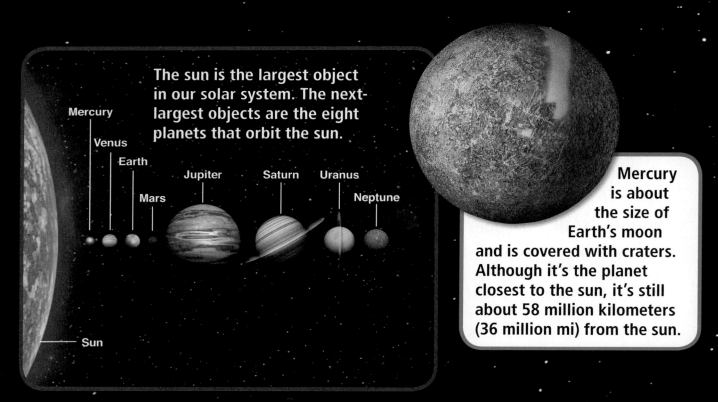

Mercury is about the size of Earth's moon and is covered with craters. Although it's the planet closest to the sun, it's still about 58 million kilometers (36 million mi) from the sun.

The Inner Planets

The inner planets are those closest to the sun. They are Mercury, Venus, Earth, and Mars. These planets are alike in many ways. They all have rocky surfaces and are smaller than most of the outer planets. Also, none of the inner planets has more than two moons.

There are also differences among the inner planets. For example, it can be 450°C on Mercury—hot enough to melt lead—while Mars's temperature never gets higher than 20°C.

Earth is the most unusual inner planet. Only Earth has liquid water on its surface and a large amount of oxygen in the atmosphere. This water and oxygen help support life on Earth.

Focus Skill COMPARE AND CONTRAST

How are the inner planets similar?

Mars is called the Red Planet because it looks fiery red from Earth. Mars is small—its diameter is only half of Earth's. It has huge dust storms that can last for months. Scientists think that at one time, Mars may have had liquid surface water.

Venus is about the same size as Earth. Venus is the third-brightest object in Earth's sky—only the sun and the moon appear brighter. Clouds of sulfuric (suhl•FYUR•ik) acid make the planet difficult to study from Earth. This radar image shows a surface made up of volcanoes, mountain ranges, highland regions, craters, and lava plains.

Earth is the largest of the inner planets. It's the only planet known to have life and the only one whose surface is mostly water. Earth's distance from the sun helps the planet maintain a temperature that supports life.

The Outer Planets and Pluto

Beyond Mars, on the far side of the asteroid belt, are the outer planets. They are Jupiter, Saturn, Uranus, and Neptune.

The outer planets have many similarities. These four planets are huge and made mostly of gases. These planets are often called the gas giants. They all have many moons, and they all are surrounded by rings that are made of dust, ice, or rock.

Pluto is unlike the outer planets. For almost 80 years Pluto was listed as the ninth planet in the solar system. In 2006, scientists met to form a new definition of a planet. They decided that a planet is a large round object in a clear orbit around a star. Because Pluto is not in a clear orbit, scientists removed it from the list of planets. They classified it as a "dwarf planet."

Focus Skill COMPARE AND CONTRAST

How is Uranus different from the other outer planets?

Jupiter—the largest planet in our solar system—has a diameter that's more than 11 times the diameter of Earth. Jupiter has at least 63 moons. For more than 300 years, a gigantic hurricane-like storm called the Great Red Spot has raged on Jupiter.

Saturn has rings that are visible from Earth through a telescope. Saturn has at least 31 moons. Its atmosphere is mostly hydrogen and helium. Like the other gas giants, Saturn has no known solid surface.

Math in Science
Interpret Data

Length of a Year

On any planet, a year is the length of time it takes that planet to orbit the sun. Here is a list of how long a year is on some planets in our solar system, compared to a year on Earth.

Planet Years

Planet	Length of Year (in Earth years)
Mars	1.9
Jupiter	11.9
Saturn	29.5
Neptune	165
Pluto*	249

*In 2006, scientists classified Pluto as a "dwarf planet."

If a person has just turned 60 on Earth, about how old is he or she in Saturn years?

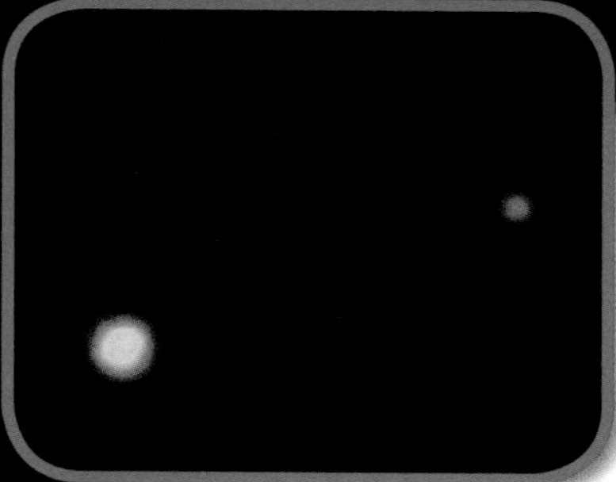

Pluto, a "dwarf planet," has a rocky core covered with nitrogen ice and small amounts of methane and carbon dioxide ices. Its atmosphere is mostly nitrogen. Pluto's largest moon is almost as large as Pluto itself. From the surface of Pluto, the sun looks like any other bright star in the sky.

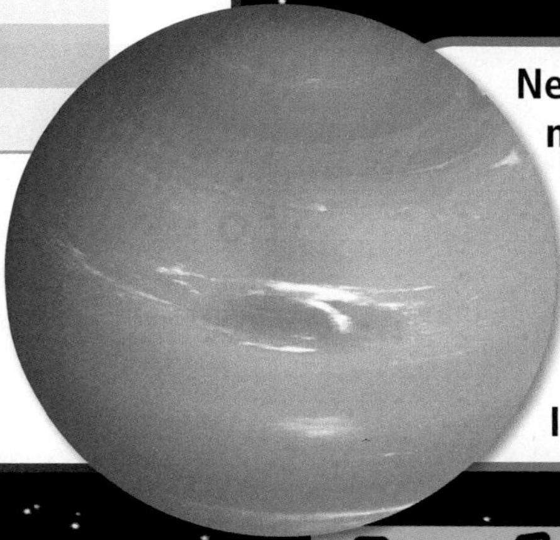

Neptune's atmosphere is mainly hydrogen and helium. It is one of the windiest places in the solar system. Winds can reach 2000 kilometers per hour (1200 mi/hr). Neptune has at least 13 moons.

Uranus is another gas giant. Uranus rotates on its side as it orbits the sun. Scientists think this may be the result of a collision with an object the size of Earth. Uranus has at least 27 moons.

Insta-Lab

Planet Sizes

Compare the approximate sizes of planets. Use a marble to represent Mercury, a table tennis ball to represent Earth, and a basketball to represent Jupiter. Which of the three balls would best represent the size of Venus?

Other Objects in the Solar System

There are objects besides planets orbiting the sun. Two types of such objects are asteroids and comets. Although both revolve around the sun, comets and asteroids are very different.

Asteroids are bits of rock and metal. Most are less than 1 kilometer (0.6 mi) across. The largest asteroid is about 1000 kilometers (620 mi) in diameter. Most asteroids revolve around the sun in a belt between Mars and Jupiter.

By contrast, a **comet** is a ball of rock, ice, and frozen gases. Most comets are less than 10 kilometers (6 mi) across, but the tails can be as much as 100,000 kilometers (62,000 mi) long. As a comet's orbit brings it close to the sun, the sun's heat may turn some of the frozen matter into gas. That gas, and dust that rises with it, then looks like a fiery tail and may be visible from Earth.

Focus Skill COMPARE AND CONTRAST

What do comets and asteroids have in common?

Some comets, like Halley's comet, become well known because their orbits bring them close to Earth.

◀ This is the asteroid Gaspra. Asteroids are harder to see from Earth than comets. A 1991 space probe took the first close-up pictures of an asteroid.

Lesson Review

Essential Question

How Do Objects Move in the Solar System?

In this lesson, you learned that our solar system is made up of the objects that revolve around our sun. Our solar system includes the inner planets, the outer planets, and other objects.

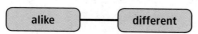

1. **Focus Skill COMPARE AND CONTRAST** Draw and complete a graphic organizer to compare and contrast the inner planets and outer planets.

alike	different

2. **SUMMARIZE** Write a summary of this lesson. Begin with this sentence: *Mercury is the planet closest to the sun.*

3. **DRAW CONCLUSIONS** Why hasn't life been found on any of the other planets in the solar system?

4. **VOCABULARY** Write a definition for *solar system.*

Test Prep

5. **CRITICAL THINKING** Suppose you look into the sky and see a comet. What can you conclude about the comet?

6. What separates the inner planets from the outer planets?
   A. asteroid belt
   B. comets
   C. Earth
   D. Venus

Make Connections

Writing

Expository Writing

Research a planet other than Earth. Write a travel guide that could be used by people who might visit that planet. Tell about the sights they would see or what a typical day might be like.

Math

Solve a Problem

Use the table in the Investigate to find the diameters of the planets in our solar system. Make a bar graph that compares their diameters.

Literature

Ecosystems

Read a short story about life on another planet or about space travel. Decide whether the story could really happen. Report to the class on what you read.

LESSON 3

Essential Question

What Other Objects Can Be Seen in the Sky?

Investigate how constellations appear in the sky.

Read and Learn about other stars and objects in the sky.

Fast Fact

Deep Space

Images from the Hubble Space Telescope show distant objects in detail. They show space objects, such as the Omega Nebula, that are very far from Earth. In the Investigate, you will make your own telescope.

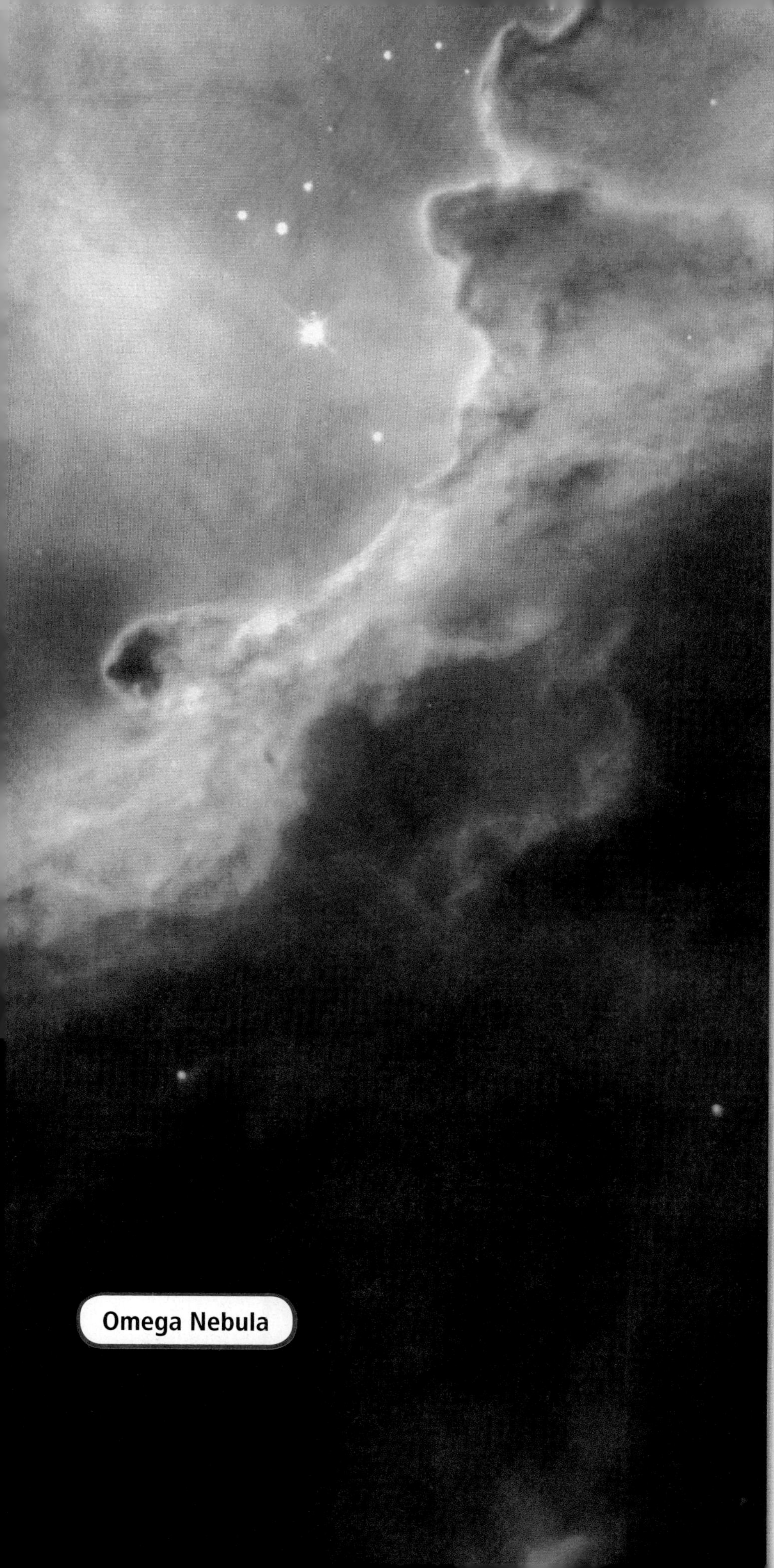

Omega Nebula

Vocabulary Preview

star [STAR] A huge ball of superheated gases (p. 432)

sun [SUHN] The star at the center of our solar system (p. 432)

constellation [kahn•stuh•LAY•shuhn] A pattern of stars that form an imaginary picture or design in the sky (p. 434)

galaxy [GAL•uhk•see] A huge system of many stars, gases, and dust (p. 434)

universe [YOO•nuh•vers] Everything that exists in space (p. 434)

Investigate

Shining Constellations

Guided Inquiry

Start with Questions

Planetariums display constellations indoors, so people can see them clearly.

- What might block a person's view of stars outdoors?
- Why might people have named constellations?

Investigate to find out. Then read to find out more.

Prepare to Investigate

Inquiry Skill Tip

When you plan and conduct a simple investigation, make sure you write your plan down. That way you can check your procedure as you go.

Materials

- black construction paper
- sharp pencil
- reference book of constellations

Make a Data Chart

Constellation	Story

Follow This Procedure

1. Work with your partner to find and research a constellation.
2. Use the pencil to mark the constellation on your sheet of black construction paper.
3. Use the sharp point of your pencil to poke a small hole where you placed each dot for a star.
4. Ask you teacher to place your sheet of construction paper with your constellation on an overhead projector. Ask your classmates to identify the constellation.
5. Explain the story that is related to your constellation. Discuss the constellations that your classmates chose to present. **Record** your information on a chart.

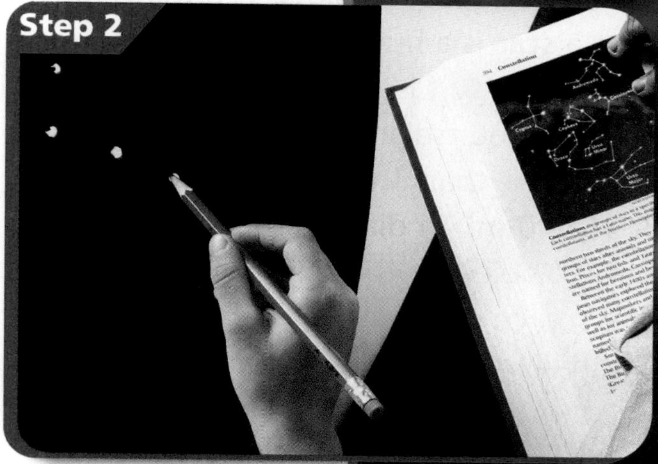

Draw Conclusions

1. What did you observe when your piece of construction paper was placed on the overhead projector?
2. **Inquiry Skill** Navigators used constellations to help them guide ships before there were accurate tools to do so. They observed the movement of the stars in the sky. How would you **plan and conduct a simple investigation** to find out if the appearance of the stars changed with your location?

Independent Inquiry

Find your constellation in the night sky. Observe the movement of the constellation through the sky for a month.

Read and Learn

VOCABULARY
star p. 432
sun p. 432
constellation p. 434
galaxy p. 434
universe p. 434

SCIENCE CONCEPTS
- what stars and galaxies are
- what constellations are

Focus Skill MAIN IDEA AND DETAILS
Look for the details that support each main idea.

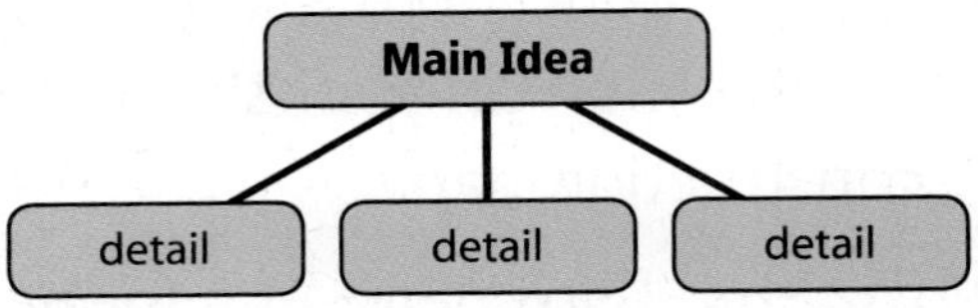

The Sun and Other Stars

You have probably looked up at the stars in the night sky and noticed their different sizes and colors. You may know that a **star** is a huge ball of superheated gases. The **sun** is a star that is at the center of our solar system.

At more than 1 million kilometers (621,000 mi) in diameter, the sun is the largest object in the solar system. It is the source of most of the energy on Earth—without it life could not exist.

From Earth, the sun looks like a ball of light. Like other stars, it is made up of gases, mostly hydrogen and helium.

The sun sometimes has dark spots called sunspots on its surface. They do not give off as much light and heat energy as the rest of the sun's surface. The red streams and loops are solar flares, gases that shoot out from the sun. These hot fountains of gas often begin near a sunspot and extend tens of thousands of kilometers into space. Both sunspots and solar flares last only a few days.

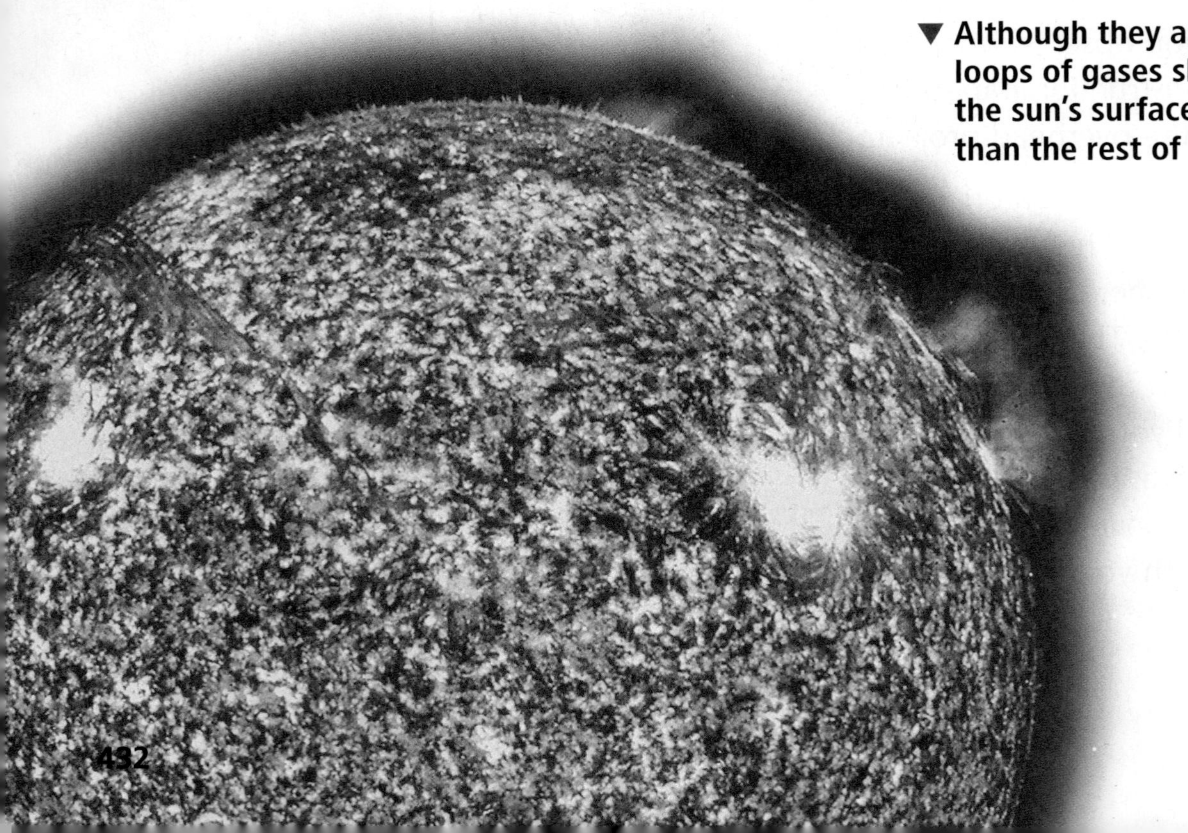

▼ **Although they appear fiery, the loops of gases shooting from the sun's surface are cooler than the rest of the sun.**

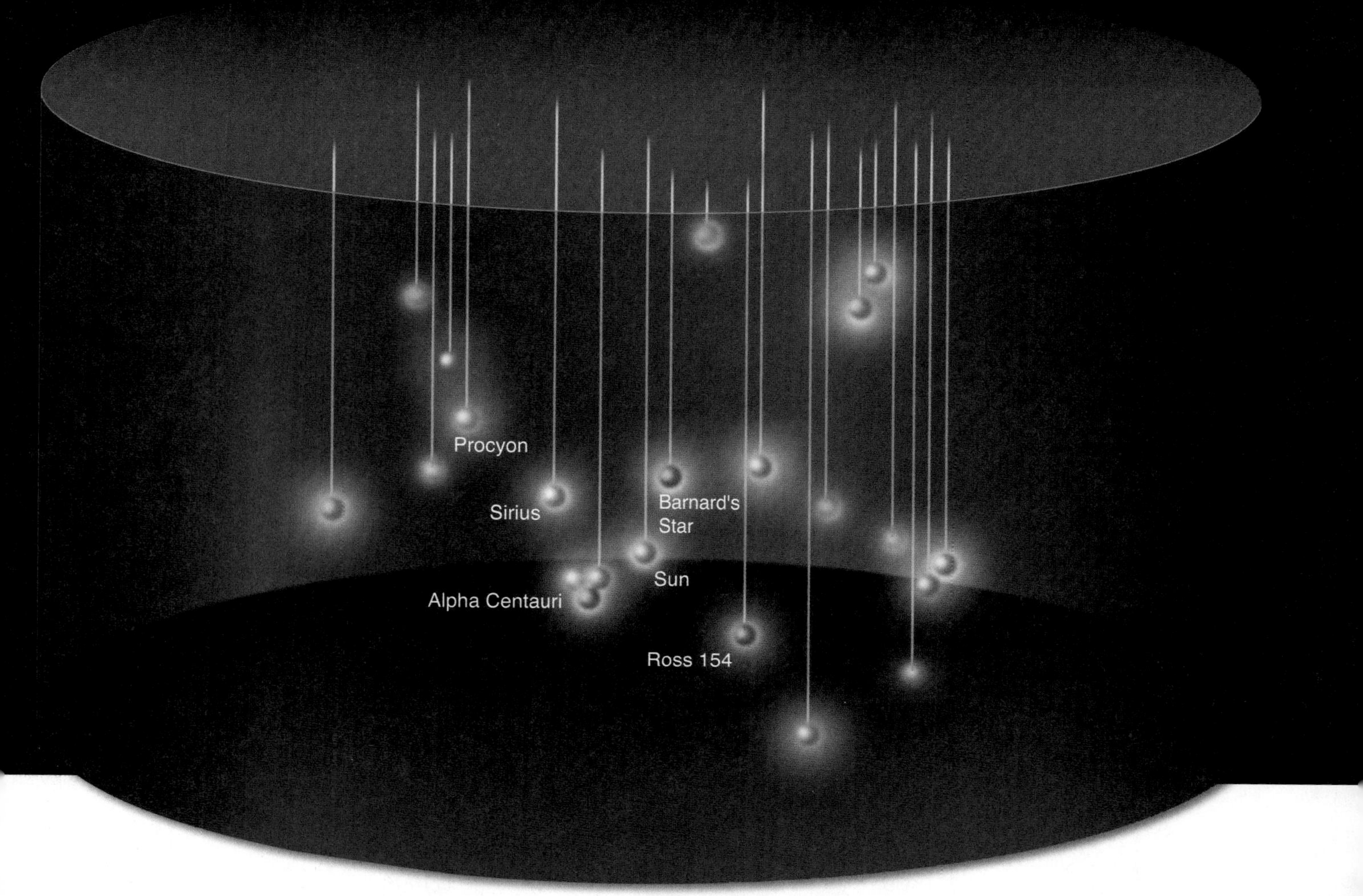

▲ **This map shows the positions of the 20 nearest stars. The three closest to our solar system make up Alpha Centauri (AL•fuh sen•TAW•ry). From Earth, Alpha Centauri looks like one star.**

Stars' colors tell us about the stars' temperatures. Red stars are the coolest and blue the hottest. The sun, a medium-size yellow star, is between the hottest and the coolest.

Stars go through stages. They form from clouds of spinning dust and gas, which gravity squeezes. When the mass is squeezed enough, changes take place that form a star. The mass of the star then begins to change into light and heat. Over billions of years, most of the mass of the star is converted to light and heat.

Focus Skill MAIN IDEA AND DETAILS

What does a star's color tell about the star?

Groups of Stars

Have you ever seen the Big Dipper in the night sky? The Big Dipper belongs to a group of stars called Ursa Major. These stars form a **constellation**, a group of stars that form an imaginary picture in the sky. In ancient times, people often gave names to these imaginary star pictures. Constellations are helpful to people because their patterns serve as landmarks in the night sky. For hundreds of years, sailors have used them to find their way.

Have you seen a bright band of stars on a clear summer night? If so, you were looking at the Milky Way, the galaxy in which our solar system lies. A **galaxy** is a huge system of gases, dust, and stars. Galaxies contain billions of stars. Our sun is on the edge of the Milky Way galaxy. Constellations are made up of stars in our own galaxy. The Milky Way is only one of the millions of galaxies in the universe. The **universe** is everything that exists in space.

There are many galaxy shapes. The Milky Way is a spiral (SPY•ruhl) galaxy. A barred spiral galaxy has two main arms. Some galaxies look like balls or eggs. Other galaxies have no regular shape.

Focus Skill **MAIN IDEA AND DETAILS**

What are two ways in which people classify groups of stars?

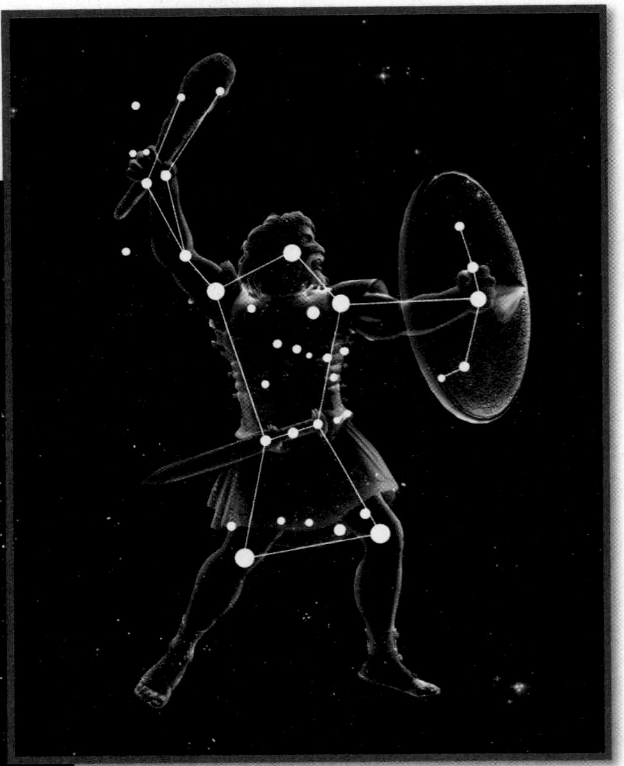

▲ **This is a drawing of Orion, a hunter in Greek myths.**

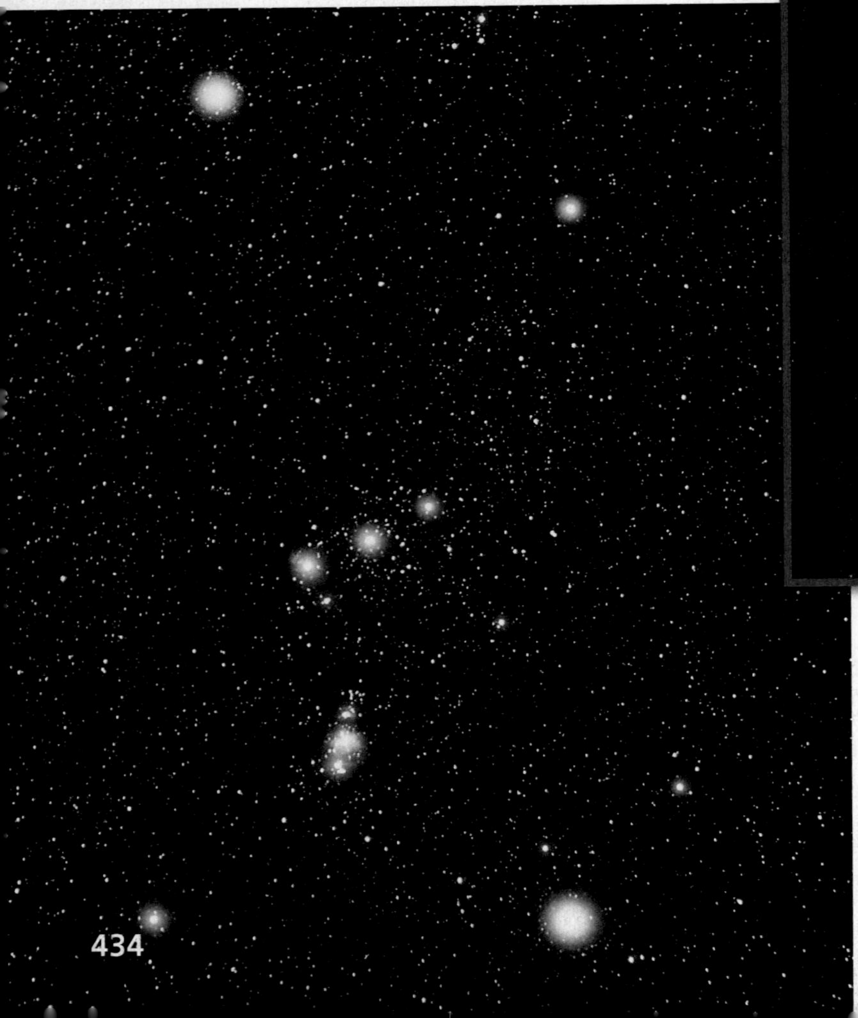

◀ **This is how the constellation Orion appears in the night sky.**

This barred spiral galaxy has two main arms branching out from it.

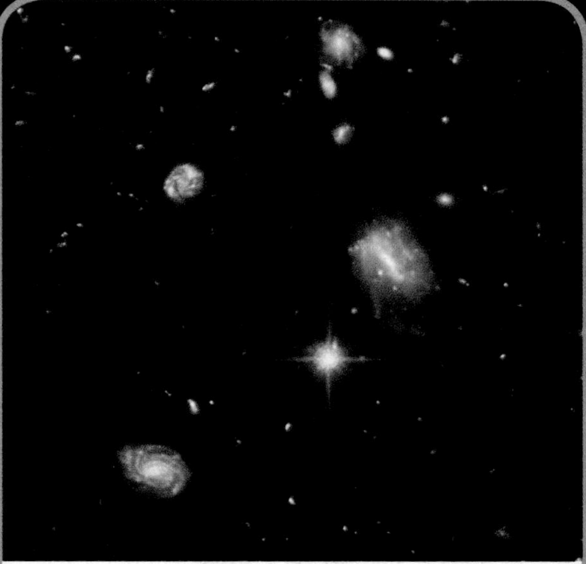

This photo, taken by the Hubble Space Telescope, shows some of the many galaxies in the universe.

Insta-Lab

Make a Constellation Model

Use a pencil point or toothpick to poke a "constellation" in a piece of aluminum foil. Use a rubber band to fasten the foil to the end of a paper towel tube. Look through the tube to see your constellation. Turn the tube while you look through it. What planetary motion are you modeling when you turn the tube?

Seasonal Star Positions

Each day, the sun appears to rise in the east, move across the sky, and set in the west. The same is true for stars at night. However, what is actually moving is Earth.

The positions of the stars appear to change with the seasons, too. In winter, you may see Orion clearly in the night sky. A few months later, Orion may no longer be visible.

This, too, is due to Earth's movement. As Earth revolves around the sun, we see different parts of space at different times of the year.

To see Orion in the same place you saw it last winter, you must wait until next winter. It will be visible again when Earth reaches that part of its orbit of the sun.

Where you live determines the constellations you will see. In the Northern Hemisphere, people see different sets of constellations from those people see in the Southern Hemisphere. People who live near the equator can see some constellations of both hemispheres.

Focus Skill MAIN IDEA AND DETAILS

Explain why constellations seem to change their locations.

◀ While some of the constellations you see change from season to season, others are visible all year round. They simply appear to move through the sky during the course of a night.

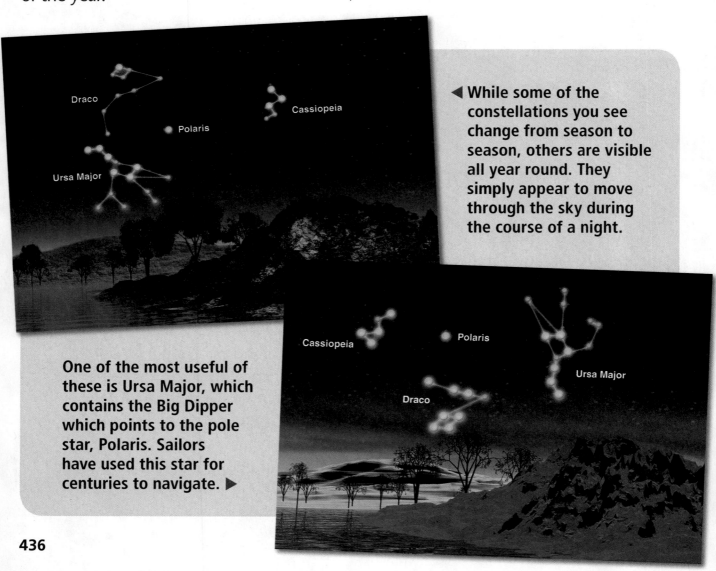

One of the most useful of these is Ursa Major, which contains the Big Dipper which points to the pole star, Polaris. Sailors have used this star for centuries to navigate. ▶

Lesson Review

Essential Question

What Other Objects Can Be Seen in the Sky?

In this lesson, you learned that there are many stars. Some of them appear to form patterns in the sky that we call constellations. The position of the stars in the sky seems to change because of Earth's movement through space.

1. **Focus Skill MAIN IDEA AND DETAILS** Draw and complete a graphic organizer to describe the properties of stars.

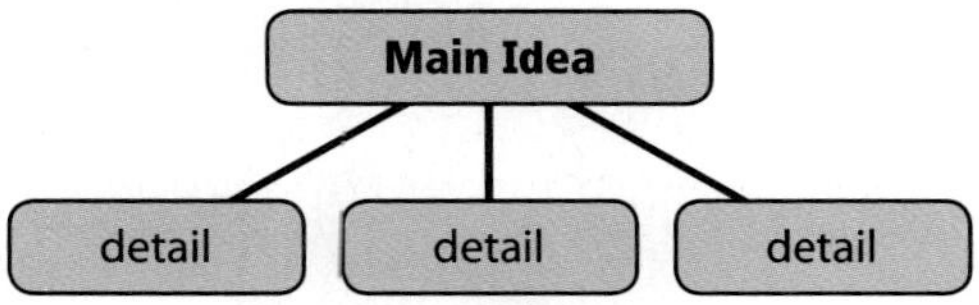

2. **SUMMARIZE** Write a summary of this lesson. Begin with this sentence: *The sun is the star at the center of our solar system.*

3. **DRAW CONCLUSIONS** If the sun were a red star or a blue star, how would it be different?

4. **VOCABULARY** Use the terms *star, galaxy,* and *universe* in a sentence about objects in space.

Test Prep

5. **CRITICAL THINKING** How were constellations useful to sailors long ago? When might they be useful to sailors today?

6. Which **best** describes the sun?
   A. small star
   B. medium-size star
   C. large star
   D. very large star

Make Connections

Writing

Expository Writing

Choose a constellation in the illustration of the winter sky. Write a **paragraph** explaining how to find it on a winter night.

Math

Solve a Problem

Earth is 150 million km from the sun. Scientists refer to this distance as 1 AU, or 1 astronomical unit. Neptune is 30 AUs from the sun. How many km is that?

Social Studies

Careers in Space

The United States began to explore space in the 1960s. Research space-related careers, and report to the class.

WATER WORLD

Over the years, many people have dreamed of going to Mars. The day when travel to Mars is possible is coming closer. Robot spacecraft have already traveled there. Those spacecraft have made many amazing discoveries.

One of the most recent spacecraft to journey to the fourth rock from the sun is *Mars Odyssey.* Photos taken by *Mars Odyssey* show that Mars has water. Because it is very cold on Mars, the water is frozen. Most of the water is frozen under the surface of Mars.

Lots of Lakes

Even though lots of ice crystals are mixed in with the Martian soil, Mars doesn't have as much water as Earth. Mars has buried lakes of water, not buried oceans of water. In fact, some scientists think that if you could collect all the water on Mars, it would fill a lake about twice the size of Lake Michigan.

There is evidence that some of the frozen water locked under the surface of Mars might melt every once in a while. Some of the water is only 46 centimeters (18 in.) below the surface. Molten rock deep beneath the surface of Mars might heat the ice. The water may then flow onto the surface.

A Grand Canyon?

Photos taken by *Mars Odyssey* show long, dark streaks on the walls of some canyons. The streaks might indicate areas where water recently flowed down the canyon walls.

Not all scientists agree, however. Many scientists say wind blowing across Mars caused the streaks. Scientists have long known about powerful wind storms on Mars. Some of those storms blow across the surface for months at a time.

Even if liquid water and life do not exist on Mars today, many scientists still want to explore the red planet. "I'm interested in Mars because it's probably the most fascinating planet in the solar system besides Earth, and probably the only one that could have ever supported other forms of life," said one NASA scientist.

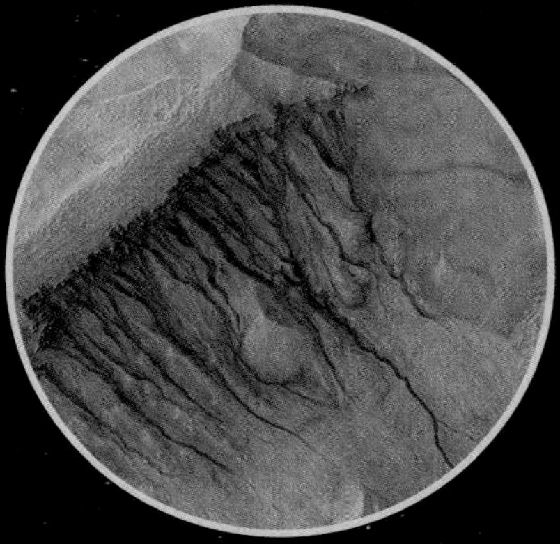

Some scientists say these dark lines were caused by streams of water flowing down a canyon wall.

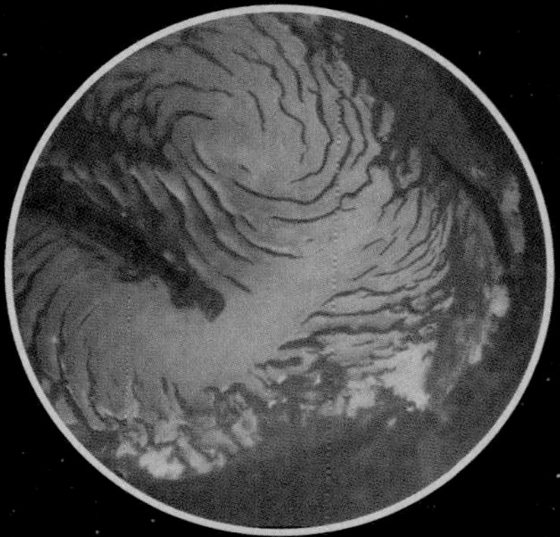

Frozen carbon dioxide covers the North Pole of Mars.

The *Mars Odyssey* spacecraft studies Mars. Photos by the spacecraft show that ice exists on Mars.

Think and Write

1. What would life on Earth be like if Earth had as little water as there is on Mars?
2. How have satellites helped us learn about other planets?

Spin-In Find out more. Log on to **www.hspscience.com**

CHAPTER 10

Review and Test Preparation

Vocabulary Review

Use the terms below to complete the sentences. The page numbers tell you where to look in the chapter if you need help.

axis p. 410	**comet** p. 426
orbit p. 410	**star** p. 432
telescope p. 412	**sun** p. 432
moon p. 414	**galaxy** p. 434
solar system p. 422	**universe** p. 434
planet p. 422	

1. The star at the center of our solar system is the _______.

2. The path an object takes around another object is its _______.

3. A star and a group of objects that revolve around it make up a _______.

4. The imaginary line through both poles of a planet is its _______.

5. A small mass of rock, ice, and frozen gases that orbits the sun is a _______.

6. A large object that revolves around a star is a _______.

7. An enormous ball of superheated gases in space is a _______.

8. Everything that exists in space is part of the _______.

9. A large system of stars, dust, and gas is a _______.

10. A natural object that revolves around a planet is a _______.

11. A device that helps people view distant objects is a _______.

Check Understanding

Write the letter of the best choice.

12. **MAIN IDEA AND DETAILS** Which detail is true of the sun?

Focus Skill

A. It's a ball of hydrogen and helium.
B. It's a ball of oxygen and hydrogen.
C. It's a ball of helium and phosphorus.
D. It's a ball of carbon dioxide and oxygen.

13. **COMPARE AND CONTRAST** How are asteroids and comets different?

Focus Skill

F. Asteroids are much smaller than comets.
G. Comets orbit the sun, while asteroids orbit Earth.
H. Comets are made up of rock, ice, and frozen gases, while asteroids are made up of rock and metals.
J. Asteroids are pieces of Earth, while comets are pieces of the sun.

14. Which **best** describes the sun's location in the universe?
   A. near the barred spiral galaxy
   B. at the edge of the solar system
   C. at the edge of a galaxy called the Milky Way
   D. in the center of a galaxy called Alpha Centauri

15. Samantha must label this diagram of the sun.

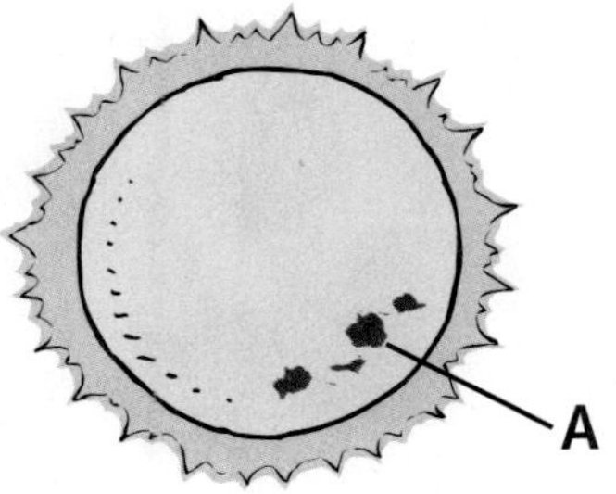

Which label should she use to identify area A?
   F. bits of rock   **H.** spinning dust
   G. oxygen   **J.** sunspot

16. What does this illustration **best** show?

   A. why Earth rotates
   B. why planets orbit the sun
   C. why the moon has phases
   D. why Earth has seasons

Inquiry Skills

17. You **used numbers** to help you understand distances in space. What other ideas in this chapter did using numbers help you understand?

18. How could **measuring** the orbit of a comet help scientists understand when it will next be visible from Earth?

Critical Thinking

19. If you look at the moon every night for a month, you can see it change shape. These changes in appearance are the phases of the moon. Why are there phases of the moon?

The Big Idea

20. Suppose that you have been asked to do a presentation about our solar system. You are to present information about the planets and show where they are located in space. Make a labeled drawing of the solar system. Include the nine planets and the sun. Write a paragraph that explains how the inner planets and the outer planets are different.

UNIT D EARTH SCIENCE

Visual Summary

Tell how each picture shows the **Big Idea** for its chapter.

CHAPTER 9

Big Idea

Water moves in a regular cycle that influences the weather.

CHAPTER 10

Big Idea

Objects in space, including Earth and its moon, move in regular and observable patterns.

PHYSICAL SCIENCE

Kentucky Standards

SC-04-1.1.1 Students will explain how matter, including water, can be changed from one state to another.

SC-04-1.2.1 Students will interpret or represent data related to an object's straight-line motion in order to make inferences and predictions of changes in position and/or time.

SC-04-1.2.2 Students will infer causes and effects of pushes and pulls (forces) on objects based on representations or interpretations of straight-line movement/motion in charts, graphs, and qualitative comparisons.

SC-04-1.2.3 Students will:
- explain that sound is a result of vibrations, a type of motion;
- describe pitch (high, low) as a difference in sounds that are produced and relate that to the rate of vibration.

SC-04-4.6.3 Students will evaluate a variety of models/representations of electrical circuits (open, closed, series, and/or parallel) to:
- make predictions related to changes in the system;
- compare the properties of conducting and non-conducting materials.

SC-04-4.6.4 Students will:
- analyze models/representations of light in order to generalize about the behavior of light.
- represent the path of light as it interacts with a variety of surfaces (reflecting, refracting, absorbing).

SC-04-4.6.5 Students will:
- identify ways that heat can be produced (e.g. burning, rubbing) and properties of materials that conduct heat better than others;
- describe the movement of heat between objects.

KENTUCKY

Kentucky Excursions and Projects

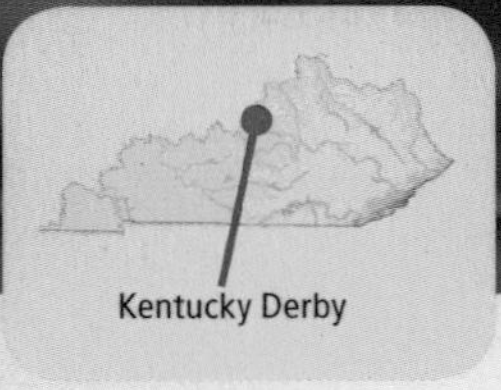

Race for the Roses

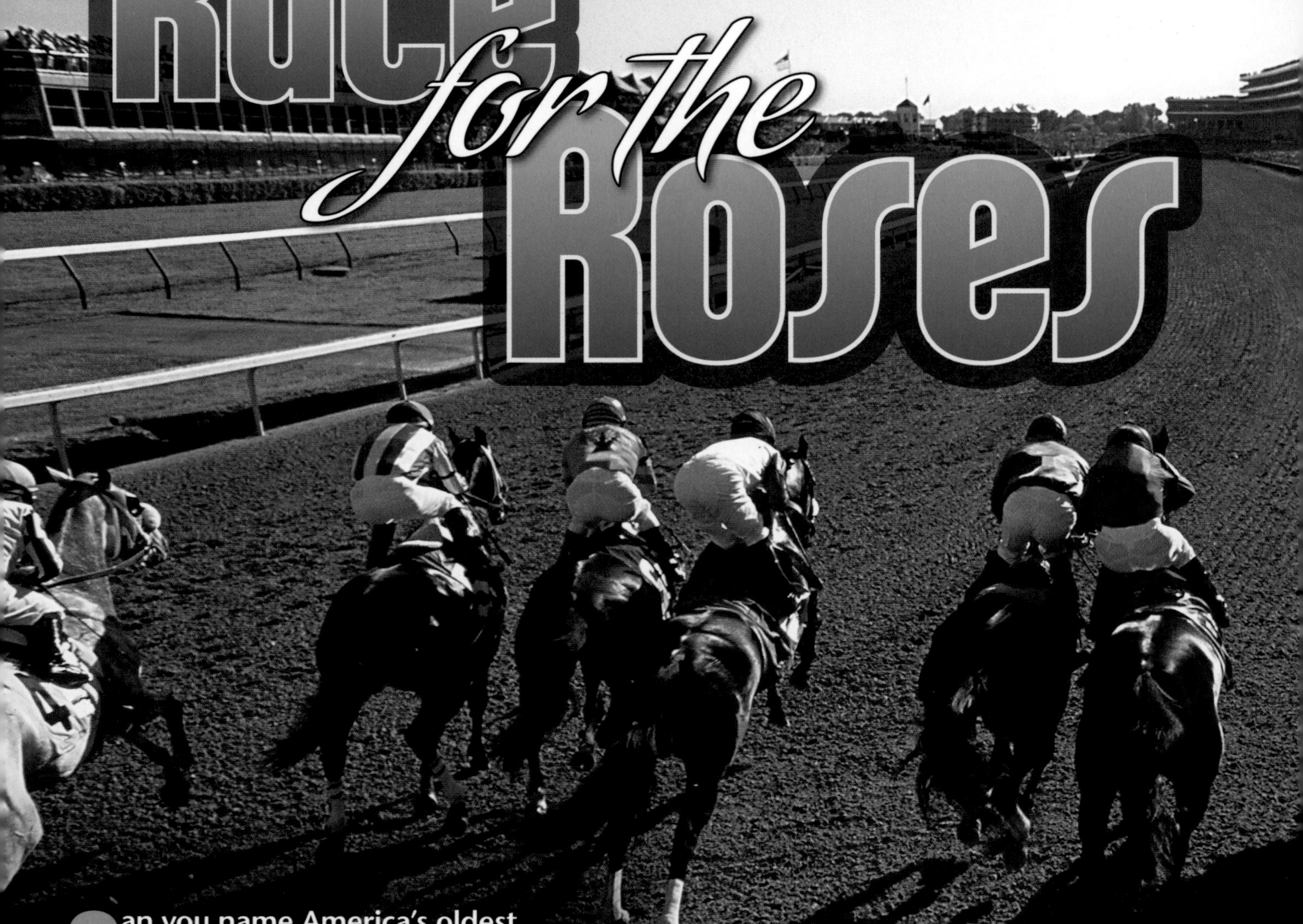

Can you name America's oldest sporting event? It's the Kentucky Derby! Since 1875, this race has been held on the first Saturday of May. Each year, thousands of people travel to Churchill Downs for the race. Many enjoy the Kentucky Derby Festival and its steamboat races, hot-air balloon festival, and colorful parade.

The Race

The highlight of the Festival is the Kentucky Derby. Spectators watch a group of three-year-old horses gallop around the Churchill Downs track at great speeds. Derby winners often complete the $1\frac{1}{4}$-mile race in two minutes or less!

Close Finishes

Sometimes, two horses reach the finish line at almost the same time. That happened at the 1933 Derby. As the horses approached the finish line, their riders pushed and jostled one another. The "fighting finish" ended with one horse beating another by about 2 inches.

▼ **Modern technology tells us who won this race!**

Photo Finish

Modern technology has provided a way to help determine Derby winners. Cameras aimed at the finish line quickly take a series of photographs. Film inside the camera moves at about the same speed as the horses. As a result, the moving horses do not appear as a blur in the photos made from the film. Race officials can view the photographs to determine which horse crossed the finish line first.

Think and Write

1. **Scientific Inquiry** The height of a horse is measured in hands. One hand equals 4 inches. What is your height expressed in hands?
2. **Scientific Inquiry** A furlong is a unit of length equal to $\frac{1}{8}$ mile. The track at Churchill Downs is $1\frac{1}{4}$ miles long. What is the length of the track expressed in furlongs?

Kentucky Excursions

Adam Matthews Balloon Festival

Balloons float with the wind. Most hot-air balloon flights occur right after sunrise or just before sunset, when the wind is calmest.

Would you like to take a ride in a hot-air balloon? If so, you should visit the Adam Matthews Balloon Festival. The three-day festival is held in Louisville, Kentucky, each September.

What You Can Do

People from all over the country attend the festival. They watch balloons being "put up," or inflated, to heights as great as 100 feet. When dusk falls, visitors get a glimpse of "balloon glow." That happens when nearly 100 balloons light up the darkening sky. Festival visitors also watch the balloons compete in races across the sky. Those who are daring enough can enjoy a balloon ride.

What You Can Learn

If you attend the festival, visit the Balloon Education Center. The displays inside the center explain what causes the colorful balloons to float across the sky, how balloon pilots steer the balloons, and what people have to do to get a pilot's license. You can stand inside a typical balloon basket and take an imaginary ride without leaving the ground.

A burner heats air inside the balloon. The balloon is buoyed up because the warm air inside it is less dense than the cool air surrounding it.

Think and Write

1. **Science and Technology** When it's time to land a hot-air balloon, the pilot pulls on a cord. A small vent opens at the top of the balloon. How does this cause the balloon to move downward?
2. **Scientific Thinking** Suppose the cord breaks, and pulling on it does not open the vent. What could the pilot do to make the balloon move downward toward the ground?

Procedure

1. Cut two 3-inch squares from aluminum foil. Crumple one square into a ball. Fold up the edges of the second square so it is shaped like a boat.
2. Place the ball in a glass filled with water. Place the boat in a second glass filled with water. Observe.
3. Did the same things occur? What causes any differences?
4. Would the results differ if you placed 5 pennies in the boat-shaped foil? Explain why or why not.

Kentucky Theatre

If you are like many people, you probably enjoy going to the movies. The sounds and sights you observe make you feel as if you are part of the show. Theaters in the early 1900s used equipment that appealed to the customer's senses, too. One of those early theaters—the Kentucky Theatre, in Lexington—is still open.

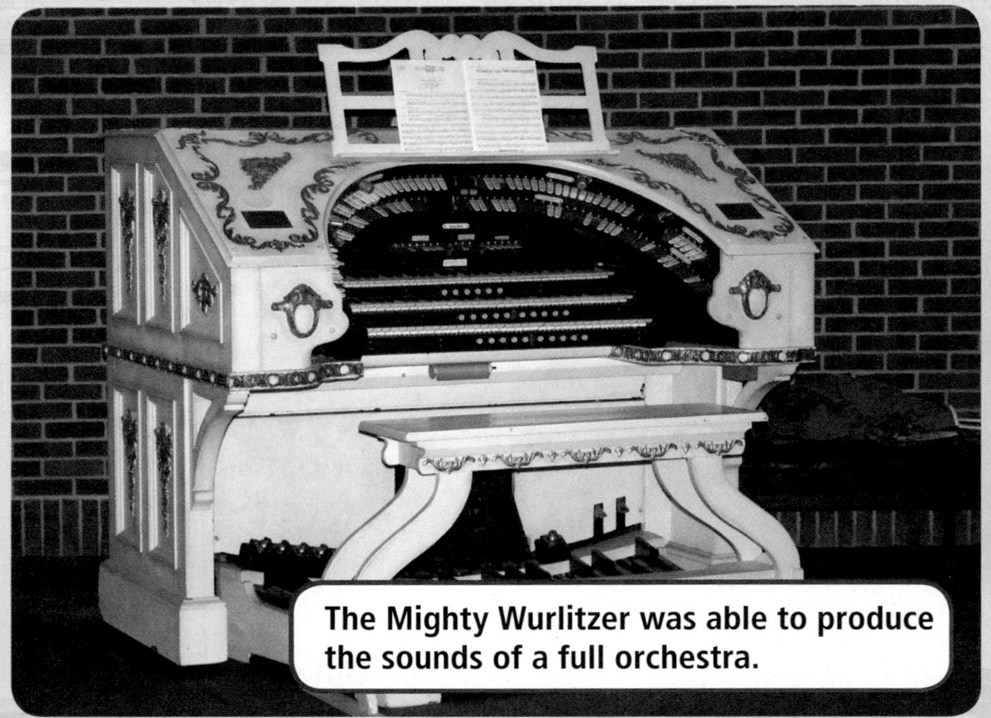

The Mighty Wurlitzer was able to produce the sounds of a full orchestra.

The Mighty Wurlitzer Pipe Organ

When the Kentucky Theatre first opened in 1922, movies did not have any sound. Viewers discovered what the actors thought or said by reading words on the screen. To make movie-viewing more enjoyable, a huge pipe organ was placed in the theater. The organ, called the Mighty Wurlitzer, produced the sounds of many different instruments. The organ also created sound effects, such as thunder and train whistles. As the movie rolled, an organist played the Mighty Wurlitzer. The great organ produced sounds that matched what was being shown on the screen. Being able to hear as well as see the action made customers enjoy seeing movies at the Kentucky Theatre.

How a Pipe Organ Works

Like other pipe organs, the Mighty Wurlitzer produced sound when air moved through pipes. A fan inside a pipe organ blows air into a collection area called a wind chest. When the organist presses a key, an electric signal goes out. Air released from the wind chest travels into certain pipes. The tones produced are determined by the size of the pipes the air is forced through.

Think and Write

1. **Scientific Thinking** What must occur within the pipes of the Mighty Wurlitzer for sound to be produced?
2. **Science and Technology** Could the Mighty Wurlitzer produce sound without electricity? Explain why or why not.

Project Water Mass

Materials

- water
- 10-mL glass vial with cap
- 10-mL graduated cylinder
- balance
- paper and pencil
- freezer

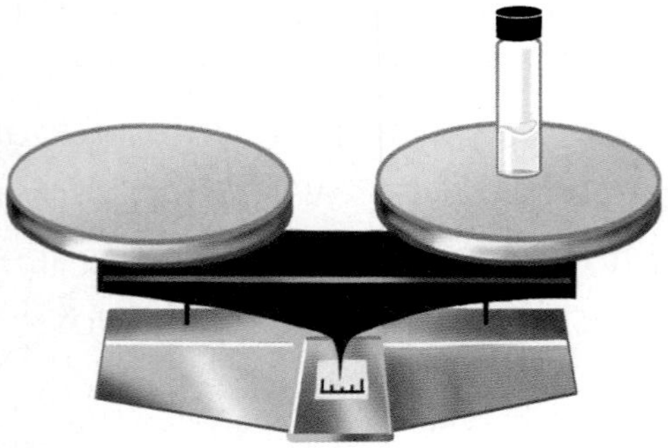

Procedure

1. Measure 3 mL of water. Pour the water into a vial, and put the cap on.
2. Place the capped vial on the balance, and find its mass to the nearest 0.1 g. Record your measurement.
3. Place your vial in the freezer until the water in the vial is completely frozen.
4. Place the vial of ice on the balance, and find its mass to the nearest 0.1 g. Record your measurement.
5. Melt the ice completely by warming the vial with your hands.
6. When the ice has melted, find the mass of the vial and water to the nearest 0.1 g. Record your measurement.
7. Perform the following calculations:

   (Mass of vial + water before freezing) – (mass of vial + ice) = change in mass

   (Mass of vial + ice) – (mass of vial + water after melting) = change in mass

Draw Conclusions

1. What was the change in mass from water to ice?
2. What was the change in mass from ice to water?

UNIT E
PHYSICAL SCIENCE

Matter and Energy

Unit Inquiry

Color and Light Energy Absorption

Matter and energy are constantly interacting with each other. Light and heat are two forms of energy that interact differently with different types of matter. Does the color of an object affect the amount of energy it absorbs? Plan and conduct an experiment to find out.

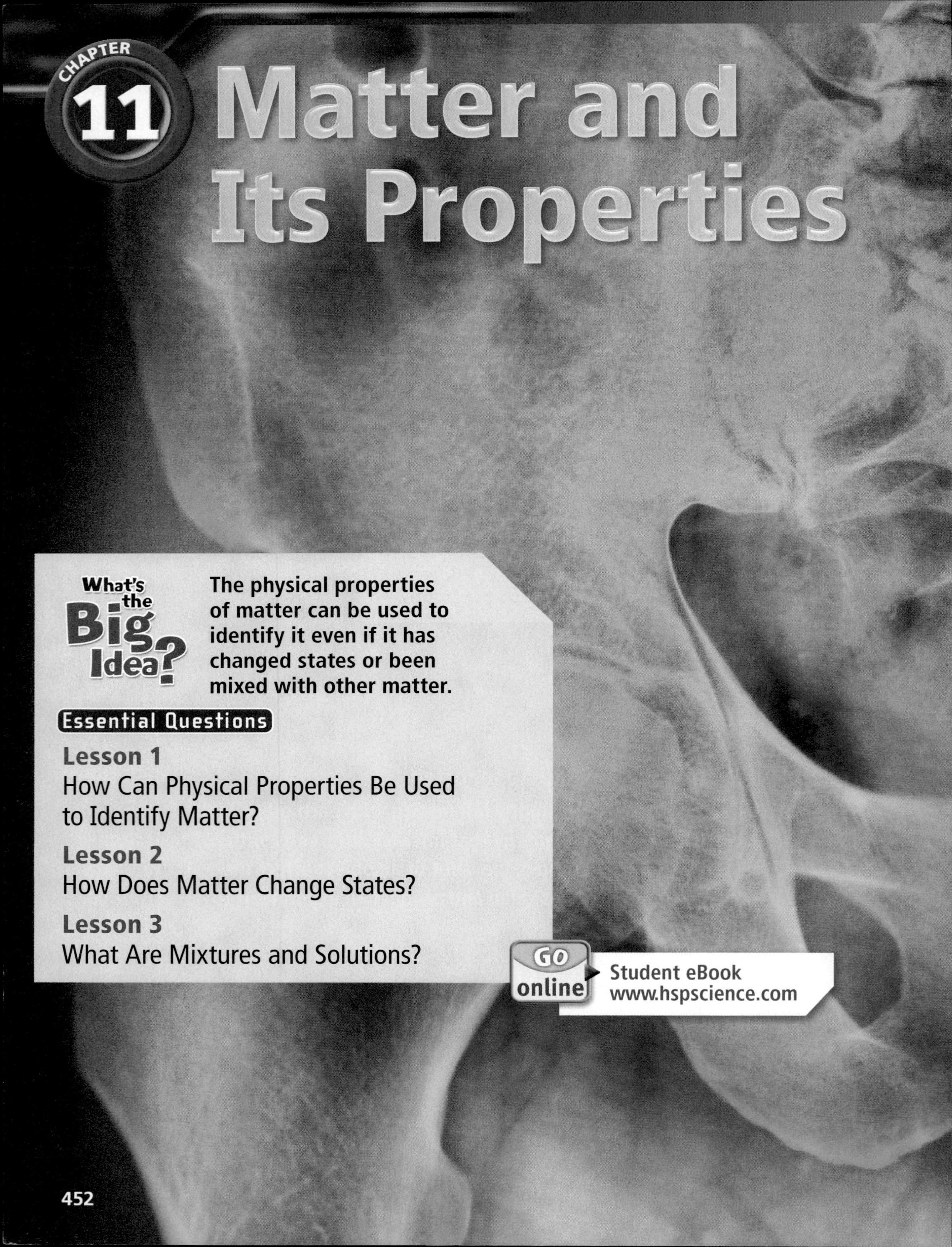

CHAPTER 11

Matter and Its Properties

What's the Big Idea?

The physical properties of matter can be used to identify it even if it has changed states or been mixed with other matter.

Essential Questions

Lesson 1
How Can Physical Properties Be Used to Identify Matter?

Lesson 2
How Does Matter Change States?

Lesson 3
What Are Mixtures and Solutions?

GO online Student eBook www.hspscience.com

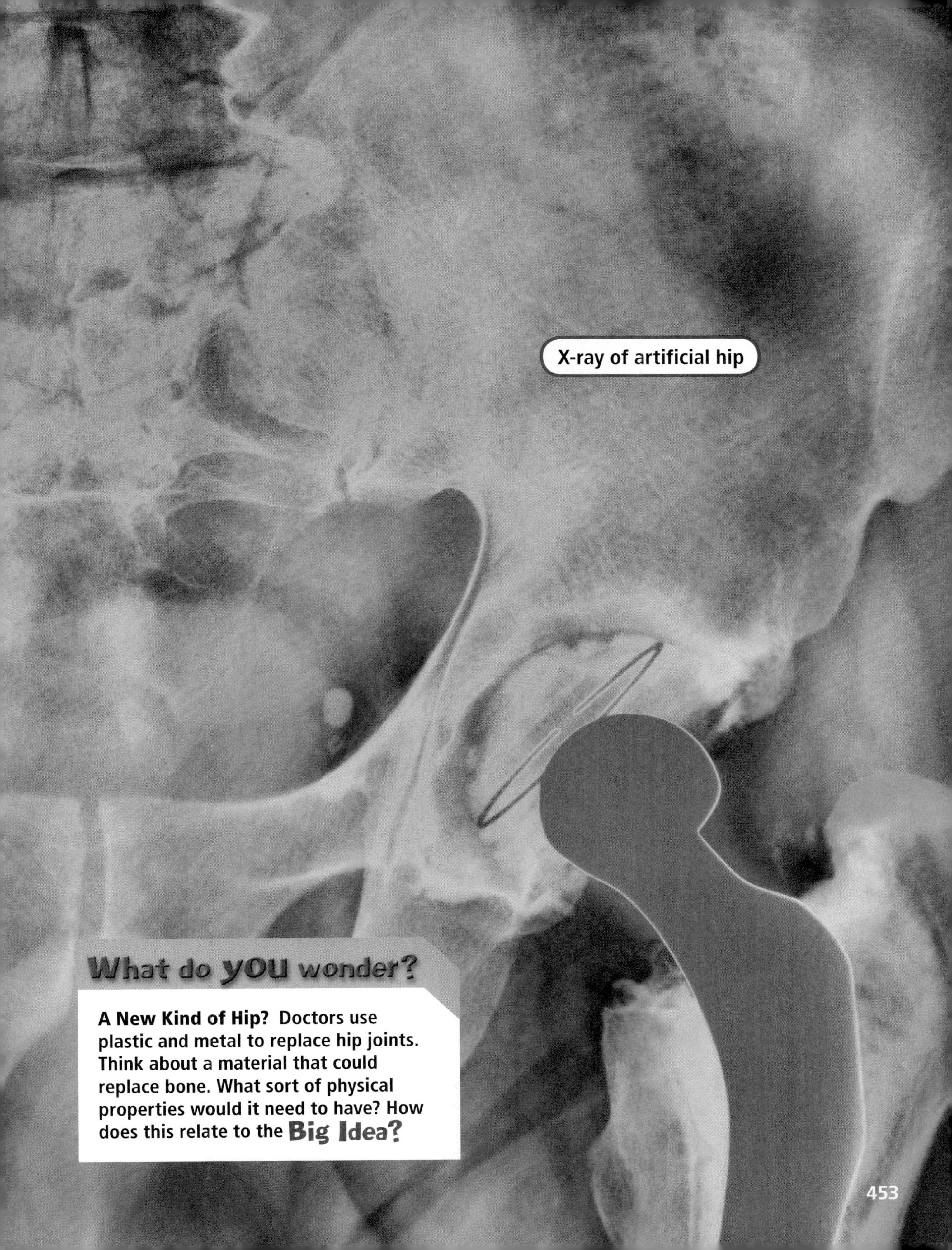

X-ray of artificial hip

What do YOU wonder?

A New Kind of Hip? Doctors use plastic and metal to replace hip joints. Think about a material that could replace bone. What sort of physical properties would it need to have? How does this relate to the **Big Idea?**

LESSON 1

Essential Question

How Can Physical Properties Be Used to Identify Matter?

Investigate the densities of different liquids.

Read and Learn the physical properties of matter.

Fast Fact

Amazing Water

Density affects the floating of liquids and solids. Water is unusual. It's less dense when it is solid ice than when it is liquid water. That's why ice floats on water. No other common material has this property of being denser as a liquid than as a solid. In the Investigate, you will find the densities of three liquids. Amazing water is one of them.

Density test

Vocabulary Preview

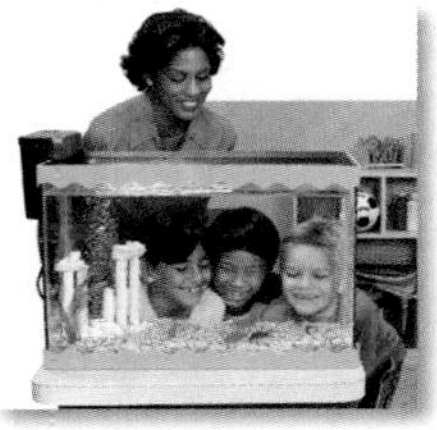

matter [MAT•er] Anything that has mass and takes up space (p. 458)

mass [MAS] The amount of matter in an object (p. 459)

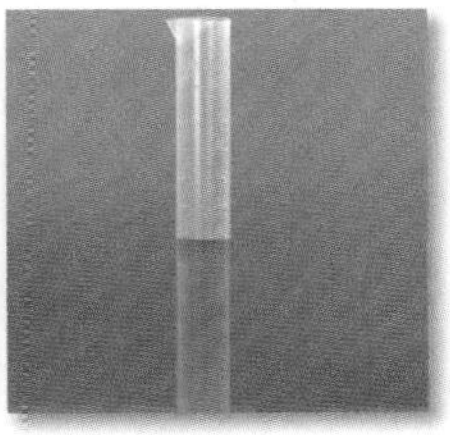

volume [VAHL•yoom] The amount of space an object takes up (p. 460)

density [DEN•suh•tee] The amount of matter in an object compared to the space it takes up (p. 460)

Measuring the Densities of Liquids

Guided Inquiry

Start with Questions

Something in this water is reflecting light. The rainbow is only on the surface of the water.

- What is causing the rainbow?
- Why hasn't it mixed with the water?

Investigate to find out. Then read to find out more.

Prepare to Investigate

Inquiry Skill Tip

Displayed data should be easy for viewers to understand. Make sure your charts are clear.

Materials

- graduated cylinder
- vegetable oil
- balance
- corn syrup
- water

Make an Observation Chart

Liquid	Mass (cylinder only) (g)	Mass (cylinder and liquid) (g)	Mass (liquid only) (g)	Volume (mL)	Density (g/mL)
Water				10	
Corn syrup				10	
Vegetable oil				10	

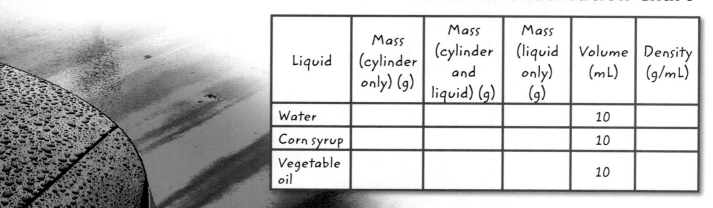

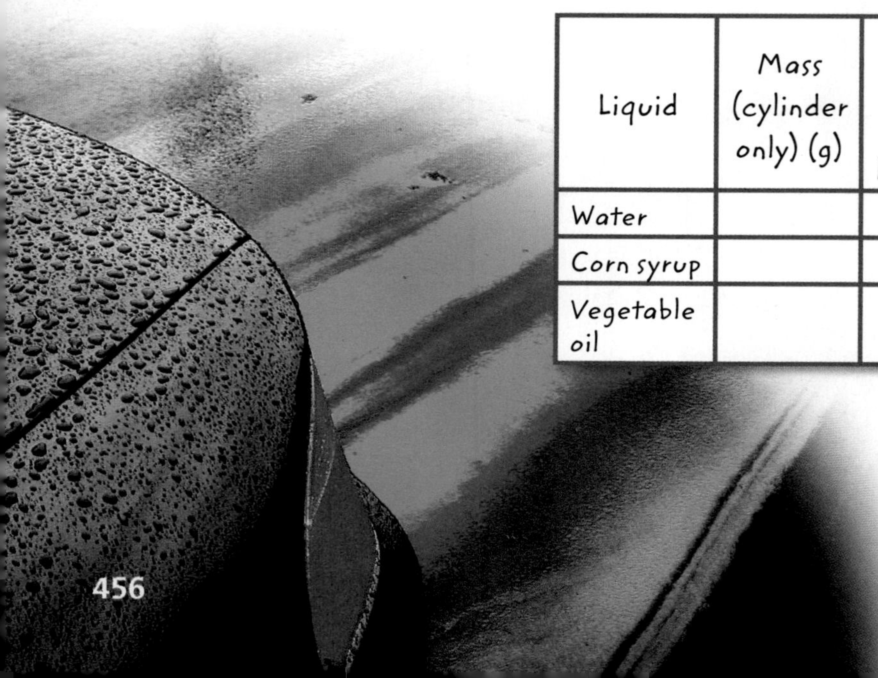

Follow This Procedure

1. Make sure the graduated cylinder is empty, clean, and dry. Then use the balance to find its mass. **Record** the mass.
2. Add 10 mL of water to the graduated cylinder. **Measure** and **record** the mass of the cylinder again. Empty the cylinder and dry it.
3. Repeat Step 2, using 10 mL of vegetable oil.
4. Repeat Step 2, using 10 mL of corn syrup.
5. Subtract the mass of the empty cylinder from each of the masses you **measured** in Steps 2, 3, and 4. **Record** each result.
6. To find the densities, divide the mass of each liquid by its volume, 10 mL. **Record** and **compare** the densities.

Step 1

Step 2

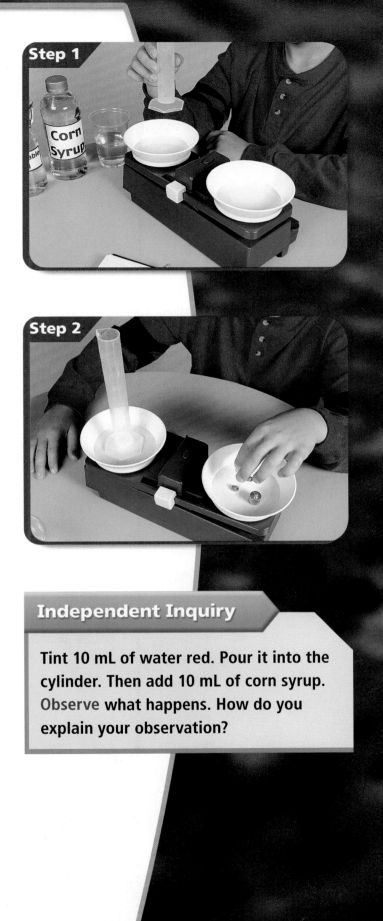

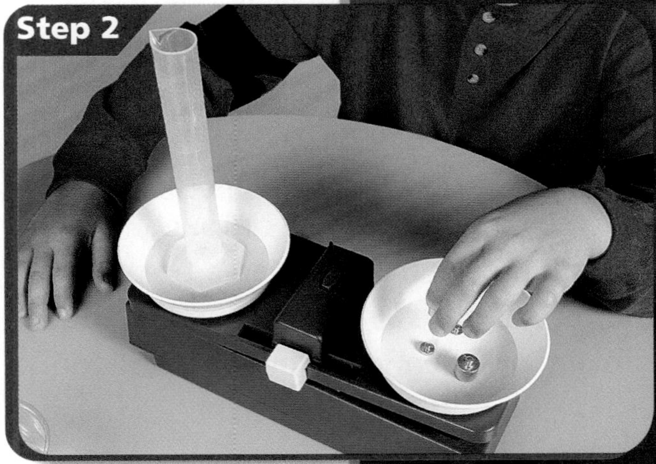

Draw Conclusions

1. Which liquid has the greatest density? Which has the least? Compare the amount of matter in each liquid sample.
2. **Inquiry Skill** Display data by making a bar graph that shows the density of each liquid you measured.

Independent Inquiry

Tint 10 mL of water red. Pour it into the cylinder. Then add 10 mL of corn syrup. Observe what happens. How do you explain your observation?

Read and Learn

VOCABULARY
matter p. 458
mass p. 459
volume p. 460
density p. 460

SCIENCE CONCEPTS
- ▶ how physical properties can be used to identify substances
- ▶ how density can be determined

Focus Skill MAIN IDEA AND DETAILS
Find out how physical properties help identify matter.

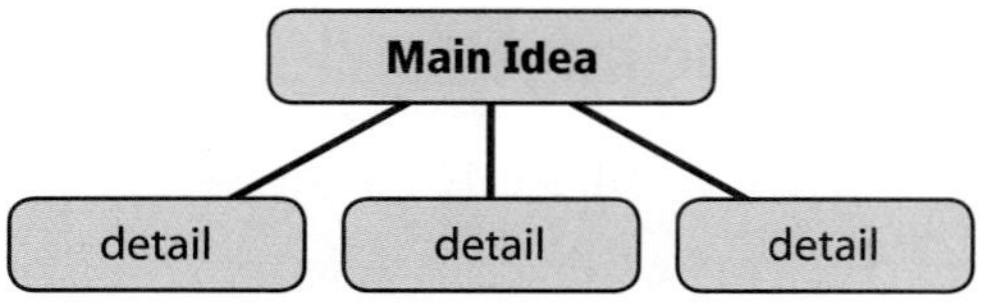

Matter

What is matter? Just about everything! Everything that takes up space is **matter**. This includes you, your skateboard, the clothes you're wearing, and the sidewalk under you. Breakfast cereal is matter. Your bowl, your spoon, and the milk you pour on the cereal are all matter, too.

If you can taste, smell, or touch something, it's matter. Even a breeze is matter, because air takes up space. You prove that when you blow up a balloon. The air you blow into the balloon pushes out the balloon's sides. The air inside the balloon takes up space.

Some things exist without taking up space, so they are not matter. What is not matter? Heat, light, and ideas are examples of things that are *not* matter. Even though they exist, they don't take up any space.

Focus Skill MAIN IDEA AND DETAILS
Define *matter*, and name three examples.

◀ **What do you have in common with a skateboard?**

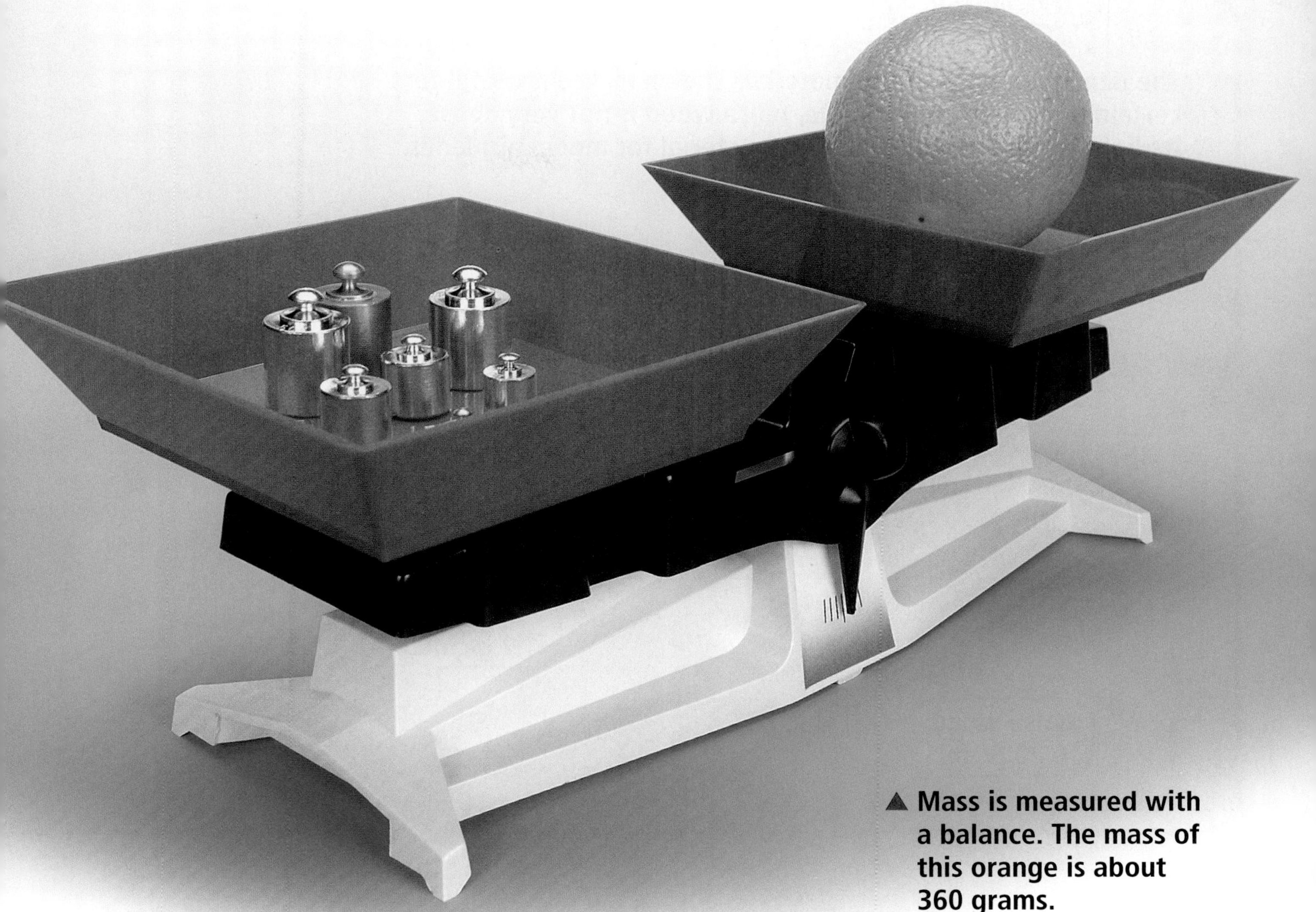

▲ Mass is measured with a balance. The mass of this orange is about 360 grams.

Mass

Matter not only takes up space but also has mass. **Mass** is the amount of matter something contains. A heavy object has more mass than a light object. Finding mass is a way of measuring matter.

All matter is made of tiny particles. You can see them only under the strongest microscopes. In general, the more particles an object has, the more mass it has. The more mass it has, the heavier it is.

A golf ball and a table tennis ball both are made of matter. The balls are about the same size. However, the golf ball is heavier because it has more mass.

The mass of an object is one of its physical properties. A physical property is something you can observe or measure. You can measure mass. Other physical properties include an object's appearance and texture.

Focus Skill MAIN IDEA AND DETAILS

Define *mass.* Name one object with a lot of mass and one with little mass.

Density

The density of each of the materials shown makes it useful for certain purposes. For example, balsa wood is not very dense. Its light weight makes it an ideal material for model airplanes.

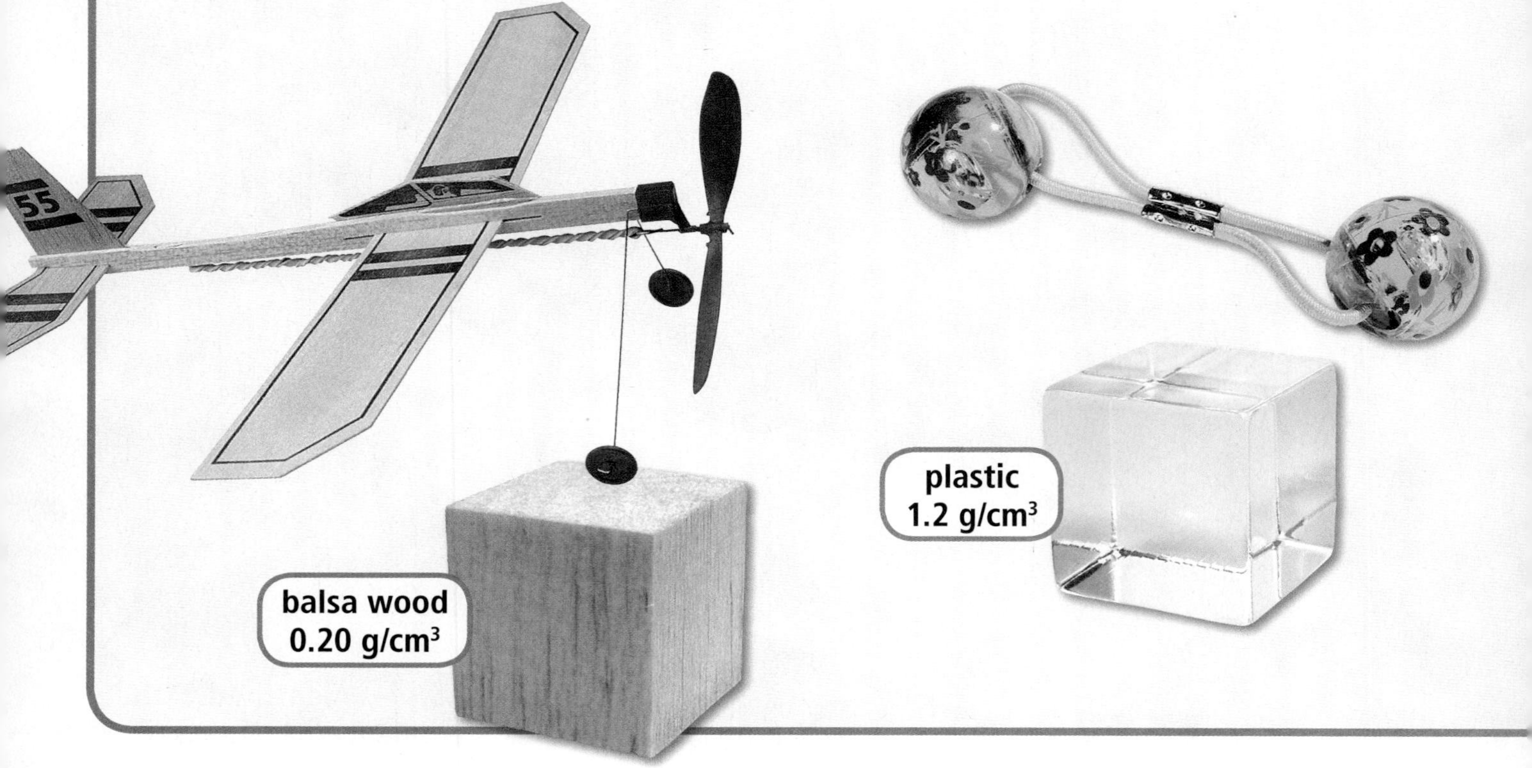

Volume and Density

Volume is the amount of space that matter takes up. Some objects, such as a blown-up balloon, have little mass (few particles). Yet a balloon takes up a lot of space. A marble has more mass but takes up little space. How can we show this relationship between mass and space?

The answer is density. **Density** is the amount of matter in an object compared to the space it takes up. In the Investigate, you measured density. You divided the masses of three liquids by their volumes.

To find the density of this liquid, divide its mass by its volume, 50 mL.

Each liquid had the same volume but a slightly different mass. This showed that each liquid had a different density.

You can find the density of a solid object by dividing its mass by its volume. For example, a certain wooden block has a mass of 20 grams. Its volume is 10 cubic centimeters (cm^3). When you divide its mass by its volume, the answer is 2 grams per cubic centimeter—2 g/cm^3. So, the block has a density of 2 grams per cubic centimeter.

Focus Skill **MAIN IDEA AND DETAILS**

How are mass and density different?

Insta-Lab

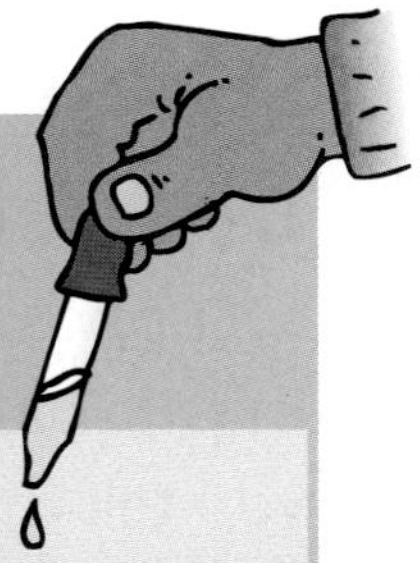

Wet Test

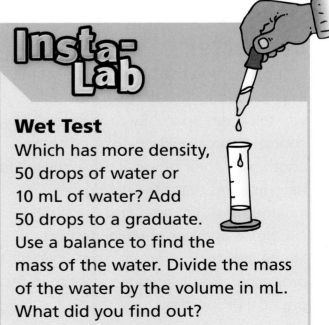

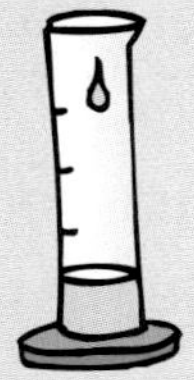

Which has more density, 50 drops of water or 10 mL of water? Add 50 drops to a graduate. Use a balance to find the mass of the water. Divide the mass of the water by the volume in mL. What did you find out?

▲ The foil is shiny and thin. It crushes easily.

The foam tube is soft and green. It bends easily. ▶

The glass is clear. It breaks easily. ▶

You can tell these objects apart by their physical properties.

Other Properties of Matter

Suppose two marbles have the same mass, volume, and density. How can you tell them apart? By their colors, of course! You can tell one object from another by their physical properties. You have learned that physical properties include mass, volume, and density.

Color is another physical property. Shape and texture are two more physical properties. You use your senses to detect physical properties.

In the next lesson, you will learn that another physical property of matter is state. Matter might be a liquid, a solid, or a gas.

The ability to transfer heat and electricity is another physical property. Some substances, such as copper, transfer heat and electricity easily. Others, such as plastic, do not.

You use physical properties to identify objects and substances every day.

Focus Skill MAIN IDEA AND DETAILS

What physical properties could you use to describe a rock?

Lesson Review

Essential Question

How Can Physical Properties Be Used to Identify Matter?

In this lesson, you learned that the physical properties of matter can be used to tell what it is. Mass, volume, and density are properties of matter. Other properties include color and shape.

1. Focus Skill MAIN IDEA AND DETAILS Draw and complete a graphic organizer to describe the physical properties of matter.

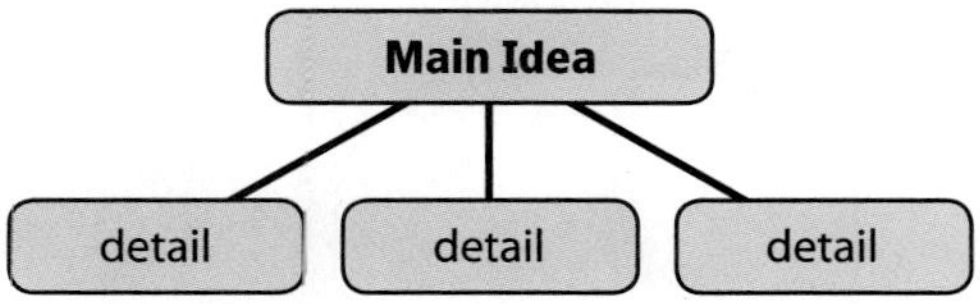

2. **SUMMARIZE** Write a paragraph to describe the physical characteristics of your science textbook.

3. **DRAW CONCLUSIONS** Two clear bags each contain a different unknown object. What physical properties can you use to tell the objects apart?

4. **VOCABULARY** In a sentence or two, explain why you must measure mass before you can determine density.

Test Prep

5. **CRITICAL THINKING** Which senses help you determine an object's physical properties?

6. Which physical property can be the same for both a large marble and a small one?
   A. color
   B. mass
   C. volume
   D. weight

Make Connections

Writing

Informative Writing

Suppose you are a scientist who has discovered a new substance. Write a **report** to describe its physical properties.

Math

Find the Density

A green ball has a mass of 100 grams and a volume of 200 cubic centimeters. A yellow ball has a mass of 50 grams and a volume of 10 cubic centimeters. Which ball has the greater density?

Physical Education

Catch This!

You can use an air pump to change the density of air inside a soccer ball or basketball. What happens when you pump more air into an inflated ball?

LESSON 2

Essential Question

How Does Matter Change States?

Investigate how water behaves at different temperatures.

Read and Learn about the different states of matter.

Fast Fact

Frozen Art

Every March, ice artists like this one gather at the World Ice Art Championships in Fairbanks, Alaska. The artists depend on changing states of matter to shape and polish the giant sculptures. In the Investigate, you will have a chance to observe changes of state.

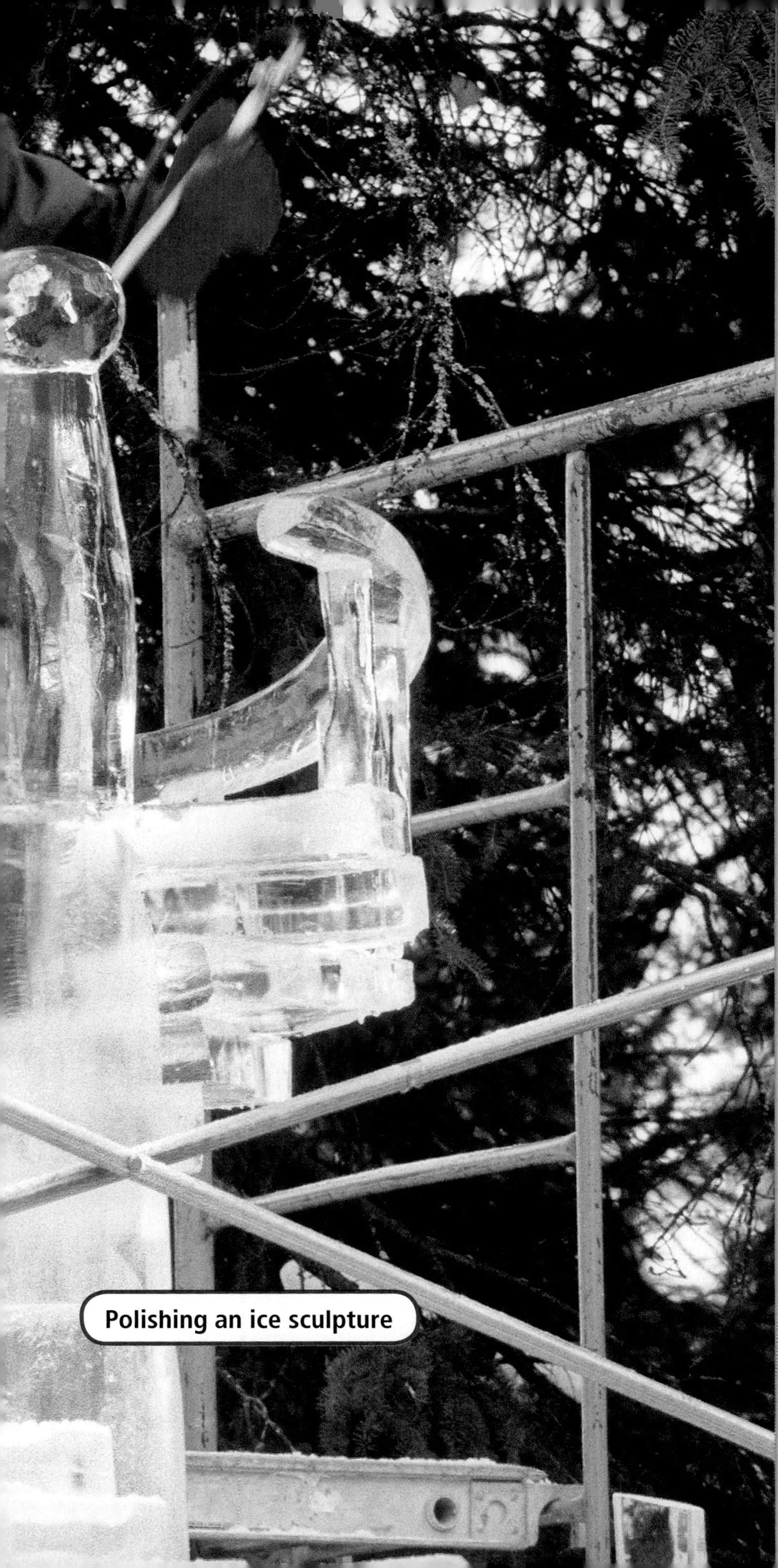

Polishing an ice sculpture

Vocabulary Preview

state of matter [STAYT UHV MAT•er] One of three forms (solid, liquid, and gas) that matter can exist in (p. 468)

solid [SAHL•id] The state of matter that has a definite shape and a definite volume (p. 468)

liquid [LIK•wid] The state of matter that has a definite volume but no definite shape (p. 469)

gas [GAS] The state of matter that does not have a definite shape or volume (p. 469)

Melt, Boil, Evaporate

Guided Inquiry

Start with Questions

A chef is going to use this butter for cooking.

- What is happening to the butter?
- Is it still butter when it turns into a liquid?

Investigate to find out. Then read to find out more.

Prepare to Investigate

Inquiry Skill Tip

Remember, when you are inferring, you are not making a random guess. Look at your information and find a reasonable solution.

Materials

- 4 ice cubes
- hot plate
- safety goggles
- oven mitts
- pan
- graduated cylinder

Make an Observation Chart

Description:	
Prediction:	
Volume:	
Prediction:	

Follow This Procedure

1. Draw the ice cubes and describe their physical properties. Tell how they look and feel.

2. CAUTION: **Put on safety goggles.** Put the ice in the pan. Your teacher will carefully heat the pan. If you must touch the handle, use oven mitts. Predict the changes you expect to see in the ice cubes.

3. When the ice cubes melt, your teacher will pour the hot water into the graduated cylinder. Record its volume.

4. Use oven mitts as you pour the water back into the pan. Your teacher will put it on the hot plate again. Let the water boil. Predict what will happen this time.

   CAUTION: **Remember to turn off your hot plate.** Remove the pan from the heat before it is dry. Place the pan on a burn-proof surface.

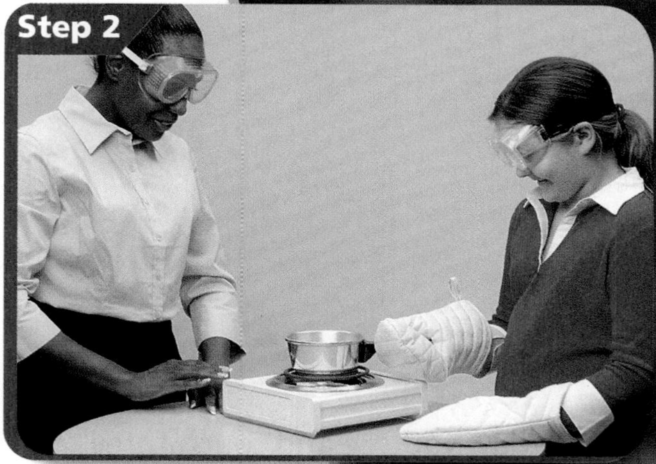

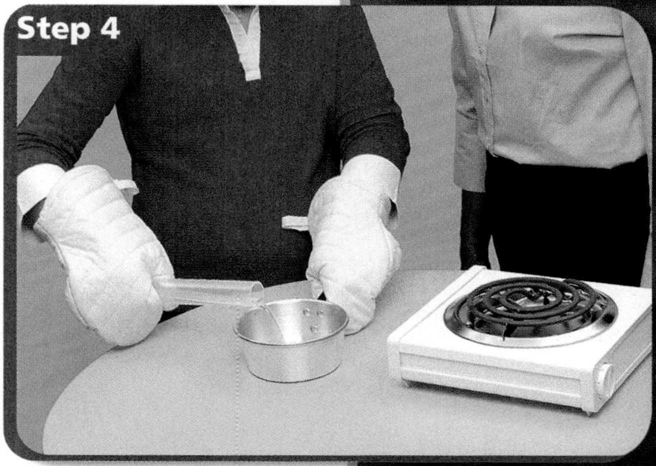

Draw Conclusions

1. What caused the water to change?
2. **Inquiry Skill** Infer where the water is now. When it evaporated, what did the liquid water become?

Independent Inquiry

Using oven mitts, pick up an ice cube in each hand. Push the cubes together while still wearing the oven mitts. Explain what you observe.

VOCABULARY

state of matter p. 468
solid p. 468
liquid p. 469
gas p. 469

SCIENCE CONCEPTS

- what three states of matter are
- how temperature can change the state of a substance without matter being lost or gained

Focus Skill CAUSE AND EFFECT

Look for things that cause changes in a state of matter.

cause → effect

States of Matter

Every day, you see and touch three **states of matter**: solid, liquid, and gas. But why is an apple solid, while milk is liquid? What makes the air you breathe a gas? The answer lies in the particles that you read about earlier.

All matter is made of particles. The way those particles are arranged determines whether the matter is a solid, a liquid, or a gas.

In a **solid**, the particles are packed together in a tight pattern. This pattern gives solids an exact shape, so the solid takes up a certain amount of space. When you roll a bowling ball, the particles stay tightly packed. As a result, the ball does not change its shape.

You learned that the particles in matter are always moving. Particles in solids are packed too tightly to move around. They vibrate in place instead.

Solids

Gems and bowling balls are solids. Their particles are packed together in tight patterns that give the objects their shape.

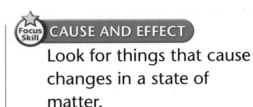

Liquids

Liquids take the shape of their containers and have definite volume.

Gases

Gases take the shape of their containers but have no definite volume.

Particles in **liquids** have more movement. They slide around, taking the shape of their container. A liquid also takes up a certain amount of space. However, if you spill a liquid, its shape changes as its particles slide around.

A **gas** has no definite shape or volume. Particles move fastest in a gas. When you open a container and release a gas into the air, its particles move away quickly. That's why you smell perfume after it is sprayed. Then the scent gets weaker because the perfume's gas particles move away and spread out.

Focus Skill CAUSE AND EFFECT

What causes solids to keep their shape?

Insta-Lab

Spaces and Places

Fill a glass with water until the water bulges above the top. Next, slowly sprinkle 2 teaspoons of salt into the glass. The glass is full of water, so where does the salt go?

Changes in the States of Water

Water clearly shows how heating and cooling change the states of matter. Heat makes particles in matter move faster. If ice gains energy, its particles move faster. They begin to slide around each other. The solid loses its shape and becomes a liquid.

Particles in the liquid move around and take the shape of the container. If you pour the liquid into another container, the liquid particles take its shape. The volume of the water stays the same.

If you keep adding heat to the water, its particles move even faster. They evaporate into a gas—water vapor. The gas particles bounce into each other and spread out in all directions.

Cooling the gas particles slows their movement. The particles condense into a liquid. If the liquid gets cold enough, the particles freeze into solid ice again.

Although heat changes the state of matter, it does not change the amount of matter.

Focus Skill **CAUSE AND EFFECT** **How does heat change the state of water?**

Science Up Close

Heat Makes the Difference

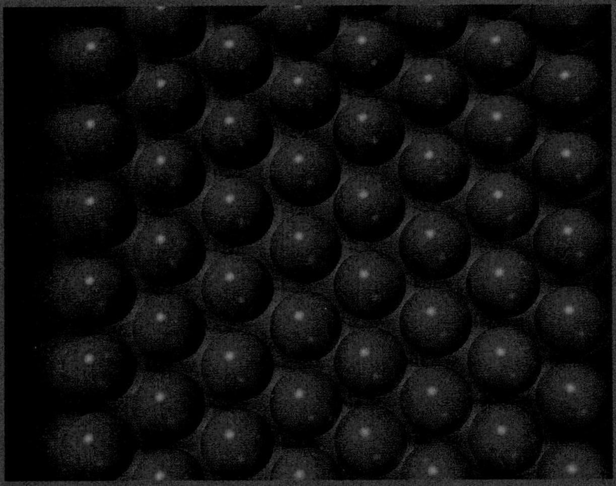

Ice is water in its solid state. The particles in a solid are arranged in a tight, evenly spaced pattern. The particles still vibrate.

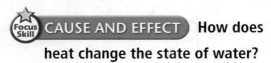

As ice warms, it melts into a liquid—water. As the particles warm up, they move and slide around one another. The even spaces between the particles become different-size spaces.

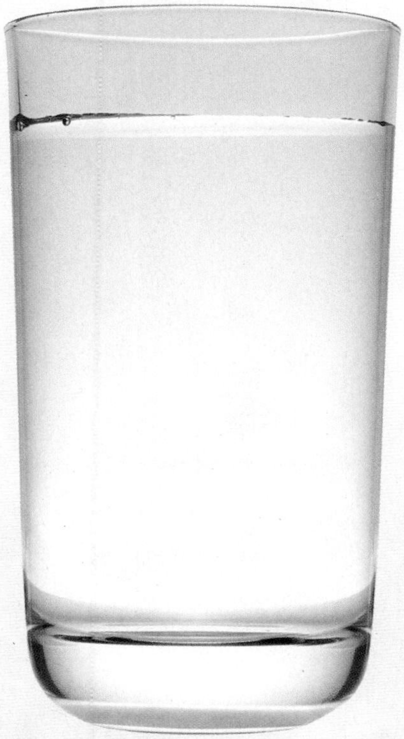

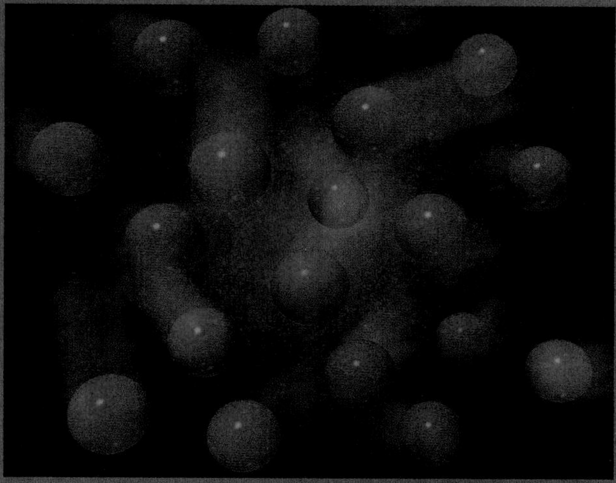

As the water is heated, the particles move faster and faster. The liquid boils and becomes a gas. The particles bounce off one another and fly out of the spout. If this water vapor cools, it will condense back into tiny drops of water.

Other Materials Change States

Water is not the only material that changes states. Some materials change states in different ways. For example, dry ice is the solid form of carbon dioxide. Carbon dioxide changes directly from a solid into a gas.

Some gases change directly into solids. One example of a solid that forms this way is frost. Solid crystals of frost form from water vapor in the air.

Focus Skill CAUSE AND EFFECT

What causes dry ice to change state?

Math in Science
Interpret Data

Freezing and Boiling Points

Almost anything will melt or boil if its temperature gets high enough or low enough. Which of these substances would be useful in an industry in which resistance to heat is important?

Substance	Melting Point	Boiling Point
Iron	1538°C (2800°F)	2862°C (5184°F)
Mercury	–39°C (–38°F)	357°C (675°F)
Nitrogen	–209°C (–344°F)	–196°C (–321°F)
Oxygen	–218°C (–360°F)	–183°C (–297°F)

Dry ice changes from a solid directly into a gas.

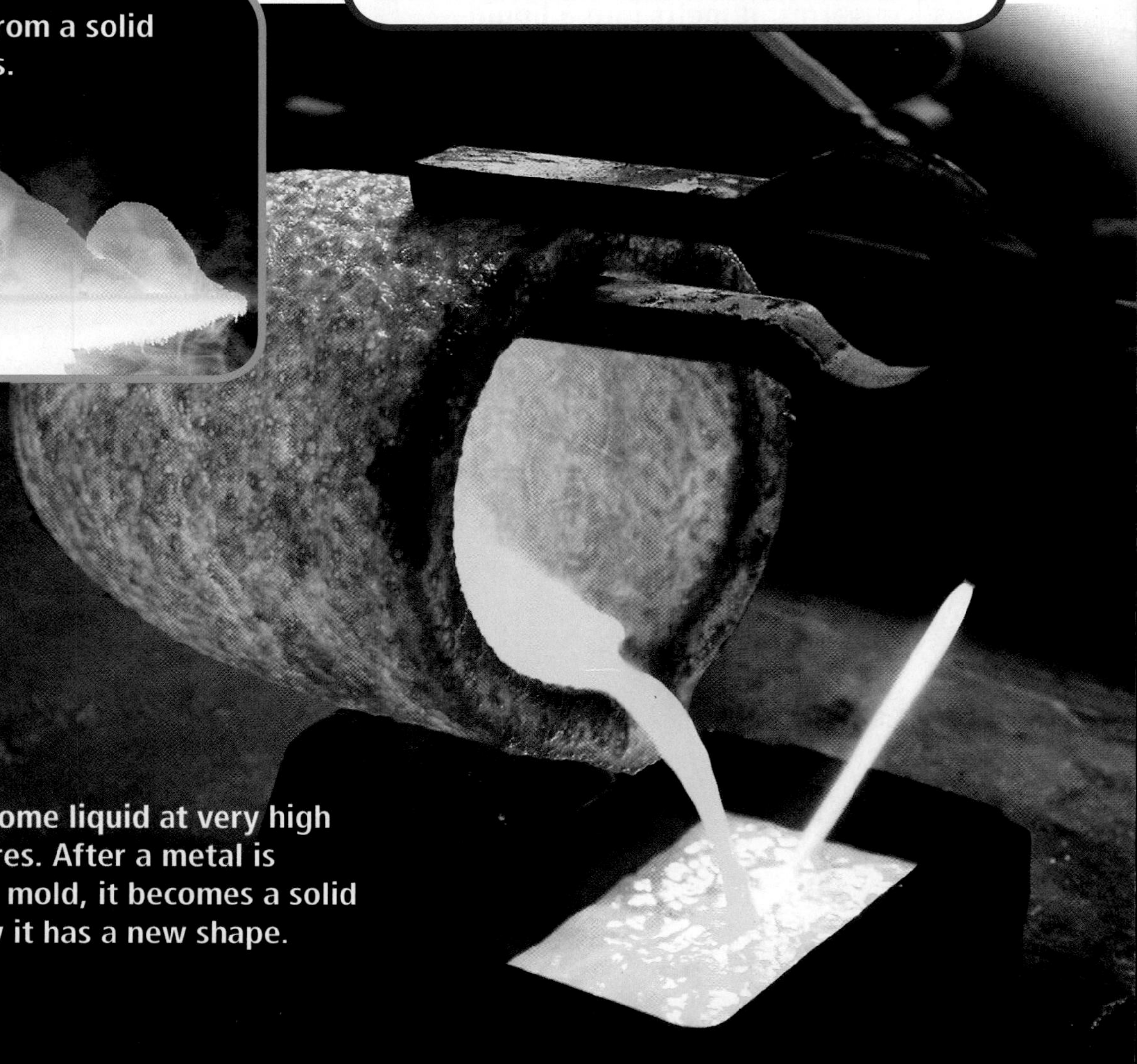

Metals become liquid at very high temperatures. After a metal is cooled in a mold, it becomes a solid again. Now it has a new shape.

Essential Question

How Does Matter Change States?

In this lesson, you learned that matter can have solid, liquid, or gas form. Some materials can take different forms, depending on conditions.

1. Focus Skill **CAUSE AND EFFECT** Draw and complete a graphic organizer to show how water can change states from gas to solid.

2. **SUMMARIZE** Using the lesson vocabulary terms, write three sentences that describe how water changes states.

3. **DRAW CONCLUSIONS** What do you think happens when gas particles cool?

4. **VOCABULARY** Make a crossword puzzle that has the vocabulary terms as answers. Write clear clues for the words.

Test Prep

5. **CRITICAL THINKING** How can you change the states of water?

6. In which state of water are the particles the most organized?
   A. ice
   B. gas
   C. liquid
   D. water vapor

Make Connections

Writing

Expository Writing

Suppose you are a drop of water. Write a story about how you experience all three states of matter in one day.

Math

Using Numbers

The metal mercury melts at about –40°C and boils at about 360°C. In which state is mercury at room temperature? How do you know?

Language Arts

Name Origins

We use two temperature scales: Celsius and Fahrenheit. Find out when and how these scales were created and named.

LESSON 3

Essential Question

What Are Mixtures and Solutions?

Investigate which solids will dissolve.

Read and Learn about mixtures and solutions.

Fast Fact

Salty, Salty Seas
Most lakes have fresh water, but some lakes are saltier than the ocean. Mono Lake, in California, has salts and minerals dissolved in it. In warm weather, its water evaporates, leaving behind some of the salts and minerals. When the lake's water level drops, a crust of minerals forms along its shore. In the Investigate, you will find out how salt and other solids dissolve in water.

Salt crust on tufa tower

Vocabulary Preview

mixture [MIKS•cher] A blending of two or more types of matter that are not chemically combined (p. 478)

solution [suh•LOO•shuhn] A mixture in which two or more substances are mixed completely (p. 480)

solubility [sahl•yoo•BIL•uh•tee] A measure of how much of a material will dissolve in another material (p. 481)

suspension [suh•SPEN•shuhn] A kind of mixture in which particles of one ingredient are floating in another ingredient (p. 482)

Investigate

Which Solids Will Dissolve?

Guided Inquiry

Start with Questions

These tablets dissolve with lots of bubbles when you put them in water.

- What are the bubbles?
- What happens to the matter in the tablets when they dissolve?

Investigate to find out. Then read to find out more.

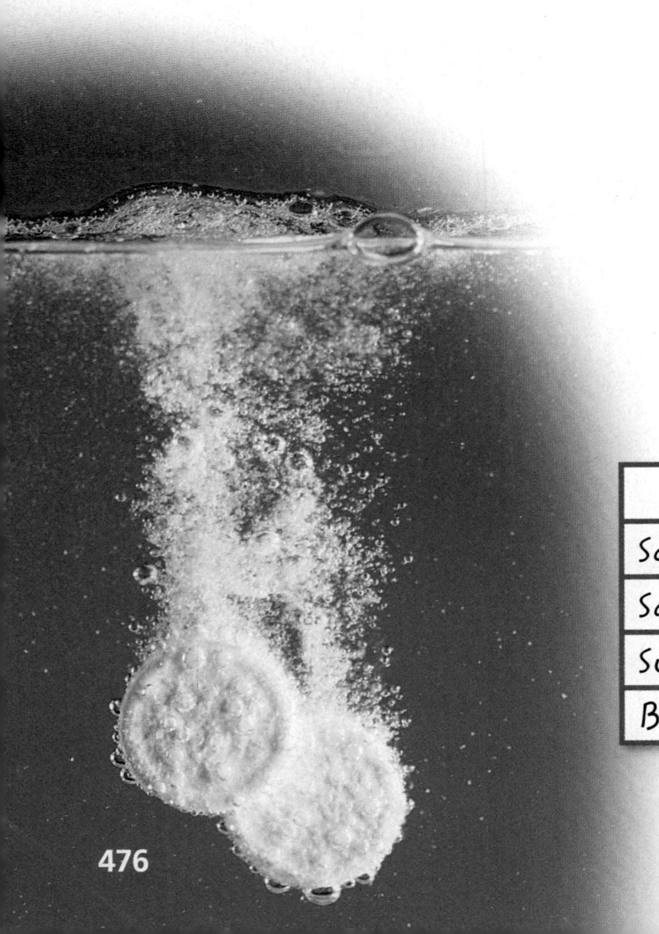

Prepare to Investigate

Inquiry Skill Tip

Each simple investigation you plan should be designed to find the answer to just one question. Changing more than one variable can change the results.

Materials

- water
- teaspoon
- sand
- 4 clear containers
- stirrer
- salt
- sugar
- baking soda

Make an Observation Chart

Material	Before Stirring	After Stirring
Sand		
Salt		
Sugar		
Baking soda		

Follow This Procedure

1. Half-fill each container with water.
2. Put 1 spoonful of sand into one container. **Observe** and **record** what happens.
3. Stir the mixture for 1 minute, and then **record** what you see.
4. Repeat Steps 2 and 3, using salt, sugar, and baking soda. **Observe** and **record** all the results.

Draw Conclusions

1. Which solid dissolved the most? Which did not dissolve at all?

2. **Inquiry Skill** Scientists often **plan a simple investigation** to test an idea quickly. What idea did this activity test? What is another simple investigation you could do with these materials?

Independent Inquiry

Dissolve table sugar and powdered sugar in separate containers of water. Compare how quickly the two kinds of sugar dissolve. Explain your results.

VOCABULARY
mixture p. 478
solution p. 480
solubility p. 481
suspension p. 482

SCIENCE CONCEPTS
- how a mixture, a solution, and a suspension differ
- about differences in how substances dissolve

Focus Skill MAIN IDEA AND DETAILS
Look for details about mixtures.

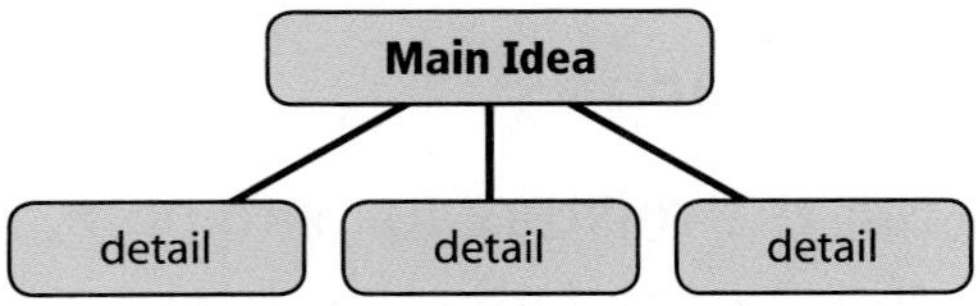

Mixtures

Do you like salad? Salad is a **mixture**. A mixture is two or more substances that are combined without being changed. These substances can be separated from each other again. For example, if you don't like onions, you can take them out of your salad.

Mixtures can contain different amounts of the substances. Your salad might have a lot of lettuce and just a little bit of onion.

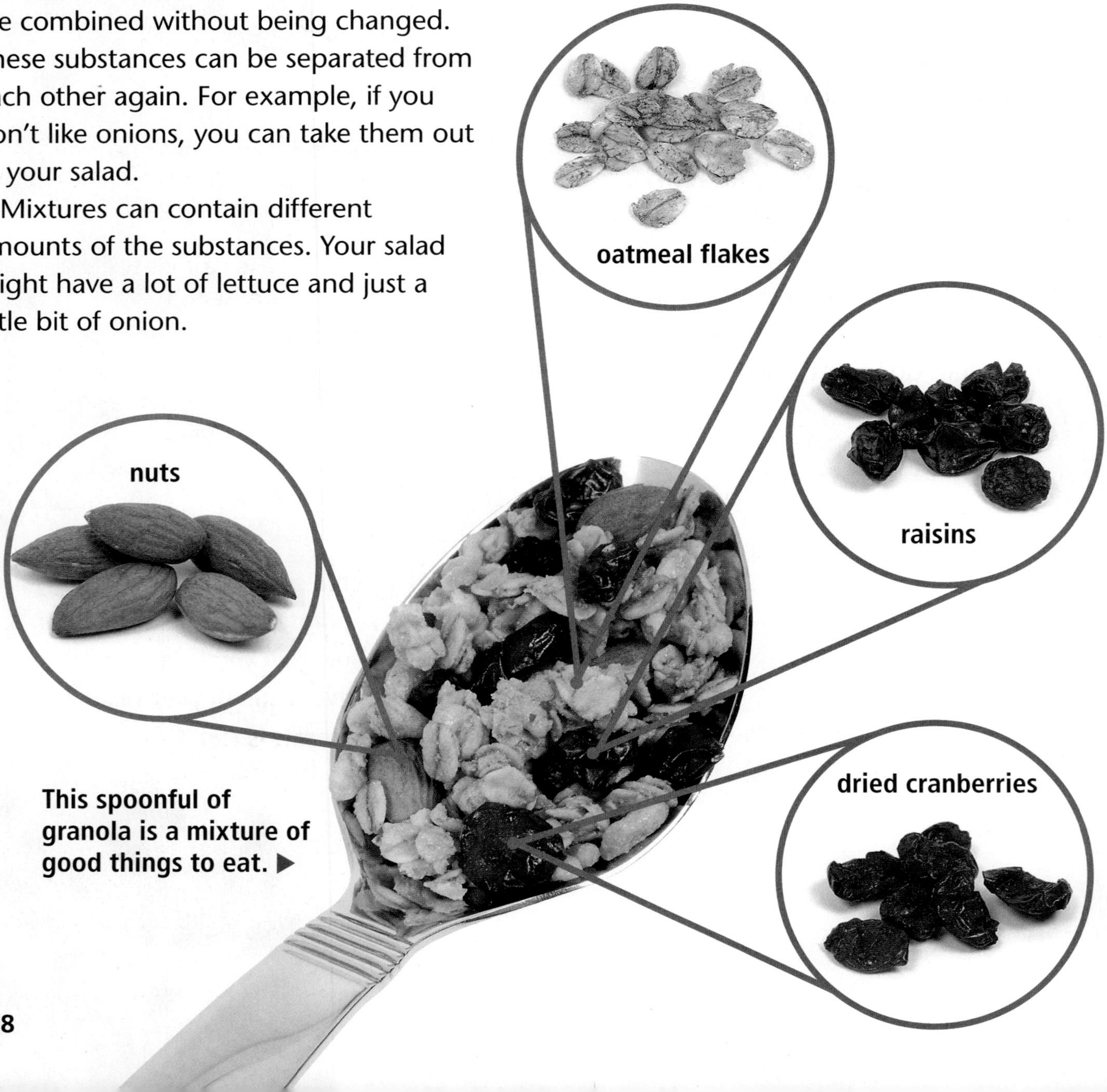

This spoonful of granola is a mixture of good things to eat. ▶

Not all mixtures are made of solids. Salt water is a mixture of a solid and a liquid. Fog is a mixture of water drops and air. Air itself is a mixture of nitrogen, oxygen, carbon dioxide, and other gases.

The pictures show how one mixture can be separated. The mixture begins as a pile of rocks, dust, salt, and bits of iron. First, larger rocks and particles are strained from the mixture. Only the smaller particles can pass through the holes in the strainer.

Next, a magnet draws out the iron bits. Then, water is added to the remaining mixture. The wet dust and salt are poured through a filter. Water and dissolved salt pass through. The dust is left behind.

Finally, the salty water is heated. The water boils away, leaving the salt behind.

All the substances in the original mixture are separated. Being in the mixture did not change them.

Focus Skill MAIN IDEA AND DETAILS

Define the term *mixture,* and name three examples.

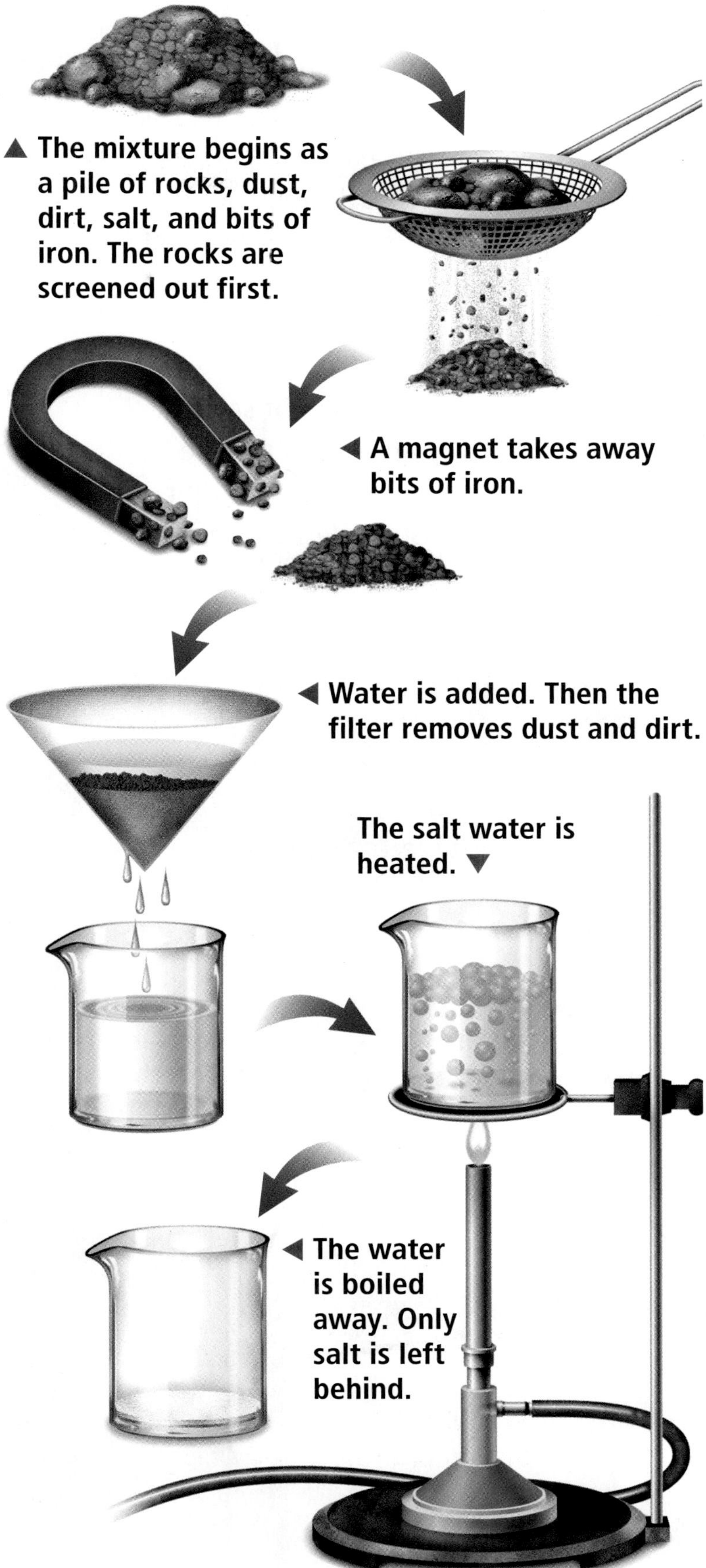

▲ **The mixture begins as a pile of rocks, dust, dirt, salt, and bits of iron. The rocks are screened out first.**

◀ **A magnet takes away bits of iron.**

◀ **Water is added. Then the filter removes dust and dirt.**

The salt water is heated. ▼

◀ **The water is boiled away. Only salt is left behind.**

Solutions

A **solution** is a kind of mixture. In a solution, different kinds of matter are mixed completely with each other. Salt water is a solution. The salt and the water are so evenly mixed that you can't see the salt. You can tell it is there by tasting the water. The air you breathe is also a solution.

On the other hand, a bowl of salad is not a solution. You can always tell the ingredients apart. The tomatoes might all be on top. Most of the lettuce might be on the bottom.

When a solid forms a solution with a liquid, the solid dissolves in the liquid. In the Investigate, you found that salt dissolves easily in water. The water particles pull the salt particles away from one another. All the particles are moving, so the salt particles spread evenly through the water.

However, sand doesn't dissolve in water. Water can't pull sand particles apart. Instead, they fall to the bottom. Sand in water is not a solution.

Focus Skill MAIN IDEA AND DETAILS

Why is pizza a mixture but not a solution?

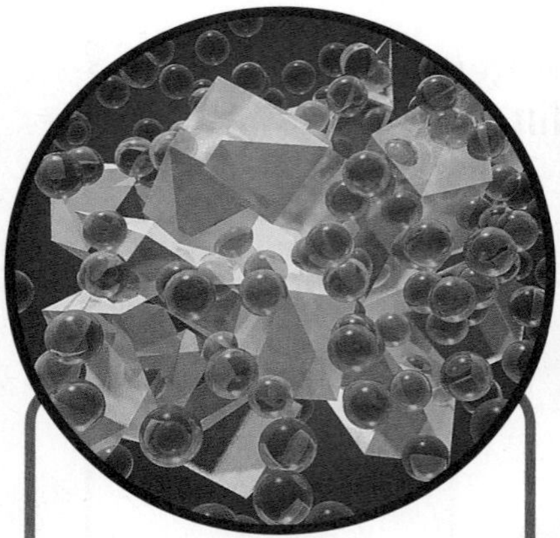

Sugar crystals are added to water.

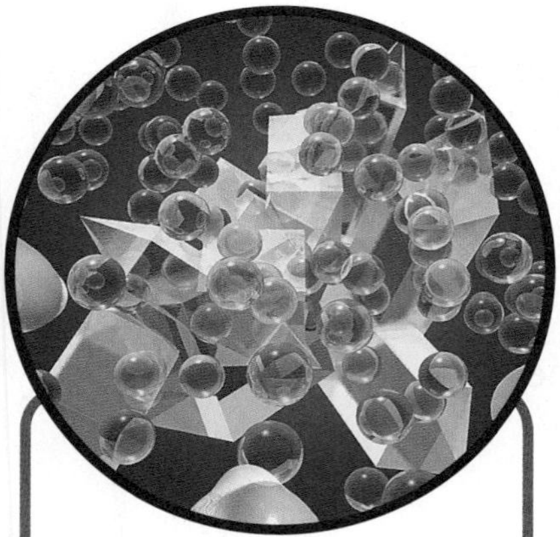

Water particles start pulling the sugar crystals apart.

The water has dissolved the sugar. The sugar bits are now too small to see, but you can taste them.

What would happen if sand dissolved in water as easily as salt does?

This salt was once dissolved in ocean water. After the water evaporated, particles of solid salt were left.

Solubility

You found in the Investigate that substances dissolve differently. **Solubility** (sahl•yoo•BIL•uh•tee) is a measure of how much of one material will dissolve in another. For example, 204 grams (7.2 oz) of sugar will dissolve in 100 milliliters (3.4 fl oz) of water at room temperature. So, sugar has a solubility of 204 g/100 mL. However, no sand will dissolve in water. Sand has a solubility of zero.

Focus Skill **MAIN IDEA AND DETAILS**

Name two things besides sand that are not soluble in water.

Insta-Lab

Cool, Warm, or Hot?

Pour 10 mL of cold water into one cup. Into another, pour 10 mL of lukewarm water, and into a third, pour 10 mL of hot water. Add a small spoonful of sugar to each cup, and stir. In which cup of water does the most sugar dissolve?

Other Mixtures

In some mixtures, the ingredients are not spread out evenly. When these mixtures sit, some of the ingredients settle to the bottom. Other ingredients rise to the top. This kind of mixture is called a **suspension**. Particles of one ingredient are suspended, or floating, in another ingredient. Some suspensions you can eat are shown here.

If you have taken a walk on a foggy day, you have walked through a suspension. Drops of water are suspended in the air. If you dip water out of a muddy creek, you will see a suspension. Bits of soil are suspended in the water.

Focus Skill MAIN IDEA AND DETAILS **How can you tell whether a mixture is a suspension?**

You must shake the orange juice container because the pulp settles out of the juice. ▶

You must also shake most salad dressings. Otherwise, you might have just oil on your salad! ▶

Fog is a suspension of water droplets in air.

Lesson Review

Essential Question

What Are Mixtures and Solutions?

In this lesson, you learned mixtures and solutions are both combinations of materials. Mixtures do not change the material. Solutions do change the material.

1. Focus Skill **MAIN IDEA AND DETAILS** Draw and complete a graphic organizer with details about mixtures.

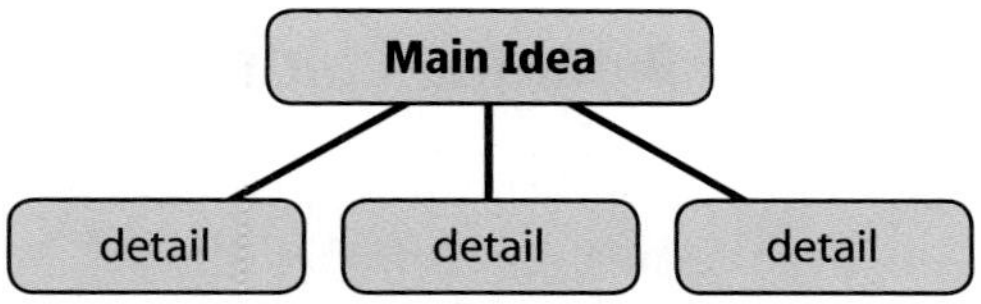

2. **SUMMARIZE** Write a summary of this lesson. Begin with this sentence: *Sand does not dissolve in water.*

3. **DRAW CONCLUSIONS** Why is lemonade that is made from a powdered mix a solution and not a suspension?

4. **VOCABULARY** Write two sentences. Use all four vocabulary words.

Test Prep

5. **CRITICAL THINKING** Name two mixtures you have eaten in the past week. Explain whether each is a simple mixture, a solution, or a suspension.

6. Which of these is a mixture?
   A. apple
   B. broccoli
   C. carrot stick
   D. ham sandwich

Make Connections

Writing

Expository Writing

Suppose you are out walking on a rainy day. Write a **description** of what you see, and mention at least four mixtures. Include one solution and one suspension in your description.

Math

Make a Bar Graph

Use a graph to show the solubility of each of these substances in 100 mL of water at room temperature: sugar, 204 g; salt, 36 g; baking soda, 7 g; and sand, 0 g.

Social Studies

The Bronze Age

Bronze is a mixture of the metals tin and copper. Find out why people mix these two metals. Then research the Bronze Age. Find out what years it covered, and name an important event from that time.

Marie Curie

Marie Curie (1867–1934) was a French scientist. She changed science and was the first woman to win the Nobel Prize.

Curie worked with Pierre, her husband. Together, they discovered the element radium. They also explored the idea of radiation. Now, doctors use radiation to find and treat diseases.

Marie Curie was born in Warsaw, Poland, on November 7, 1867. Her father taught high school physics and inspired her to study science. Later, Curie moved to France, where she met and married Pierre Curie.

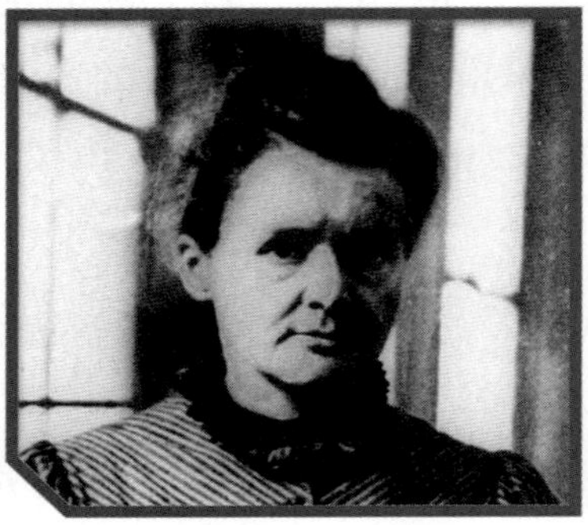

▶ **MARIE CURIE**

▶ Chemist

▶ Nobel Prize for Physics, 1903

Think and Write

1. How might science have changed when Marie Curie won the Nobel Prize?
2. Why is working with radiation important?

Career Nuclear Medicine Technologist

A nuclear medicine technologist uses radiation. Patients swallow a liquid that has a safe dose of radioactive material in it. The technologist uses special cameras to take 3-D pictures that show where the liquid is. The pictures can tell a doctor if there are problems.

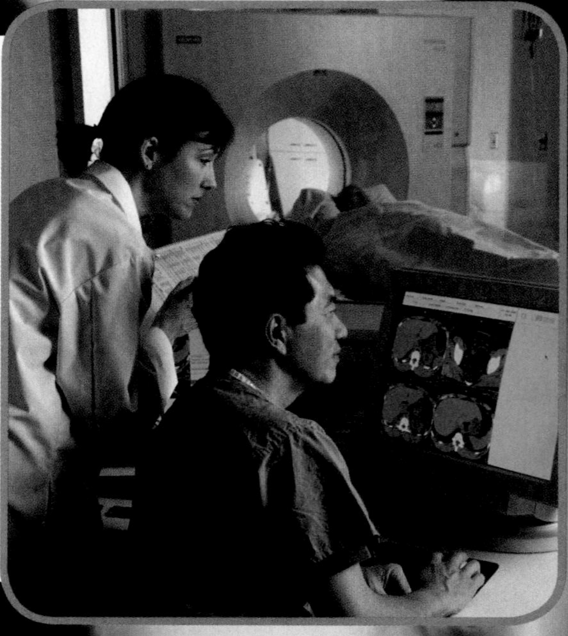

▶ **PETER DAUM**

▶ Environmental scientist

Peter Daum

In 1991, the United States government sent chemist Peter Daum to the Middle East. Daum was not there to fight in the first Persian Gulf War, however. He was sent there to study the environmental effects of the oil fires set by the retreating Iraqi army during the war.

Daum works for the U.S. Department of Energy's Brookhaven Laboratory. He studies pollution that is in Earth's atmosphere.

When Daum is at home in the United States, he and other scientists spend a lot of time flying in a plane that is an airborne laboratory. The plane's equipment can measure the levels of pollutants in the air.

They measure everything from aerosols to ultraviolet radiation. They must also decide where to fly to collect their information. If they are looking in the wrong place, they may not be able to gather the data that they need.

Once Peter Daum and his fellow scientists have the information, they must interpret it. Their conclusions are what law-makers use to make decisions about air pollution. Peter Daum has said that this is the hardest part of his job!

Think and Write

1. What does Peter Daum study?
2. Why is it important to know how much pollution is in the air?

CHAPTER 11

Review and Test Preparation

Vocabulary Review

Use the terms below to complete the sentences. The page numbers tell you where to look in the chapter if you need help.

mass p. 459
volume p. 460
density p. 460
state of matter p. 468
solid p. 468
liquid p. 469
solubility p. 481
suspension p. 482

1. When some solids get warm enough, they become a _______.
2. When a liquid gets cool enough, it becomes a _______.
3. Mass divided by volume is _______.
4. The amount of a substance that can be dissolved in another substance is the measure of its _______.
5. Gas is one _______.
6. If particles settle out of a mixture, the mixture is a _______.
7. The amount of space an object takes up is its _______.
8. _______ is the measure of the amount of matter an object has.

Check Understanding

Write the letter of the best choice.

9. Which of these is made of matter?
   A. a dream
   B. a book
   C. happiness
   D. an idea

10. Which of these is a mixture?
   F. pail of sand and soil
   G. copper wire
   H. ring of pure gold
   J. pinch of salt

11. **MAIN IDEA AND DETAILS** (Focus Skill) Which of these is an example of a solution?
   A. granola
   B. iced tea
   C. pizza
   D. salad

12. Which of these has no definite volume?
   F. gas
   G. liquid
   H. matter
   J. solid

13. **CAUSE AND EFFECT** (Focus Skill) Which of these probably has the **most** mass?
   A. apple
   B. balloon
   C. brick
   D. golf ball

14. Which term best describes the contents of this glass?

   F. density
   G. mass
   H. suspension
   J. volume

15. Which is a measure of how closely particles are packed together?
   A. density
   B. matter
   C. solubility
   D. volume

16. Which has mass and takes up space?
F. height
G. matter
H. volume
J. weight

Inquiry Skills

17. **Compare** the arrangement of particles in a solid with the arrangement of particles in a gas.

18. Two boxes are the same size and have the same density. What can you **infer** about their masses?

Critical Thinking

19. You have a red box and a black box that are exactly the same size. The red box is heavier than the black one. What does this tell you about the physical properties of the boxes?

20. **The Big Idea** The air around us is a mixture of nitrogen, oxygen, carbon dioxide, and other gases. This morning, the air outside looked like Picture A to the right. Right now, the air outside looks like Picture B. Use the terms *solution* and *suspension* to describe the air this morning and the air right now. Explain how air can be a mixture, a solution, and a suspension.

Picture A

Picture B

CHAPTER 12 Changes in Matter

What's the Big Idea?

Matter can undergo both physical and chemical changes.

Essential Questions

Lesson 1
What Is Matter Made Of?

Lesson 2
What Are Physical Changes in Matter?

Lesson 3
How Does Matter React Chemically?

GO online Student eBook www.hspscience.com

What do YOU wonder?

Beached? The shrinking Aral Sea left this ship behind. What happened to the sea floor? What changes are happening to the outside of the ship? How does this relate to the **Big Idea?**

LESSON 1

Essential Question

What Is Matter Made Of?

Investigate mixing solutions.

Read and Learn what matter is made of.

Fast Fact

Tiny Circles

Each of the little peaks on the oval marks an iron atom. Iron atoms are tiny. It would take more than 40 million iron atoms to make a 1-cm-long line. In the Investigate, you will observe a way that matter can change.

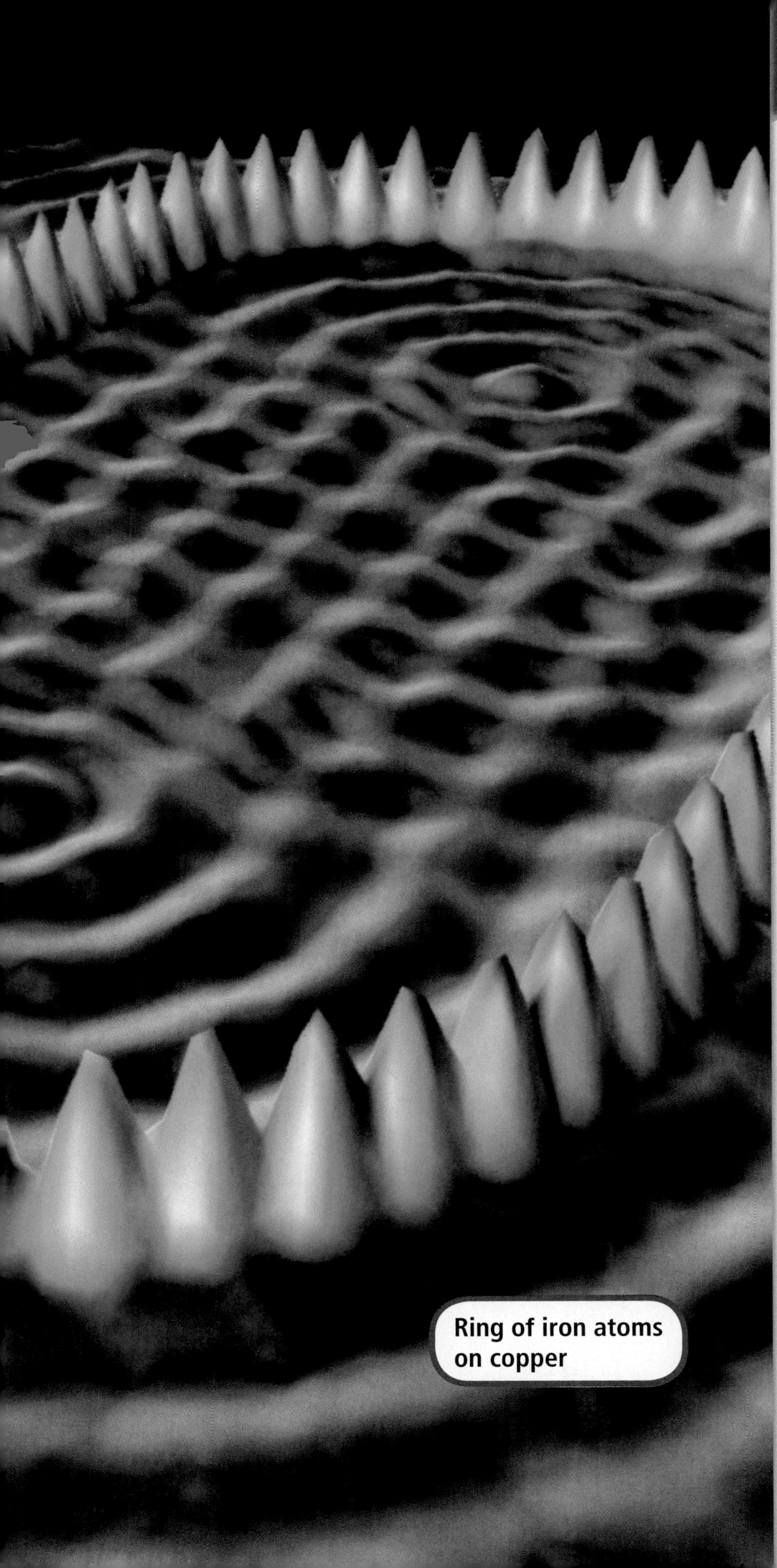

Ring of iron atoms on copper

Vocabulary Preview

atom [AT•uhm] The smallest unit of an element that has all the properties of that element (p. 496)

element [EL•uh•muhnt] A substance made up of only one kind of atom (p. 498)

Investigate

A Solution to the Problem

Guided Inquiry

Start with Questions

Chefs follow recipes when they are cooking. This cook is mixing salt into the pan.

- How does the heat of the burner affect the salt?
- Is this a mixture or a solution?

Investigate to find out. Then read to find out more.

Prepare to Investigate

Inquiry Skill Tip

The conclusions you draw might not support your hypothesis. That is OK. Do not change your conclusions. Instead, make a new hypothesis and test again.

Materials

- iodized salt
- kosher salt
- sea salt
- granulated sugar
- powdered sugar
- brown sugar
- 6 spoons
- 6 paper plates
- 6 plastic cups
- water

Make an Observation Chart

Sample	Color	Texture	Grain Size	Reaction in Water
Iodized salt				

Follow This Procedure

1. Place a small amount of each kind of salt and each kind of sugar on its own plate.
2. **Compare** each sample's color and texture. **Record** your **observations**.
3. **Compare** the grain sizes of the samples. **Record** your **observations**.
4. Place the same amount of water in each of six cups. Use a clean spoon to place the same amount of each sample in its own cup. Stir. **Record** your **observations**.

Draw Conclusions

1. Which samples—the light-colored ones or the darker-colored ones—mixed into the water more quickly?
2. Which samples—the ones with larger grains or the ones with smaller grains—mixed into water more quickly?
3. **Inquiry Skill** Scientists interpret data to **draw conclusions**. What can you conclude about how color and grain size affect the speed with which a sample mixes into water?

Independent Inquiry

Sequence the samples by how quickly they mixed into water. Predict where sugar cubes will fit in your list. Test your prediction.

VOCABULARY
atom p. 496
element p. 498

SCIENCE CONCEPTS
- that matter is made up of atoms
- that an element is a substance made up of just one kind of atom

Focus Skill MAIN IDEA AND DETAILS
Look for details about atoms.

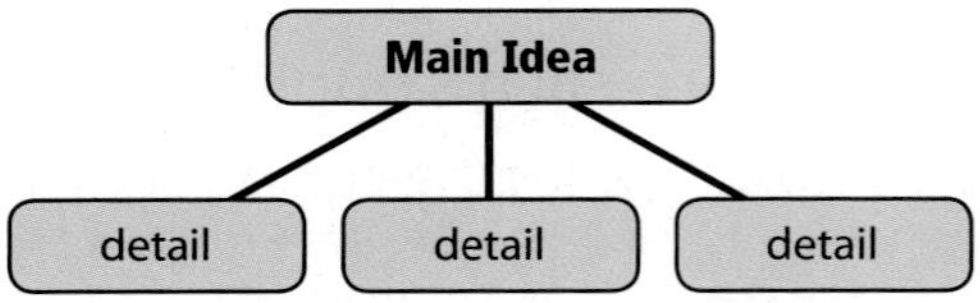

Basic Properties of Matter

What do your bed, the water in the ocean, and the air in your classroom all have in common? Not much, really. In fact, they have only one thing in common—they are all examples of matter. As you learned earlier, matter is anything that has mass and takes up space.

Sunlight is not matter. A light room does not have more mass than a dark room has. An idea also is not made of matter. Your brain doesn't take up more space when you think hard.

What is matter made of, though? You know that it has different properties. How does it come together to make the things you see and touch?

Like matter, these toy pieces can be put together to form objects of many shapes and sizes. Each object has mass and takes up space. ▶

The soccer ball at the right has more mass than the one at the left. Where does the extra mass come from? ▶

Air is around you every day. You need it to breathe. You know it is matter. The two balls on this page show that you can squeeze different amounts of it into a container.

The fact that you can squeeze more and more air into a container is evidence of that. This hints at the size of the particles of matter. You can't see the particles. With an air pump, you can pack more and more of them into the same space. They must be very small.

Other properties of matter are also hints. Substances have properties such as solubility, mass, and hardness. As you learned in the Investigate, some materials act differently when mixed with water. You also know that metal knives are heavier and harder than plastic ones. So, some particles must be heavier or hold together more tightly. These differences are because the tiny particles that make up each substance are different. In the rest of this lesson, you'll learn more about these particles.

Focus Skill MAIN IDEA AND DETAILS

How do you define *matter*?

Insta-Lab

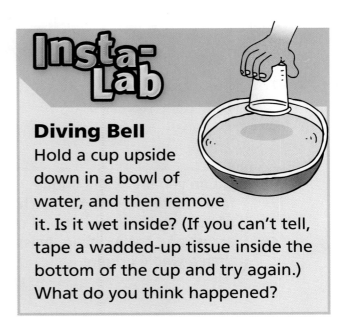

Diving Bell

Hold a cup upside down in a bowl of water, and then remove it. Is it wet inside? (If you can't tell, tape a wadded-up tissue inside the bottom of the cup and try again.) What do you think happened?

Particles of Matter

More than 2000 years ago, a Greek thinker named Democritus (dih•MAHK•ruh•tuhs) had an idea about matter. Democritus said that all matter is made up of tiny particles, or bits. He said that different kinds of matter are made up of different kinds of particles. And he thought that these particles could not be split endlessly into smaller parts.

Democritus didn't experiment or test his ideas in any way. Still, it turns out that he was partly right. We now know that matter can be broken down only so far. If you divide something into smaller and smaller particles, you end up with an atom. An **atom** is the smallest possible particle of a substance.

Science Up Close

1 **How small can something get? Start with a bag of charcoal briquets. It is about $\frac{1}{2}$ m long, and it has a fair amount of mass.**

2 **It's easy to break down the contents of the bag into smaller parts. This is one briquet. It is about 5 cm square, and it has a small mass.**

3 **Can you break the briquet into smaller pieces? Yes. Each of the large chunks is 1 or 2 cm across and has a smaller mass than a whole briquet.**

As you might guess, an atom is very small. It's really, really small. In fact, it's so small that you can't see it. Even with a regular microscope you couldn't see an atom. Why not? Because single atoms are too small to reflect light! So there's no way you can see a single atom at all unless you use a special microscope.

Democritus made up the word *atom.* It comes from a word that means "cannot be divided." Think about a tank of oxygen. You can divide all the oxygen inside into smaller and smaller parts. But when you get to an oxygen atom, you have to stop. If you break it up further, it won't be oxygen anymore.

Focus Skill **MAIN IDEA AND DETAILS**

What is an atom?

For more links and animations, go to **www.hspscience.com**

4 **If you break the chunks further, you end up with dust. A dust grain is very tiny. It's so small that you can barely see it. Look at it under a microscope. You'll see that even it can be broken into smaller pieces.**

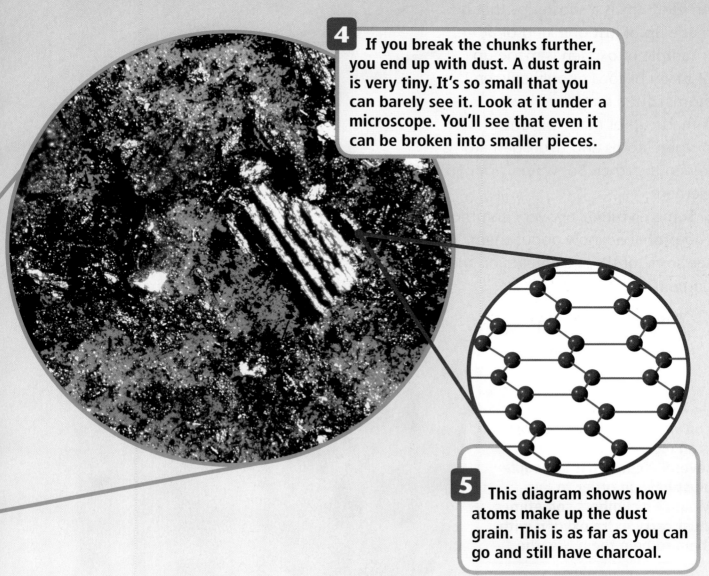

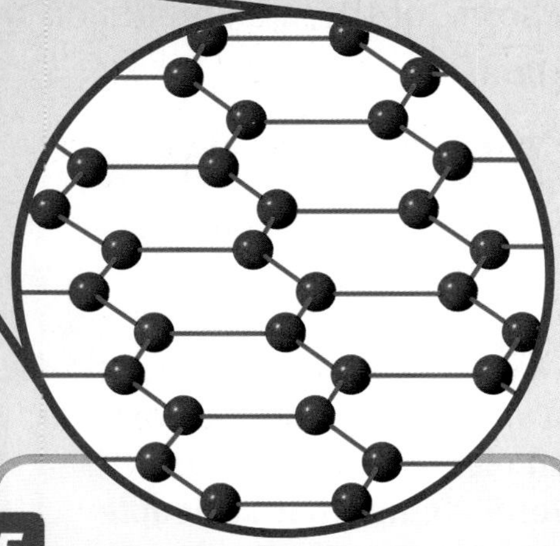

5 **This diagram shows how atoms make up the dust grain. This is as far as you can go and still have charcoal.**

Elements

You just read that if you were to break all the oxygen inside a tank into smaller and smaller parts, you would end up with an oxygen atom. What if you did the same thing with a drop of water? Would you end up with a single water atom? No, because there is no such thing as an atom of water. The smallest possible particle of water is made up of two different kinds of atoms—two hydrogen atoms and one oxygen atom.

Hydrogen and oxygen are elements. An **element** is a substance that is made up of just one kind of atom. A sample of oxygen is made up of many billions of only oxygen atoms. But a sample of water is made up of many billions of oxygen atoms and hydrogen atoms joined together. So, water is not an element.

Some elements are very common, and you probably know about them. You can see some of these elements on these two pages.

Focus Skill **MAIN IDEA AND DETAILS**

What is an element?

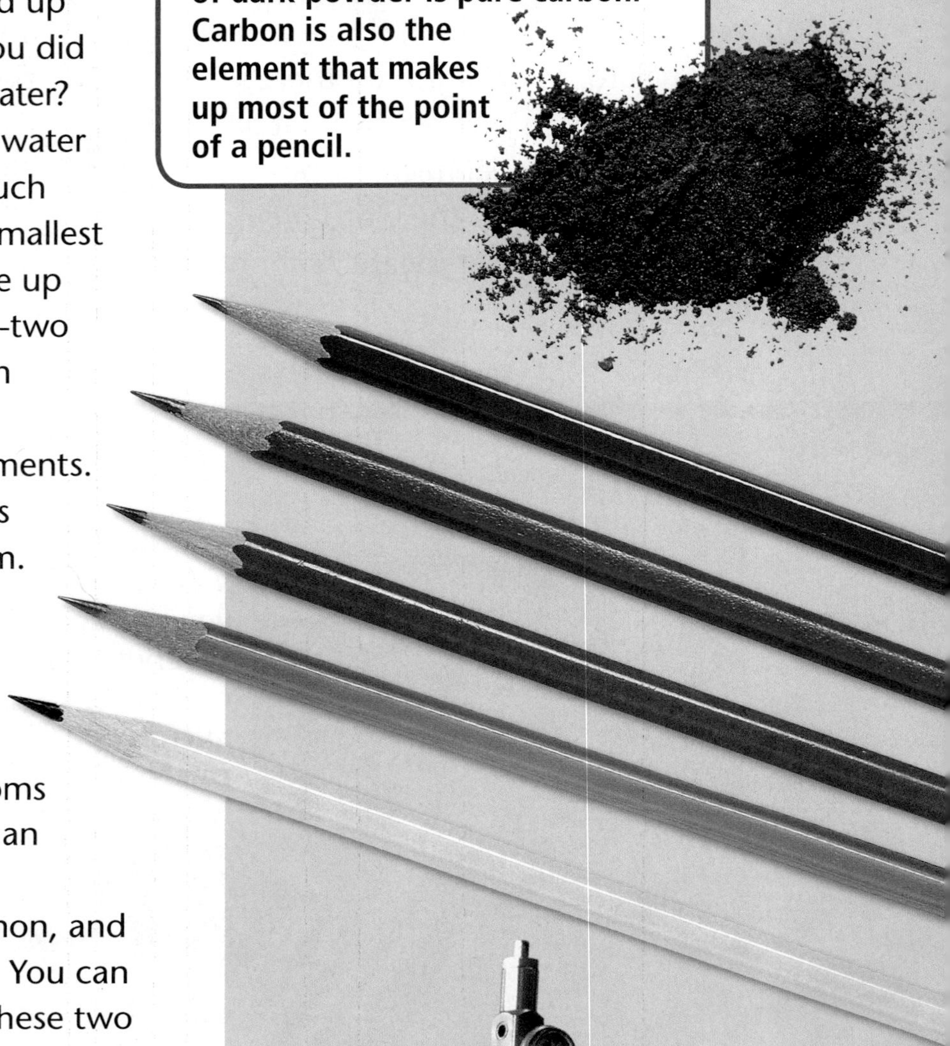

Remember the atoms in charcoal? They are carbon atoms. The pile of dark powder is pure carbon. Carbon is also the element that makes up most of the point of a pencil.

You've already read that oxygen is an element. It is one of several elements that people must have in order to live. Mountain climbers sometimes must carry extra oxygen with them to help them breathe.

Have you ever seen a mercury switch inside a thermostat? As you can see, mercury is a shiny, silver-colored element.

Iron is another common element. You probably see things made of iron every day. You may also see things made of steel. Steel is made up of iron and a small amount of carbon.

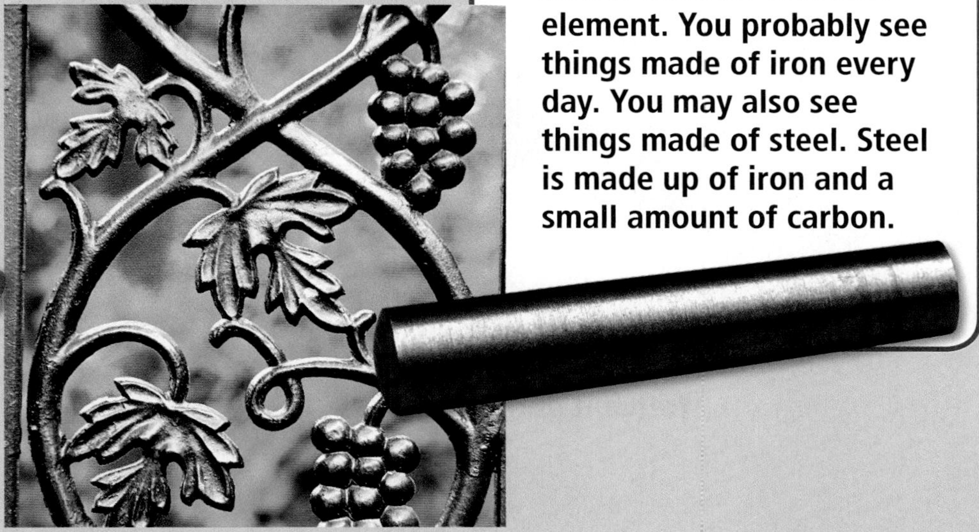

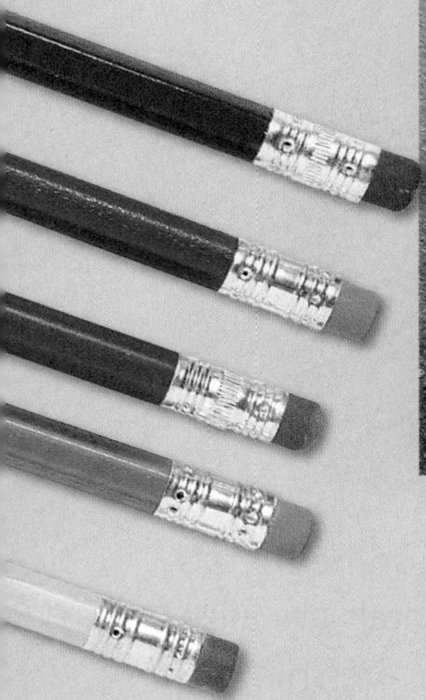

Another shiny, silver-colored element is silver. Silver is somewhat rare. Many people call forks and spoons "silverware." However, only expensive silverware is really made of silver.

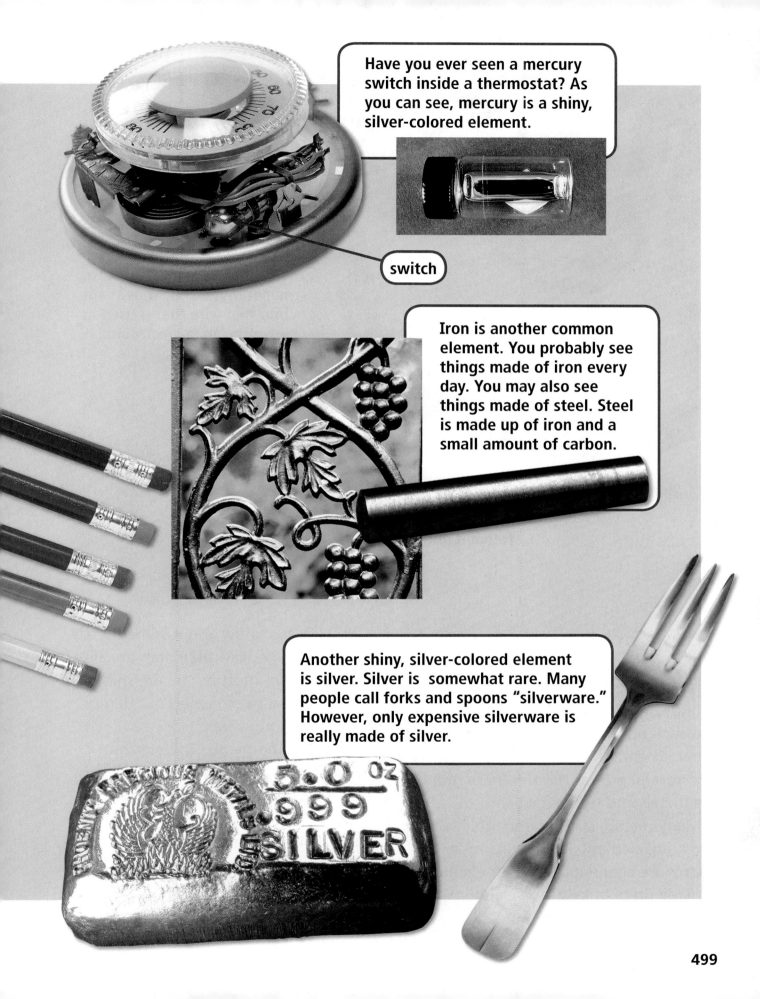

▲ **Gold is an element. It is also a metal. It can be drawn out into thin wire that is used in jewelry and in electronics.**

Sulfur is another element. It is a nonmetal. If you try to stretch it out, it breaks. ▶

Some Groups of Elements

You've probably noticed that scientists classify things into groups. Forming groups helps people see how things are like each other and different from each other. Scientists have classified elements into several groups. Two of these groups are metals and nonmetals.

Many metals, such as iron, gold, and silver, are elements. However, not all metals are elements. Steel, for example, is made up of at least two elements, iron and carbon.

You already know about some metals. What are some ways all metals are alike? For one thing, most metals are shiny. They can also be stretched out thin or drawn into long wires.

How are nonmetals different from metals? Nonmetals aren't shiny. They're dull. They can't be stretched out thin. Most nonmetals are brittle. They break instead of stretching. Some nonmetals, such as oxygen, aren't even solids.

Focus Skill MAIN IDEA AND DETAILS

Name two groups of elements.

Essential Question

What is Matter Made of?

In this lesson, you learned that matter has different properties. It is made of tiny atoms. Each element is made up of only one kind of atom.

1. **Focus Skill MAIN IDEA AND DETAILS** Draw and complete a graphic organizer to show the details of particles of matter.

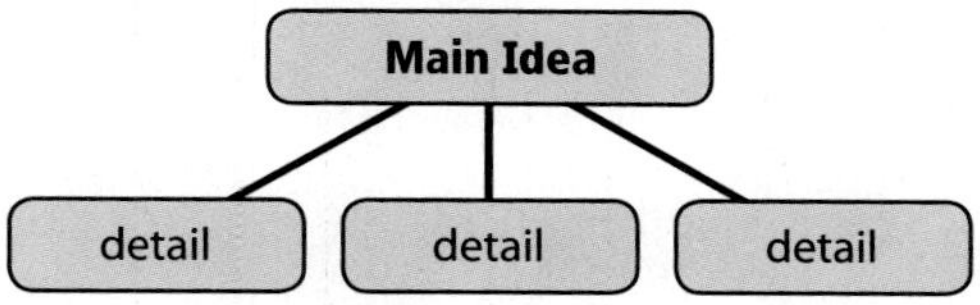

2. **SUMMARIZE** Write a sentence that describes the relationship beween elements and atoms.

3. **DRAW CONCLUSIONS** The scientific name for table salt is sodium chloride. Why do you think it has this name?

4. **VOCABULARY** Write two sentences using the lesson vocabulary words. Then write your own definition for each term.

Test Prep

5. **CRITICAL THINKING** Why is "anything you can touch and pick up" not a good definition of *matter*?

6. Which is the smallest particle of an element?
   A. atom
   B. bit
   C. chunk
   D. grain

Make Connections

Writing

Expository Writing
Imagine that you have been shrunk down to the size of an atom. Write a short **story** about what you see and do.

Math

Solve a Problem
You have read that you would have to line up more than 40 million iron atoms to get a line of them 1 cm long. How do you write the numeral for 40 million?

Social Studies

Explore the History of Science
Did everyone accept Democritus' ideas about atoms 2000 years ago? Do some research. Then write a paragraph about people's reactions to Democritus' ideas.

LESSON 2

Essential Question

What Are Physical Changes in Matter?

Investigate the physical properties of liquids.

Read and Learn about physical changes in matter.

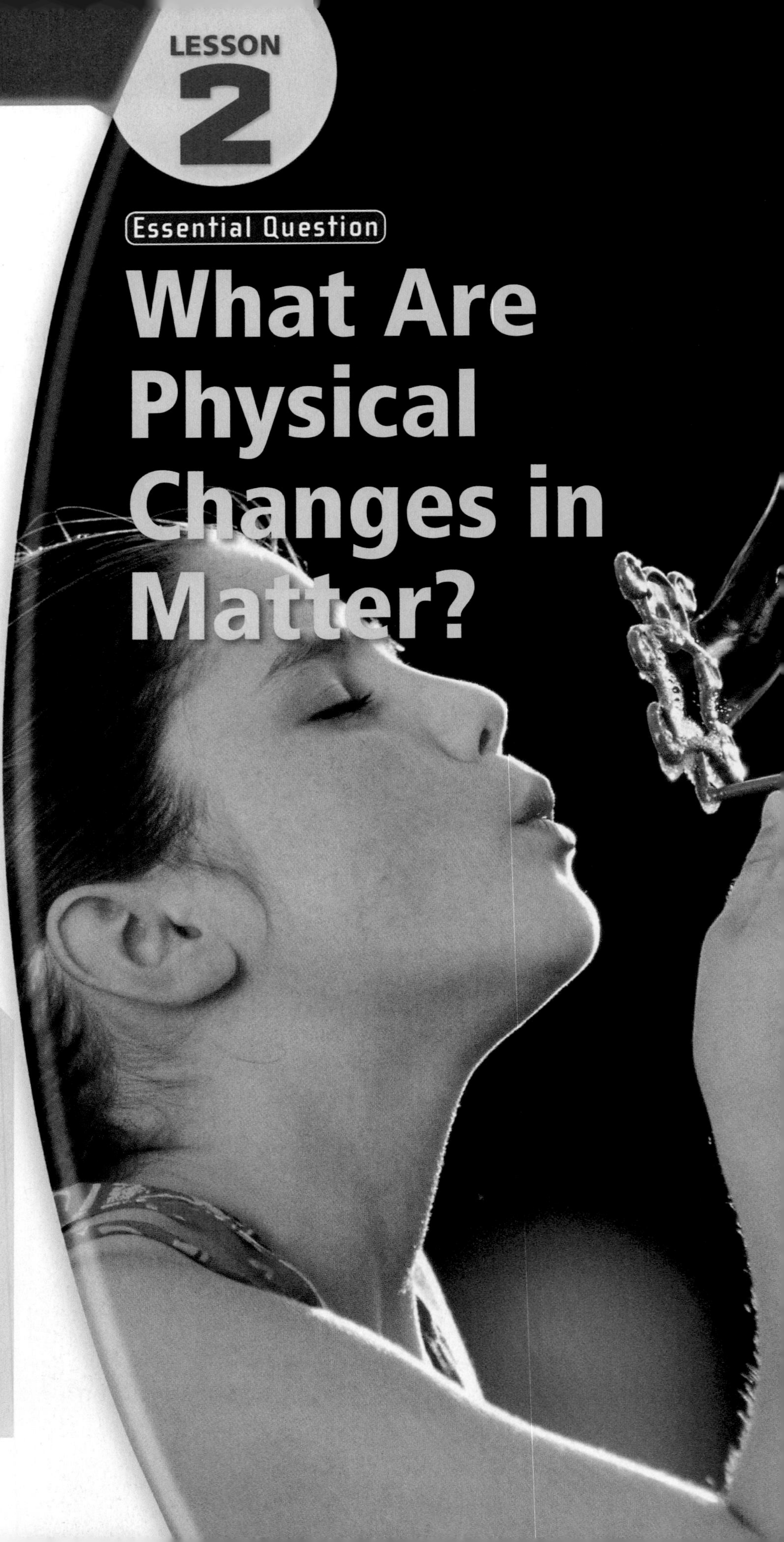

Fast Fact

Bubble Life Span
A scientist once kept a bubble in a jar for three months! It never popped, but it eventually shrank down until the air in the bubble was gone. The shape of the bubble changed, but the substance didn't. In the Investigate, you will observe changes in three liquids over time.

Vocabulary Preview

change of state [CHAYNJ uhv STAYT] A physical change that occurs when matter changes from one state to another, such as from a liquid to a gas (p. 506)

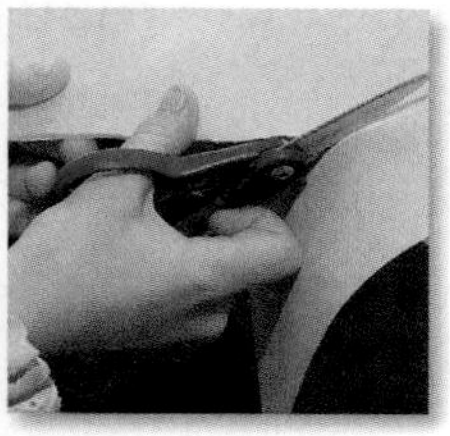

physical change [FIZ•ih•kuhl CHAYNJ] A change in matter from one form to another that doesn't result in a different substance (p. 508)

Drop by Drop

Guided Inquiry

Start with Questions

Have you ever been to the ocean and tasted the salt water? Salt water has evaporated and left this residue on the shore.

- What is the residue made of?
- Why didn't it evaporate with the water?

Investigate to find out. Then read to find out more.

Prepare to Investigate

Inquiry Skill Tip

When you think of your hypothesis, make sure it addresses the question you are trying to answer. If it is too vague, your experiment will not test it well.

Materials

- 3 droppers
- water
- vegetable oil
- rubbing alcohol
- 3 plates
- safety goggles

Make an Observation Chart

Observation	Water	Oil	Alcohol
1			
2			
3			
4			
5			
6			
7			
8			
9			

Follow This Procedure

1. CAUTION: **Wear safety goggles.** Place 3 drops of water on one plate, 3 drops of vegetable oil on the second plate, and 3 drops of rubbing alcohol on the third plate. Use a different dropper for each liquid.
2. **Record** your **observations** of each liquid.
3. Repeat Step 2 every half hour for the rest of the school day.

Step 1

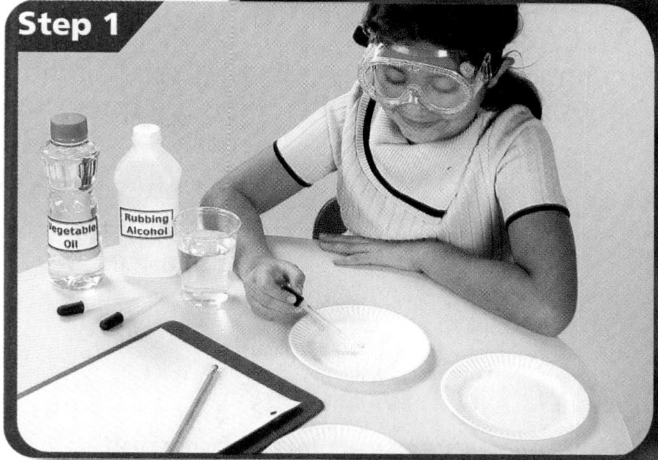

Step 2

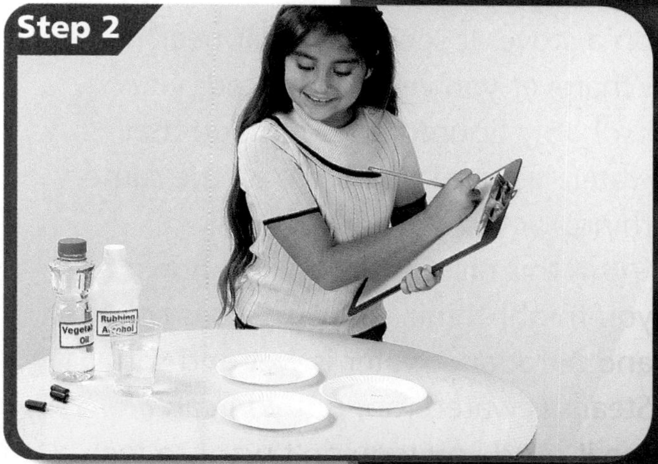

Draw Conclusions

1. What did you observe at the end of the day?
2. **Inquiry Skill** When scientists give a possible explanation for what they observe, we say they are making a **hypothesis**. Then the scientists test the **hypothesis**. What **hypothesis** can you make from your observations?

Independent Inquiry

What could you do to test your hypothesis? Plan and carry out an investigation to find out.

Read and Learn

VOCABULARY
change of state, p. 506
physical change, p. 508

SCIENCE CONCEPTS
- that solid, liquid, and gas are three states of matter
- that physical changes do not make new substances

Focus Skill COMPARE AND CONTRAST
Look for similarities and differences in states of matter.

alike — different

States of Matter

Have you ever seen ice cubes melt in a glass? The ice becomes water. Or maybe you've seen water boil away on a stove. It seems to disappear. Whatever you've experienced, you probably figured out long ago that water, ice, and steam are all the same thing.

But this fact isn't as easily known as
ou might think. After all, ice is cold
d hard, and water is wet and soft.
m is water, too, but you can't
And you wouldn't want to feel
—it's very hot.
w is it that water can have
ns that are so different?
ery substance on Earth
a solid, as a liquid, or as a
called the *three states*

tate occurs when a
s from one state to
ge of state has its

arm by sitting
e surrounded
its states. ▶

Liquid
The particles of water in this glass are close to one another. They move quickly and slide past each other easily.

If a solid is heated enough, it will eventually turn into a liquid. This is called *melting.* If a liquid is cooled enough, it will turn into a solid. This is called *freezing.*

If a liquid is heated enough, it will turn into a gas. This is called *boiling.* If a gas cools, it will turn into a liquid. This is called *condensing.*

You know that all matter is made up of tiny particles. These particles are always moving. Since ice, water, and steam are all the same substance, they are made up of the same kind of particles.

The difference between them is in the way the particles move. Ice particles don't move around at all; they just vibrate in place. Water particles move easily. Steam particles very quickly fly all over the place.

Focus Skill **COMPARE AND CONTRAST** **How are the particles of ice, water, and steam different? How are they the same?**

Solid
The particles of ice are locked in place, although they're still vibrating.

Gas
The particles of air in this balloon are far apart and are moving very quickly.

ysical Changes

Look at the pictures of the icicles melting and the water boiling. What do they have in common? They both show a change of states.

Now look at the pictures on the next page. One sheet of paper is being shredded, another sheet of paper is being cut, and wood is being carved with a chain saw. Those pictures have something in common with the pictures on this page. Do you know what it is?

The paper and wood are being changed, but none of these changes is a change of states. All the pictures on these two pages show **physical changes**. A physical change is a change that does not result in a new substance. Changes of states are examples of physical changes. So are shredding, cutting, and carving.

Both of these pictures show physical changes taking place.

The water is boiling into steam, a gas you cannot see. Water and steam are two forms of the same thing. ▼

▲ The icicles are melting and becoming water. Ice and water are two forms of the same thing.

The shredder is changing paper into many thin strips of paper. ▼

The scissors are changing a large sheet of paper into two smaller pieces of paper. ▶

This artist is using a chain saw to change a log into a deer statue and wood chips. ▼

How do you know that a change of states is a physical change? Well, you know that ice, water, and steam are all different forms of the same thing. If ice changes to water or water changes to steam, no new substance is made. So, that change is a physical change.

After you shred a sheet of paper, what do you get? You get shreds of paper. And when you cut a sheet of paper in two, you get two smaller pieces of paper. The size and shape are different, but they are all still paper.

The chain saw makes lots and lots of wood chips. They're small, but they're still wood. Since wood is not being changed into another substance, the change is a physical change.

Focus Skill COMPARE AND CONTRAST **What do all physical changes have in common?**

Insta-Lab

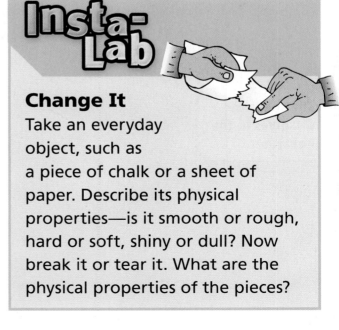

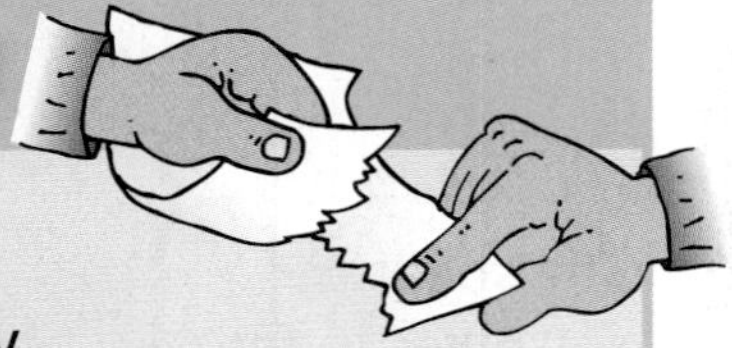

Change It

Take an everyday object, such as a piece of chalk or a sheet of paper. Describe its physical properties—is it smooth or rough, hard or soft, shiny or dull? Now break it or tear it. What are the physical properties of the pieces?

Dissolving

You know that a change of states is a kind of physical change. This picture shows another kind of physical change—dissolving. The sugar dissolves in, or becomes evenly mixed into, the hot water in the jar.

How can you tell that dissolving is a physical change? You can let the water in the jar evaporate, which is another physical change. After the water evaporates, the sugar is left behind in the beaker. The sugar doesn't change into another substance. It's still there.

COMPARE AND CONTRAST (Focus Skill)

How is dissolving like evaporating?

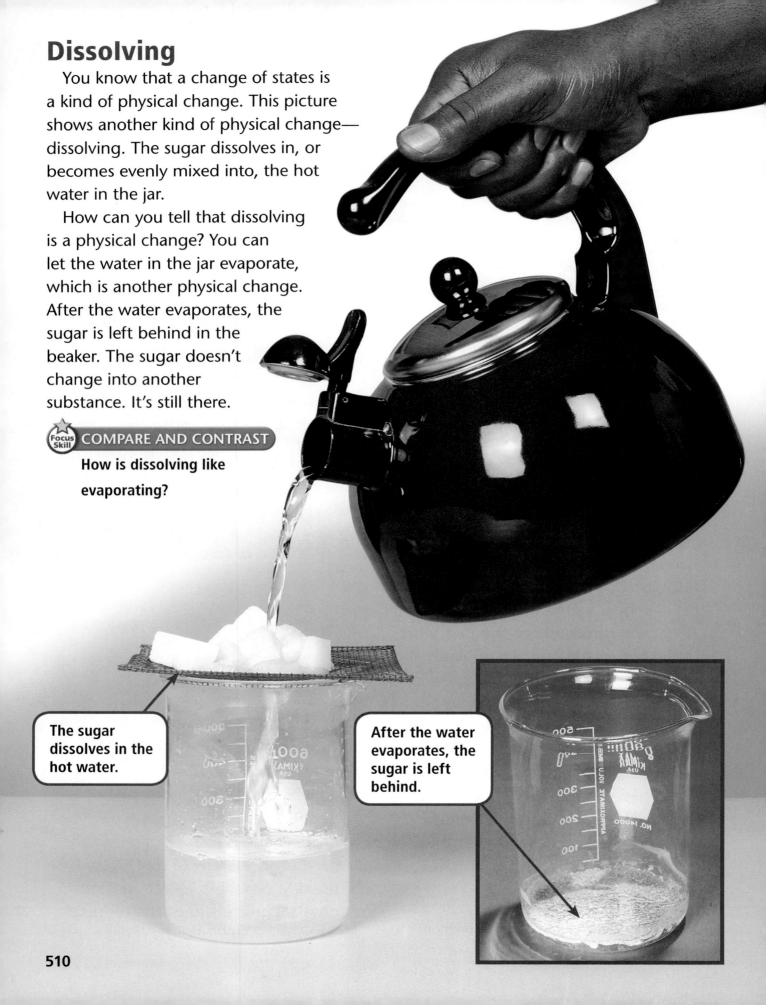

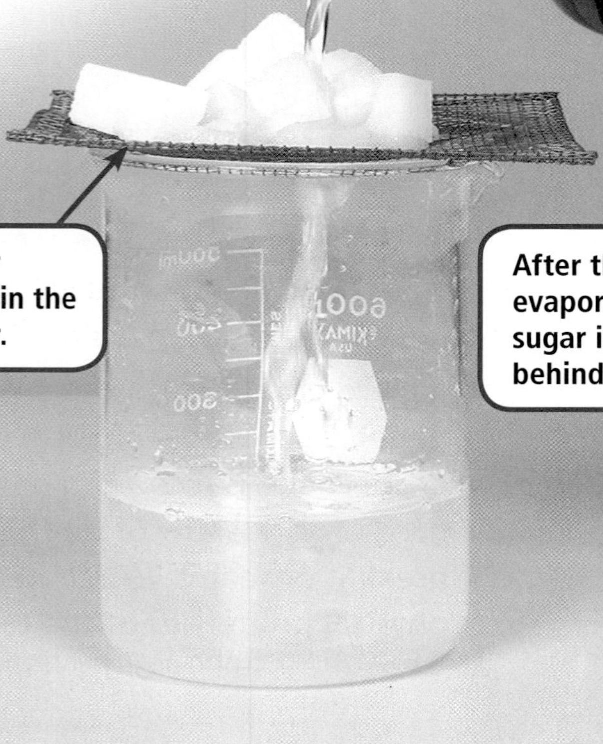
The sugar dissolves in the hot water.

After the water evaporates, the sugar is left behind.

Lesson Review

Essential Question

What Are Physical Changes in Matter?

In this lesson, you learned that a change of state is a physical change. So is shredding and cutting. Dissolving is also a physical change because no new substance is formed.

1. **Focus Skill COMPARE AND CONTRAST** Draw and complete a graphic organizer to compare and contrast the states of matter.

   alike — different

2. **SUMMARIZE** Write a paragraph that describes three states of matter.

3. **DRAW CONCLUSIONS** A glass falls to the floor and smashes into hundreds of tiny pieces. Is this a physical change? Why or why not?

4. **VOCABULARY** Write a fill-in-the-blank sentence for each vocabulary term. Show the right answers.

Test Prep

5. **CRITICAL THINKING** A cook adds oil to vinegar and then mixes it to make salad dressing. Is this a physical change? Why or why not?

6. Which might occur if you heat a substance?
   A. boiling
   B. freezing
   C. shredding
   D. none of these

Make Connections

Writing

Expository Writing

Imagine that you are helping a younger student learn about science. Write a short **explanation** of the changes that occur when a substance goes through a change of states.

Math

Estimate Measurements

Nancy combines 950 mL of vinegar with 800 mL of oil. About how many liters is that in all?

Health

Food Changes

When you eat, your body changes food so that you can digest it. Make a diagram that shows two places in the body in which food undergoes a physical change. (Hint: Read about digestion.)

LESSON 3

Essential Question

How Does Matter React Chemically?

Investigate what water does to steel wool.

Read and Learn about chemical changes in matter.

Fast Fact

Bang! Zoom!
The energy released by two chemical reactions is enough to lift the space shuttle into orbit. Believe it or not, the substance that is made by one reaction is water. In the Investigate, you will find out about another reaction that involves water.

Shuttle launch

Vocabulary Preview

physical property [FIZ•ih•kuhl PRAHP•er•tee] A trait that involves a substance by itself (p. 517)

chemical property [KEM•ih•kuhl PRAHP•er•tee] A property that involves how a substance interacts with other substances (p. 517)

chemical change [KEM•ih•kuhl CHAYNJ] A reaction or change in a substance, produced by chemical means, that results in a different substance (p. 518)

chemical reaction [KEM•ih•kuhl ree•AK•shuhn] A chemical change (p. 518)

compound [KAHM•pownd] A substance made of two or more different elements that have combined chemically (p. 518)

Investigate

Wet Wool

Guided Inquiry

Start with Questions

This lock is not going to open!

- What is the reddish brown material?
- Where did it come from if the lock was not made of it?

Investigate to find out. Then read to find out more.

Prepare to Investigate

Inquiry Skill Tip

When you draw your conclusions, make sure they answer the question that started your investigation.

Materials

- 3 pieces of steel wool
- water
- 2 paper plates
- bowl

Make an Observation Chart

Day	Dry Steel Wool	Wet Steel Wool	Steel Wool in Water
1			
2			
3			
4			
5			

Follow This Procedure

1. Put one piece of steel wool on a plate.
2. Soak another piece of steel wool in water. Then put it on the other plate.
3. Fill a bowl with water, and put the third piece of steel wool in the water. Make sure none of it sticks out above the water.
4. Place all three samples in the same area, away from direct sunlight. Examine them every day for a week. **Record** your **observations**.

Step 2

Step 3

Draw Conclusions

1. How do the three samples compare?
2. **Inquiry Skill** Scientists can **draw conclusions** from the results of their experiments. What two things can you conclude caused the changes?

Independent Inquiry

What do you predict will happen if you place the three samples in direct sunlight? Carry out a test to find out.

Read and Learn

VOCABULARY
physical property, p. 517
chemical property, p. 517
chemical change, p. 518
chemical reaction, p. 518
compound, p. 518

SCIENCE CONCEPTS
- ▶ that one or more new substances are produced during a chemical change

Focus Skill **COMPARE AND CONTRAST**
Compare chemical changes to physical changes.

alike — different

Chemical and Physical Properties

How would you describe a pencil? You might say that it's yellow, that it's long and thin, and that it has six sides. You might say that you use it to write, and that the tip breaks easily.

All of these descriptions have something in common—they all describe the pencil by itself.

Can you also describe something in relation to another substance? Yes, you can. You can describe something by the way it interacts with other substances.

Think about the wood in the pencil. If there is oxygen near the wood and the temperature is hot enough, the wood will burn. So, another description of the pencil might be "It burns if there is oxygen near it and the temperature is very high."

	Physical Properties	
	• colorless • odorless • liquid at room temperature	• boils at 100°C • melts at 0°C
	• shiny • soft • silver in color	• boils at 2163°C • melts at 962°C
	• shiny • hard • grayish silver in color	• boils at 2861°C • melts at 1538°C
	• dull • brittle • yellow	• boils at 445°C • melts at 115°C

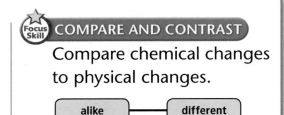

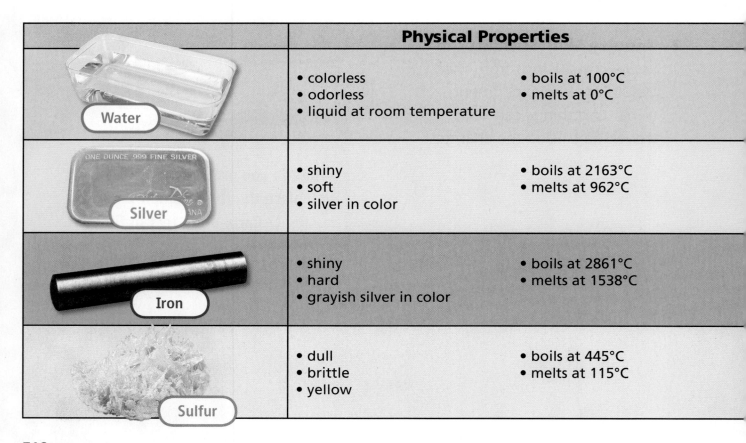

So, now you know two different ways to describe a substance. One way is to tell about its physical properties. **Physical properties** are traits that involve a substance by itself.

Another way to describe a substance is to tell about its chemical properties. **Chemical properties** are properties that involve how a substance interacts with other substances.

Look at the table. You're probably familiar with most of these substances. You're probably also familiar with some of these changes. Have you ever seen rusted iron or tarnished silver?

Focus Skill COMPARE AND CONTRAST

How are physical properties different from chemical properties?

Math in Science
Interpret Data

Boiling Mad

Which substance in the graph has the highest boiling point? Which has the lowest boiling point?

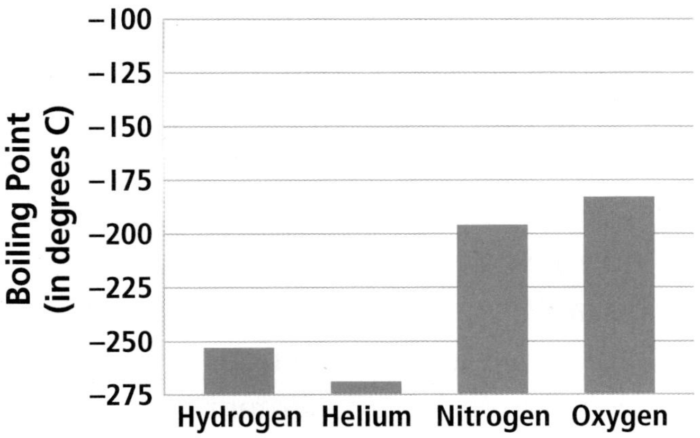

Chemical Properties
• reacts with calcium metal to release hydrogen gas • many substances dissolve easily in it
• does not react with many other substances • does not react with air • reacts with ozone or sulfur to form tarnish
• reacts easily with many other substances • reacts with oxygen to form the minerals hematite and magnetite • reacts with oxygen in presence of water to form rust
• reacts with any liquid element • reacts with any solid element except gold and platinum • reacts with oxygen to form sulfur dioxide, a form of air pollution

◀ **Notice that under *Chemical Properties,* one particular word is used in nearly every line. That word is *react* or *reacts.* What does that word mean in science? Well, it's a big topic, and you'll start reading about it on the next page.**

Chemical Changes

You know that hydrogen and oxygen are usually gases. Do you know what happens when hydrogen burns? It combines with oxygen to form water.

This change results in a new substance—water. Clearly the formation of water is not a physical change. A physical change does not result in a new substance. This change is a chemical change. A **chemical change** is a change that results in one or more new substances. Another term for a chemical change is a **chemical reaction**. Now you know what the word *react* or *reacts* means in the table on the previous page. It means "goes through a chemical change."

You know that an element is something made up of only one kind of atom. Since water is made up of hydrogen and oxygen atoms, it is not an element. It's a compound. A **compound** is made up of two or more different elements that have chemically combined.

Focus Skill COMPARE AND CONTRAST **How is a chemical change different from a physical change?**

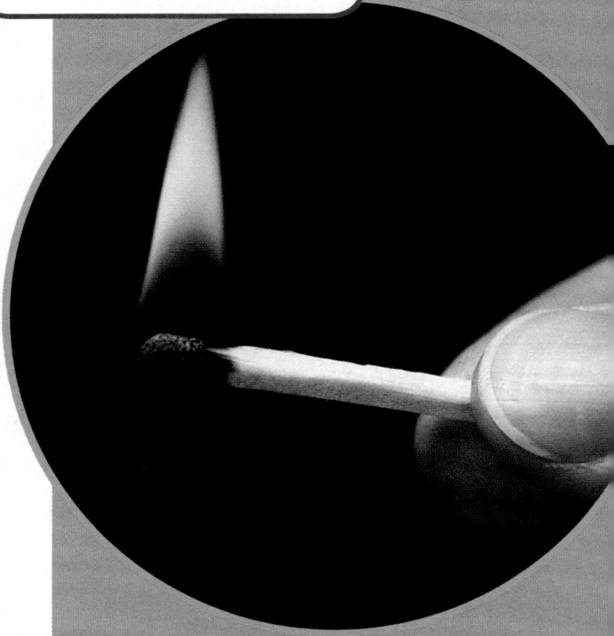

Sulfur in the match head is what helps the match light quickly.

Iron reacts with oxygen in the presence of water to form rust.

Insta-Lab

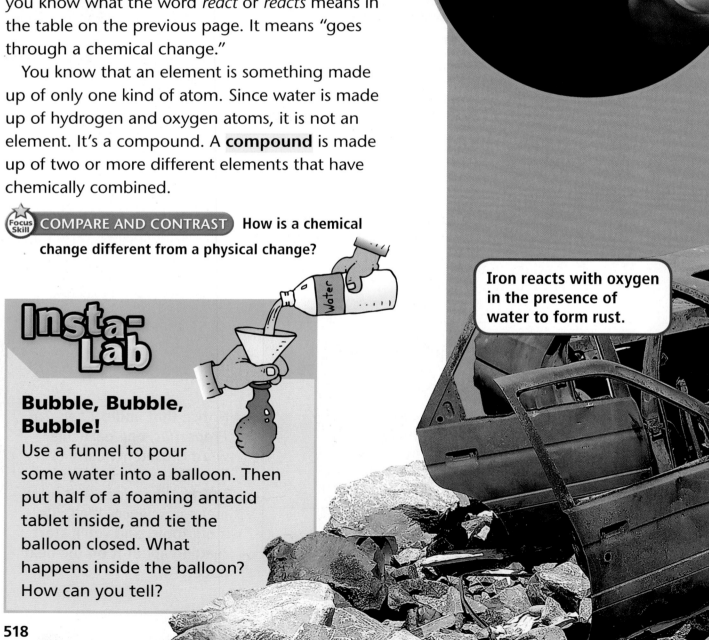

Bubble, Bubble, Bubble!

Use a funnel to pour some water into a balloon. Then put half of a foaming antacid tablet inside, and tie the balloon closed. What happens inside the balloon? How can you tell?

Silver reacts with sulfur to form tarnish. This helps you know that either sulfur or compounds that contain sulfur were in the air.

Sulfur reacts with oxygen to form sulfur dioxide. Often, *reacts with oxygen* means that the substance burns.

Recognizing Chemical Changes

Water is made up of two gases—oxygen and hydrogen. They react to form a liquid. It's easy to understand that a chemical reaction took place. The water is a liquid, not a gas!

There are clues that help you know that chemical changes are probably taking place. You can read about some of them in the table below. But remember that none of these clues is perfect. When water freezes, it becomes solid—a new physical property. But freezing is a physical change, not a chemical change.

Before bread dough is baked, it's white or very pale tan.

After the bread is baked, its crust is dark brown. That's because baking causes a chemical change.

Focus Skill COMPARE AND CONTRAST

Suppose you bake bread. Suppose you draw with a marker on paper. How are the changes in color that occur different from *each other*?

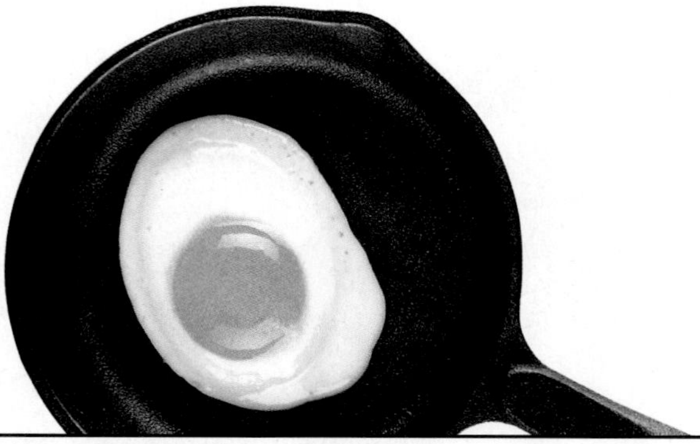

The smell of eggs frying tells you that a chemical change is taking place. So does seeing the egg yolk change from a runny liquid to a solid. ▶

Clues to Chemical Changes

Clue	Example	Description
Color Change	Bread dough baking	Changes from white to brown
Smell	Eggs rotting	Gives off a terrible smell
New Physical Property	Iron rusting	Changes from hard and silvery to brittle and reddish brown
Substance Given Off	Wood burning	Smoke is released into the air
Heat Given Off	Sulfur burning	Fire is hot

Lesson Review

Essential Question

How Does Matter React Chemically?

In this lesson, you learned that some changes are chemical changes. When a chemical change has taken place, a new substance is formed.

1. Focus Skill **COMPARE AND CONTRAST** Draw and complete a graphic organizer to show how chemical and physical changes are alike and different.

alike	different

2. **SUMMARIZE** Write a list of properties showing that a chemical change has taken place.

3. **DRAW CONCLUSIONS** A car engine uses gasoline and oxygen. The exhaust given off has water and the gas carbon dioxide. Does a chemical reaction occur? Explain.

4. **VOCABULARY** Use each of the lesson vocabulary terms in a sentence.

Test Prep

5. **CRITICAL THINKING** Explain why the burning of wood results in chemical changes. List as many clues as you can.

6. Which is a chemical property of a substance?
   A. the color it is
   B. whether it floats
   C. whether it burns when oxygen is present
   D. what its melting temperature is

Make Connections

Writing

Expository Writing

It is often easier to remember something you've learned if you describe it to someone else. Write a **friendly letter** telling a relative what you learned in this lesson.

9÷3 Math

Estimate Sums

A lab has 22 grams of iron, 14 g of sulfur, 31 g of sodium, and 29 g of potassium. Estimate the total mass of these four chemicals.

Art

Illustrate a Reaction

Choose one of the chemical reactions described in this lesson. Draw or paint a picture illustrating this reaction.

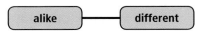

Maria Goeppert-Mayer

DR. MARIA GOEPPERT-MAYER (1906–1972)

- Professor, University of California at San Diego
- Nobel Prize for Physics, 1963

When Maria Goeppert was born in 1906, a science education was very difficult for women to obtain. She worked hard to overcome prejudice and, with her family's support, she finally finished her doctorate in theoretical physics in Germany in 1930.

She married chemist Joseph Edward Mayer, and they moved to America. Dr. Goeppert-Mayer worked for several universities, but only as a volunteer with no pay. Universities at that time would not hire women to teach physics. Nevertheless, they respected her work and encouraged her to continue her research on the structure of the nuclei of atoms. She published many important papers and even wrote a textbook during her time as a voluntary professor.

Finally, when she was 53 years old, she was hired as a professor at the Institute for Nuclear Studies, in Chicago. Later, she became a professor of physics at the University of California at San Diego. She continued her research on her own. In 1963, she was awarded the Nobel Prize for Physics. She is only the second woman in history to win the Nobel Prize for Physics. The first was Marie Curie in 1903.

Think and Write

1. Why was it difficult for a woman in Maria Goeppert-Mayer's time to get a science education and employment as a scientist?
2. Dr. Goeppert-Mayer is an example of scientific achievement. In what other way is Dr. Goeppert-Mayer an example to women who want to study science?

France Anne Córdova

▶ **FRANCE ANNE CÓRDOVA**

▶ Chancellor at the University of California at Riverside

▶ former NASA Chief Scientist

France Anne Córdova was the first woman and the youngest person ever to be the Chief Scientist for NASA. She is now a Chancellor at the University of California at Riverside. She has received many honors and awards, including being named one of the 100 Most Influential Hispanics by *Hispanic Business Magazine.*

Córdova has a degree in English, has been on archaeological digs, and has published a Mexican food cookbook! She is a person of many interests and talents. However, she focuses her scientific career on researching pulsars and identifying faint wavelengths of light, and she is a leader on scientific teams working with satellites.

Think and Write

1. Why might France Anne Córdova's many interests help her be a better scientist?
2. Do you think France Anne Córdova is a good scientific role model? Explain.

Career Welder

Welders join pieces of metal together permanently by using heat or pressure. Some welders work in industry and manufacturing, and some welders create artistic metal sculptures.

CHAPTER 12 Review and Test Preparation

Vocabulary Review

Write the term that fits each definition or description. Some terms may be used twice. The page numbers tell you where to look in the chapter if you need help.

atom p. 496
element p. 498
change of state p. 506
physical change p. 508
physical property p. 517
chemical property p. 517
chemical change p. 518
chemical reaction p. 518
compound p. 518

1. A substance having atoms of more than one element that are combined chemically is a _______.

2. A _______ describes a substance by itself.

3. A _______ results in a new substance.

4. How a substance reacts with other substances is known as a _______.

5. Melting or freezing is a _______.

6. Another name for *chemical change* is _______.

7. The process of boiling is a _______.

8. A substance having just one kind of atom is an _______.

9. The smallest possible particle of an element is an _______.

10. A _______ does not result in a new substance.

Check Understanding

Write the letter of the best choice.

11. What is all matter made of?

A. atoms
B. oxygen
C. water
D. wood

12. Which statement about atoms is true?

F. They are all the same.
G. Just one kind is in a compound.
H. You see them with just your eyes.
J. They are too small to be seen with an ordinary microscope.

13. The diagrams show iron, oxygen, carbon dioxide, and hydrogen.

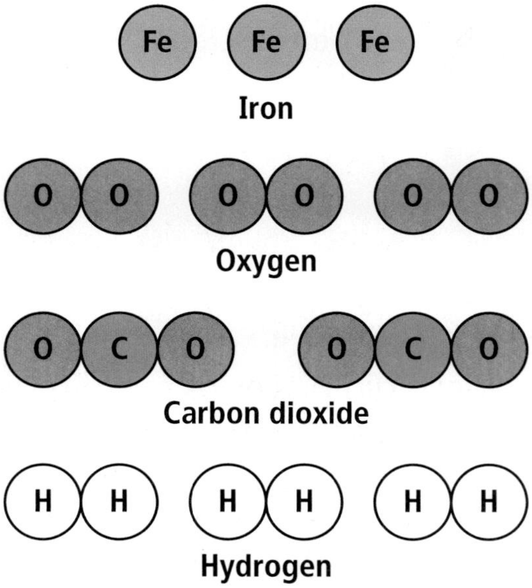

Which of these is a compound?

A. iron **C.** carbon dioxide
B. oxygen **D.** hydrogen

14. An element is made up of how many kinds of atoms?

F. none **H.** two
G. one **J.** two or more

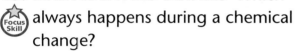

15. **MAIN IDEA AND DETAILS** Which always happens during a chemical change?

Focus Skill

A. Matter disappears.
B. A smell is produced.
C. A gas is formed.
D. A new substance is produced.

16. **COMPARE AND CONTRAST** How are physical properties and chemical properties similar?

Focus Skill

F. They both describe how one substance reacts with another.
G. They both describe a substance.
H. They both describe the size of a substance.
J. They both describe a substance by itself.

Inquiry Skills

17. You're watching a chemist work. She mixes a green powder with a blue liquid and then heats the mixture. A yellow gas rises out of the beaker. When she is done, all that remains in the beaker is a crumbly orange solid. Did a chemical reaction take place? Explain your **conclusion**.

18. Next, the chemist places a whitish solid in a beaker and heats it. Before long, the solid has turned into a clear liquid. **Hypothesize** what might happen if she continues to heat the beaker.

Critical Thinking

19. Can butter have a change of state? Why do you think this?

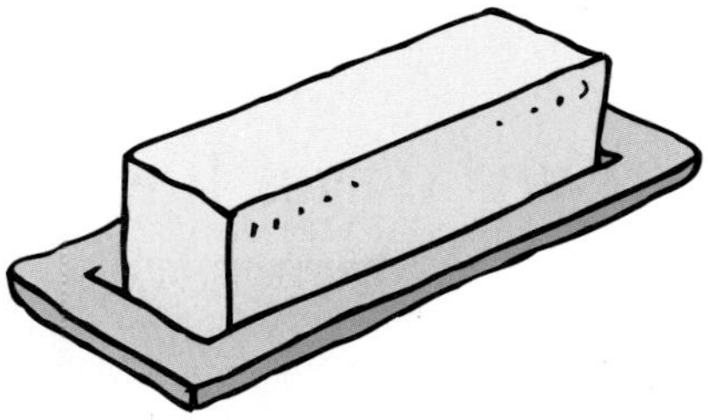

20. Suppose you leave a metal hand tool in a garden for a few weeks. Your area gets rain several times. When you finally pick up the tool, you see orange-brown spots on it. What are the spots? Explain what caused the orange-brown spots on the tool.

The Big Idea

CHAPTER 13 Sound

What's the Big Idea?

Vibrations cause sounds, which travel in wave form.

Essential Questions

Lesson 1
What Is Sound?

Lesson 2
What Are the Properties of Waves?

Lesson 3
How Do Sound Waves Travel?

Go online
Student eBook
www.hspscience.com

What do YOU wonder?

Out Loud? When people design a concert hall, their goal is to provide high-quality sound to every person in the hall. How do you think the sound differs between the first and last rows in this hall? How does this relate to the **Big Idea?**

LESSON

1

Investigate sound and vibrations.

Read and Learn what sound is.

Essential Question

What Is Sound?

Fast Fact

Listen to the Drums!
Every year, the people of Ako, Japan, hold a festival that honors warriors of long ago. Drums are a major part of that festival. The largest of the drums can be about 1 to 2 meters (3 to 6 ft) across. Hitting a drum is one way to make a sound. In the Investigate, you'll explore other ways to make sounds.

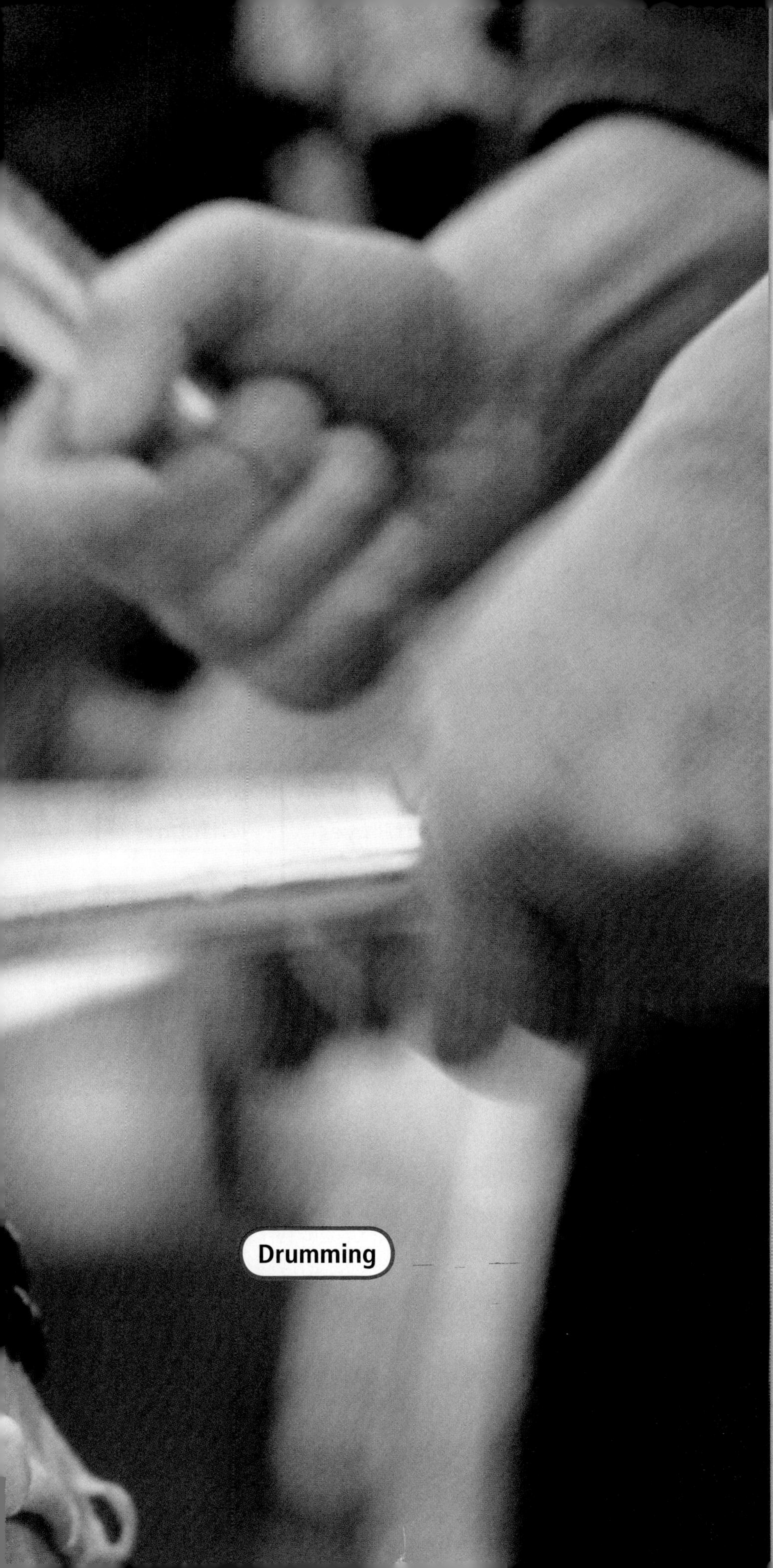

Vocabulary Preview

vibration [vy•BRAY•shuhn] A quick back-and-forth motion (p. 532)

pitch [PICH] A measure of how high or low a sound is (p. 534)

intensity [in•TEN•suh•tee] A measure of how loud or soft a sound is (p. 535)

Investigate

Feel the Vibes

Guided Inquiry

Start with Questions

The string of this piano is vibrating very quickly because the small hammer has hit it.

- Does it make a sound?
- How does the length of the string change the sound?

Investigate to find out. Then read to find out more.

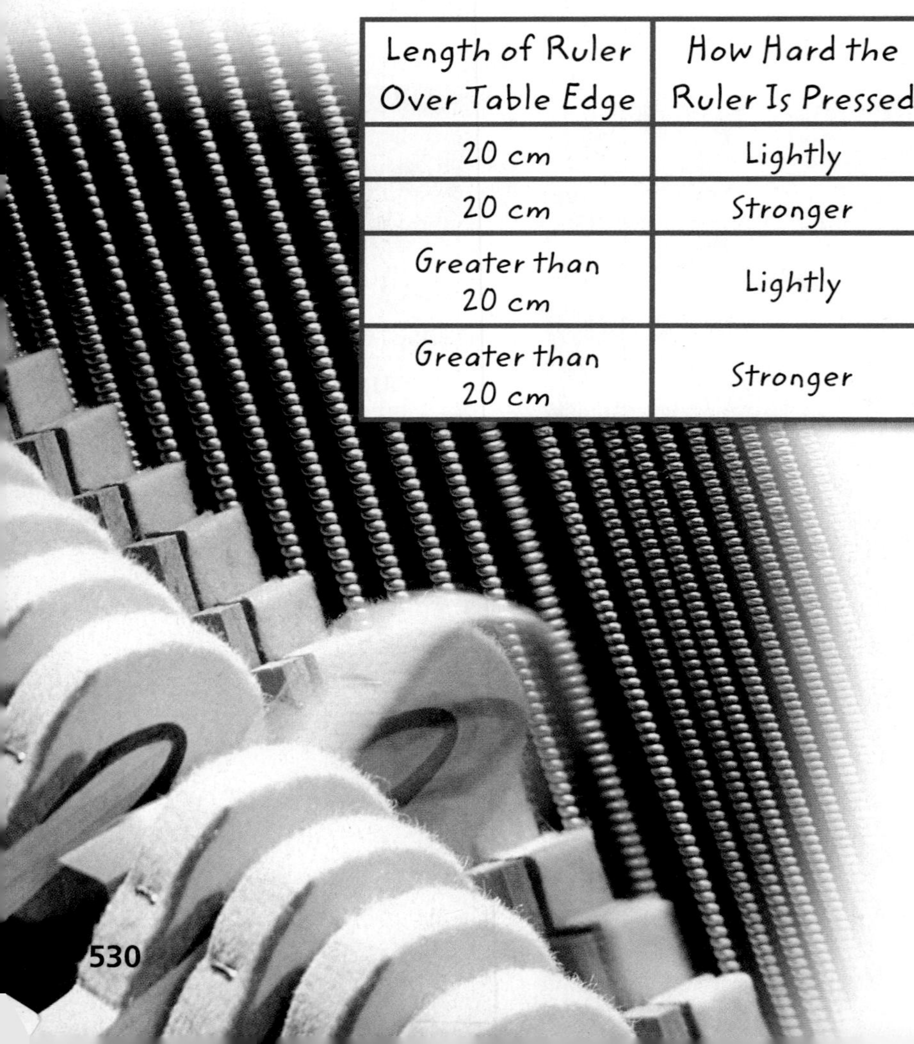

Prepare to Investigate

Inquiry Skill Tip

Keep your hypothesis as simple as possible. Complicated explanations are difficult to test with simple investigations.

Materials

- plastic ruler

Make an Observation Chart

Length of Ruler Over Table Edge	How Hard the Ruler Is Pressed	Observations with Eyes	Observations with Ears
20 cm	Lightly		
20 cm	Stronger		
Greater than 20 cm	Lightly		
Greater than 20 cm	Stronger		

Follow This Procedure

1. Place a ruler on a desk or table. Let 20 cm of the ruler stick out over the edge.
2. With one hand, firmly press down on the end that is on the tabletop. With the other hand, flick the other end of the ruler.
3. **Observe** the ruler with your eyes. **Record** your observations.
4. Repeat Step 2. **Observe** the ruler with your ears. **Record** your observations.
5. Change the strength with which you flick the end of the ruler. **Observe** the results and **record** your observations.
6. Move the ruler to change the length that hangs over the edge of the tabletop. Repeat Steps 2–5. **Observe** the results and **record** your observations.

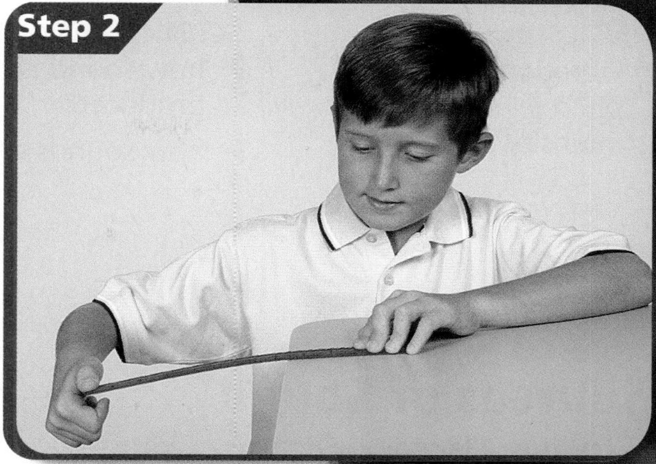

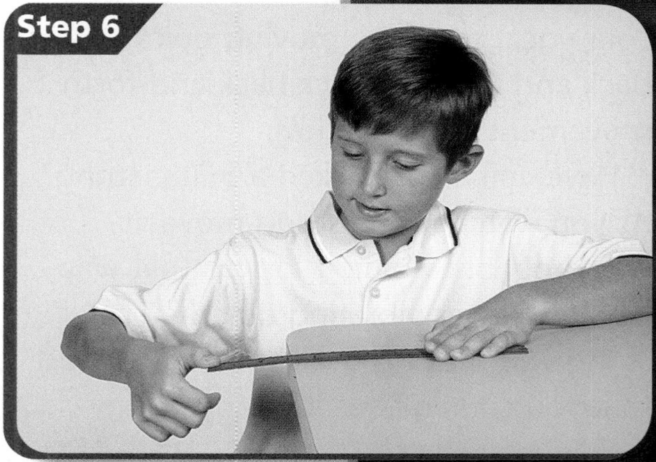

Draw Conclusions

1. What did you observe in Step 3? In Step 4? How do you think these observations are related?
2. **Inquiry Skill** Hypothesize how changing the ruler affects the sound it makes. Tell how you would test your hypothesis.

Independent Inquiry

Place one ear on the tabletop, and cover the other ear with your hand. Have a partner repeat Steps 1 and 2. What do you observe?

Read and Learn

VOCABULARY
vibration p. 532
pitch p. 534
intensity p. 535

SCIENCE CONCEPTS
- how sound is produced
- how sounds can vary

Focus Skill — MAIN IDEA AND DETAILS

Find details about the nature of sound.

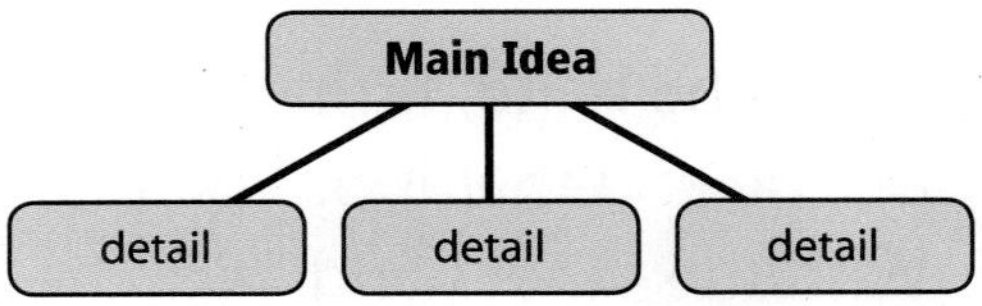

Sources of Sound

Try this. Place your hand on your throat, and hum softly. What do you feel? You may feel slight movements. Your vocal cords are moving quickly back and forth. A quick back-and-forth movement is a **vibration**.

Have you ever plucked a guitar string? As you watched the string move, it was probably a blur. It looked that way because it was vibrating quickly. The string was moving back and forth so fast that you couldn't see it clearly.

In the Investigate, you made the ruler vibrate. You also changed how much or how little the ruler vibrated. What do a moving ruler, a plucked guitar string, and your humming throat all have in common? They all make sounds, and they all vibrate.

When something vibrates, the air around it vibrates, too. Then the vibrations move through the air. They travel out in all directions. When they reach your ear, you hear them as sounds.

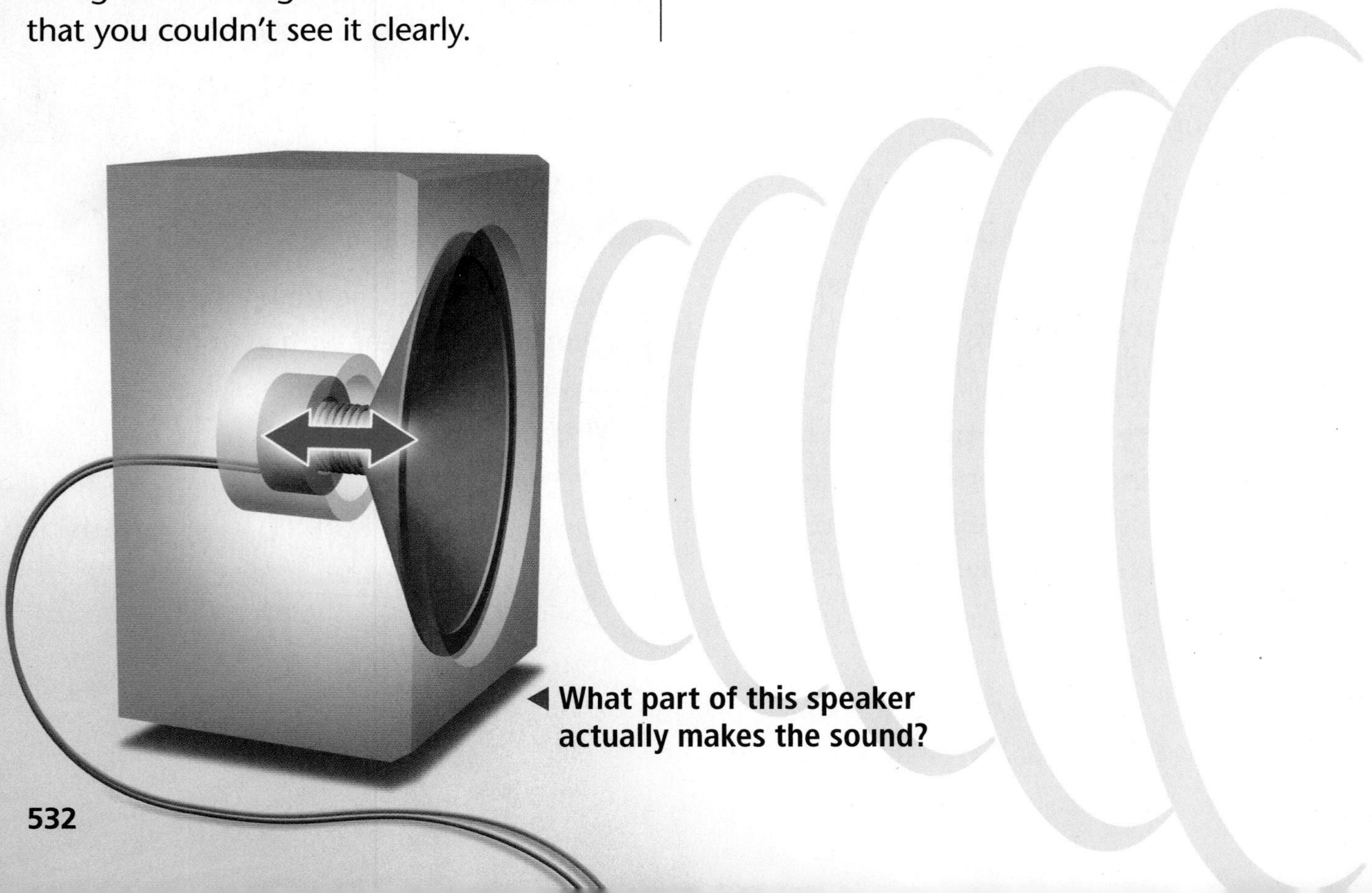

◀ **What part of this speaker actually makes the sound?**

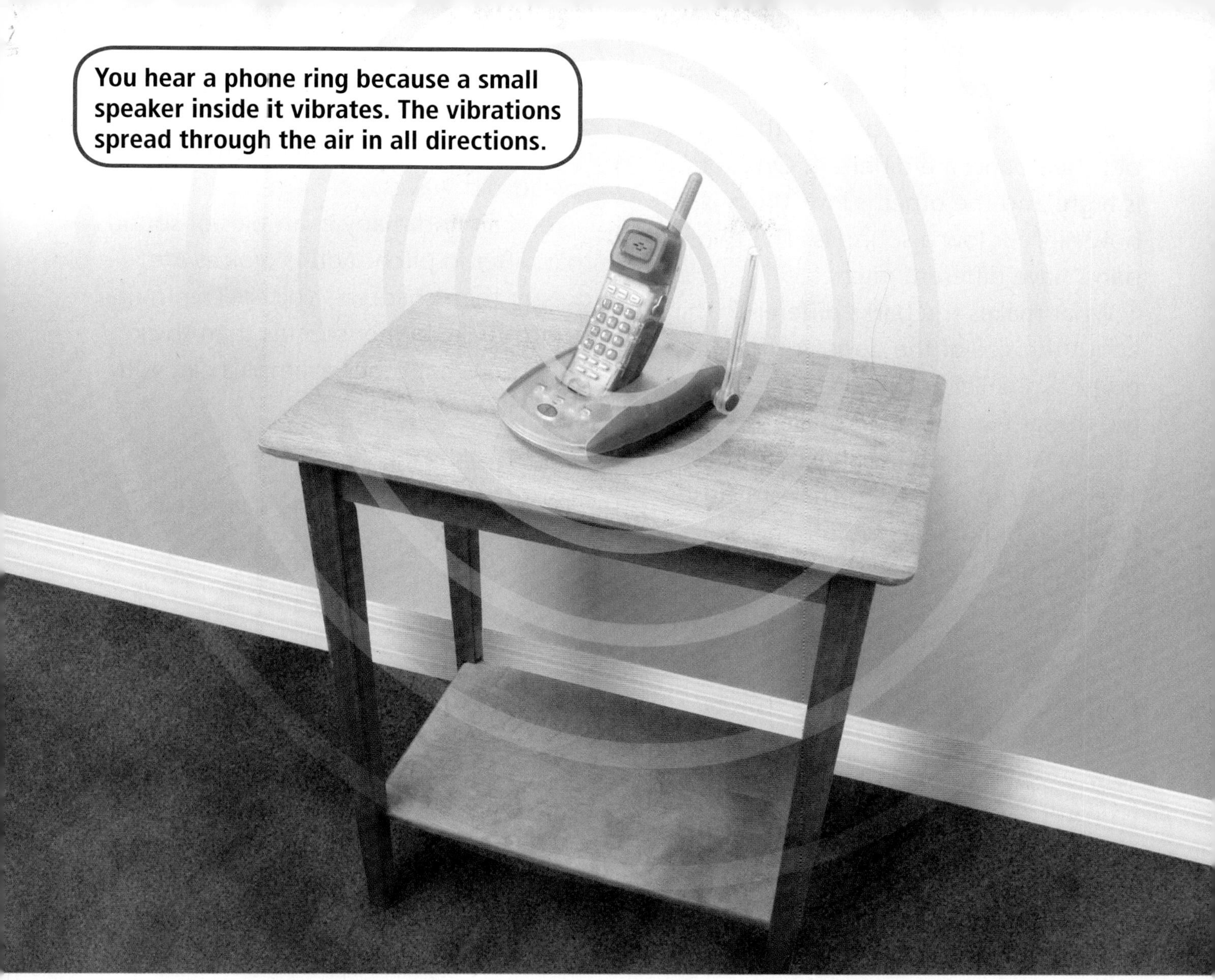

You hear a phone ring because a small speaker inside it vibrates. The vibrations spread through the air in all directions.

Sound travels through the air, but it can also travel through other materials. You can hear sounds through a liquid when you swim underwater. In the Independent Inquiry activity, you heard sounds traveling through a solid tabletop. You can hear all those sounds because vibrations can travel through liquids and solids, as well as through gas mixtures like air.

The vibrations that carry sounds are called *sound waves.* When sound waves reach your ear, they make parts inside your ear vibrate. Then a signal travels to your brain, which converts the signal so you can hear it.

Sounds can be loud or soft, high or low, but they are all carried by sound waves. You'll learn that the properties of the waves are what make sounds different from each other.

Focus Skill MAIN IDEA AND DETAILS

How is sound produced?

Pitch

Little dogs and big dogs both bark, but their barks are different. One sound is high, and the other is low. **Pitch** is how high or low a sound is. The two barks have different pitches.

What makes the barks different? Think about the size of the dogs. A smaller dog has smaller vocal cords, parts in the throat that vibrate. Smaller objects usually vibrate faster than larger ones. They make sound waves that are close together. Big objects vibrate more slowly. They produce sound waves that are more spread out. When the sound waves reach your ears, the close-together waves sound higher than the spread-out waves.

You can find many examples of sounds that differ in pitch. Adults' voices are deeper than children's voices. Thin guitar strings make higher sounds than thick ones do. What other examples can you think of?

Focus Skill MAIN IDEA AND DETAILS

What waves make high-pitched sounds?

This bird's tiny vocal cords make a high sound. ▶

◀ Long, thick bass strings make a low sound.

What can you infer about the strings on the left side of the piano?

▼ **How are the sounds from a jet engine different from the sounds that are produced by a pin as it bounces on a table?**

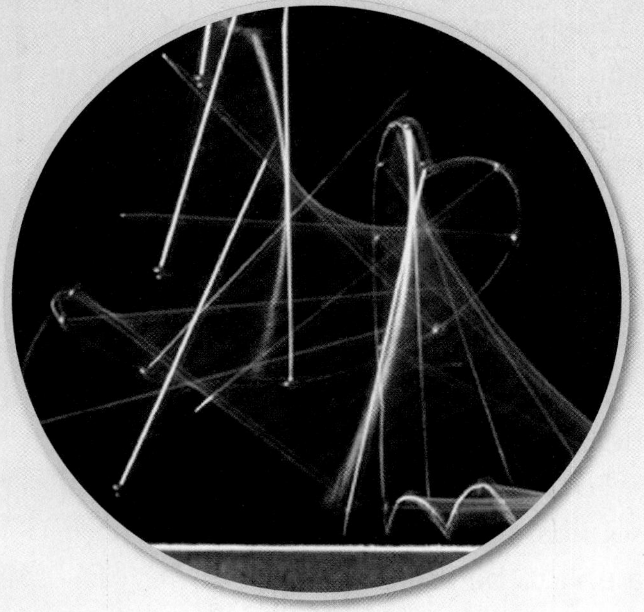

Intensity

Imagine that you drop a small paperback book on the floor. Then you drop a huge encyclopedia. How would the sounds differ? The encyclopedia would make a much louder sound than the paperback. These sounds would differ in **intensity**—the measure of how loud or soft a sound is.

But what makes such sounds different? You can probably guess that the difference is in the sound waves. Sound waves have a certain amount of energy. A heavier book would have more energy when it hits the floor, so it would produce sound waves with more energy.

When a door closes slowly, it produces sound waves. But when the door slams shut, it produces higher-energy sound waves. The sound waves you produce when you whisper don't have as much energy as the sound waves you produce when you shout. You hear sound waves with more energy as louder sounds.

Focus Skill **MAIN IDEA AND DETAILS**

What kind of waves make soft sounds?

Insta-Lab

Hands-On Vibrations!

Place two fingers gently on your upper throat. Now hum. Hum high notes and low notes. Hum loudly and softly. Say something and then shout it. What changes do you notice in your throat each time?

Measuring Sound Intensity

You know a loud sound when you hear it, but how could you measure how loud it is? Scientists measure sound intensity by using a unit called a bel. The bel was named after Alexander Graham Bell. He invented the telephone, but he also studied sound and hearing.

For most common sounds, the bel is too big a unit to be useful. Most sounds are measured in decibels. A decibel (dB) is one-tenth of a bel.

You'd probably think that a 20-dB sound is twice as loud as a 10-dB sound. But it isn't. A 20-dB sound is ten times as loud as a 10-dB sound. Any difference of 10 dB means that one sound is ten times as loud as another.

Focus Skill MAIN IDEA AND DETAILS

What unit is used to measure the intensity of most sounds?

Math in Science
Interpret Data

How many times the loudness of rustling leaves are the sounds of a residential area at night?

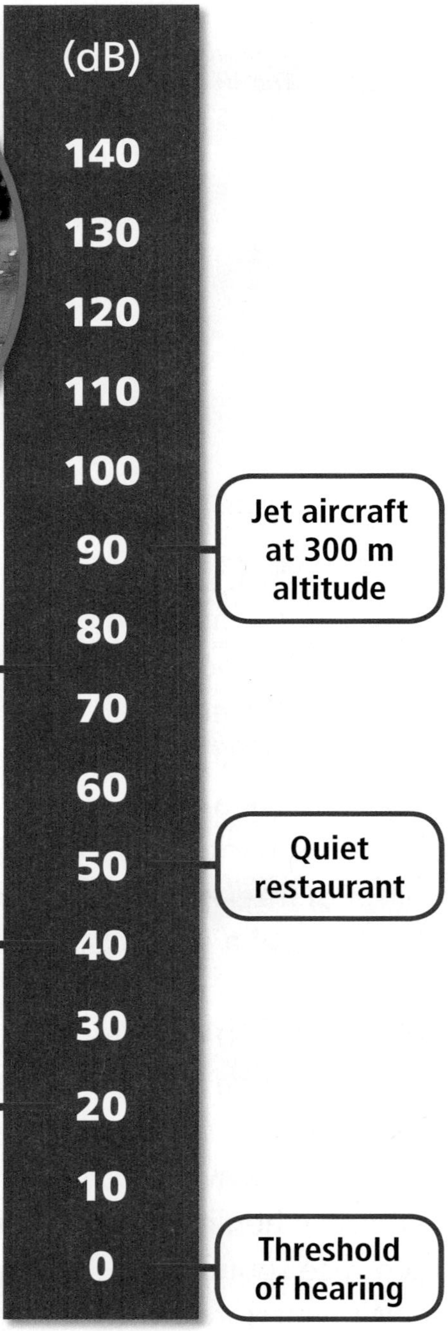

Lesson Review

Essential Question

What Is Sound?

In this lesson, you learned that sound is caused by vibrations. Sound can travel, in waves, through many substances. Pitch and intensity are properties of sound.

1. Focus Skill **MAIN IDEA AND DETAILS** Draw and complete a graphic organizer that describes the different ways in which you can measure sound.

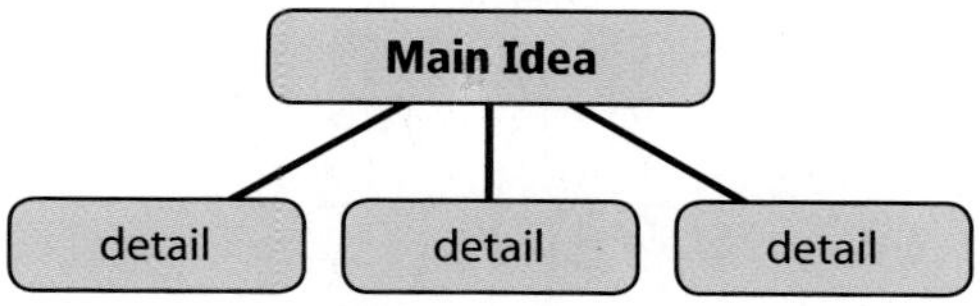

2. **SUMMARIZE** Write a sentence to define sound.

3. **DRAW CONCLUSIONS** If you strike a piano key hard and hold it, the note takes some time to die out. Why?

4. **VOCABULARY** Use each of the lesson vocabulary words in a separate sentence.

Test Prep

5. **CRITICAL THINKING** If you tap the longest bar on a xylophone, it makes a sound. As you go up the scale to the shorter bars, the pitch of the sound rises. Why?

6. What converts waves into sound?
   A. air
   B. your ear
   C. your brain
   D. vibration

Make Connections

Writing

Expository Writing

Explaining something to someone else can often help you understand it better yourself. Write a **friendly letter** to a relative or friend. In the letter, explain the sound you heard at a concert.

Math

Compare Whole Numbers

Two bells are vibrating. The first bell vibrates 16,597 times each second. The second bell vibrates 16,832 times each second. Which bell has a higher pitch? Why?

Language Arts

Sound Poetry

Poetry uses the sounds of words. Write a poem about sounds and how they travel. Include sounds differing in pitch and intensity for an audience to chant with you.

LESSON 2

Essential Question

What Are the Properties of Waves?

Investigate sound vibrations with strings.

Read and Learn about the properties of waves.

Fast Fact

Take Note

Guitar strings produce different notes because they vibrate at different speeds. When a guitar is in tune, the string that makes the lowest sound vibrates 164.8 times a second. The string that makes the highest sound vibrates 659.2 times a second. Most people can "vibrate" (tap) a finger only about 10 times a second. In the Investigate, you'll observe the vibration of rubber "strings."

Plucking a guitar string

Vocabulary Preview

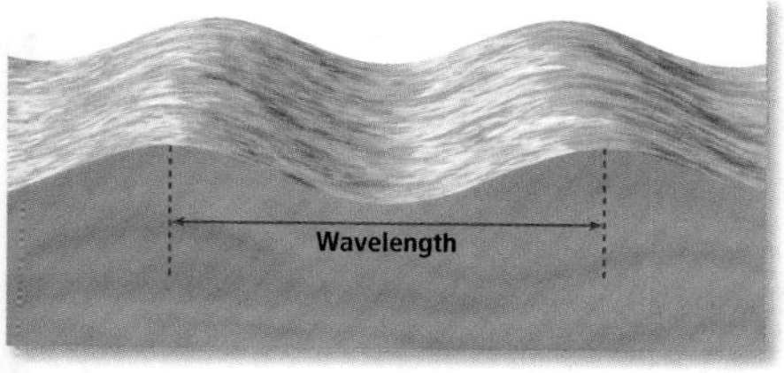

wavelength [WAYV•length] The distance between a point on one wave and the identical point on the next wave (p. 543)

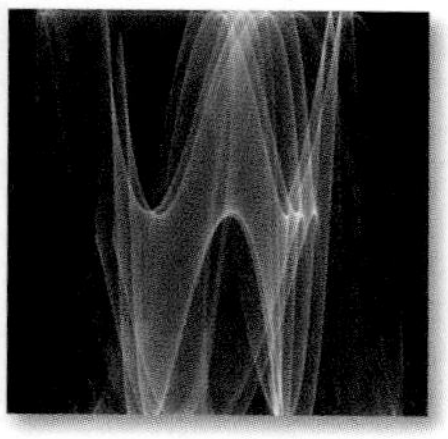

frequency [FREE•kwuhn•see] A measure of the number of waves that pass in a second (p. 543)

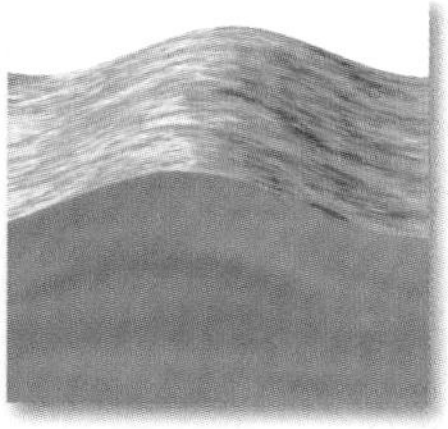

amplitude [AM•pluh•tood] A measure of the amount of energy in a wave (p. 543)

Investigate

Feel the Vibes II

Guided Inquiry

Start with Questions

A harp has strings like a guitar or piano. The harpist has plucked a string to make a sound.

- How is that sound traveling?
- Why does the string keep vibrating?

Investigate to find out. Then read to find out more.

Prepare to Investigate

Inquiry Skill Tip

Using numbers can help you keep quantities in order. Having a number tells you when a measurement is larger than another measurement.

Materials

- safety goggles
- pencil
- foam cup
- thin rubber band
- 2 paper clips
- ruler
- tape
- thick rubber band

Make an Observation Chart

Rubber Band	Mark on Ruler	Distance Pulled	Observations

Follow This Procedure

1. CAUTION: **Put on safety goggles.** Use a pencil to poke a hole in the bottom of a cup.
2. Thread a thin rubber band onto a paper clip. Put them in the cup, and then pull the rubber band through the hole.
3. Place the cup upside down on a table. Tape a ruler to the cup as shown in the picture, with the 1-cm mark at the top. Pull the end of the rubber band over the end of the ruler, and tape it to the back.
4. Pull the rubber band to one side, and then let it go. Observe the sound. Record your observations.
5. Repeat Step 4, but this time, pull the rubber band farther.
6. Use one finger to press the rubber band against the 2-cm mark and then the 4-cm mark. Repeat Step 4 each time.
7. Repeat Steps 2–6, using the thick rubber band.

Draw Conclusions

1. Compare the sounds you made.
2. **Inquiry Skill** How did using the numbers on the ruler help you give a reason for the sounds that you made?

Step 2

Step 3

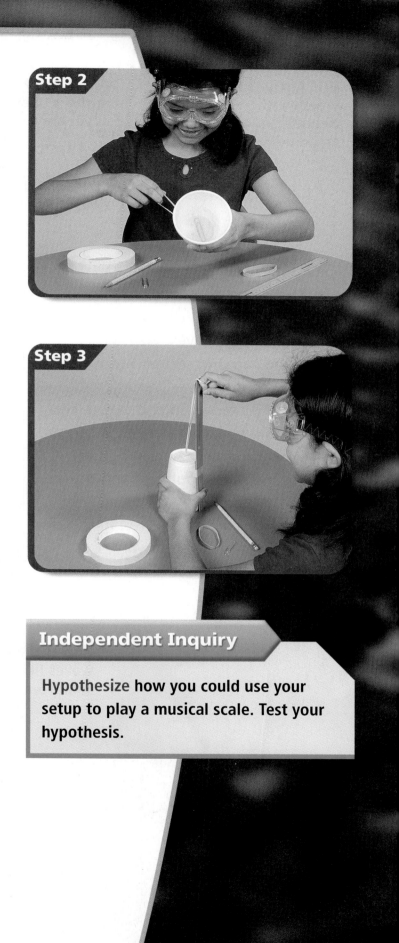

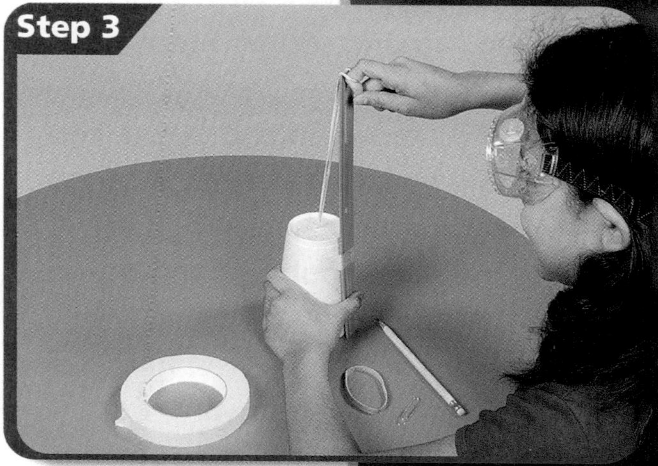

Independent Inquiry

Hypothesize how you could use your setup to play a musical scale. Test your hypothesis.

Read and Learn

VOCABULARY
wavelength p. 543
frequency p. 543
amplitude p. 543

SCIENCE CONCEPTS
- ▶ what the properties of waves are
- ▶ how frequency relates to pitch
- ▶ how amplitude relates to volume

Focus Skill **MAIN IDEA AND DETAILS**
Look for details about the nature of waves.

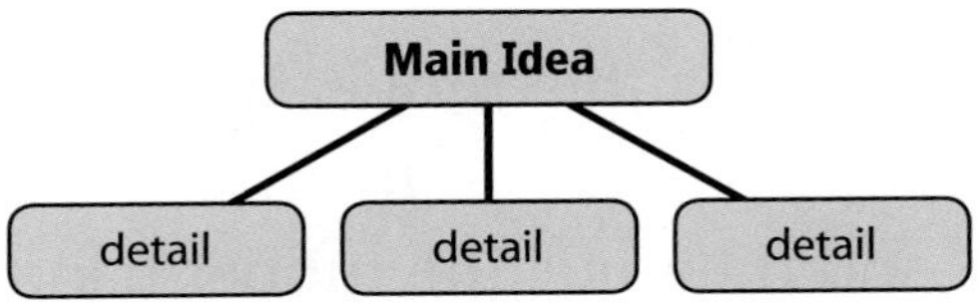

Sound Waves

Have you ever watched the water along the shore of an ocean or a lake? Then you've seen waves. Waves also travel in air, carrying sound. But water waves and sound waves are different.

Water waves move up and down. You can see this if you look at a raft when a passing boat makes waves. When the waves hit the raft, it bobs up and down.

Waves that move up and down like this are called *transverse waves.* In the ocean, the waves travel forward, but the water moves up and down. The two directions cross each other. The word *transverse* means "across."

Sound waves are different. Have you ever played with a spring toy? If you hold one end of the spring and move it forward and back, you create waves. What you see is a bunching up of some coils that moves down to the end of the spring and back. That's a wave, although it doesn't move up and down. Waves that move this way, along the travel direction of the waves, are *longitudinal waves. Longitudinal* means "along." Spring-toy waves move along the spring.

◀ **How is the movement of water waves like the movement of sound waves?**

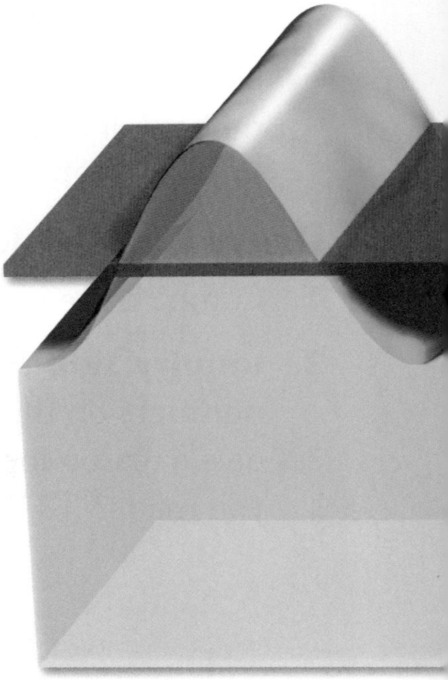

If you wanted to describe waves, how would you begin? You could start with length. You'd choose a point on one wave, such as the top of a water wave. Then you'd measure to the same point on the next wave. The distance between the two points is the **wavelength**.

Another property you can use to describe waves is **frequency**—the number of waves that pass in a second. If you were to count water waves as they crash on a beach, you'd be measuring the waves' frequency.

You could also describe how much energy waves have. This property is called **amplitude**. For transverse waves, such as water waves, the amplitude is how tall the waves are. For longitudinal waves, such as sound waves, the amplitude is how tightly bunched the particles or sections are.

Focus Skill MAIN IDEA AND DETAILS

Name three properties of waves.

▼ **For longitudinal waves, one wavelength is the distance from one bunched-up section to the next.**

▼ **For transverse waves, you measure amplitude from the rest position to the top of the wave. The red surface shows the rest position.**

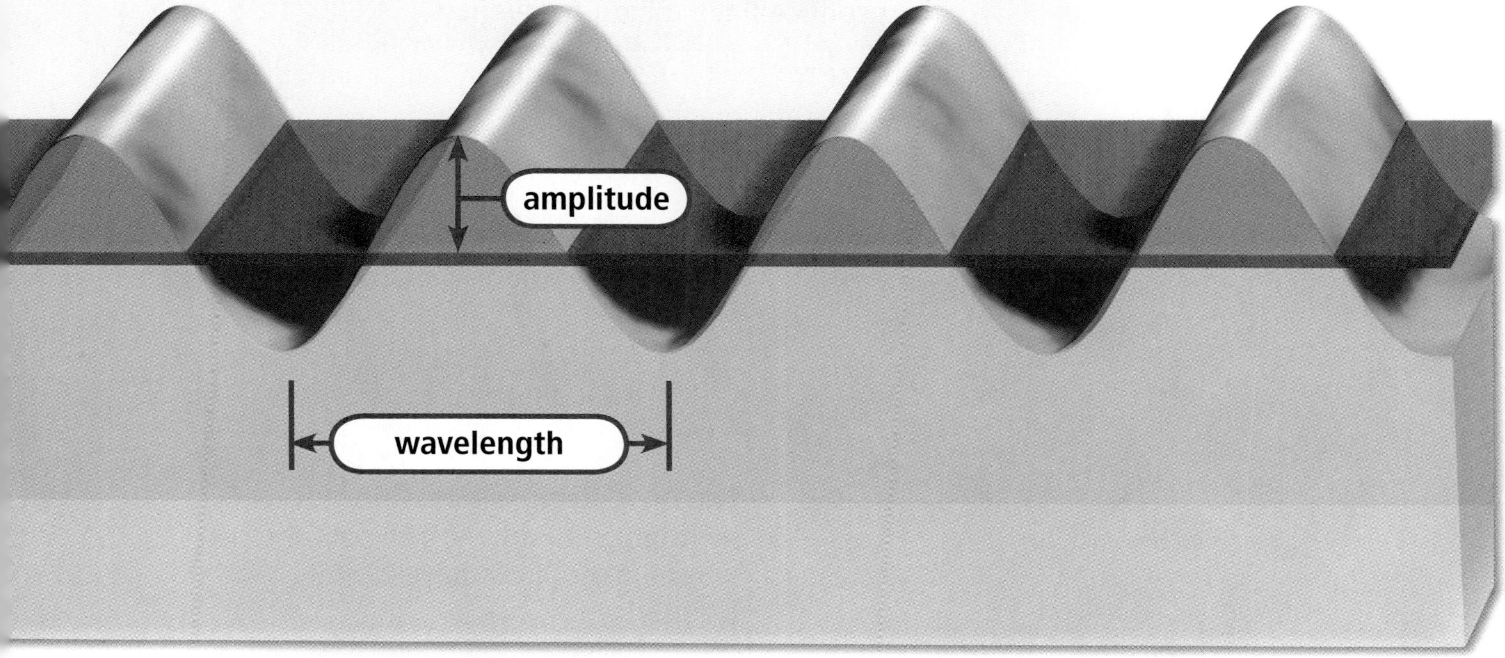

Frequency and Pitch

Imagine that you could see sound waves moving past you. If you were amazingly fast, you could check their frequency by counting how many waves go by each second. If the waves were close together, more would pass by during each second. That would mean that the frequency of the waves is high.

Remember, an object that vibrates quickly produces sound-wave peaks that are close together. The waves have a shorter wavelength than the waves produced by objects that vibrate slowly.

When the wave peaks are close together, the sound has a high pitch. As you can see, frequency and pitch are related. When the sound waves reach your ears, the waves with close-together peaks have a high-pitched sound. The higher the frequency of the waves, the higher the pitch of the sound.

Focus Skill **MAIN IDEA AND DETAILS**

How are frequency and pitch related?

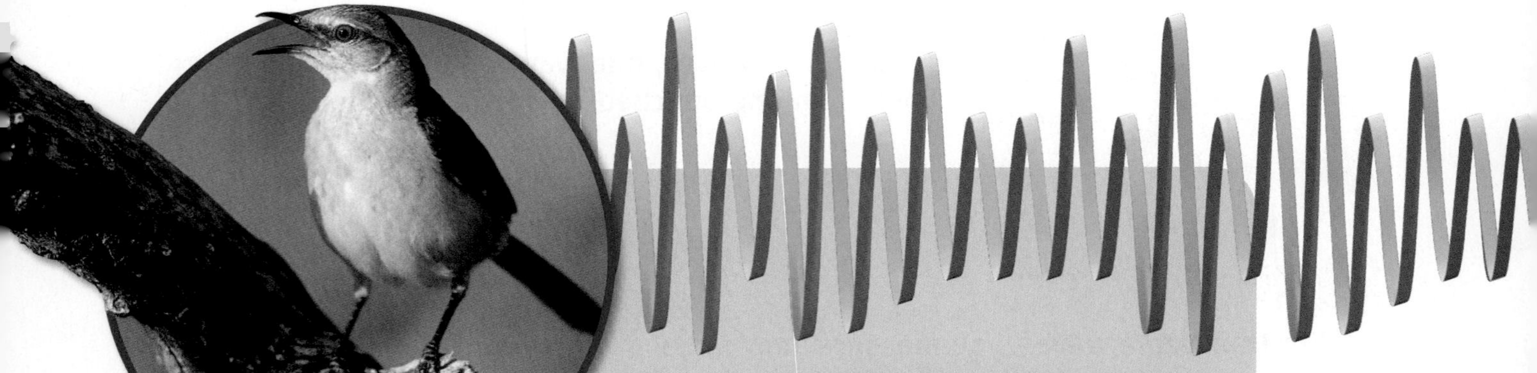

◀ A bird's vocal cords are short, so they vibrate quickly. The sound waves they produce have a high frequency.

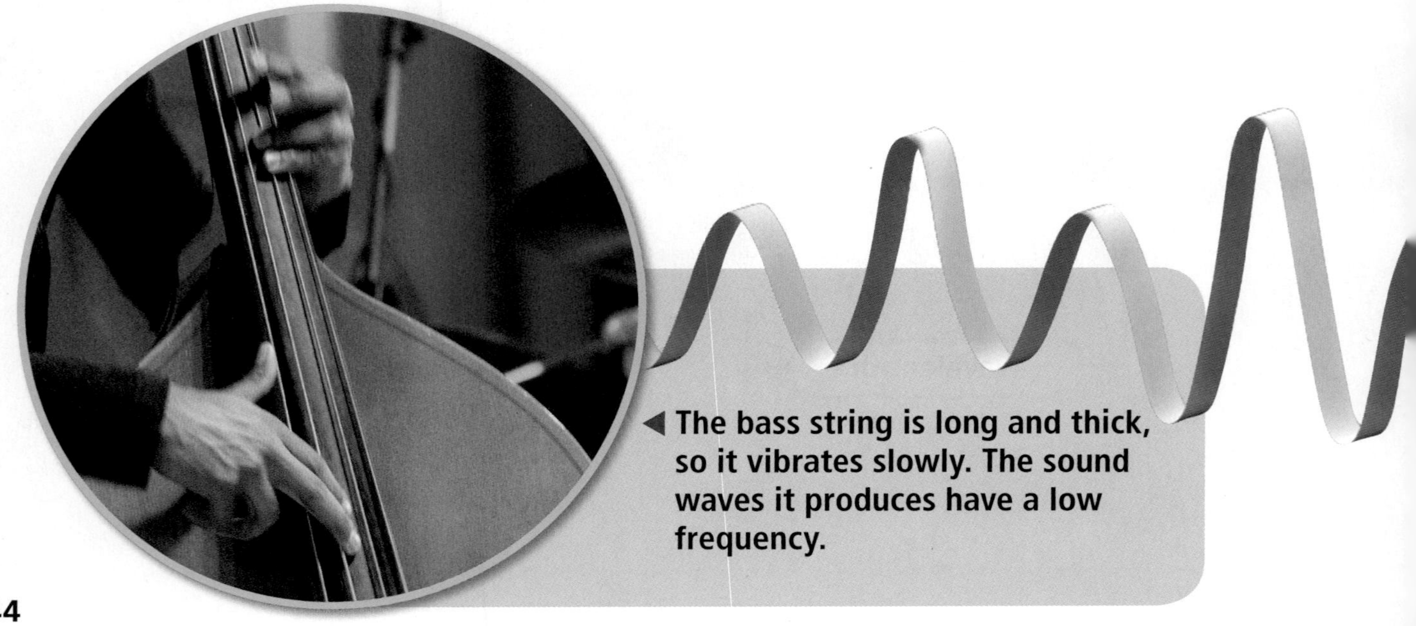

◀ The bass string is long and thick, so it vibrates slowly. The sound waves it produces have a low frequency.

Amplitude and Loudness

You know that sound waves with more energy make a louder sound. And you've learned that amplitude is a measure of how much energy a wave has. Put those two statements together, and what do you get? Sound waves with larger amplitudes are louder.

Imagine that you're tossing stones into a pond. First, you throw in a pebble. It hits the water with little energy and makes a small "bloop" sound. It also makes small ripples in the water. Both the sound waves and the water waves have small amplitudes.

Then, you throw in a big rock. It hits the water with a lot of energy. It makes a loud splashing sound and big ripples in the water. Both types of waves produced by the big rock have large amplitudes.

Focus Skill MAIN IDEA AND DETAILS

How does the amplitude of sound waves relate to their intensity?

A pin has very little energy when it hits a table. It produces sound waves with very small amplitudes. ▶

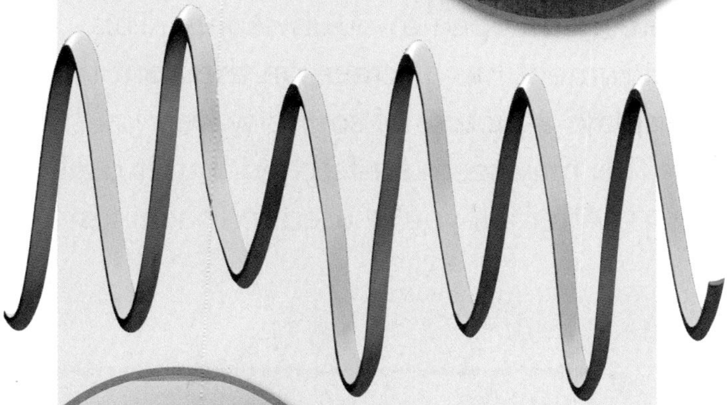

◀ A jet engine has a lot of energy. It produces sound waves with very large amplitudes.

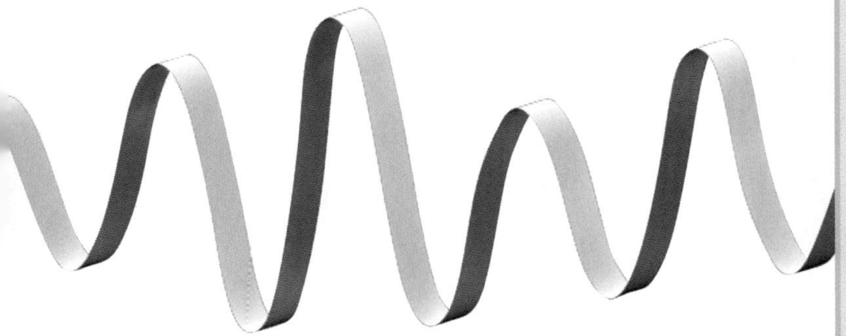

Insta-Lab

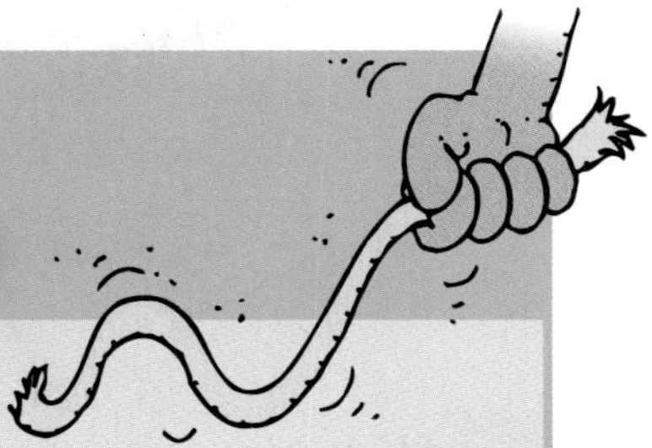

Making Waves

Tie one end of a rope to a tree, a doorknob, or anything that's roughly 1 meter off the ground. Move the rope to make transverse waves. Change the amplitude and frequency of the waves.

Measuring Sound Waves

You now know several properties of sound waves—wavelength, frequency, and amplitude. But how do you measure those properties? After all, you can't just hold a ruler up to a sound wave. It's very hard to count things you can't see! Fortunately, technology has a solution.

To measure sound waves, you can use an oscilloscope (uh•SIL•uh•skohp). This instrument has a screen on the front that displays a picture of sound waves.

This may seem far-fetched, but it really isn't. After all, you're used to machines that take in sound waves and change them into magnetic code on a tape or into laser marks on a disc.

An oscilloscope isn't all that different. Like a tape recorder or a CD recorder, it has a microphone. The microphone picks up sound waves in the air, and the oscilloscope changes them into pictures on the screen, like those shown below.

Focus Skill **MAIN IDEA AND DETAILS**

What machine can be used to measure the properties of sound waves?

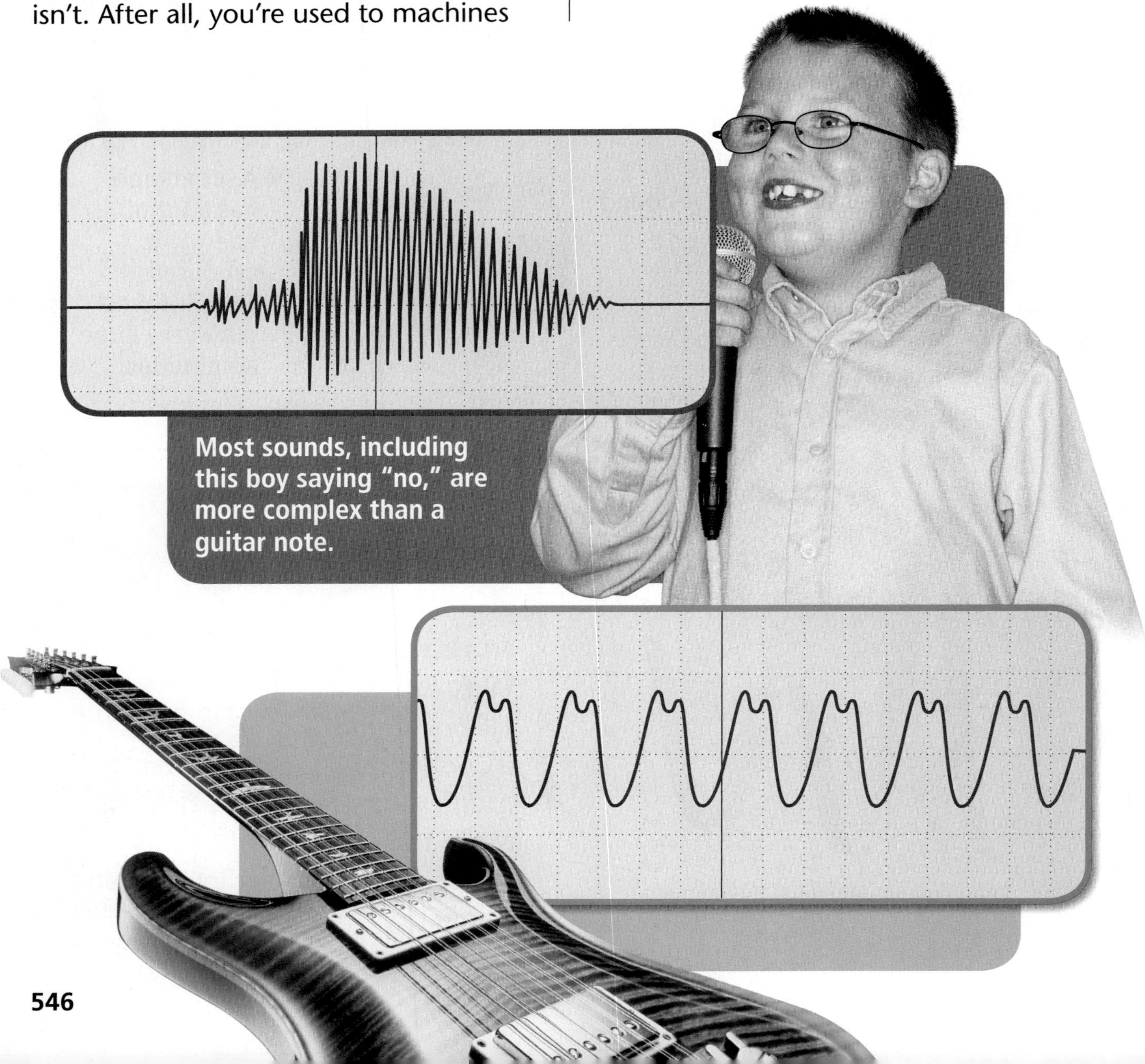

Most sounds, including this boy saying "no," are more complex than a guitar note.

Essential Question

What Are the Properties of Waves?

In this lesson, you learned that sound waves have the properties of wavelength and frequency, which are related to pitch. Sound waves with greater amplitude are louder.

1. Focus Skill **MAIN IDEA AND DETAILS** Draw and complete a graphic organizer that shows sound wave properties.

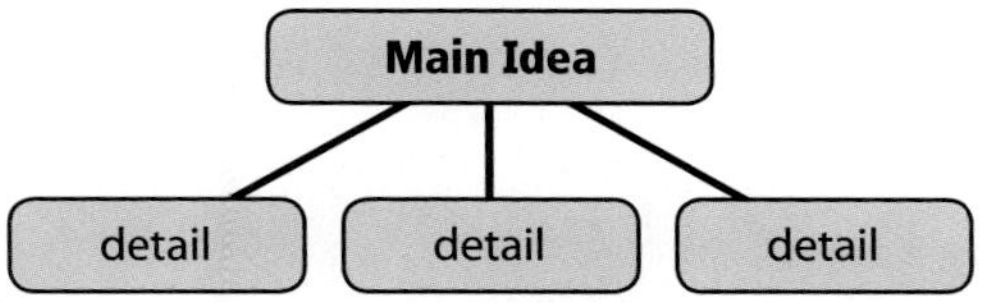

2. **SUMMARIZE** Write a paragraph that describes the properties of sound waves.

3. **DRAW CONCLUSIONS** You hit a key on the left side of a piano. Then you hit a key on the right side harder. Compare the sound waves.

4. **VOCABULARY** Draw and label a picture to show the wavelength and amplitude of a transverse wave.

Test Prep

5. **CRITICAL THINKING** How are the amplitudes of sound waves and of water waves related?

6. Which of the following machines can be used to measure sound waves?

   A. CD burner
   B. microphone
   C. oscilloscope
   D. tape recorder

Make Connections

Writing

Expository Writing
Imagine that you're playing the piano. Your brother says he doesn't understand why some strings produce higher notes than other strings. Write a brief **explanation**.

9÷3 Math

Name Decimals
You strike a B key on a piano. The sound wave that is produced has a wavelength of 0.69 m. Write the word form of this decimal.

Music

Notes and Frequencies
There is a direct relationship between frequency and the notes of a scale. Research this topic. Then write the names for the notes of a scale. Beside each name, write its frequency.

LESSON 3

Essential Question

How Do Sound Waves Travel?

Investigate how sound travels through solids.

Read and Learn about how sound travels.

Fast Fact

Sing Me a Song
Humpback whales communicate underwater by using sound. Scientists call the sounds whale songs. Those sounds are among the loudest made by any animal on Earth. In the Investigate, you'll study how sound travels through different materials.

Humpback whale

Vocabulary Preview

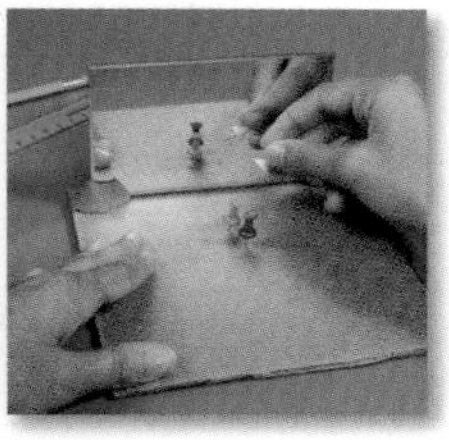

reflection [rih•FLEK•shuhn] The bouncing of light, sound, or heat off an object (p. 554)

absorption [ab•ZAWRP•shuhn] The taking in of light or sound energy by an object (p. 555)

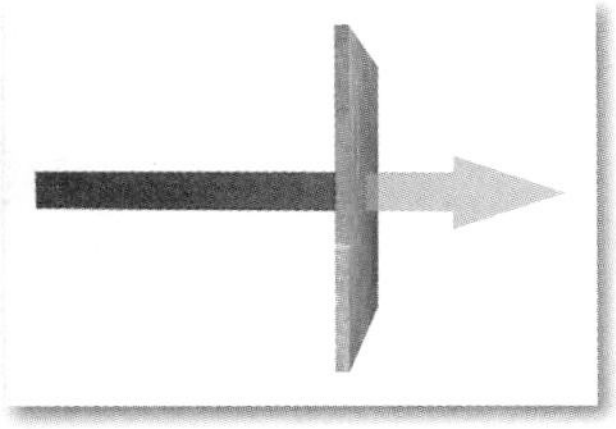

transmission [tranz•MISH•uhn] The passing of light or sound waves through a material (p. 556)

Investigate

Do You Hear What I Hear?

Guided Inquiry

Start with Questions

When you hear a knock, you know someone is at the door!

- How can you hear the knock through the material of the door?
- Does the sound change from one side of the door to the other?

Investigate to find out. Then read to find out more.

Prepare to Investigate

Inquiry Skill Tip

It is important to identify your variable so that you know what changes to make to your experiment. If you change the wrong thing, other variables can change.

Materials

- 2 × 4 pine board
- cardboard tube
- paper cup
- water

Make an Observation Chart

Material	Observations
Desktop through air	
Ear against desktop	
Ear against board	
Ear against cardboard tube	
Ear against empty cup	
Ear against cup with water	

Follow This Procedure

1. Have a partner rub a fingernail on a desktop. Listen, and **record** your **observations**. Press one ear against the desktop, and listen to the rubbing again. **Record** your **observations**.
2. Have your partner hold a board. Press your ear against one end of the board. Then have your partner, at the other end, lightly rub a fingernail against the wood. Listen, and **record** your **observations**.
3. Hold one end of a cardboard tube to your ear. Have your partner lightly rub a fingernail on the other end of the tube. Listen, and **record** your **observations**.
4. Press the side of a paper cup against your ear. Have your partner lightly rub a fingernail on the other side of the cup. Listen, and **record** your **observations**.
5. Fill the cup with water, and repeat Step 4.

Step 2

Step 4

Draw Conclusions

1. What differences did you observe in the sounds?
2. **Inquiry Skill** Identify the variable that you changed in this Investigate. What variable did you observe?

Independent Inquiry

Can you observe how sound travels through a liquid other than water? Plan and conduct a simple investigation to find out.

VOCABULARY
reflection p. 554
absorption p. 555
transmission p. 556

SCIENCE CONCEPTS
- how the human ear works
- how sound waves react when they strike a surface

Focus Skill COMPARE AND CONTRAST
Look for differences in the way sound waves interact with objects.

alike — different

Hearing Sounds

When a rocket is launched into space, it makes a huge roar. The engines vibrate, sending out sound waves in all directions. But how do you actually hear the sound?

First, the sound waves have to travel through matter to your ear. Usually, they travel through air.

In space, there is no air. Once the rocket engine is out in space, it's completely silent. If you flew past it, you wouldn't hear any sound at all. Out in space, sound waves have nothing to travel through.

But here on Earth, air carries the sound from the rocket to your ears. When the vibrations reach one of your ears, they make your eardrum vibrate. Those vibrations travel through bones and tissues until they reach your inner ear. There, special cells change the vibrations into electrical signals. These signals travel along a nerve to your brain. A special part of your brain recognizes the electrical signals. You hear the loud noise from the rocket.

Focus Skill COMPARE AND CONTRAST

How is hearing on Earth different from hearing in space?

▼ **How does the sound of the alarm travel to the girl's right ear? How does it travel to her left ear?**

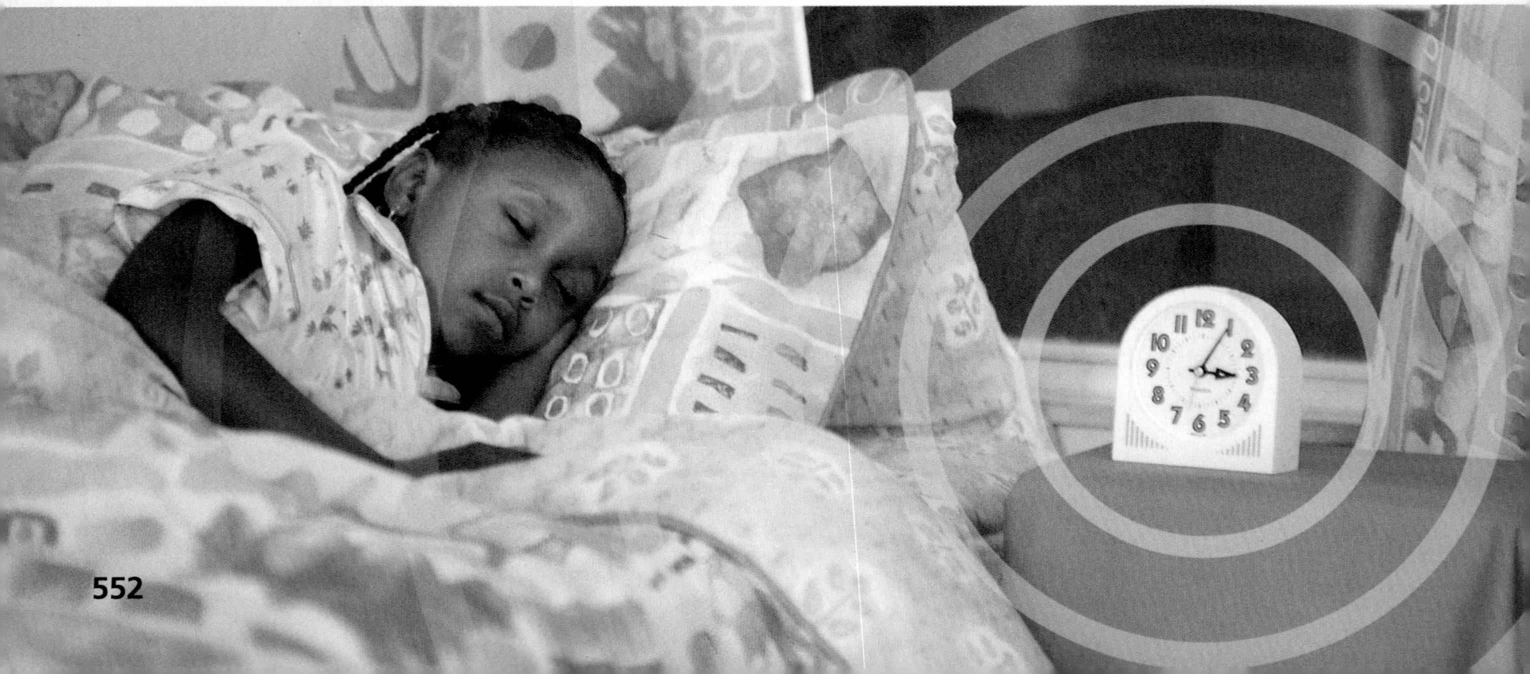

For more links and animations, go to **www.hspscience.com**

How Hearing Works

The way sound travels from the air to become signals in your brain is complex. Follow the numbers, and then read the other information.

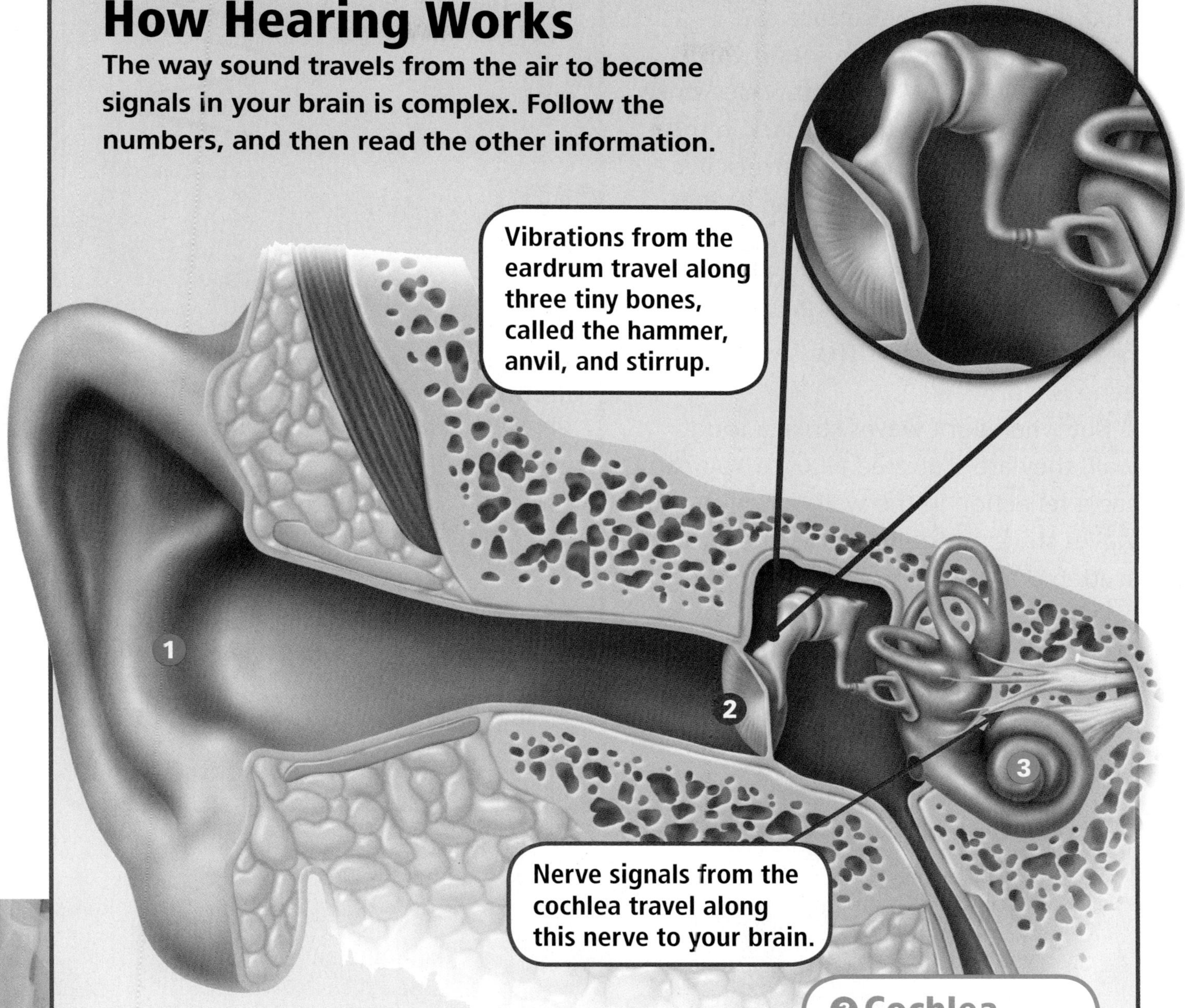

Vibrations from the eardrum travel along three tiny bones, called the hammer, anvil, and stirrup.
1
2
3
Nerve signals from the cochlea travel along this nerve to your brain.

❶ Outer ear

Your outer ear catches sound waves and funnels them inward to your eardrum.

❷ Eardrum

The sound waves make your eardrum vibrate.

❸ Cochlea

Bones pass vibrations to a snail-shaped organ called the cochlea (KAHK•lee•uh). Hairlike cells inside change vibrations into nerve signals.

Reflection

What happens when a sound wave strikes a surface other than your ear? That depends on the surface.

It's helpful to compare sound waves and light waves. When light waves strike a mirror, they are reflected back in the same pattern in which they struck it. That's why you see a reflection. When sound waves strike a smooth, flat surface, they are also reflected back in the same pattern. The result is that you hear the sound again. That's what an echo is.

But when light waves strike a rough wall, they are scattered all over. You can't see a reflection in the wall. When sound waves strike a rough surface, they are scattered all over, too.

Whether they echo or not, the sound waves are bouncing off the surface, a process called **reflection**.

Focus Skill COMPARE AND CONTRAST **What is different about the two ways sound waves can reflect off a surface?**

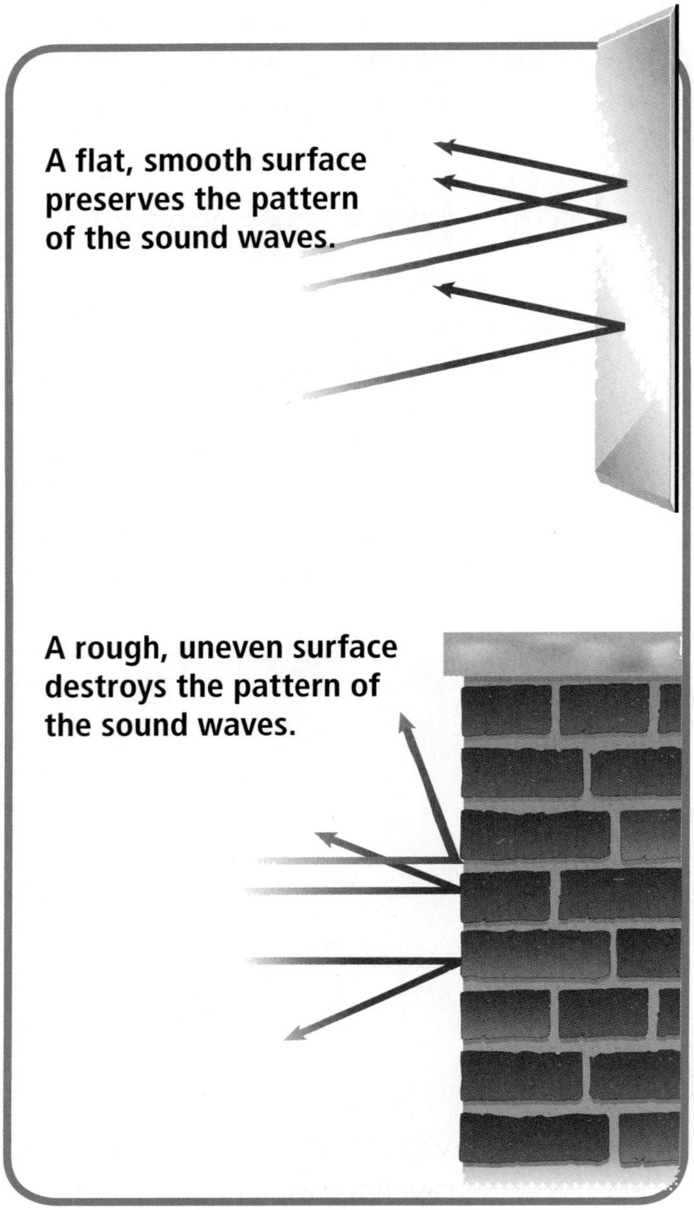

A flat, smooth surface preserves the pattern of the sound waves.
A rough, uneven surface destroys the pattern of the sound waves.

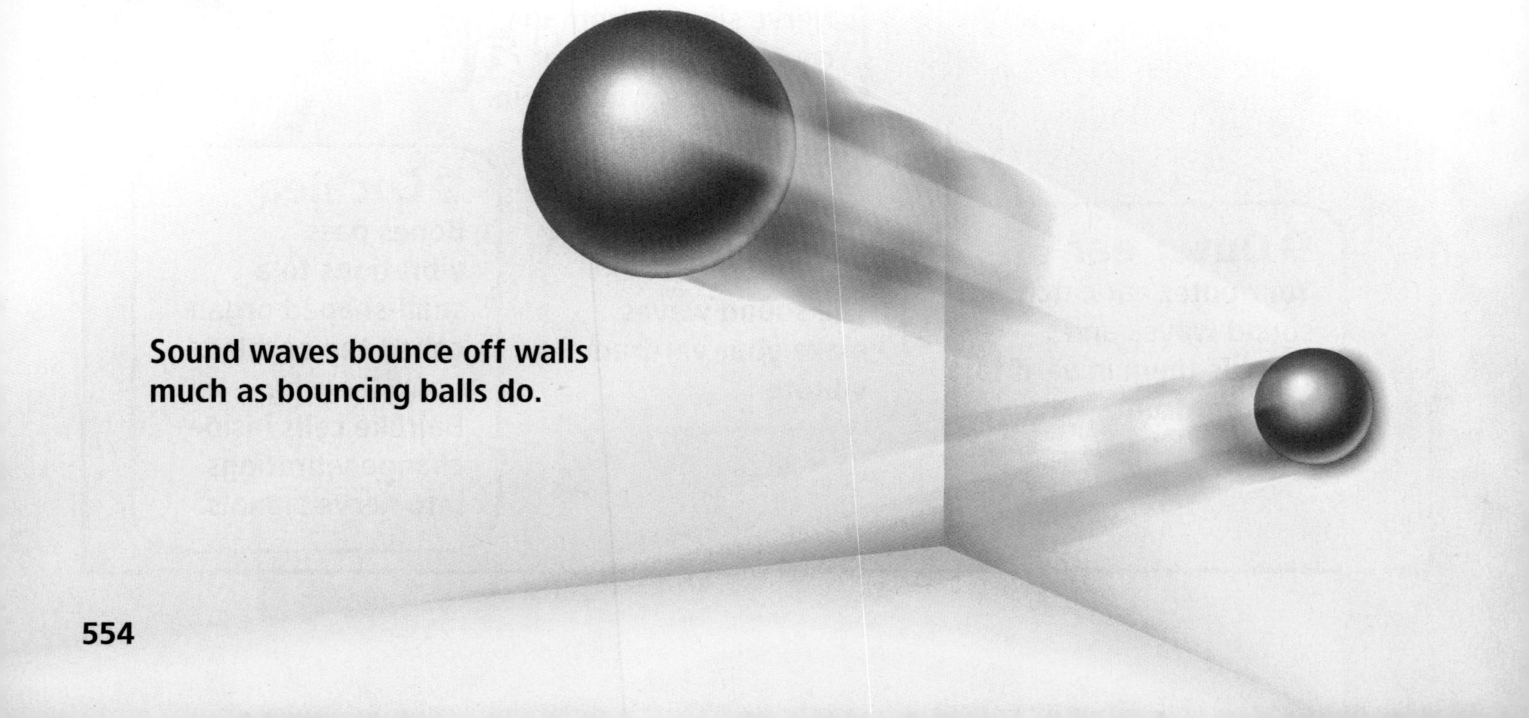

Sound waves bounce off walls much as bouncing balls do.

This anechoic (an•eh•KOH•ik), or "without echoes," chamber is carefully designed to absorb any sounds that are made inside it.

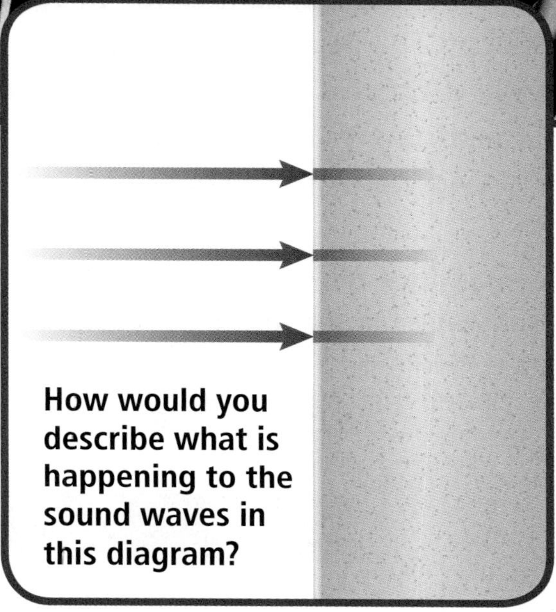

How would you describe what is happening to the sound waves in this diagram?

Absorption

Imagine making a loud sound in a bare room. You hear the sound reflecting off the hard floors and walls. What a noisy place!

But what if you make the same sound in a room with carpets and curtains? This time, you don't hear any echoes. This room seems much more quiet, because the carpets and the curtains take in the sound. They stop the sound waves from reflecting or traveling any farther. This process is called **absorption**.

What happens to a sound wave that is absorbed? It just dies out. There is no more vibration and no more sound.

This can be very useful. Imagine that you're trying to read and your neighbor is running noisy power tools. If materials in the walls of your home absorb the loud sounds, the sounds can't travel to your ears. Then you can have some peace and quiet!

Focus Skill COMPARE AND CONTRAST **How is absorption different from reflection?**

Insta-Lab

Quiet, Please

Find something that makes a steady, even sound, such as a clock that ticks loudly. Place your hands over your ears. Can you still hear the sound? Place other materials over your ears to see how well they conduct or absorb sound waves.

Transmission

You know that the parts of your ear don't reflect sound. And they don't absorb sound, either. If they did, how would you hear the sounds around you?

You can hear sounds when sound waves keep vibrating through some kinds of material. They travel through air or other matter, all the way to your inner ear. The sound waves keep moving along—a process called **transmission**. Your eardrum transmits, or moves along, the sound waves to the hammer, then to the anvil and the stirrup, and finally to the cochlea.

Have you ever heard someone talking in the next room, even though the door was closed? The sound waves were transmitted through the air in that room, through the wall, through the air in your room, and then into your ear. Materials that can vibrate are materials that can transmit sounds.

Focus Skill COMPARE AND CONTRAST **How is transmission similar to absorption? How is it different from absorption?**

How does this diagram relate to the example of someone talking in the next room?

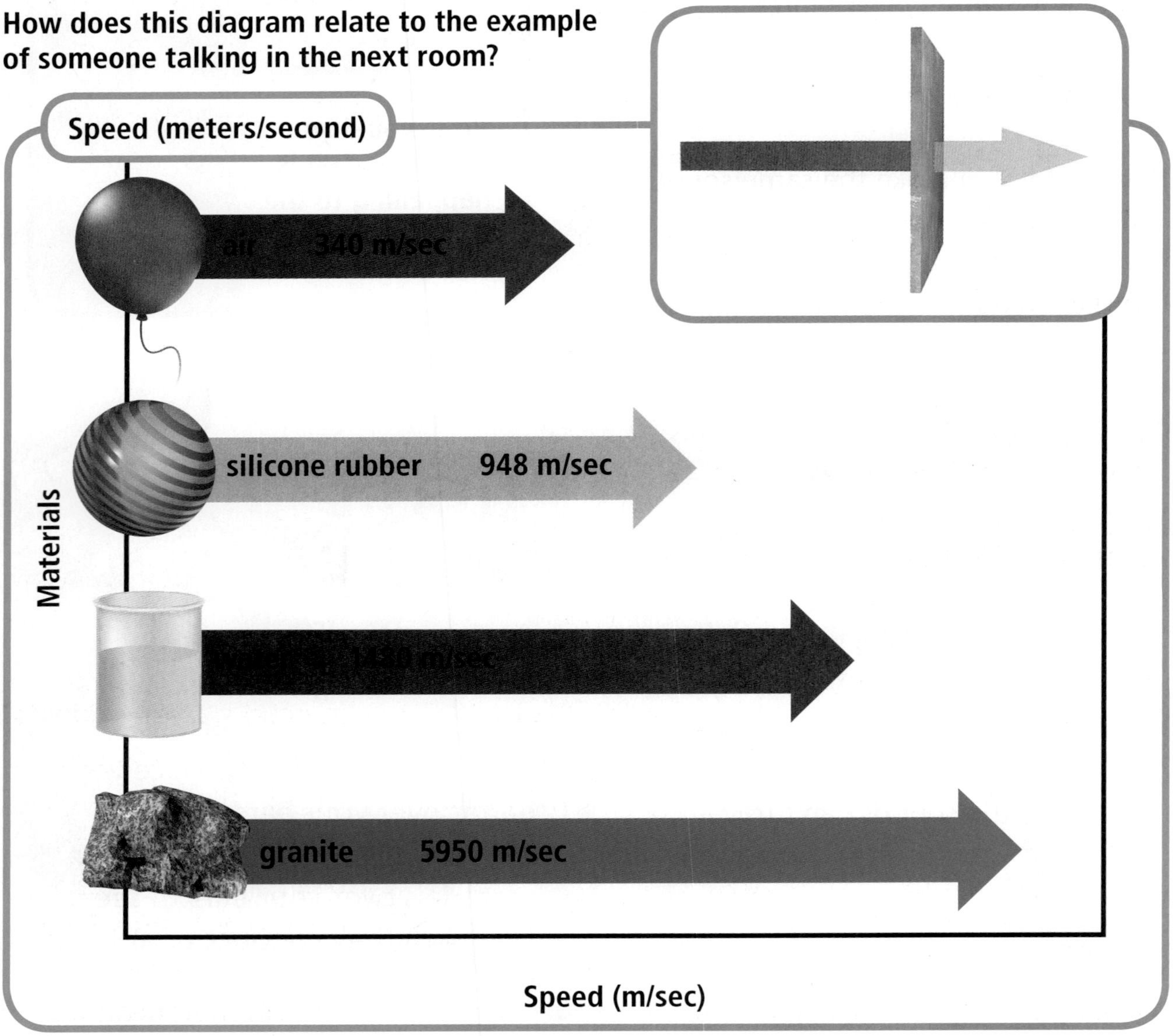

Essential Question

How Do Sound Waves Travel?

In this lesson, you learned that sound waves must have something to travel through. Usually, they travel through air, but they can also travel through other matter such as solids and liquids. This can change the sound.

1. Focus Skill COMPARE AND CONTRAST Draw and complete a graphic organizer to show what happens when sound is reflected or absorbed.

   alike — different

2. **SUMMARIZE** Summarize this lesson by writing one sentence that summarizes each section.

3. **DRAW CONCLUSIONS** As people get older, some of the hairlike cells in their cochleas die off. How might that affect their hearing?

4. **VOCABULARY** Write a dictionary definition of each vocabulary word.

Test Prep

5. **CRITICAL THINKING** Why do people often hear echoes in the mountains?

6. Which would do the best job of absorbing sounds?

   A. air
   B. blankets
   C. rocks
   D. water

Make Connections

Writing

Expository Writing

Some people find it easier to understand words than pictures. Look back at the diagram in Science Up Close. Then write an **explanation** that conveys the same information.

Math

Round Whole Numbers

A human cochlea has about 35,000 hairlike cells in it. To what place has that number been rounded?

Health

Protect Your Hearing

Infections and accidents that damage the ear usually affect hearing. Do some research on hearing. Then write a brief report describing what people can do to protect their hearing.

Michael Nyberg

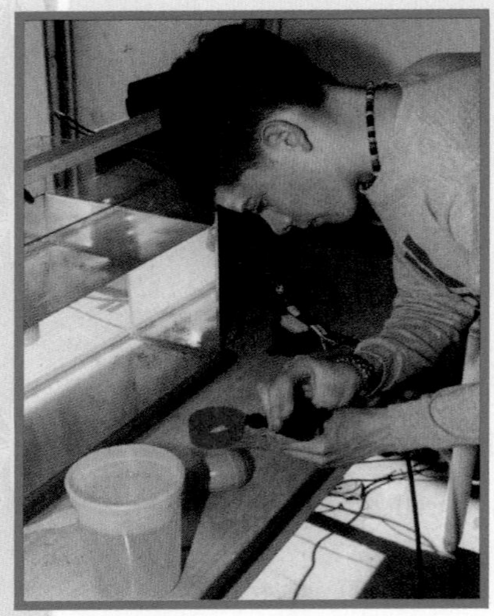

Michael Nyberg lives in an area where mosquitoes are a big problem. After visiting a sound lab in Michigan, Michael decided that he could fight mosquitoes with sound.

Michael placed mosquito larvae in a fish tank and hooked up a loudspeaker. The teen scientist used the speaker to send sound waves through the water in the tank.

"The sound vibrations caused air sacs, which are like lungs, inside the larvae to explode," Michael said. "When the air sacs exploded, the larvae died." Now some pest companies are hoping to use Michael's idea to fight mosquitoes.

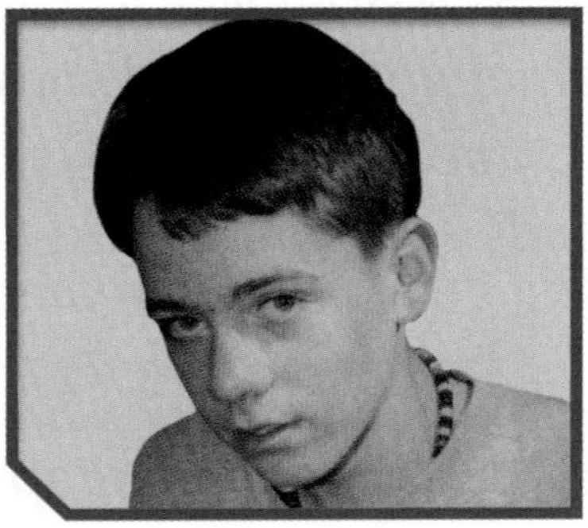

▶ **MICHAEL NYBERG**

▶ Inventor

Think and Write

1. How did Michael Nyberg get his idea?
2. How might it help pest companies fight mosquitoes?

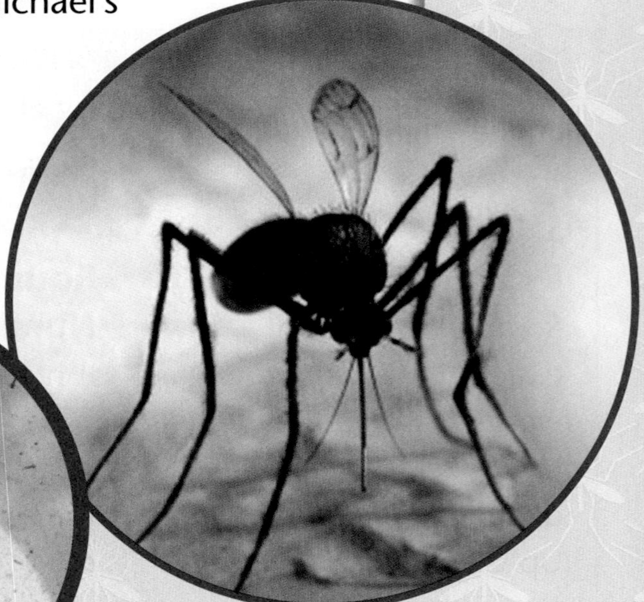

larvae

▶ **JOHN BROOKS SLAUGHTER**

▶ Used computers to solve problems in the ocean and the environment

John Brooks Slaughter

As a boy, John Brooks Slaughter loved to read science magazines. He enjoyed building the projects they described. His father bought radios for him to repair and sell. The money from repairs helped pay for college. John was the only African American student in his engineering class.

After college, Slaughter developed computer programs to analyze electrical signals. His knowledge of electricity helped solve problems involving the ocean and the environment. He has won many awards related to his job. However, his real interest is in education.

Today, Slaughter works to encourage young people to study science and math. He is excited about engineering. He hopes more young people will develop an interest in science!

Think and Write

1. How did Slaughter begin his study of electrical energy?
2. What is he most interested in now?

Career Audio Engineer

Do you like music? Audio engineers make music sound its best on a recording. They also make sure you can hear people talking in movies and television shows. Audio engineers work with computers to make sure sounds can be heard.

CHAPTER 13 Review and Test Preparation

Vocabulary Review

Use the terms below to complete the sentences. One term will be used twice. The page numbers tell you where to look in the chapter if you need help.

vibration p. 532
pitch p. 534
intensity p. 535
wavelength p. 543
frequency p. 543
amplitude p. 543
reflection p. 554
absorption p. 555
transmission p. 556

1. A word that means "bouncing off" is _______.

2. Quick back-and-forth motion is called _______.

3. The distance from the rest position to the top of a wave is called the wave's _______.

4. How high or low a note sounds is called its _______.

5. The process of a sound wave's traveling through matter is called _______.

6. The measure of the loudness of a sound is called _______.

7. The number of waves that pass a certain point in one second is called the _______.

8. The process of taking in and stopping a sound is called _______.

9. The distance from the top of one wave to the top of the next wave is called the _______.

10. An echo in the mountains can be an example of a sound's _______ off of cliffs.

Check Understanding

Write the letter of the best choice.

Use the diagram to answer Questions 11–13.

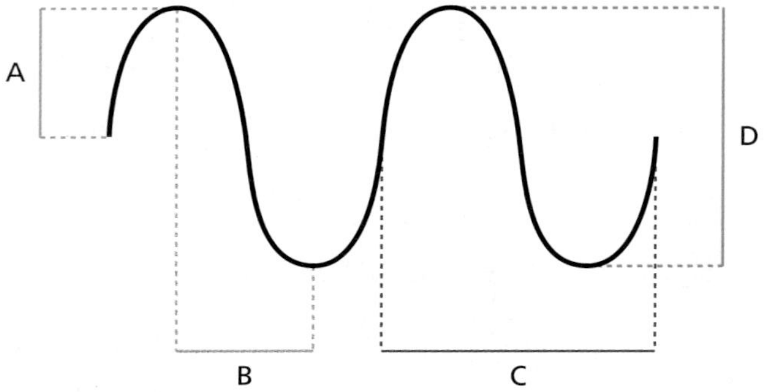

11. What kind of wave is shown?
A. a longitudinal wave
B. a transverse wave
C. a sound wave
D. a water wave

12. Which shows the amplitude of the wave?
F. A
G. B
H. C
J. D

13. Which shows the wavelength of the wave?

A. A
B. B
C. C
D. D

14. **COMPARE AND CONTRAST** One bell produces sound waves with a greater amplitude than those of another bell. How do the sounds of the two bells differ?

F. The first bell sounds higher.
G. The first bell sounds lower.
H. The first bell is louder.
J. The first bell is softer.

15. What unit is most often used to measure the intensity of a sound?

A. bel
B. centimeter
C. decibel
D. meter

16. **MAIN IDEA AND DETAILS** Where are sound waves changed into electrical signals that travel to your brain?

F. the eardrum
G. the hammer
H. the stirrup
J. the cochlea

Inquiry Skills

17. Ronald is taking out the trash. He drops a trash can lid, and it makes a huge crash. A second later, he hears an echo of that crash. What can you **infer** about Ronald's surroundings? Explain.

18. Janel is looking at a musical instrument she's never seen before. It has five strings. The thickest string is on the left, and the strings get thinner to the right. **Predict** which string will produce the lowest note. Explain your **prediction**.

Critical Thinking

The Big Idea

19. Imagine that you want to give a friend a chirping toy bird as a gift. Describe how you will wrap the toy so that the sound can't be heard until the gift is opened. Tell what happens to the sound when you wrap the toy that way.

20. Dr. Jeffers places an oscilloscope and a microphone inside a vacuum chamber. He then removes all the air from the chamber. Outside the chamber is a CD player. Dr. Jeffers plays a recording of a single, pure note—a G. What should appear on the screen of the oscilloscope? Explain. Inside the vacuum chamber is another CD player. Using a remote control, Dr. Jeffers plays a recording of another note—an A. Now what should appear on the screen of the oscilloscope? Explain.

CHAPTER 14

Light and Heat

What's the Big Idea?

Light and heat are useful forms of energy.

Essential Questions

Lesson 1
How Does Light Behave?

Lesson 2
How Can Heat Be Transferred?

Lesson 3
How Is Heat Produced and Used?

GO online
Student eBook
www.hspscience.com

What do YOU wonder?

Light Bright? Laser light can be used to cut wood and metals. Some lasers get so hot that they can burn right through steel. How do you think light makes things hotter? How does this relate to the **Big Idea?**

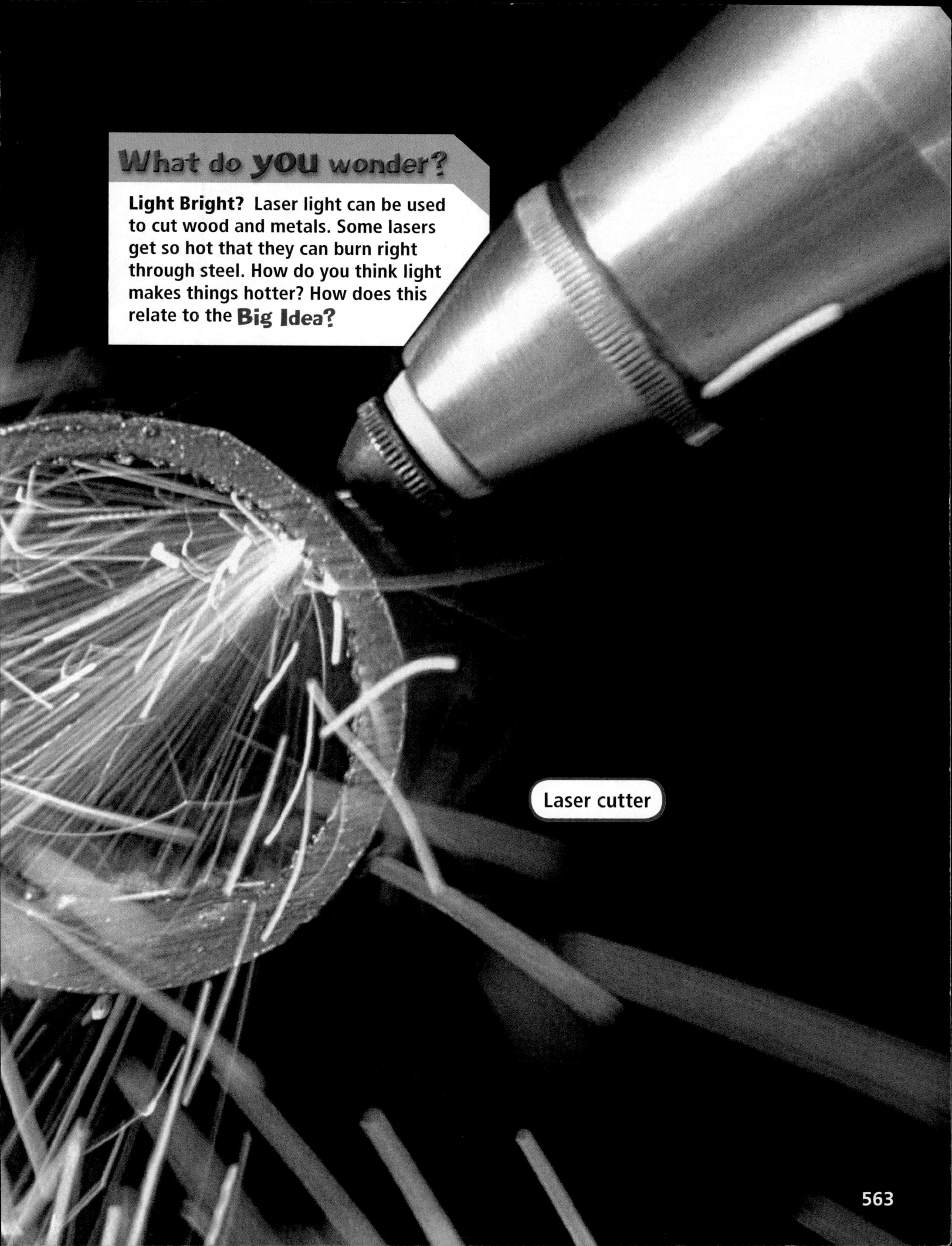

LESSON
1

Essential Question

How Does Light Behave?

Investigate how light travels.

Read and Learn how light behaves.

Fast Fact

Chain of Candles

How many candles do you see? Light bounces from mirror to mirror and back again. Every bounce makes you see another candle. In the Investigate activity, you will find out about the path of a beam of light.

Reflected candles

Vocabulary Preview

light [LYT] A form of energy that can travel through space and lies partly within the visible range (p. 568)

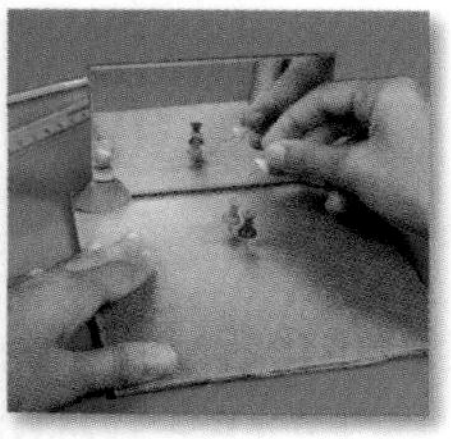

reflection [rih•FLEK•shuhn] The bouncing of light, sound, or heat off an object (p. 569)

refraction [rih•FRAK•shuhn] The bending of light when it moves from one kind of matter to another (p. 571)

Investigate

How Light Travels

Guided Inquiry

Start with Questions

The light from this boy's flashlight forms a circle on the wall.

- Why is the circle larger than the flashlight?
- How does the light get from the flashlight to the wall?

Investigate to find out. Then read to find out more.

Prepare to Investigate

Inquiry Skill Tip

Drawing diagrams of your results can help you communicate your results. Be sure that your diagrams make sense and are organized well.

Materials

- ruler
- small lamp without a lampshade
- clay
- 3 index cards
- pencil

Make an Observation Chart

Setup 1	Setup 2
Setup 3	Setup 4

Follow This Procedure

1. Using a ruler, draw lines on each card from corner to corner to make a large X.
2. Use a pencil to make a hole at the center of each X. Stack the cards, and use the pencil to make sure all the holes are at the same height.
3. Make a clay stand for each card. Stand the cards on the desk, one in front of the other and a few centimeters apart.
4. Place a lamp on the desk, and turn it on. Look through the holes in the cards. Move the cards until you can see the light bulb through all the holes at once. Draw a diagram to show your setup.
5. Move the cards to new places. Each time you move them, draw a diagram to show your setup. Try to **observe** the light through the holes each time.

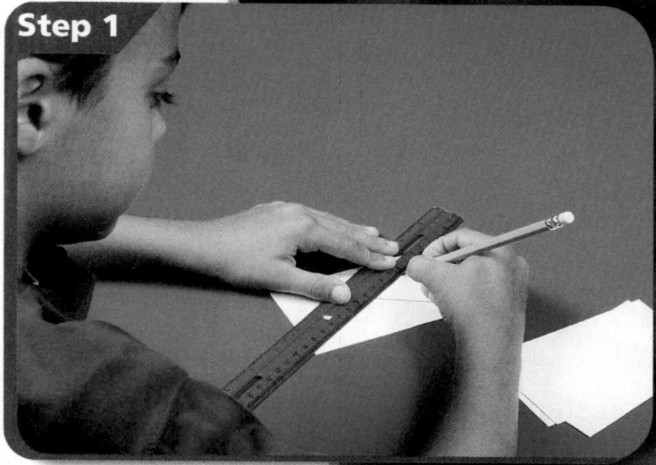
Step 1

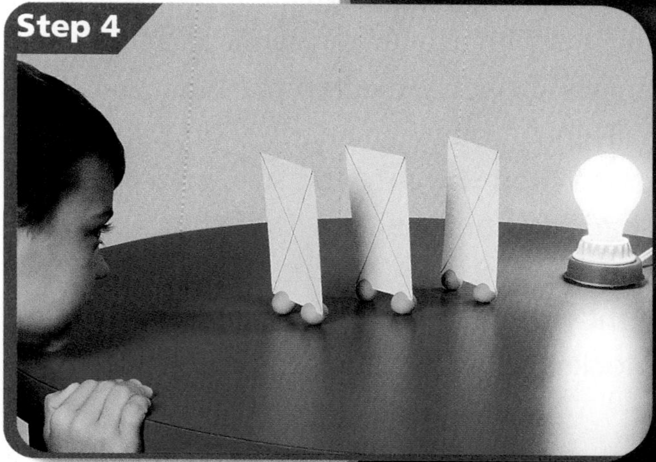
Step 4

Draw Conclusions

1. In what position were the cards when you were able to see the light bulb?
2. **Inquiry Skill** How did drawing diagrams help you **communicate** your results?

Independent Inquiry

Would your results be the same if the cards were not on a level surface? Plan and conduct a simple investigation to find out.

Read and Learn

VOCABULARY
light p. 568
reflection p. 569
refraction p. 571

SCIENCE CONCEPTS
- how matter affects the path of light
- how the eye receives light

Focus Skill CAUSE AND EFFECT
Look for ways in which matter affects light.

cause → effect

Properties of Light

Remember how warm you feel when you stand in the sun? **Light** is a form of energy that can travel through space. Light from the sun gives plants the energy they need to make food. Animals get their energy from plants and from animals that have eaten plants.

Think about your shadow on a sunny day. When you face the sun, your shadow is behind you. That's because you are blocking the path of some of the light. The dark area where the light is blocked is your shadow.

Light travels in straight lines until it hits something. When the light hit you, its path was blocked. Light doesn't go around corners. That's why the area behind you was dark.

Think back to the Investigate. The only time you could see the light bulb was when the holes in the cards were in a straight line. If you moved one card out of line, it blocked the light. When you tried to look at the light through the holes, you saw the card, not the light.

Focus Skill CAUSE AND EFFECT
What causes a shadow?

This stop sign makes a shadow because it blocks light from the sun. As the sun's position in the sky changes, the size and position of the shadow change.

▲ **When the surface of water is smooth, it acts just like the regular mirror does, as you can see in this reflecting pool.**

Reflection

When you comb your hair, do you look in a mirror to make sure you look okay? What you see in the mirror is called an image. You can see your image because light bounces off the mirror and back to you.

When light hits an object, the light bounces off the surface of the object. The bouncing of light off an object is called **reflection**.

Most objects have rough surfaces. You can't see an image in something with a rough surface, such as cloth, because the roughness makes light reflect in many different directions. A mirror or a calm lake has a smooth, flat surface. Almost all the light reflects in the same direction. This is the kind of reflection that allows you to see yourself.

Your image in a mirror looks just like you—except for one thing. It's backward! Images in a mirror are reversed from left to right.

Focus Skill CAUSE AND EFFECT **What causes a mirror to reflect an image?**

Absorption

Not all of the light that hits an object is reflected. You know that light passes through glass. That's why you can see through glass. *Transparent* materials let most of the light that hits them pass through. Glass, water, and many kinds of plastic are transparent.

Translucent (tranz•LOO•suhnt) materials let some of the light that hits them pass through, but they also absorb or scatter some of the light. This is why you can't see through them clearly. Wax paper, frosted glass, and some kinds of plastic are translucent.

Can you see through a metal door or a brick wall? Of course not! The reason is that these materials absorb or reflect all of the light. No light passes through them. *Opaque* (oh•PAYK) materials do not allow light to pass through. Metal, brick, and wood are opaque.

Focus Skill CAUSE AND EFFECT **Why can't you see through opaque materials?**

The dark red vase on the left is opaque. The middle vase is transparent. The vase on the right is translucent. ▼

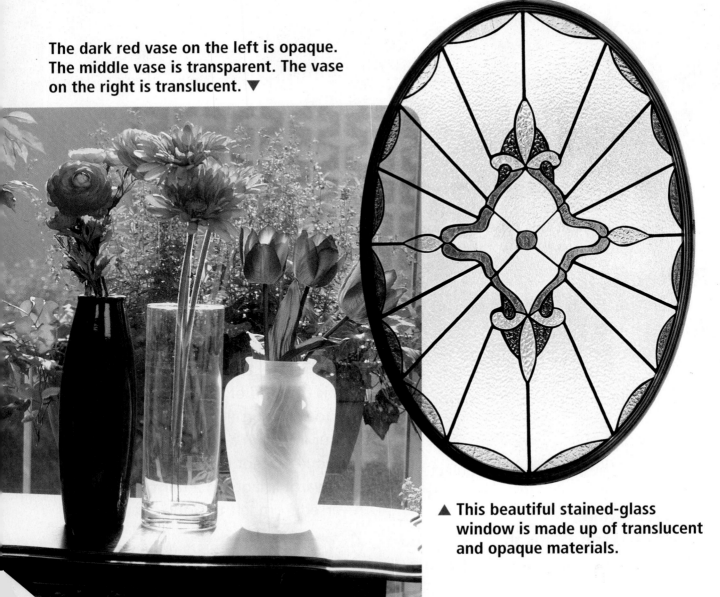

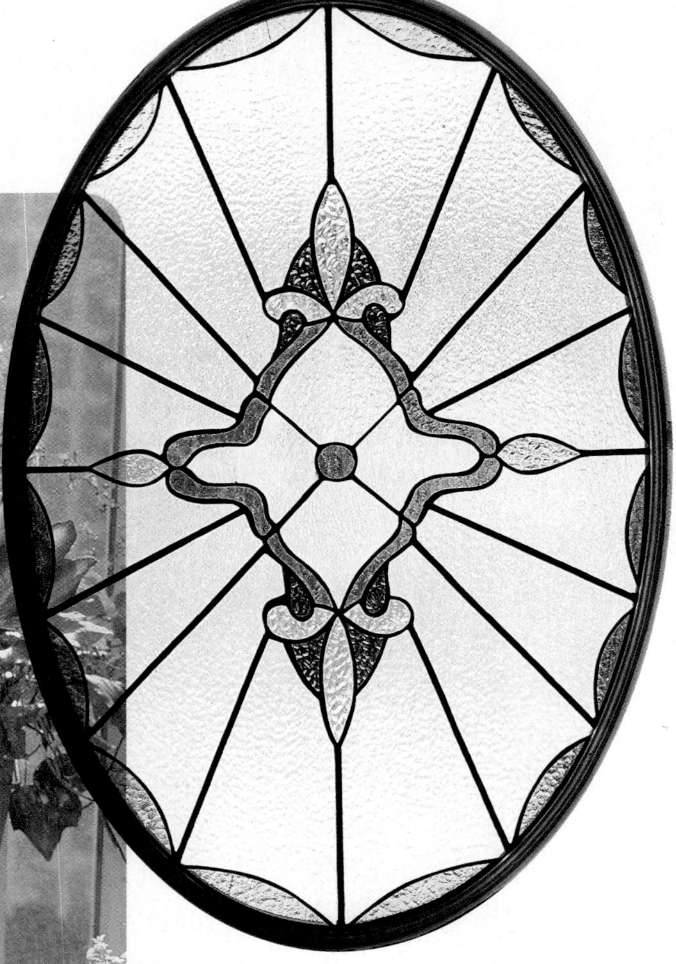

▲ This beautiful stained-glass window is made up of translucent and opaque materials.

▲ When a beam of light enters water, it slows down. If it hits at an angle, the light bends. Light travels faster in air than in water.

▲ A beam of light doesn't bend if it enters the water straight on.

Refraction

Have you ever used a net to catch a fish in a tank? You probably had a hard time telling where the fish was. That's because your eyes were fooled by the direction the light came from.

Light reflecting off the fish passed through the water, into the air, and to your eye. When the light moved from the water to the air, its speed changed. The change in speed made the beam of light bend. The bending of light is called **refraction** (rih•FRAK•shuhn).

Focus Skill **CAUSE AND EFFECT**

What causes refraction?

Insta-Lab

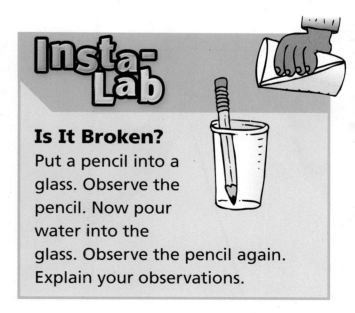

Is It Broken?

Put a pencil into a glass. Observe the pencil. Now pour water into the glass. Observe the pencil again. Explain your observations.

Seeing Light

Light is all around you. The sun gives off light. So do streetlights and desk lamps. Light also bounces off objects. When light bouncing from an object reaches your eyes, you see the object.

How do you see light? It enters the front of the eye and passes through an opening called the pupil. Around this opening is the iris, the colored part of the eye. The iris controls how much light can pass into the eye. When light is bright, the iris makes the pupil small. When light is dim, the iris makes the pupil large so that more light can enter.

The transparent lens of your eye bends the rays of light to make them focus, or meet, on the retina, at the back of your eye. A nerve carries information about the light to your brain. Your brain tells you what you're seeing.

Focus Skill **CAUSE AND EFFECT** **What causes an image to form inside the eye?**

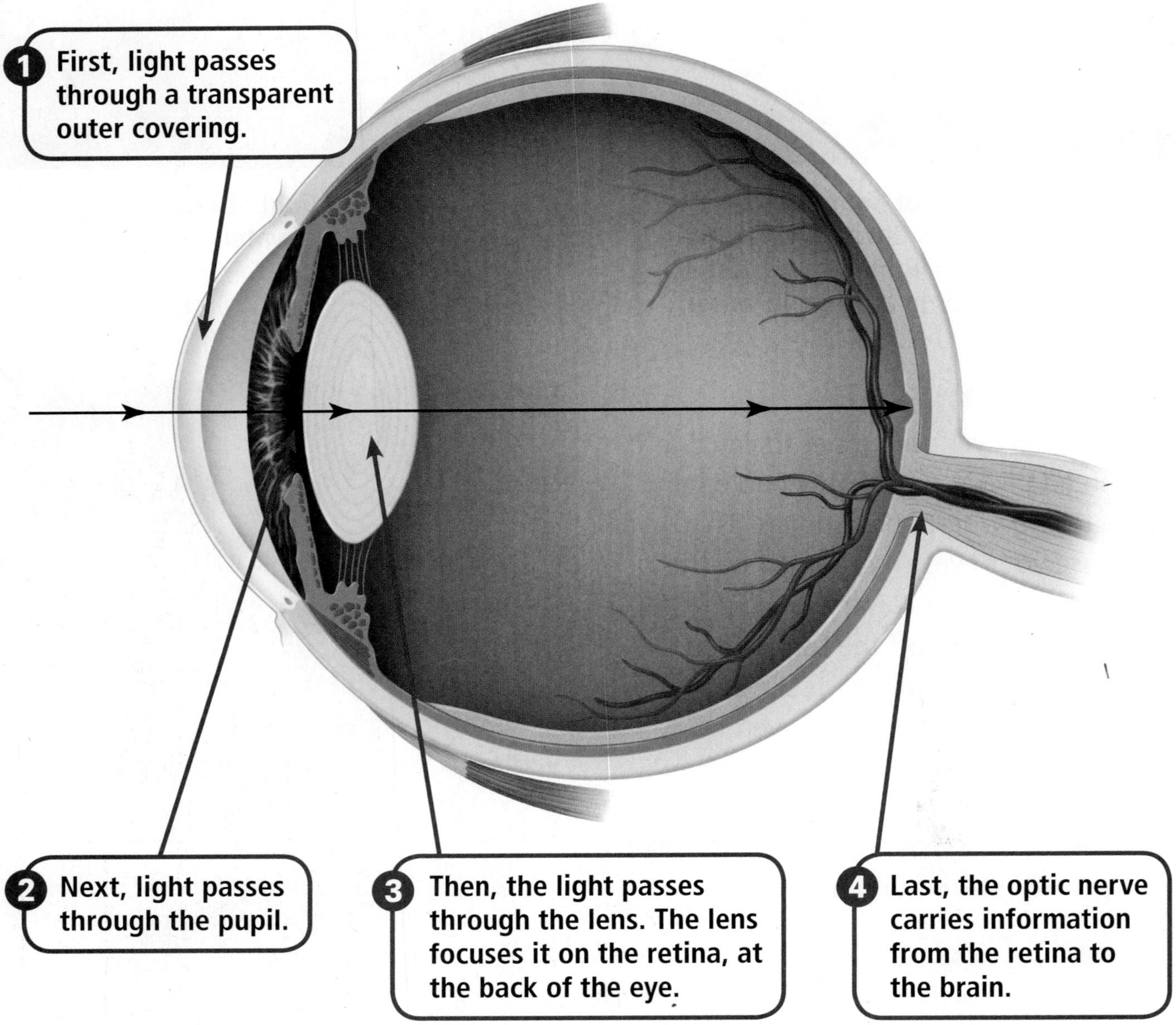

1 First, light passes through a transparent outer covering.
2 Next, light passes through the pupil.
3 Then, the light passes through the lens. The lens focuses it on the retina, at the back of the eye.
4 Last, the optic nerve carries information from the retina to the brain.

Lesson Review

Essential Question

How Does Light Behave?

In this lesson, you learned that light travels in straight lines. You learned that light can be reflected or absorbed and that both change how you see things. Light can also be refracted, which changes how things look.

1. Focus Skill CAUSE AND EFFECT Draw and complete a graphic organizer to show what happens when light hits matter.

2. **SUMMARIZE** Write two sentences that describe light absorption.

3. **DRAW CONCLUSIONS** Why can't you see around corners?

4. **VOCABULARY** Write a paragraph that shows how the vocabulary terms in this lesson are related.

Test Prep

5. **CRITICAL THINKING** You put your arm into a tank of water. Why does your arm look broken?

6. Which part of the eye controls the amount of light that enters?
   A. pupil
   B. iris
   C. lens
   D. retina

Make Connections

Writing

Expository Writing

Think about a time when you have seen a lake, a pond, or even a puddle reflect a scene. Write a **paragraph** that describes the scene and its reflection.

Math

Compare Lengths

A sign is 200 cm tall. Its shadow is 100 cm long at 10 A.M. What ratio compares the sign's height to the shadow's length? Will the ratio be greater or smaller just after sunrise?

Art

Sun Sculpture

Use what you know about how light moves to make a sculpture. The sculpture should change in some way due to sun movement. For example, its color or shadow shapes may change.

LESSON 2

Essential Question

How Can Heat Be Transferred?

Investigate how to build a thermometer.

Read and Learn how heat can be transferred.

Fast Fact

Seeing Temperature
A thermogram (THER•muh•gram) is a picture that shows how hot things are. Blue and black show the coldest objects. Yellow and red show the hottest objects. You can tell that the car has just been driven because the tires and engine are hot. In the Investigate, you will build a device that uses a much older method to measure temperature.

Thermogram of a house and driveway

Vocabulary Preview

heat [HEET] The flow of thermal energy from one object to another (p. 579)

conduction [kuhn•DUHK•shuhn] The movement of heat between two materials that are touching (p. 580)

convection [kuhn•VEK•shuhn] The movement of heat in liquids and gases from a warmer area to a cooler area (p. 581)

radiation [ray•dee•AY•shuhn] The movement of heat without matter to carry it (p. 582)

Investigate

Build a Thermometer

Guided Inquiry

Start with Questions

This thermometer tells the cook the temperature inside the turkey. The temperature tells the cook if the turkey is cooked.

- How does the heat change the turkey?
- How does the heat get to the inside of the turkey?

Investigate to find out. Then read to find out more.

Prepare to Investigate

Inquiry Skill Tip

Predictions can help you decide how to test something. Write down all your predictions so you can use them to guide your experimentation.

Materials

- apron
- food coloring
- modeling clay
- funnel
- tape
- water
- clear plastic drinking straw
- clear plastic 1-L bottle with narrow mouth

Make an Observation Chart

Thermometer originally
Thermometer in a warm place

Follow This Procedure

1. Put on an apron. Add water to a bottle until it is about one-third full.
2. Add two or three drops of food coloring. Swirl the bottle to mix the color evenly.
3. Put a straw in the bottle. Hold the straw so that the end is half-way down in the water. Tape the straw in place at the neck of the bottle.
4. Use clay to seal the top of the bottle so that no air can get in or out. *Do not squeeze the bottle.*
5. Make a drawing of your thermometer. Show the water level in the straw.
6. Put the thermometer in a warm place for five minutes. **Observe** the water level in the straw. Make a drawing to **record** this observation.

Step 3

Step 4

Draw Conclusions

1. Did the water level in the straw change when the thermometer was in a warm place? If so, how did it change?

2. **Inquiry Skill** Suppose you put your thermometer in a cold place, such as a refrigerator. **Predict** what would happen.

Independent Inquiry

Predict which places in your classroom will be the warmest and coolest. Then plan and conduct a simple investigation to check.

Read and Learn

VOCABULARY
heat p. 579
conduction p. 580
convection p. 581
radiation p. 582

SCIENCE CONCEPTS
- how temperature and heat are different
- ways in which heat moves

Focus Skill MAIN IDEA AND DETAILS

Look for ways heat can move.

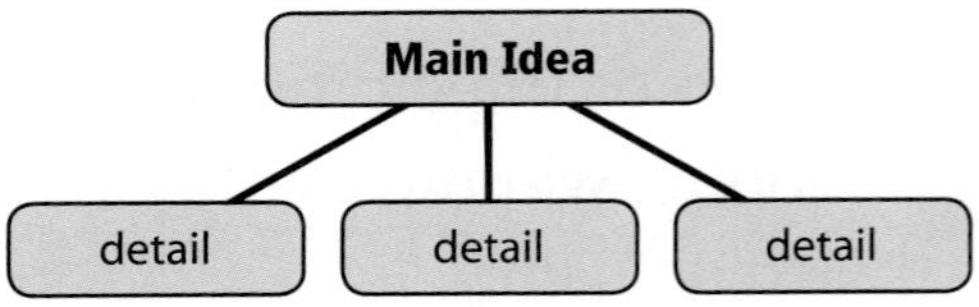

Temperature and Heat

You step outside on a bright summer day and feel the hot air right away. You look up at the thermometer. It shows that the temperature is 33°C (92°F). No wonder you feel hot! A thermometer measures the temperature of matter—in this case, the air outdoors. Temperature is the measure of how hot or cold something is.

The particles in matter are always moving. The more energy they have, the more they move. The particles in a solid can't move very far. They vibrate in place. In a liquid or a gas, the particles can move faster and farther. Temperature is actually the measure of the average energy of this movement.

On a hot day, particles in the air have more energy than they do on a cooler day. The air particles move faster. This gives them a higher temperature.

◀ **A thermometer measures temperature. It tells how hot or cold matter is.**

Which has a higher temperature—steaming tea in a teapot or water in a swimming pool? If you said the tea, you'd be right. It's much hotter than the water in the pool.

Which has more energy—the tea or the water in the pool? Even though it's cooler, the water in the pool has more thermal energy. Thermal energy is the total amount of energy in an object. There is a much larger amount of matter in the pool, so the total of its energy is larger. The tea in the teapot is a small amount of matter. It has less total energy.

It's a hot day, so you jump into the swimming pool. Ahh, you feel cooler already! And you are cooler. Energy is moving from your body into the water. The term for this transferred energy is **heat**. Heat always moves from matter that is warmer to matter that is cooler. In the pool, as the heat from your body moves into the cool water, you cool off.

Focus Skill **MAIN IDEA AND DETAILS**

How does heat move?

▼ **The small mass of liquid in this teapot has a high temperature.**

▼ **The liquid in this wading pool is cool. However, its total thermal energy is greater than that of the liquid in the teapot because the pool water has much more mass.**

Conduction

Have you ever left a metal spoon in a bowl of hot soup? When you touched the spoon handle, it felt hot. The handle of the spoon wasn't in the soup, so how did it get hot? Heat moved from the soup into the spoon. Then it moved along the spoon until the whole spoon was hot.

Heat travels by **conduction** through materials that are touching. The heat from the soup moved by conduction to the handle of the spoon and then from the spoon to your fingers.

Some materials conduct heat better than others. Most metals conduct heat well. Other materials do not conduct well at all. A foam cup, for example, is a poor conductor of heat. Glass, air, water, and wood also do not conduct heat well.

Focus Skill **MAIN IDEA AND DETAILS**

What kinds of matter conduct heat well?

Math in Science
Interpret Data

Heat Conductors

The table lists some metals in order of how well they conduct heat. The best conductor is listed first. Some steel cooking pots have a thin layer of copper on the bottom. Why do you think they are made that way?

Conductivity	Metal
good	Silver
	Copper
	Steel
poor	Lead

The blacksmith's forge warms the pieces of metal. Heat spreads through the metal by conduction. ▼

Convection

The particles in liquids and gases move constantly. The movement of heat in liquids and gases from a warmer area to a cooler area is called **convection**.

Warm liquid or gas is forced up by cooler liquid or gas. When water boils in a pot, the water near the heat source gets hot first and is forced up by the cooler water. Then the cool water gets hot and is forced up. This happens over and over in a circular current, or flow. This is an example of convection.

Focus Skill MAIN IDEA AND DETAILS

What kinds of matter carry heat by convection?

Insta-Lab

Hot Air

Cut a spiral shape from a sheet of construction paper. Make a hole in its center. Tie thread through the hole. Hold the spiral above a warm desk lamp. What happens? Why? Next, hold the spiral beside the lamp. What happens? Why?

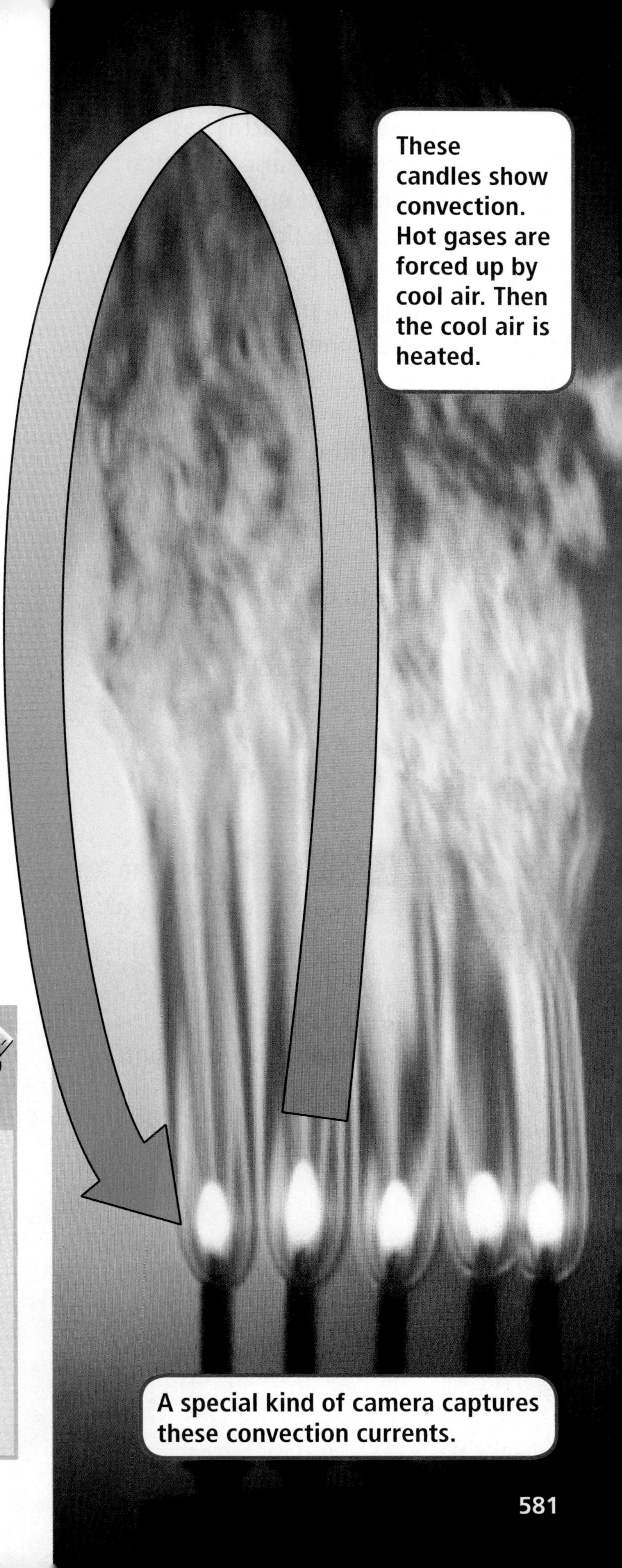

These candles show convection. Hot gases are forced up by cool air. Then the cool air is heated.

A special kind of camera captures these convection currents.

Radiation

You have seen that matter has heat energy. You have also seen that matter can carry heat energy. Solids carry heat by conduction. Liquids and gases carry heat by convection. What happens, then, in a place where there is no matter? Can heat pass through space without matter to carry it? Yes, it can.

You know that the sun warms Earth. Heat travels from the sun to Earth's surface. Almost all of that distance is through space. The movement of heat without matter to carry it is **radiation**.

Radiation can take place when matter is present, too. You don't have to touch a hot stove to know it's hot. You can feel the heat when you hold your hand near it. You feel that heat by radiation.

Focus Skill MAIN IDEA AND DETAILS **How can heat move without matter to carry it?**

▼ Heat from the wires in a toaster moves to a slice of bread by radiation. The glowing wires of the toaster also give off light.

▼ This is a regular photograph of an elephant.

▼ This photograph shows how heat radiates from the body of an elephant.

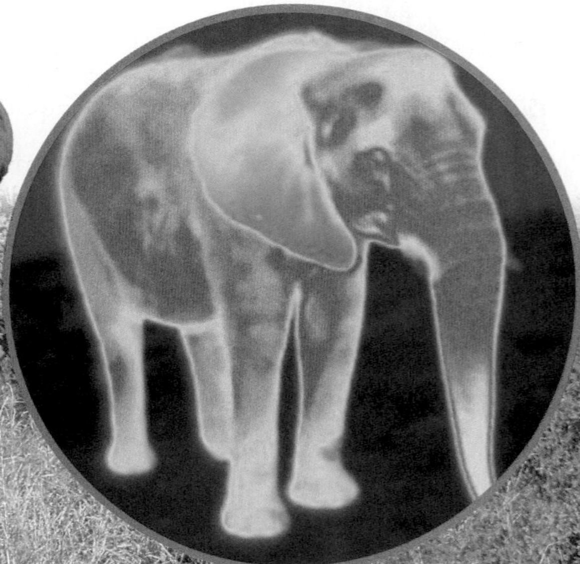

Lesson Review

Essential Question

How Can Heat Be Transferred?

In this lesson, you learned that heat moves from hot objects to cooler ones. It can move in three different ways: conduction, convection, and radiation.

1. Focus Skill **MAIN IDEA AND DETAILS** Draw and complete a graphic organizer explaining how heat moves.

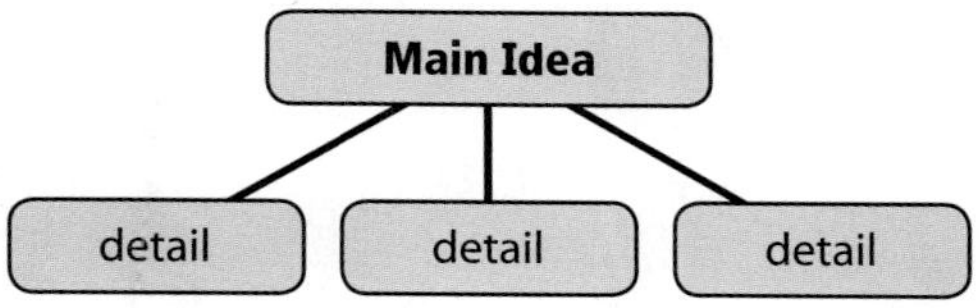

2. **SUMMARIZE** Write a sentence that describes conduction.

3. **DRAW CONCLUSIONS** How is radiation different from conduction and convection?

4. **VOCABULARY** Draw a picture to illustrate the lesson vocabulary.

Test Prep

5. **CRITICAL THINKING** Two glasses hold water at 22°C. One holds 250 mL. The other holds 350 mL. Which glass holds more thermal energy? Explain.

6. Which material conducts heat well?
   A. brick
   B. glass
   C. plastic
   D. silver

Make Connections

Writing

Expository Writing

Write a **personal story** about a very hot day and what you did to cool off. Explain why what you did cooled you off.

Math

Measure Temperature

Fill an ice cube tray with water. Place a thermometer in one section. Put the tray in a freezer. Just as the water freezes, measure the temperature. What is it?

Social Studies

Time Line

Find out who invented the first thermometer and who developed the two temperature scales. Make a time line that shows what you learned.

LESSON 3

Essential Question

How Is Heat Produced and Used?

Investigate how solar energy heats.

Read and Learn how heat is produced and used.

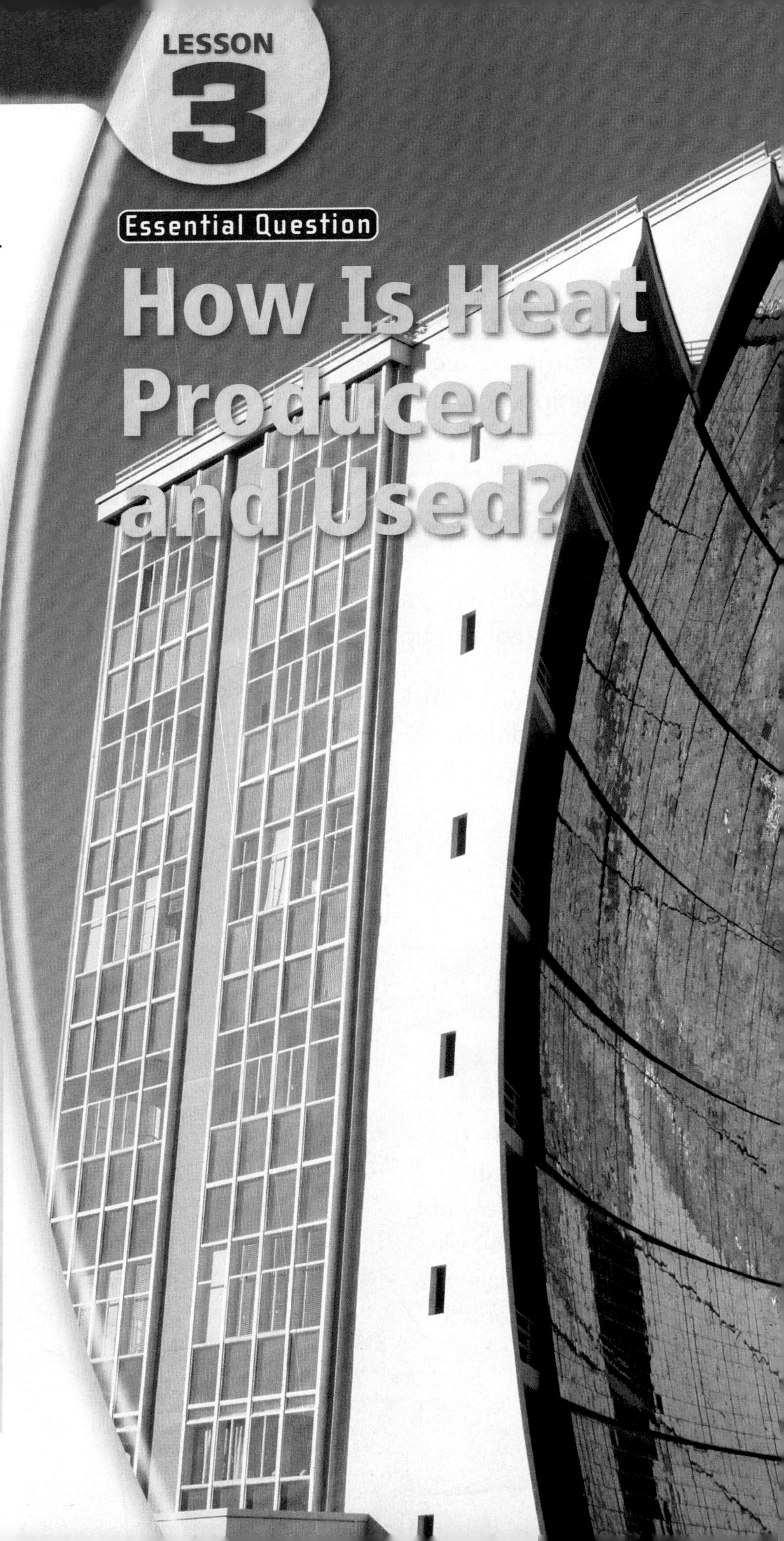

Fast Fact

Collecting Sunlight

This building is designed to collect energy from the sun. Its curved wall is covered with 9130 mirrors. They reflect sunlight toward a single point on a tower in front of them. This point can reach temperatures as high as 3800°C (almost 7000°F)! In the Investigate, you'll use a curved reflector to make your own "hot spot."

Mirrors of a solar furnace

Vocabulary Previe

energy transfer [EN•er•jee TRANS•fer] A change of energy from one form to another (p. 589)

waste heat [WAYST HEET] Heat that can't be used to do useful work (p. 592)

Build a Solar Hot Spot

Guided Inquiry

Start with Questions

This meal was cooked by the energy of the sun!

- How can sunlight provide heat?
- Why is the solar cooker shaped the way it is?

Investigate to find out. Then read to find out more.

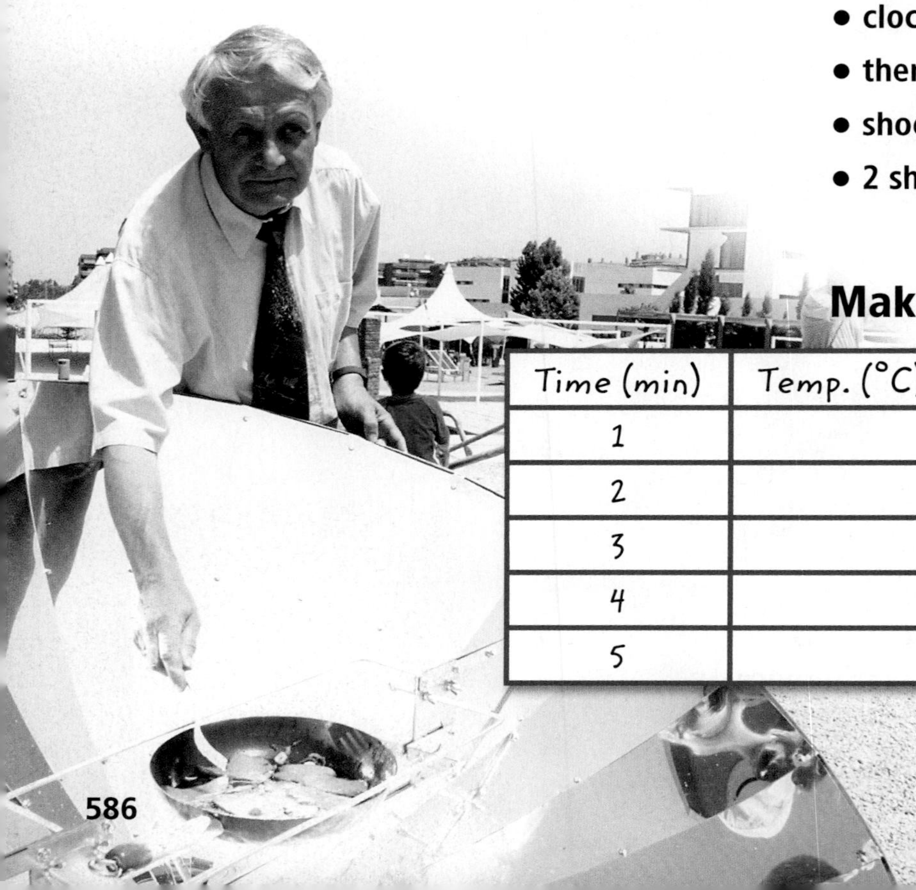

Prepare to Investigate

Inquiry Skill Tip

Look only at the data you have collected when you are interpreting your data. Don't base your results on what you expect or what other students may have measured.

Materials

- poster board
- scissors
- clock or watch
- thermometer
- shoe-box lid
- 2 sheets of graph paper
- aluminum foil
- string
- glue
- hole punch
- ruler

Make an Observation Chart

Time (min)	Temp. (°C)	Time (min)	Temp. (°C)
1		6	
2		7	
3		8	
4		9	
5		10	

Follow This Procedure

1. CAUTION: **Be careful when using scissors.** Cut a piece of poster board 10 cm by 30 cm. Glue foil to one side. Let it dry for at least 10 minutes.

2. Place a thermometer in a shoe-box lid.

3. Place the lid in sunlight. Record the temperature each minute for 10 minutes.

4. Punch a hole 2 cm from the middle of each 10-cm side of the poster board. Use string to pull these sides toward each other until they are about 20 cm apart. Then tie the string to hold the shape.

5. Put the curved reflector in the shoe-box lid, with the thermometer in its center. Repeat Step 3.

6. Make line graphs of the data from Steps 3 and 5. Show time on the horizontal axis and temperature on the vertical axis.

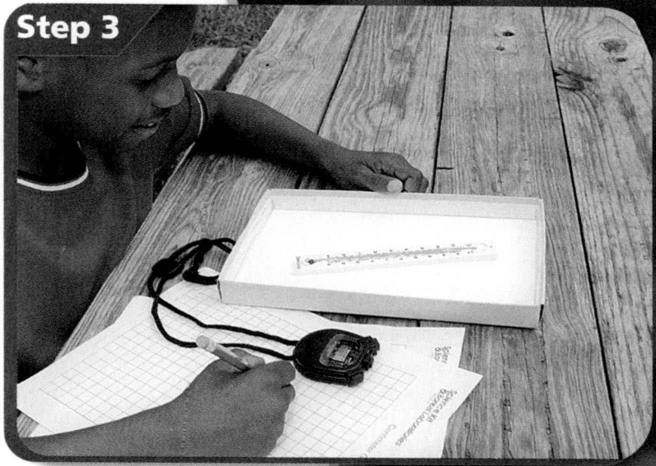

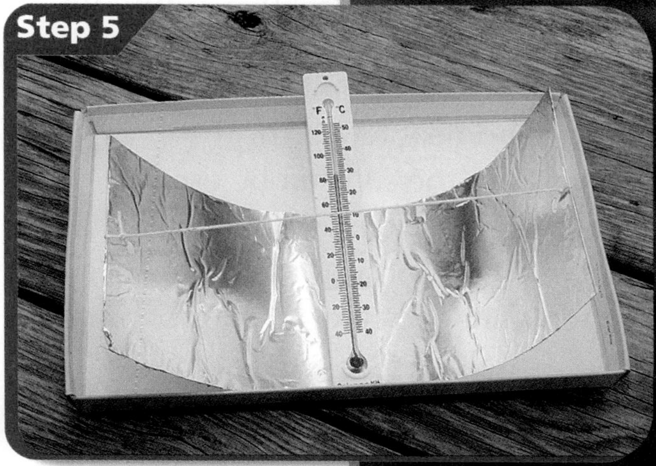

Draw Conclusions

1. Describe the temperature changes shown on each graph.
2. **Inquiry Skill** Interpret the data. What do you infer caused the differences in the temperatures on the two graphs?

Independent Inquiry

Repeat the experiment, using black construction paper instead of foil. Make a chart to compare your results. Explain the difference in your results from the two surfaces.

Read and Learn

VOCABULARY
energy transfer p. 589
waste heat p. 592

SCIENCE CONCEPTS
- how heat energy is transferred to other forms of energy
- how people use heat

Focus Skill MAIN IDEA AND DETAILS

Look for examples of how heat is produced and used.

Main Idea
detail | detail | detail

Heat Sources

Did you know that you can absorb heat just by going outside? During the day, even if it's cloudy, energy from the sun reaches Earth. It warms you, and it warms Earth. The sun is the main source of light and heat for Earth.

Heat from the sun can be used in other ways. In the Investigate, you made a curved reflector. You used it to collect the sun's energy. Large groups of mirrors can do the same thing. This is how some solar power plants work. The mirrors reflect light onto a tower. The tower contains materials that collect the heat. The heat is used to make electricity.

Have you ever noticed something that looks like a window propped up on the roof of a house? That's a solar panel. Solar panels collect and store heat from the sun. This heat is used to warm water for use in the home.

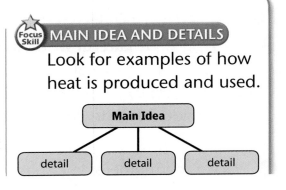

Solar Two, in California, was a power plant. The mirrors reflected the sun's energy onto the tower, which collected the heat.

▲ **When a fuel such as wood is burned, it gives off light and heat.**

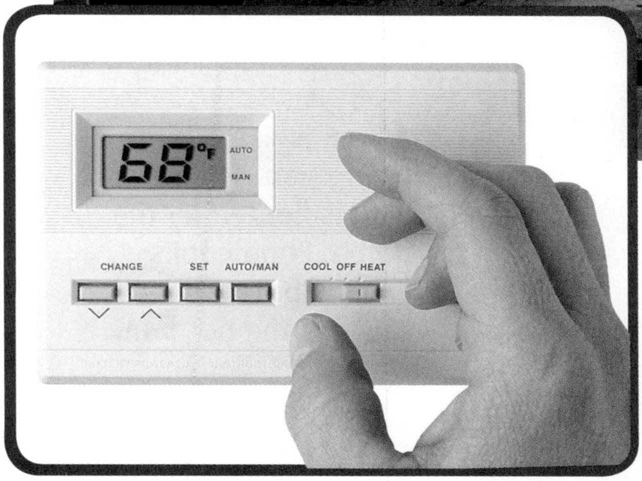

◀ **A thermostat (THER•muh•stat) allows a person to control how much heat the furnace sends into the rooms.**

Some homes collect heat from the sun naturally because they have large windows that face the sun. In many areas, however, the sun doesn't provide enough heat to keep a whole house warm. In those areas, houses have to be warmed by changing other forms of energy to heat. The change of energy from one form to another is called **energy transfer**.

Fuels are sources of energy to make heat. Wood and any other materials that burn are fuels. Many homes have furnaces that burn oil or natural gas. A furnace warms water or air. As the warmed material is pumped through the house, it gives off its heat to the rooms.

Other homes don't have fuel-burning furnaces. Instead, they have electric heaters in each room, usually along the bottom of a wall. When electricity flows through wires, the wires get hot. The wires in the heaters in each room warm the home.

Focus Skill **MAIN IDEA AND DETAILS**

What are three sources of heat?

Using Heat

People use heat in many ways. You already know that it's used to warm homes. Heat is also used to warm water for bathing and washing dishes. Heat is used to dry clothes, either in a dryer or outside on a line in the sun. If the clothes are wrinkled, heat from an iron makes the cloth smooth again.

Heat is also used to make changes in matter. People do this every day at home when they cook. Some stoves burn natural gas. Other stoves use electricity. Food is put into a pan, and the pan is put on top of the stove or in the oven. Heat from the stove moves into the pan. Then the heat moves into the food, making it hot and causing changes in its matter.

Heat also changes matter in factories. For example, metals such as iron and brass are heated until they melt. Then the liquid metals are poured into molds. When the metals cool, they harden and have the shapes of the molds. Plastics are molded in a similar way.

◀ **A wok is like a large frying pan. The whole wok is heated by the flame. Food cooks quickly because it touches the hot pan.**

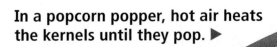

In a popcorn popper, hot air heats the kernels until they pop. ▶

Science Up Close

Motion from Heat

A heat engine burns fuel to produce heat. Then the engine transfers the heat into the energy of motion. Steam engines are heat engines.

In a steam engine, fuel is burned to heat water. The water boils, making steam.

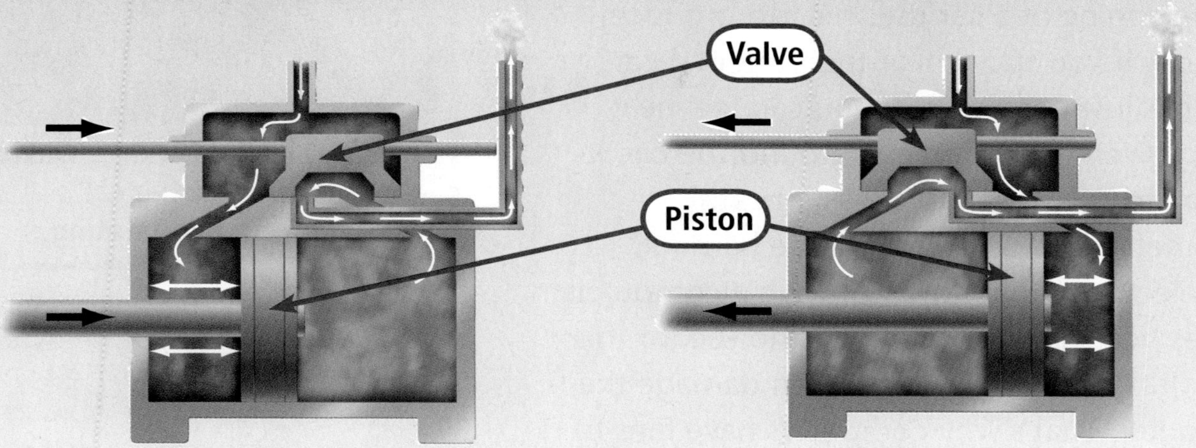

First, a valve lets hot steam into the left side. The steam pushes the piston to the right. The valve lets out cooler steam from the right side.

Then, the valve opens to let steam into the right side. The steam pushes the piston back. This left-right cycle repeats.

For more links and animations, go to **www.hspscience.com**

Heat can be used to produce motion. In some power plants, heat is used to boil water. This heat may come from burning fuel or from the sun. The boiling water becomes steam. The expanding steam pushes the blades of fanlike machines called turbines (TER•binz). The energy of the turbines' motion is changed to electricity. When that electricity gets to your home, you can turn it back into heat by turning on the stove.

Focus Skill MAIN IDEA AND DETAILS **What are four ways heat is used in the home?**

Insta-Lab

Zap It!

Do this experiment on a sunny day. CAUTION: **Put on safety goggles.** Take a kernel of popcorn and a raisin outside. Set both on concrete or brick in the sun. Hold a hand lens so that it focuses a small dot of light on the kernel. Wait one minute. Repeat with the raisin. What happens? Why?

Waste Heat

As you have learned, making heat often involves burning a fuel. People burn fuels to heat homes and to make car engines work. Most electricity is made in power plants that burn fuel. When fuel is burned, not all of the heat it produces can be put to use. The heat that can't be used to do work is **waste heat**.

The engine of a car uses heat to produce motion. If you stand near the front of a car that has just been driven, you can feel heat being given off into the air around the car. It doesn't do any work. It's waste heat.

Sometimes, waste heat can be harmful. The electricity that flows through a computer makes heat. The computer has no use for this heat. If the heat builds up, it can damage the computer. That's why computers have fans to remove the waste heat.

Focus Skill MAIN IDEA AND DETAILS **What is waste heat?**

A car radiator collects waste heat to protect the car's engine from overheating.

A light bulb turns energy to light and heat. The heat is waste heat.

The computer fan moves hot air. The heat sink conducts heat away from chips. ▼

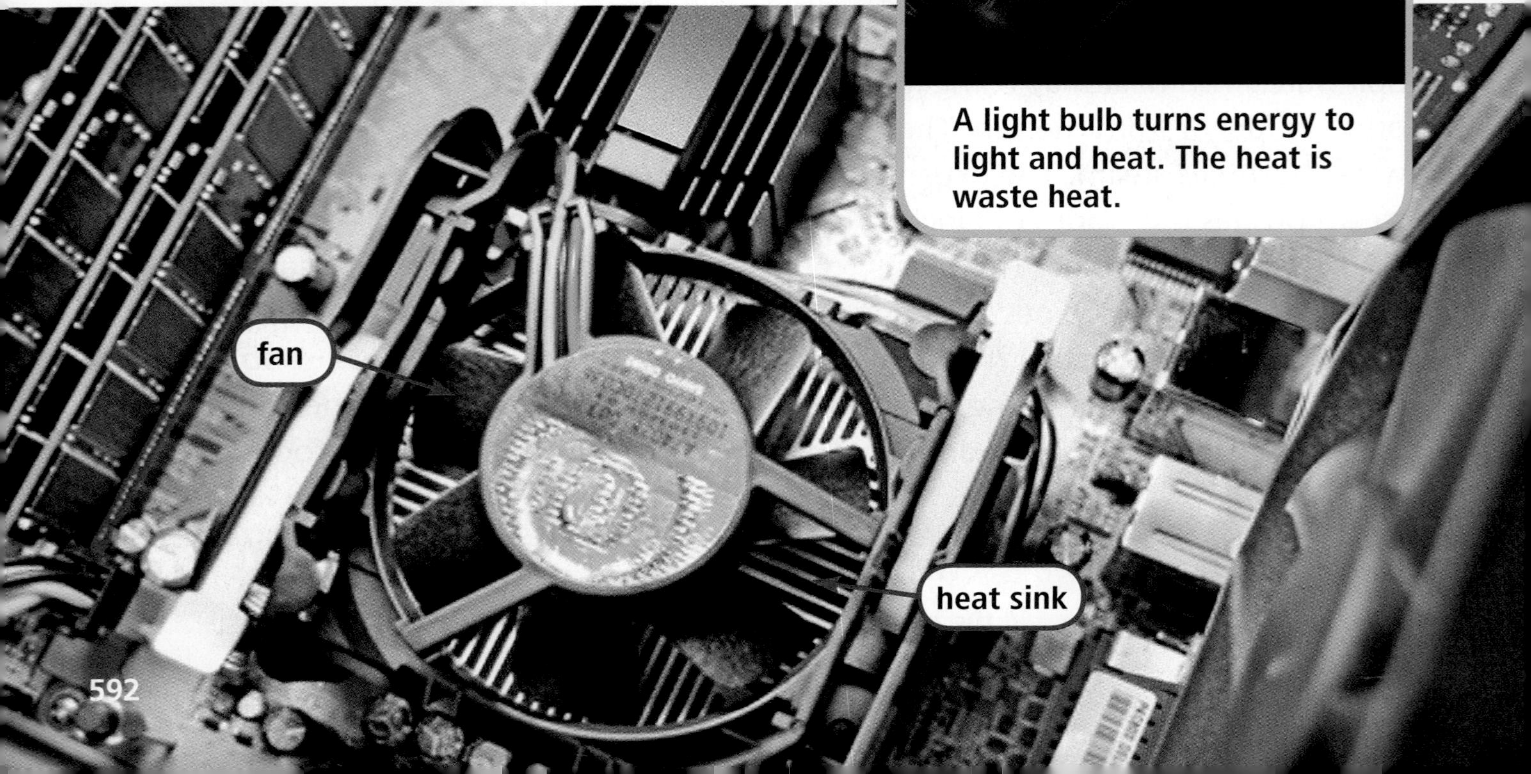

Essential Question

How Is Heat Produced and Used?

In this lesson, you learned that heat can be produced from the sun and by burning fuels. Heat is used to cook, to warm homes, and to produce other kinds of energy.

1. Focus Skill **MAIN IDEA AND DETAILS** Draw and complete a graphic organizer to show some sources of heat.

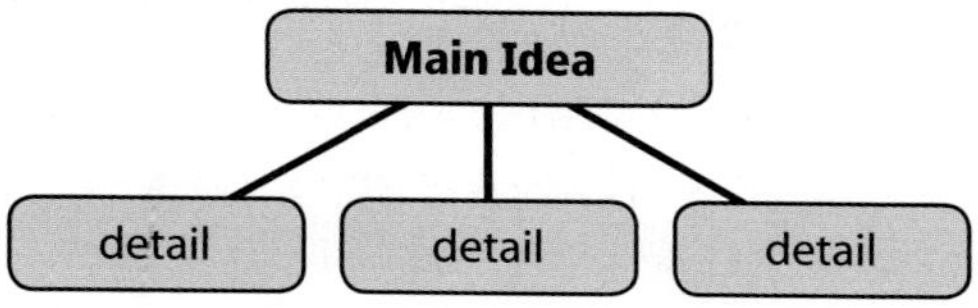

2. **SUMMARIZE** Write a sentence describing waste heat.

3. **DRAW CONCLUSIONS** Why does a car engine need a radiator?

4. **VOCABULARY** Give two examples of energy transfer.

Test Prep

5. **CRITICAL THINKING** If you sit in the sun, you will feel warmer in dark-colored clothing than in light-colored clothing. Explain how energy transfer causes this effect.

6. Which property must be different between two objects for heat to be transferred from one to the other?
   A. mass
   B. shape
   C. temperature
   D. volume

Make Connections

Writing

Persuasive Writing

Imagine that you sell furnaces to homeowners. Write a **business letter** explaining why your furnaces are the best ones to buy.

Math

Make a Bar Graph

About nine-tenths of the energy that some light bulbs use produces heat instead of light. Make a bar graph showing how much of a light bulb's energy makes light and how much makes heat.

Physical Education

Overheated!

Your body also produces waste heat. If it builds up, overheating can lead to heatstroke. Research heatstroke. Make a poster about its signs and the treatment for it.

Heat from Earth

How does your family heat the house when it's cold outside? They might use oil. They might burn gas. Some people heat their homes by using thermal heat.

In Iceland, pools of naturally heated water called hot springs warm homes and greenhouses. People also go there to swim. Hot springs are places where heat from deep inside Earth comes to the surface and warms pools of water. This heating process is caused by *geothermal energy.*

Hot springs can be found around the world. In Iceland, homes and greenhouses are warmed by heat from hot springs. People in Iceland aren't the only ones to use Earth's heat to warm or cool their houses, however.

Several feet below the ground, the soil temperature stays at an almost constant temperature. Depending on the location, the temperature of the soil below the surface ranges from 7 to 24 degrees Celsius (45 to 75 degrees Fahrenheit). During winter, the ground temperature is usually warmer than the air temperature above ground. In the summer, the ground temperature is usually cooler than the air temperature above ground. Those temperature differences can be used to make indoor temperatures warm or cool.

To make use of the temperature differences, a house must be equipped with a heat pump. A heat pump is connected to pipes buried in the ground. A special liquid moves through the pipes and into the heat pump. In the winter, the pump brings heat from the ground into the house. In the summer, the heat from the house is carried by the liquid to the underground pipes. Ducts carry the heated or cooled air throughout the house.

Think and Write

1. How else could geothermal energy be used?
2. Do you know of any other places where hot springs are found?

Hot springs and geothermal power plants rely on heat from deep inside Earth.

Spin-In™ Find out more. Log on to **www.hspscience.com**

CHAPTER 14 Review and Test Preparation

Vocabulary Review

Match the terms to the definitions below. The page numbers tell you where to look in the chapter if you need help.

light p. 568
reflection p. 569
refraction p. 571
heat p. 579
conduction p. 580
convection p. 581
radiation p. 582
energy transfer p. 589
waste heat p. 592

1. Heat that can't be used to do work is _______.

2. The bending of light is called _______.

3. The change of energy from one form to another is called _______.

4. Heat flows through a liquid or a gas by _______.

5. _______ is a form of energy that travels in straight lines.

6. The bouncing of light off an object is called _______.

7. Heat travels through solids that are touching by _______.

8. _______ moves heat through space, where there is no matter.

9. Transferred thermal energy is called _______.

Check Understanding

Write the letter of the best choice.

10. In which container does the water have the most thermal energy?

A. Beaker 1
B. Beaker 2
C. Beaker 3
D. They're equal.

11. MAIN IDEA AND DETAILS Which of the following removes waste heat?
Focus Skill
F. car radiator
G. furnace
H. heat engine
J. turbine

12. CAUSE AND EFFECT Which causes an image to form inside the eye?
Focus Skill
A. The cornea is transparent.
B. The lens bends light rays.
C. The pupil changes size.
D. The optic nerve leads to the brain.

13. Which of these is translucent?

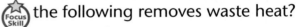

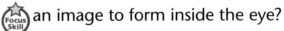

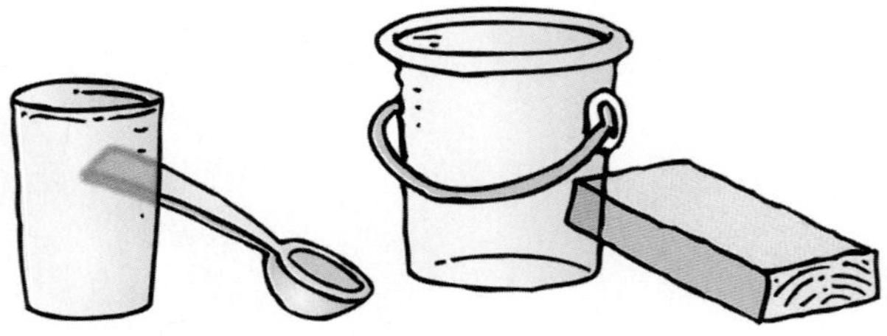

F. **G.** **H.** **J.**

14. Which energy transfers are taking place?

A. light to heat and electricity
B. electricity to heat and light
C. heat to light and electricity
D. waste heat to light and electricity

15. Kira walked by the stove and said, "Wow! That's hot!" What allowed her to feel how hot the stove was without touching it?
F. conduction
G. fuel
H. radiation
J. refraction

16. Which does a thermometer measure?
A. number of particles of matter
B. total energy of movement of particles of matter
C. fuel energy of particles of matter
D. average energy of movement of particles of matter

Inquiry Skills

17. **Predict** what will happen to the handle of a metal spoon when you put the spoon into a cup of hot cocoa. Explain your answer.

18. Suppose you measure temperature in two cups. Each holds 250 mL of water. Both begin at 80°C. Over time, Cup A cools more quickly than Cup B. What **conclusion** can you draw about what each cup is made of?

Critical Thinking

The Big Idea

19. Lenses in eyeglasses change the direction of light rays to help the lens of the eye form an image inside the eye. What process takes place in the eyeglass lenses? Explain your answer.

20. You are helping with the dishes after supper, and you notice that the pots have wooden handles. What is the reason for wooden handles on a pot? What other materials might be used to make pot handles?

UNIT E PHYSICAL SCIENCE

Visual Summary

Tell how each picture shows the **Big Idea** for its chapter.

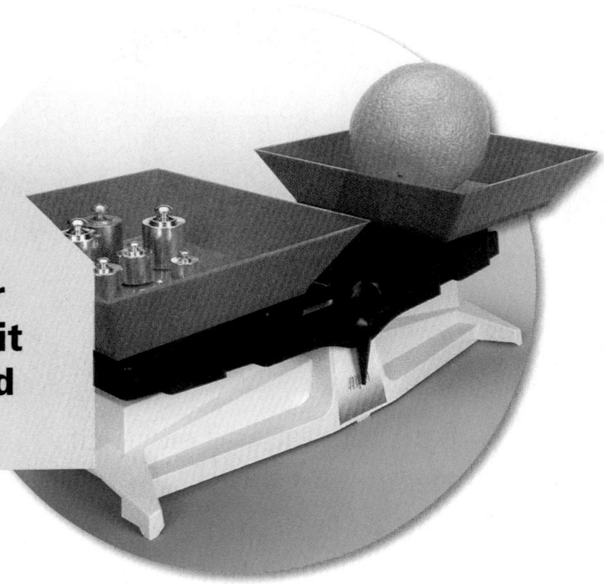

CHAPTER 11

Big Idea

The physical properties of matter can be used to identify it even if it has changed states or been mixed with other matter.

CHAPTER 12

Big Idea

Matter can undergo both physical and chemical changes.

CHAPTER 13

Big Idea

Vibrations cause sounds, which travel in wave form.

CHAPTER 14

Big Idea

Light and heat are useful forms of energy.

Forces and Motion

UNIT F
PHYSICAL SCIENCE

Unit Inquiry

Test the Shape and Size of Sails

Sailboats have large sails that catch the wind, which causes the boats to move. The sails on a ship can be many shapes and sizes. What kind of sail is able to catch the most wind and make a boat move the fastest? Plan and conduct an experiment to find out.

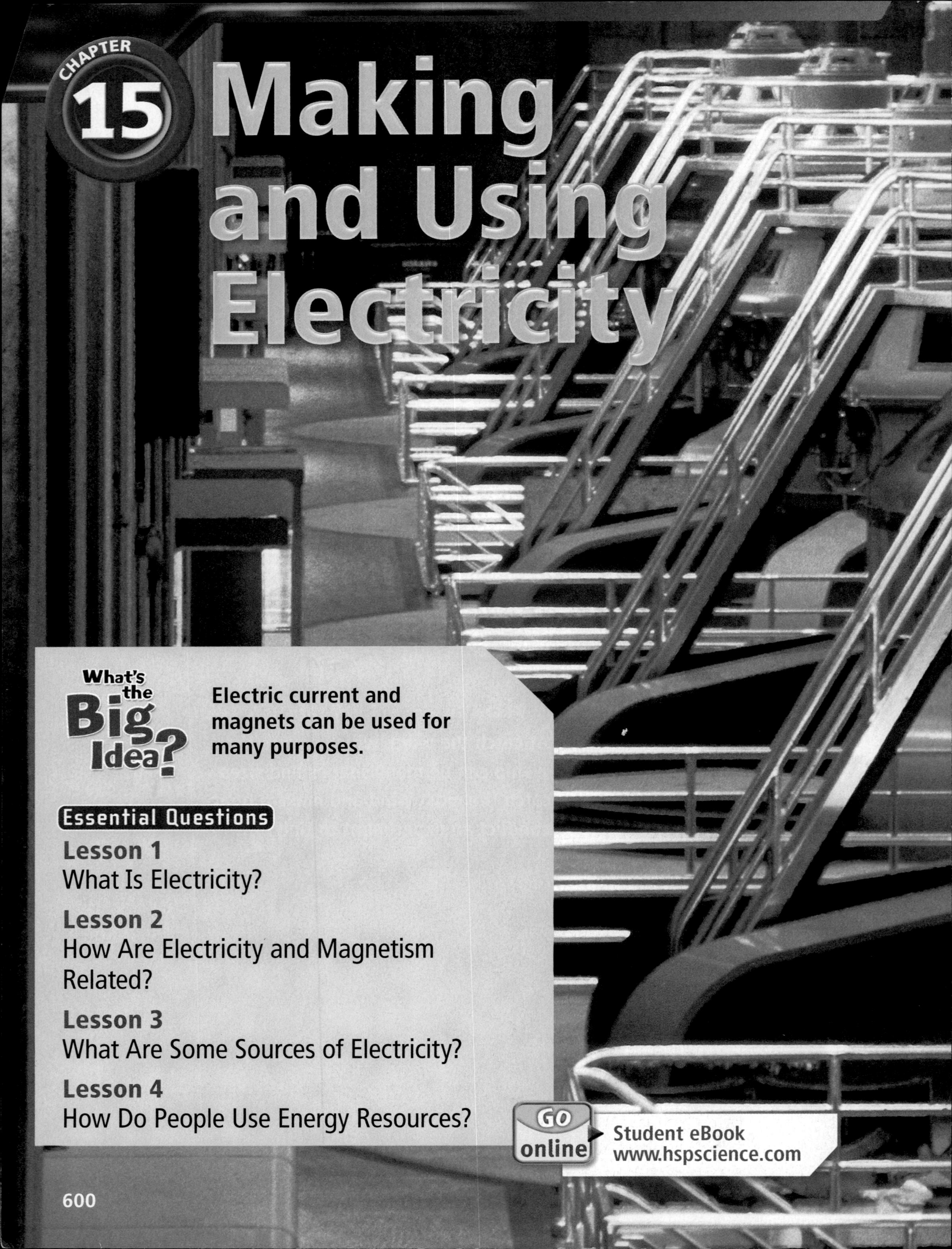

CHAPTER 15

Making and Using Electricity

What's the Big Idea?

Electric current and magnets can be used for many purposes.

Essential Questions

Lesson 1
What Is Electricity?

Lesson 2
How Are Electricity and Magnetism Related?

Lesson 3
What Are Some Sources of Electricity?

Lesson 4
How Do People Use Energy Resources?

GO online ▸ Student eBook www.hspscience.com

Turbines below a dam

What do YOU wonder?

Turning Wheels? These huge machines are turbines and generators. They produce electricity. What might that electricity be used for? How does this relate to the **Big Idea?**

LESSON 1

Essential Question

What Is Electricity?

Investigate how to light a light bulb.

Read and Learn about electricity and how electric charges move.

Fast Fact

Ceramic Insulators
Some insulators are made of a ceramic material through which electricity can't flow. Sparks heat the air to 3000°C (5400°F) or more around the insulators shown here! In the Investigate, you'll see what kinds of paths let electricity flow.

Ceramic insulator

Vocabulary Preview

static electricity [STAT•ik ee•lek•TRIS•uh•tee] An electrical charge that builds up on an object (p. 606)

current electricity [KER•uhnt ee•lek•TRIS•uh•tee] A steady movement of charges through certain materials (p. 608)

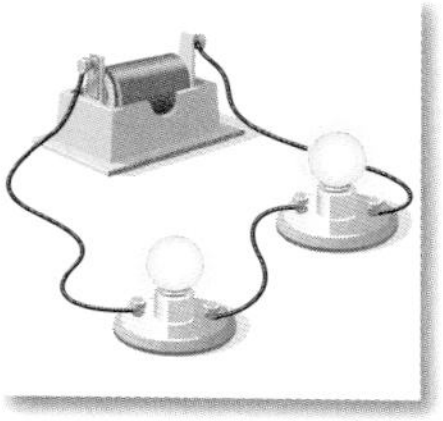

series circuit [SIR•eez SER•kit] A circuit that has only one path for an electric current to follow (p. 610)

parallel circuit [PAIR•uh•lel SER•kit] A circuit that has more than one path for an electric current to follow (p. 610)

conductor [kuhn•DUK•ter] Materials that let electric charges travel through them easily (p. 612)

insulator [IN•suh•layt•er] A material that does not let current electricity move through it easily (p. 612)

Light a Bulb

Guided Inquiry

Start with Questions

This girl is turning off the light before she leaves the room.

- Why isn't the light bulb always on?
- How does the light switch work?

Investigate to find out. Then read to find out more.

Prepare to Investigate

Inquiry Skill Tip

Record your data accurately. Mistakes in your data mean your conclusions will be incorrect.

Materials

- D-cell battery
- flashlight bulb
- masking tape
- insulated electric wire, about 30 cm, with ends stripped

Make an Observation Chart

Best Result:

Follow This Procedure

CAUTION: **Don't touch the sharp ends of the wire!**

1. Using these materials, how can you make the bulb light? Predict the kind of setup that will make the bulb light.
2. Draw a picture of your prediction.
3. Test your prediction. Put the materials together the way your drawing shows.
4. Record your results. Beside your drawing, write *yes* if the bulb lit. Write *no* if it didn't.
5. Make more predictions and drawings. Test them all. Record the results of each try. Draw the setup that works the best.

Draw Conclusions

1. How must the materials be put together to make the bulb light?

2. **Inquiry Skill** Look at your drawings and notes. How did you record data? Scientists publish their results so that others can check them. Could someone use your records to double-check your tests? Explain.

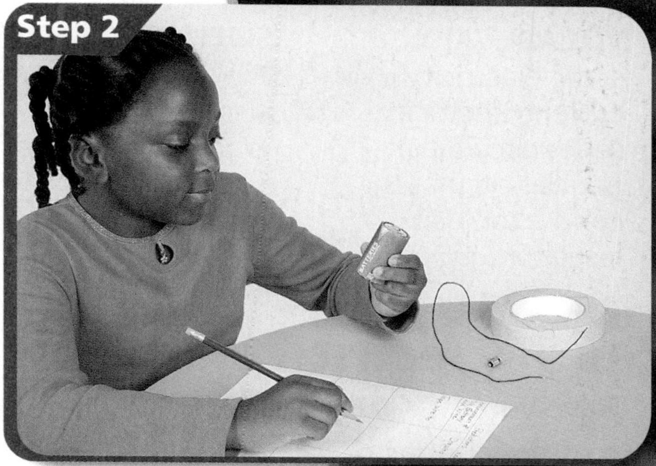

Step 2

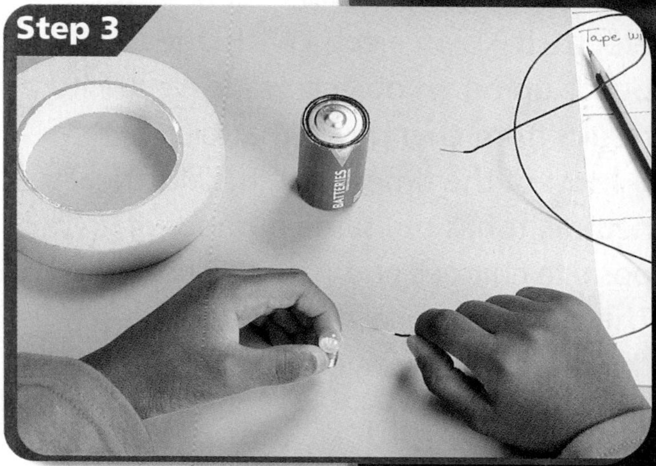

Step 3

Independent Inquiry

Predict the kind of setup that will light two bulbs at the same time. Test your prediction.

Read and Learn

VOCABULARY
static electricity p. 606
current electricity p. 608
series circuit p. 610
parallel circuit p. 610
conductor p. 612
insulator p. 612

SCIENCE CONCEPTS
- what electricity is
- how electricity moves

Focus Skill SEQUENCE
Look for the steps by which electricity is generated and the ways it moves.

Static Electricity

Have you ever pulled your sweater out of the clothes dryer and found your socks stuck to it? If so, you have seen static electricity in action. **Static electricity** is an electrical charge that builds up on an object. Static electricity results from changes in matter.

Most of the time, matter is electrically neutral. It has the same number of positive charges and negative charges. The charges cancel each other out, so the matter has no electrical charge.

In the dryer, your socks rub against other clothes. Some clothes gain negative charges. These clothes end up with a negative electrical charge. Other clothes lose negative charges and end up with a positive electrical charge.

Objects with opposite charges attract, or pull, each other. That's why your socks stick to your sweater. Objects with the same charge repel, or push away, each other.

Static electricity stays in an object until something happens to remove it. Pulling your socks off your sweater forces charges to move.

◀ **What electric charges make this girl's hair stand on end?**

Objects with the same charges move away from each other. What happens if their charges are different? ▼

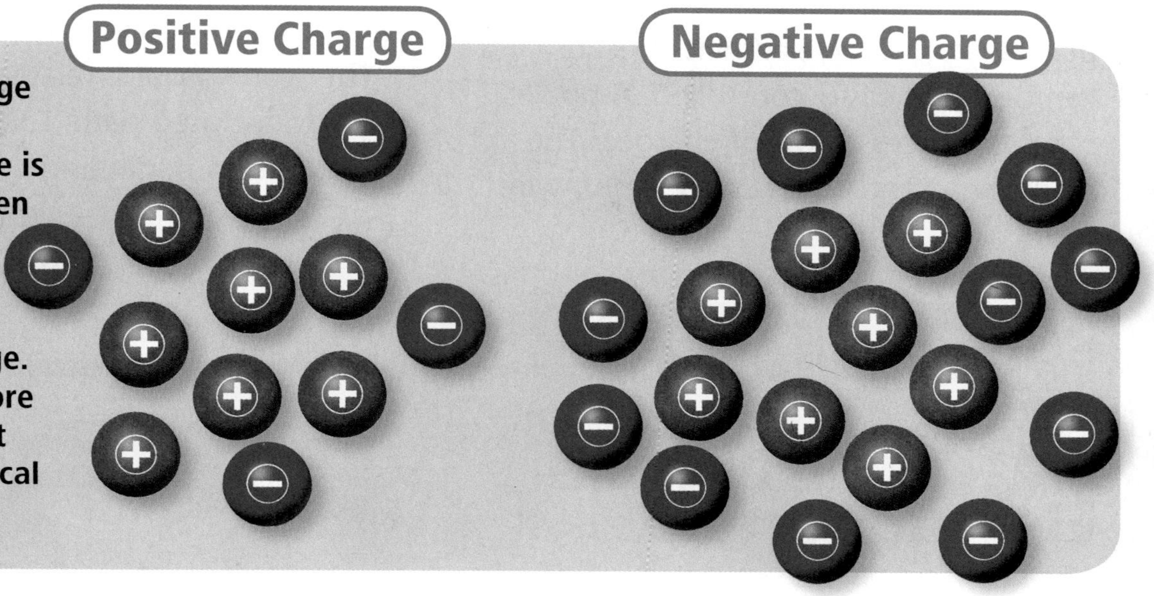

A positive charge is labeled ⊕. A negative charge is labeled ⊖. When an object has more ⊕s than ⊖s, it has a ⊕ electrical charge. When it has more ⊖s than ⊕s, it has a ⊖ electrical charge.

You hear a crackle of sparks as extra negative charges move between the sweater and the socks. Then the socks aren't charged anymore.

Lightning is caused by static electricity. During a storm, ice crystals in clouds rub together and gain negative charges. The ground beneath the negative cloud takes on a positive charge. Soon the difference in charges becomes large. Negative charges move from the clouds to the ground as a giant spark. Flash! You see lightning.

Focus Skill SEQUENCE **Explain the sequence of events that leads to a flash of lightning.**

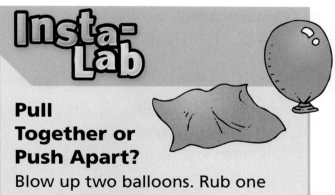

Insta-Lab

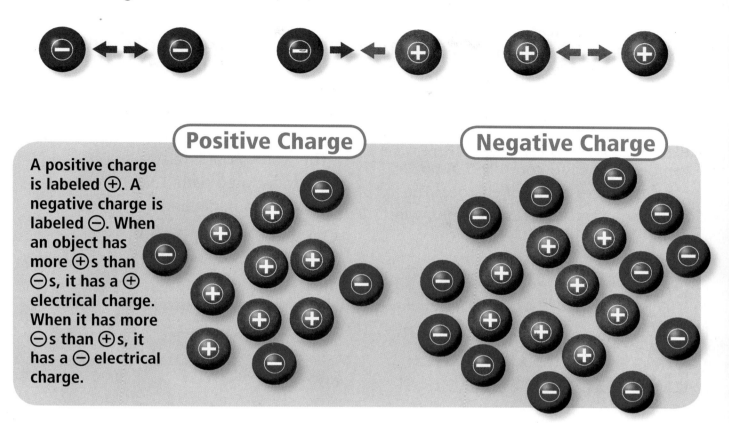

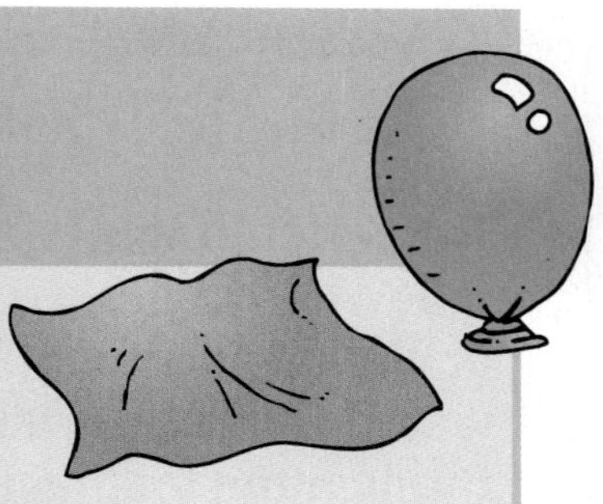

Pull Together or Push Apart?

Blow up two balloons. Rub one with wool. Hold it up to a wall. What happens? Tie a string to each balloon. Rub the balloons together. Hold them by their strings. Put them close together. What happens? Why?

Current Electricity

Static electricity is one form of electricity. Another form is **current electricity**, or a steady stream of charges. In current electricity, an electric current moves through a material such as a copper wire.

Current electricity is more useful to people than static electricity because it can be more easily controlled. A power plant produces a flow of charges. The plant then sends the current along wires to homes and businesses, where people use it to provide light and heat and to run machines.

In the Investigate, you lit a bulb by using an electric current. The battery was the source of the current. The current moved along a path that linked the battery and bulb. The path that an electric current follows is a circuit.

The word *circuit* is related to *circle* and refers to a closed path. Like a circle, a circuit has no beginning or end.

Science Up Close

Water Current and Electric Current

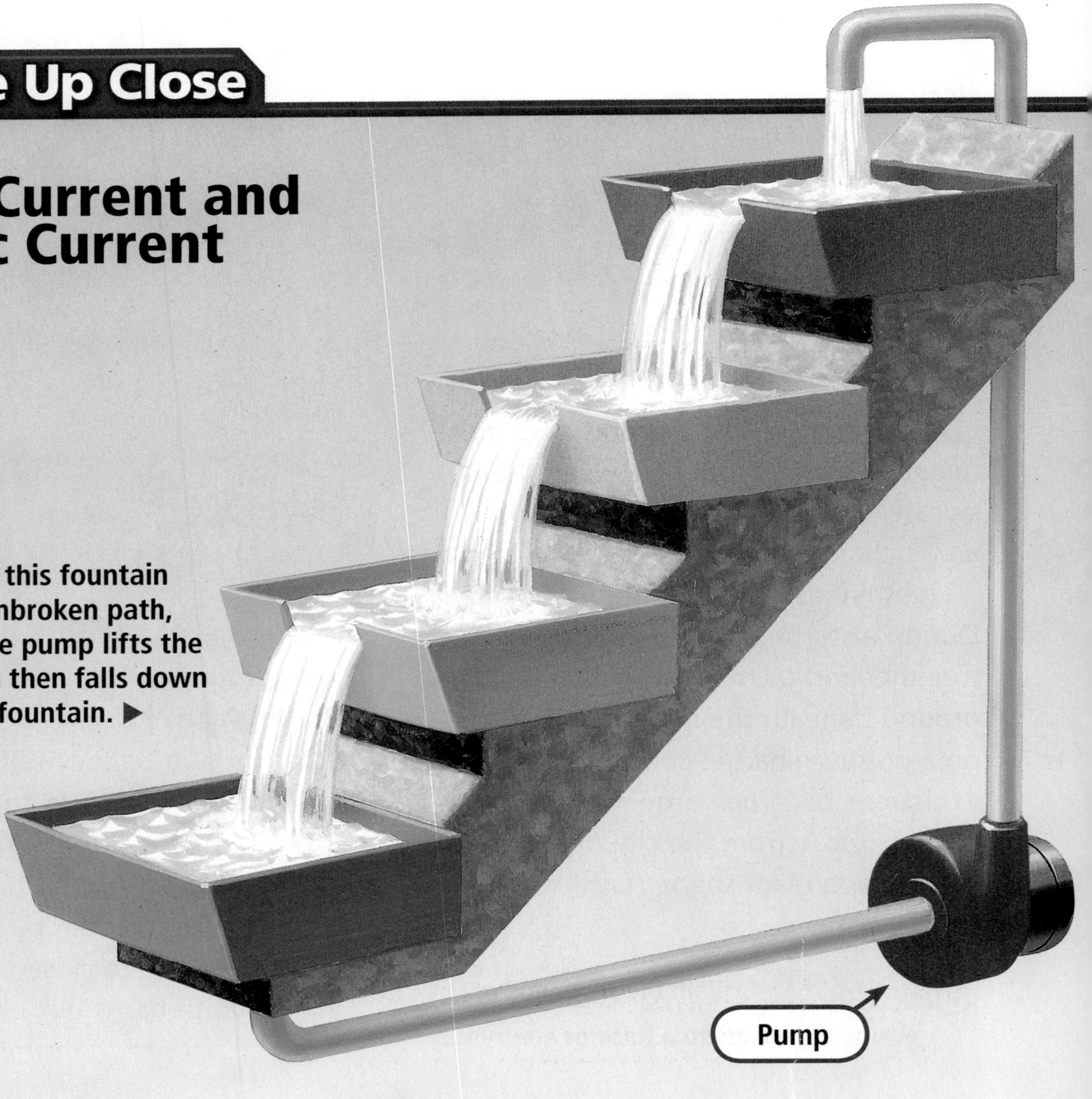

The water in this fountain follows an unbroken path, or circuit. The pump lifts the water, which then falls down through the fountain. ▶

Charges flow around a circuit without starting or stopping. For any electrical machine to work, the circuit must be complete, or closed.

In the Investigate, the bulb lit only when the path of wire connecting it to the battery was closed. You needed a circuit with no gaps in it. Unhooking a wire at any point broke the circuit, leaving it incomplete, or open. Then the bulb stayed dark because no electric current flowed through it.

Light bulbs aren't the only things that work when they are part of a closed circuit. Turning the key in a car's ignition closes a circuit. The closed circuit starts the car's engine. Pushing the power button on a computer closes a circuit and starts the computer. Closing an electrical circuit can make a doorbell ring or the beaters of an electric mixer spin.

Focus Skill SEQUENCE **What happens when a driver presses on the steering wheel to honk the horn of a car?**

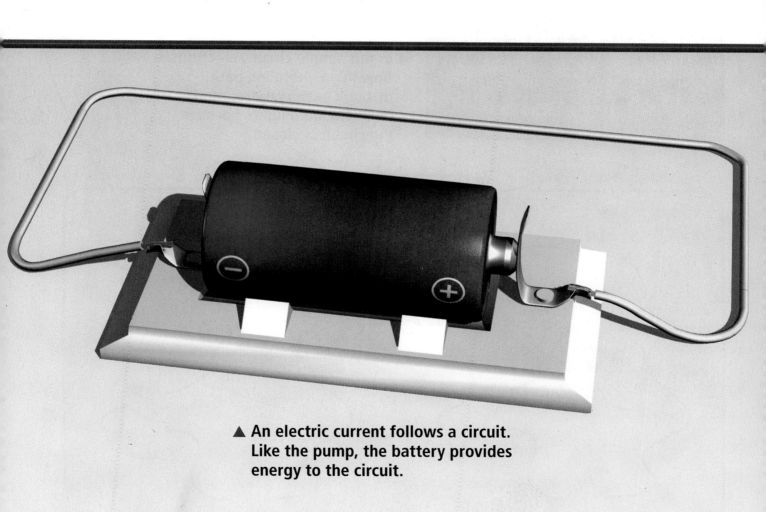

▲ **An electric current follows a circuit. Like the pump, the battery provides energy to the circuit.**

For more links and animations, go to **www.hspscience.com**

Electrical Circuits

Electrical circuits are not all laid out in the same way. A circuit that has only one path for the current to follow is a **series circuit**.

A simple example has two bulbs, one battery, and wires. The current flows in a path from the battery, through the first bulb, through the second bulb, and back to the battery. While both bulbs are in place and undamaged, they glow. But the flow of charges stops if either bulb burns out or is unscrewed. If one part of a series circuit fails, the whole circuit fails.

A **parallel circuit** has more than one path for the electric current to follow. If something stops charges from moving along one path, they can take another.

In the pictures of a parallel circuit, you can see two closed paths. The current can travel through both bulbs and light them both. If one bulb is missing or damaged, however, the current can still travel through the other bulb.

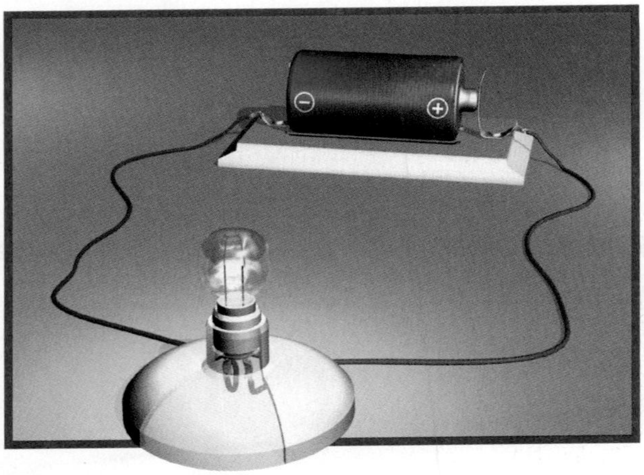

◀ **In this simple circuit, electrons flow in an unbroken path through battery, wires, and bulb. The bulb lights because the circuit is closed.**

Series Circuit

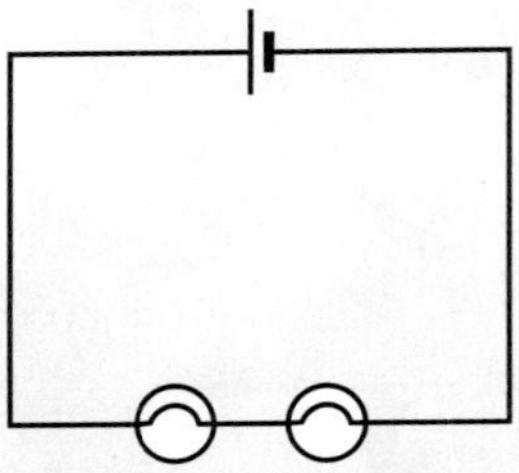

◀ **More than one item can be powered along a series circuit.**

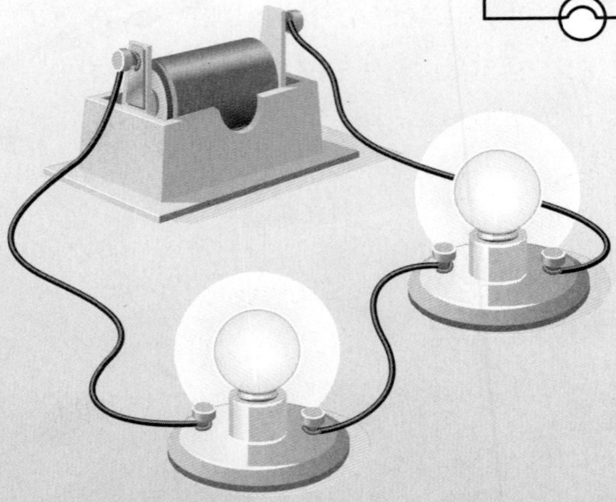

▲ **A closed series circuit can light two bulbs.**

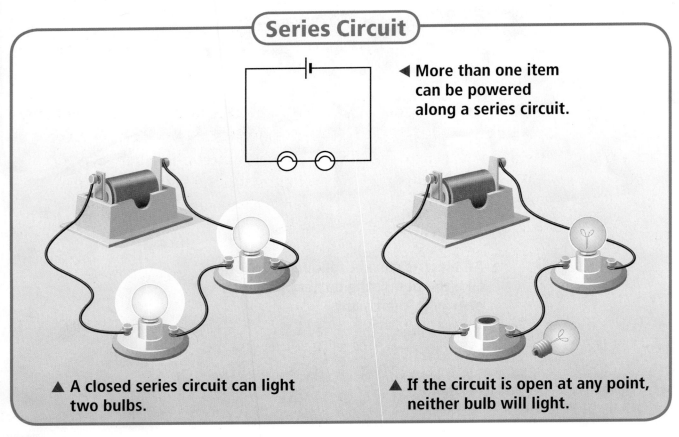

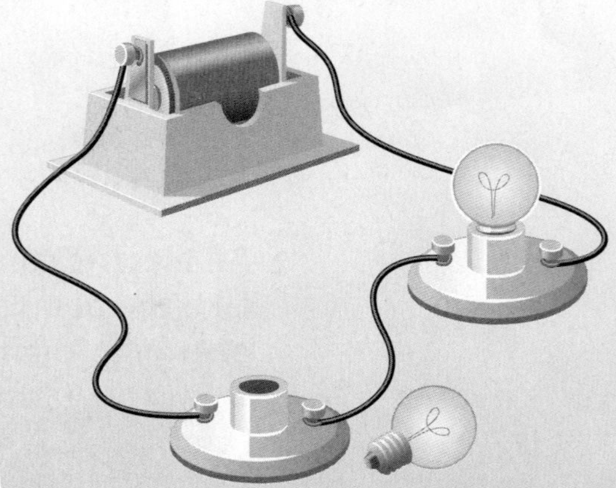

▲ **If the circuit is open at any point, neither bulb will light.**

Parallel Circuit

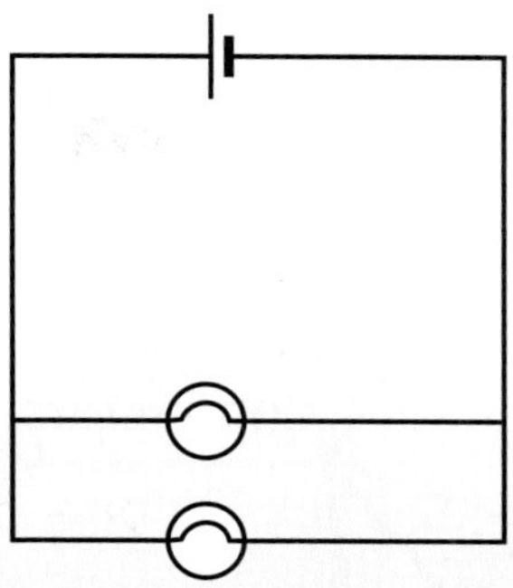

◀ A parallel circuit has more than one path.

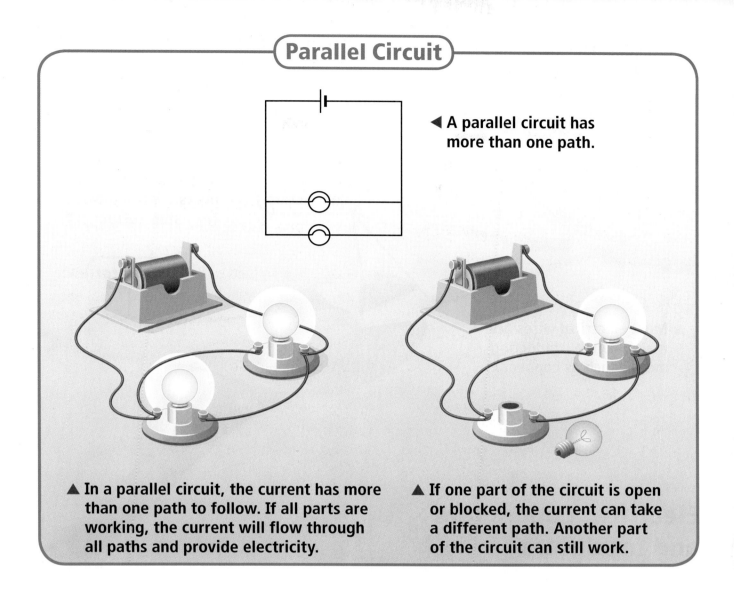

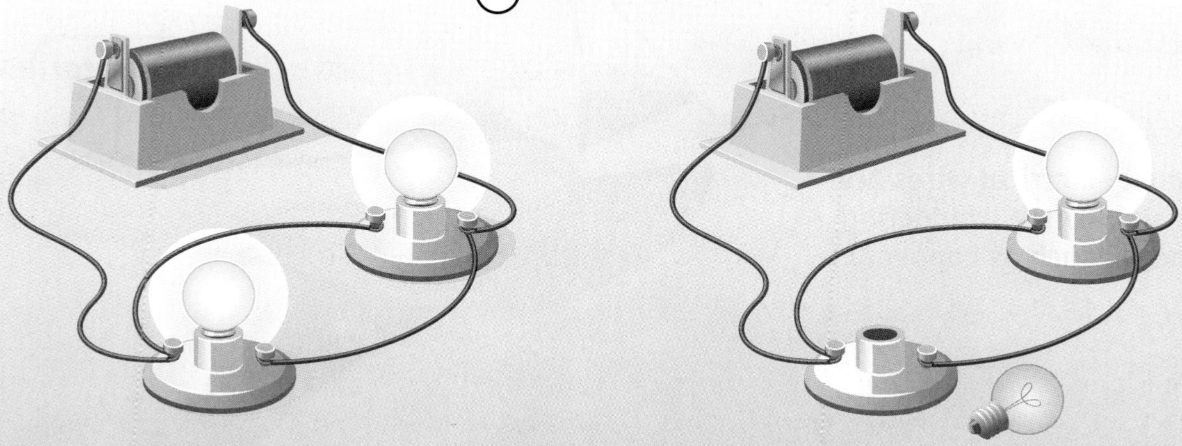

▲ **In a parallel circuit, the current has more than one path to follow. If all parts are working, the current will flow through all paths and provide electricity.**

▲ **If one part of the circuit is open or blocked, the current can take a different path. Another part of the circuit can still work.**

Breaking one path doesn't stop the current. When one part of a parallel circuit fails, other parts of the circuit continue to work. The electric current still has a path along which it can travel.

Think of electrical circuits as streets in a city. A series circuit is like a single street that goes around in a circle. If the street is blocked at any point, all traffic stops. A parallel circuit is more like several streets that cross one another. If traffic backs up on one street, cars and buses can turn and take a different route.

Series and parallel circuits make many devices work. In a flashlight, a series circuit lets current flow between the batteries and the bulb. Homes and schools have many lights. These lights are wired in parallel circuits. Any of these lights can work alone, or many can work at the same time. If one light burns out or is turned off, the others can still work because the electric current travels through parallel circuits.

Focus Skill SEQUENCE **Describe the path of current in a two-bulb series circuit.**

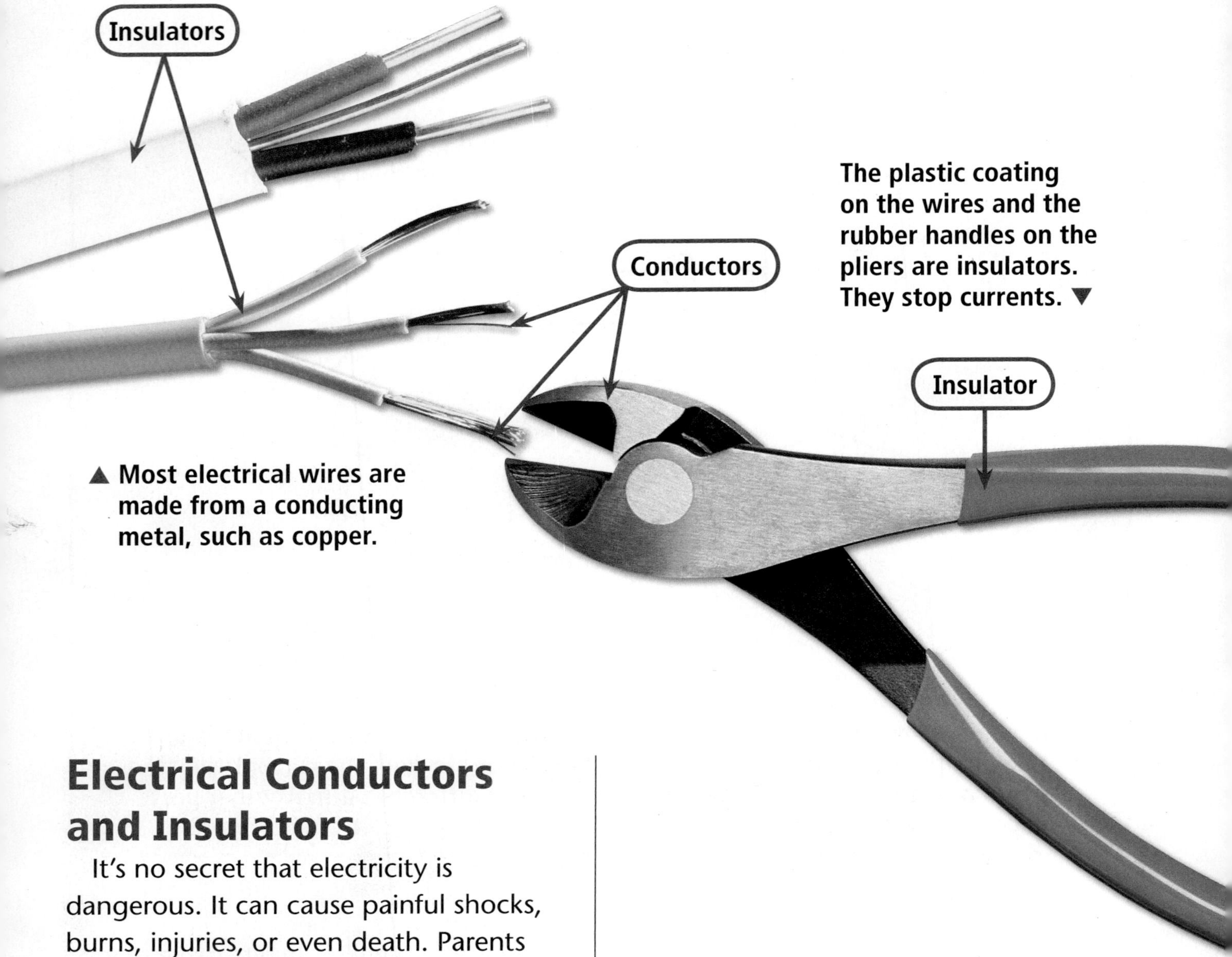

The plastic coating on the wires and the rubber handles on the pliers are insulators. They stop currents. ▼

▲ Most electrical wires are made from a conducting metal, such as copper.

Electrical Conductors and Insulators

It's no secret that electricity is dangerous. It can cause painful shocks, burns, injuries, or even death. Parents often put plastic covers over wall outlets. The covers stop small children from poking their fingers into the outlets. Yet it's safe to touch the electrical cord of a lamp or an appliance. Have you ever wondered why?

The answer is connected with the properties of materials. Some materials, called **conductors**, let electric charges move through them easily. Other materials, called **insulators**, do not.

Most metals are good conductors of electricity. That's why the working parts of an electrical outlet are metal. Most electrical wires are metal, too—usually copper. You should never touch any bare metal electrical wires at home. The electrical cords of appliances have a coating of plastic or rubber around the metal wire to protect you when you handle them. Plastic and rubber are good insulators. Many everyday things do their jobs safely and well because of the way insulators and conductors work together.

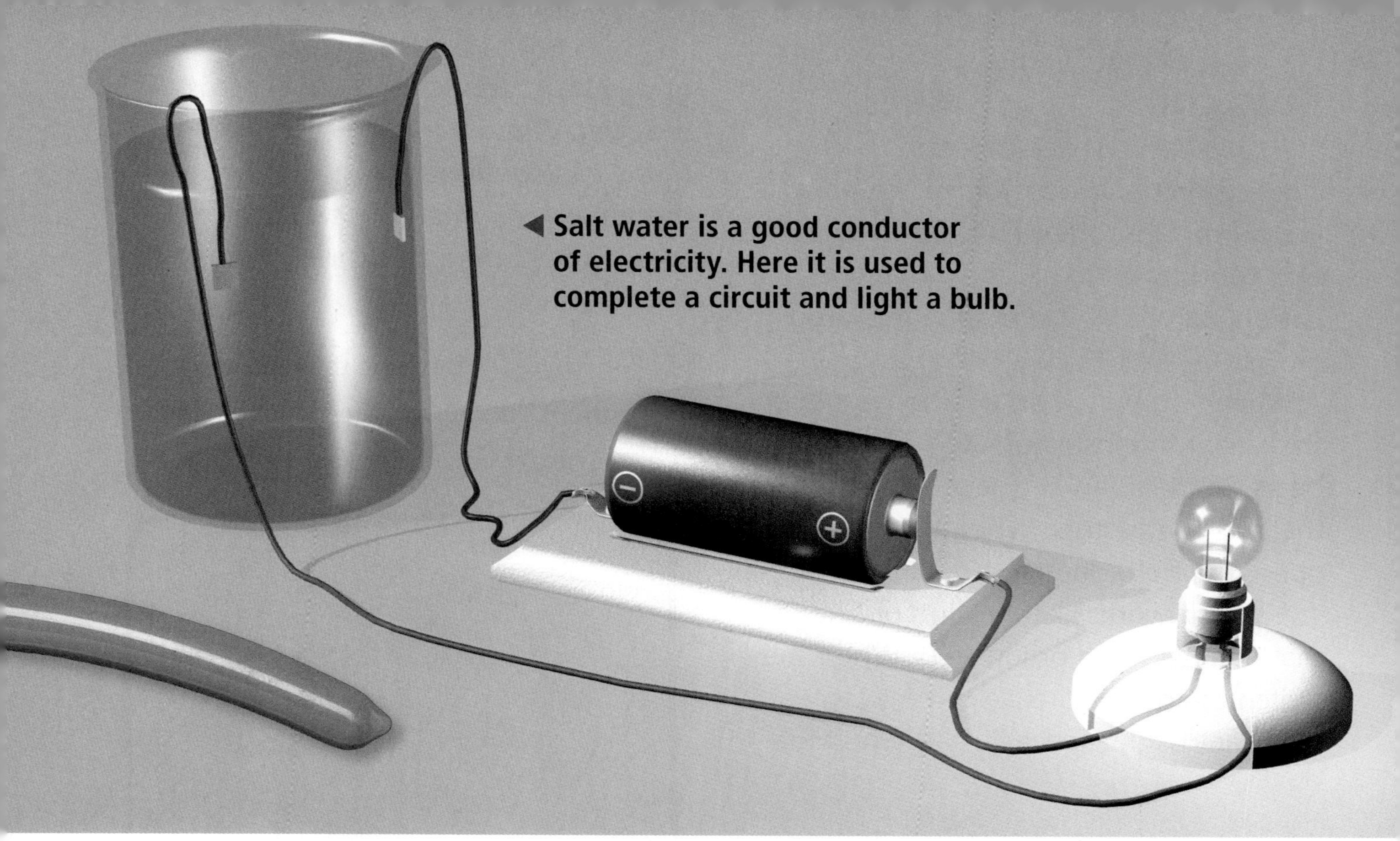

◀ **Salt water is a good conductor of electricity. Here it is used to complete a circuit and light a bulb.**

Light comes from a bulb because an electric current makes a thin wire inside it glow. ▶

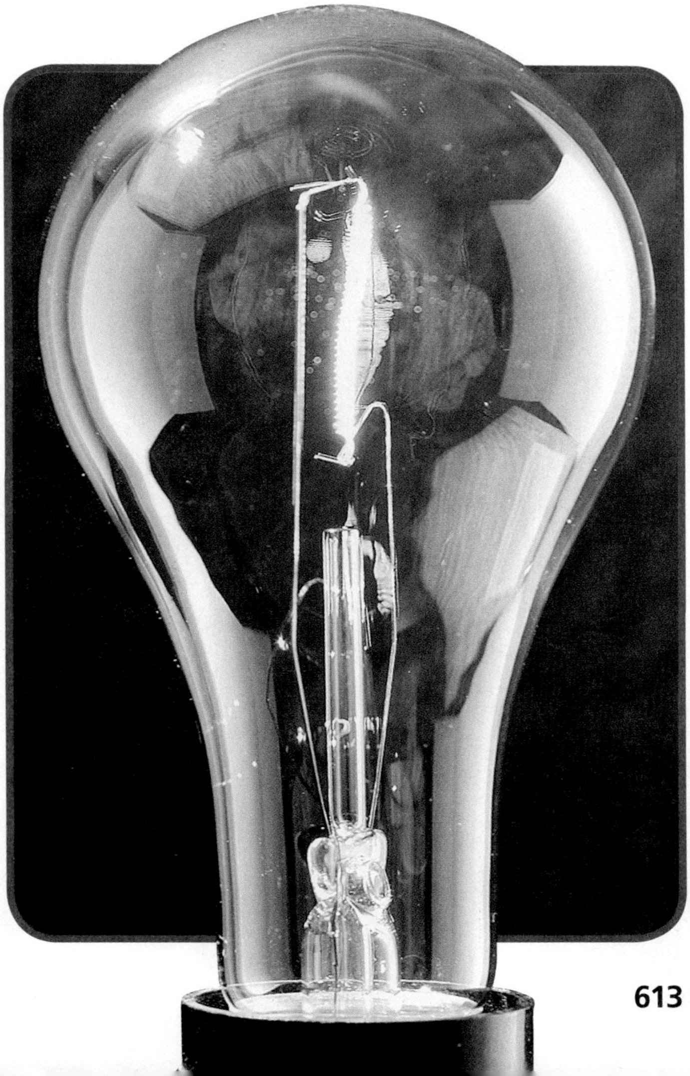

If you look at the bottom of a light bulb, you will see the small metal tip that conducts the current from the socket into the bulb. Just above the tip, you will see a black band. This band is an insulator. It does not allow the current to flow from the metal tip to the metal screw threads above it.

Focus Skill SEQUENCE **What happens when a current reaches a conductor? What happens when it reaches an insulator?**

Switches

A switch is a device that opens or closes a circuit. When you switch on a lamp, you close the circuit. You allow two conductors to touch so that the current can flow. The bulb in the lamp glows.

When you switch off a lamp, you open the circuit. An insulator—which may be as simple as an air space—separates the two conductors. When the circuit is open, the bulb doesn't glow.

A switch works like the kind of bridge that can be raised or lowered. When the switch opens the circuit, current can't travel across the space, just as when the bridge is up, traffic can't travel across the river. When the bridge is lowered, traffic can continue across the river. In the same way, when the switch closes the circuit, current can travel through it once again.

Focus Skill SEQUENCE **Describe the flow of current through an electric heater when the heater is switched on.**

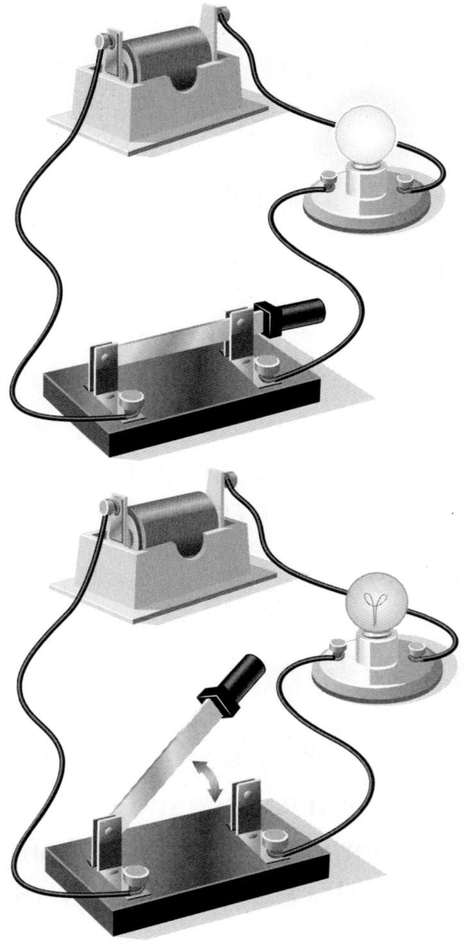

Find the switches in these pictures. Why is the bulb glowing in one circuit but not the other?

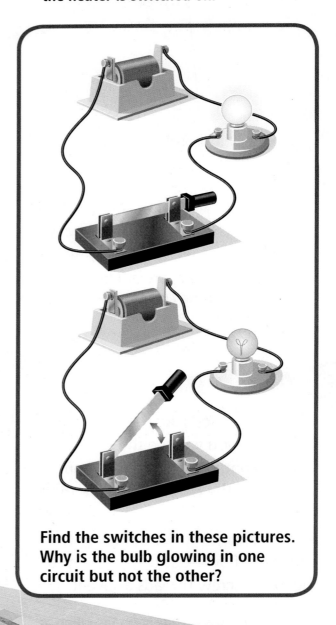

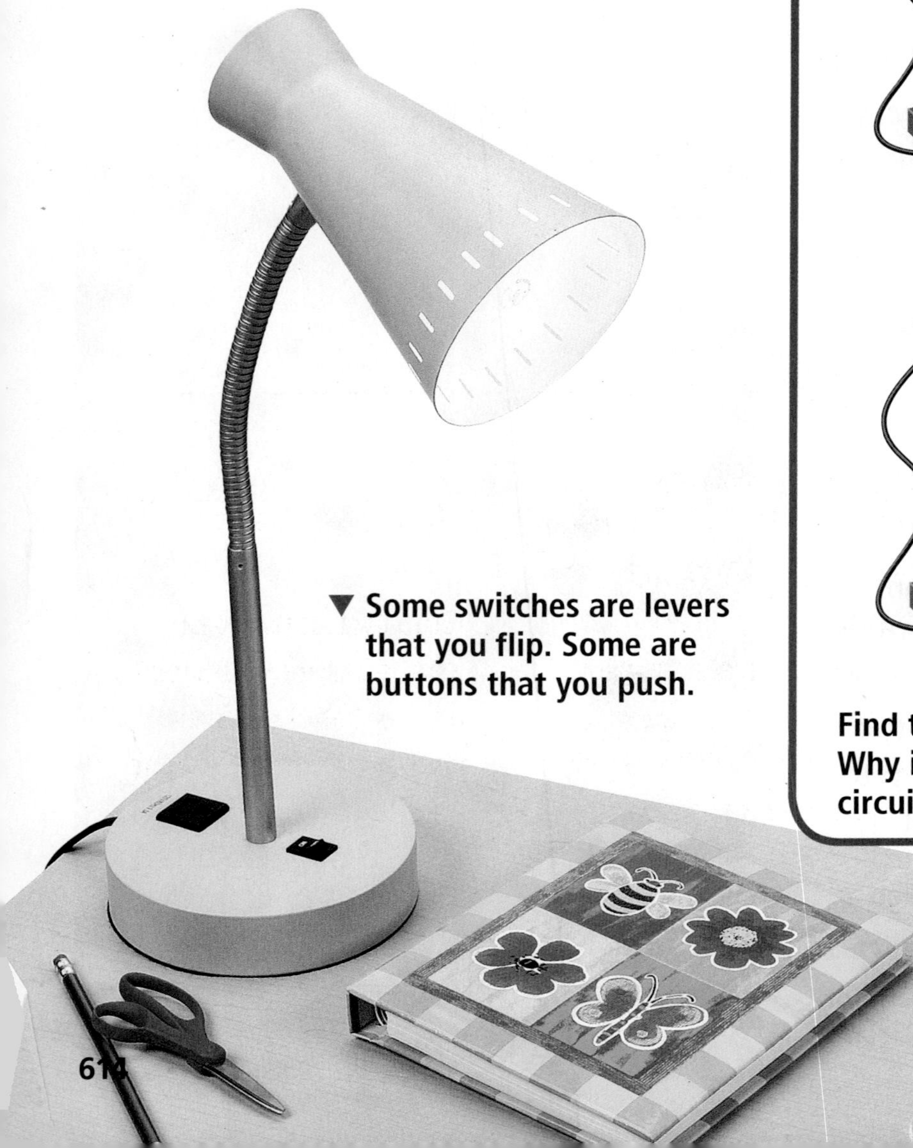

▼ **Some switches are levers that you flip. Some are buttons that you push.**

Lesson Review

Essential Question

What is electricity?

In this lesson, you learned that electricity is made of positive and negative charges. It can flow through circuits. Some materials conduct electricity well and some do not.

1. **Focus Skill SEQUENCE** Draw and complete a graphic organizer to show the path of electricity through a series circuit.

2. **SUMMARIZE** Write a summary of this lesson. Begin with this sentence: *Electrical charges can be positive or negative.*

3. **DRAW CONCLUSIONS** Suppose you want to decorate a room for a party. You plan to buy strings of lights. Which type of circuit would be better to use? Why?

4. **VOCABULARY** How are insulators and conductors different? Why are both important?

Test Prep

5. **CRITICAL THINKING** How are static electricity and current electricity alike? How are they different?

6. What does a switch bring together?
   A. circuits
   B. conductors
   C. currents
   D. charges

Make Connections

Writing

Expository Writing

Write a **report** about a charge that travels through a circuit. Tell how it moves from an energy plant—where electricity is generated—to the lights in your home and back to the energy plant.

Math

Compare Whole Numbers

We measure electric energy in units called watts. Which light bulb do you think would burn brighter—a 100-watt bulb or a 60-watt bulb? Explain.

Music

Compose a Tune

Connect some bells and buzzers in series and parallel circuits with switches. Use the switches to make the bells and buzzers play a rhythm or a tune.

LESSON 2

Essential Question

How Are Electricity and Magnetism Related?

Investigate how electricity makes a magnet.

Read and Learn how magnetism and electricity are related.

Fast Fact

Mighty Magnets!
The world's strongest magnets are made of the metals iron and neodymium (nee•oh•DIM•ee•uhm) with boron. A tiny, 50-mm (2-in.) magnet made of these materials can lift 30 kg (66 lb)! This sculpture uses pairs of these strong magnets. In the Investigate, you'll learn how to make a different kind of magnet.

Magnetic sculpture

Vocabulary Preview

magnet [MAG•nit] An object that attracts iron and a few other (but not all) metals (p. 620)

---

magnetic poles [mag•NET•ik POHLZ] The parts of a magnet at which its force is strongest (p. 622)

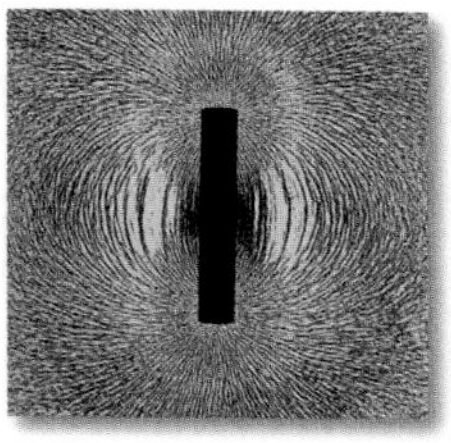

magnetic field [mag•NET•ik FEELD] The space around a magnet in which the force of the magnet acts (p. 623)

---

electromagnet [ee•lek•troh•MAG•nit] A temporary magnet caused by an electric current (p. 624)

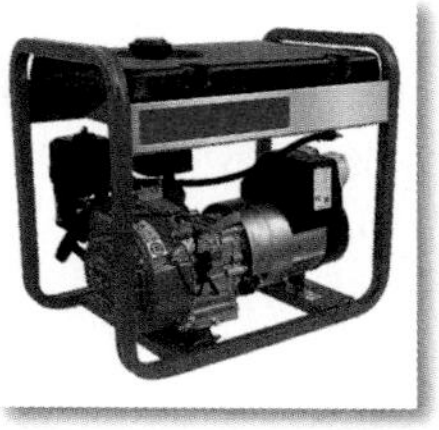

generator [JEN•er•ayt•er] A device that produces an electric current (p. 626)

---

electric motor [ee•LEK•trik MOHT•er] A device that changes electrical energy to energy of motion (p. 627)

Investigate

Can Electricity Make a Magnet?

Guided Inquiry

Start with Questions

This doorbell has chimes that sound when someone pushes the button outside the door.

- How does electricity make these chimes ring?
- Why don't the chimes ring all the time?

Investigate to find out. Then read to find out more.

Prepare to Investigate

Inquiry Skill Tip

When you compare things, remember to look for both similarities and differences.

Materials

- bar magnet
- small compass
- sheet of cardboard
- tape
- D-cell battery
- 30-cm length of insulated wire with stripped ends

Make an Observation Chart

Bar Magnet	Battery

Follow This Procedure

1. Move a bar magnet around a compass. **Observe** what the compass needle does. Put the magnet away.
2. Tape the battery to the cardboard. Tape one end of the wire to the flat end of the battery. Leave the other end loose.
3. Tape the wire to the cardboard in a loop, as shown in the picture.
4. Place the compass on top of the wire. **Observe** the direction in which the compass needle points.
5. Touch the loose end of the wire to the free end of the battery. **Observe** what the compass needle does. **Record** your observations on a chart.

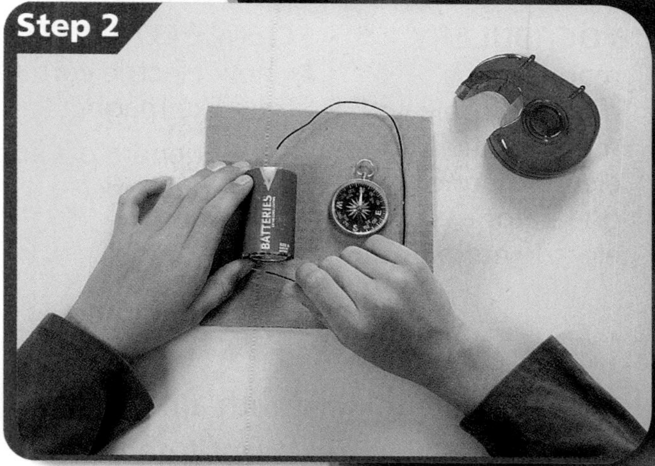

Step 2

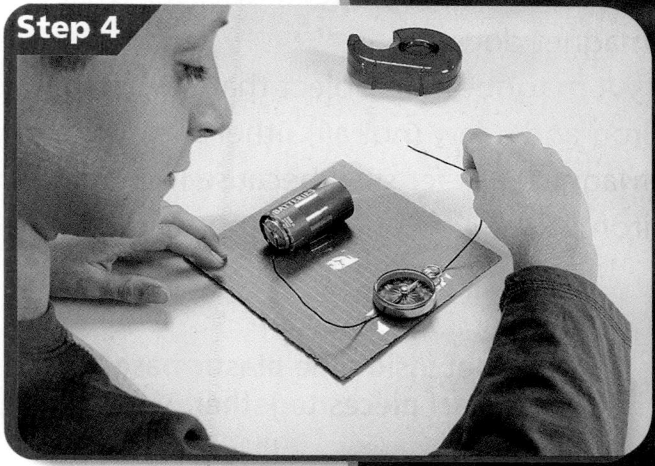
Step 4

Draw Conclusions

1. How does a magnet affect a compass needle?
2. How does an electric current affect a compass needle?
3. **Inquiry Skill** Compare electricity and magnetism. How are they alike?

Independent Inquiry

Repeat Steps 4 and 5 with the compass *under* the wire. Compare your observations.

Read and Learn

VOCABULARY
magnet p. 620
magnetic pole p. 622
magnetic field p. 623
electromagnet p. 624
generator p. 626
electric motor p. 627

SCIENCE CONCEPTS
- how electric currents are like magnets
- how generators and motors work

Focus Skill COMPARE AND CONTRAST
Look for ways in which magnets and electric currents are alike and different.

Magnets

Have you ever played with a magnet? If you haven't, you may want to now! As you move a magnet around and bring it close to objects, you can discover what a magnet does.

A **magnet** is an object that attracts iron and a few (not all) other metals. Magnets attract steel because it contains iron. When you bring an iron object or a steel object close to a magnet, the object moves toward the magnet. Try this for yourself. Place a steel paper clip near a magnet. What happens? Try the same thing with a plastic paper clip. How do your results compare?

All magnets attract iron, but they may not look alike. Some magnets are shaped like bars. Others are U-shaped. Some magnets that stick to refrigerator doors are thin, flat shapes.

A magnet inside the plastic base holds these steel pieces together. ▼

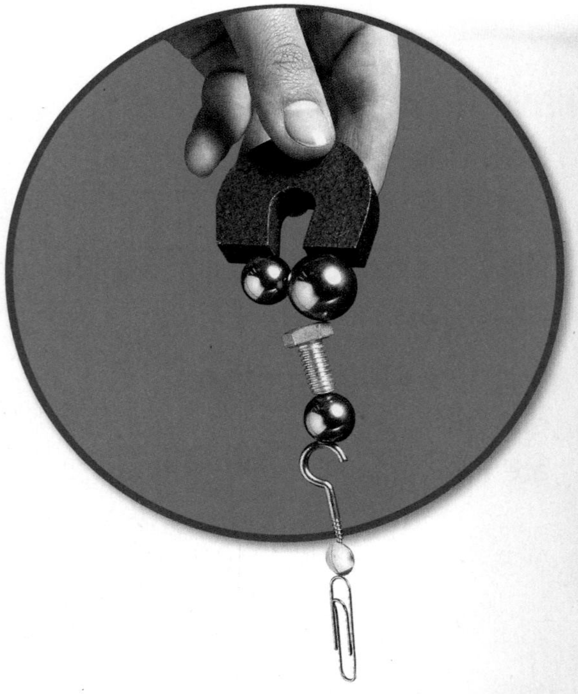

▲ The horseshoe magnet attracts these metal objects. What metal do the objects contain?

Some magnets are shaped like bars.

Why do these plastic letters stick to this refrigerator door? ▶

Distance affects the strength of a magnet's attraction. A small steel object that is close to a magnet moves toward it. However, if the same object is farther away, it will not move toward the magnet.

Other forces can overcome the force of a magnet. Refrigerator magnets stick well to the door, but you can easily pull them off.

Barriers can interfere with a magnet's pull, too. A refrigerator magnet may hold one or two sheets of paper to the door, but if you put too many sheets under it, the magnet will fall.

Magnets can make some other objects magnetic. For example, if you rub a needle over a magnet several times in the same direction, the needle will become magnetic enough to pick up other needles.

Focus Skill COMPARE AND CONTRAST **How are all magnets alike? How are they different?**

Magnetic Poles and Magnetic Fields

A magnet has two places at which its force is the strongest. Each of these is called a **magnetic pole**, or *pole* for short. If you tie a string around the middle of a bar magnet and let it swing, one end will point north. That end is the magnet's north-seeking pole. It is often marked with an *N*. The end that points south is often marked *S*.

Forces between magnetic poles act like forces between electrical charges. Opposite poles attract, and like poles repel. If you hold two S poles or two N poles near each other, they push apart. If you hold an N pole and an S pole near each other, they attract.

Magnets of every shape have N and S poles. Try holding two round refrigerator magnets close together. If you turn them in one direction, they attract each other. If you turn them in the other direction, they repel each other.

Magnets keep their poles even if you change their shape. If you cut a bar magnet into pieces, each piece would be a magnet with both an N pole and an S pole.

Magnetic Poles

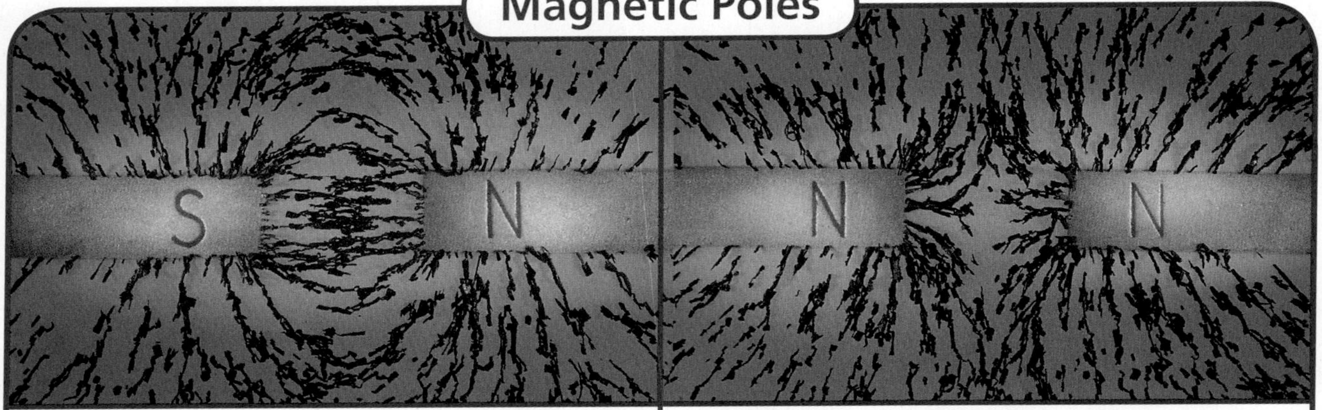

Putting the opposite poles of magnets near each other causes the magnets to pull toward each other.

Putting the like poles of magnets near each other causes the magnets to push away from each other.

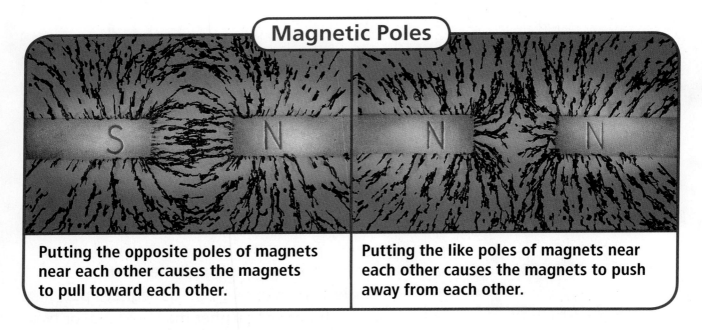

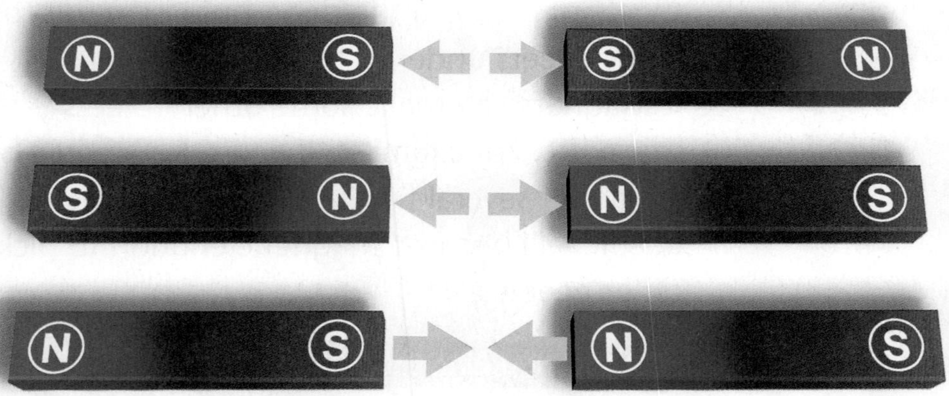

◀ **All magnets have N and S poles. Poles that are the same repel, or push apart. Poles that are opposite attract, or pull together.**

Magnetic Field

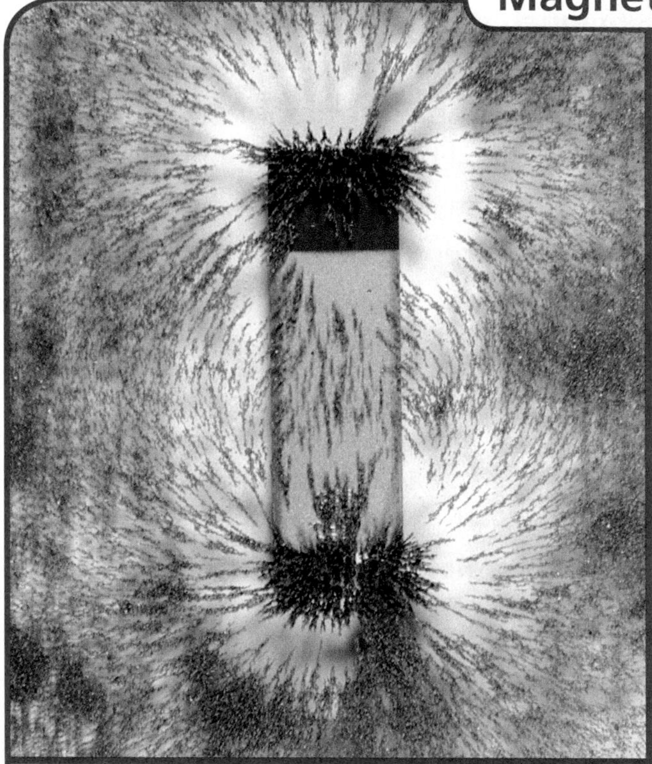

A bar magnet moves iron filings into the shape of the magnet's field.

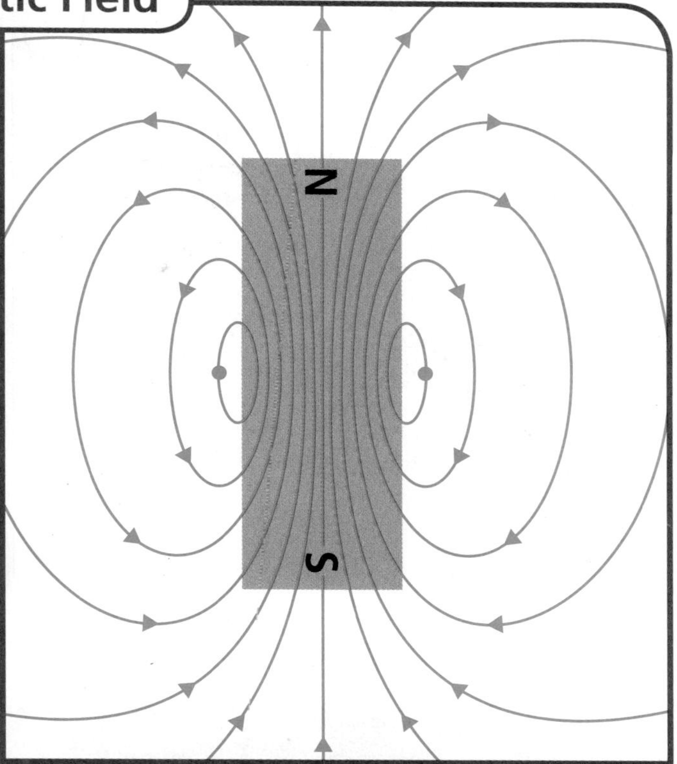

The shape of a magnetic field depends on the shape of the magnet. A magnetic field forms loops all around this bar magnet.

You can use a compass to see a magnet's force. If you put a compass close to a bar magnet, the needle will point toward the magnet's N pole and away from the magnet's S pole.

A **magnetic field** is the space around a magnet in which the force of the magnet acts. If you put iron filings around the magnet, you will be able to see the shape of the magnet's field. The filings will form circles that start and end at the poles, where the magnet's pull is the strongest.

Focus Skill **COMPARE AND CONTRAST**

How are a magnet's magnetic force and magnetic field different?

Insta-Lab

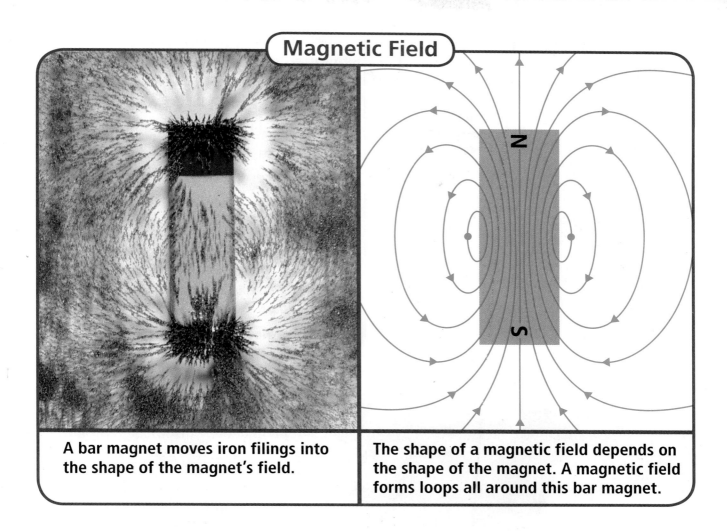

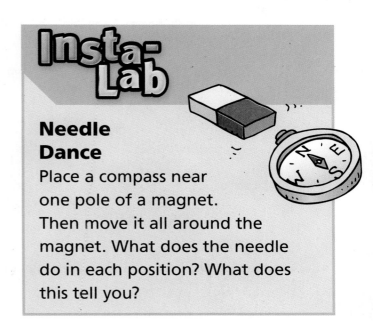

Needle Dance

Place a compass near one pole of a magnet. Then move it all around the magnet. What does the needle do in each position? What does this tell you?

Electromagnets

In the Investigate, you saw that a current of electricity causes a magnetic force. You showed that electricity and magnetism are related.

Actually, an electric current produces a magnetic field around a wire. You can't see the field, but it circles the wire. The field around a single wire is weak. The field around many wires close together is strong. When coils wrap around an iron core, such as a nail, the core becomes an **electromagnet**.

An electromagnet is a temporary magnet. It has a magnetic force only when an electric current moves through the wire. The electromagnet does not work if the current is switched off.

With many coils of wire and a strong current, electromagnets can be made very strong. In junkyards, such electromagnets lift many tons of scrap iron and steel.

Focus Skill COMPARE AND CONTRAST

How are a magnet and an electromagnet alike? How are they different?

A steel nail is not normally a magnet, but it becomes one when an electric current runs around it. How can you tell that this nail is now a magnet? What would happen if you took one of the wire ends off the battery?

Math in Science
Interpret Data

In one experiment, a student built and tested an electromagnet. This graph shows the results. What hypothesis was the student testing? How did the student measure the magnet's strength? What conclusion can you draw from this graph?

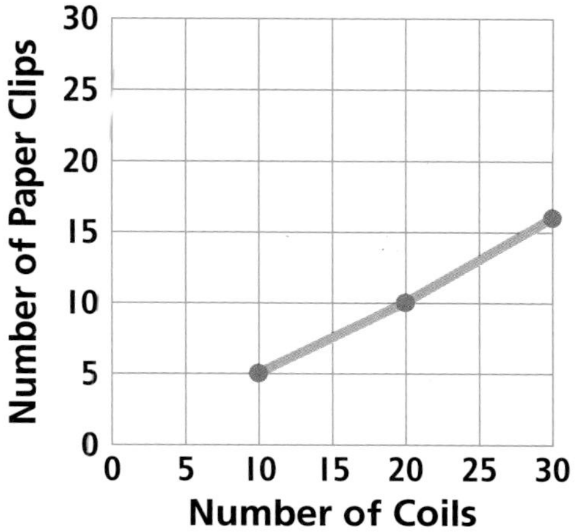

▲ **This powerful electromagnet is being used to move scrap iron in a junkyard.**

▼ **This is an MRI (magnetic resonance imaging) machine in a hospital. It uses a magnetic field to take pictures of the brain, the muscles, and other soft tissues inside the body.**

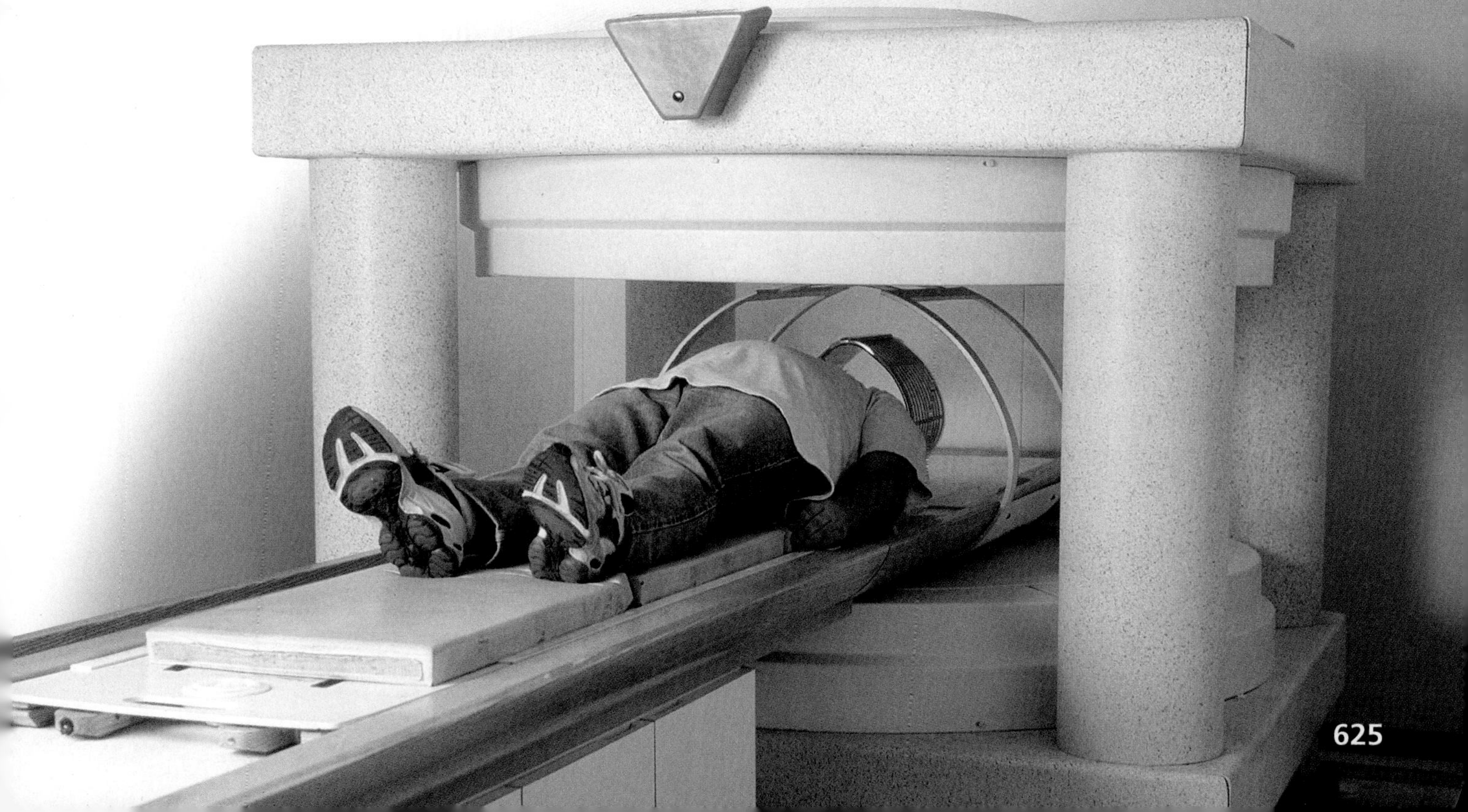

Generators and Motors

Electricity can produce a magnetic field. Luckily for us, the reverse is also true—a magnetic field can produce electricity. If you move a coil of wire near a magnet, current electricity flows in the wire. That is how a **generator**, a device that produces an electric current, works.

Any source of energy that can turn a coil of wire in a magnetic field can produce electricity. Hand-cranked generators use human power to turn the coil. During a power failure, you might use a gasoline-powered generator to produce electricity for lights.

Power plants in large cities use many huge generators to produce enough electricity to meet people's needs. Most power plants burn coal, oil, or natural gas. The fuel heats water until it turns to steam. The steam's pressure turns a turbine. A turbine is a machine that produces electricity. The turbine spins a coil inside the field of a magnet to produce electricity. Then the electricity is sent out along power lines to homes and businesses.

Generators use motion to produce electricity. Can electricity produce motion?

Generators

◀ **This small, simple generator doesn't turn the coil inside a magnet. Instead, it turns a magnet around a coil. The result is the same—an electric current is generated.**

This hand-cranked generator uses "people power" to produce electricity. ▶

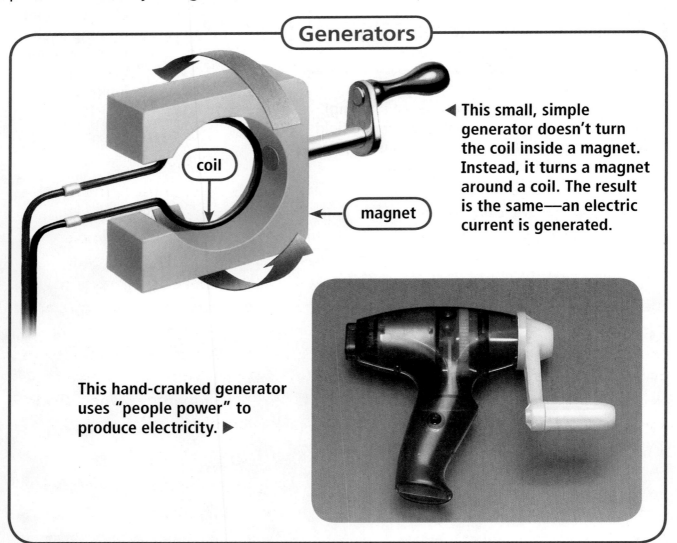

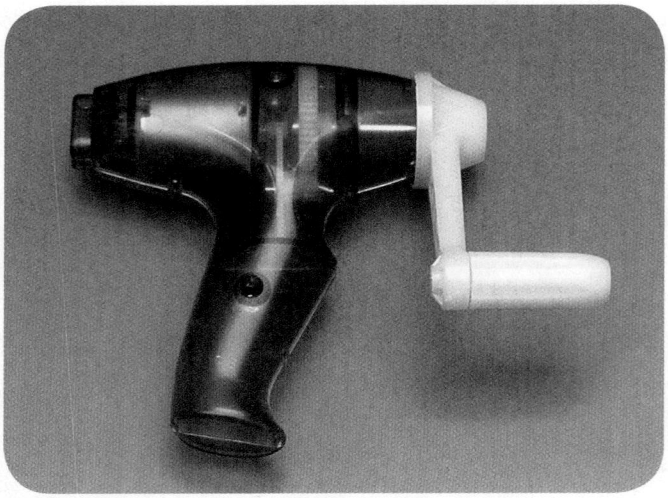

Motors

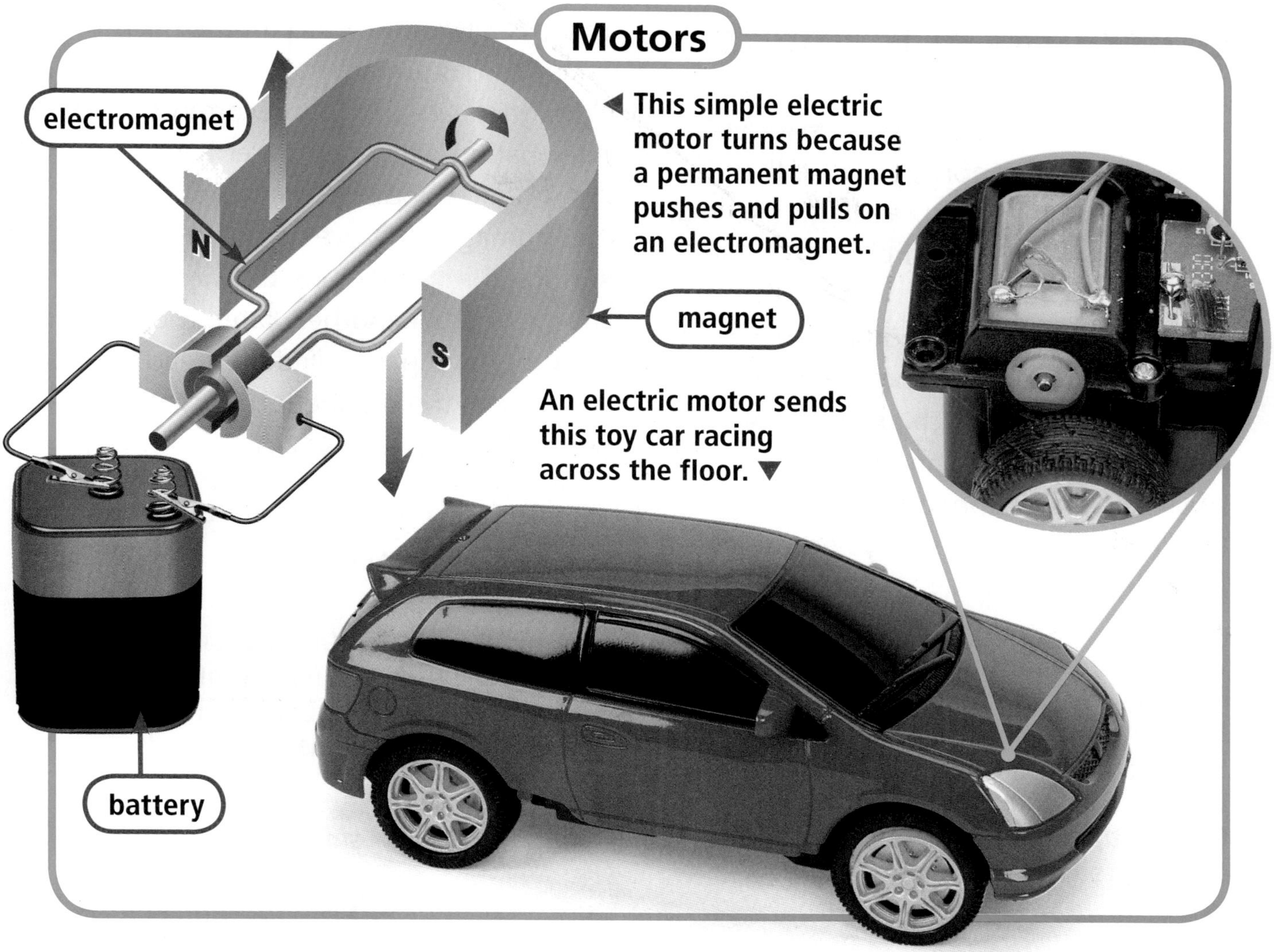

◀ This simple electric motor turns because a permanent magnet pushes and pulls on an electromagnet.

An electric motor sends this toy car racing across the floor. ▼

If you have ever seen someone use a mixer or an electric drill, you know that the answer is yes. Such tools have an electric motor in them. An **electric motor** is a device that changes electrical energy into mechanical energy.

In some motors, an electromagnet lies between the poles of a permanent magnet. Like all magnets, the electromagnet has an N pole and an S pole. The poles are pushed away from the like poles of the permanent magnet. They are pulled toward the opposite poles of the permanent magnet.

The motor's shaft turns until the poles of the electromagnet are near the opposite poles of the permanent magnet. Then the current of the electromagnet reverses. Its N pole becomes its S pole, and its S pole becomes its N pole. The shaft turns again. The current keeps reversing, and the shaft keeps spinning.

Electric motors do many useful things. They start cars. They run CD players. The next time you turn on a fan, thank the inventors of motors!

Focus Skill COMPARE AND CONTRAST

How are a generator and a motor alike? How are they different?

Other Uses of Magnets

Generators and motors aren't the only devices that work because of magnets. Compasses point north because they respond to Earth's natural magnetic field. This helps people find their way on land and at sea.

Magnets are used in computers, compact disc players, and magnetic recording devices, such as VCRs. They are also inside headphones, stereo speakers, and telephone receivers. Doorbells and phones ring because of magnets. Even the strip on the back of a credit card is a magnet.

Magnets are used for recording information. On a computer hard drive or floppy disk, for example, electromagnets move across the disk's surface. They make one disk area more magnetic than another. Later, the disk spins under a part called the head. The head reads the magnetic information.

Focus Skill **COMPARE AND CONTRAST**

How are a videotape and a computer hard drive alike?

◀ On this computer hard drive, information is stored as a pattern of magnetic fields.

When the head inside the VCR records, an electromagnet "writes" a magnetic field on the videotape. When the tape is played back, the magnetic field on the tape produces an electrical signal. ▼

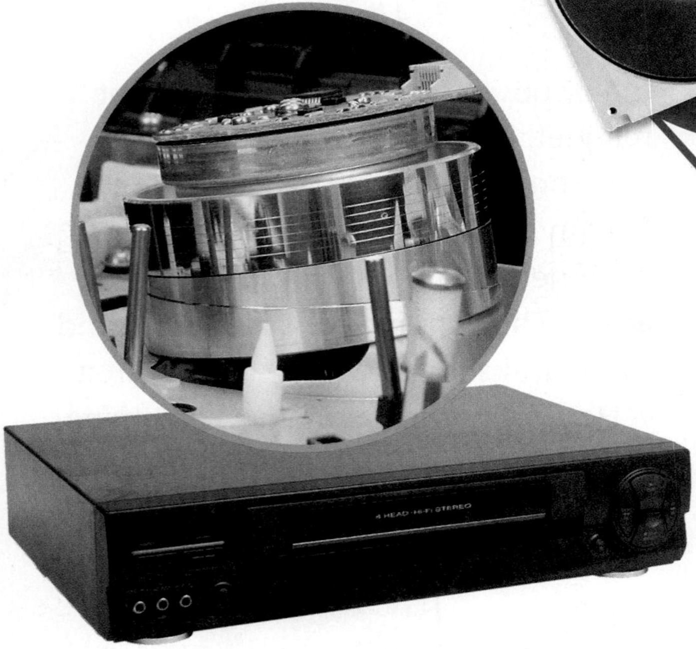

▲ A VCR (video cassette recorder) uses electricity and magnetism to record sounds and pictures.

Computers have magnets inside. ▼

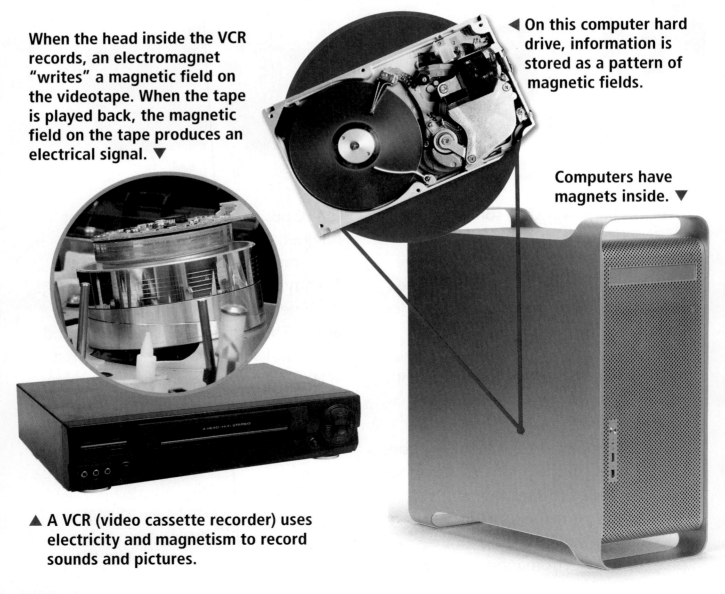

Lesson Review

Essential Question

How are electricity and magnetism related?

In this lesson, you learned that magnetism is a force that attracts iron. Magnetism and electricity can make an electromagnet. Electromagnets are used for many things.

1. **Focus Skill COMPARE AND CONTRAST** Draw and complete a graphic organizer to compare and contrast magnets and electromagnets.

   alike — different

2. **SUMMARIZE** Write a summary of this lesson. Begin with this sentence: *Magnets have two poles.*

3. **DRAW CONCLUSIONS** Tell why the relationship between electricity and magnetism is important.

4. **VOCABULARY** Use *magnetic pole* and *magnetic field* in a sentence to explain magnetic forces.

Test Prep

5. **CRITICAL THINKING** Why is an electromagnet not a permanent magnet?

6. If you turn the N poles of two magnets toward each other, what will they do?
   A. attract
   B. produce electricity
   C. repel
   D. spin

Make Connections

Writing

Expository Writing

Write a **paragraph** for a friend. Tell your friend how an electric motor works.

9÷3 Math

Make a Bar Graph

Test the strength of one magnet by measuring how many paper clips it can pick up. Then test two, three, and four magnets stuck together. Does it matter how the magnets are put together? Make a bar graph of your results.

Social Studies

History of Names

Electricity is measured in amperes, coulombs, ohms, watts, and volts. Find out more about the famous scientists whose names are used for these units of measurement. Share what you learn with the class.

LESSON 3

Essential Question

What Are Some Sources of Electricity?

Investigate how energy changes forms.

Read and Learn about sources of electricity.

Fast Fact

Where Does It Come From?

Wind farms provide the energy to produce only a small fraction of the electricity used in the United States. In the Investigate, you'll see two kinds of energy.

Vocabulary Preview

potential energy [poh•TEN•shuhl EN•er•jee] Energy that an object has because of its position or its condition (p. 634)

kinetic energy [kih•NET•ik EN•er•jee] The energy of motion (p. 635)

hydroelectric power [hy•droh•ee•LEK•trik POW•er] Electrical energy made by using the kinetic energy of falling water (p. 636)

geothermal energy [jee•oh•THER•muhl EN•er•jee] Heat that comes from the inside of Earth (p. 637)

solar energy [SOH•ler EN•er•jee] The power of the sun (p. 638)

Investigate

The Ups and Downs of Energy

Guided Inquiry

Start with Questions

This roller coaster is making its way to the top of a hill.

- What will happen when it reaches the top?
- Why does it move faster down the hill than up the hill?

Investigate to find out. Then read to find out more.

Prepare to Investigate

Inquiry Skill Tip

When you experiment, be sure to identify and control variables. Remember that you must change only one variable. Otherwise your experiment will not reliably test your hypothesis.

Materials

- piece of lightweight poster board, about 30 cm × 70 cm
- ruler
- ballpoint pen
- books
- masking tape
- marble

Make an Observation Chart

Our Roller Coaster

Follow This Procedure

1. Build a "roller coaster" for the marble. Using the ruler, draw a line along each long edge of the piece of poster board, about 1 cm from the edge. Press hard with the ballpoint pen. Fold the edges up along the lines to make walls to keep the marble from rolling off the sides.
2. Place the poster board between two stacks of books so that it forms a valley. Tape the ends of the poster board to the books.
3. Hold a marble at the top on one side. Let it go, and observe what happens. Does it go past the bottom and all the way up the other side? Hypothesize about what affects the marble's path.
4. Change your setup as needed so that the marble goes all the way up the hill the way a roller coaster car does. Draw a picture of your roller coaster.

Draw Conclusions

1. What was the source of energy for the marble?
2. **Inquiry Skill** To make a roller coaster that worked, you had to change a variable. Which variable did you change? Explain.

Independent Inquiry

Plan and conduct an investigation. **Determine whether the weight of a marble affects the way the marble rolls.**

Read and Learn

VOCABULARY
potential energy p. 634
kinetic energy p. 635
hydroelectric power p. 636
geothermal energy p. 637
solar energy p. 638

SCIENCE CONCEPTS
- how energy changes form
- how people produce electricity from other forms of energy

Focus Skill MAIN IDEA AND DETAILS
Look for forms and sources of energy.

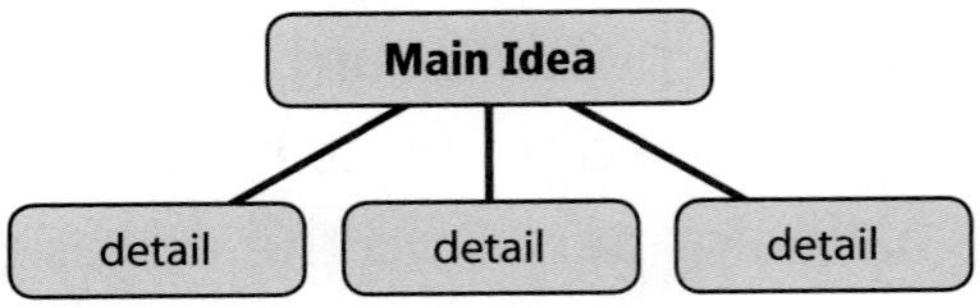

Potential and Kinetic Energy

You can't always see energy, but you know it's there. A pot of water boils on the stove. An egg fries in a pan. Cooking takes a lot of energy. So does moving around. Jet airplanes speeding between cities use energy. So do birds soaring through the sky.

Anytime something gets warmer, gets cooler, or moves, energy is being changed from one form to another. Often you can see or feel the effects of released energy. For example, your body gets energy from food. This energy keeps you alive and provides power for all you do. The energy stored in the food is released in your body. The gasoline used in a car also has stored energy. Burning the fuel releases the energy.

Objects can also have energy because of their position or because of what is done to them. A roller coaster car at the top of a hill has energy. A rubber band has energy when it is stretched. These are both examples of **potential energy**, or energy due to an object's position or condition.

◀ **The bicycle's position at the top of the hill gives it potential energy. It can coast down the hill.**

Kinetic energy is the energy of motion. This bicycle and rider have some kinetic energy. They are moving slowly. ▶

This bicycle and rider have greater kinetic energy. They are moving faster. ▶

You can't always see evidence of potential energy, but you can guess that it exists when an object is in a high place or in a stretched condition. When an object moves, it has **kinetic energy**, or the energy of motion. You can see evidence of kinetic energy.

How are potential and kinetic energy related? Suppose you push a bicycle up a hill. At the top, the bicycle has potential energy because of its position. It can coast down the hill. If it does, its potential energy will change to kinetic energy as it rolls downhill.

You can measure kinetic energy. The faster an object moves, the more kinetic energy it has. For example, if you pedal a bicycle slowly, your kinetic energy is less than if you race it at top speed.

Focus Skill MAIN IDEA AND DETAILS

What are two main differences between potential and kinetic energy?

Hydroelectric Power

Another good example of potential and kinetic energy is a waterfall. At the top of a waterfall, the water has potential energy. When it falls, it gains kinetic energy. People use dams to change the kinetic energy of falling water into electrical energy called **hydroelectric power**.

Many hydroelectric power plants are on rivers. A dam blocks the flow of the river. A reservoir (REZ•er•vwar), or human-made lake, forms behind the dam. To produce electricity, water is released. The falling water flows through and turns a large, fanlike turbine. The turning turbine causes a generator to spin.

Another kind of dam stores energy by pumping water from a lower reservoir to a higher one. When electricity is needed, the water is released.

A huge dam can produce enough electricity to supply a big city. A small dam can produce enough for a farm or ranch.

Focus Skill **MAIN IDEA AND DETAILS**

What is hydroelectric power?

▼ Turbines inside dams change the kinetic energy of falling water into electricity.

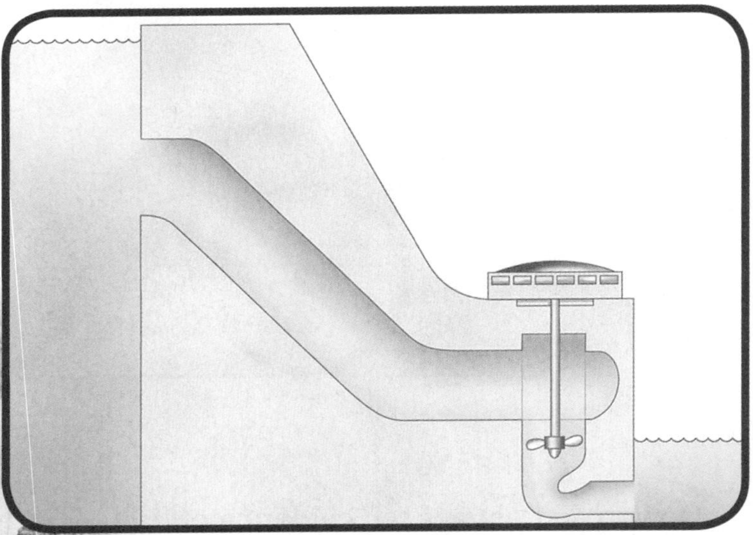

▲ As water flows down from the reservoir, it turns the turbine. The turbine turns the generator, which produces an electric current.

Inside a geothermal plant, heat from below ground is used to make steam that turns turbines.

▲ The Geysers Power Plant in Calistoga, California, is the world's largest producer of electricity from geothermal energy.

Geothermal Energy

It might surprise you to learn that people can use the heat inside Earth. You know that Earth is hot deep underground. Heat from inside Earth is called **geothermal energy**.

In some places, reservoirs of hot water lie 3 kilometers (2 mi) or more below Earth's surface. A deep well can reach the hot water. Then people can pump up the water and use it to heat buildings.

Not all geothermal heat pumps must go so deep. In winter, the upper 3 meters (10 ft) of the ground is warmer than the air. In summer, it is cooler than the air. Pipes can move heat between the ground and a building to warm or cool the building.

Geothermal energy can be used to produce electricity. Most power plants burn coal, oil, or natural gas to produce heat to turn water to steam. The steam turns turbines, and the turbines spin generators. Geothermal power plants don't need to burn fuel for heat. The heat is ready to use right from the ground.

Focus Skill MAIN IDEA AND DETAILS

What is geothermal power?

Solar Power

You feel heat and see light—two forms of energy—when you go outside on a sunny day. People can use **solar energy**, or the energy of sunlight, to meet some of their energy needs.

Solar energy can heat buildings without any special equipment. The south side of a building gets more sunlight than the other sides. Big windows on the south side can let in sunlight to heat the building.

Solar energy can also heat water. A flat solar panel, or collector, on a roof stores water in clear tubes. The sun shines on this water and heats it. Then the hot water is pumped inside the building for people to use.

Solar energy can also be used to produce electricity. Solar cells use sunlight to produce electricity. This solar power is used to run many devices, including watches, calculators, and outdoor garden lights.

Focus Skill MAIN IDEA AND DETAILS

What is solar power?

◀ **Solar cells change the sun's energy to electrical energy to power this highway emergency phone.**

Insta-Lab

Solar Heating

Take two empty soft drink cans. Put a thermometer into each can, and seal the opening around it with clay. Tape white paper around one can and black paper around the other. Leave the cans on their sides in the sun. What happens? Why?

Essential Question

What are some sources of electricity?

In this lesson, you learned that energy can be potential or kinetic. It can come from hydroelectric power, geothermal power, or solar power.

1. Focus Skill **MAIN IDEA AND DETAILS** Draw and complete a graphic organizer showing different kinds of energy.

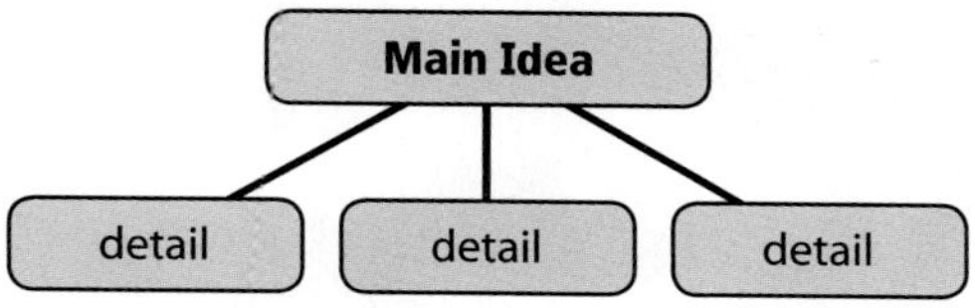

2. **SUMMARIZE** Write two sentences to support this sentence: *Potential energy is always there.*

3. **DRAW CONCLUSIONS** What energy source do you think people will use most in the future? Explain.

4. **VOCABULARY** Write a sentence to explain the difference between potential and kinetic energy.

Test Prep

5. **CRITICAL THINKING** Tell how a dam is used to produce electricity.

6. Which energy source can provide both direct heat and electricity?
   A. a turbine
   B. falling water
   C. sun
   D. wind

Make Connections

Writing

Expository Writing

Write a **paragraph** about ways to classify energy. Give examples of different forms of energy. Tell why they are important and how people use them.

Math

Using Angles

Earth's surface absorbs the most solar energy when the sun's rays shine straight down. It absorbs less when the rays strike the surface at a slant. Draw pictures of two solar water heaters on roofs. Show one that would work well and one that wouldn't.

Health

Sun Safety

The sun is a good source of energy, but it also causes risks to human health. Research the dangers of too much exposure to sunlight. Make a list of sun safety rules to post in the classroom.

LESSON 4

Essential Question

How Do People Use Energy Resources?

Investigate how you use energy.

Read and Learn how people use energy resources.

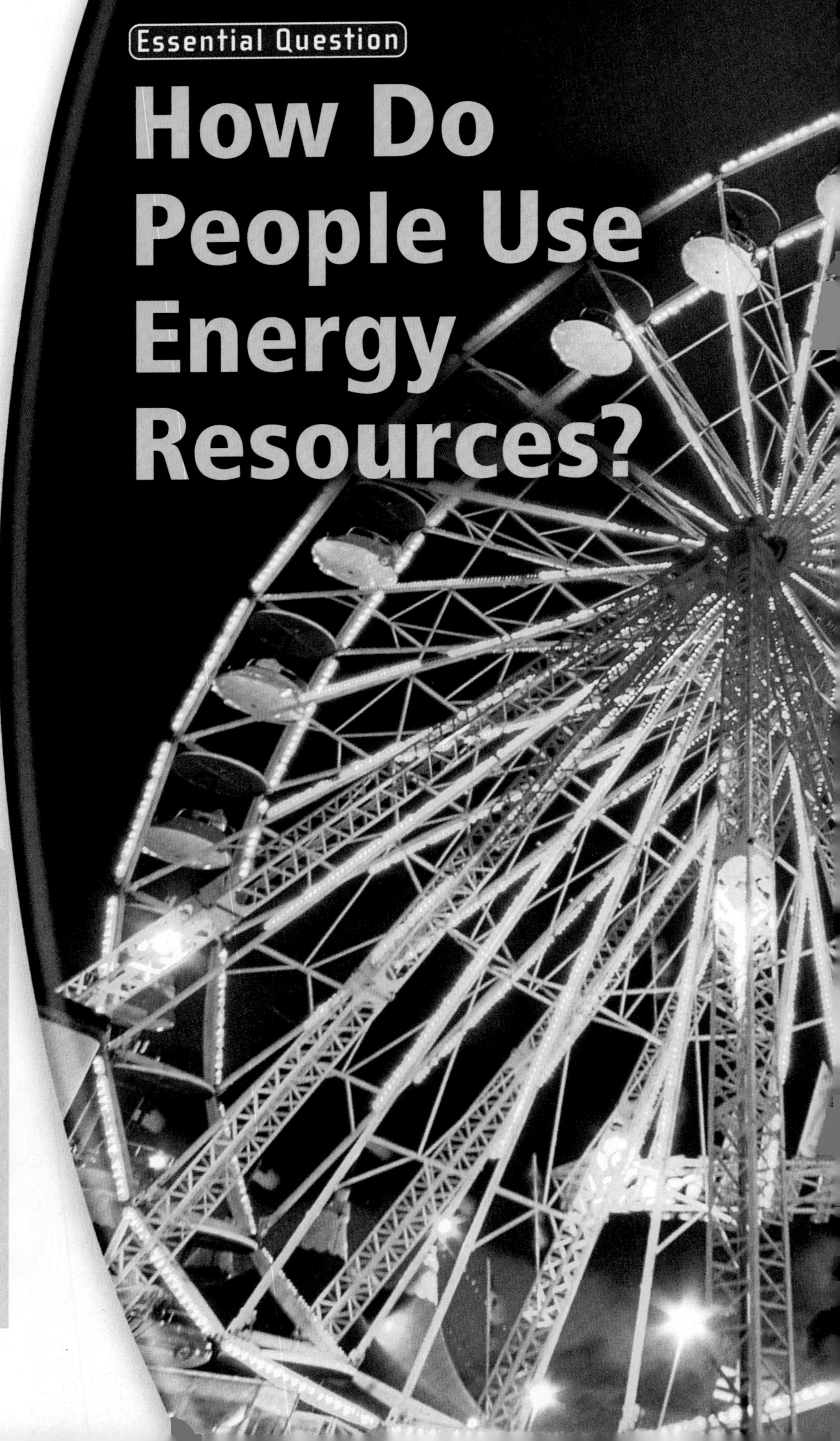

Fast Fact

Think Trillions!
Energy is measured in kilowatt-hours (kWh). A 100-watt light bulb burning for 10 hours uses 1 kilowatt-hour of electricity. Electric plants in the United States generate nearly 4 trillion kilowatt-hours of electricity every year! In the investigation, you'll examine some sources of energy.

Vocabulary Preview

chemical energy
[KEM•ih•kuhl EN•er•jee]
Energy that can be released by a chemical reaction (p. 646)

mechanical energy
[muh•KAN•ih•kuhl EN•er•jee]
The total potential and kinetic energy of an object (p. 647)

Investigate

Energy Sources and Uses

Guided Inquiry

Start with Questions

The water in this tea kettle is boiling. It is ready to make tea!

- What is the steam?
- What made the water boil?

Investigate to find out. Then read to find out more.

Prepare to Investigate

Inquiry Skill Tip

Classifying things can help you organize your ideas and thoughts. Remember to classify every item according to the same standards.

Materials

- colored construction paper (5 yellow and 5 blue)
- pens, pencils, drawing materials

Make an Observation Chart

Uses of Energy	Sources of Energy

Follow This Procedure

1. On each blue card, write *Uses of Energy.* On each yellow card, write *Sources of Energy.*
2. With your classmates, brainstorm ways you use energy every day. Choose five of these ways, and draw a picture of each on a separate blue card. Label each picture with a word or two.
3. Determine the source of energy for each use you named. Draw and label the sources on the yellow cards.
4. Match your energy source cards with your energy use cards.
5. Mix up your cards, exchange sets with a classmate, and work to match up the sources and uses. Make a chart to share your results.

Step 1

Step 2

Draw Conclusions

1. In what ways do you and your classmates use energy? What are the sources of the energy you use?
2. **Inquiry Skill** Sort your cards to classify the uses and sources of energy you listed. Give reasons for the way you sorted the cards.

Independent Inquiry

Make cards that show how energy moves and changes from a source through one use of it. Communicate this sequence to your classmates.

VOCABULARY

chemical energy p. 646

mechanical energy p. 647

SCIENCE CONCEPTS

- ways people use energy
- ways people can save energy

Focus Skill **MAIN IDEA AND DETAILS**

Look for details about ways people use energy.

Main Idea → detail | detail | detail

Uses of Electricity

Can you imagine a world without electricity? Strange as it may seem, people have been using electricity for only a short time. Thomas Edison made his first successful electric light bulb in 1879. The first electric power plant opened that same year. That may seem like a long time ago to you, but it's a short time in human history.

The refrigerator was invented in 1913. Microwave ovens were invented in the 1950s, but few people had them before 1970. The first wind farm for making electricity started working in 1980.

◀ **We use electricity to light our homes, schools, and businesses. Can you imagine living without electric lights?**

The heater uses electricity to heat a room. In what other ways do we use electricity for heat? ▼

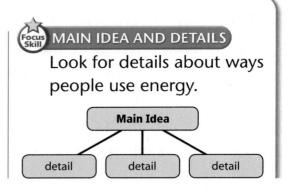

In computer speakers, electricity is changed to sound energy.

Today, we often take electricity for granted. We use it in our homes and in businesses. About one-third of the electricity used in the United States is used in homes. It warms and cools rooms. It heats water for showers. It cooks food, and it keeps food cold to preserve it.

Businesses such as stores and offices use another one-third of our energy. Like homes, these businesses use electricity for heating, cooling, and light. They also use it to run machines, such as computers and photocopiers. Businesses use electricity to keep offices clean and to provide services to their customers.

Another one-third of our electricity is used in manufacturing businesses. Workers in factories use electricity to make or prepare many of the products we buy. For example, in food processing factories, electricity runs the canning and freezing equipment.

Electricity is used to mine metals and to drill for and refine oil. It is used to make cars, trains, and airplanes. It's hard to imagine what life was like before people learned to use electricity!

Focus Skill MAIN IDEA AND DETAILS **How is electricity used in homes and businesses?**

Uses of Chemical Energy

Electricity is an important form of energy. However, it is not the only one we use. We use the energy stored in gasoline to move the cars and airplanes that take people from one place to another. Gasoline also fuels trucks, ships, and trains that carry goods.

Chemical energy is energy stored in the arrangement of particles of matter. Gasoline, which is made from oil, has chemical energy. So do coal and natural gas. Coal, oil, and natural gas all formed inside Earth from the remains of ancient plants and animals. The remains decayed under great pressure millions of years ago.

Because they come from ancient living things, these fuels are called fossil fuels. Fossil fuels remained underground for centuries. Then, people started mining coal and drilling for oil. Today, we burn huge amounts of fossil fuels.

Chemical energy can be changed into other forms of energy. Many power plants burn fossil fuels to change their stored chemical energy into heat.

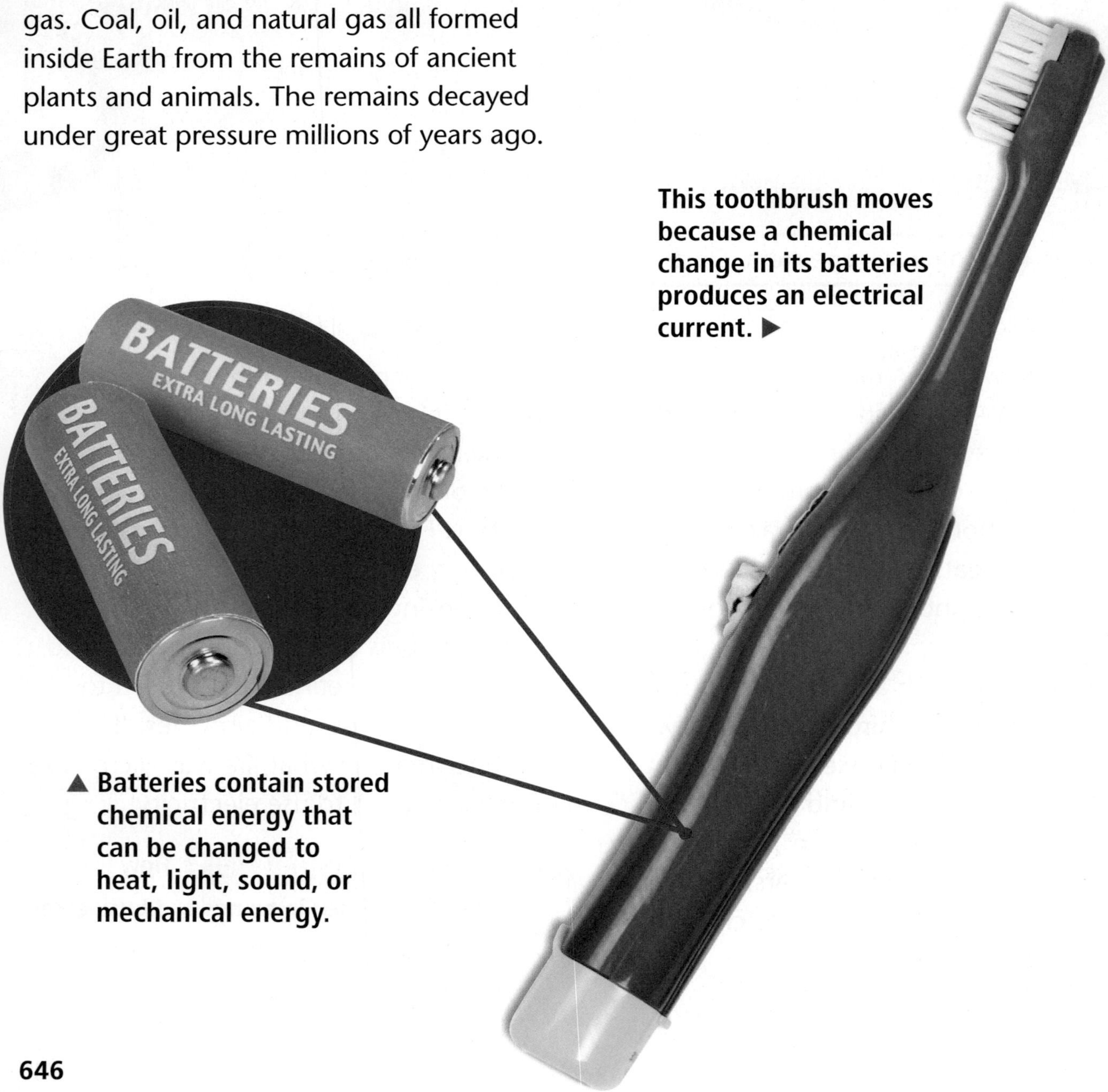

This toothbrush moves because a chemical change in its batteries produces an electrical current. ▶

▲ Batteries contain stored chemical energy that can be changed to heat, light, sound, or mechanical energy.

When it is finished, this combustion turbine will work like a jet engine. It will burn natural gas to generate electricity. ▶

◀ This portable generator uses gasoline, which has stored chemical energy. Burning it releases the energy.

The heat is used to produce steam to turn the turbines that generate electricity. Car engines burn gasoline to change its chemical energy into mechanical energy. **Mechanical energy** makes machine parts move.

Chemical energy is what makes batteries work. A chemical change inside the battery releases charges from atoms. The current causes CD players to make sound or battery-operated toys to move.

Focus Skill MAIN IDEA AND DETAILS **Explain two ways people use chemical energy.**

Insta-Lab

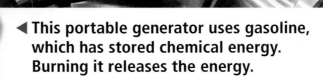

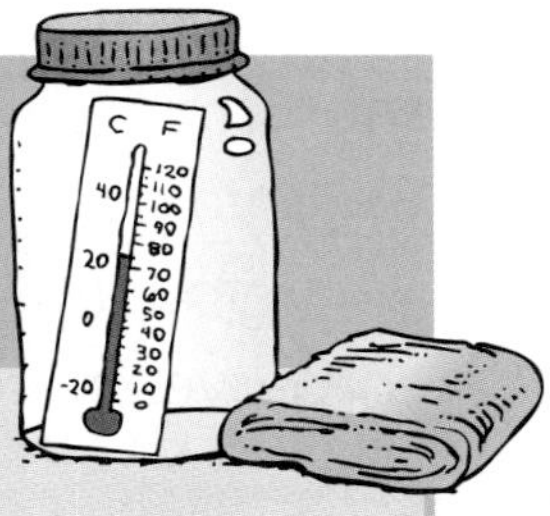

Chemical Energy

Wrap a dry pad of steel wool around the base of a thermometer. Put them together into a clear jar, and close it. Wait 5 minutes. Read the temperature. Remove the pad and thermometer from the jar. Soak the pad in vinegar for 1 minute. Squeeze out the extra vinegar, and wrap the pad around the base of the thermometer again. Put them back in the jar and close it. Wait 5 minutes. Read the temperature again. What happens? How can you explain it?

Energy Conservation

Most of the energy you use comes from burning fossil fuels. Today, people are using Earth's stores of energy faster than ever. Fossil fuels were formed millions of years ago. When they have been used up, it will take millions of years for more to form.

When fossil fuels are gone, we will need other energy sources to take their place. It will take time to develop new energy sources, so we must make the fossil fuels last as long as possible. We can do this by conserving, or using less of them.

How can you help with this? You can turn off the TV when you aren't watching it. You can take shorter showers or use cooler water. Talk about ways you can save energy at school. See what you and your classmates can do to conserve energy.

Focus Skill MAIN IDEA AND DETAILS

Tell why people should conserve energy.

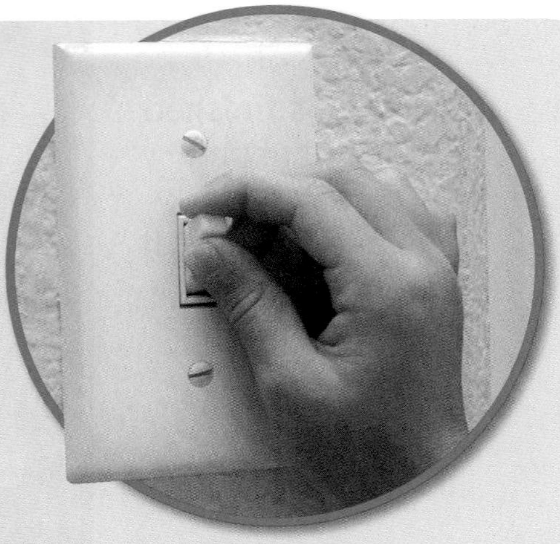

▲ **Turning off lights that you are not using is a good way to conserve energy.**

▲ **Insulation in attics and walls helps save energy. Insulated buildings lose less heat in winter and stay cooler in summer than uninsulated ones.**

◀ **This car may look ordinary, but it isn't. It's a "hybrid" car. A hybrid car's engine uses both gasoline and electricity.**

Lesson Review

Essential Question

How do people use energy resources?

In this lesson, you learned that people use energy resources to provide things like light and heat and to run machines. People use chemical energy in the form of batteries. Conserving energy helps conserve resources.

1. **Focus Skill MAIN IDEA AND DETAILS** Draw and complete a graphic organizer to show how people use chemical energy.

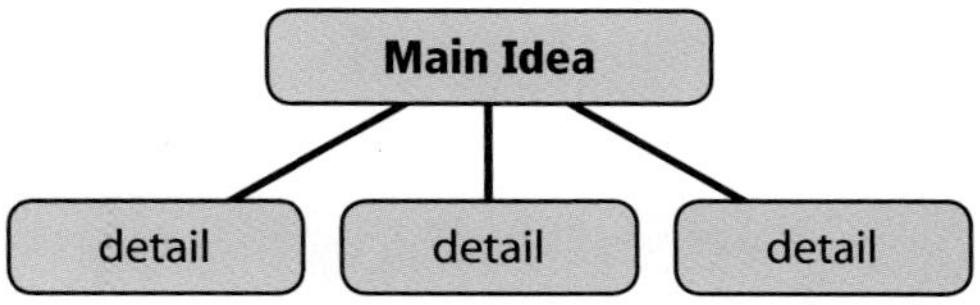

2. **SUMMARIZE** Write a list of ways you can conserve energy.

3. **DRAW CONCLUSIONS** Which kind of energy is most important? Why?

4. **VOCABULARY** Use the terms *chemical energy* and *mechanical energy* to explain how a battery-operated toy works.

Test Prep

5. **CRITICAL THINKING** List some things your class can do at school to conserve energy.

6. In which form is energy stored inside a battery?
   A. chemical
   B. electrical
   C. kinetic
   D. mechanical

Make Connections

Writing

Persuasive Writing

Write a **letter** you could send to the editor of your local newspaper. Explain why you think people in your community should work harder to conserve energy.

Math

Solve a Problem

Energy use is measured in kilowatt-hours (kWh). *Kilo-* means "one thousand," so 1 kWh equals 1,000 watts used for 1 hour. How long would five 100-watt bulbs need to burn to use 1 kWh?

Literature

Write a Poem

Use a thesaurus to find words related to energy. Use them to write a rhyming poem about ways people can conserve energy. Trade poems with a partner, and read them aloud. Display your poems on a bulletin board.

Lewis Latimer

Without the help of Lewis Latimer (1848–1929), you would have to read at night by candlelight. Latimer helped design the electric light bulb.

In the early 1880s, Thomas Edison invented an electric lamp. Electricity passed through a thin thread of carbon to make light. The thread was inside a glass bulb. The thin thread burned out after only a few days.

Latimer worked to design a light bulb that would last longer. In 1882, he succeeded. He later was awarded patents for the new design.

▶ **LEWIS LATIMER**

▶ Inventor

Think and Write

1. Why might Latimer have worked to improve the light bulb?
2. Why is it important for light bulbs to last a long time?

Career Power Plant Technician

Electricity plays a huge role in our daily lives. The people who make electricity possible are the power plant technicians. They control and monitor the machines that generate the electricity to power homes, schools, and businesses. The technicians also control the complex network of circuits that carries the electricity.

▶ **BENJAMIN FRANKLIN**

▶ Co-author of the Declaration of Independence

▶ Inventor

Benjamin Franklin

Curious is the word that best describes Benjamin Franklin! He was fascinated by storms and suspected that lightning was an electric current. His famous experiment with a kite and a key helped him prove it.

Franklin explained electricity in words we still use today: *charge, discharge, positive, negative, conductor,* and *electric shock.* He experienced electric shock firsthand, describing it as "a universal blow through my whole body."

In his 40s, Franklin figured out how to make a battery, but he saw no use for it. He also invented the lightning rod. A metal spike on top of a building is connected by wire to the ground. During a storm, electric charges collect on its point. They then flow along the wire to the ground instead of destroying the building.

Ben Franklin designed the lightning rod that protects the Maryland State House. This lightning rod is 8.5 meters (27.9 ft) tall.

Think and Write

1. What did Franklin's experiments show people about lightning?
2. How do you think Franklin's discoveries have helped later scientists studying electricity?

Modern lightning rod

CHAPTER 15 Review and Test Preparation

Vocabulary Review

Use the terms below to complete the sentences. The page numbers tell you where to look in the chapter if you need help.

static electricity p. 606	**magnet** p. 620
current electricity p. 608	**electromagnet** p. 624
series circuit p. 610	**generator** p. 626
parallel circuit p. 610	**potential energy** p. 634
conductor p. 612	**kinetic energy** p. 635

1. An object that attracts iron is a _______.

2. The charge that builds up on an object is _______.

3. A circuit that has only one path for electricity to follow is a _______.

4. The energy of motion is _______.

5. A device that produces an electric current is a _______.

6. A material that electricity can flow through easily is a _______.

7. An _______ is a temporary magnet.

8. Electricity that flows along a wire is _______.

9. The energy an object has because of its position is _______.

10. A circuit that has two or more paths that electricity can follow is a _______.

Check Understanding

Write the letter of the best choice.

11. **COMPARE AND CONTRAST** (Focus Skill) What is one way in which all magnets are alike?

A. They stick to aluminum cans.
B. They attract iron.
C. They need a current to work.
D. They have one or two poles.

12. **MAIN IDEA AND DETAILS** (Focus Skill) What kind of energy does water at the top of a dam have?

F. chemical
G. kinetic
H. mechanical
J. potential

13. How do charges move in a circuit?

A. along two or more paths
B. along a loop with no beginning and no end
C. through an insulator
D. up and down

14. What energy source is used to produce most of the electricity we use today?

F. fossil fuels
G. geothermal energy
H. falling water
J. wind

15. Which pair is made up of two things that work in opposite ways?

A. bar magnet and horseshoe magnet
B. chemical energy and mechanical energy
C. generator and motor
D. solar energy and geothermal energy

16. What does an electromagnet have that a bar magnet does not have?

F. attraction for iron
G. magnetic field
H. two poles
J. wire coil

Inquiry Skills

17. The needle of a compass moves when you put a bar of metal close to it. What can you **infer** from this observation?

18. A student team builds two electromagnets. The students use 20 coils of wire in one of the electromagnets. They use 40 coils in the other. Everything else is the same. **Compare** the strengths of the two electromagnets.

Critical Thinking

The Big Idea

19. Suggest a practical use for an electromagnet. Explain why it would be a good use for the magnet.

20. Suppose you woke up one morning and one use of electricity had disappeared. How would your life change? How would your community change?

CHAPTER 16

Forces and Motion

What's the Big Idea? Motion can be measured and described. It is influenced by forces such as gravity.

Essential Questions

Lesson 1
How Is Motion Described and Measured?

Lesson 2
What Is Acceleration?

Lesson 3
Why Is the Force of Gravity Important?

GO online Student eBook www.hspscience.com

What do YOU wonder?

Fluid Motion? This photograph shows each stage of the gymnast's movement. The camera recorded tiny changes in her position. How do you know the gymnast moved? How does this relate to the **Big Idea?**

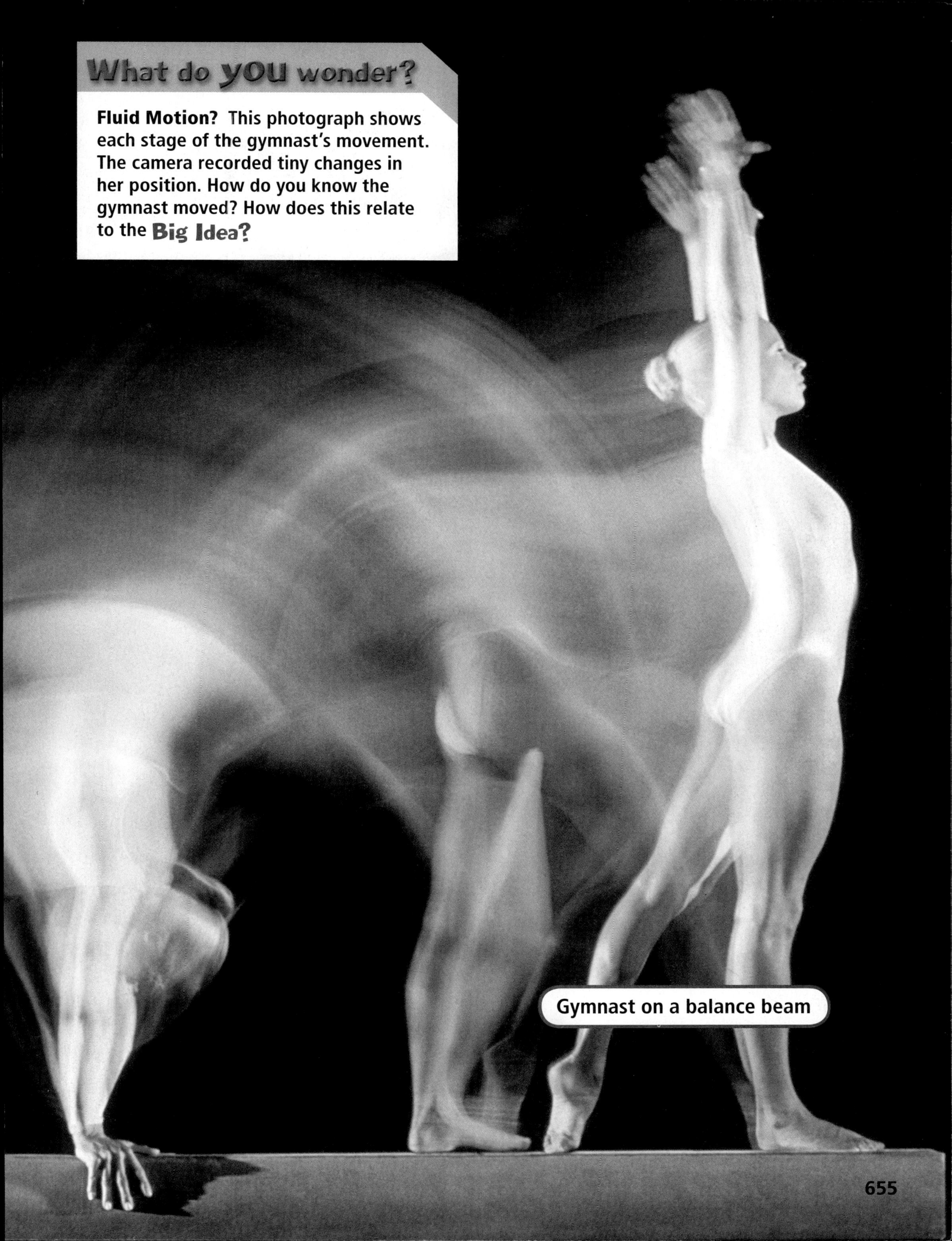

Gymnast on a balance beam

LESSON 1

Investigate how to give directions.

Read and Learn how motion is described and measured.

Essential Question

How Is Motion Described and Measured?

Fast Fact

Higher Speed Means Higher Risk

On a highway, cars often go as fast as 120 kilometers per hour (75 mi/hr). High-speed accidents are much more deadly than low-speed ones. A driver is 15 times as likely to die in a crash that takes place at 80 kilometers per hour (50 mi/hr) as in one that takes place at 40 kilometers per hour (25 mi/hr). In the Investigate, you'll describe moving at a very low speed.

Traffic turning a corner

Vocabulary Preview

position [puh•ZISH•uhn] The location of an object (p. 660)

motion [MOH•shuhn] A change of position of an object (p. 660)

speed [SPEED] The measure of an object's change in position during a unit of time (p. 662)

Walk This Way

Guided Inquiry

Start with Questions

This old map might lead the right person to a treasure.

- How do you know what the map shows?
- What information would make the location more clear?

Investigate to find out. Then read to find out more.

Prepare to Investigate

Inquiry Skill Tip

If you do not communicate clearly with people, they will not understand you. Then neither of you will get what you need.

Materials

- paper
- pencil

Make an Observation Chart

Landmark	Direction of Movement

Follow This Procedure

1. Choose a location in your school. The location could be an exit door or a bench, for example. A person going there from your classroom should have to make some turns.
2. Start walking to the selected location. As you walk, **record** the way you move. Include distance, where you turn, landmarks, and how fast you move.
3. Return to the classroom. On a sheet of paper, write directions to the location. Use your notes to add details. Don't name the location. Your partner should follow the directions and match your speed.
4. Get feedback from your partner about how well your directions worked. Use the feedback to improve your directions. Then follow the improved directions.
5. Switch roles with your partner, who should repeat Steps 1–4. Record information about good directions.

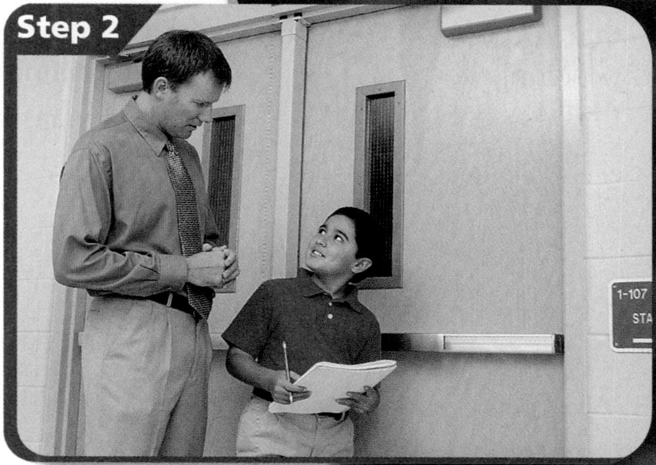

Draw Conclusions

1. How did your partner know how far and how fast to walk and where to turn?
2. **Inquiry Skill** Tell why the revised directions and a good experiment plan are examples of clear **communication**.

Independent Inquiry

Draw a map to your location. Trade maps with a new partner. Compare using a map to using written directions.

VOCABULARY
position p. 660
motion p. 660
speed p. 662

SCIENCE CONCEPTS
- how to define motion
- how to measure speed

Focus Skill COMPARE AND CONTRAST
Look for similarities and differences between motion and speed.

alike — different

Changing Position

Where are you located right now? Are you *at* your desk? *Under* a light? To the *right* of a door, or *2 meters (6 ft) away from* the board? Words such as these describe your position. **Position** is the location of an object.

Every object has a position. The position of your nose is the center of your face. How would you describe the position of the doorway in your classroom? These positions don't change.

But sometimes, an object's position does change. When it does, the object is in motion. **Motion** is a change in the position of an object.

There are many kinds of motion. You can walk forward or backward. An elevator goes up and down. A pendulum swings from side to side. Things may move quickly or slowly. They may follow a straight, curved, or circular path. But whenever something moves, its position changes.

◀ The soccer players are in constant motion. Their positions are always changing.

The still pictures don't show the actual motion of the boats, but you can tell that the boats moved. How do you know? Without even thinking about it, you interpret an object's change of position as motion. ▶

In the boat race pictures, have the boats in the second picture moved from where they were in the first picture?

You can tell that the boats have moved, because their positions have changed. In the first picture, the boats were close to the docks. They were to the right of the man with the flag. In the second picture, the boats have moved past the man with the flag. The docks can't be seen anymore.

You sensed the boats' motion by looking at the shore and assuming it was still. In other words, you used the shore as your *frame of reference.* Relative to the shore, the boats have moved.

You can change your frame of reference. You might say you're not moving when you're sitting at your school desk. But change your frame of reference to the solar system. Now you realize that you're spinning and moving around the sun with Earth. You're moving at about 1000 kilometers per hour (600 mi/hr)!

Focus Skill COMPARE AND CONTRAST

How are the boat and the shore different frames of reference for the rowers?

Measuring Motion

How fast can you run? If you run faster than your friend, your speed is greater. **Speed** tells you how the position of an object changes during a certain amount of time.

You can use words like *fast* and *slow* to describe speed. Fast-moving objects change their position quickly. Slow-moving objects change their position slowly. But you can be more exact if you use numbers and units, such as 10 meters per second or 5 miles per hour.

To find an object's speed, you need to measure two things. You need to measure distance. This distance is the change in the object's position. You also need to measure the time it takes the object to move through the distance.

Once you have both the distance and time measurements, you can find the object's speed with this formula:

speed = distance ÷ time

In other words, find speed by dividing the movement distance by the time it takes to move that distance.

For example, suppose you're going by car to a campground for a vacation. You travel 225 kilometers in 3 hours. You can find your speed this way:

225 km ÷ 3 hr = 75 km/hr

◀ **In a close race, times can be nearly the same. Judges use precise stopwatches to measure time in tenths or hundredths of a second to determine who is fastest.**

To know speed, you must know two other things—distance and time. In a race, the distance is the same for all the runners, but their times vary.

▲ **The police officer uses a radar gun to measure the speeds of cars moving toward him.**

For drivers, speed is often measured in miles per hour. ▼

When you know the speed of an object, you know how much distance it can move in a certain amount of time.

Suppose an insect moves 100 centimeters per second (40 in./sec). This means that in 1 second, it can travel 100 centimeters (40 in.). Does that seem fast? It is fast, for an insect. An insect that moves this fast probably has wings!

Speed tells you only how quickly or slowly an object moves. It doesn't tell you the direction of the motion.

Focus Skill **COMPARE AND CONTRAST**

Which travels faster—a bicycle that travels 24 kilometers in 1 hour or a bicycle that travels 48 kilometers in 2 hours?

Insta-Lab

Fast Walk, Slow Walk

Compare walking speeds. Mark off a distance of at least 10 m. Walk that distance twice while measuring the time. Cover the distance first in 10 seconds and then in 15 seconds. How do you determine how quickly you need to walk?

Comparing Speeds

Suppose you're watching a horse race between Lightning and Thunder. Lightning's speed so far is 55 kilometers per hour (34 mi/hr). Thunder's speed so far is 60 kilometers per hour (37 mi/hr). The race is half over. Can you say which horse is moving faster right now? You might guess Thunder. But you need more information to be sure.

You have just learned that speed is the total distance divided by time. This formula gives *average* speed. For example, you saw how to find the average speed during a 3-hour car trip. You can also measure speed over a shorter time. The speedometer of a car shows the car's speed moment by moment.

Now let's go back to the horse race. Thunder has a greater average speed so far. However, Lightning could be moving faster at this moment. To be sure, you have to watch the race closely and compare the horses' positions. If Lightning is catching up to Thunder, you know Lightning is running faster now.

Focus Skill COMPARE AND CONTRAST

How is speed at one moment different from average speed?

Math in Science
Interpret Data

Top Speeds of Vehicles

The graph shows the fastest speed for each type of vehicle. Which vehicle is fastest? Slowest?

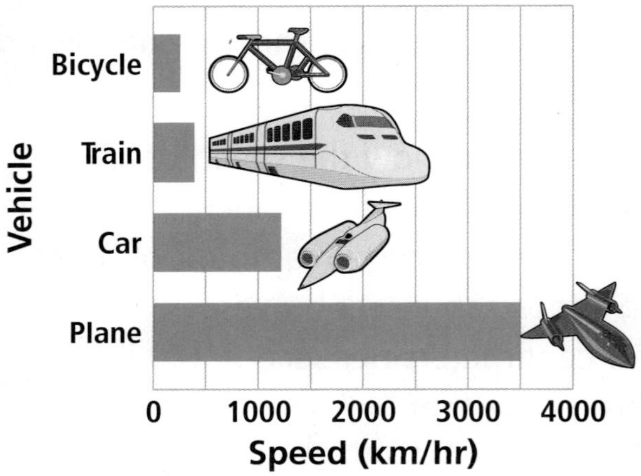

Can you tell from the pictures whether the horse in front was running faster? Explain. ▶

Lesson Review

Essential Question

How is motion described and measured?

In this lesson, you learned that a change in position indicates motion. Motion can be measured by speed and distance.

1. Focus Skill COMPARE AND CONTRAST Draw and complete a graphic organizer to show how speed at one moment is different from average speed.

alike — different

2. **SUMMARIZE** Use the lesson vocabulary terms to explain change of position.

3. **DRAW CONCLUSIONS** A top spins in place without changing its location. Is it moving? Why or why not?

4. **VOCABULARY** Write one question for each of the terms *position, motion,* and *speed.* Trade questions with a partner, and answer your partner's questions.

Test Prep

5. **CRITICAL THINKING** What does it mean to say that the average speed of a car is 35 miles per hour?

6. What is the speed of a dog that runs 9 meters in 3 seconds?
   A. 3 meters per second
   B. 9 meters per second
   C. 12 meters per second
   D. 27 meters per second

Make Connections

Writing

Descriptive Writing

Write a paragraph about how you experience motion. **Describe** examples of each of these kinds of motion: forward, backward, back-and-forth, side-to-side, and rotating.

9÷3 Math

Speed Fact Family

Write the related fact-family members for this formula.

speed = distance ÷ time

Physical Education

Sprint the Distance

Go outside with a partner. Take a meterstick, masking tape, and a stopwatch. Mark off a distance of at least 10 meters (33 ft). Walk or run while your partner times you. Use the formula to find your speed.

LESSON 2

Essential Question

What Is Acceleration?

Investigate how a ball moves and changes direction.

Read and Learn about acceleration.

Fast Fact

Tennis Serves
Stopping and returning a tennis serve can be a real challenge. The world's fastest serve was a sizzling 239.8 kilometers per hour (149 mi/hr)! In the Investigate, you'll see how a force changes the motion of an object such as a table tennis ball.

Tennis player

Vocabulary Preview

velocity [vuh•LAHS•uh•tee] The measure of the speed and direction of the motion of an object (p. 670)

acceleration [ak•sel•er•AY•shuhn] Any change in the speed or direction of an object's motion (p. 671)

force [FAWRS] A pull or push of any kind (p. 672)

inertia [in•ER•shuh] The property of matter that keeps an object at rest or keeps it moving in a straight line (p. 674)

Which Way the Ball Blows

Guided Inquiry

Start with Questions

The sails on this boat are moving the boat across the water.

- What is making the sails full?
- Is the boat's speed constant?

Investigate to find out. Then read to find out more.

Prepare to Investigate

Inquiry Skill Tip

Taking accurate measurements will give you important information. Measure the same way each time so that your measurements can be compared.

Materials

- ruler
- masking tape, 10-cm strip
- table tennis ball
- straw

Make an Observation Chart

	Observations
Step 2	
Step 3	
Step 4	

Follow This Procedure

1. Put the strip of tape on a table or on your desktop. Place a table tennis ball at one end of the tape.

2. Blow through a straw onto the ball. Blow gently and steadily. Make the ball roll along the tape. **Observe** whether the ball rolls in the direction in which you blow.

3. Return the table tennis ball to the end of the tape. Blow on the ball at a right angle to the tape. **Observe** whether the ball rolls in the direction in which you blow.

4. Roll the ball gently. Blow on the ball in a direction different from where the ball is rolling. **Observe** what happens.

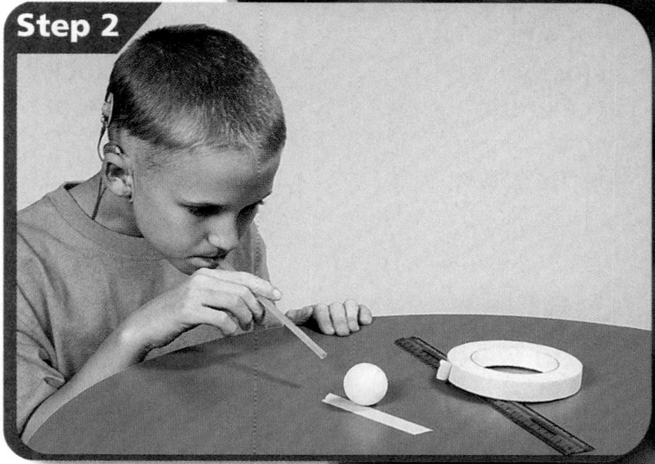

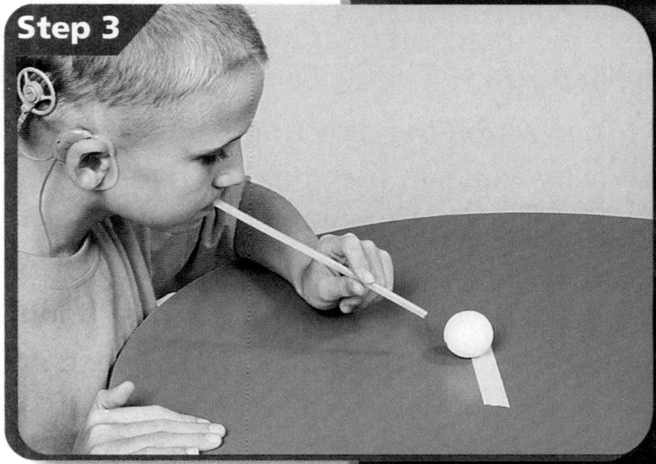

Draw Conclusions

1. In what direction did you blow to make the ball roll along the tape? To make it roll at right angles to the tape?

2. **Inquiry Skill** What tools could you use to **measure** the motion of the ball?

Independent Inquiry

Blow on the ball in one direction. Have a partner blow at right angles to the direction in which you blow. Observe the path of the ball.

Read and Learn

VOCABULARY
velocity p. 670
acceleration p. 671
force p. 672
inertia p. 674

SCIENCE CONCEPTS
- how velocity relates to acceleration
- how forces cause acceleration

Focus Skill CAUSE AND EFFECT
Look for ways in which forces cause acceleration.

cause → effect

Velocity

If you were asked to describe the motion of a bird, a bike, or a train, you'd probably tell how fast it was going. You'd probably also mention its direction. When you tell both the speed and the direction of an object, you give its **velocity**.

To describe the direction part of velocity, you can use compass directions or words such as *right, left, up,* and *down.* For example, suppose you're riding a bicycle at 30 kilometers per hour (19 mi/hr) toward the west. Your speed is 30 kilometers per hour. But your velocity is 30 kilometers per hour, west.

Two objects with the same speed have different velocities if they are moving in different directions. While your velocity is 30 kilometers per hour, west, your friend's velocity might be 30 kilometers per hour, north.

Velocity includes both speed and direction. A rocket's velocity is at least 11 kilometers per second (7 mi/sec), up. These riders' velocity is 24 kilometers per hour (15 mi/hr), east.

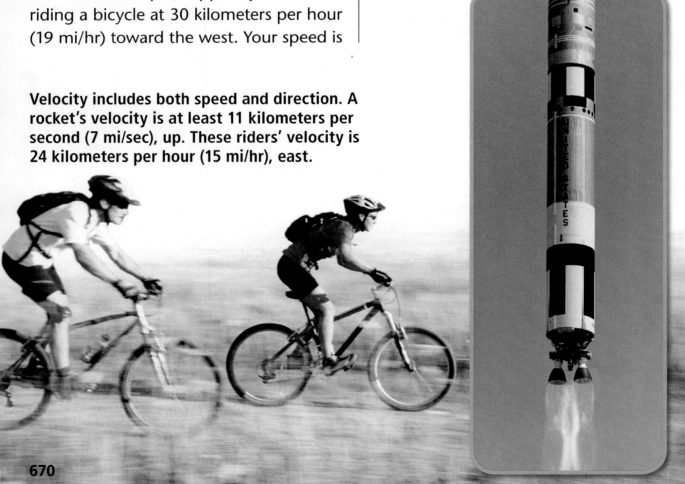

Acceleration may be a change in speed, direction, or both. This boat is changing direction. This skier is changing both speed and direction.

Changing Velocity

Like your bicycle, objects don't always move steadily in one direction. They stop and start, slow down and speed up, and turn. These changes are examples of *acceleration*. **Acceleration** is any change in the speed or direction of an object's motion. So acceleration is any change of velocity.

Think about what happens to your bicycle when you ride it. It accelerates when it speeds up and rolls away from a stop sign. It also accelerates when it slows to a stop at a stop sign. Slowing down is acceleration, just as speeding up is. If the bicycle moves in a circle at a constant speed of 10 kilometers per hour (6 mi/hr), is it accelerating? Yes, it is. It is always turning in the circle—changing direction—so it is always accelerating.

You can measure acceleration. The larger the change in speed, the larger the acceleration. Getting a car up to top speed is a larger acceleration than doing so for your bicycle. Stopping a large jet plane that is moving at top speed is a larger acceleration than doing so for a car.

Focus Skill CAUSE AND EFFECT **What is one change that causes an acceleration?**

More Force, More Acceleration

When forces push or pull in the same direction, they simply add up. Suppose you double the force on an object by pushing it twice as hard. Then you double its acceleration as well.

▲ **The athletes push the sled, and it accelerates.**

◀ **More athletes push this sled with more force. Its acceleration is greater than that of the sled shown above.**

Force and Acceleration

Push a door, and it moves. Pull the door, and it moves the other way. Pushes and pulls of all kinds are **forces**. Forces are measured in newtons (N).

Forces change motion. If a soccer ball is still, it stays still until a force moves it. If you kick the soccer ball, it keeps moving in the same direction until a force changes its motion. Any change of speed or direction requires a force. In other words, *forces cause acceleration.*

The direction in which an object moves depends on the direction of the force that is used on the object. You used a force on the table tennis ball in the Investigate. The ball rolled in the direction in which you blew.

What if there's more than one force? In that case, the forces work together. You saw this in the Independent Inquiry. The ball rolled in a direction between the direction of your force and the direction of your partner's force. Two forces of the same size but opposite in direction cancel out each other. Forces that cancel out each other are called balanced forces.

▲ This sled is pulled by six dogs. The sled with more dogs is pulled harder. It accelerates more than the other sled.

◀ One dog pulls this sled.

For more links and animations, go to **www.hspscience.com**

How does the size of a force affect acceleration? If you tap a basketball with your finger, it may roll a little. You've used a small force. But if you kick the ball hard, it takes off. You've used a large force. A larger force results in a larger acceleration. For example, a windmill's blades are turned by the wind. A gentle breeze turns them slowly. A strong wind spins them so fast that they're a blur!

Focus Skill CAUSE AND EFFECT **What causes the speed or direction of objects to change?**

Insta-Lab

Spring-Scale Follow the Leader

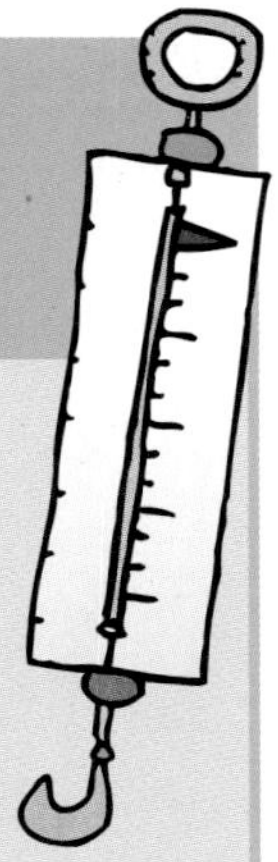

You will need a spring scale and a box. Hook the scale to the box. Drag the box. What happens when the scale shows a large reading? What happens when it reads zero?

Mass and Acceleration

Which would you rather move by pushing—a bicycle or a car? Pushing the bicycle would take much less force. You'd need to push the car much harder to get it moving.

The acceleration of an object depends on its mass. It takes more force to accelerate a large mass than to accelerate a small mass. This is because all matter has inertia. **Inertia** is the property of matter that keeps it moving in a straight line and keeps unmoving matter at rest. A truck has more inertia than a motorcycle. It needs a bigger engine, because more force is needed to get it moving quickly.

The more mass an object has, the more inertia it has. And the more inertia an object has, the harder it is to change its motion.

Focus Skill CAUSE AND EFFECT

Why is it harder to get a loaded wheelbarrow moving than an empty one?

The boy is throwing each ball equally hard. Which ball accelerates more when the boy throws it—the basketball or the tennis ball? Why?

Lesson Review

Essential Question

What is acceleration?

In this lesson, you learned that velocity is both speed and direction. Acceleration is a change in velocity. Forces change motion.

1. **Focus Skill CAUSE AND EFFECT** Draw and complete a graphic organizer to show five things that can cause acceleration.

   cause → effect

2. **SUMMARIZE** Write a summary of this lesson. Begin with this sentence: *Slowing down is acceleration.*

3. **DRAW CONCLUSIONS** Describe the acceleration of a downhill skier.

4. **VOCABULARY** Describe an everyday situation in which you might notice forces. Use the terms *velocity, acceleration, force,* and *inertia.*

Test Prep

5. **CRITICAL THINKING** A polar bear walks toward the North Pole. It walks 15 kilometers in 1 hour. What is the bear's velocity?

6. The acceleration of an object depends on the size of the force used on it and what other property?

   A. color
   B. mass
   C. temperature
   D. volume

Make Connections

Writing

Narrative Writing

Write an action-packed adventure **story** that describes motion and uses the vocabulary from this lesson.

9÷3 Math

Compare Accelerations

A car goes from 0 to 100 kilometers per hour in 10 seconds. Another car slows from 100 to 0 kilometers per hour in 10 seconds. Compare these accelerations.

Social Studies

History of Science

Use library resources to learn more about Isaac Newton. Explain what Newton's second law of motion is and how it relates to the ideas in this lesson.

LESSON 3

Essential Question

Why Is the Force of Gravity Important?

Investigate circular motion.

Read and Learn about the force of gravity.

Fast Fact

What Goes Up . . .
The same force that pulls sky divers to Earth keeps planets in their orbits around the sun. In the Investigate, you'll learn how an object can travel a circular path like the orbits of the planets.

Sky divers in a double ring

Vocabulary Preview

gravity [GRAV•ih•tee] The force of attraction between Earth and other objects, an expression of gravitation (p. 681)

---

gravitation [grav•ih•TAY•shuhn] A force that acts between any two objects and pulls them together (p. 681)

weight [WAYT] A measure of the gravitational force acting on an object (p. 682)

friction [FRIK•shuhn] A force that resists motion between objects that are touching (p. 683)

Investigate

Making Circular Motion

Guided Inquiry

Start with Questions

This student is playing tetherball. The ball is on a rope that winds around a pole.

- Why does the ball move up or down as it moves around the pole?
- Why does the ball keep moving in a circle around the pole?

Investigate to find out. Then read to find out more.

Prepare to Investigate

Inquiry Skill Tip

Sometimes the only way to find out why something happens is to conduct an experiment. That is the only way you can be sure how your variables will affect each other.

Materials

- safety goggles
- rubber stopper
- string, 1-m length
- tape
- cardboard tube

Make an Observation Chart

Direction of Pull	Direction of Stopper

Follow This Procedure

1. **CAUTION: Put on safety goggles.** Tie a stopper to one end of a string.
2. Put tape over the string on the stopper to hold the string in place. Be sure the stopper is securely fastened. Thread the string through a tube.
3. Go outdoors. Stand where you have a clear space 3 meters around you in all directions.
4. Holding the string, move the tube to whirl the stopper in a circular path over your head. Hold the string securely. You may want to wrap it once around your hand. Don't hit anything with the stopper! The circular path of the stopper should be level with the ground.
5. **Observe** the direction in which you are pulling the string as the stopper moves around the circle.

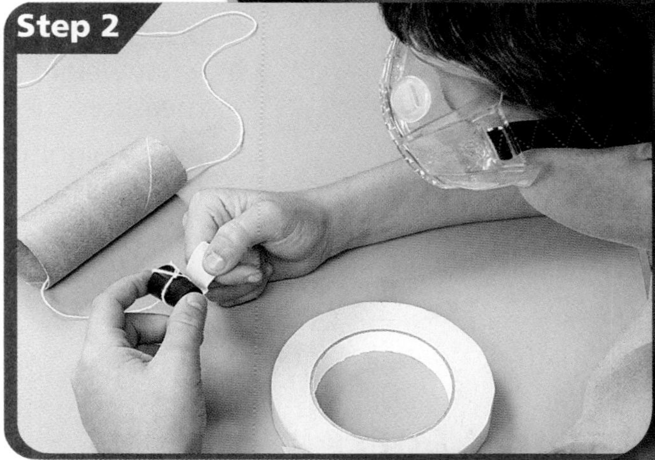
Step 2

Step 4

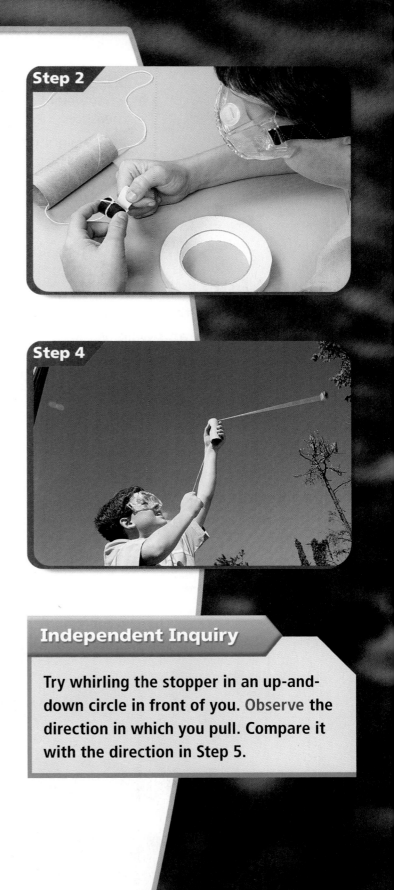

Draw Conclusions

1. In what direction did you pull the string to keep the stopper moving in a circle?
2. **Inquiry Skill** What materials would you need for an **experiment** to test the hypothesis that spinning the stopper faster requires a stronger pull?

Independent Inquiry

Try whirling the stopper in an up-and-down circle in front of you. Observe the direction in which you pull. Compare it with the direction in Step 5.

VOCABULARY
gravity p. 681
gravitation p. 681
weight p. 682
friction p. 683

SCIENCE CONCEPTS
- what weight measures
- how weight differs from mass

Focus Skill MAIN IDEA AND DETAILS
Look for details about gravity, gravitation, and weight.

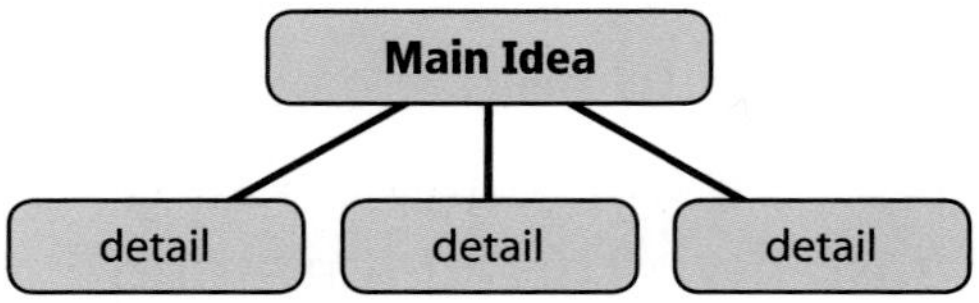

Natural Forces

Every day, you use the force of your muscles to sit, stand, and walk. What other forces do you use every day? You've seen how magnets interact. You've also explored electric charges. You use electric devices and machines with magnets all the time.

The force between electric charges is one of the most important in nature. It holds together tiny particles of matter. These particles are so small that you don't see how electricity affects their motion.

You do see the result of electric force when it pulls and pushes charged objects. For example, you've probably seen a balloon stick to a wall after you rubbed it against fabric or your hair.

Focus Skill MAIN IDEA AND DETAILS
Give an example of how you used the force of your muscles today.

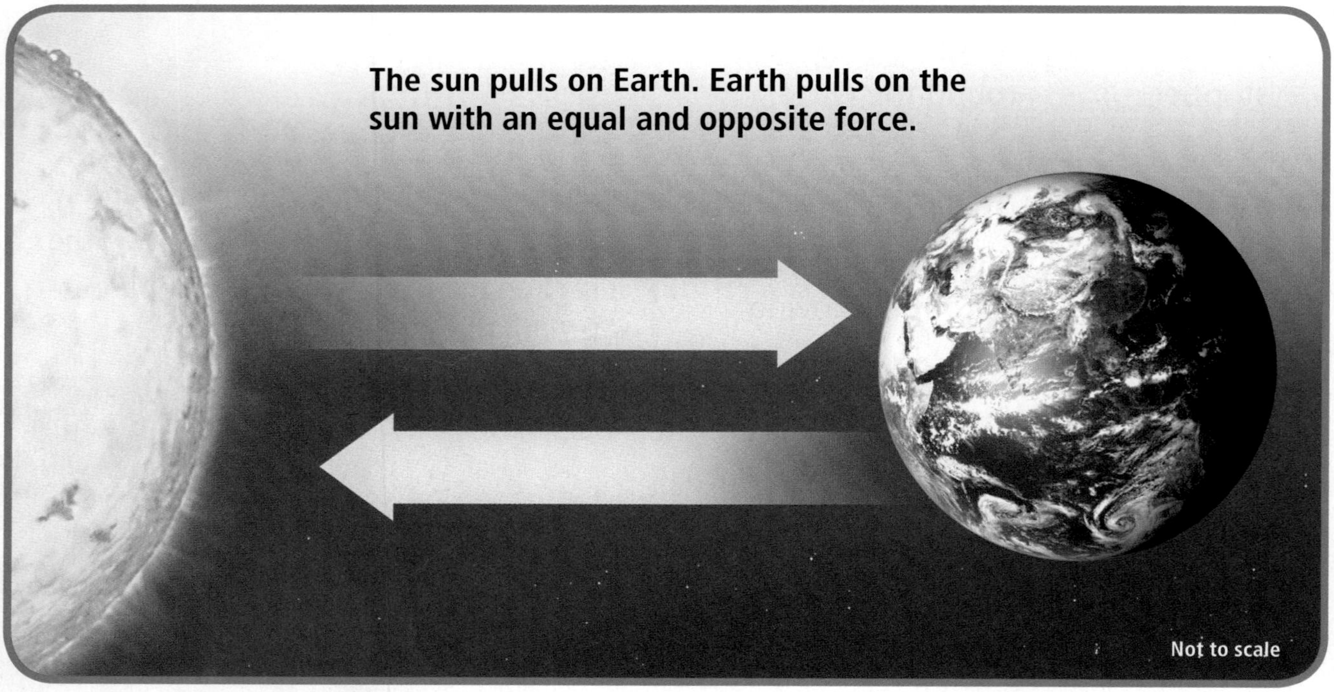

The sun pulls on Earth. Earth pulls on the sun with an equal and opposite force.

Gravity

Besides the force of your own muscles, gravity is probably the force you notice most. **Gravity** is the force that pulls things toward Earth. If you toss a ball upward, gravity pulls it back down to the ground.

Gravity is an effect of gravitation. **Gravitation** is a force that acts between all masses and causes them to attract one another. It acts everywhere, all the time. Gravitation helps hold the moon in its orbit around Earth. It pulls the moon and Earth toward each other. This pull prevents the moon from flying off in a straight line because of its inertia. It is similar to the pull that held the stopper in its path in the Investigate.

Gravitation also holds Earth in its orbit around the sun. The other planets, too, are held in their orbits by gravitation.

The larger and closer two masses are, the more gravitation affects them. Sometimes, the force is very weak, but it's always there. Earth's gravitation affects you more than any other object's, because Earth is so large and so close to you.

Focus Skill MAIN IDEA AND DETAILS

What keeps the moon in a circular path?

▼ **Gravity is the force that pulls you toward Earth. Roller coasters use this force to provide thrills.**

Weight

How can you measure the force of gravity on an object? Simple—just weigh the object on a scale.

An object's **weight** is the gravitational force acting on it. Because it is a force, weight is measured in newtons (N). One newton is about the weight of an apple, or just under a quarter of a pound.

Don't confuse weight with mass—they aren't the same thing. Mass is the amount of matter in an object. It's measured on a balance, not on a scale. The unit of mass is the gram.

Your weight is the gravitational force acting on you. So your weight would change if you were away from Earth's gravity. The moon's gravitational force is less than Earth's. On the moon, you would weigh only one-sixth of what you weigh on Earth. Your mass, however, is the same wherever you are.

This bear cub weighs about 27 newtons (about 6 pounds). The cub is being weighed with a spring scale. The child weighs 271 newtons (61 lb). She's being weighed on a doctor's scale.

Focus Skill MAIN IDEA AND DETAILS

Is a person on a diet trying to lose weight or mass? Explain your reasoning.

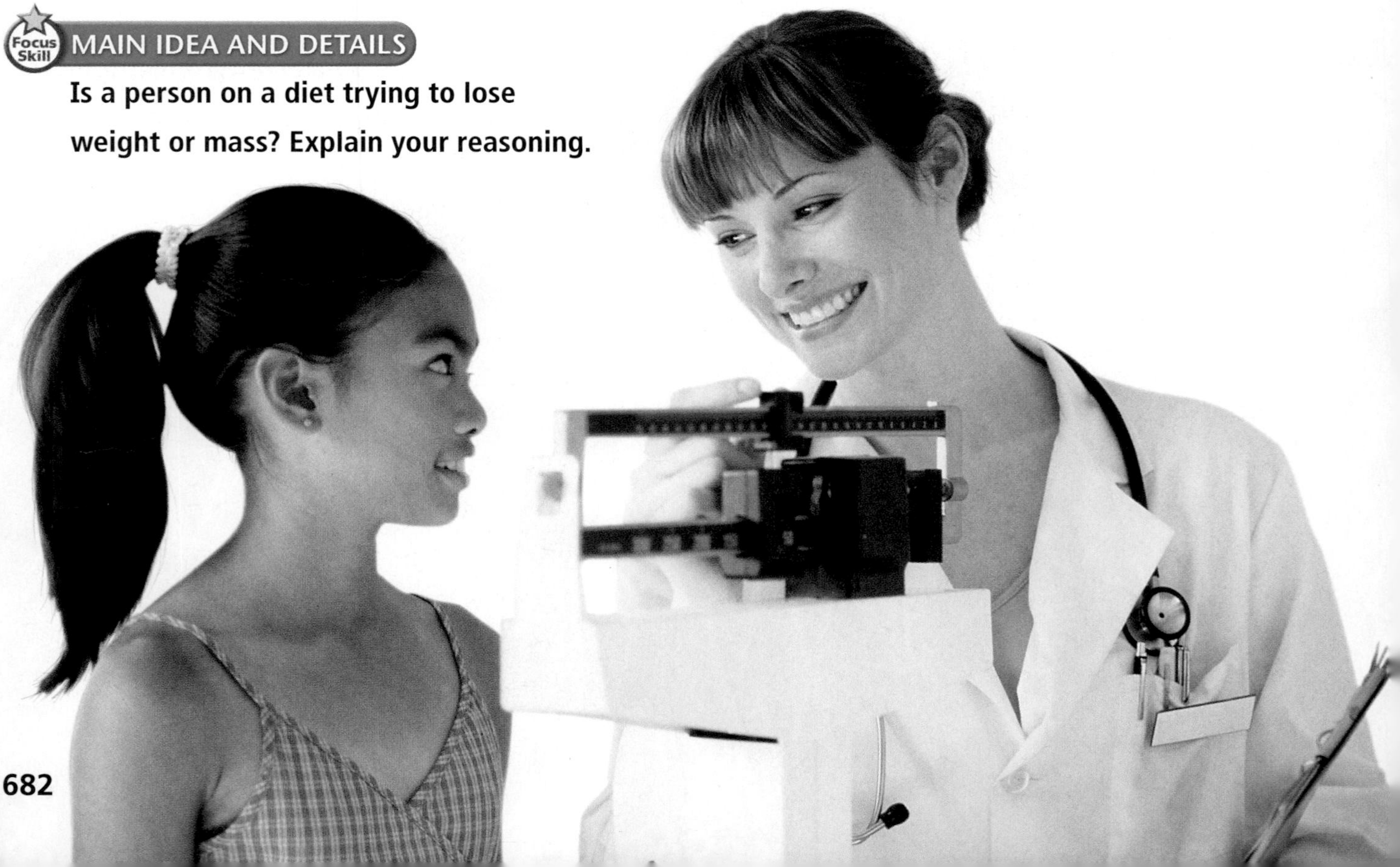

▲ **A bike's brakes use friction to slow down the bike, to stop it, or to keep it from moving in the first place.**

Friction

Have you ever heard tires squeal when a car stopped suddenly? That sound is caused by another familiar force—friction. **Friction** is a force that resists the motion of objects, relative to each other, when the objects are touching. Friction changes kinetic energy to heat. Over time, friction slows down motion and stops it. Friction is measured in newtons, just like other forces.

The force of friction is always present when one surface touches another. Often, friction is useful. For example, your bike slows down when you apply the brakes. The brakes are rubber pads that create friction when they press against a wheel. The friction slows the wheel and finally stops it.

Sports shoes have rubber soles that increase friction. This helps keep you from slipping while you run and play.

Focus Skill MAIN IDEA AND DETAILS

If your friend pushes you to the right, in what direction does friction act?

Insta-Lab

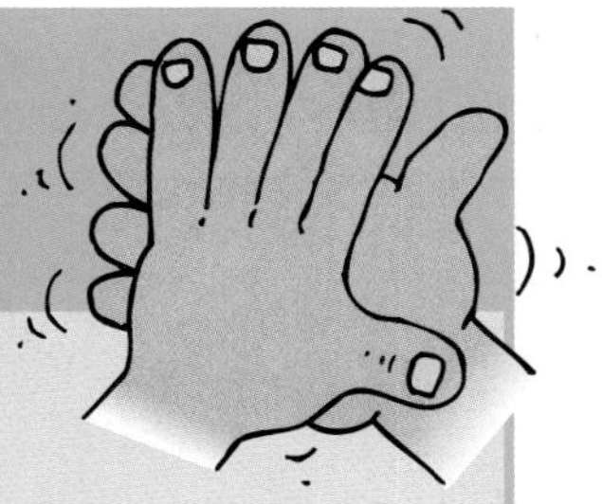

Get the Feel of Friction

Rub your hands together. Put a drop of cooking oil on your hands, and rub them together again. Now put on some rubber gloves, and rub your hands together. How is the friction different each time?

Controlling Friction

Friction acts between any two surfaces. For example, it slows or stops motion of the parts within machines. Friction causes machines to lose energy as waste heat. Did you notice your hands warm up when you rubbed them together in the Insta-Lab?

Friction is useful when you want to brake your bicycle. However, surfaces wear out quickly when a lot of friction is present. So friction can also be a problem. People reduce friction by making surfaces smooth. Also, surfaces may be covered with oil or another slippery material to reduce friction.

Several moving parts of a bicycle are oiled to reduce friction. The chain, gears, and pedals are oiled. The oil allows the moving parts to slide smoothly over one another.

Focus Skill MAIN IDEA AND DETAILS

What are two ways that friction can be controlled?

Water on a water slide reduces friction, making the ride faster and more exciting. ▶

The bike rider oils his chain and gears to reduce friction and make his ride easier. ▼

The surfer waxes his board to increase the friction between the board and his feet. ▼

Essential Question

Why is the Force of Gravity Important?

In this lesson, you learned that gravity is a natural force that pulls things toward Earth. Gravity is why weight exists. Friction also acts on matter.

1. Focus Skill **MAIN IDEA AND DETAILS** Draw and complete a graphic organizer showing how gravity is related to weight.

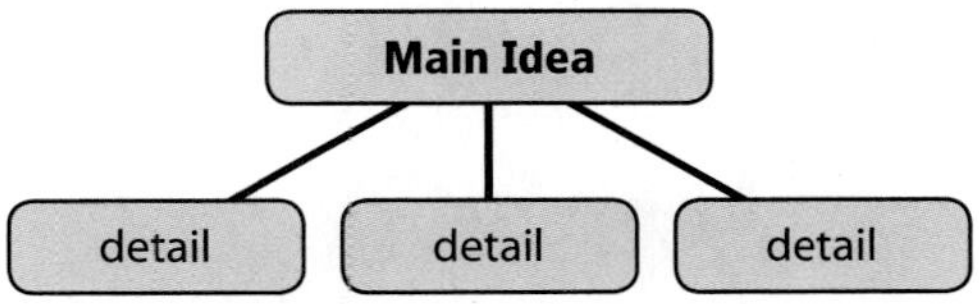

2. **SUMMARIZE** Write two sentences to define weight and friction.

3. **DRAW CONCLUSIONS** Explain how friction keeps nails from falling out of walls.

4. **VOCABULARY** Use the vocabulary terms from this lesson to make a word puzzle.

Test Prep

5. **CRITICAL THINKING** What happens to motion when friction is reduced?

6. What does weight measure?
   A. electrical force
   B. friction
   C. gravity
   D. acceleration

Make Connections

Writing

Expository Writing

Write about a product that reduces or increases friction. **Explain** how the product works and why people need it.

Math

Solve a Problem

You push an eraser forward with a force of 2 newtons. The eraser doesn't move. What is the force of the friction acting on the eraser?

Music

Make a Glass Sing

The friction between a wet finger and the rim of a thin-walled glass can make a pleasing sound. See if you can make music this way. Be careful! Hold the glass with one hand while you run a finger around its rim.

SCIENCE SOARS AT THE OLYMPICS

Chris Soule races down a hill on his sled to train for the Winter Olympics.

To train for the Winter Olympics, athlete Chris Soule stands at the top of a long hill holding a small sled. He springs forward, jumps on the sled, and races down the hill as fast as he can. Soule competes in a kind of Olympic sled race called skeleton. Competing in skeleton takes speed, strength, and science. That's right—science.

Shaving Time

A top skeleton racer must be fast. The athlete who finishes with the fastest time wins the race and the gold medal. "Some of the sports events are won by one-hundredth or even one-thousandth of a second," Peter Davis told *Weekly Reader.* Davis is the head of coaching and sports sciences for the United States Olympic Committee.

Racing with Science

To shave hundredths of a second off their times, many athletes have turned to science.

At the U.S. Olympic Training Facility in Lake Placid, New York, scientists called biomechanists (by•oh•MEH•kuhn•ists) use computer software to help skeleton racers improve their push starts.

To do this, scientists videotape the athletes during their push starts. The tapes are fed into a computer. The scientists can then study every movement and every angle of the athletes' bodies. They decide, for example, whether the athlete is leaning too far forward at the start or whether his or her feet are in the best position.

Virtual Training

Another training tool that's being used more and more is virtual reality. "We can set up an athletic event on a computer," Davis said. "An athlete uses video goggles to see the event and react to what is happening." By using virtual reality, athletes who compete in winter sports can train throughout the year.

Think and Write

1. Why are even small improvements important for some sports?
2. How is videotape used to help racers?

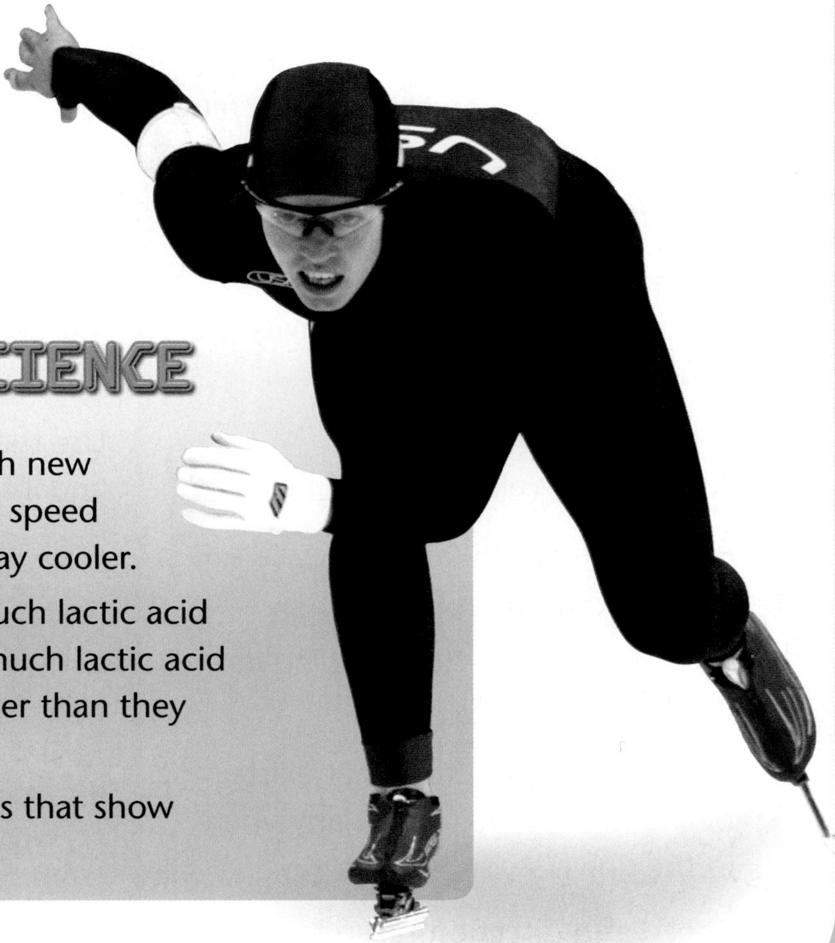

MORE SPORTS SCIENCE

- Uniforms are being made with new kinds of slick fabrics that help speed skaters perform better and stay cooler.
- Blood tests can show how much lactic acid is in an athlete's blood. Too much lactic acid makes the muscles work harder than they should.
- Skiers practice in wind tunnels that show them how to go faster.

Spin-In™ Find out more. Log on to **www.hspscience.com**

Chapter 16 Review and Test Preparation

Vocabulary Review

Use the terms below to complete the sentences. The page numbers tell you where to look in the chapter if you need help.

position p. 660
motion p. 660
speed p. 662
velocity p. 670
acceleration p. 671
force p. 672
inertia p. 674
gravitation p. 681
weight p. 682
friction p. 683

1. The force that slows or stops the motion of objects, relative to each other, when the objects are touching is _______.
2. A push or pull measured in newtons is a _______.
3. The measurement of the gravity acting on an object is the object's _______.
4. A change in velocity is _______.
5. A change in position is _______.
6. The property that describes an object's resistance to changing its motion is _______.
7. The force of attraction that exists between any two masses anywhere in the universe is _______.
8. Speed and direction taken together are _______.
9. The distance an object travels divided by the time it takes to travel is its _______.
10. An object's location is its _______.

Check Understanding

Write the letter of the best choice.

11. **MAIN IDEA AND DETAILS** What force holds the moon in its orbit around Earth?
    Focus Skill
    A. friction **C.** position
    B. gravitation **D.** weight

12. If an object has a large mass on Earth, what else does it have a lot of?
    F. inertia and volume
    G. weight and inertia
    H. weight and speed
    J. weight and volume

Use the picture to answer Questions 13 and 14.

13. A dial in the picture tells you how many kilometers per hour the car is going. What does this measure?
    A. acceleration **C.** velocity
    B. speed **D.** weight

14. What information about the car can you find by using the dial and compass together?

F. its acceleration **H.** its speed
G. its motion **J.** its velocity

15. What force is shown by Arrow 2?

A. electric force **C.** gravity
B. friction **D.** magnetic force

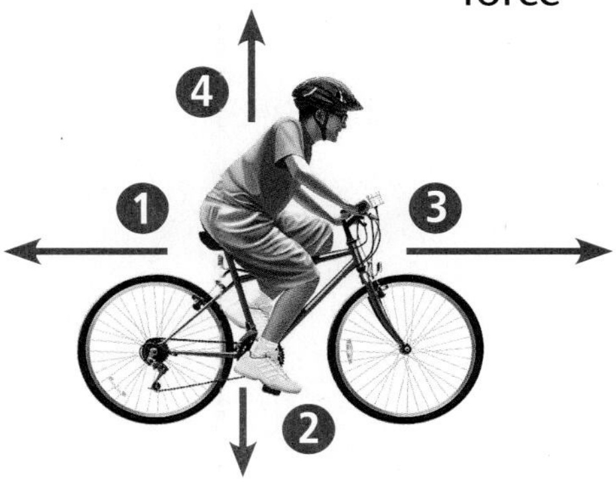

16. **CAUSE AND EFFECT** If you increase the force on an object, what do you probably also increase?

Focus Skill

F. acceleration **H.** inertia
G. gravity **J.** mass

Inquiry Skills

17. How do you **observe** friction when you erase a pencil mark?

18. A girl pulls a wagon by applying a force to it. What other force can you **infer** acts on the wagon in the opposite direction?

Critical Thinking

19. Can an object that moves at a constant speed be accelerating? Explain your answer.

The Big Idea

20. A truck, a car, and a bicycle are driving away from a stoplight. The truck uses a big engine for this acceleration. A car uses a smaller engine, and the bicycle rider uses the force of his own muscles. Why does each vehicle require a different amount of force to accelerate? Suppose each vehicle is pushed forward with a force of the same size. Which vehicle will be moving fastest after one minute? Why?

CHAPTER 17

Simple Machines

What's the Big Idea? Simple machines change the way that work is done to help people accomplish tasks.

Essential Questions

Lesson 1
How Do Simple Machines Help People Do Work?

Lesson 2
How Do a Pulley and a Wheel-and-Axle Help People Do Work?

Lesson 3
How Do Other Simple Machines Help People Do Work?

GO online ▸ Student eBook www.hspscience.com

What do YOU wonder?

Raging River? Simple machines can be found just about anywhere there are people. What simple machines is this person using? How do they relate to the **Big Idea?**

Whitewater kayaker

LESSON 1

Essential Question

How Do Simple Machines Help People Do Work?

Investigate how the force you need can change.

Read and Learn how simple machines can help people do work.

Fast Fact

Boinnng!

The two people on the left end dropped 2 meters ($6\frac{1}{2}$ ft) onto the seesaw. That sent the person on the right end flying almost 3 meters (10 ft) into the air! In the Investigate, you'll make a model that shows the forces on a seesaw.

Acrobats using a seesaw

Vocabulary Preview

work [WERK] The use of force to move an object over a distance (p. 696)

simple machine [SIM•puhl muh•SHEEN] A machine with few or no moving parts that you apply just one force to (p. 697)

lever [LEV•er] A simple machine made of a bar that pivots on a fixed point (p. 698)

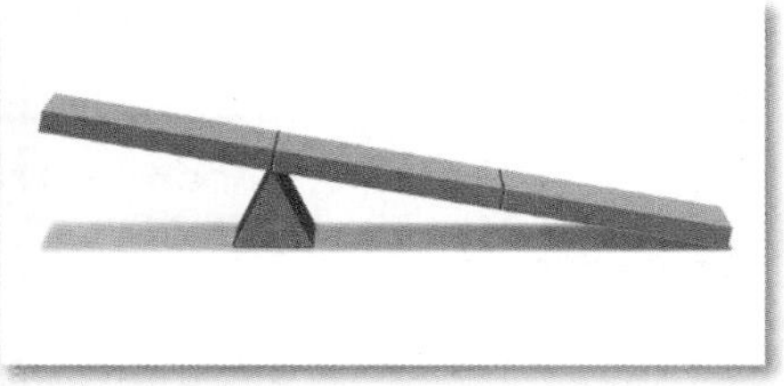

fulcrum [FUHL•kruhm] The fixed point on a lever (p. 698)

Investigate

Up and Down

Guided Inquiry

Start with Questions

These people are playing on a seesaw. One end goes up as the other end goes down.

- What makes the ends of the seesaw move?
- Is it harder to lift a person on a seesaw than it would be to lift the person alone?

Investigate to find out. Then read to find out more.

Prepare to Investigate

Inquiry Skill Tip

Using space relationships means paying attention to the position and motion of more than one thing. Make sure you are tracking both of the items you are comparing to each other.

Materials

- safety goggles
- tape
- 2 rubber bands
- wooden ruler

Make an Observation Chart

Finger Position	Length of Rubber Band Closest to 0 cm (cm)	Length of Rubber Band Closest to 30 cm (cm)	Observations
15-cm mark			
17-cm mark			
19-cm mark			
21-cm mark			

Follow This Procedure

1. CAUTION: **Put on safety goggles.** Work in groups of three. Tape a rubber band 2 cm from each end of one ruler.
2. One person should hook a finger through each rubber band and lift the ruler. This person should pull enough to keep the ruler level while a second person presses down on the 15-cm mark.
3. The third person should **measure** the length of each rubber band. **Record** your **observations** and **measurements**.
4. Repeat Steps 2 and 3, with the second person pressing on the 17-cm mark.
5. Repeat Steps 2 and 3, with the second person pressing on the 19-cm and 21-cm marks.

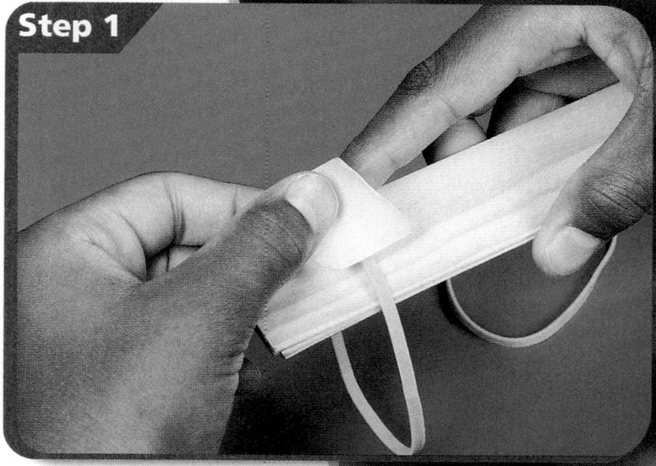
Step 1

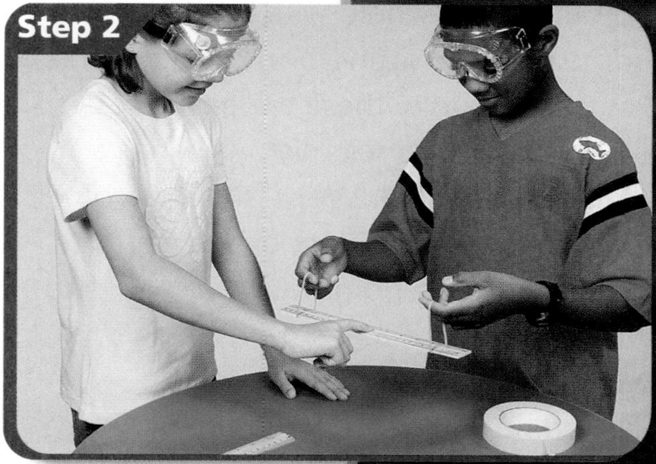
Step 2

Draw Conclusions

1. What happened as the second person pressed farther from the ruler's center?
2. **Inquiry Skill** Sometimes, scientists can learn about what they can't see by watching how it affects other things. For example, the push on the ruler affected the rubber bands. How did you **use space relationships** to observe what was happening to the ruler and rubber bands?

Independent Inquiry

What do you predict would happen if you pressed down on the 10-cm mark? Test your prediction.

Read and Learn

VOCABULARY
work p. 696
simple machine p. 697
lever p. 698
fulcrum p. 698

SCIENCE CONCEPTS
- what a scientist means by work
- what a simple machine is
- how a lever changes the way work is done

Focus Skill MAIN IDEA AND DETAILS

Look for details about levers.

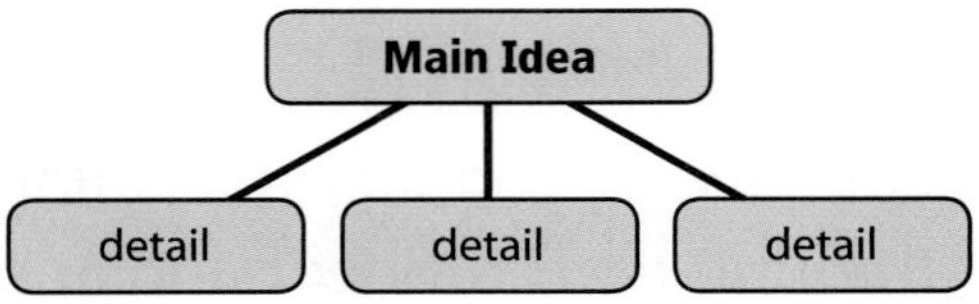

Work and Simple Machines

You do schoolwork in class and at home. You may help with work at home by baby-sitting or mowing lawns. For most people, these are examples of work. But to a scientist, *work* has a different meaning. **Work** is the use of force to move an object over a distance.

When you do homework, you have to concentrate. But to a scientist, the only work you might do is lift a pencil.

Imagine you're pushing with all your might on a door that's stuck. If it doesn't move, you're not doing work.

For work to be done, an object also has to move in the direction of the force applied to it. If you lift a box, you apply a force upward and the box moves up. That's work.

But what if you then carry the box across the room? Your arms are lifting up, but the box is moving sideways. So, your arms aren't doing any work on the box, no matter how tired they might get.

Here's another definition: A *machine* is anything that changes the way work is done.

The girl uses an upward force on the dog, and the dog moves up. The girl is having fun but is doing work, too.

A lawn mower makes the work of mowing lawns easier. It's a complex machine with many parts.

This wheelbarrow is a simple machine—a lever. The boy lifts the handles, and the pile of leaves goes up. He does the same amount of work as carrying the leaves by hand. It takes less force, but he lifts further. ▶

You just read that work is the use of force applied over a distance. A machine might change the direction of a force or the amount of force that is needed.

You probably use a lot of machines every day. Most machines have many moving parts. But some machines are very simple. In fact, they're called simple machines.

A **simple machine** is a machine with few or no moving parts to which you apply just one force. Some simple machines have very few moving parts. Others have no moving parts.

Imagine that you want to pry up a board nailed to the floor. You slide one end of a pry bar under the board and press down on the other end. After a good push, the board comes up.

The pry bar is a simple machine. You applied a force when you pushed down. The bar changed the direction of the force, and the board moved up. The bar also changed the amount of force that was needed. After all, you couldn't pry up the board with just your hands!

Focus Skill MAIN IDEA AND DETAILS **How might a machine change the way work is done?**

Levers

A **lever** is a bar that pivots on a fixed point. The fixed point is called the **fulcrum**. For example, a seesaw is a lever. The board of the seesaw is the bar, and the place in the middle, where the board pivots, is the fulcrum.

The pry bar you just read about is one kind of lever. The fulcrum was the point where the pry bar touched the floor. A force was applied at one end of the bar. The thing that moved—the board—was at the other end.

With the seesaw and the pry bar, the fulcrum is between the force and the thing that moves. But there are other kinds of levers. In a picture on the previous page, a boy lifts one end of a wheelbarrow. He applies force at that end, and the wheelbarrow pivots at the other end. The thing that is moved—the pile of leaves—is between the force and the fulcrum.

A broom is a third kind of lever. You hold the handle at one end—the fulcrum. The thing that is moved—the dirt—is at the other end. You apply force between the thing that is moved and the fulcrum.

Focus Skill **MAIN IDEA AND DETAILS**

Give three examples of a lever.

A lever is just a bar that pivots on a fulcrum. In this diagram, the fulcrum is between where you push and where the work is done. How is this lever like a seesaw?

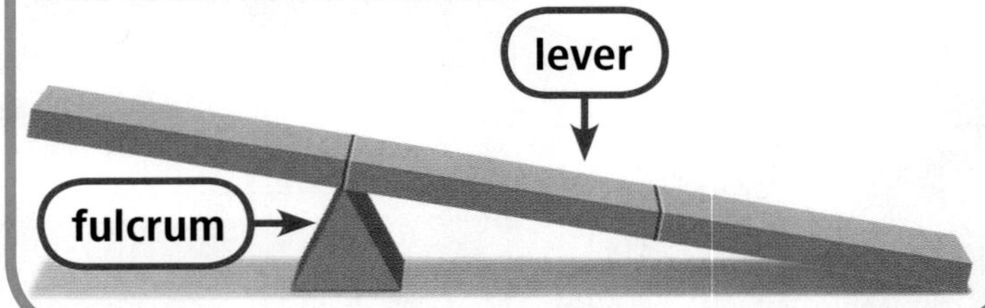

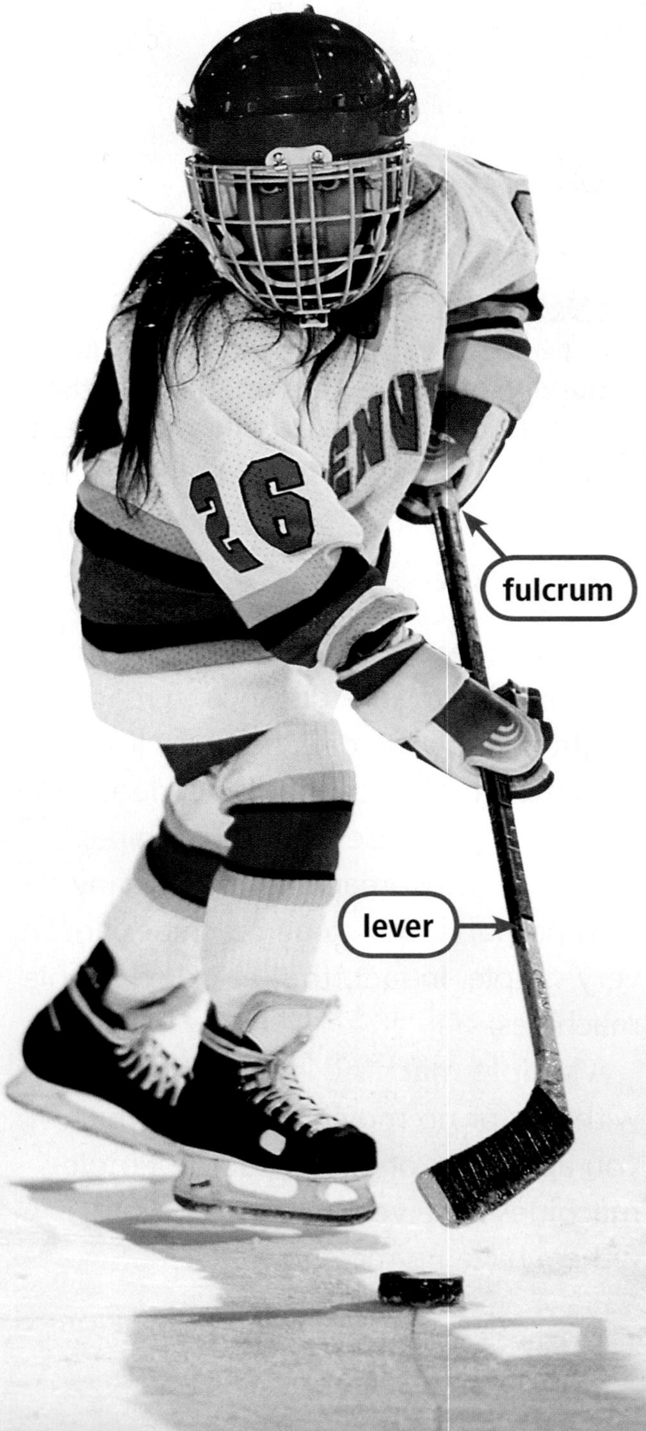

A hockey stick is one kind of lever. The girl holds one end of the stick. That's the fulcrum, where the stick pivots. The other end moves the puck. The girl applies force between the two ends. ▶

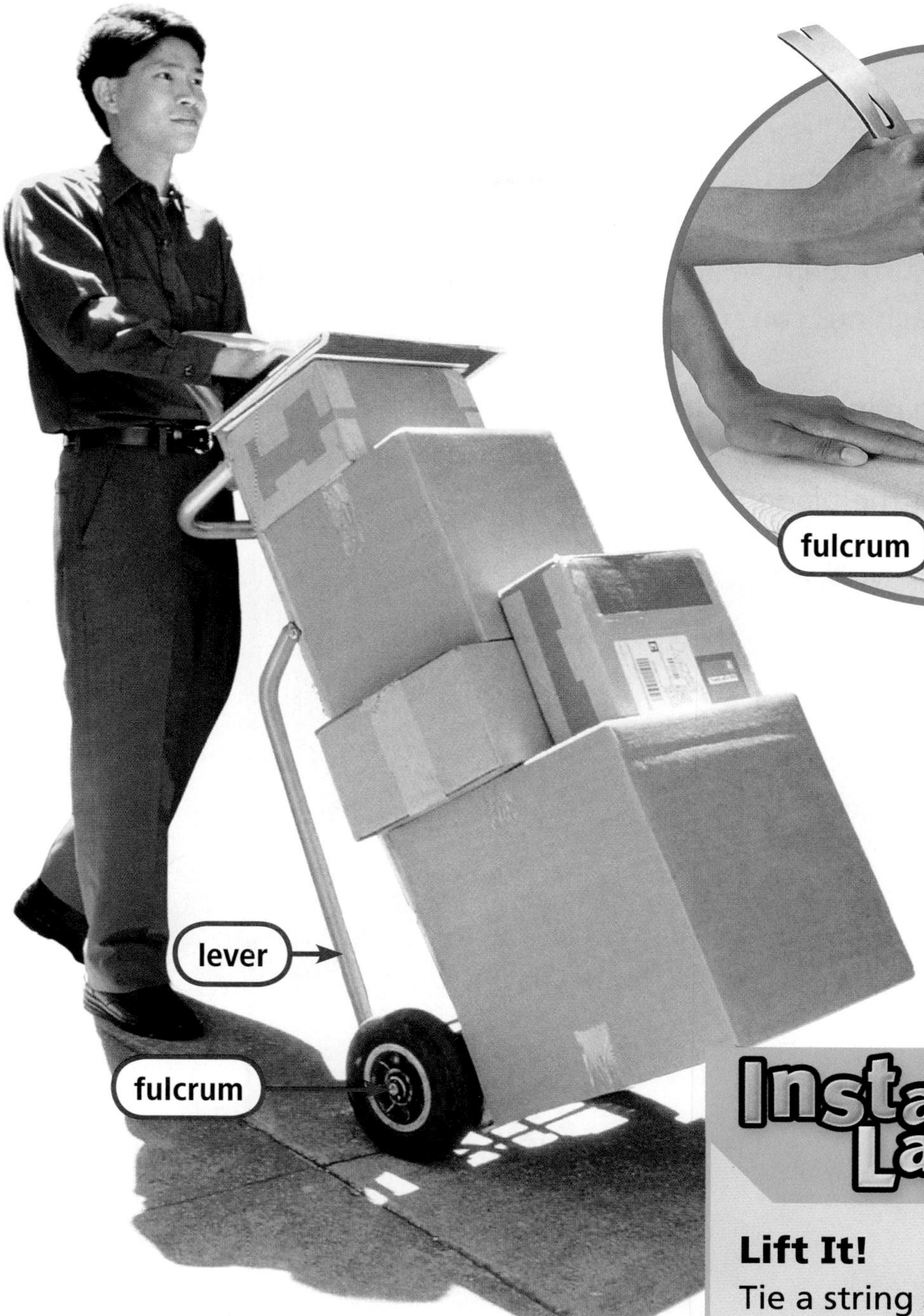

▲ When the man tips the hand truck, it acts like a lever. He applies force at one end, and the hand truck pivots on the wheels at the other end. The boxes between the ends move.

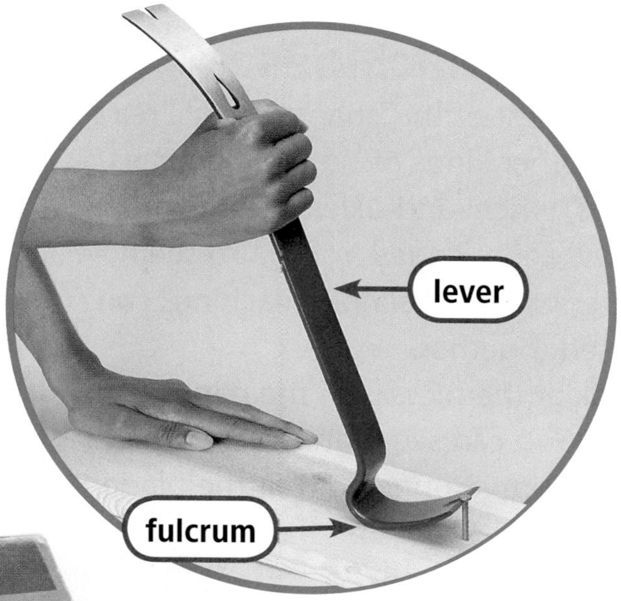

▲ Here's the pry bar that you read about. The fulcrum is where the bar pivots. You apply force at one end. The nail at the other end moves.

Insta-Lab

Lift It!

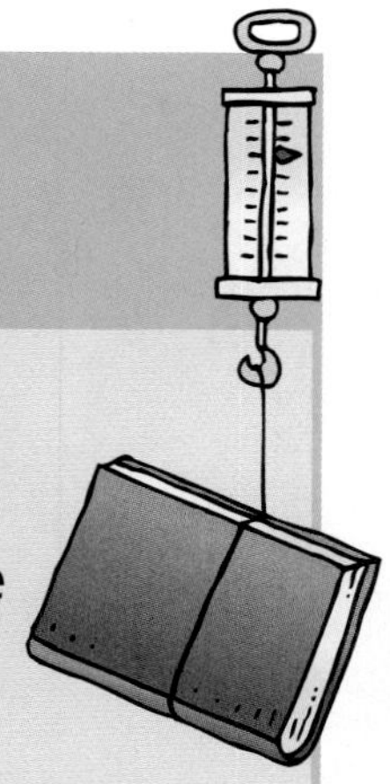

Tie a string around a book. Hook a spring scale to the string. How much force does it take to lift the book? Then move the string to one end of the book. Lift this end, leaving the other end on a table. How much force is needed to lift the book now? How is this like a wheelbarrow?

Levers with Other Simple Machines

In the rest of this chapter, you'll read about other kinds of simple machines—pulleys, wheel-and-axles, inclined planes, screws, and wedges. You'll also see how different kinds of simple machines can be used together.

Look at the picture of the paper cutter. You can see that it's a lever with the fulcrum at one end. But the blade of the paper cutter is another simple machine—a wedge. The two simple machines work together to cut paper.

A hedge clipper is made up of two levers. Each has its fulcrum between the two ends. And just as in the paper cutter, the blades are wedges.

Focus Skill **MAIN IDEA AND DETAILS**

Give an example of a lever working with another simple machine.

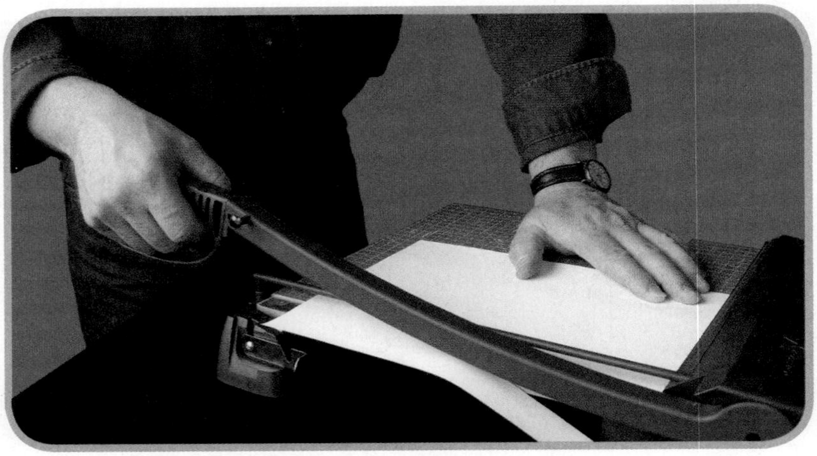

This paper cutter consists of a lever and a wedge working together. ▶

▼ This hedge clipper is made up of two levers and two wedges.

Climbing a practice wall

Vocabulary Preview

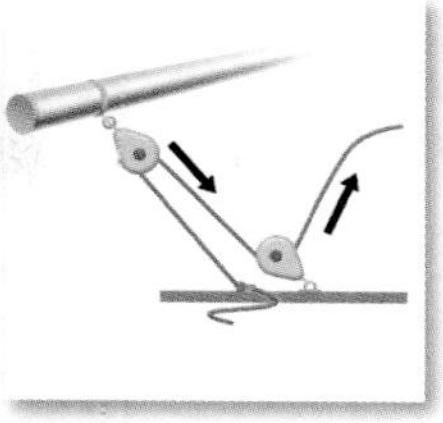

pulley [PUHL•ee] A simple machine made of a wheel with a line around it (p. 706)

wheel-and-axle [WEEL•and•AK•suhl] A simple machine made of a wheel and an axle that turn together (p. 708)

Investigate

Hoist Away

Guided Inquiry

Start with Questions

This hoist is lifting materials that would be very hard for a person to move!

- How can the machine lift these materials?
- Could the people move the materials without the machine?

Investigate to find out. Then read to find out more.

Prepare to Investigate

Inquiry Skill Tip

When you do more than one experiment, you can change more than one variable. Keep track of which variables have changed. Note what effect that has on your experiment from test to test.

Materials

- string
- book
- wire coat hanger
- ruler
- scissors
- spring scale

Make an Observation Chart

	Step 4 (Pull Down)	Step 5 (Pull Up)
Spring scale reading		
Distance spring scale moved (cm)		
Distance book moved (cm)		
Observations		

Follow This Procedure

1. Work with a partner. Tie a loop of string tightly around a book.
2. Bend a hanger into a diamond shape. Hang it from a doorknob or a coat hook.
3. Cut a 1-m length of string. Tie one end to the loop of string around the book. Pass the other end through the hanger, and attach it to the spring scale.
4. One partner should lift the book by pulling down on the spring scale. Note the reading on the spring scale. The other partner should **measure** the distance the spring scale moved and the distance the book moved. **Record** your observations and **measurements**.
5. Hook the hanger to the loop of string on the book. Untie the long string. Pass it through the hanger, and tie it to the doorknob or coat hook. Repeat Step 4, but pull up on the spring scale.

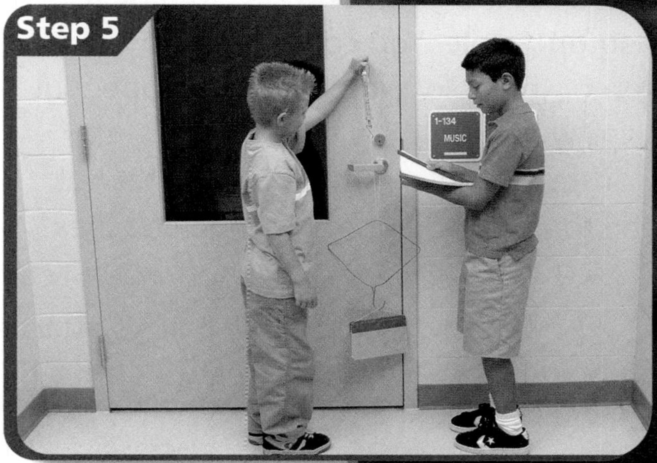

Draw Conclusions

1. How did the force needed to lift the book change?

2. **Inquiry Skill** What **variable** changed the second time?

Independent Inquiry

Experiment. **How could you use two hangers with the spring scale and string to lift the book? Try it!**

VOCABULARY
pulley p. 706
wheel-and-axle p. 708

SCIENCE CONCEPTS
- how a pulley changes the way work is done
- how a wheel-and-axle changes the way work is done

Focus Skill MAIN IDEA AND DETAILS

Look for details about pulleys and wheel-and-axles.

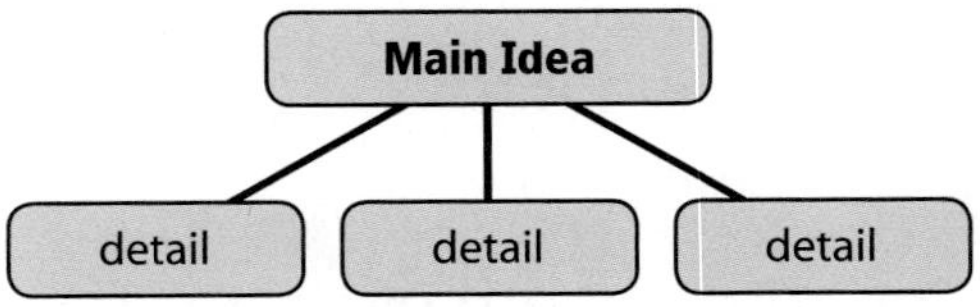

Pulleys

Changing the direction of the force can make a job much easier. For example, imagine you want to raise a flag up a pole. You could climb to the top of the pole and pull up the rope. But who would do that?

Instead, you can use a pulley that's at the top of the flagpole. A rope attaches to the flag, goes up around the wheel, and runs back down to the ground. You pull down on one end of the rope, and the other end goes up, taking the flag with it. That's easier, isn't it?

A **pulley** is a wheel with a line around it. The line might be a rope, a cord, or a chain. The wheel has a lip around its edge to keep the line from slipping off.

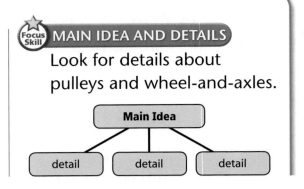

Most sailboats have pulleys attached to the sails. Pulleys enable the sails to move in different directions—up, down, and even sideways. ▼

Pulling one end of the rope in one direction moves the other end in a different direction.

As you know, all simple machines change the way work is done. A pulley changes the direction of the force. If you pull down on one end of the line, the other end goes up.

A single, fixed pulley doesn't change the amount of force needed. For example, suppose you wanted to lift a 200-newton (45-lb) box. You'd still need to lift 200 newtons, even with a pulley. Pulleys come in all sizes. A child might use a tiny pulley to open a window blind. A mechanic might use a large group of pulleys with a chain to lift an engine out of a car.

Focus Skill **MAIN IDEA AND DETAILS** **How does a pulley change the way work is done?**

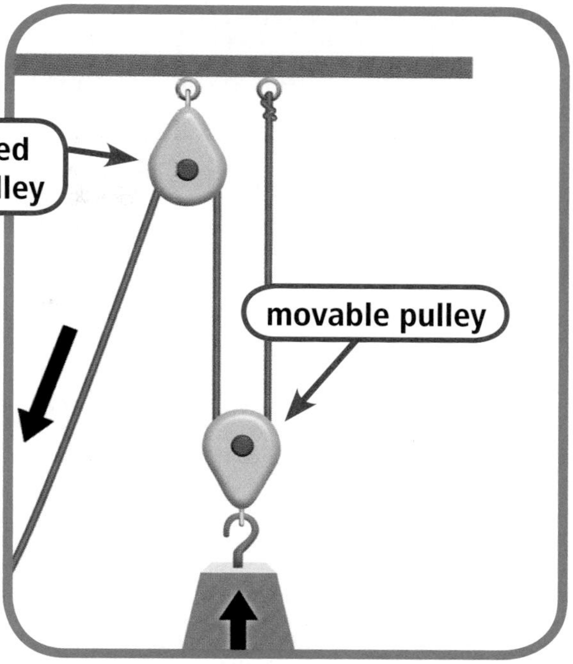

▲ **Adding pulleys can lower the force needed to do work. But, you have to pull a greater distance.**

This man is using a large group of pulleys to increase his lifting force.

Wheel-and-Axles

A wheel-and-axle is exactly what its name says—a wheel and an axle. An axle is a rod that goes into or through a wheel. You can see wheels as well as axles on wheelbarrows and on skateboards, but those wheels and those axles are not simple machines.

To be a simple machine, a **wheel-and-axle** must have a wheel and an axle that turn *together.* If you turn the axle, the wheel turns with it. If you turn the wheel, the axle turns, too.

A wheel-and-axle changes the way work is done. If you turn the wheel, the axle turns with more force. You have to move the wheel over a greater distance, but you use less force. If you move the axle, the wheel moves a greater distance. You have to use more force, but you don't have to move the axle as far.

Focus Skill MAIN IDEA AND DETAILS

What must a wheel and an axle do to be a simple machine?

▼ A wheel-and-axle can work in two ways. You can turn the wheel to make the axle move. Or you can turn the axle to make the wheel move.

Science Up Close

The Faucet: A Wheel-and-Axle in Use

Did you ever wonder how a faucet works? The water flows through a small opening inside the faucet. When a washer blocks that opening, no water can get out. If you raise the washer a little, a little water does flow. When the opening is completely unblocked, lots of water flows.

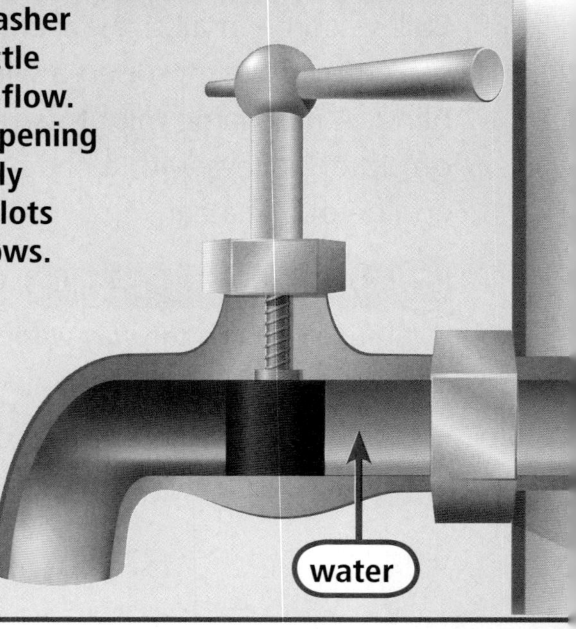

Insta-Lab

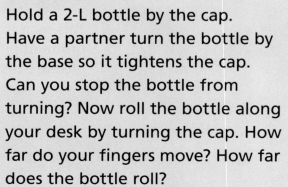

A Model Wheel-and-Axle

Hold a 2-L bottle by the cap. Have a partner turn the bottle by the base so it tightens the cap. Can you stop the bottle from turning? Now roll the bottle along your desk by turning the cap. How far do your fingers move? How far does the bottle roll?

The moving part of the faucet is a wheel-and-axle. The handle is like one spoke of a wheel. The washer is on the end of an axle. The axle moves up and down because of a screw. Without the handle, you'd have to turn the axle by hand to adjust the water. That would be hard to do. But when you turn the handle, you turn the axle, too. You can use much less force, which makes it easier to open and close the faucet.

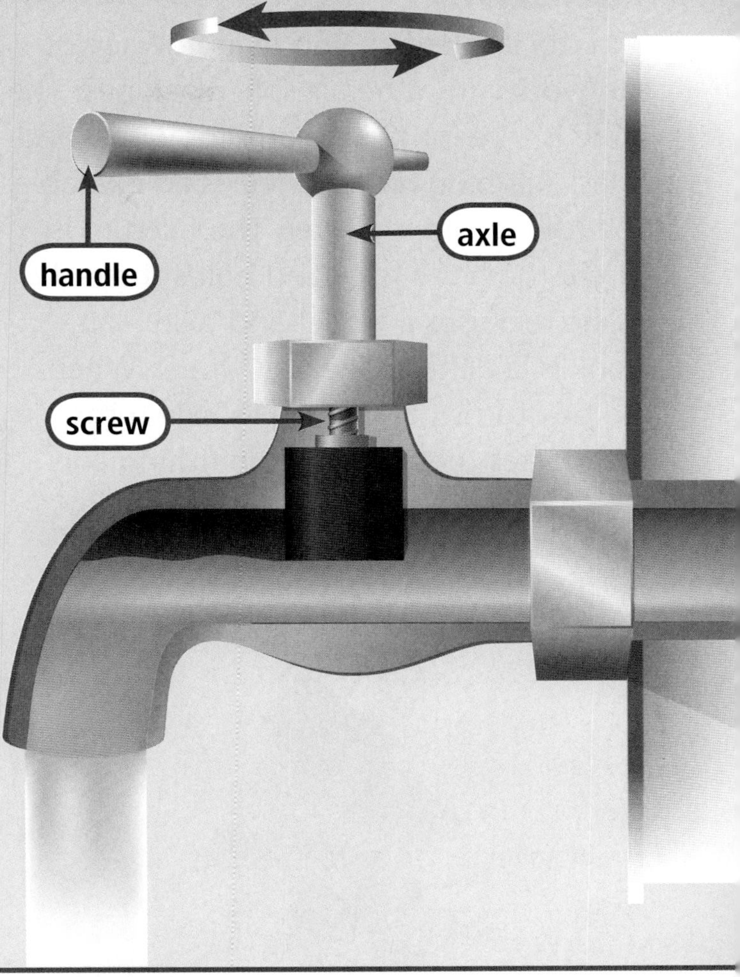

For more links and animations, go to **www.hspscience.com**

This salad spinner handle is a wheel-and-axle. The outside part is the wheel. The axle is inside. It is what moves the basket. ▶

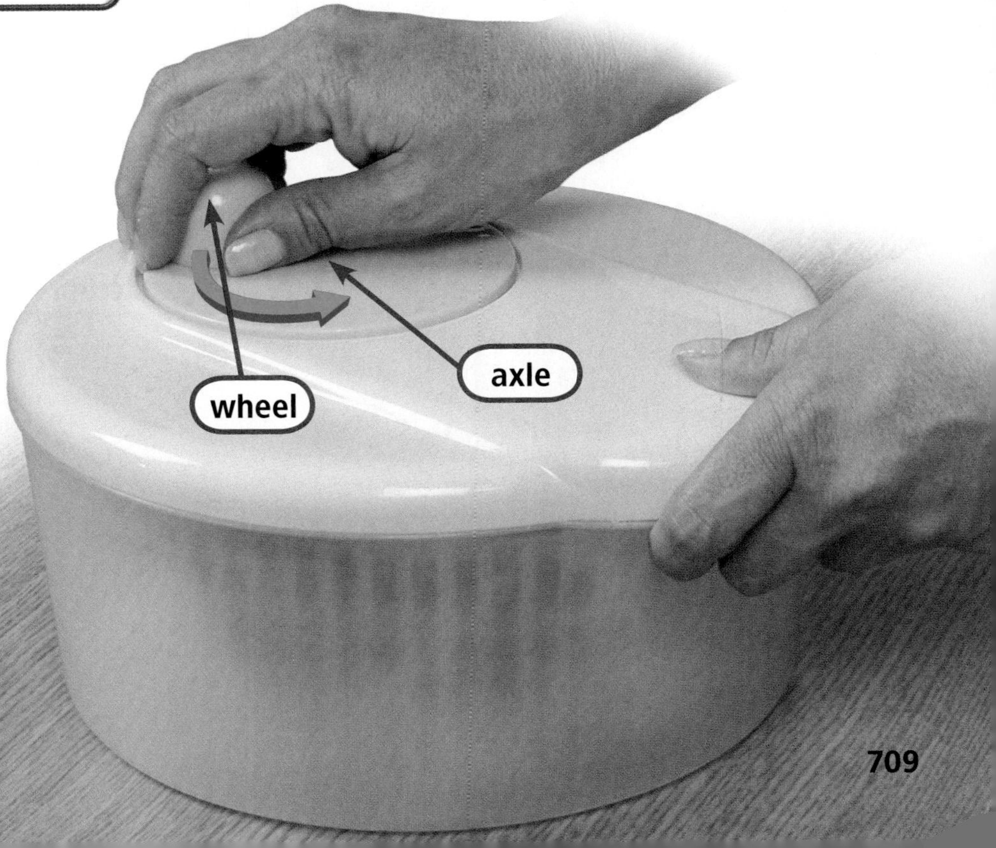

Machines Working Together

In the last lesson, you read how levers can work with other simple machines. The same is true for pulleys and for wheel-and-axles. A fishing rod and reel is an example. The fishing rod is a lever. The fulcrum is where the boy's left hand holds the rod.

The reel uses a wheel-and-axle. The crank is like the spoke of a wheel. When the boy turns the crank, the axle turns. This makes the reel wind up fishing line.

MAIN IDEA AND DETAILS **Is a rod and reel one simple machine? Explain.**

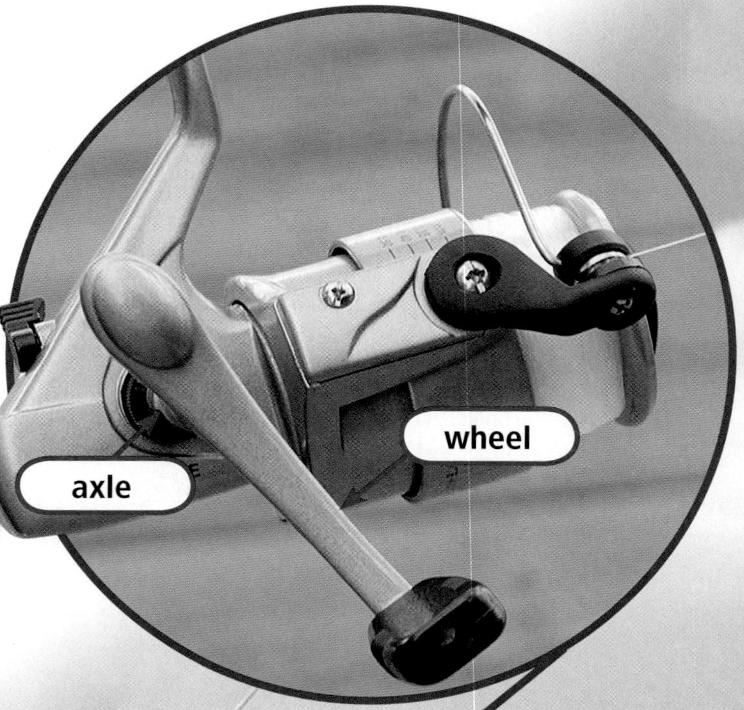

◀ This rod and reel is made up of a wheel-and-axle machine attached to a lever.

Essential Question

How Do a Pulley and a Wheel-and-Axle Help People do Work?

In this lesson, you learned that pulleys make lifting jobs easier. A wheel-and-axle can make things turn with less applied force.

1. **Focus Skill MAIN IDEA AND DETAILS** Draw and complete a graphic organizer showing parts of pulleys and wheels-and-axles.

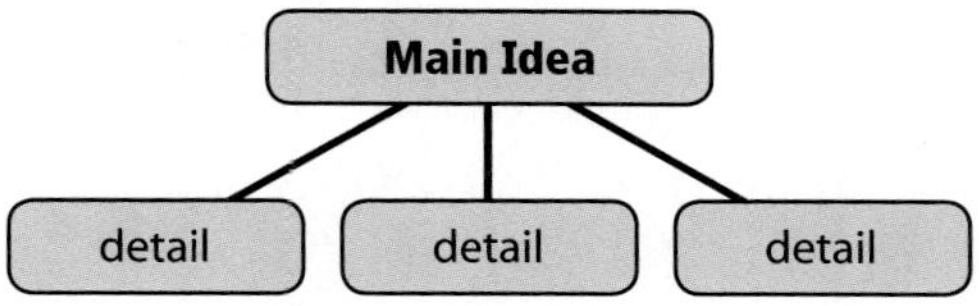

2. **SUMMARIZE** Write a summary of this lesson. Begin with this sentence: *Simple machines help us do work.*

3. **DRAW CONCLUSIONS** How does the pulley in a window blind change the way work is done?

4. **VOCABULARY** Use each of the vocabulary terms in a sentence.

Test Prep

5. **CRITICAL THINKING** How is a screwdriver an example of a wheel-and-axle?

6. Which kind of simple machine is the beater part of a mixer?
   A. pulley
   B. wheel-and-axle
   C. pulley and lever
   D. two pulleys

Make Connections

Writing

Narrative Writing

Imagine that you are the person who invented the pulley. Write a paragraph **describing** how you invented it.

Math

Define Geometric Relationships

A wheel is a short, wide cylinder, and an axle is a long, thin cylinder. What do the two cylinders of a wheel-and-axle have in common?

Social Studies

Ancient Simple Machines

Research how pulleys may have been used to help build the Egyptian pyramids. Write a paragraph or draw a picture to report what you find out.

LESSON 3

Essential Question

How Do Other Simple Machines Help People Do Work?

Investigate uphill motion.

Read and Learn about other simple machines.

Fast Fact

Screws
Machines like those shown here can move large amounts of water uphill. These are screws that each move about 38,000 liters (10,000 gal) of water each minute. In the Investigate, you'll use another kind of simple machine—a ramp—that makes lifting things easier.

Vocabulary Preview

inclined plane [IN•klynd PLAYN] A simple machine that is a slanted surface (p. 716)

screw [SKROO] A simple machine made of a post with an inclined plane wrapped around it (p. 718)

wedge [WEJ] A simple machine made of two inclined planes placed back to back (p. 720)

Investigate

Moving Up

Guided Inquiry

Start with Questions

This person is riding a skateboard on a ramp.

- What happens when the skateboarder rides up the ramp?
- What happens when the skateboarder rides down the ramp?

Investigate to find out. Then read to find out more.

Prepare to Investigate

Inquiry Skill Tip

When you interpret data, keep that separate from drawing conclusions. You need to examine all your data first.

Materials

- cardboard
- tape measure
- toy car
- scissors
- string
- spring scale

Make an Observation Chart

	Distance (cm)	Force Shown on Spring Scale (N)
Straight up		
Short ramp		
Long ramp		

Follow This Procedure

1. Use some of the cardboard to make a ramp from the floor to a chair seat. Make a second ramp, twice as long as the first. Using a tape measure, find and record the distance from the floor to the seat, both straight up and along each ramp.
2. Tie a loop of string to a toy car. Attach a spring scale to the string.
3. Hold on to the spring scale, and lift the car from the floor directly to the chair seat. Record the force shown.
4. Hold on to the spring scale, and pull the car up the short ramp from the floor to the chair seat. Record the force shown. Do the same for the long ramp.

Draw Conclusions

1. How did using the ramps affect the amount of force needed to move the car to the chair seat?
2. **Inquiry Skill** Scientists interpret data to draw conclusions. After examining your data, what conclusions can you draw?

Independent Inquiry

Predict what variables affect the force needed to lift the car. With a partner, plan and conduct a simple investigation to test your ideas.

Read and Learn

VOCABULARY
inclined plane p. 716
screw p. 718
wedge p. 720

SCIENCE CONCEPTS
▶ how an inclined plane, a wedge, and a screw change the way work is done

Focus Skill **MAIN IDEA AND DETAILS**
Look for details about inclined planes, wedges, and screws.

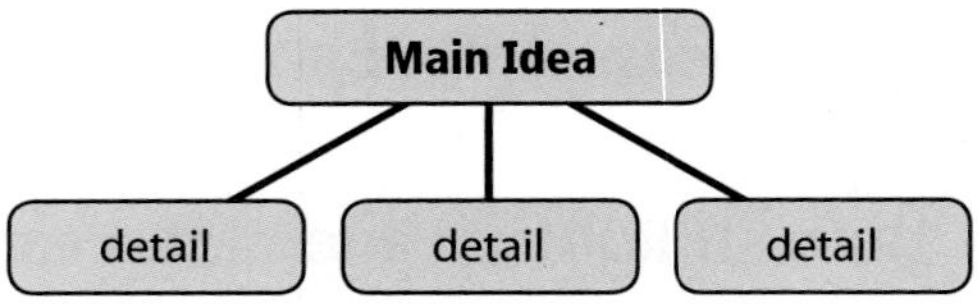

Inclined Planes

An inclined plane may be the simplest simple machine of all. An **inclined plane** is simply a slanted surface. How can a surface be a machine? It changes the way work is done. An inclined plane changes the amount of force needed, and it changes the direction of the force.

Look at the sloping shore in the picture on this page. This sloping shore is an inclined plane.

Suppose that raising the boat out of the water involves lifting it up 2 meters (7 ft). You'd need a crane to lift the boat 2 meters straight up. It's much easier to use a truck to pull the boat up the slope.

There's something else, too. A truck's engine might not be able to lift the boat straight up. But with the slope, it doesn't have to. To lift the boat 2 meters (7 ft), the truck might actually move forward 15 meters (49 ft). But the truck will use a lot less force to move the boat.

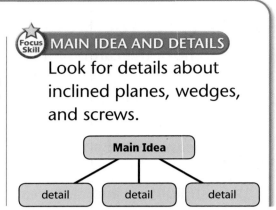

1 The truck moves forward to move the boat up.
2 The truck moves 15 meters (49 ft) to lift the boat 2 meters (7 ft), and it uses less force.

There are two ways that the sloping shore changes how the work is done in lifting the boat.

An inclined plane enables you to lift an object by using less force. But you must move that object a greater distance.

The pictures on this page show other examples of inclined planes. It may seem odd to think of something in nature as being a simple machine, but a hill is an inclined plane. Remember, an inclined plane is simply a slanted surface.

Imagine that the bikers in the two pictures are riding to the top of the same hill. The biker in the red shirt is on a steep path. He has to pedal hard to reach the top. Even so, taking the path is easier than lifting the bike straight up would be.

The biker in the striped shirt is on a path that is less steep. He doesn't have to pedal as hard to reach the top. But because the path is less steep, it's longer. He has to pedal a greater distance to reach the top of the hill.

Focus Skill MAIN IDEA AND DETAILS

How does an inclined plane change the way work is done?

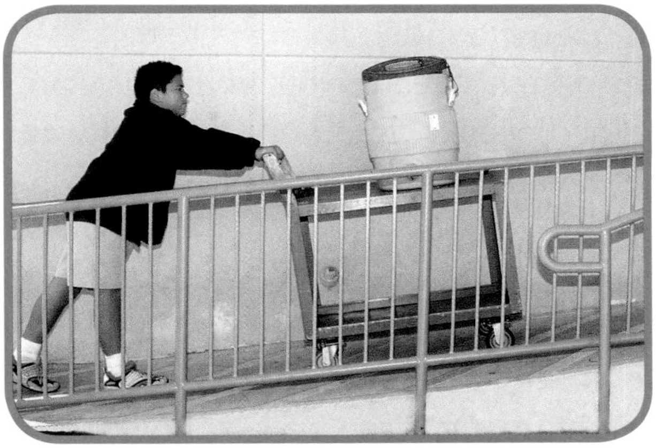

▲ **How would the work of pushing the cart be different if the ramp were steeper?**

▲ **The road is less steep than the rocky hill. It's easier to pedal along the road. But you have to travel farther to reach the hilltop.**

Screws

You've read that using an inclined plane enables you to use less force to move something, even though you must apply the force over a greater distance. A screw is another type of simple machine. It does exactly the same thing.

A **screw** is a post with threads wrapped around it. If you were to unwrap the threads, you would have an inclined plane. Or, to put it another way, the threads are an inclined plane that curls around a post.

Look at the neck of the bottle. Imagine an ant climbing from the bottom of the neck to the opening. It can climb straight up. Or it can walk along the threads. It will use less force if it follows the threads, but it will walk farther.

There are two screws here. The threads on the neck of the bottle slide along the threads on the inside of the cap. ▼

Focus Skill MAIN IDEA AND DETAILS

What is a screw?

An Inclined Plane and a Screw

Moving something up an inclined plane requires less force over a greater distance than moving it straight up.

A screw is just an inclined plane wrapped around a post. When something moves along the threads of a screw, it is actually moving along an inclined plane.

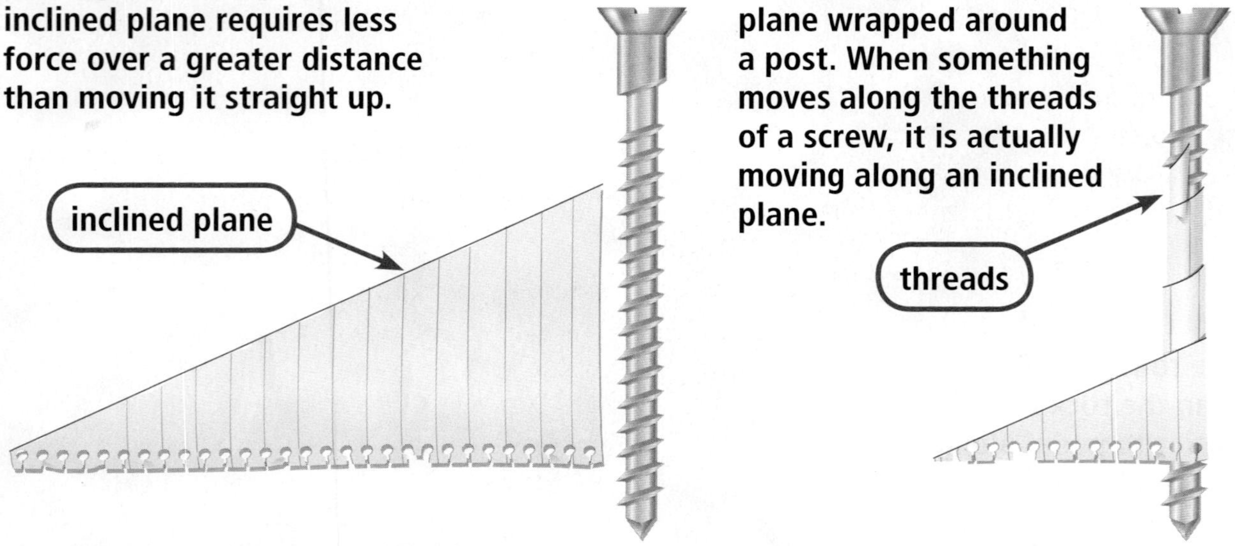

Math in Science
Interpret Data

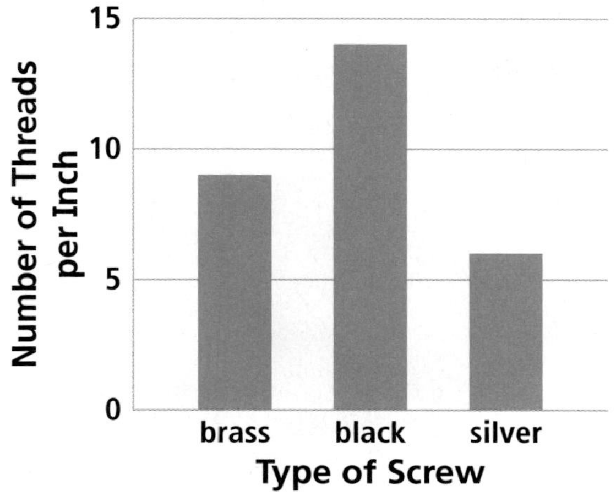

The graph describes the three kinds of screws in Beth's workshop. You know that the threads of a screw form an inclined plane. Which kind of screw has the steepest threads? Explain.

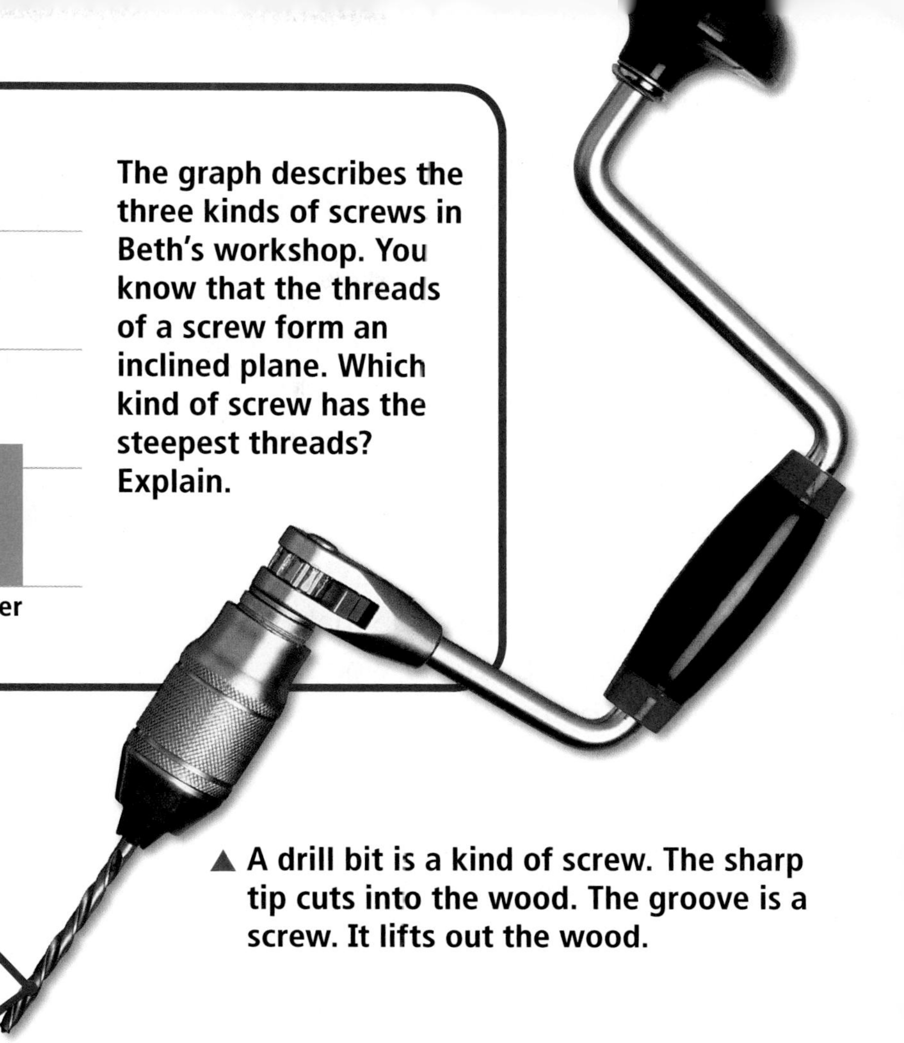

▲ A drill bit is a kind of screw. The sharp tip cuts into the wood. The groove is a screw. It lifts out the wood.

A nut and a bolt both have screw threads, like a cap and a bottle. The threads inside the nut slide along the threads on the bolt. ▶

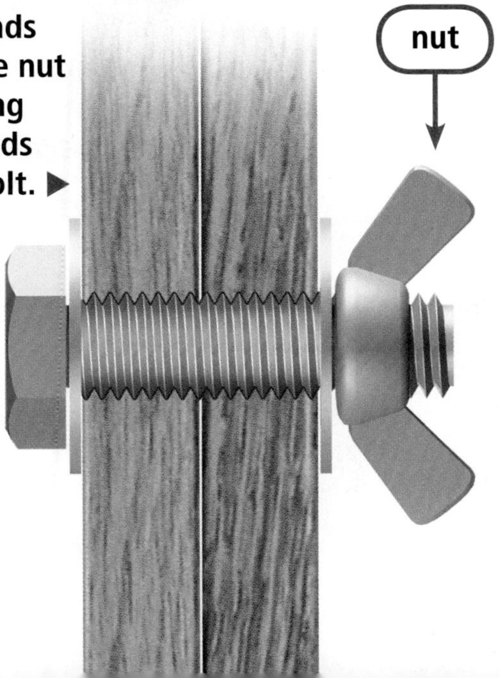

Insta-Lab

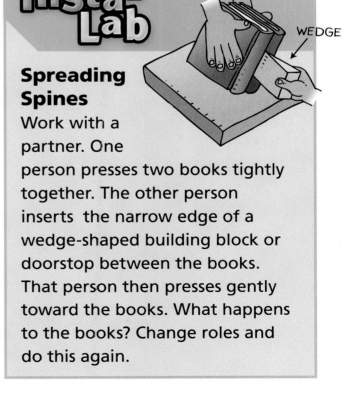

Spreading Spines

Work with a partner. One person presses two books tightly together. The other person inserts the narrow edge of a wedge-shaped building block or doorstop between the books. That person then presses gently toward the books. What happens to the books? Change roles and do this again.

Wedges

Another simple machine related to the inclined plane is the wedge. A **wedge** is two inclined planes placed back to back.

An inclined plane and a wedge both change the direction of a force. If you want to raise a heavy object, you can slide it along the slanted part of an inclined plane.

Imagine using a wedge to split wood. You stick the narrow edge into the wood. Then you use a big hammer to apply a downward force. The wedge makes that force greater. The pieces of wood are pushed apart by the slanted parts of the wedge.

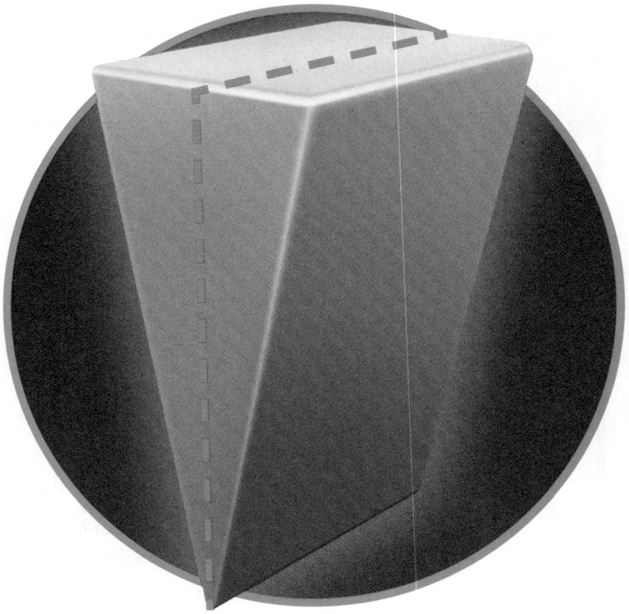

▲ A wedge is really just two inclined planes back to back.

Focus Skill MAIN IDEA AND DETAILS

How is a wedge like an inclined plane?

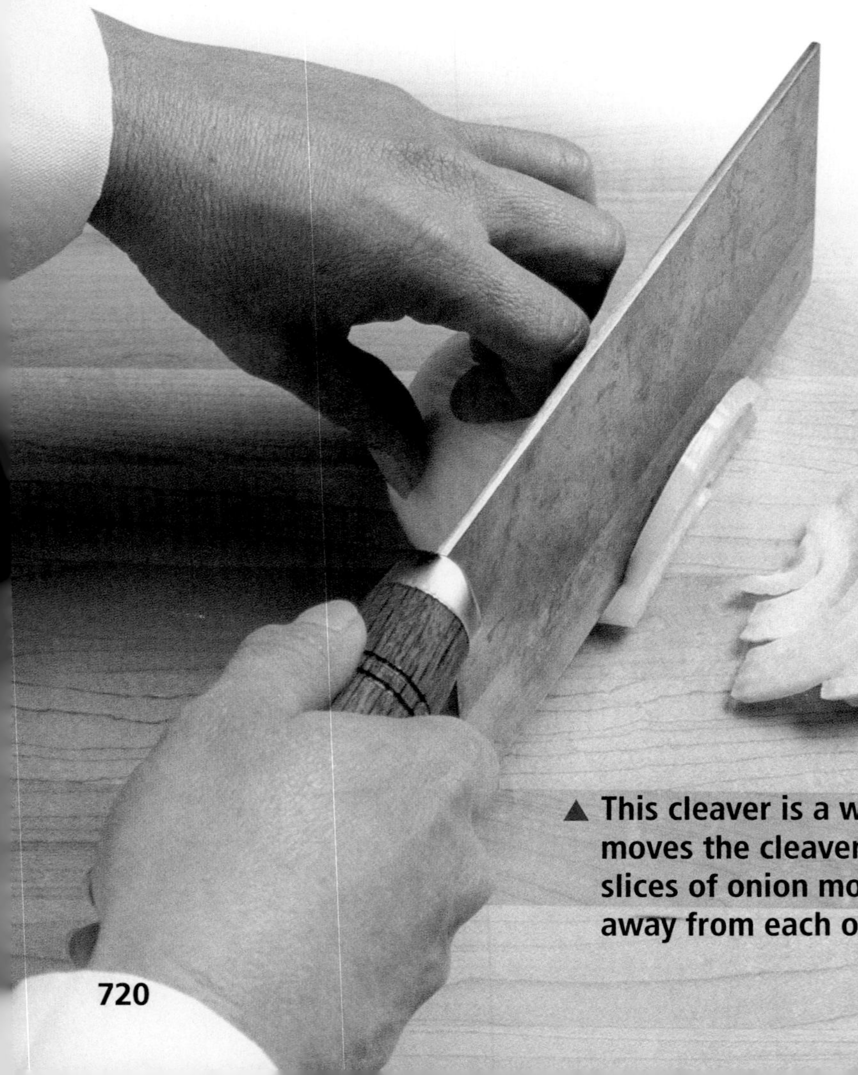

▲ This cleaver is a wedge. The cook moves the cleaver down, and the slices of onion move sideways, away from each other.

Like many blades, the blade of this tile cutter is a wedge.

Lesson Review

Essential Question

How do other simple machines help people do work?

In this lesson, you learned that inclined planes make lifting objects easier. A screw lets people use less force to move something. Wedges are two inclined planes placed back to back.

1. **Focus Skill MAIN IDEA AND DETAILS** Draw and complete a graphic organizer to describe other simple machines.

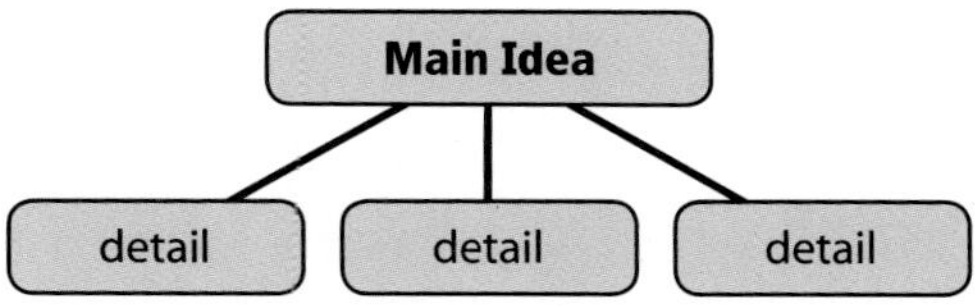

2. **SUMMARIZE** Write three sentences that sum up the lesson.

3. **DRAW CONCLUSIONS** How does the screw on a bottle cap change the direction of a force?

4. **VOCABULARY** Make a flash card for each lesson vocabulary term. Include a definition and a labeled diagram on each flash card.

Test Prep

5. **CRITICAL THINKING** One screw has many threads close together. Another screw has few threads, and they're spread out. Which screw is like a steep inclined plane? Explain.

6. Which kind of simple machine is an ax?
   A. inclined plane
   B. screw
   C. wedge
   D. ramp

Make Connections

Writing

Expository Writing

An inclined plane is like a screw and like a wedge, but it is also different from them. Write a **paragraph** comparing and contrasting an inclined plane, a screw, and a wedge.

Math

Classify Geometric Figures

Draw separate diagrams for an inclined plane, a screw, and a wedge. Label geometric figures on each diagram.

Health

Surgical Simple Machines

Research screws that are used in surgery. Write a paragraph telling what you find out.

Dean Kamen

In college, he invented a portable medicine pump that patients could use at home. Then came the IBOT—a six-wheeled wheelchair that climbs curbs and stairs. When Dean Kamen sees that people need something, he invents it.

Kamen saw that cars in cities cause traffic and pollution, so he invented the Segway Human Transporter. This two-wheeled scooter moves easily over paved surfaces and can ride over small obstacles. The rider controls speed and direction by shifting weight and turning the handlebars.

Besides inventing, Kamen spends a lot of time trying to get young people interested in science. He started FIRST, an organization that pairs high school students with engineers to create robots and invent other things. If Dean has his way, scientists and engineers will be the superheroes of the twenty-first century!

▶ **DEAN KAMEN**

▶ Inventor of the Segway and the IBOT

Think and Write

1. What does Dean Kamen look for when he thinks about a new invention?
2. A Segway causes much less pollution than a car. How could this help people who live far from cities?

▶ **JUDY LEDEN**

▶ Glider pilot

Judy Leden

Recently, Judy Leden strapped a pair of wings on her back. The 9-meter-wide (30-ft-wide) wings carried Leden about 11 meters (35 ft) into the air. Her flight lasted for 17 seconds.

Between 1490 and 1505, artist Leonardo da Vinci made several drawings of a glider. The wings that Leden used were based on da Vinci's glider. No one knew whether the glider would actually fly. Leden decided to find out.

Leden flew da Vinci's glider a total of 20 times. Leonardo da Vinci's plans seem to be a success!

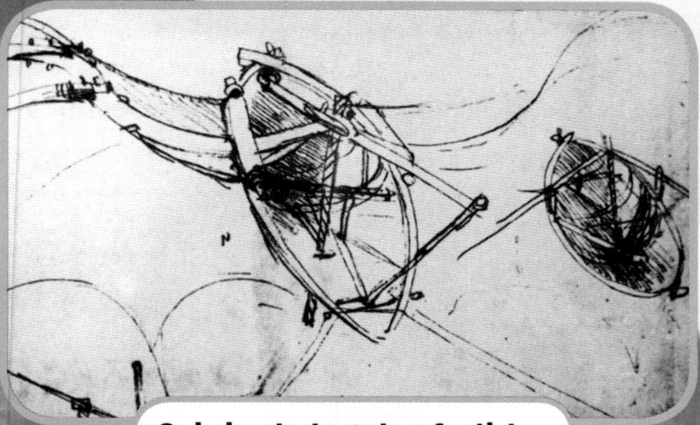

Original sketch of glider

Think and Write

1. Would it be difficult to follow very old plans to build a machine?
2. Why might testing old plans be a good way to build new technology?

Career Drafter

Drafters make drawings and plans. These plans are used to build everything from toys to buildings to spacecraft. A drafter's tools include pencils, paper, calculators, and computers.

CHAPTER 17

Review and Test Preparation

Vocabulary Review

Use the terms below to complete the sentences. The page numbers tell you where to look in the chapter if you need help.

work p. 696
simple machine p. 697
lever p. 698
fulcrum p. 698
pulley p. 706
inclined plane p. 716
screw p. 718
wedge p. 720

1. A paper cutter is made up of a wedge and a _______.

2. A hill is an example of an _______.

3. A machine with few parts that makes work easier is a _______.

4. Two inclined planes that are back to back form a _______.

5. A wheel with a rope or chain around it is a _______.

6. A post with threads wrapped around it is a _______.

7. The point where a lever pivots is the _______.

8. Using force to move an object over a distance is _______.

Check Understanding

Write the letter of the best choice.

9. Which of the following is an example of work to a scientist?
A. solving a mental math problem
B. carrying a book across the room
C. pushing against the floor
D. lifting a chair off the floor

10. Where can the fulcrum of a lever **NOT** be?
F. the end of the bar
G. the middle of the bar
H. between the middle and the end
J. not touching the bar

11. How is the screwdriver being used in this picture?

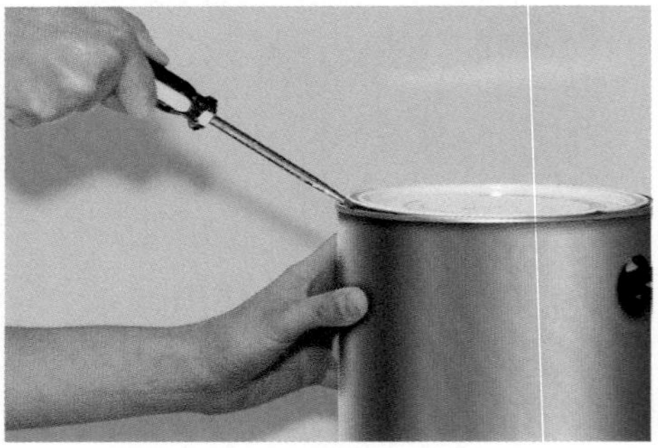

A. as a lever
B. as a screw
C. as a pulley
D. as a wheel-and-axle

12. **MAIN IDEA AND DETAILS** An inclined plane is a part of which other simple machine?

Focus Skill

F. lever
G. pulley
H. screw
J. wheel-and-axle

13. Which of the following does **NOT** change the direction of a force?

A. inclined plane
B. pulley
C. wedge
D. wheel-and-axle

14. **MAIN IDEA AND DETAILS** Which detail about an ax lets you know that it is a wedge?

Focus Skill

F. It has just one inclined plane.
G. It changes the way work is done.
H. It has two inclined planes.
J. It changes the direction of the force applied.

15. Which simple machine could you use to hold two objects together?

A. lever
B. pulley
C. screw
D. wheel-and-axle

16. Which kind of simple machine is the wheelchair resting on?

F. inclined plane
G. lever
H. pulley
J. screw

Inquiry Skills

17. Think about a spiral staircase. Which simple machine can you **compare** it to? Explain.

18. This table shows the force needed to lift a heavy box 1 meter by using four different methods. What conclusions can you draw about the distance the box traveled by **interpreting the data**?

Method Used	Force Needed
Lever	200 newtons
Inclined plane	300 newtons
Pulley	500 newtons
Lifting straight up	500 newtons

Critical Thinking

The Big Idea

19. Tamyra and Marv are loading boxes onto identical trucks. Tamyra slides the boxes up a ramp that is 1 meter long. Marv uses a ramp that is 2 meters long. Who uses more force? Explain.

20. You have to put a 20-kilogram box on a shelf. You can lift it 1 meter, or you can push it up a ramp. The ramp is 2 meters long. If you use the ramp, you'll feel as if you're moving 10 kilograms. Which method for putting the box on the shelf would you choose? Why? Which method might make you feel more tired? Explain.

UNIT F PHYSICAL SCIENCE

Visual Summary

Tell how each picture shows the **Big Idea** for its chapter.

CHAPTER 15

Big Idea

Electric current and magnets can be used for many purposes.

CHAPTER 16

Big Idea

Motion can be measured and described. It is influenced by forces such as gravity.

CHAPTER 17

Big Idea

Simple machines change the way that work is done to help people accomplish tasks.

Visit the Multimedia Science Glossary to see illustrations of these words and to hear them pronounced.
www.hspscience.com

Every entry in the glossary begins with a term and a *phonetic respelling.* A phonetic respelling writes the word the way it sounds, which can help you pronounce new or unfamiliar words. The definition of the term follows the respelling. An example of how to use the term in a sentence follows the definition.

There is a page number in ( ) at the end of each entry. It tells you where to find the term in your textbook. These terms are highlighted in yellow in the chapter in your textbook. Each entry has an illustration to help you understand the term. The Pronunciation Key below will help you understand the respellings. Syllables are separated by a bullet (•). Small, uppercase letters show stressed syllables.

Pronunciation Key

Sound	As in	Phonetic Respelling	Sound	As in	Phonetic Respelling
a	bat	(BAT)	oh	over	(OH•ver)
ah	lock	(LAHK)	oo	pool	(POOL)
air	rare	(RAIR)	ow	out	(OWT)
ar	argue	(AR•gyoo)	oy	foil	(FOYL)
aw	law	(LAW)	s	cell	(SEL)
ay	face	(FAYS)		sit	(SIT)
ch	chapel	(CHAP•uhl)	sh	sheep	(SHEEP)
e	test	(TEST)	th	that	(THAT)
	metric	(MEH•trik)		thin	(THIN)
ee	eat	(EET)	u	pull	(PUL)
	feet	(FEET)	uh	medal	(MED•uhl)
	ski	(SKEE)		talent	(TAL•uhnt)
er	paper	(PAY•per)		pencil	(PEN•suhl)
	fern	(FERN)		onion	(UHN•yuhn)
eye	idea	(eye•DEE•uh)		playful	(PLAY•fuhl)
i	bit	(BIT)		dull	(DUHL)
ing	going	(GOH•ing)	y	yes	(YES)
k	card	(KARD)		ripe	(RYP)
	kite	(KYT)	z	bags	(BAGZ)
ngk	bank	(BANGK)	zh	treasure	(TREZH•er)

Multimedia Science Glossary: **www.hspscience.com**

A

abiotic [ay•by•AHT•ik] **Of the nonliving parts of an ecosystem:** Water and rocks are *abiotic.* (214)

absorption [ab•ZAWRP•shuhn] **The taking in of light or sound energy by an object:** The sun's energy is taken in by *absorption.* (555)

acceleration [ak•sel•er•AY•shuhn] **Any change in the speed or direction of an object's motion:** Speeding up and slowing down are both *acceleration.* (671)

adaptation [ad•uhp•TAY•shuhn] **A body part or behavior that helps an organism survive:** This insect's sticklike body is an *adaptation* that makes it look like part of a tree. (132)

air mass [AIR MAS] **A large body of air that has a similar temperature and moisture level:** The blue arrows represent cool *air masses.* (392)

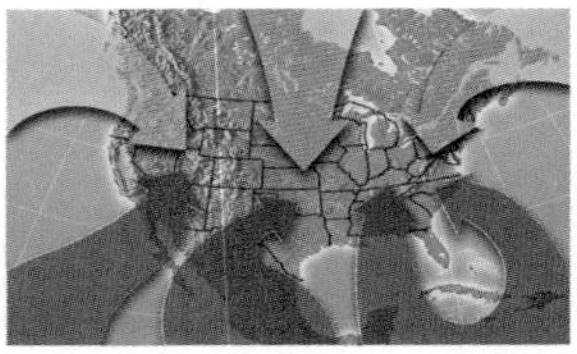

amplitude [AM•pluh•tood] **A measure of the amount of energy in a wave:** The *amplitude* of a sound wave controls the sound's loudness. (543)

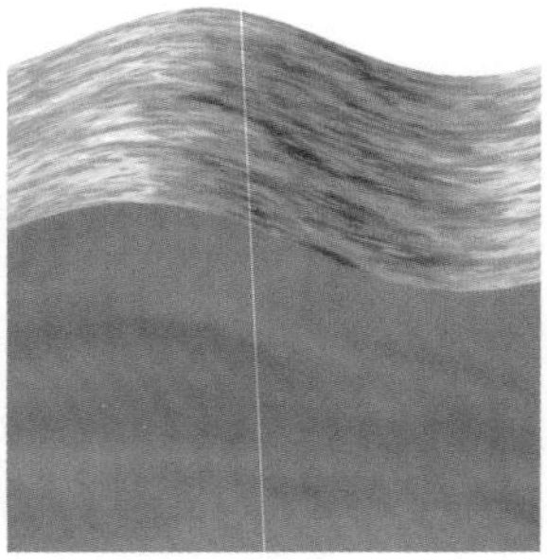

anemometer [an•uh•MAHM•uht•er] **A weather instrument that measures wind speed:** *Anemometers* measure the speed of the wind. (398)

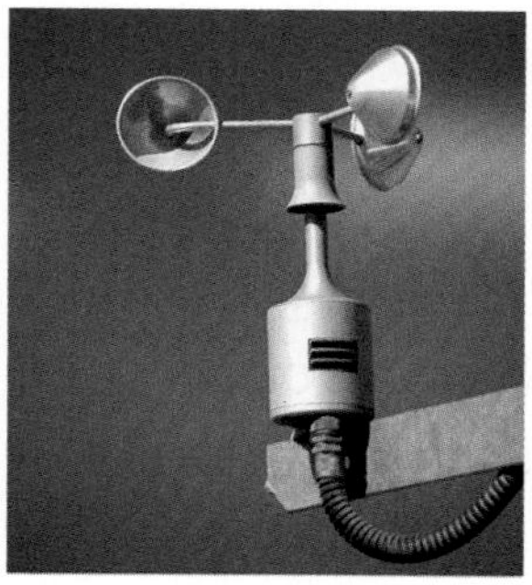

artery [ART•er•ee] **A blood vessel that carries blood away from the heart:** Inside your body, an *artery* carries oxygen-rich blood from the heart to the rest of your body. (174)

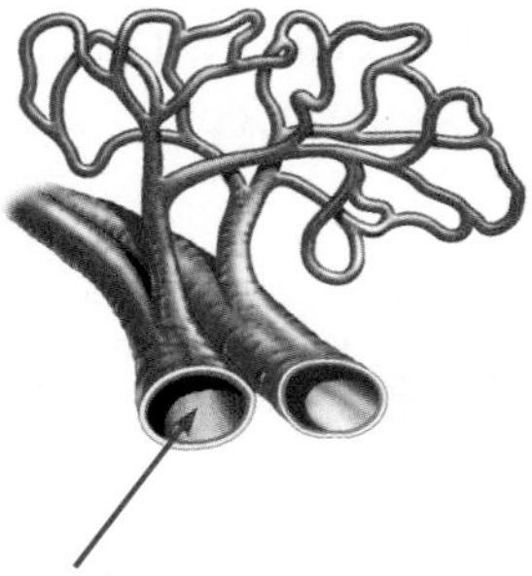

atom [AT•uhm] **The smallest unit of an element that has all the properties of that element:** Nearly all *atoms* have neutrons. (496)

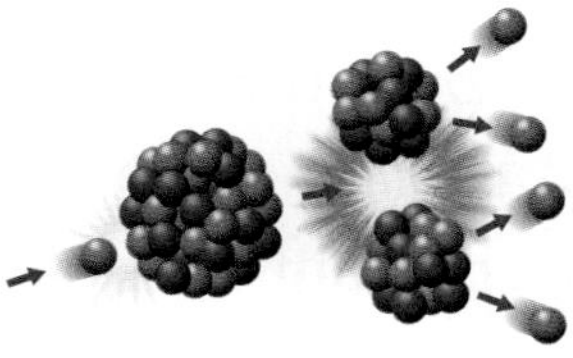

axis [AK•sis] **The imaginary line around which Earth spins as it rotates:** Every twenty-four hours, Earth spins completely on its *axis*. (410)

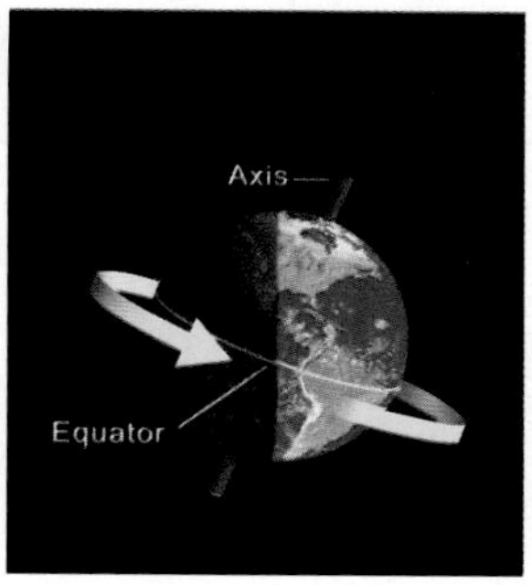

B

bacteria [bak•TIR•ee•uh] **The kingdom of one-celled living things that lack nuclei:** Some *bacteria* can make you sick. (59)

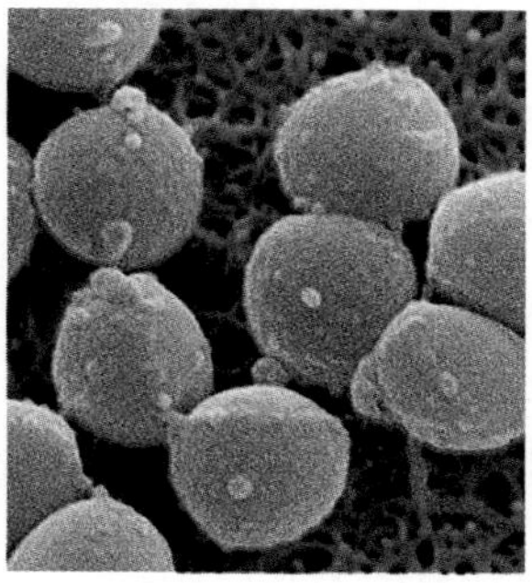

barometer [buh•RAHM•uh•ter] **A weather instrument used to measure air pressure:** The first *barometer* used mercury in a glass tube to measure air pressure. (398)

basic needs [BAY•sik NEEDZ] **Food, water, air, and shelter that an organism needs to survive:** All living organisms have *basic needs,* such as food and water. (130)

bedrock [BED•rahk] **The solid rock that forms Earth's surface:** In rocky landscapes, there is very little topsoil over the *bedrock.* (309)

biotic [by•AHT•ik] **Of the living parts of an ecosystem:** Plants, animals, and fungi are *biotic* parts of an ecosystem. (212)

bone [BOHN] **A hard organ made of a hard outer covering tissue and a softer inside tissue:** Your skeletal system includes more than 200 *bones* in different shapes and sizes. (184)

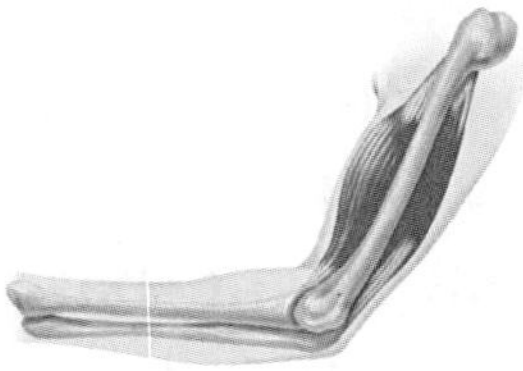

C

capillary [KAP•uh•lair•ee] **A blood vessel with very thin walls that allows oxygen and carbon dioxide to pass through:** A *capillary* is an important part of your circulatory system. (174)

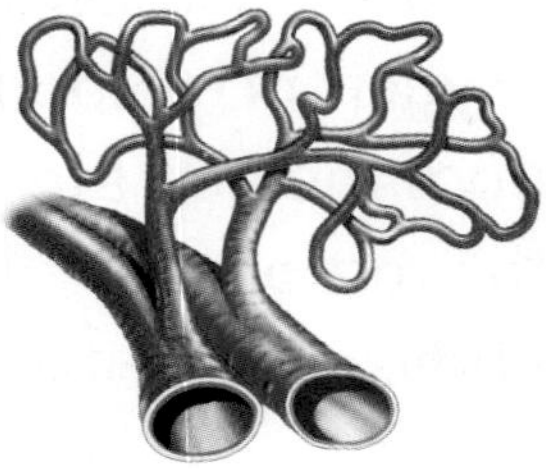

carnivore [KAHR•nuh•vawr] **An animal that eats only other animals:** *Carnivores* have sharp teeth to help them eat meat. (244)

change of state [CHAYNJ UHV STAYT] **A physical change that occurs when matter changes from one state to another, such as from a liquid to a gas:** Ice melting into water is a *change of state.* (506)

chemical change [KEM•ih•kuhl CHAYNJ] **A reaction or change in a substance, produced by chemical means, that results in a different substance:** Scientists can produce *chemical changes* in their laboratories. (518)

chemical energy [KEM•ih•kuhl EN•er•jee] **Energy that can be released by a chemical reaction:** Striking a match releases *chemical energy.* (646)

chemical property [KEM•ih•kuhl PRAHP•er•tee] **A property that involves how a substance interacts with other substances:** Flammability is one kind of *chemical property.* (517)

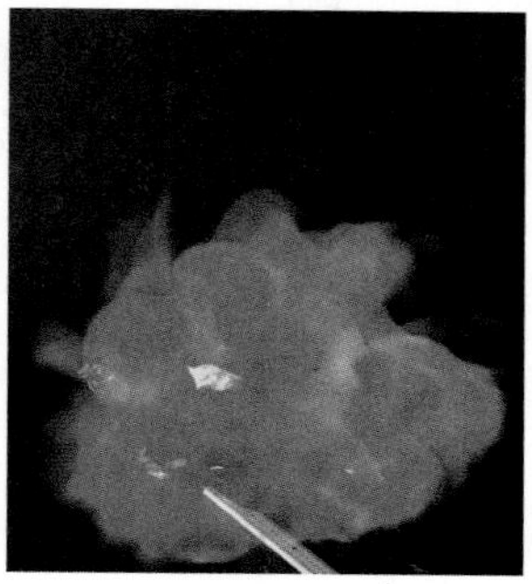

chemical reaction [KEM•ih•kuhl ree•AK•shuhn] **A chemical change:** Rusting is one kind of *chemical reaction.* (518)

clay [KLAY] **The smallest particles that make up soil:** Dirt and soil on Earth are made up of *clay.* (310)

cold front [KOHLD FRUHNT] **The boundary where a cold air mass moves under a warm air mass:** A *cold front* causes cooler weather because it pushes warm air higher into the atmosphere. (394)

comet [KAHM•it] **A ball of rock, ice, and frozen gases in space:** The orbit of a *comet* around the sun is usually irregular. (426)

community [kuh•MYOO•nuh•tee] **All the populations of organisms living together in an environment:** A *community* has many kinds of living things. (206)

compound [KAHM•pownd] **A substance made of two or more different elements that have combined chemically:** Baking soda and vinegar are *compounds.* (518)

condensation [kahn•duhn•SAY•shuhn] **The process by which a gas changes into a liquid:** Dew results from *condensation.* (367)

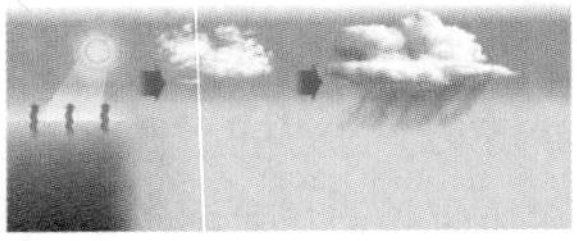

conduction [kuhn•DUK•shuhn] **The movement of heat between two materials that are touching:** The liquid is heating the metal through *conduction.* (580)

conductor
[kuhn•DUK•ter] **Materials that let electric charges or heat travel through them easily:** Metal is a good *conductor.* (612)

constellation
[kahn•stuh•LAY•shuhn] **A pattern of stars that form an imaginary picture or design in the sky:** Ursa Major is a *constellation* that many people think looks like a bear. (434)

consumer
[kuhn•SOOM•er] **A living thing that can't make its own food and must eat other living things:** Animals are *consumers.* (242)

convection
[kuhn•VEK•shuhn] **The movement of heat in liquids and gases from a warmer area to a cooler area:** *Convection* of water in the atmosphere can produce rain. (581)

current electricity
[KUR•uhnt ee•lek•TRIS•uh•tee] **A steady movement of charges through certain materials:** *Current electricity* is lighting this bulb. (608)

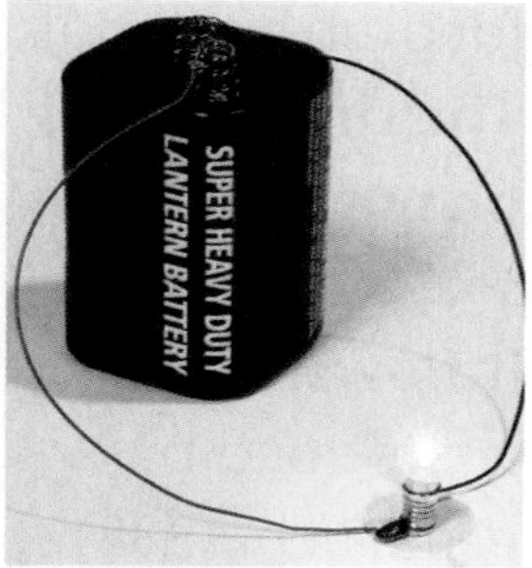

D

decomposer
[dee•kuhm•POHZ•er] **A living thing that feeds on the wastes of plants and animals:** Mushrooms are one kind of *decomposer.* (246)

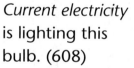

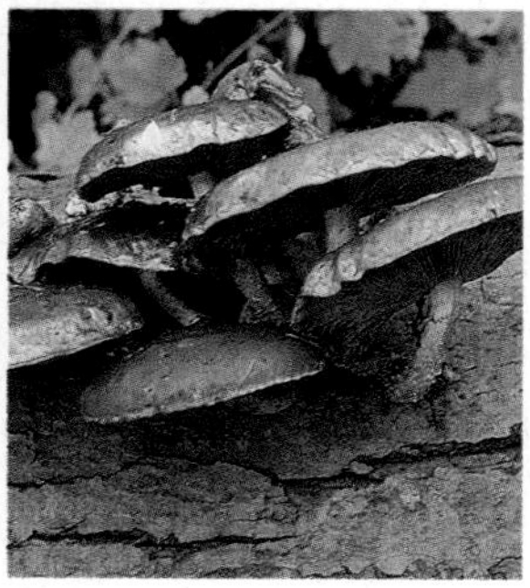

density
[DEN•suh•tee] **The amount of matter in an object compared to the space it takes up:** The rock has a higher *density* than the water, so it sinks. (460)

deposition
[dep•uh•ZISH•uhn] **The dropping of bits of rock and soil by a river as it flows:** Deltas are formed by *deposition.* (338)

diaphragm
[DY•uh•fram] **The muscle in your body that allows you to inhale and exhale:** When you breathe, you are using your *diaphragm* to inhale and exhale. (172)

direct development
[duh•REKT dih•VEL•uhp•muhnt] **A kind of growth in which an organism gets larger but doesn't go through other changes:** Kittens experience *direct development.* (116)

diversity
[duh•VER•suh•tee] **A measure of the number and variety of species in an ecosystem:** This group of shells has high *diversity.* (218)

E

earthquake
[ERTH•kwayk] **The shaking of Earth's surface caused by movement of rock in the crust:** This seismograph is recording an *earthquake.* (336)

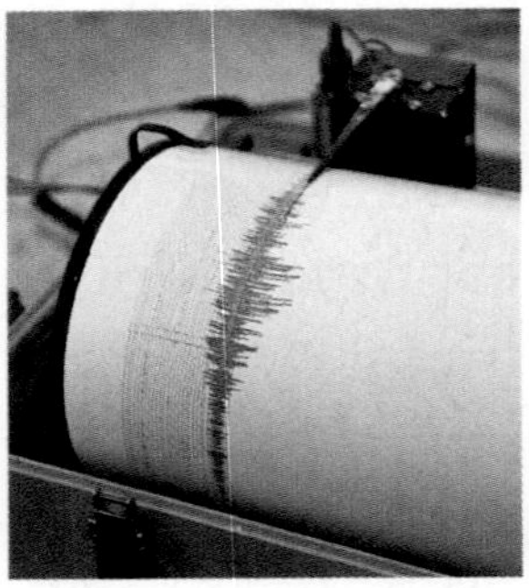

ecosystem
[EE•koh•sis•tuhm]
A community and its physical environment together: A pond is one example of an *ecosystem.* (202)

electric motor
[uh•LEK•trik MOHT•er]
A device that changes electrical energy to energy of motion: Some toys have *electric motors.* (627)

electromagnet
[ee•lek•troh•MAG•nit]
A temporary magnet caused by an electric current: You can make an *electromagnet* with a nail, some wire, and a battery. (624)

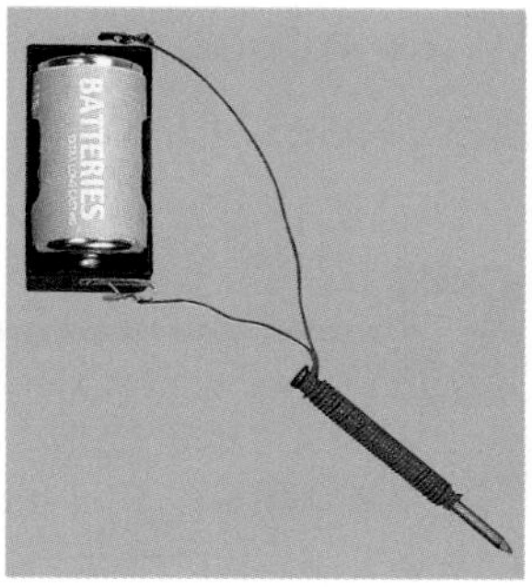

element
[EL•uh•muhnt] **A substance made up of only one kind of atom:** Copper is an *element* because it is made of only one kind of atom. (498)

energy pyramid
[EN•er•jee PIR•uh•mid] **A diagram showing how much energy is passed from one organism to the next in a food chain:** Producers are at the bottom of the *energy pyramid.* (258)

energy transfer
[EN•er•jee TRANS•fer]
A change of energy from one form to another: *Energy transfer* happens when the chipmunk eats the nut. (589)

environment
[en•VY•ruhn•muhnt]
All of the living and nonliving things that affect an organism: Many kinds of living things can share the same *environment.* (202)

erosion
[uh•ROH•zhuhn]
The process of moving sediment from one place to another: This gully was formed by *erosion.* (302)

esophagus
[ih•SAHF•uh•guhs]
A muscular tube that connects your mouth with your stomach: Food travels through the *esophagus* after being swallowed. (170)

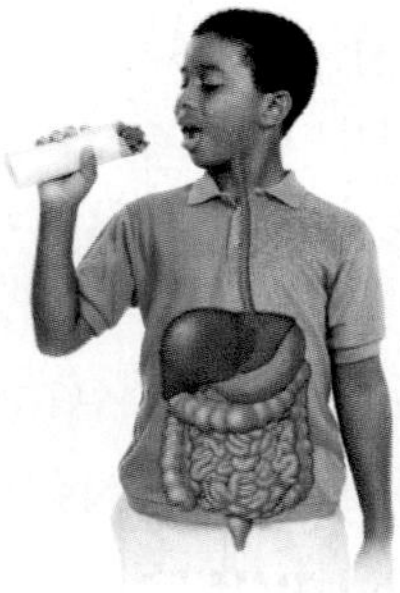

evaporation
[ee•vap•uh•RAY•shuhn] **The process by which a liquid changes into a gas:** The red arrows show *evaporation,* which is one of the steps of the water cycle. (366)

experiment
[ek•SPEHR•uh•muhnt]
A test of a hypothesis: An *experiment* has controlled variables and a dependent variable. (21)

extinction
[ek•STINGK•shuhn]
The death of all the members of a certain group of organisms: *Extinction* can happen when a habitat changes or when a food supply decreases. (156)

F

food chain
[FOOD CHAYN] **The movement of food energy in a sequence of living things:** A producer is at the bottom of every *food chain.* (254)

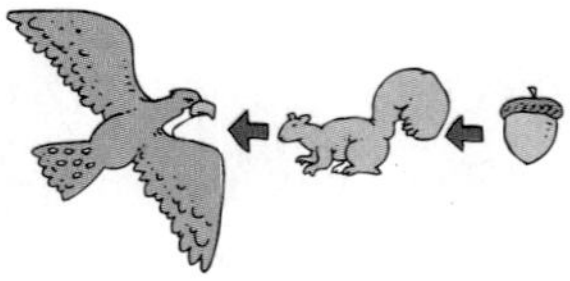

food web [FOOD WEB] **A group of food chains that overlap:** *Food webs* show interdependence in ecosystems. (256)

force [FAWRS] **A pull or push of any kind:** *Forces* affect the movement of objects. (672)

fossil [FAHS•uhl] **The remains or traces of a plant or animal that lived long ago:** We can learn about living things of long ago by studying *fossils.* (152, 346)

fossil record [FAHS•uhl REK•erd] **The information about Earth's history that is contained in fossils:** The *fossil record* helps scientists understand Earth's time line. (348)

frequency [FREE•kwuhn•see] **A measure of the number of waves that pass in a second:** The *frequency* of a sound wave determines the sound's pitch. (543)

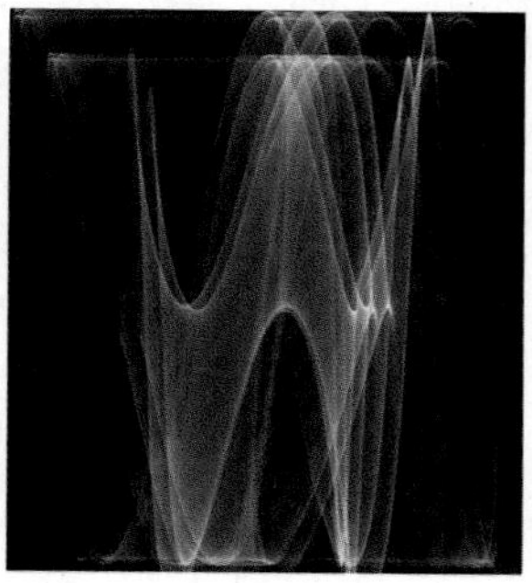

friction [FRIK•shuhn] **A force that resists motion between objects that are touching:** Rubbing your hands together causes *friction,* which warms your hands. (683)

fulcrum [FUHL•kruhm] **The fixed point on a lever:** The *fulcrum* is the pivot point on a lever. (698)

fungi [FUHN•jy] **Organisms that can't make food and can't move about:** Mushrooms are a kind of *fungus.* (70)

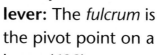

G

galaxy [GAL•uhk•see] **A huge system of many stars, gases, and dust:** Earth is part of the Milky Way *galaxy.* (434)

gas [GAS] **The state of matter that does not have a definite shape or volume:** This balloon contains helium *gas.* (469)

gene [JEEN] **The basic unit of heredity:** *Genes* are passed down from parents to offspring. (93)

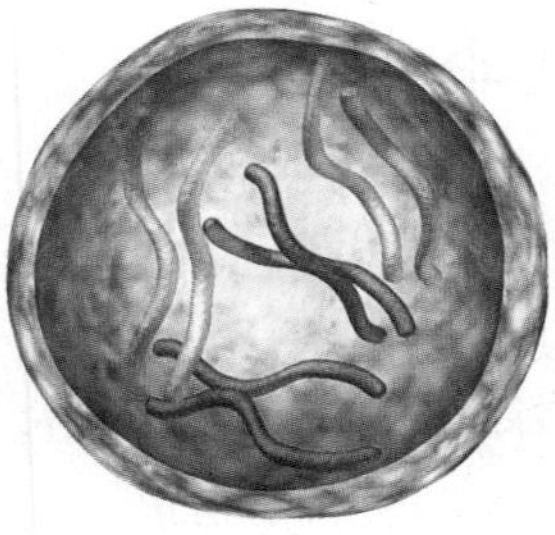

generator [JEN•er•ayt•er] **A device that makes an electric current:** People use portable *generators* when the power is out. (626)

geothermal energy [jee•oh•THER•muhl EN•er•jee] **Heat that comes from the inside of Earth:** *Geothermal energy* plants use heat from Earth's mantle to produce electricity. (637)

glacier [GLAY•sher] **A large, moving mass of ice:** *Glaciers* cover 10 percent of Earth's land area. (339)

gravitation [grav•ih•TAY•shuhn] **A force that acts between any two objects and pulls them together:** Earth's *gravitation* keeps you on the ground. (681)

gravity [GRAV•ih•tee] **The force of attraction between Earth and other objects, the expression of gravitation:** If you fall, you experience the effects of *gravity.* (681)

H

habitat [HAB•ih•tat] **An environment that meets the needs of an organism:** Different living things need different *habitats.* (252)

habitat restoration [HAB•ih•tat res•tuh•RAY•shuhn] **Returning a natural environment to its original condition:** *Habitat restoration* is important for repairing damaged ecosystems. (227)

hail [HAYL] **Round pieces of ice formed when frozen rain is coated with water and refreezes:** *Hail* falls in summer thunderstorms. (375)

heat [HEET] **The flow of thermal energy from one object to another:** These steel bars have been exposed to a lot of *heat.* (579)

herbivore [HER•buh•vawr] **An animal that eats only plants, or producers:** Cows are *herbivores.* (244)

heredity [huh•RED•ih•tee] **The process by which traits are passed from parents to offspring:** Genes are the basic unit of *heredity.* (92)

hibernation [hy•ber•NAY•shuhn] **A dormant, inactive state in which normal body activities slow:** When an animal goes into *hibernation,* its breathing and heartbeat slow down and its body temperature drops. (143)

horizon [huh•RY•zuhn] **A layer in the soil:** Some soils have many *horizons,* while others have few. (308)

humus [HYOO•muhs] **The remains of decayed plants or animals in the soil:** *Humus* helps plants to grow. (308)

hurricane [HER•ih•kayn] **A large tropical storm with wind speeds of at least 74 miles per hour:** *Hurricanes* form over warm ocean waters. (376)

hydroelectric power [hy•droh•ee•LEK•trik POW•er] **Electrical energy made by using the kinetic energy of falling water:** A *hydroelectric power* station converts the energy of this water to electricity. (636)

hypothesis [hy•PAHTH•uh•sis] **A statement of what you think will happen and why:** Scientists carry out an experiment to test a *hypothesis.* (21)

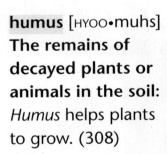

I

igneous rock [IG•nee•uhs RAHK] **A type of rock that forms from melted rock that cools and hardens:** Granite is one kind of *igneous rock.* (282)

inclined plane [IN•klynd PLAYN] **A simple machine that is a slanted surface:** A ramp is a type of *inclined plane.* (716)

inertia [in•ER•shuh] **The property of matter that keeps an object at rest or keeps it moving in a straight line:** It takes a lot of force to start a space shuttle moving because of *inertia.* (674)

inference [IN•fer•uhns] **An untested conclusion based on your observations:** An *inference* can help you build a hypothesis to test. (18)

instinct [in•stinkt] **A behavior that an animal begins life with:** Young birds respond to their parents by *instinct.* (142)

insulator [IN•suh•layt•er] **A material that does not let current electricity move through it easily:** Styrofoam is a common *insulator.* (612)

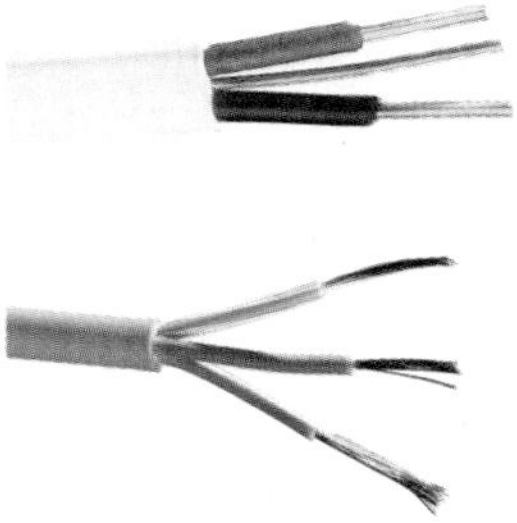

intensity [in•TEN•suh•tee] **A measure of how loud or soft a sound is:** A fire engine has a much higher *intensity* than a whisper. (535)

invertebrates [in•VER•tuh•brits] **The group of animals without a backbone:** This octopus is an *invertebrate.* (78)

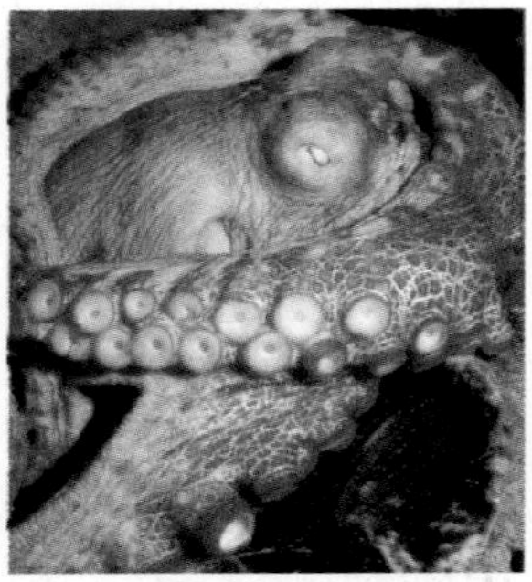

J

joint [JOYNT] **A place in the body where two bones meet:** Your knees and elbows are *joints.* (184)

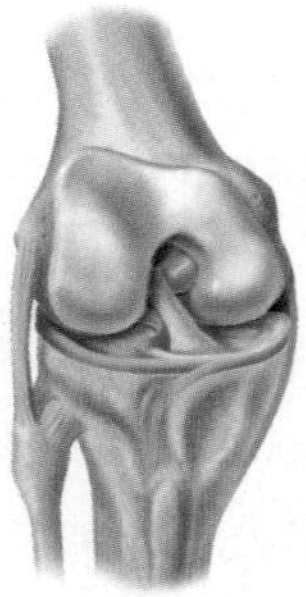

K

kinetic energy [kih•NET•ik EN•er•jee] **The energy of motion:** When you move, you have *kinetic energy.* (635)

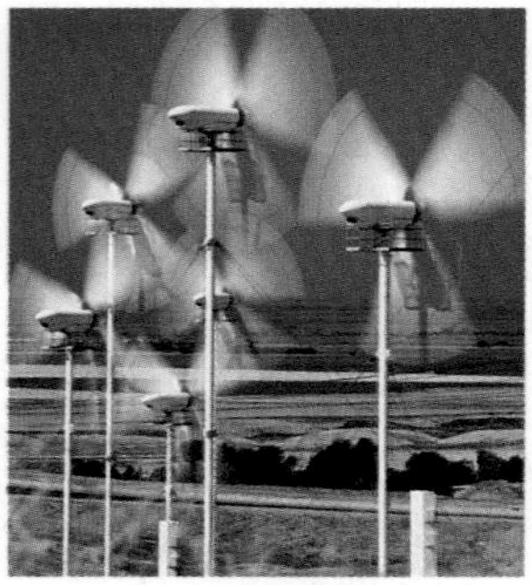

L

land breeze [LAND BREEZ] **A breeze that moves from the land to the water:** A *land breeze* cycles warm air from the land to the water. (384)

landform [LAND•fawrm] **A natural feature on Earth's surface:** Mountains and valleys are two different types of Earth's *landforms.* (324)

learned behavior [LERND bee•HAYV•yer] **A behavior that an organism doesn't begin life with:** In nature, parents teach their offspring *learned behaviors.* (146)

lever [LEV•er] **A simple machine made of a bar that pivots on a fixed point:** *Levers* can help you do more work with less force. (698)

life cycle [LYF CY•kuhl] **All the stages a living thing goes through:** The *life cycle* of the tadpole continues until it becomes an adult frog. (104)

light [LYT] **A form of energy that can travel through space and lies partly within the visible range:** The sun produces *light* energy. (568)

liquid [LIK•wid] **The state of matter that has a definite volume but no definite shape:** Water is one kind of *liquid.* (469)

M

magnet [MAG•nit] **An object that attracts iron and a few other (but not all) metals:** This *magnet* is strong enough to attract a paper clip even through three sheets of paper. (620)

magnetic field [mag•NET•ik FEELD] **The space around a magnet in which the force of the magnet acts:** The metal filings show where the *magnetic field* is. (623)

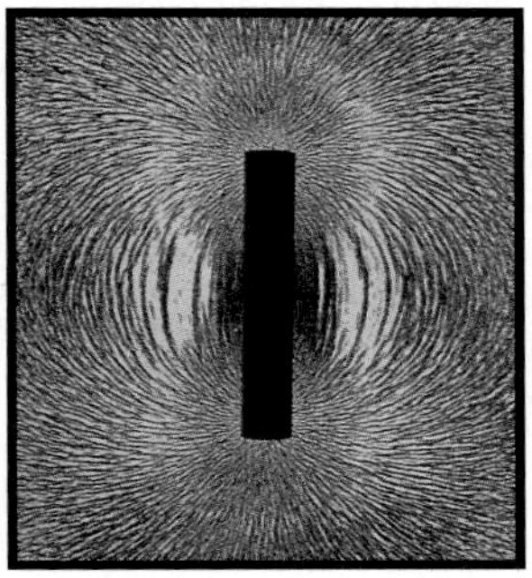

magnetic poles [mag•NET•ik POHLZ] **The parts of a magnet at which its force is strongest:** Every magnet has two *magnetic poles.* (622)

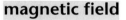

mass [MAS] **The amount of matter in an object:** A balance is used to measure how much *mass* an object has. (459)

matter [MAT•er] **Anything that has mass and takes up space:** *Matter* can be described by physical properties. (458)

mechanical energy [muh•KAN•ih•kuhl EN•er•jee] **The total potential and kinetic energy of an object:** A spring's *mechanical energy* is the total of stored energy combined with the energy it releases when moving. (647)

metamorphic rock [met•uh•MAWR•fik RAHK] **A type of rock that forms when heat or pressure change an existing rock:** Gneiss is a *metamorphic rock.* (284)

metamorphosis [met•uh• MAWR• fuh•sis] **Major changes in the body form of during the life cycle of an animal:** Caterpillars experience *metamorphosis* and become butterflies. (118)

microscope [MY•kruh•skohp] **A tool that makes an object look several times bigger than it is:** You might find this kind of *microscope* in your science lab at school. (8)

microscopic [my•kruh•SKAHP•ik] **Too small to be seen with the eyes alone:** A microscope enables you to see *microscopic* objects, like plant and animal cells. (55)

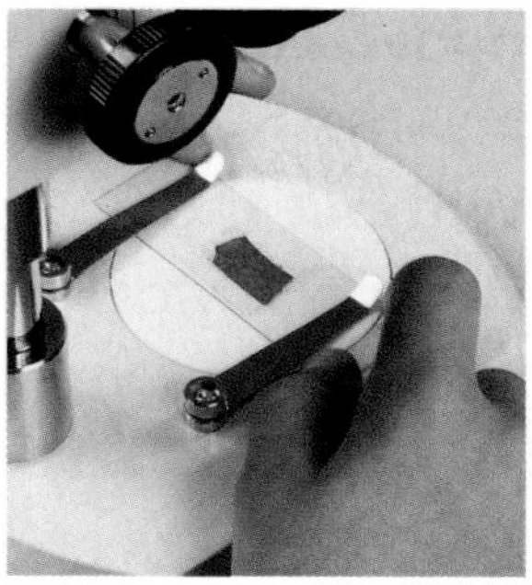

migration [my•GRAY•shuhn] **The movement of animals from one region to another and back:** Some birds travel thousands of miles during *migration*. (144)

mineral [MIN•er•uhl] **A solid substance that occurs naturally in rocks or in the ground:** Amethyst is a *mineral*. (280)

mixture [MIKS•chuhr] **A blending of two or more types of matter that are not chemically combined:** Lemonade is a *mixture* of water, sugar, and lemon juice. (478)

moon [MOON] **Any natural body that revolves around a planet:** The *moon* orbits Earth about every 4 weeks. (414)

motion [MOH•shuhn] **A change of position of an object:** This student is in *motion*. (660)

mountain [MOUNT•uhn] **An area that is higher than the land around it:** *Mountains* are one of Earth's natural landforms. (324)

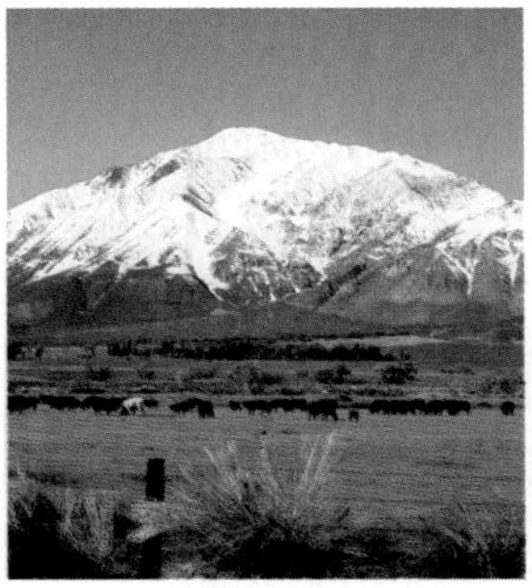

muscle [MUHS•uhl] **An organ that is made of bundles of long fibers and works with bones to help you move:** You need the *muscles* in your body to run, jump, and move. (186)

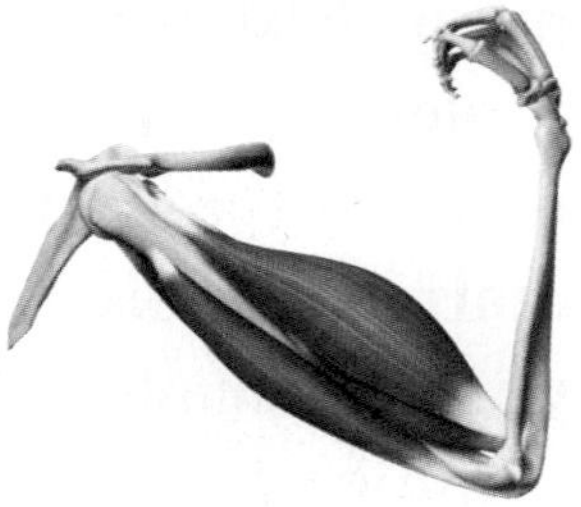

N

natural selection [NACH•uhr•uhl suh•LEK•shuhn] **A process in which the best adapted organisms in an ecosystem are able to survive and reproduce:** *Natural selection* is responsible for the survival of giraffes with long necks. (135)

niche [NICH] **The role of an organism in its habitat:** Every living thing has a *niche.* (253)

nonvascular [nahn•VAS•kyuh•ler] **Without tubes or channels:** Moss is a *nonvascular* plant. (68)

O

observation [ahb•zuhr•VAY•shuhn] **Information that you gather with your senses:** You can make an *observation* with your eyes or ears. (18)

omnivore [AHM•nih•vawr] **An animal that eats both plants and other animals:** A bear is an *omnivore.* (244)

orbit [AWR•bit] **The path of one object in space around another object:** It takes 365.25 days for Earth to complete its *orbit* around the sun. (410)

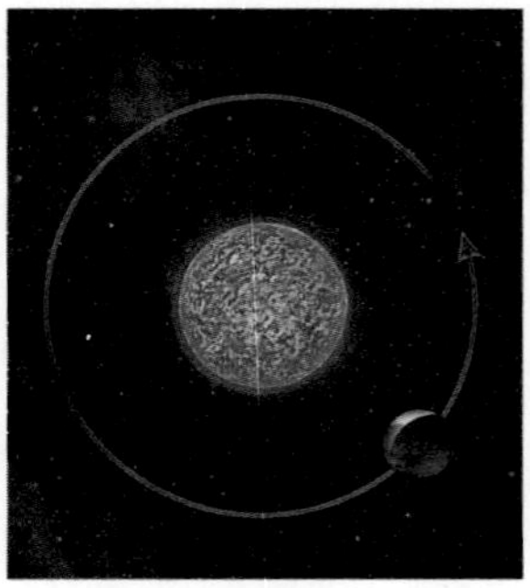

organ [AWR•guhn] **A body part made of different kinds of tissues that work together to perform a particular job:** Your heart, liver, and stomach are *organs.* (169)

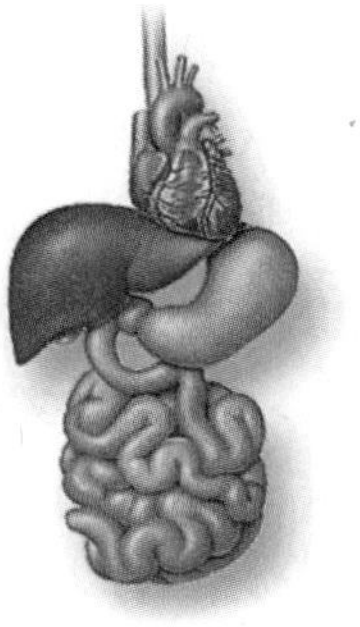

organism [AWR•guh•niz•uhm] **A living thing:** Plants and animals are *organisms.* (54)

P

pan balance [PAN BAL•uhns] **A tool that measures mass:** The *pan balance* shows that the masses of these objects are equal. (10)

parallel circuit [PAR•uh•lel SER•kit] **A circuit that has more than one path for an electric current to follow:** If one bulb in a *parallel circuit* goes out, the others stay on. (610)

phases [FAYZ•uhz] **The different shapes that Earth's moon seems to have:** The moon *phases* change as the moon orbits Earth. (414)

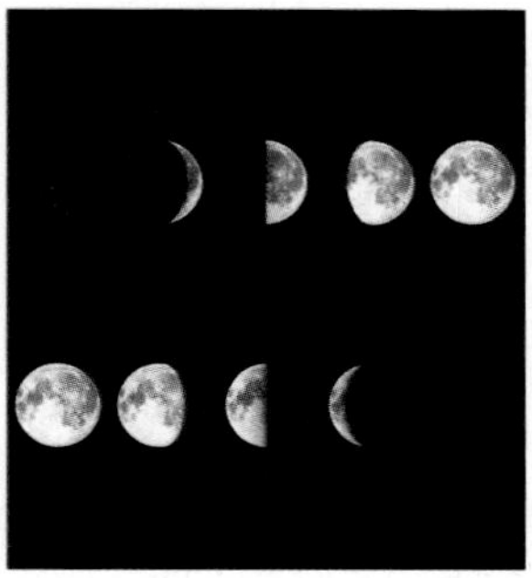

photosynthesis [foht•oh•SIN•thuh•sis] **The process that plants use to make sugar:** Plants need light and water to perform *photosynthesis.* (102)

physical change [FIZ•ih•kuhl CHAYNJ] **A change in matter from one form to another that doesn't result in a different substance:** The cutting of paper is a *physical change.* (508)

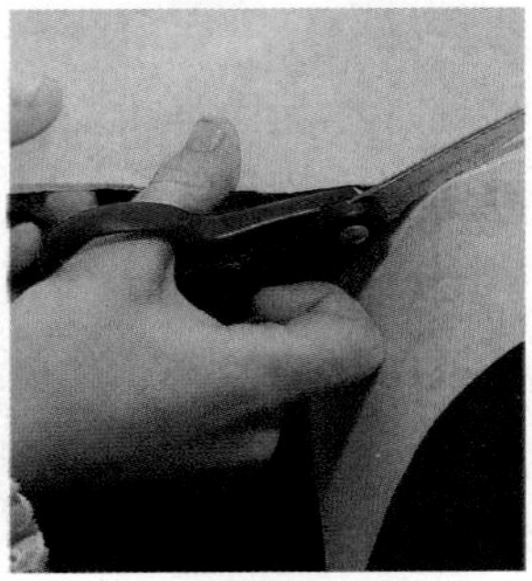

physical property [FIZ•ih•kuhl PRAHP•er•tee] **A trait that involves a substance by itself:** Some of the *physical properties* of this lizard are its color and shape. (517)

pitch [PICH] **A measure of how high or low a sound is:** Sounds with a very high *pitch* can hurt your ears. (534)

planet [PLAN•it] **A large object that moves around a star:** Earth is one of the *planets* that orbit the sun. (422)

pollution [puh•LOO•shuhn] **Waste products that damage an ecosystem:** Oil spills are a source of water *pollution.* (226)

population [pahp•yuh•LAY•shuhn] **All the individuals of the same kind living in the same environment:** Available resources limit animal *populations.* (204)

position [puh•ZISH•uhn] **The location of an object:** An object's *position* will change if a force is applied to it. (660)

potential energy [poh•TEN•shuhl EN•er•jee] **Energy that an object has because of its position or its condition:** Being on top of a hill increases *potential energy.* (634)

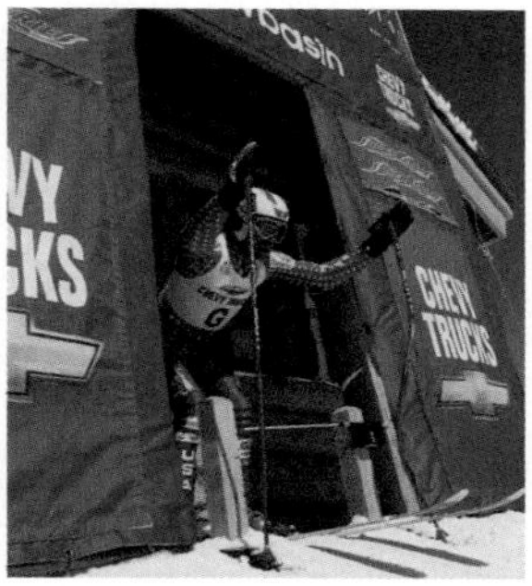

precipitation [pree•sip•uh•TAY•shuhn] **Water that falls to Earth:** *Precipitation* can be solid, like snow, or liquid, like rain. (364)

predator [PRED•uh•ter] **A consumer that eats prey:** Bobcats are *predators.* (254)

prey [PRAY] **Consumers that are eaten by predators:** Rabbits are one kind of *prey.* (254)

producer [pruh•DOOS•er] **A living thing, such as a plant, that can make its own food:** Grasses are *producers.* (242)

protist [PROHT•ist] **One of the kingdoms of living things that can be one-celled:** An amoeba is a *protist*—it has only one cell. (60)

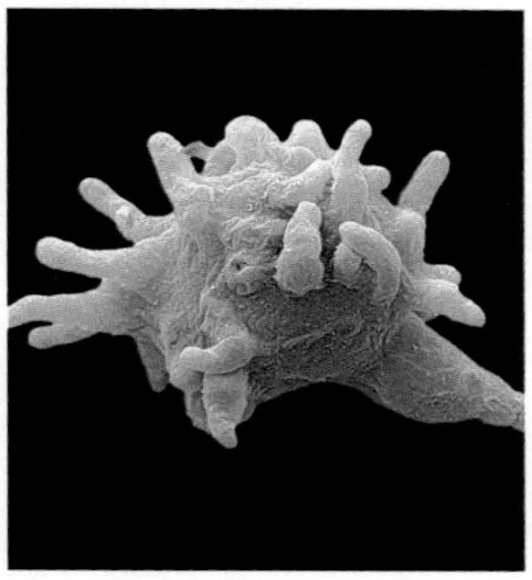

pulley [PUHL•ee] **A simple machine made of a wheel with a line around it:** You can lift heavy objects with the help of a *pulley.* (706)

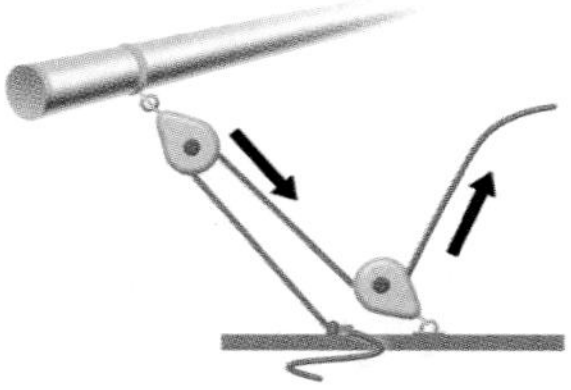

R

radiation [ray•dee•AY•shuhn] **The movement of heat without matter to carry it:** Hot objects cool through *radiation.* (582)

rain [RAYN] **Precipitation that is liquid water:** Some forest areas receive a lot of *rain.* (374)

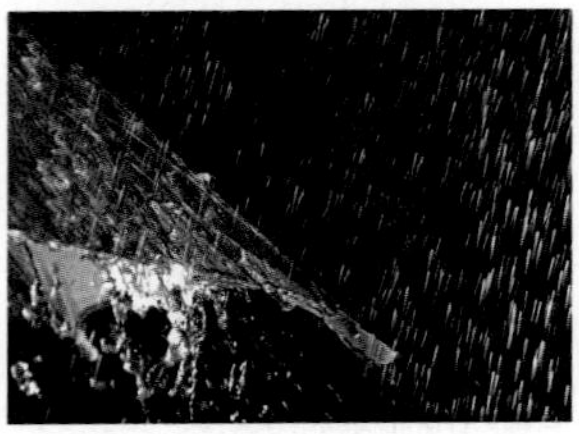

rain shadow [RAYN SHAD•oh] **The area on the side of a mountain range that gets little or no rain or cloud cover:** The *rain shadow* is the drier, less fertile side of the mountain. (386)

reflection [rih•FLEK•shuhn] **The bouncing of light, sound, or heat off an object:** *Reflection* allows you to see objects in a mirror. (554, 569)

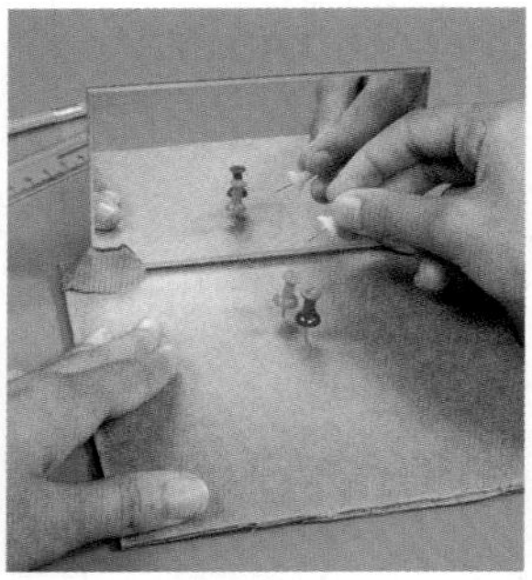

refraction [rih•FRAK•shuhn] **The bending of light when it moves from one kind of matter to another:** *Refraction* causes the straw to appear broken. (571)

rock [RAHK] **A solid substance made of one or more minerals:** *Rocks* come in all shapes and sizes. (280)

rock cycle [RAHK SY•kuhl] **The sequence of processes that change rocks from one type to another over long periods:** In the *rock cycle,* the same minerals may become different rocks. (290)

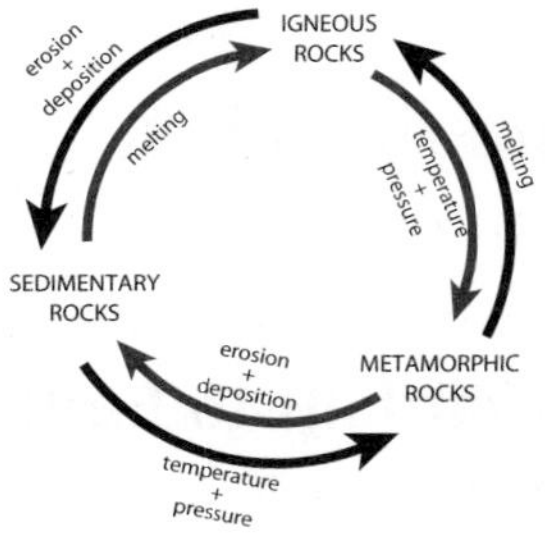

S

sand [SAND] **The largest particles that make up soil:** When rocks are broken down into very small pieces, they become *sand.* (310)

scientific method [sy•uhn•TIF•ik METH•uhd] **A way that scientists find out how things work and affect each other:** The student is using the *scientific method* to answer a question about how freezing affects rocks. (30)

screw [SKROO] **A simple machine made of a post with an inclined plane wrapped around it:** *Screws* are often used to hold things together. (718)

sea breeze [SEE BREEZ] **A breeze that moves from the water to the land:** A *sea breeze* can cool the land close to the shore. (384)

sedimentary rock [sed•uh•MEN•ter•ee RAHK] **A type of rock that forms when layers of sediment are pressed together:** Sandstone is one kind of *sedimentary rock.* (283)

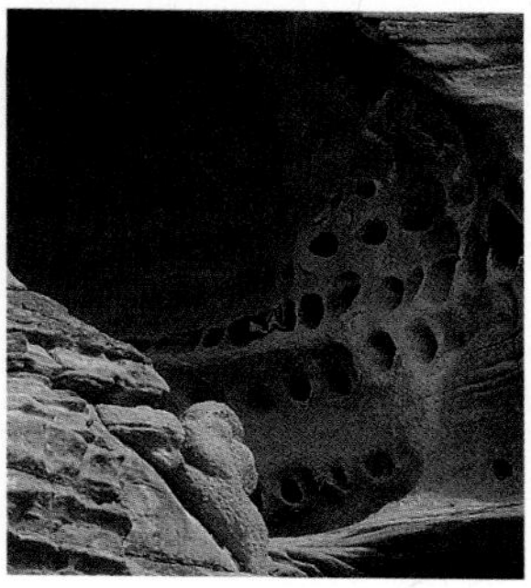

series circuit [SIR•eez SER•kit] **A circuit that has only one path for an electric current to follow:** If one bulb in a *series circuit* goes out, the others also go out. (610)

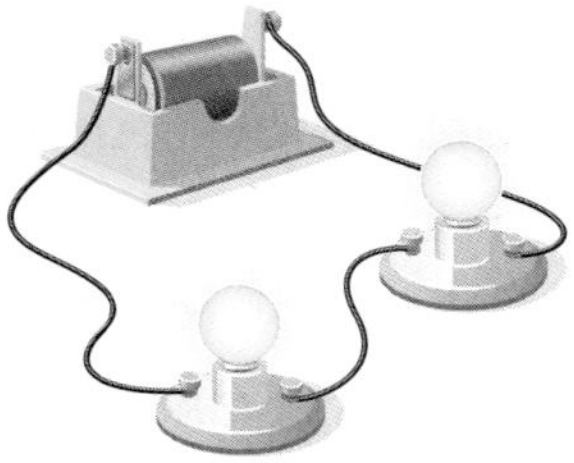

simple machine [SIM•puhl muh•SHEEN] **A machine with few or no moving parts that you apply just one force to:** A screwdriver is a wheel–and–axle, which is a kind of *simple machine.* (697)

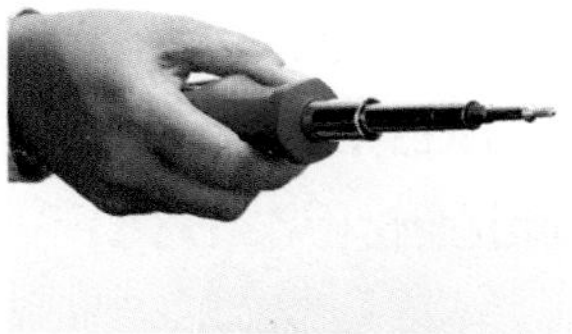

sleet [SLEET] **Precipitation made when rain falls through freezing-cold air and turns to ice:** *Sleet* makes sidewalks very slippery. (375)

snow [SNOH] **Precipitation caused when water vapor turns directly into ice and forms ice crystals:** Flakes of *snow* are ice crystals. (375)

solar energy [SOH•ler EN•er•jee] **The power of the sun:** Solar panels store *solar energy* and convert it to electricity. (638)

solar system [SOH•ler SIS•tuhm] **A group of objects in space that revolve around a central star:** The *solar system* is made up of the planets that orbit the sun. (422)

solid [SAHL•id] **The state of matter that has a definite shape and a definite volume:** Ice is one example of a *solid.* (468)

solubility [sahl•yoo•BIL•uh•tee] **A measure of how much of a material will dissolve in another material:** The drink mix has high *solubility.* (481)

solution [suh•LOO•shuhn] **A mixture in which two or more substances are mixed completely:** The air you breathe is a *solution.* (480)

speed [SPEED] **The measure of an object's change in position during a unit of time:** The *speed* of the racecar is found by knowing how far and how fast the racecar traveled. (662)

spinal cord [SPY•nuhl KAWRD] **A tube of nerves that runs through your backbone to your brain:** The nerves in your *spinal cord* control the movement in your body. (182)

spring scale [SPRING SKAYL] **A tool that measures forces, such as weight:** You can find *spring scales* in the produce department at some grocery stores. (11)

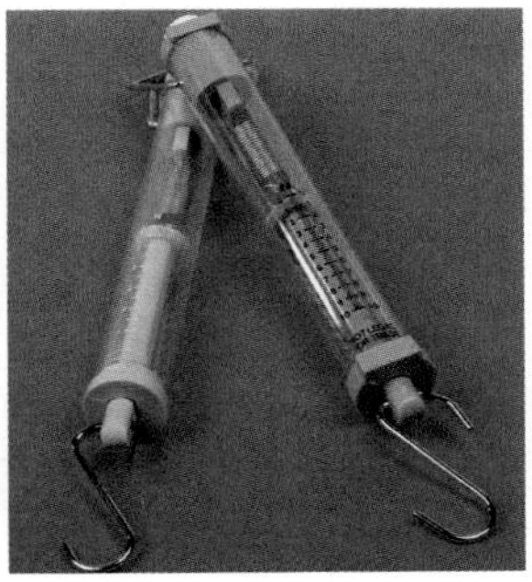

standard measure [STAN•derd MEZH•er] **An accepted measurement:** A meter is a *standard measure* of length. (6)

star [STAR] **A huge ball of superheated gases:** There are many *stars* in the night sky. (432)

state of matter [STAYT UHV MAT•er] **One of three forms (solid, liquid, and gas) that matter can exist in:** Ice is a solid *state of matter.* (468)

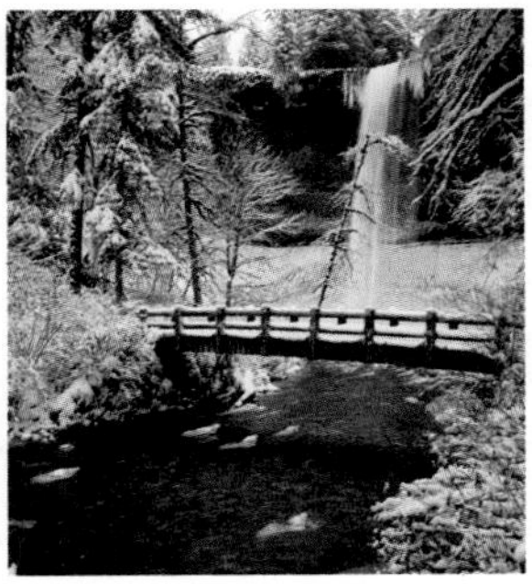

static electricity [STAT•ik ee•lek•TRIS•uh•tee] **An electrical charge that builds up on an object:** *Static electricity* might make your clothes stick together. (606)

stomach [STUHM•uhk] **A baglike organ in which food is mixed with digestive juices and squeezed by muscles:** Your *stomach* breaks down the food you eat into energy. (170)

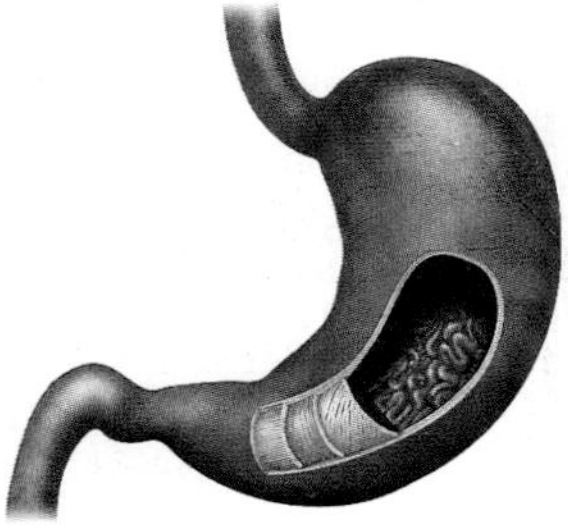

sun [SUHN] **The star at the center of the solar system:** The *sun* provides light and heat energy to our solar system. (432)

suspension [suh•SPEN•shuhn] **A kind of mixture in which particles of one ingredient are floating in another ingredient:** Salad dressing, with oil and vinegar, is a *suspension.* (482)

T

telescope [TEL•uh•skohp] **A device people use to observe distant objects with their eyes:** This girl can see the stars in the sky through her *telescope.* (412)

tissue [TISH•oo] **A group of cells of the same type that work together to perform a certain job:** All of the organs and muscles in your body are made up of *tissue.* (168)

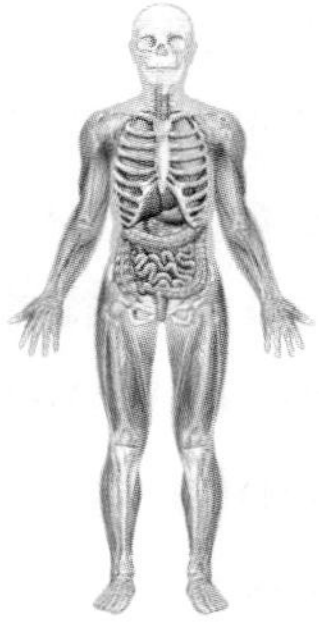

topography [tuh•PAHG•ruh•fee] **The shape of landforms in an area:** The *topography* of this area includes hills. (326)

tornado [tawr•NAY•doh] **A fast-spinning spiral of wind that touches the ground:** The inside of a *tornado* has very low air pressure. (376)

trait [TRAYT] **A characteristic that makes one organism different from another:** The different *traits* of these flowers help you tell them apart. (92)

transmission [tranz•MISH•uhn] **The passing of light or sound waves through a material:** The *transmission* of sound is faster through water than air. (556)

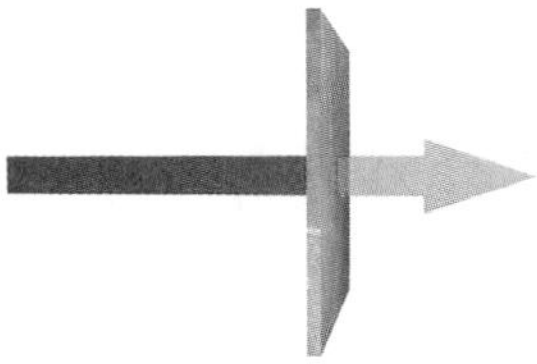

U

universe [YOO•nuh•vers] **Everything that exists in space:** Many galaxies make up the *universe.* (434)

V

vascular [VAS•kyuh•ler] **Having tubes or channels:** *Vascular* plants are made up of root, stem, and leaf systems. (66)

vein [VAYN] **A blood vessel that carries blood back to the heart from another part of the body:** Any *vein* in your body carries blood to your heart. (174)

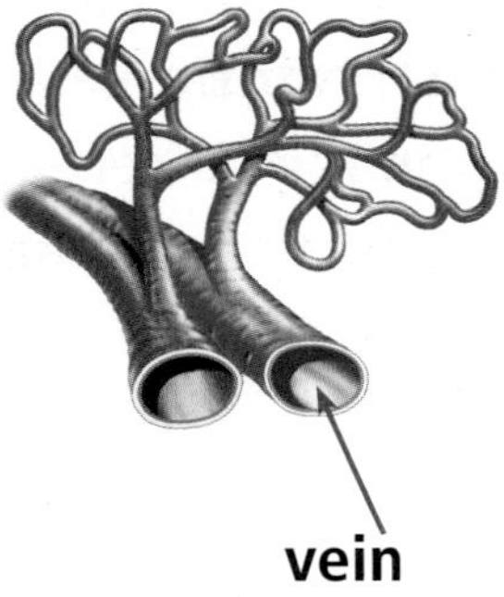

velocity [vuh•LAHS•uh•tee] **The measure of the speed and direction of motion of an object:** *Velocity* describes the direction of motion as well as the speed. (670)

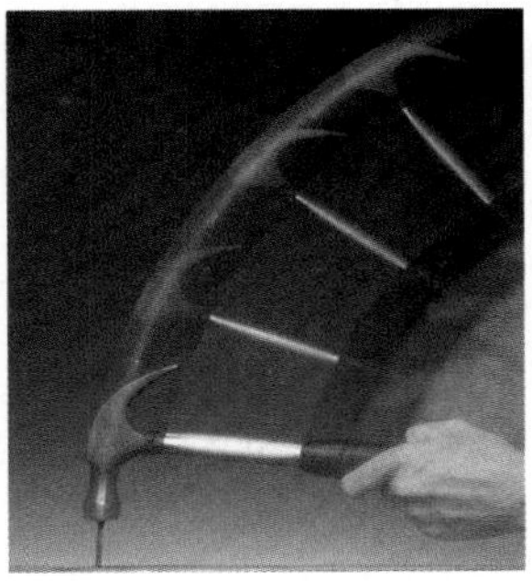

vertebrates [VER•tuh•brits] **The group of animals with a backbone:** The leopard is a powerful, fast *vertebrate.* (76)

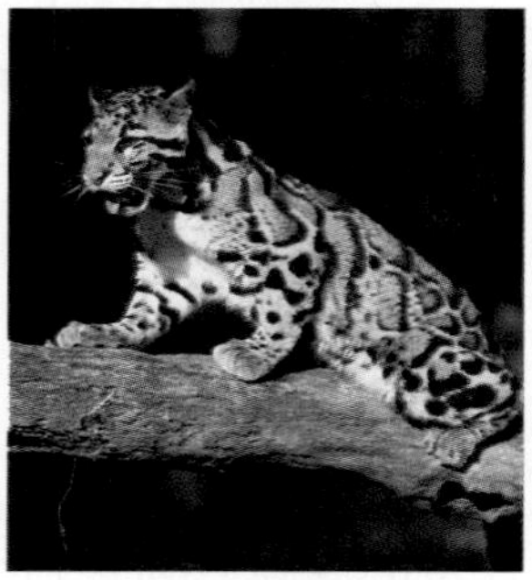

vibration [vy•BRAY•shuhn] **A quick back-and-forth motion:** *Vibration* of certain materials can create sound. (532)

volcano [vahl•KAY•noh] **A mountain that forms as lava flows through a crack onto Earth's surface:** The lava from the *volcano* was thick and flowed slowly. (336)

volume [VAHL•yoom] **The amount of space an object takes up:** You can measure how much *volume* a liquid has by using a graduated cylinder. (460)

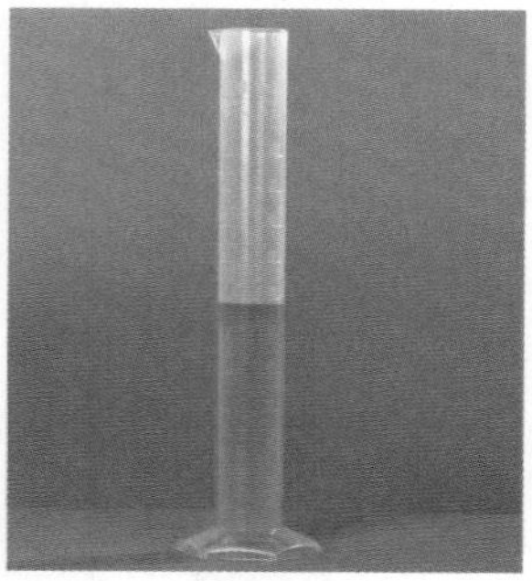

W

warm front [WAWRM FRUHNT] **The boundary where a warm air mass moves over a cold air mass:** A cold front causes a *warm front* to rise, cooling the weather for an area. (394)

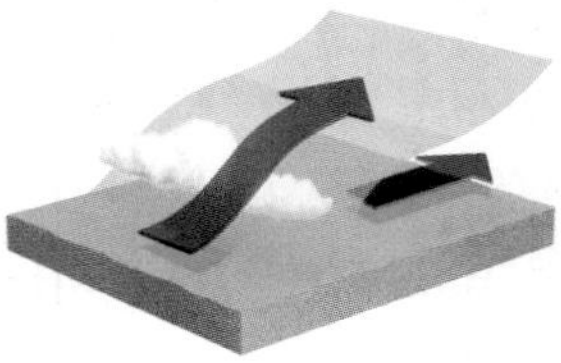

waste heat [WAYST HEET] **Heat that can't be used to do useful work:** The heat that radiates from a car engine is *waste heat.* (592)

water cycle [WAW•ter SY•kuhl] **The movement of water from the surface of Earth into the air and back again:** The *water cycle* includes evaporation and precipitation. (364)

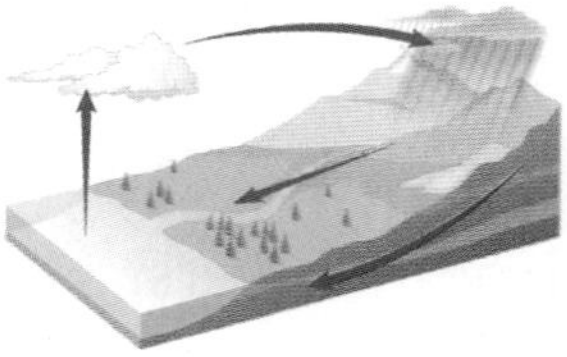

wavelength [WAYV•length] **The distance between a point on one wave and the identical point on the next wave:** The *wavelength* of visible light determines its color. (543)

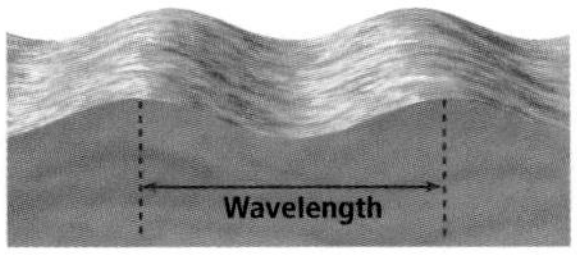

weathering [WETH•er•ing] **The breaking down of rocks on Earth's surface into smaller pieces:** *Weathering* has formed a hole in this sandstone, making an arch. (298)

wedge [WEJ] **A simple machine made of two inclined planes placed back-to-back:** An ax is a useful *wedge.* (720)

weight [WAYT] **A measure of the gravitational force acting on an object:** Your *weight* would be different on the moon because the gravitational force is different there. (682)

wheel-and-axle [WEEL•AND•AK•suhl] **A simple machine made of a wheel and an axle that turn together:** A doorknob is a *wheel-and-axle* that you use every day. (708)

work [WERK] **The use of force to move an object over a distance:** Pushing is a kind of *work.* (696)

Index

A

B

C

G

H

I

J

M

P

Q

R

U

V

W

KEY: (*t*) top, (*b*) bottom, (*l*) left, (*r*) right, (*c*) center, (*bg*) background, (*fg*) foreground

Introduction

x–1 (*c*) S Frink/Masterfile; 2 (*c*) AP Photo/NASA; 9 (inset) Sinclair Stammers/Science Photo Library; 11 (*c*) AP Photo/David J. Phillip; 12 (inset) Bartomeu Amengual/Age Fotostock; 26 (*c*) National Research Council Canada; (inset) Mark Gibson/Index Stock Imagery, Inc.; 30 (*bc*) Robert Llewellyn/CORBIS.

Unit A

39 (*bg*) Corel Stock Photo Library; 48–49 Stuart Westmoreland/CORBIS; 50 (*c*) Robert Winslow/Animals Animals; 52 Bob Krist/CORBIS; 54 (*r*) BSIP Agency/Index Stock Imagery; (*l*) Eric V. Grave/Photo Researchers; (*bg*) Garry Black/Masterfile; 55 (*r*) Bill Beatty/Visuals Unlimited; (*c*) Wally Eberhart/Visuals Unlimited; (*b*) Adam Jones/Visuals Unlimited; 56 (*l*) Biophoto Associates/Photo Researchers; 57 (*r*) LSHTM/Photo Researchers; 58 (*tl*) Jan Hinsch/Photo Researchers; (*cl*) Biophoto Associates/Photo Researchers; (*bg*) Astrid & Hanns-Frieder Michler/Photo Researchers; 59 (*cl*) Tom Adams/Visuals Unlimited; (*cr*) Science Photo Library/Photo Researchers; (*bl*) Dr. Kari Lounatmaa/Photo Researchers; 60 (*tr*) M.I. Walker/Photo Researchers; (*cl*) Microfield Scientific LTD/Photo Researchers; 62 (*bg*) Freeman Patterson/Masterfile; (*c*) Dan Suzio/Photo Researchers; 64 Malcolm Freeman/Alamy; 66 (*br*) Steve Satushek/Getty Images; 68 (inset) Norman Owen Tomalin/Bruce Coleman; (*bg*) David Noton/Masterfile; 69 (*tr*) James Richardson/Visuals Unlimited; (*tl*) Henry Robison/Visuals Unlimited; 70 (*tr*) Robert Pickett/CORBIS; (*tcr*) SciMAT/Photo Researchers; (*cr*) Carolina Biological/Visuals Unlimited; (*bc*) Jacqui Hurst/CORBIS; (*br*) E. R. Degginger/Color-Pic; (*bg*) CORBIS; 72 Roger Archibald/Animals Animals; 74 Adrian Sherratt/Alamy; 76 (*bl*) Frans Lanting/Minden Pictures; (*br*) Ken Lucas/Ardea London; 77 (*tl*) Michael & Patricia Fogden/Minden Pictures; 78 (*tl*) OSF/Mantis W.F./Animals Animals; (*cl*) Paul Sutherland/Independent Photography Network; (*cl*) Alex Fradkin/Images.com/Independent Photography Network; 79 (*tl*) Lightwave Photography/Animals Animals; (*cl*) Roger de la Harpe/Animals Animals; 80 (*r*) Pascal Goetgheluck/Ardea; 82 (*t*) James H. Robinson/Photo Researchers; (*b*) Getty Images; 83 (*t*) Getty Images; (inset) Getty; 86–87 Bill Curtsinger/Getty Images; 88 John Daniels/Ardea; 90 Petra Wegner/Alamy; 92 (*b*) Getty Images; 93 (*t*) Rob Lewine/Corbis; (*cr*) Getty Images; 94 (*tl*) Ray Kachatorian/Getty Images; (*tr*) Gio Barto/Getty Images; (*bl*) AGE Fotostock; (*bc*) H. & D. Zielske/Peter Arnold, Inc.; (*br*) Jonathan Nourok/PhotoEdit; 95 (*tl*) Phil Degginger/Animals Animals; (*tcl*) Klein/Hubert/Peter Arnold; (*tc*) Burke/Triolo Productions/Getty Images; (*tcr*) Jack Milchanowski/Visuals Unlimited; (*tr*) Frans Lanting/Minden Pictures; (*cr*) Arthur Morris/Visuals Unlimited; 96 (*tr*) E. A. Janes/AGE Fotostock; (*cr*) Bruce Coleman, Inc.; (*bl*) John Anderson/Animals Animals; (*br*) Cheryl Ertlet/Visuals Unlimited; 98 Dwight Kuhn; 100 Plantography/Alamy; 103 (*cr*) Brian Sullivan/Visuals Unlimited; 104 (*bl*) Brent Bergherm/AGE Fotostock; (*bc*) Rachel Weill/Getty Images; (*br*) Carltons/Getty Images; 106 (*cl*) Michael Gadomski/Photo Researchers; (*br*), (*cr*) Dwight Kuhn; 108 (*l*) Santiago Fernandez/AGE Fotostock; (*r*), (*cl*) Alamy Images; (*cr*) Dwight Kuhn; (*bg*) Bernard Photo Productions/Animals Animals; 110 Ray Coleman/Visuals Unlimited; 112 John Cornell/Visuals Unlimited; 114 (*tr*) SuperStock; (*bl*) Georgette Douwma/Getty Images; (*br*) Zigmund Leszczynski/Animals Animals; 115 (*l*) Curtis Richter/Alamy Images; (*r*) Morales/AGE Fotostock; 116 (*r*) Cosmos Blank/Photo Researchers; (*cl*) Norbert Rosing/Getty Images; (*bl*) Tom Brakefield/Corbis; 117 (*tl*) Susan Solie Patterson/Corbis; (*tr*) David Zelick/Getty Images; (*cl*) Photodisc/Getty Images; (*c*) Photodisc/Getty Images; (*cr*) Hans-George Gaul/Getty Images; 118 (*cl*), (*cr*) & (*bl*) Dwight Kuhn; (*br*) Patti Murray/Animals Animals; 124 Dave Watts/Nature Picture Library; 126 Luiz C. Marigo/Peter Arnold; 128 Arthur Morris/CORBIS; 130 Peter Arnold/Peter Arnold, Inc.; 131 (*cr*) E & P Bauer/Bruce Coleman, Inc.; (*br*) Gil Lopez Espina/Visuals Unlimited; 131 (*cl*) Masa Ushioda/Bruce Coleman, Inc.; 132 (*cl*) Jean Paul Ferrero/Ardea London; (*cr*) Lynn Stone/Animals Animals; (*bl*) Michael & Patricia Fogden/Minden Pictures; (*br*) David Moore/Alamy Images; 133 (*t*) Chase Swift/Corbis; (*tcr*) Alan G. Nelson/Animals Animals; 134 Konrad Zelazowski/Alamy; 135 (*t*) David Fox/Jupiter Images; 135 (*tr*) Kim Taylor/npl/Minden Pictures; 136 (*cl*) Brad Mitchell/Alamy Images; (*b*) Robert W. Domm/Visuals Unlimted; 138 Francois Gohier/Ardea; 140 Daniel J Cox/Getty Images; 142 (*bl*) Bernard Castelein/Nature Picture Library; (*bcr*) Hanne & Jens Eriksen/Nature Picture Library; 143 (*tr*) Patti Murray/Animals Animals; (*tcr*) Georgette Douwma/Nature Picture Library; (*cr*) Dietmar Nill/Nature Picture Library; (*bl*) Jennifer Loomis/Animals Animals; (*br*) Doug Wechsler/Animals Animals; 144 (*tr*) Nigel Bean/Nature Picture Library; (*br*) Bob Cranston/Animals Animals; 145 (*tr*) Staffan Widstrand/Nature Picture Library; (*bcr*) Arthur Morris/Corbis; 146 (*tr*) Ray Richardson/Animals Animals; (*c*) Michael Habicht/Animals Animals; (*bl*) M. Watson/Ardea; 148 Tammy L. Johnson/Florida Museum of Natural History; 150 L. K. Broman/Photo Researchers, Inc.; 152 (*bg*) Mitsuaki Iwago/Minden Images; (*cr*) Paul A. Souders/CORBIS; (*br*) Roger Harris/Science Photo Library; 153 (*t*)(*bg*) SuperStock; (*tl*) Jeff Gage/Florida Museum of Natural History; (*cr*) Peter Scoones/Science Photo Library; (*br*) Dr. Schwimmer/Bruce Coleman, Inc.; 154 (*bg*) Carol Havens/Corbis; (*br*) Kevin Schafer/Corbis; 155 (*tl*) E.R. Degginger/Bruce Coleman, Inc.; (*tc*) Barry Runk/Stan/Grant Heilman Photography; (*tr*) Ken Lucas/Visuals Unlimited; (*bl*) Patti Murray/Animals Animals; (*bcl*) D.Robert & Lorri Franz/Corbis; (*br*) David Cavagnaro/Visuals Unlimited; 156 (*cl*) Gianni Dagli Orti/CORBIS; (*cr*) Hulton Archive/Getty Images; (*b*) Ron Testa/The Field Museum; 162 Amwell/Getty Images; 164 Susumu Nishinaga/Science Photo Library; 166 Sean Justice/Getty Images; 169 (*tr*) Manfred Kage/Peter Arnold, Inc.; 178 Andy Wong/AP Photo; 180 Will & Deni McIntyre/Getty Images.

Unit B

196–197 Fritz Polking/Visuals Unlimited; 198 Bob Thomas/Getty Images; 200 luedke & sparrow/Getty Images; 202 (*cr*) Bob & Clara Calhoun/Bruce Coleman; (*br*) Beth Davidow/Visuals Unlimited; 202 (*b*) Cathy Melloan/PhotoEdit; 203 (*t*) E. R. Degginger/Bruce Coleman, Inc.; (*cl*) George Sanker/Bruce Coleman, Inc.; 204 (*t*) Dennis MacDonald/PhotoEdit; (*tl*) Dennis MacDonald/PhotoEdit; 205 (*bl*) Steve Maslowski/Visuals Unlimited; (*b*) Kenneth Fink/Bruce Coleman, Inc.; 206 (*cl*) Jeremy Woodhous/Getty Images; 208 Karl Kummels/SuperStock; 210 Lindsay Hebberd/CORBIS; 212 (*c*) Jerome Wexler/Visuals Unlimited; (*bl*) Adam Jones/Visuals Unlimited; (*br*) Rob Simpson/Visuals Unlimited; 213 David L. Shirk/Animals Animals; 217 (*tr*) Greg Neise/Visuals Unlimited; (*tl*) Julie Eggers/Bruce Coleman, Inc.; (*cl*) Adam Jones/Visuals Unlimited; (*cr*) Richard Thom/Visuals Unlimited; (*bl*) Patrick Endres/Visuals Unlimited; (*br*) Eastcott-Momatiuk/The Image Works; 220 Jim Richardson/Corbis; 222 Chris Howes/Wild Places Photography/Alamy; 224 (*bl*) Dennis Brack/IPN; (*b*) Joel Sartore/Getty Images; (*tl*) Micheal Rose/Photo Researchers; (*tr*) Stuart Westmorland/Coribs; (*cl*) Coribs; (*cr*) Masterfile; 226 (*tcr*) Susan Van Etten/Photo Edit; (*r*) Mark Richards/PhotoEdit; (*bcr*) Steve Maslowski/Visuals Unlimited; (*br*) Rick Poley/Visuals Unlimited; 227 (*tl*) Cary Wolinsky/IPN; (*tr*) Nancy Richmond/The Image Works; 228 (*br*) Lester Lefkowitz/Getty Images; 228 (*bl*) Werner Otto/Alamy; 229 (*tl*) Bert Wiklund; 229 (*tr*) Bert Wiklund; 230 (*cr*) Frank Ordonez/Syracuse Newspapers/The Image Works; (*bl*) Corbis; 232 (*t*) Assign Nature Conservation Foundation; (*b*) Corbis; 233 (*tr*) Fritz Reiss/Associated Press, (*br*) AFP/Getty Images; (*bg*) Anthony Bannister/Photo Researchers; 236–237 Tom and Pat Leeson; 238 Kim Taylor/Bruce Coleman, Inc.; 243 (*tl*) Darrell Gulin/Corbis; (*tr*) Lynn Stone/Animals Animals; (*br*) D. Robert & Lorri Franz/Corbis; 245 (*tc*) Lynn Stone/Animals Animals; (*cl*) Kevin Schafer/Corbis; (*cr*) Bob Barber/Barber Nature Photography; (*bl*) Michael Fogden/Animals Animals; 246 (*cr*) Wolfgang Kaehler/Corbis; (*cl*) Ken Lucas/Visuals Unlimited; (*b*) Jim Brandenburg/Minden Picures; 247 (*br*) D.Hurst/Alamy Images; 248 CDC/PHIL/Corbis; 252 (*cr*) Gerry Ellis / Minden Pictures; (*b*) Royalty-Free/Corbis; (*br*) Darrell Gulin/Corbis; 252 (*tr*) ZSSD/Minden Pictures; 253 (*tl*) Corbis; (*tr*) Dale Sanders/Masterfile; (*c*) Andrew J. Martinez/Photo Researchers; (*br*) Dale Sanders/Masterfile; 254 (*bl*) M. Timothy O'Keefe/Bruce Coleman, Inc.; (*br*) Doug Perrine/SeaPics.com; (*bg*) Wolfgang Kaehler/CORBIS; 255 (*tl*) Jim Zipp/Photo Researchers; (*tc*) Bill Brooks/Masterfile; (*cr*) Barry Runk/Stan/Grant Heilman Photography; (*bl*) Joe McDonald/CORBIS; 265 (*bg*) Corel Stock Photo Library.

Unit C

274–275 Keren Su/CORBIS; 276 Kerrick James/Getty Images; 278 Steve Satushek/Getty Images; 280 (*bl*) Herve Berthoule/JACANA/Science Photo Library; (*bc*) Mark A. Schneider/Visuals Unlimited; (*br*) Bildagentur/Alamy Images; 281 (*tl*) Arnold Fisher/Science Photo Library; (*cl*) Marli Miller/Visuals Unlimited; 281 (*tr*) Marli Miller/Visuals Unlimited; (*cr*) Michael Barnett/Science Photo Library; 282 (*cl*), (*tcr*), (*cr*), & (*bl*) Wally Eberhart/Visuals Unlimited; (*br*) Sciencephotos/Alamy Images; 283 (*tl*) Glenn Oliver/Visuals Unlimited; (*tr*) E.R. Degginger/Color-Pic; (*cl*) Joyce Photographics/Photo Researchers; (*cr*) Wally Eberhart/Visuals Unlimited; 284 (*tcr*) A. J. Copley/Visuals Unlimited; (*bcr*),(*bl*) Wally Eberhart/Visuals Unlimited; (*br*) Joyce Photographics/Photo Researchers; 286 Ronen Zilberman/AP Photo; 292 (*tr*) Ed Degginger/Color-Pic; (*bl*) Albert J. Copley/Visuals Unlimited; 294–295 (*tr*) John Lawrence/Getty Images; 296 slayman.com/Alamy; 298 (*bcr*) Peter Kubal/Pan Photo; (*b*) Claire Selby/Animals Animals; 299 (*bg*) AP PHOTO; 300 (*cl*) Freeman Patterson/Masterfile; (*b*) George and Monserrate Schwartz/Alamy Images; 301 (*t*) Masterfile; (*cr*) John Kieffer/Peter Arnold, Inc.; 302 (*r*) Jim Wark/Airphoto; (*bl*) Greg Probst; 304 Louie Psihoyos/IPN; 306 mediacolor's/Alamy; 310 (*b*) Wally Eberhart/Visuals Unlimited; 311 (*tc*) Roland Liptak/Alamy Images (*tr*) Peter Griffith/Masterfile; 311 (*tl*) Jim Craigmyle/CORBIS; (*fg*) Diane Hirsch/Fundamental Photographs; 312 (*bl*) Nigel Cattlin/Alamy Images; (*br*) Jeff Morgan/Alamy Images; 313 (*br*) Dorothea Lange/Library of Congress; 314 Roger Wood/Corbis; 314–315 Stone/Getty Images; 318–319 Mediacolor's/Alamy Images; 320 G. Alan Nelson Outdoor Photography; 324 (*bl*) Paul A. Souders/Corbis; (*br*) Darrell Gulin/Corbis; 325 (inset) Gary Yeowell/Getty Images; (*bg*) Josef Beck/Getty Images; 326 (*bg*) James Strachan/Getty Images; (inset) AirphotoNA.com; 327 (*t*) NASA/Corbis, 327 (*b*) David Muench/Corbis; 328 (*cr*) Photri/Topham/The Image Works; (*b*) Douglas Peebles; 330 Jean-Paul Ferrero/Ardea; 335 (*bg*) David Paterson/Getty Images; 336 (*bg*) Bernhard Edmaier/Science Photo Library; 337 (*tr*) David Butow/Corbis SABA; (*br*) David Hume Kennerly/Getty Images; 338 (*tr*) Ernest Manewal/Index Stock Imagery; (*br*) Pat O'Hara/CORBIS; 339 (*tr*) Arnulf Husmo/Getty Images; (*tl*) Harvey Lloyd/Getty Images; 340 (*bg*) M. T. O'Keefe/Robertstock.com; (inset) Mark Gibson/Index Stock Imagery; 342 James L. Amos/Corbis; 344 Frans Lanting/Minden Pictures; 346 (*bg*) Runk/Schoenberger/Grant Heilman Photography, Inc.; 347 (*tl*) Francois Gohier/Photo Researchers; (*tr*) Eberhard Grames/Bilderberg/Peter Arnold, Inc.; (*c*) Imagenes de Nuestro Mundo; 348 (inset) Indiana Dept. of Natural Resources/Falls of the Ohio State Park; (*b*) Indiana Dept. of Natural Resources/Falls of the Ohio River; 349 (*cr*) Sinclair Stammers/Photo Researchers; 352 (*bg*) Bill Frymire; 353 (*b*) William J. Smith/Associated Press.

Unit D

358–359 SuperStock; 360 Jeff Greenberg/The Image Works; 370 David Sailors/CORBIS; 372 Matthias Rietschel/AP Images; 374 (*b*) Royalty-Free/CORBIS; (*tr*) Oote Boe/Alamy Images; (*cr*) Layne Kennedy/Dembinksy Photo Assoc.; 375 (*b*) Rob Atkins/Getty Images; 376 (*tr*) Royalty-Free/CORBIS; (*bl*) Alaska Stock Images; 377 (*bg*) Royalty-Free/CORBIS; 378 (*cl*) Gene Rhoden; (*cr*) Micheal Heller/911 Pictures; (*bl*) Silver Image; (*br*) Richard

Cummins/CORBIS; 380 Alan R. Mcller/Getty Images; 382 Tom Brakefield/SuperStock; 385 (*cr*) NOAA/AP Photo; 388 Gene Rhoden/Peter Arnold, Inc.; 390 Mel Yates/Getty Images; 395 (*tl*) Eastcott/Momatiuk/The Image Works; (*tr*) Tom Dietrich/Getty Images; (*cl*) John Eastcott & Yva Momatiuk/Getty Images; (*cr*) George Post/Photo Researchers; (*b*) Getty Images; (*tc*) Paul Seheult; (*tcr*) Burke/Triolo Productions/Getty Images; (*c*) David Young-Wolff/Photo Edit; (*bg*) Eye Ubiquitous/CORBIS; 404–405 David Nunuk/Photo Researchers; 406 Warren Flagler/Index Stock Imagery; 408 Adam Jones/Getty Images; 412 (*bl*) Lester Lefkowitz/Getty Images; 412 (*br*) Photolibrary/Alamy; 413 (*cr*) NASA/Roger Ressmeyer/CORBIS; 413 (inset) Roger Ressmeyer/CORBIS; 413 (*t*) Science Faction; 417 (*bl*) Gianni Dagli Orti/CORBIS; 418 NASA/JPL/Space Science Institute; 420 Charles C Place/Getty Images; 422 (*bg*) StockTrek/Getty Images; (*bcr*) USGS /Photo Researchers; 423 (*tr*) US Geological Survey/Photo Researchers; (*bcr*) Getty Images; 424 (*tr*) NASA; (*c*) Getty Images; (*bl*) STScl/NASA/Photo Researchers; 426 (*c*) Jerry Lodriguss/Photo Researchers; (*bl*) Reuters/CORBIS; 428 Reuters/CORBIS; 430 Russell Gordon; 432 (*bl*) GoodShoot/SuperStock; 434 (*bl*) John Chumack/Photo Researchers; 435 (*bg*) Celestial Image Co./Photo Researchers; (*bl*) NASA; 438–439 All photos NASA; 443 (*bg*) Digital Stock.

Unit E

452–453 Science Photo Library/Photo Researchers; 454 Steve Shott/DK Images; 456 Peter Steiner/Alamy; 460 (*tl*) PhotoDisc/Getty Images; 461 (*tc*) Getty Images; (*tr*) Charles D. Winters/Photo Researchers; 462 (*cr*) Flat Earth/FotoSearch; 464 Patrick J. Endres/AlaskaPhotoGraphics; 466 Felicia Martinez/PhotoEdit; 468 (*bl*) Charles D. Winters/Photo Researchers; (*br*) Mike Hipple/Index Stock Imagery; 469 (*tl*) David Bishop/FoodPix/Getty Images; (*tc*) Spencer Jones/FoodPix/Getty Images; 470 (*br*) Keate/Masterfile; 471 (*bl*) Keate/Masterfile; (*br*) Japack Company/CORBIS; 472 (*bg*) Charles O'Rear/CORBIS; (*cl*) Charles D. Winters/Photo Researchers; 474 David Whitten/Index Stock Imagery/PictureQuest; 476 Brand X Pictures/Alamy; 481 (*bg*) Peter French/Bruce Coleman; 482 (*bg*) Tim Fitzharris/Minden Pictures; 484 (*bg*) Corel Stock Photo Library -Royalty Free; 485 (*t*) Daum photos; (*b*) Layne Kennedy/Corbis; 487 (*bc*) Daryl Benson/Masterfile; (*br*) John Warden/Index Stock Imagery; 488–489 Gerd Ludwig/VISUM/The Image Works; 490 M.F. Crommie, C.P. Lutz, D.M. Eigler/IBM; 492 Food Features/Alamy; 497 (*cl*) Richard Megna/Fundamental Photographs; 498 (*tr*) Charles D. Winters/Photo Researchers; (*bl*) Bill Aron/Photo Edit; (*br*) Tony O'Brien/The Image Works; 499 (*tr*) Russ Lappa/Photo Researchers; (*bc*) Jeff J. Daly/Fundamental Photographs; 499 (*c*) Richard Cummins/CORBIS; (*cr*) Tom Pantages/AGPix; (*br*) Ryan McVay/Getty Images; 500 (*tl*) Elio Ciol/CORBIS; (*cr*) Richard Treptow/Photo Researchers; 502 Rommel/Masterfile; 504 Tony Hamblin; Frank Lane Picture Agency/CORBIS; 506 (*tcr*) Gary Buss/Getty Images; (*br*) Joseph Van Os/Getty Images; 507 (*cr*) Royalty-Free/CORBIS; 508 (*l*) Kjell Sandved/Bruce Coleman; (*br*) Michael Dalton/Fundamental Photographs; 509 (*tl*) PhotoDisc/Getty Images; (*cr*) Bonnie Kamin/PhotoEdit; 512 NASA/Science Photo Library; 514 age fotostock/SuperStock; 516 (*tc*) Scott Haag; (*bc*) Tom Pantages/AGPix; (*b*) Andrew Lambert Photography/Science Photo Library/Photo Researchers; 518 (*tr*) SuperStock; (*br*) Fife/Photo Researchers; 395 (*br*) Richard Megna/Fundamental Photographs; 520 (*tr*) Grant Heilman/Grant Heilman Photography; (*cr*) Grant Heilman/Grant Heilman Photography; (*bc*) Burke/Triolo/Brand X Pictures/PictureQuest; 522 (*tr*) Bettmann/CORBIS; 522 (*bg*) Chad Baker/Getty Images; 523 (*br*) Corel Stock Photo Library - Royalty Free; 523 (*tl*) Courtesy of the University of California; 523 (*bg*) Ian McKinnell/Alamy; 526–527 Jean Pragen/Getty Images; 528 David Schmidt/Masterfile; 530 Richard Megna/Fundamental Photographs; 534 (*cl*) Rob Lacey/Vividstock/Alamy Images; (*cr*) Jeremy Woodhouse/Getty Images; (*b*) CORBIS; 535 (*tl*) Iain Davidson Photographic/Alamy Images; (*tr*) Ted Kimsman/Photo Researchers; 536 (*tc*) Alan Schein Photography/CORBIS; (*bl*) John Foxx/Alamy Images; 538 CORBIS; 540 John D. Norman/CORBIS; 542 (*bl*) Japack Company/CORBIS; 544 (*cl*) Jeremy Woodhouse/Getty Images; (*bl*) Rob Lacey/Vividstock/Alamy Images; 546 (*cr*) Russell Underwood/CORBIS; (*bl*) James Noble/CORBIS; 548 Tim Davis/CORBIS; 550 age fotostock/SuperStock; 555 (*t*) Roger Ressmeyer/CORBIS; 558 (*tl*), (*cl*), (*br*) Julie Wolf Alissi; (*bl*) Will Crocker/Getty Images; 562–563 Maximillian Stock LTD/Science Photo Library; 564 Loren Winters/Visuals Unlimited; 569 (*tr*) Robert Harding Picture Library LTD/Alamy Images; (*cr*) Rolf Bruderer/Masterfile; 570 (*cr*) Grant Heilman Photography; 571 (*tr*), (*tl*) Richard Megna/Fundamental Photographers; 574 Ted Kinsman/Photo Researchers; 576 Michael Newman/PhotoEdit; 578 (*bl*) Grant Heilman Photography; 579 (*cr*) Peter Bowater/Photo Researchers; (*b*) Big Cheese Photo/PictureQuest; 580 (*b*) Grant Heilman Photography; 581 (*r*) Clouds Hill Imaging LTD/Science Photo Library; 582 (*tr*) David Michael Zimmerman/CORBIS; (*bl*) Stephen J. Krasemann/Photo Researchers; br) Ted Kinsman/Photo Researchers; 584 Paul Almasy/CORBIS; 586 Paco Ayala/Age Fotostock; 588 (*b*) CORBIS; 589 (*t*) IPS Agency/Index Stock Imagery; (*cl*) Michael Keller/Index Stock Imagery; 590 (*cl*) Rachel Weill/FoodPix; 591 (*tr*) R. Ian Lloyd/Masterfile; 592 (*tr*) Lon C. Diehl/PhotoEdit; (*b*) Pasieka/Science Photo Library; 592 (*cr*) Randy Faris/CORBIS; 294–595 Hans Strand/Corbis.

Unit F

600–601 Mark Gibson/Visuals Unlimited; 602 Robert Essel NYC/CORBIS; 606 (*b*) Science Museum, London/Topham-HIP/The Image Works; 612 (*tl*) Andrew Lambert Photography/Photo Researchers; (*cr*) Image Farm Inc./Alamy Images; 613 (*br*) Loren Winters/Visuals Unlimited; 616 Bruce Gray; 618 Jenn Heacox-Alberts; 620 (*br*) Peter Arnold/Peter Arnold, Inc.; 621 (*bg*) Digital Vision/Getty Images; (*tl*) Tony Freeman/Photo Edit; 622 (*cr* & *cl*) Richard Megna/Fundamental Photographs; 623 (*tl*) Biodisc/Visuals Unlimited; 624 (*b*) Tony Freeman/Photo Edit; 625 (*t*) Jeremy Walker/Photo Researchers; 625 (*b*) Jack Plekan/Fundamental Photographs; 626 (*br*) Tom Pantages; 628 (*tc*) David Young-Wolff/Photo Edit; 628 (*c*) Robert Mathena/Fundamental Photographs; 630 Martin Miller/Visuals Unlimited; 632 Wm. Baker/GhostWorx Images/Alamy; 636 (*bl*) Jeff Greenberg/Visuals Unlimited; 637 (*t*) Martin Bond/Science Photo Library; 638 (*c*) Martin Bond/Peter Arnold, Inc.; (*bl*) Pegasus/Visuals Unlimited; 640 Angelo Cavalli/Getty Images; 642 Masterfile Royalty Free; 644 (*bl*) Digital Vision/AGE Fotostock; 645 (*tc*) H. Spichtinger/Masterfile; 647 (*tr*) Maximillian Stock LTD/Phototake; (*tl*) Kawasaki Motors Corporation USA; 648 (*tr*) Felicia Martinez/Photo Edit; (*cr*) Anne Dowie/Index Stock Imagery; (*bl*) Peter Arnold/Peter Arnold, Inc.; 650 (*bg*) age fotostock/SuperStock; 651 (*tl*) National Portrait Gallery, Smithsonian Institution/Art Resource, NY, (*br*) Peter Gridley/Getty Images, (*l*) Florida Images/Alamy; 654–655 Adastra/Getty Images; 656 Macduff Everton/CORBIS; 658 Jon Riley/Jupiter Images; 660 (*b*) Jim Cummins/CORBIS; 662 (*bc*) C Squared Studios/Getty Images; (*b*) David Young-Wolff/PhotoEdit; 663 (*tl*) Leslie O'Shaushnessy/Visuals Unlimited; (*cr*) Spencer Grant/PhotoEdit; 664 (*br*), (*bcl*) Dennis MacDonald/PhotoEdit; 666 Lori Adamski Peek/Getty Images; 674 (*b*) Jim Craigmyle/CORBIS; (*br*) CORBIS; 675 (*tr*) Bill Bachmann/PhotoEdit; (*tcl*) Jonathan Nourok/PhotoEdit; 672 (*tcl*) Wally McNamee/CORBIS; (*tr*) Chris Trotman/Duomo/CORBIS; 673 (*tc*), (*tcl*) Lon C. Diehl/PhotoEdit; 676 Tom Sanders/CORBIS; 681 (*b*) Bill Bachmann/PhotoEdit; 682 (*tr*) Roy Morsch/Bruce Coleman; (*b*) Jose Luis Pelaez, Inc./CORBIS; 683 (*cl*) Kelly-Mooney Photography/CORBIS; (*bl*) Richard Hutchings/PhotoEdit; (*bg*) Michael Ferguson; 686 Matthew Stockman/Getty Images; 687 Robert LaBerge/Getty Images; 692 (*b*) Farley Lewis/Photo Researchers; 694 Digital Archive Japan/Alamy; 697 (*t*) Grant Heilman Photography; 698 (*r*) William Sallaz/Duomo/CORBIS; 699 (*tl*) Cindy Charles/Photo Edit; 700 (*c*) Lon C. Diehl/Photo Edit; (*bl*) Zefa/Masterfile; 704 Sandra Baker/Getty Images; 706 (*b*) Farley Lewis/Photo Researchers; 707 (*tr*) Ted Spiegel/CORBIS; (*br*) Philip Gould/CORBIS; 712 Will Funk/Alpine Aperture; 714 Kayte M. Deioma/PhotoEdit; 716 (*b*) Richard Cummins/CORBIS; 717 (*tr*) Tony Freeman/Photo Edit; (*bcl*) David Young-Wolff/Photo Edit; (*br*) Lori Adamski Peek/Getty Images; 719 tr) Image Farm/PictureQuest; (*cl*) Tom Schierlitz/Getty Images; 720 (*bl*) Marshall Gordon/Cole Group/Getty Images; 722 (*bg*) AFP/Getty Images; 723 (*bg*) Siede Preis/Getty Images.

All other photos © Harcourt School Publishers. Harcourt Photos provided by the Harcourt Index, Harcourt IPR, and Harcourt photographers: Weronica Ankarorn, Victoria Bowen, Eric Camden, Doug Dukane, Ken Kinzie, April Riehm, and Steve Williams.

KENTUCKY SCIENCE STANDARDS CURRICULUM MAP

Program of Studies: Understandings	Program of Studies: Skills and Concepts	Related Core Content for Assessment	*Kentucky HSP Science*, Grade 4, Locations and Page Numbers
	Enduring Knowledge-Understandings: (Inquiry and Research-Intermediate) Students will understand that • collaboration involves sharing new ideas with others. Shared knowledge is a community-building process, and the meaning of research/investigation takes on greater relevance in the context of the learner's society. Comparing notes, discussing conclusions, and sharing experiences are all examples of this process in action		**Getting Ready for Science** Lesson 1 What Are Tools for Inquiry?, pp. 2–13
SC-4-EU-U-5 Students will understand that a model of something can never be exactly like the real thing, but can be used to learn something about the real thing.	**Enduring Knowledge-Understandings: (Inquiry and Research-Intermediate)** Students will understand that • many methods of and sources for investigation exist, including interview, observation, survey, viewing, experimenting, and critical reading. The ability to synthesize meaning is the creative spark that forms new knowledge • inquiry integrates elements and processes of reading, writing, research, creative and critical thinking, and logic, and involves communicating findings through a product • collaboration involves sharing new ideas with others. Shared knowledge is a community-building process, and the meaning of research/investigation takes on greater relevance in the context of the learner's society. Comparing notes, discussing conclusions, and sharing experiences are all examples of this process in action		Lesson 2 What Are Inquiry Skills?, pp. 14–25

Program of Studies: Understandings	Program of Studies: Skills and Concepts	Related Core Content for Assessment	*Kentucky HSP Science*, Grade 4, Locations and Page Numbers
SC-4-STM-U-5 Students will understand that scientists pay more attention to claims about how something works when the claims are backed up with evidence that can be confirmed. **SC-4-ET-U-6** Students will understand that seeing how a model works after changes are made to it may suggest how the real thing would work if the same thing were done to it.	**Enduring Knowledge-Understandings: (Inquiry and Research-Intermediate)** Students will understand that • the inquiry process is used to investigate topics or questions important to the researcher. Questions are redefined throughout the learning process. The researcher may revise the question, refine a line of query, or go in a direction that the original question did not anticipate • reflection is ongoing and integral to the inquiry and research processes and involves taking the time to look back at the question, the research strategy, and the conclusions made. The learner evaluates, makes observations, and possibly makes new decisions • collaboration involves sharing new ideas with others. Shared knowledge is a community-building process, and the meaning of research/investigation takes on greater relevance in the context of the learner's society. Comparing notes, discussing conclusions, and sharing experiences are all examples of this process in action **SC-4-STM-S-8** Students will write clear descriptions of their designs and experiments, present their findings (when appropriate) in tables and graphs (designed by the students) **SC-4-STM-S-9** Students will analyze the designs and investigations of themselves and others to see if following the same procedures would produce similar results and conclusions (scientific validity)		Lesson 3 What Is the Scientific Method?, pp. 26–35

	SC-4-I-S-1, SC-4-I-S-2, SC-4-I-S-3	SC-04-3.4.1, SC-04-3.4.2, SC-04-4.7.2	**Life Science** Kentucky Excursions and Projects, pp. 40–46
SC-4-UD-U-1 Students will understand that things in the environment are classified as living, nonliving and once living. **SC-4-UD-U-2** Students will understand that characteristics of living things can be used to sort them into various groups: the characteristics chosen to establish the grouping depend on the reason for the grouping. **SC-4-UD-U-3** Students will understand that organisms have different structures that are used for different functions. Observations of the structures of a certain organism can be used to predict how that organism functions or where it might live.	**SC-4-UD-S-1** Students will compare the concepts of living, once living and nonliving **SC-4-UD-S-2** Students will analyze the structures and related functions of a variety of plants and animals in order to establish classification schemes **SC-4-UD-S-5** Students will answer student-generated questions about the diversity of living things using information from a variety of print and non-print sources	SC-04-3.4.1 Students will: • **compare the different structures and functions of plants and animals that contribute to the growth, survival and reproduction of the organisms;** • **make inferences about the relationship between structure and function in organisms.** **Each plant or animal has structures that serve different functions in growth, survival and reproduction. For example, humans have distinct body structures for walking, holding, seeing and talking. Evidence about the relationship between structure and function should be used to make inferences and draw conclusions.** **DOK 3** *SC-04-3.4.2* *Students will understand that things in the environment are classified as living, nonliving and once living. Living things differ from nonliving things. Organisms are classified into groups by using various characteristics (e.g., body coverings, body structures).*	**Chapter 1 Classifying Living Things** Lesson 1 How Are Living Things Classified?, pp. 50–61
SC-4-UD-U-2 Students will understand that characteristics of living things can be used to sort them into various groups: the characteristics chosen to establish the grouping depend on the reason for the grouping. **SC-4-UD-U-3** Students will understand that organisms have different structures that are used for different functions. Observations of the structures of a certain organism can be used to predict how that organism functions or where it might live.	**SC-4-UD-S-2** Students will analyze the structures and related functions of a variety of plants and animals in order to establish classification schemes **SC-4-UD-S-5** Students will answer student-generated questions about the diversity of living things using information from a variety of print and non-print sources	*SC-04-3.4.2* *Students will understand that things in the environment are classified as living, nonliving and once living. Living things differ from nonliving things. Organisms are classified into groups by using various characteristics (e.g., body coverings, body structures).*	Lesson 2 How Are Plants and Fungi Classified?, pp. 62–71 Lesson 3 How Are Animals Classified?, pp. 72–81
SC-4-UD-U-4 Students will understand that offspring resemble their parents because the parents have a reliable way to transfer information to the next generation. **SC-4-UD-U-5** Students will understand that some likenesses between parents and offspring are inherited (e.g. eye color) and some likenesses are learned (e.g. speech patterns in people).	**SC-4-UD-S-4** Students will identify, observe and compare some characteristics of organisms that are passed from the parents (e.g., color of flower petals) and others that are learned from interactions with the environment (e.g., learning to ride a bike) **SC-4-UD-S-5** Students will answer student-generated questions about the diversity of living things using information from a variety of print and non-print sources	SC-04-3.4.4 **Students will identify some characteristics of organisms that are inherited from the parents and others that are learned from interactions with the environment.** **Observations of plants and animals yield the conclusion that organisms closely resemble their parents at some time in their life cycle. Some characteristics (e.g., the color of flowers, the number of appendages) are passed to offspring. Other characteristics are learned from interactions with the environment, such as the ability to ride a bicycle, and these cannot be passed on to the next generation. Explorations related to inherited versus learned characteristics should offer opportunities to collect data and draw conclusions about various groups of organisms.** **DOK 2**	**Chapter 2 Life Cycles** Lesson 1 What Is Heredity?, pp. 88–97

Program of Studies: Understandings	Program of Studies: Skills and Concepts	Related Core Content for Assessment	*Kentucky HSP Science,* Grade 4, Locations and Page Numbers
SC-4-UD-U-6 Students will understand that all living things are produced from other living things. They grow and then eventually die. Before they die most living things create offspring, allowing their kind to continue.	**SC-4-UD-S-3** Students will investigate and compare life cycles, especially reproductive characteristics (e.g., gestational periods, germination rates, number of offspring) and life expectancies of plants and animals to make inferences and/or draw conclusions about their populations **SC-4-UD-S-5** Students will answer student-generated questions about the diversity of living things using information from a variety of print and non-print sources	SC-04-3.4.3 **Students will compare a variety of life cycles of plants and animals in order to classify and make inferences about an organism.** **Plants and animals have life cycles that include the beginning of life, growth and development, reproduction and death. The details of a life cycle are different for different organisms. Models of organisms' life cycles should be used to classify and make inferences about an organism.** **DOK 3**	Lesson 2 What Are Some Plant Life Cycles?, pp. 98–109 Lesson 3 What Are Some Animal Life Cycles?, pp. 110–119
SC-4-UD-U-3 Students will understand that organisms have different structures that are used for different functions. Observations of the structures of a certain organism can be used to predict how that organism functions or where it might live. **SC-4-I-U-1** Students will understand that all living things depend on their environment and other organisms within it for their survival. Certain patterns of behavior or physical features may help an organism survive in some environments yet perish in others.	**SC-4-UD-S-5** Students will answer student-generated questions about the diversity of living things using information from a variety of print and non-print sources **SC-4-I-S-1** Students will observe, document and explain the cause and effect relationships existing between organisms and their environments	SC-04-3.4.1 **Students will:** **• compare the different structures and functions of plants and animals that contribute to the growth, survival and reproduction of the organisms;** **• make inferences about the relationship between structure and function in organisms.** **Each plant or animal has structures that serve different functions in growth, survival and reproduction. For example, humans have distinct body structures for walking, holding, seeing and talking. Evidence about the relationship between structure and function should be used to make inferences and draw conclusions.** **DOK 3**	**Chapter 3 Adaptations** Lesson 1 How Do the Bodies of Animals Help Them Meet Their Needs?, pp. 126–137
SC-4-UD-U-5 Students will understand that some likenesses between parents and offspring are inherited (e.g. eye color) and some likenesses are learned (e.g. speech patterns in people). **SC-4-I-U-1** Students will understand that all living things depend on their environment and other organisms within it for their survival. Certain patterns of behavior or physical features may help an organism survive in some environments yet perish in others.	**SC-4-UD-S-4** Students will identify, observe and compare some characteristics of organisms that are passed from the parents (e.g., color of flower petals) and others that are learned from interactions with the environment (e.g., learning to ride a bike) **SC-4-UD-S-5** Students will answer student-generated questions about the diversity of living things using information from a variety of print and non-print sources **SC-4-I-S-1** Students will observe, document and explain the cause and effect relationships existing between organisms and their environments **SC-4-3.4.4** Students will identify some characteristics of organisms that are inherited from the parents and others that are learned from interactions with the environment.	SC-04-3.4.4 **Students will identify some characteristics of organisms that are inherited from the parents and others that are learned from interactions with the environment.** **Observations of plants and animals yield the conclusion that organisms closely resemble their parents at some time in their life cycle. Some characteristics (e.g., the color of flowers, the number of appendages) are passed to offspring. Other characteristics are learned from interactions with the environment, such as the ability to ride a bicycle, and these cannot be passed on to the next generation. Explorations related to inherited versus learned characteristics should offer opportunities to collect data and draw conclusions about various groups of organisms.** **DOK 2**	Lesson 2 How Do the Behaviors of Animals Help Them Meet Their Needs?, pp. 138–147

SC-4-BC-U-1 Students will understand that the structures and characteristics of fossils provide information about the nature of an organism, the environmental conditions where/when it lived and how it is related to organisms still alive today. **SC-4-BC-U-2** Students will understand that scientists ask many questions about the world around them, but not all of their questions can be investigated in a scientific way. Part of the job of a scientist is to focus only on questions that can be scientifically tested. **SC-4-BC-U-3** Students will understand that scientists pay more attention to claims when they are supported with evidence that can be confirmed through scientific investigation.	**SC-4-BC-S-1** Students will examine fossils and representations of fossils to make comparisons among organisms that lived long ago and organisms of today and draw conclusions about the nature of the organisms and basic environments represented by fossils **SC-4-BC-S-2** Students will describe reasons why some differences in organisms give individuals an advantage in surviving and reproducing **SC-4-BC-S-3** Students will answer student-generated questions about how/why organisms and the environment have changed over time using information from a variety of print and non-print sources to support claims/provide evidence for conclusions **SC-4-BC-S-4** Students will analyze claims and information based on the credibility of the source and ability to confirm with multiple sources	SC-04-3.5.1 **Students will use representations of fossils to:** **• draw conclusions about the nature of the organisms and the basic environments that existed at the time;** **• make inferences about the relationships to organisms that are alive today.** **Fossils found in Earth materials provide evidence about organisms that lived long ago and the nature of the environment at that time. Representations of fossils provide the basis for describing and drawing conclusions about the organisms and basic environments represented by them.** **DOK 3**	Lesson 3 How Do Living Things of the Past Compare with Those of Today?, pp. 148–157
		SC-04-3.4.1 **Students will:** **• compare the different structures and functions of plants and animals that contribute to the growth, survival and reproduction of the organisms;** **• make inferences about the relationship between structure and function in organisms.** **Each plant or animal has structures that serve different functions in growth, survival and reproduction. For example, humans have distinct body structures for walking, holding, seeing and talking. Evidence about the relationship between structure and function should be used to make inferences and draw conclusions.** **DOK 3**	**Chapter 4 The Human Body** Lesson 1 How Does Your Body Get Oxygen and Nutrients?, pp. 164–177 Lesson 2 How Does Your Body Think and Move?, pp. 178–189

Program of Studies: Understandings	Program of Studies: Skills and Concepts	Related Core Content for Assessment	*Kentucky HSP Science*, Grade 4, Locations and Page Numbers
SC-4-ET-U-1 Students will understand that ecosystems are defined by the relationships that occur within them. These relationships can be determined through observation of the organisms and their environment. **SC-4-ET-U-2** Students will understand that light and heat from the sun are essential to sustaining most life on earth. Plants change energy from the sun's light into energy that is used as food by the plant.	**SC-4-ET-S-1** Students will observe/construct, analyze patterns and explain basic relationships of plants and animals in an ecosystem (e.g., food webs) **SC-4-ET-S-2** Students will analyze food webs in order to draw conclusions about the relationship between the sun's heat and light and sustaining most life on Earth	**SC-04-4.6.2** **Students will:** **• analyze data/evidence of the Sun providing light and heat to earth;** **• use data/evidence to substantiate the conclusion that the Sun's light and heat are necessary to sustaining life on Earth.** **Simple observations, experiments and data collection begin to reveal that the Sun provides the light and heat necessary to maintain the temperature of Earth. Evidence collected and analyzed should be used to substantiate the conclusion that the sun's light and heat are necessary to sustain life on Earth.** **DOK 3** *SC-04-3.4.2* *Students will understand that things in the environment are classified as living, nonliving and once living. Living things differ from nonliving things. Organisms are classified into groups by using various characteristics (e.g., body coverings, body structures).*	**Chapter 5 Understanding Ecosystems** Lesson 1 What Are the Parts of an Ecosystem?, pp. 198–207
SC-4-I-U-2 Students will understand that environmental relationships extend beyond food (e.g. shelter, seed transport). **SC-4-I-U-4** Students will understand that *beneficial* and *harmful* are relative terms: any single action can be both beneficial and harmful to different organisms in an ecosystem.	**SC-4-I-S-1** Students will observe, document and explain the cause and effect relationships existing between organisms and their environments **SC-4-I-S-2** Students will use evidence and observations to make predictions/draw conclusions about how changes in the environment affect the plants' and animals' ability to survive **SC-4-I-S-4** Students will describe and provide examples of how *beneficial* and *harmful* are relative terms	**SC-04-4.7.1** **Students will make predictions and/or inferences based on patterns of evidence related to the survival and reproductive success of organisms in particular environments.** **The world has many different environments. Distinct environments support the lives of different types of organisms. When the environment changes, some plants and animals survive and reproduce and others die or move to new locations. Examples of environmental changes resulting in either increase or decrease in numbers of a particular organism should be explored in order to discover patterns and resulting cause and effect relationships between organisms and their environments (e.g., structures and behaviors that make an organism suited to a particular environment). Connections and conclusions should be made based on the data.** **DOK 3**	Lesson 2 What Factors Influence Ecosystems?, pp. 208–219
SC-4-I-U-3 Students will understand that people impact their environment in both beneficial and harmful ways. Some of these impacts can be predicted, while others cannot. **SC-4-I-U-4** Students will understand that *beneficial* and *harmful* are relative terms: any single action can be both beneficial and harmful to different organisms in an ecosystem.	**SC-4-I-S-3** Students will observe, document and describe human interactions that impact the local environment **SC-4-I-S-4** Students will describe and provide examples of how *beneficial* and *harmful* are relative terms **SC-4-I-S-5** Students will evaluate the consequences of changes caused by humans or other organisms, and propose solutions to real life situations/dilemmas **SC-4-I-S-6** Students will use evidence (obtained through investigative and/or non investigative research) to support or defend positions on real world environmental problems	**SC-04-4.7.2** **Students will:** **• describe human interactions in the environment where they live;** **• classify the interactions as beneficial or harmful to the environment using data/evidence to support conclusions.** **All organisms, including humans, cause changes in the environment where they live. Some of these changes are detrimental to the organism or to other organisms; other changes are beneficial (e.g., dams benefit some aquatic organisms but are detrimental to others). By evaluating the consequences of change using cause and effect relationships, solutions to real life situations/dilemmas can be proposed.** **DOK 3**	Lesson 3 How Do Humans Affect Ecosystems?, pp. 220–231

SC-4-ET-U-1 Students will understand that ecosystems are defined by the relationships that occur within them. These relationships can be determined through observation of the organisms and their environment. **SC-4-ET-U-2** Students will understand that light and heat from the sun are essential to sustaining most life on earth. Plants change energy from the sun's light into energy that is used as food by the plant.	**SC-4-ET-S-1** Students will observe/construct, analyze patterns and explain basic relationships of plants and animals in an ecosystem (e.g., food webs) **SC-4-ET-S-2** Students will analyze food webs in order to draw conclusions about the relationship between the sun's heat and light and sustaining most life on Earth	SC-04-4.6.1 **Students will analyze patterns and make generalizations about the basic relationships of plants and animals in an ecosystem (food chain).** **Plants make their own food. All animals depend on plants. Some animals eat plants for food. Other animals eat animals that eat the plants. Basic relationships and connections between organisms in food chains, including the flow of energy, can be used to discover patterns within ecosystems.** **DOK 2**	**Chapter 6 Energy Transfer in Ecosystems** Lesson 1 What Are the Roles of Living Things?, pp. 238–247 Lesson 2 How Do Living Things Get Energy?, pp. 248–259
		SC-04-2.3.2, SC-04-2.3.4, SC-04-2.3.5, SC-04-2.3.1	**Earth Science** Kentucky Excursions and Projects, pp. 266–272
SC-4-EU-U-1 Students will understand that classifying Earth materials according to their properties allows decisions to be made about their usefulness for various purposes. **SC-4-EU-U-3** Students will understand that the surface of the Earth is always changing through both fast and slow processes. These changes may be steady, repetitive or irregular. Careful analysis of data from past events allows the prediction of expected consequences when similar events happen again. **SC-4-EU-U-5** Students will understand that a model of something can never be exactly like the real thing, but can be used to learn something about the real thing.	**SC-4-EU-S-1** Students will use the properties of earth materials to make and support decisions about using them for different purposes (e.g., growing plants, building materials, fuel) **SC-4-EU-S-4** Students will describe and compare the processes, factors involved and consequences of slow changes to earth's surface (e.g., erosion and weathering) **SC-4-EU-S-7** Students will analyze and interpret information from a variety of sources (e.g., print based, models, video) to construct reasonable explanations from direct and indirect evidence	SC-04-2.3.1 **Students will:** • **classify earth materials by the ways that they are used;** • **explain how their properties make them useful for different purposes.** **Earth materials provide many of the resources humans use. The varied materials have different physical properties that can be used to describe, separate, sort and classify them. Inferences about the unique properties of the earth materials yield ideas about their usefulness. For example, some are useful as building materials (e.g., stone, clay, marble), some as sources of fuel (e.g., petroleum, natural gas), or some for growing the plants we use as food.** **DOK 2**	**Chapter 7 The Rock Cycle** Lesson 1 What Are the Types of Rocks?, pp. 276–285
SC-4-EU-U-3 Students will understand that the surface of the Earth is always changing through both fast and slow processes. These changes may be steady, repetitive or irregular. Careful analysis of data from past events allows the prediction of expected consequences when similar events happen again. **SC-4-EU-U-5** Students will understand that a model of something can never be exactly like the real thing, but can be used to learn something about the real thing.	**SC-4-EU-S-4** Students will describe and compare the processes, factors involved and consequences of slow changes to earth's surface (e.g., erosion and weathering) **SC-4-EU-S-7** Students will analyze and interpret information from a variety of sources (e.g., print based, models, video) to construct reasonable explanations from direct and indirect evidence	SC-04-2.3.2 **Students will describe and explain consequences of changes to the surface of the Earth, including some common fast changes (e.g., landslides, volcanic eruptions, earthquakes), and some common slow changes (e.g., erosion, weathering).** **The surface of the Earth changes. Some changes are due to slow processes such as erosion or weathering. Some changes are due to rapid processes such as landslides, volcanic eruptions and earthquakes. Analyzing the changes to identify cause and effect relationships helps to define and understand the consequences.** **DOK 3**	Lesson 2 What Is the Rock Cycle?, pp. 286–293

Program of Studies: Understandings	Program of Studies: Skills and Concepts	Related Core Content for Assessment	*Kentucky HSP Science,* Grade 4, Locations and Page Numbers
SC-4-EU-U-3 Students will understand that the surface of the Earth is always changing through both fast and slow processes. These changes may be steady, repetitive or irregular. Careful analysis of data from past events allows the prediction of expected consequences when similar events happen again.	**SC-4-EU-S-4** Students will describe and compare the processes, factors involved and consequences of slow changes to earth's surface (e.g., erosion and weathering) **SC-4-EU-S-5** Students will describe and compare contributing factors and consequences of fast changes to earth's surface (e.g., landslides, earthquakes, floods)	SC-04-2.3.2 **Students will describe and explain consequences of changes to the surface of the Earth, including some common fast changes (e.g., landslides, volcanic eruptions, earthquakes), and some common slow changes (e.g., erosion, weathering).** **The surface of the Earth changes. Some changes are due to slow processes such as erosion or weathering. Some changes are due to rapid processes such as landslides, volcanic eruptions and earthquakes. Analyzing the changes to identify cause and effect relationships helps to define and understand the consequences.** DOK 3	Lesson 3 How Do Weathering and Erosion Affect Rocks?, pp. 294–303
SC-4-EU-U-1 Students will understand that classifying Earth materials according to their properties allows decisions to be made about their usefulness for various purposes.	**SC-4-EU-S-1** Students will use the properties of earth materials to make and support decisions about using them for different purposes (e.g., growing plants, building materials, fuel)	SC-04-2.3.1 **Students will:** **• classify earth materials by the ways that they are used;** **• explain how their properties make them useful for different purposes.** **Earth materials provide many of the resources humans use. The varied materials have different physical properties that can be used to describe, separate, sort and classify them. Inferences about the unique properties of the earth materials yield ideas about their usefulness. For example, some are useful as building materials (e.g., stone, clay, marble), some as sources of fuel (e.g., petroleum, natural gas), or some for growing the plants we use as food.** DOK 2	Lesson 4 What Is Soil?, pp. 304–313
SC-4-EU-U-1 Students will understand that classifying Earth materials according to their properties allows decisions to be made about their usefulness for various purposes. **SC-4-EU-U-5** Students will understand that a model of something can never be exactly like the real thing, but can be used to learn something about the real thing.	**SC-4-EU-S-1** Students will use the properties of earth materials to make and support decisions about using them for different purposes (e.g., growing plants, building materials, fuel) **SC-4-EU-S-7** Students will analyze and interpret information from a variety of sources (e.g., print based, models, video) to construct reasonable explanations from direct and indirect evidence	SC-04-2.3.1 **Students will:** **• classify earth materials by the ways that they are used;** **• explain how their properties make them useful for different purposes.** **Earth materials provide many of the resources humans use. The varied materials have different physical properties that can be used to describe, separate, sort and classify them. Inferences about the unique properties of the earth materials yield ideas about their usefulness. For example, some are useful as building materials (e.g., stone, clay, marble), some as sources of fuel (e.g., petroleum, natural gas), or some for growing the plants we use as food.** DOK 2	**Chapter 8 Changes to Earth's Surface** Lesson 1 What Are Some of Earth's Landforms?, pp. 320–329

SC-4-EU-U-3 Students will understand that the surface of the Earth is always changing through both fast and slow processes. These changes may be steady, repetitive or irregular. Careful analysis of data from past events allows the prediction of expected consequences when similar events happen again. **SC-4-EU-U-5** Students will understand that a model of something can never be exactly like the real thing, but can be used to learn something about the real thing.	**SC-4-EU-S-4** Students will describe and compare the processes, factors involved and consequences of slow changes to earth's surface (e.g., erosion and weathering) **SC-4-EU-S-5** Students will describe and compare contributing factors and consequences of fast changes to earth's surface (e.g., landslides, earthquakes, floods) **SC-4-EU-S-7** Students will analyze and interpret information from a variety of sources (e.g., print based, models, video) to construct reasonable explanations from direct and indirect evidence	**SC-04-2.3.2** **Students will describe and explain consequences of changes to the surface of the Earth, including some common fast changes (e.g., landslides, volcanic eruptions, earthquakes), and some common slow changes (e.g., erosion, weathering).** **The surface of the Earth changes. Some changes are due to slow processes such as erosion or weathering. Some changes are due to rapid processes such as landslides, volcanic eruptions and earthquakes. Analyzing the changes to identify cause and effect relationships helps to define and understand the consequences. DOK 3**	Lesson 2 What Causes Changes to Earth's Landforms?, pp. 330–341
SC-4-BC-U-1 Students will understand that the structures and characteristics of fossils provide information about the nature of an organism, the environmental conditions where/when it lived and how it is related to organisms still alive today.	**SC-4-BC-S-1** Students will examine fossils and representations of fossils to make comparisons among organisms that lived long ago and organisms of today and draw conclusions about the nature of the organisms and basic environments represented by fossils **SC-4-BC-S-2** Students will describe reasons why some differences in organisms give individuals an advantage in surviving and reproducing **SC-4-BC-S-3** Students will answer student-generated questions about how/why organisms and the environment have changed over time using information from a variety of print and non-print sources to support claims/provide evidence for conclusions	**SC-04-3.5.1** **Students will use representations of fossils to:** **• draw conclusions about the nature of the organisms and the basic environments that existed at the time;** **• make inferences about the relationships to organisms that are alive today.** **Fossils found in Earth materials provide evidence about organisms that lived long ago and the nature of the environment at that time. Representations of fossils provide the basis for describing and drawing conclusions about the organisms and basic environments represented by them. DOK 3**	Lesson 3 What Are Fossils?, pp. 342–351
SC-4-EU-U-3 Students will understand that the surface of the Earth is always changing through both fast and slow processes. These changes may be steady, repetitive or irregular. Careful analysis of data from past events allows the prediction of expected consequences when similar events happen again.	**SC-4-EU-S-7** Students will analyze and interpret information from a variety of sources (e.g., print based, models, video) to construct reasonable explanations from direct and indirect evidence	**SC-04-2.3.3** **Students will make generalizations and/or predictions about weather changes from day to day and over seasons based on weather data.** **Weather changes from day to day and over seasons. Weather can be described by observations and measurable quantities such as temperature, wind direction, wind speed and precipitation. Data can be displayed and used to make predictions. DOK 3**	**Chapter 9 The Water Cycle** Lesson 1 What Is the Water Cycle?, pp. 360–369

Program of Studies: Understandings	Program of Studies: Skills and Concepts	Related Core Content for Assessment	*Kentucky HSP Science,* Grade 4, Locations and Page Numbers
SC-4-EU-U-2 Students will understand that weather data can be organized and represented in ways that reveal patterns needed for making predictions about the future, but the weather is so complex that it cannot always be predicted beyond being more or less likely to occur. **SC-4-EU-U-3** Students will understand that the surface of the Earth is always changing through both fast and slow processes. These changes may be steady, repetitive or irregular. Careful analysis of data from past events allows the prediction of expected consequences when similar events happen again.		**SC-4-EU-U-5** **Students will understand that a model of something can never be exactly like the real thing, but can be used to learn something about the real thing.** **SC-04-2.3.3** **Students will make generalizations and/or predictions about weather changes from day to day and over seasons based on weather data.** **Weather changes from day to day and over seasons. Weather can be described by observations and measurable quantities such as temperature, wind direction, wind speed and precipitation. Data can be displayed and used to make predictions.** **DOK 3**	Lesson 2 How Is the Water Cycle Related to Weather?, pp. 370–379
SC-4-EU-U-3 Students will understand that the surface of the Earth is always changing through both fast and slow processes. These changes may be steady, repetitive or irregular. Careful analysis of data from past events allows the prediction of expected consequences when similar events happen again.	**SC-4-EU-S-7** Students will analyze and interpret information from a variety of sources (e.g., print based, models, video) to construct reasonable explanations from direct and indirect evidence	**SC-04-2.3.3** **Students will make generalizations and/or predictions about weather changes from day to day and over seasons based on weather data.** **Weather changes from day to day and over seasons. Weather can be described by observations and measurable quantities such as temperature, wind direction, wind speed and precipitation. Data can be displayed and used to make predictions.** **DOK 3**	Lesson 3 How Do Land Features Influence the Water Cycle?, pp. 380–387
SC-4-EU-U-2 Students will understand that weather data can be organized and represented in ways that reveal patterns needed for making predictions about the future, but the weather is so complex that it cannot always be predicted beyond being more or less likely to occur.	**SC-4-EU-S-2** Students will analyze weather data to make predictions about future weather **SC-4-EU-S-3** Students will assess the accuracy of weather predictions and the evidence used to support the predictions made by each other and meteorologists	**SC-04-2.3.3** **Students will make generalizations and/or predictions about weather changes from day to day and over seasons based on weather data.** **Weather changes from day to day and over seasons. Weather can be described by observations and measurable quantities such as temperature, wind direction, wind speed and precipitation. Data can be displayed and used to make predictions.** **DOK 3**	Lesson 4 How Can Weather Be Predicted?, pp. 388–399

SC-4-EU-U-4 Students will understand that a variety of models of the sun, earth, moon system are needed to explain the observed patterns of their relative motions, since people are not able to see from the outside how this system is constructed. **SC-4-EU-U-5** Students will understand that a model of something can never be exactly like the real thing, but can be used to learn something about the real thing.	**SC-4-EU-S-6** Students will explore, design and evaluate a number of models (e.g., physical, analogous, conceptual) of Earth-Sun and Earth-Sun-Moon systems for benefits, limitations and accuracy (e.g., scale, proportional relationships) **SC-4-EU-S-7** Students will analyze and interpret information from a variety of sources (e.g., print based, models, video) to construct reasonable explanations from direct and indirect evidence	SC-04-2.3.4 **Students will identify patterns, recognize relationships and draw conclusions about the Earth-Sun system by interpreting a variety of representations/models (e.g., diagrams, sundials, distance of sun above horizon) of the sun's apparent movement in the sky.** **Changes in movement of objects in the sky have patterns that can be observed, described and modeled. The Sun appears to move across the sky in the same way every day, but the Sun's apparent path changes slowly over seasons. Data collected can be used to identify patterns, recognize relationships and draw conclusions about the Earth and Sun system.** **DOK 3** *SC-04-2.3.5* *Students will understand that the moon moves across the sky on a daily basis much like the Sun. The observable shape of the moon can be described as it changes from day to day in a cycle that lasts about a month.*	**Chapter 10 Planets and Other Objects in Space** Lesson 1 How Do Earth and Its Moon Move?, pp. 406–417
SC-4-EU-U-4 Students will understand that a variety of models of the sun, earth, moon system are needed to explain the observed patterns of their relative motions, since people are not able to see from the outside how this system is constructed. **SC-4-EU-U-5** Students will understand that a model of something can never be exactly like the real thing, but can be used to learn something about the real thing.	**SC-4-EU-S-6** Students will explore, design and evaluate a number of models (e.g., physical, analogous, conceptual) of Earth-Sun and Earth-Sun-Moon systems for benefits, limitations and accuracy (e.g., scale, proportional relationships) **SC-4-EU-S-7** Students will analyze and interpret information from a variety of sources (e.g., print based, models, video) to construct reasonable explanations from direct and indirect evidence	**SC-04-2.3.4** **Students will identify patterns, recognize relationships and draw conclusions about the Earth-Sun system by interpreting a variety of representations/models (e.g., diagrams, sundials, distance of sun above horizon) of the sun's apparent movement in the sky.** **Changes in movement of objects in the sky have patterns that can be observed, described and modeled. The Sun appears to move across the sky in the same way every day, but the Sun's apparent path changes slowly over seasons. Data collected can be used to identify patterns, recognize relationships and draw conclusions about the Earth and Sun system.** **DOK 3**	Lesson 2 How Do Objects Move in the Solar System?, pp. 418–427 Lesson 3 What Other Objects Can Be Seen in the Sky?, pp. 428–437
SC-4-MF-U-4, SC-4-STM-U-4	**SC-4-MF-S-4, SC-4-STM-S-4**	**SC-04-1.2.3**	**Physical Science** Kentucky Excursions and Projects, pp. 444–450
SC-4-STM-U-5 Students will understand that scientists pay more attention to claims about how something works when the claims are backed up with evidence that can be confirmed.	**SC-4-STM-S-1** Students will identify matter as solids, liquids and gases **SC-4-STM-S-2** Students will gather information including temperature, magnetism, hardness and mass using appropriate tools to identify physical properties of matter **SC-4-STM-S-6** Students will investigate student-generated questions about the properties of matter and uses of matter with particular properties. Students will design and build objects that require different properties of materials **SC-4-STM-S-8** Students will write clear descriptions of their designs and experiments, present their findings (when appropriate) in tables and graphs (designed by the students) **SC-4-STM-S-9** Students will analyze the designs and investigations of themselves and others to see if following the same procedures would produce similar results and conclusions (scientific validity)		**Chapter 11 Matter and Its Properties** Lesson 1 How Can Physical Properties Be Used to Identify Matter?, pp. 454–463

Program of Studies: Understandings	Program of Studies: Skills and Concepts	Related Core Content for Assessment	*Kentucky HSP Science,* Grade 4, Locations and Page Numbers
SC-4-STM-U-3 Students will understand that properties of materials may change if the materials become hotter or colder. **SC-4-STM-U-4** Students will understand that if water is turned into ice and then the ice is allowed to melt, the amount of water is the same as it was before freezing. When liquid water "disappears" it is not really gone, it has turned into a gas (vapor). **SC-4-STM-U-5** Students will understand that scientists pay more attention to claims about how something works when the claims are backed up with evidence that can be confirmed.	**SC-4-STM-S-4** Students will conduct tests, compare data and draw conclusions about physical properties of matter including states of matter, conduction and buoyancy **SC-4-STM-S-3** Students will investigate and describe how the physical properties of water change as heat energy is added or removed **SC-4-STM-S-8** Students will write clear descriptions of their designs and experiments, present their findings (when appropriate) in tables and graphs (designed by the students) **SC-4-STM-S-9** Students will analyze the designs and investigations of themselves and others to see if following the same procedures would produce similar results and conclusions (scientific validity)	SC-04-1.1.1 **Students will explain how matter, including water, can be changed from one state to another.** **Materials can exist in different states—solid, liquid and gas. Some common materials, such as water, can be changed from one state to another by heating or cooling. Resulting cause and effect relationships should be explored, described and predicted.** **DOK 3**	Lesson 2 How Does Matter Change States?, pp. 464–473
SC-4-STM-U-2 Students will understand that when a new material is made by combining two or more materials the new material often has properties that are different from the original materials. **SC-4-STM-U-5** Students will understand that scientists pay more attention to claims about how something works when the claims are backed up with evidence that can be confirmed.	**SC-4-STM-S-5** Students will predict and describe patterns of properties in matter, such as how materials will interact with each other and how they can be changed **SC-4-STM-S-8** Students will write clear descriptions of their designs and experiments, present their findings (when appropriate) in tables and graphs (designed by the students) **SC-4-STM-S-9** Students will analyze the designs and investigations of themselves and others to see if following the same procedures would produce similar results and conclusions (scientific validity		Lesson 3 What Are Mixtures and Solutions?, pp. 474–483
SC-4-STM-U-5 Students will understand that scientists pay more attention to claims about how something works when the claims are backed up with evidence that can be confirmed.	**SC-4-STM-S-1** Students will identify matter as solids, liquids and gases **SC-4-STM-S-2** Students will gather information including temperature, magnetism, hardness and mass using appropriate tools to identify physical properties of matter **SC-4-STM-S-8** Students will write clear descriptions of their designs and experiments, present their findings (when appropriate) in tables and graphs (designed by the students) **SC-4-STM-S-9** Students will analyze the designs and investigations of themselves and others to see if following the same procedures would produce similar results and conclusions (scientific validity)		**Chapter 12 Changes in Matter** Lesson 1 What Is Matter Made Of?, pp. 490–501

SC-4-STM-U-1 Students will understand that things can be done to materials to change some of their properties, but not all materials respond the same way to what is done to them. **SC-4-STM-U-3** Students will understand that properties of materials may change if the materials become hotter or colder. **SC-4-STM-U-4** Students will understand that if water is turned into ice and then the ice is allowed to melt, the amount of water is the same as it was before freezing. When liquid water "disappears" it is not really gone, it has turned into a gas (vapor). **SC-4-STM-U-5** Students will understand that scientists pay more attention to claims about how something works when the claims are backed up with evidence that can be confirmed.	**SC-4-STM-S-4** Students will conduct tests, compare data and draw conclusions about physical properties of matter including states of matter, conduction and buoyancy **SC-4-STM-S-3** Students will investigate and describe how the physical properties of water change as heat energy is added or removed **SC-4-STM-S-8** Students will write clear descriptions of their designs and experiments, present their findings (when appropriate) in tables and graphs (designed by the students) **SC-4-STM-S-9** Students will analyze the designs and investigations of themselves and others to see if following the same procedures would produce similar results and conclusions (scientific validity)	SC-04-1.1.1 **Students will explain how matter, including water, can be changed from one state to another.** **Materials can exist in different states--solid, liquid and gas. Some common materials, such as water, can be changed from one state to another by heating or cooling. Resulting cause and effect relationships should be explored, described and predicted. DOK 3**	Lesson 2 What Are Physical Changes in Matter?, pp. 502–511
SC-4-STM-U-1 Students will understand that things can be done to materials to change some of their properties, but not all materials respond the same way to what is done to them. **SC-4-STM-U-2** Students will understand that when a new material is made by combining two or more materials the new material often has properties that are different from the original materials. **SC-4-STM-U-3** Students will understand that properties of materials may change if the materials become hotter or colder. **SC-4-STM-U-5** Students will understand that scientists pay more attention to claims about how something works when the claims are backed up with evidence that can be confirmed.	**SC-4-STM-S-5** Students will predict and describe patterns of properties in matter, such as how materials will interact with each other and how they can be changed **SC-4-STM-S-8** Students will write clear descriptions of their designs and experiments, present their findings (when appropriate) in tables and graphs (designed by the students) **SC-4-STM-S-9** Students will analyze the designs and investigations of themselves and others to see if following the same procedures would produce similar results and conclusions (scientific validity)	SC-04-1.1.1 **Students will explain how matter, including water, can be changed from one state to another.** **Materials can exist in different states—solid, liquid and gas. Some common materials, such as water, can be changed from one state to another by heating or cooling. Resulting cause and effect relationships should be explored, described and predicted. DOK 3**	Lesson 3 How Does Matter React Chemically?, pp. 512–521

Program of Studies: Understandings	Program of Studies: Skills and Concepts	Related Core Content for Assessment	*Kentucky HSP Science,* Grade 4, Locations and Page Numbers
SC-4-MF-U-3 Students will understand that sound is produced by the vibration of matter, and the rate of vibration affects the pitch of the sound.	SC-4-MF-S-3 Students will investigate how the rate of vibration of an object changes the pitch (high-low) of the sound it produces SC-4-MF-S-5 Students will answer student-generated questions through investigative and non-investigative processes about what affects motion and sound using information from a variety of print and non-print sources	SC-04-1.2.3 **Students will:** **• explain that sound is a result of vibrations, a type of motion;** **• describe pitch (high, low) as a difference in sounds that are produced and relate that to the rate of vibration.** **Vibration is a type of motion that can be observed, described, measured and compared. Sound is produced by vibrating objects. The pitch of the sound can be varied by changing the rate of vibration. The relationship between rates of vibration and produced sounds can be described and graphed.** DOK 3	**Chapter 13 Sound** Lesson 1 What Is Sound?, pp. 528–537 Lesson 2 What Are the Properties of Waves?, pp. 538–547 Lesson 3 How Do Sound Waves Travel?, pp. 548–557
SC-4-ET-U-4 Students will understand that light interacts with different kinds of matter in different ways and those interactions can be predicted based on the type of matter involved.	SC-4-ET-S-7 Students will represent the path of light as it interacts with a variety of surfaces (reflecting, refracting, absorbing) SC-4-ET-S-8 Students will make predictions/inferences about the behavior of light as it interacts with materials of differing properties SC-4-ET-S-9 Students will answer student-generated questions about forms of energy (e.g., heat, light, sound, magnetic effects) using information from a variety of print and non-print sources	SC-04-4.6.4 **Students will:** **• analyze models/representations of light in order to generalize about the behavior of light;** **• represent the path of light as it interacts with a variety of surfaces (reflecting, refracting, absorbing).** **Light can be observed as traveling in a straight line until it strikes an object. Light can be reflected by a shiny object (e.g., mirror, spoon), refracted by a lens (e.g., magnifying glass, eyeglasses), or absorbed by an object (e.g., dark surface).** DOK 3	**Chapter 14 Light and Heat** Lesson 1 How Does Light Behave?, pp. 564–573
SC-4-ET-U-5 Students will understand that heat is a form of energy that results when another form of energy is transformed. Heat flows through different materials at different rates, and it naturally flows from warmer areas to cooler ones.	SC-4-ET-S-4 Students will identify events/situations that result in some energy being transformed into heat (e.g., rubbing hands together, lighting a bulb, running a car engine) SC-4-ET-S-5 Students will identify and compare how heat is transferred through different materials in order to make predictions and draw conclusions about the heat conductivity of materials (e.g., compare the 'hotness' of wooden spoons, metal spoons, plastic spoons when exposed to higher temperatures) SC-4-ET-S-9 Students will answer student-generated questions about forms of energy (e.g., heat, light, sound, magnetic effects) using information from a variety of print and non-print sources	SC-04-4.6.5 **Students will:** **• identify ways that heat can be produced (e.g. burning, rubbing) and properties of materials that conduct heat better than others;** **• describe the movement of heat between objects.** **Heat can be produced in many ways such as burning or rubbing. Heat moves from a warmer object to a cooler one by contact (conduction) or at a distance. Some materials absorb and conduct heat better than others. Simple investigations can illustrate that metal objects conduct heat better than wooden objects.** DOK 2	Lesson 2 How Can Heat Be Transferred?, pp. 574–583

SC-4-ET-U-5 Students will understand that heat is a form of energy that results when another form of energy is transformed. Heat flows through different materials at different rates, and it naturally flows from warmer areas to cooler ones. **SC-4-ET-U-6** Students will understand that seeing how a model works after changes are made to it may suggest how the real thing would work if the same thing were done to it.	**SC-4-ET-S-4** Students will identify events/situations that result in some energy being transformed into heat (e.g., rubbing hands together, lighting a bulb, running a car engine) **SC-4-ET-S-6** Students will design and conduct investigations/experiments to compare properties of conducting and non-conducting materials (both heat and electrical), documenting and communicating (speak, draw, write, demonstrate) observations, designs, procedures and results of scientific investigations **SC-4-ET-S-9** Students will answer student-generated questions about forms of energy (e.g., heat, light, sound, magnetic effects) using information from a variety of print and non-print sources	SC-04-4.6.5 **Students will:** **• identify ways that heat can be produced (e.g. burning, rubbing) and properties of materials that conduct heat better than others;** **• describe the movement of heat between objects.** **Heat can be produced in many ways such as burning or rubbing. Heat moves from a warmer object to a cooler one by contact (conduction) or at a distance. Some materials absorb and conduct heat better than others. Simple investigations can illustrate that metal objects conduct heat better than wooden objects. DOK 2**	Lesson 3 How Is Heat Produced and Used?, pp. 584–593
SC-4-ET-U-3 Students will understand that electrical energy can be used for a variety of purposes. Many electrical systems share some common features, including a source of energy, a closed conducting path and a device that performs a function by utilizing that energy.	**SC-4-ET-S-3** Students will demonstrate open and closed circuits, and series and parallel circuits using batteries, bulbs and wires; analyze models of a variety of electrical circuits in order to predict changes to the systems **SC-4-ET-S-9** Students will answer student-generated questions about forms of energy (e.g., heat, light, sound, magnetic effects) using information from a variety of print and non-print sources	SC-04-4.6.3 **Students will evaluate a variety of models/representations of electrical circuits (open, closed, series, and/or parallel) to:** **• make predictions related to changes in the system;** **• compare the properties of conducting and non-conducting materials.** **Electricity in circuits can produce light, heat and sound. Electrical circuits require a complete conducting path through which an electrical current can pass. Analysis of a variety of circuit models creates an opportunity to make predictions about circuits, as well as to demonstrate an understanding of the concepts of open and closed circuits and basic conducting and non-conducting materials. DOK 3**	**Chapter 15 Making and Using Electricity** Lesson 1 What Is Electricity?, pp. 602–615
SC-4-ET-U-3 Students will understand that electrical energy can be used for a variety of purposes. Many electrical systems share some common features, including a source of energy, a closed conducting path and a device that performs a function by utilizing that energy.	**SC-4-ET-S-6** Students will design and conduct investigations/experiments to compare properties of conducting and non-conducting materials (both heat and electrical), documenting and communicating (speak, draw, write, demonstrate) observations, designs, procedures and results of scientific investigations **SC-4-ET-S-9** Students will answer student-generated questions about forms of energy (e.g., heat, light, sound, magnetic effects) using information from a variety of print and non-print sources	SC-04-4.6.3 **Students will evaluate a variety of models/representations of electrical circuits (open, closed, series, and/or parallel) to:** **• make predictions related to changes in the system;** **• compare the properties of conducting and non-conducting materials.** **Electricity in circuits can produce light, heat and sound. Electrical circuits require a complete conducting path through which an electrical current can pass. Analysis of a variety of circuit models creates an opportunity to make predictions about circuits, as well as to demonstrate an understanding of the concepts of open and closed circuits and basic conducting and non-conducting materials. DOK 3**	Lesson 2 How Are Electricity and Magnetism Related?, pp. 616–629 Lesson 3 What Are Some Sources of Electricity?, pp. 630–639
SC-4-ET-U-3 Students will understand that electrical energy can be used for a variety of purposes. Many electrical systems share some common features, including a source of energy, a closed conducting path and a device that performs a function by utilizing that energy.	**SC-4-ET-S-9** Students will answer student-generated questions about forms of energy (e.g., heat, light, sound, magnetic effects) using information from a variety of print and non-print sources		Lesson 4 How Do People Use Energy Resources?, pp. 640–649

Program of Studies: Understandings	Program of Studies: Skills and Concepts	Related Core Content for Assessment	*Kentucky HSP Science,* Grade 4, Locations and Page Numbers
-4-MF-U-1 tudents will understand that an object's motion can be described as its change in position over time and can be represented in a variety of ways. **SC-4-MF-U-4** Students will understand that things vary greatly in their motion. Some things move so fast they cannot be seen, while others are so slow that we cannot see that they are moving at all. Technology enables people to observe these fast or slow movements. **SC-4-MF-U-5** Students will understand that recording and representing information about the motion of objects in a variety of ways makes that data useful in supporting explanations, even long after it was originally collected.	**SC-4-MF-S-4** Students will use tools and resources, such as stopwatches, sonic rangers, microscopes, computer simulations/animations and video clips, to observe motions that are hard to see or quantify and compare the usefulness/limitations of such tools **SC-4-MF-S-5** Students will answer student-generated questions through investigative and non-investigative processes about what affects motion and sound using information from a variety of print and non-print sources	SC-04-1.2.1 **Students will interpret or represent data related to an object's straight-line motion in order to make inferences and predictions of changes in position and/or time.** **An object's motion can be described by measuring its change in position over time such as rolling different objects (e.g., spheres, toy cars) down a ramp. Collecting and representing data related to an object's motion provides the opportunity to make comparisons and draw conclusions. DOK 3**	**Chapter 16 Forces and Motion** Lesson 1 How Is Motion Measured and Described?, pp. 656–666
SC-4-MF-U-2 Students will understand that forces (pushes and pulls) cause changes in the direction or speed of something moving; the greater the force on an object, the greater its change in motion.	**SC-4-MF-S-1** Students will measure and record changes (using appropriate charts, graphs) in the position and motion of an object to which a force has been applied **SC-4-MF-S-2** Students will make inferences about the size of forces or the change in motion produced by various forces **SC-4-MF-S-5** Students will answer student-generated questions through investigative and non-investigative processes about what affects motion and sound using information from a variety of print and non-print sources	SC-04-1.2.1 **Students will interpret or represent data related to an object's straight-line motion in order to make inferences and predictions of changes in position and/or time.** **An object's motion can be described by measuring its change in position over time such as rolling different objects (e.g., spheres, toy cars) down a ramp. Collecting and representing data related to an object's motion provides the opportunity to make comparisons and draw conclusions. DOK 3**	Lesson 2 What Is Acceleration?, pp. 667–675
SC-4-MF-U-2 Students will understand that forces (pushes and pulls) cause changes in the direction or speed of something moving; the greater the force on an object, the greater its change in motion.	**SC-4-MF-S-5** Students will answer student-generated questions through investigative and non-investigative processes about what affects motion and sound using information from a variety of print and non-print sources	SC-04-1.2.1 **Students will interpret or represent data related to an object's straight-line motion in order to make inferences and predictions of changes in position and/or time.** **An object's motion can be described by measuring its change in position over time such as rolling different objects (e.g., spheres, toy cars) down a ramp. Collecting and representing data related to an object's motion provides the opportunity to make comparisons and draw conclusions. DOK 3**	Lesson 3 Why Is the Force of Gravity Important?, pp. 676–685
SC-4-MF-U-2 Students will understand that forces (pushes and pulls) cause changes in the direction or speed of something moving; the greater the force on an object, the greater its change in motion.	**SC-4-MF-S-2** Students will make inferences about the size of forces or the change in motion produced by various forces **SC-4-MF-S-5** Students will answer student-generated questions through investigative and non-investigative processes about what affects motion and sound using information from a variety of print and non-print sources		**Chapter 17 Simple Machines** Lesson 1 How Do Simple Machines Help People Do Work?, pp. 692–701 Lesson 2 How Do a Pulley and a Wheel-and-Axle Help People Do Work?, pp. 702–711 Lesson 3 How Do Other Simple Machines Help People Do Work?, pp. 712–721

YOUNG When flamingo chicks hatch, their feathers are gray.

FLIGHT Flamingos have to run a few steps before they can take off and fly.

Joints Sometimes it looks as if flamingos can bend their knees backward, but the joints in the middle of flamingos' legs are actually ankles. Their knees are higher up, underneath their feathers.

Behavior Flamingos often stand on one foot, but scientists aren't quite sure why.

Feeding Flamingos feed with their heads upside down.